EVERYTHING UNDER THE SUN

EVERYTHING UNDER THE SUN

THE COMPLETE GUIDE TO PINK FLOYD

MIKE CORMACK

First published 2024

The History Press
97 St George's Place, Cheltenham,
Gloucestershire, GL50 3QB
www.thehistorypress.co.uk

© Mike Cormack, 2024

The right of Mike Cormack to be identified as the Author
of this work has been asserted in accordance with the
Copyright, Designs and Patents Act 1988.

All rights reserved. No part of this book may be reprinted
or reproduced or utilised in any form or by any electronic,
mechanical or other means, now known or hereafter invented,
including photocopying and recording, or in any information
storage or retrieval system, without the permission in writing
from the Publishers.

British Library Cataloguing in Publication Data.
A catalogue record for this book is available from the British Library.

ISBN 978 1 80399 535 9

Typesetting and origination by The History Press
Printed and bound in Great Britain by TJ Books Limited, Padstow, Cornwall.

'The only thing that is important is whether it moves you or not'
Roger Waters

'All we've been trying to do is make music that will move people'
David Gilmour

*Dedicated to George Smith and Bill Cormack,
who shine on, and to my father, who started it all*

*With thanks to Darren Mackay, Thomas Ulrik Larsen,
Wang Huihua and Jenny Cormack*

CONTENTS

Preface   9

Introduction   13

Chapter 1: The Songs
I   Explorations 1967–72   19
II   Exaltations 1973–79   110
III   Echoes 1982–2022   187

Chapter 2: Chronology   255

Chapter 3: Bootleg Guide   297

Chapter 4: Interviews
Guy Pratt   385
James Guthrie   392
Steve Mac   399

PREFACE

Pink Floyd have always been a part of my life. I'm a second-generation fan: my dad and uncles were always playing the albums, and I was lucky enough, or simply predisposed, to inherit their taste. Though Pink Floyd are sometimes dismissed as a nice middle-class band expressing middle-class anxieties,* my male relatives were working-class guys who had gone to sea at a young age (Dad and George in the fishing, and Billy in the Merchant Navy). That's what you did in our neck of the woods in northern Scotland. All three were all practical guys, dismissive of anything pretentious, but passionate about art and culture – though they'd hate it to be put that way. They loved big solid entertaining books, like those by Stephen King, James Clavell and J.R.R. Tolkien. Musically they were prog rockers who still liked a good tune; they all liked, say, Mike Oldfield, Deep Purple, Led Zeppelin and The Doors, more than they liked Van Der Graaf Generator or King Crimson, though they were also fans of Kraftwerk, Captain Beefheart and Jethro Tull. They had interesting diversions into areas such as classical (Billy liked Gilbert and Sullivan, and Rossini), the blues (George explored this deeply, enthused by *The Blues Brothers*), and ambient music (Dad liked Brian Eno and The Orb, though neither George nor Billy ever really made the leap to electronic music beyond Kraftwerk). They all despised jazz and detested punk – a trendy spasm to them – while the odd folky album could be found in their collections, Christy Moore or Nick Drake rather than Donovan (the Led Zeppelin *III* influence, probably).

This all filtered down to me. It was naturally strongest from my dad, though the route was circuitous. My parents split up when I was 6, my dad lived here and there, then returned and married again, when I was about 11, making a living as a low-end hash dealer. There is an etiquette about buying hash: you're supposed to be sociable with it – like, we're all on the same level, man, have a toke and mellow out, man. So when I visited he would always have music on rather than the TV, as people would come round to buy their scores and half-scores of

---

* For example – 'Having grown up listening to Radiohead, I never quite saw the point of Pink Floyd. It was enough to have one group of upper-middle-class glum-wits, stooped over their guitars, telling us how awful the world is – and it's all the fault of those bloody humans! – without having another, older, even more ponderous version darkening my stereo ... Pink Floyd seemed the ultimate bloke's band: alienated, moody, so pathologically averse to the life-affirming pleasure of a simple pop song that they'd long disappeared up their own dark side.' (Lynsey Hanley, 'Posh Rock', *New Statesman*, 7 November 2005).

resin and share a joint or two. There was nothing glamorous or *Scarface* in any of this. Being the child of a perennial pot-head is nothing like as bad as being the child of an alcoholic, but you get a bit frustrated at everyone sitting about doing nothing and constantly having to make tea or coffee for everyone because they are too gouchy to move. However, Dad always wanted me to visit, and I felt obliged. And this all took place in a nondescript two-bedroom council house in a small town in northern Scotland. It was all ordinary, mundane.

As a peripatetic guy, Dad had a huge range of pirated C90 tapes, carefully labelled – he was the kind of guy who would visit friends with a bunch of blank cassettes in case they had anything good, whereas George and Billy, as more settled family men, had major vinyl collections and quality Hi-Fis. So I absorbed a great deal when visiting him in those days. I had started to develop my own music collection by then (first album: Guns N' Roses' *Appetite For Destruction*, on my 9th birthday), but was always willing to listen, and anyway he, of course, had control of the stereo. So I picked up everything from Pink Floyd to Can to Peter Tosh to the Velvet Underground to AC/DC to Tangerine Dream to Brian Eno to Kraftwerk to Queen to The Doors to Genesis to Nick Drake to Hawkwind to dub poet Mikey Smith* to Captain Beefheart to Black Sabbath to Marillion to Rush to Dianno-era Iron Maiden.† It might not have been the typical childhood, but as a musical education it was absolutely first class.

Although basically a pot-head allergic to work and responsibility, Dad always made it his mission to convert the people around him to what he liked: Gandalf with a spliff instead of a staff. The underground music that he venerated was completely absent from mainstream TV and radio, and so was passed around by word of mouth and through the connections they raised. For example, Led Zeppelin opened the door to *Lord of the Rings*, then still a cult, underground book; Iron Maiden led to Frank Herbert's *Dune*; the Velvet Underground to Andy Warhol, pop art and Nico; and Roxy Music and Brian Eno led to ambient music. That's how it was for working-class guys with intellectual interests. This was their higher education, sitting getting stoned and enjoying something a bit deeper than the Top 40. These were people for whom Glastonbury (before it became mainstream and corporate) was Mecca, John Peel their patron saint.

Pink Floyd were always the favourite band of my relatives by some considerable margin. Why? They were all intelligent and they responded to music that had depth but didn't go overboard in asserting its musical ability (only Billy was into Rick Wakeman, for example). Pink Floyd were nice middle-class boys and so never needed to justify themselves as artists – the fatal error of many a once-hungry rock band. *The Wall* in particular seized the imagination. It was high art for people who didn't like anything fancy. It had a complex psychological narrative, and crushing riffs, soaring solos and highly literate lyrics. It was

---

* John Peel played poems from Smith's *Mi Cyaan Believe It* (1982) album in his BBC Radio 1 show.
† The gaps interest me now: no David Bowie? No Television? No Joy Division or The Smiths or The Cure? No Beatles or Rolling Stones?

nightmarishly dark, but said at the end if we all came together and were nice to each other that things would be better. It mocked authority figures from schoolteachers to doctors to tour managers. It evoked the dribbling lust of a young man, and said women could tear you apart. It was everything for an angry young man. *Dark Side* was more a sonic journey; *Wish You Were Here* was melancholy waves of sound; *Piper* was gaily frivolous (perfect for mushroom season, though Billy had never even taken a puff of a joint). Pink Floyd perfectly suited them and they were hopelessly, passionately devoted fans of the group. George to this day pretty much always wears jeans and Pink Floyd T-shirts, though he's comfortably retired after a successful career in the oil industry.

So I was lucky: I had ingested all this before I was even in my teens. My own Pink Floyd journey began with *The Wall*. George had the VHS cassette (as well as *Live At Pompeii*) and sometimes I'd watch it, when about 9 years old. It was staggering. There was no text on the back of the VHS box so I could barely make head nor tail of it, simply enjoying the animation and feeling the horror of Pink's decline into madness and fascism. Later, when I was maybe 11, the local John Menzies had what must have been a re-release, with some explanation actually on the cassette box. I was a tremendous shop-browser in those days, since I never had any money, and studied the box every time I visited, which was every weekend. Things started to click, and when I watched it subsequently, I started to understand the metaphorical point of the scenes and so the lyrics took on greater meaning.

The great leap came when I was 15, when I borrowed practically every album and worked my way through them. *Animals* swiftly became my favourite, an opinion I've rarely changed. The live side of *Ummagumma* has moved up in recent years; *Obscured by Clouds* gets more listens than it used to; *The Final Cut* I respect rather than enjoy, although some people whose musical taste I value rate it highly; *The Division Bell* rises and falls; I still think *Wish You Were Here* is slightly overrated, though clearly I'm in the minority here. And ever since then Pink Floyd have featured very heavily on my musical playlist. I own most of the albums on vinyl, have seen David Gilmour and Roger Waters play live, and read whatever books or magazines I can on the group.

All of which is to say that Pink Floyd have always been a huge part of my life. Their sonic ambition, lyrical dexterity, and structural ability are unparalleled in rock music. They inspire emotions that only religion once described – the sense of the numinous in 'Comfortably Numb', the transcendence of 'Wish You Were Here' and 'Eclipse', the desperate isolation of 'Is There Anybody Out There?' and 'Nobody Home', the mystery and majesty of 'Echoes', the bittersweet nostalgia of 'Fat Old Sun', the feeling of rebirth in 'Coming Back to Life'. I simply cannot tire of their music – even after writing this book. They astonish and intrigue and move you like no other group.

Shine on.

INTRODUCTION

No rock group has ever seized the imagination like Pink Floyd. In a field normally primarily concerned with sex, relationships, war and aggression, the self and others, Pink Floyd have explored space, psychosis, pastoralism, isolation, absence, business ethics, transcendence, death, madness, empathy, inertia, communication difficulties, war and the psychology of fascism. They have done so with a range of music perhaps surpassing anyone in the rock canon, from folky acoustic rural homages to ambient rhythms to orchestral grandiosity to ass-kicking hard rock. Yet there is something we can call 'Floydian': moderately-paced, spacious, repetitively melodic, coloured by the Farsifa keyboard, with lyrics of unusual verbal felicity about the human condition. This is not to say that Pink Floyd were formulaic: few bands have stretched themselves and worked so hard to improve their recorded output and their live performances. Many rock bands are spent creative forces after a few albums; Pink Floyd did not hit their golden period until their eighth album, sustaining it across three further works which remain among the highest-selling and most critically esteemed records ever made.

The context is important in understanding Pink Floyd. In the mid-1960s, rock 'n' roll was a juvenile art, but groups like The Beatles and The Who worked to develop it into a more mature artform, with increasing musical, recording and lyrical sophistication. The distance from The Beatles' album closers 'Twist And Shout' and 'Tomorrow Never Knows' was just three years, demonstrating the incredible rate at which the genre was developing. The Who, similarly, moved the album towards a symphonic piece with *Tommy* (1969), inaugurating the concept album as full thematically and musically integrated work (The Beatles' 1967 album *Sgt. Pepper*, often considered the first rock concept album, is not unified lyrically, instead really only having an overture and a curtain-closer). However, in the jazz world, Miles Davis had moved the album from being a disparate collection of individual tracks to a thematic whole, as on the acclaimed albums *Kind of Blue* (1959) and *Sketches of Spain* (1960). The LP, in rock as in jazz, was moving closer to becoming an integrated artistic unity, like a classical music symphony.

In this context Pink Floyd began in 1965. Starting as an R&B cover band based in London, and taking their name from two Piedmont blues musicians, the group developed rapidly during 1966 residencies at the Marquee club (in Wardour Street, Soho) and UFO (at Tottenham Court Road). Early bootlegs[*] show setlists of basic R&B and Bo Diddley-style rock, with Barrett singing in an American style very far from his English manner on *The Piper at the Gates of Dawn*. However, they had artistic and musical backgrounds exceeding these floundering derivative efforts. Barrett was an art student coming from an intellectual middle-class family (his father was a noted doctor). Wright was privately educated, had learned the trumpet and trombone as well as guitar and piano while still a schoolboy, and was steeped in jazz rather than R&B. Waters' parents were teachers and left-wing political activists. So while their first steps were naturally rudimentary, it was equally unsurprising that their subsequent efforts should have greater artistic ambitions.

Yet while their first album is a very singular psychedelic masterpiece, the group's subsequent efforts demonstrate the balkanisation of rock music that had occurred in the late 1960s: towards a populist singalong style that eventually became glam rock; the electric thunder that became heavy metal; and the experimental progressive rock of groups like Yes, Genesis, Rush and King Crimson, as well, of course, as Pink Floyd. For a time it was perfectly acceptable to have twenty-minute multi-sectional epics and choirs and orchestras and lyrical themes drawn from any manner of esoteric philosophies. The more far out the better, man. Given this room to grow, and initially touring very hard too,[†] Pink Floyd gradually developed songwriting chops, an astonishing lyrical facility, and a jaw-dropping live spectacle. The integration of guitarist and vocalist David Gilmour didn't really occur until three years into his career in the band, with 1971's *Meddle* album. But that heralded one of the greatest streaks of creativity in rock history, easily comparable with The Beatles' *Revolver–Sgt Pepper–White Album–Abbey Road* and The Rolling Stones' *Beggars Banquet–Let It Bleed–Sticky Fingers–Exile on Main Street* sequences.[‡] Once the group had truly found their voice, the albums *Dark Side of the Moon* (1973), *Wish You Were Here* (1975), *Animals* (1977) and *The Wall* (1979) display some of the most profound and moving writing in rock music as well as some of the most dazzlingly creative music. Perhaps more than any other albums in rock music, these four integrate lyrical depth with verbal dexterity and musically visionary songs, creating integrated artistic unities that retain the power to enthral and deeply move the listener fifty years on.

But career peaks do not last, and as intra-band relationships fragmented then collapsed during and following *The Wall*,[§] so the work too declined. *The Final Cut* (1983), *A Momentary Lapse of Reason* (1987), *The Division Bell* (1994) and *The*

---

[*] Partially reproduced on disc 1 of the *Early Years 1965-72* boxset. It includes 'I'm A King Bee', the sole cover on any music officially released by Pink Floyd.

[†] See Chronology. The group performed 183 concerts in 1967, including three in one day on 25 March.

[‡] As well as, say, *Radioactivity-Trans Europe Express-The Man Machine-Computer World* by Kraftwerk, or *In A Silent Way-Bitches Brew-A Tribute To Jack Johnson-Live/Evil* (amongst others) by Miles Davis, if you want to go beyond rock music.

[§] I have no intention of recounting the various ongoing tiffs between Waters and Gilmour, or Waters' political opinions except as they pertain to the song being discussed.

Endless River (2014): all have their moments, all have their fans, all have sold millions around the world. Yet I think there is a clear arc to the career of Pink Floyd, as I shall argue in the song analyses that follow. But then, quite understandably, some fans are most passionate about the fervent creativity of the group's early years, while others adore the brilliant savaging of Thatcherite Britain and lament for those traumatised by war in *The Final Cut*, or fondly recall discovering the group from *A Momentary Lapse of Reason*, or are hardcore Syd Barrett devotees. There are many paths to Pink Floyd. So here, across 187 recorded tracks and fifteen albums, across 1,160 gigs from New Zealand to Canada, from 1967 to 2022, is the career of rock's most devastatingly emotional and articulate band.

Note on the Selection

For this book I have chosen to only record and critique the canonical songs from official albums, singles and various stray tracks. These comprise:

- the singles: 'Arnold Layne' b/w 'Candy and a Currant Bun' (1967), 'See Emily Play' b/w 'Scarecrow' (1967), 'Apples and Oranges' b/w 'Paint Box' (1967), 'It Would Be So Nice' b/w 'Julia Dream' (1968), 'Point Me at the Sky' b/w 'Careful with that Axe, Eugene' (1968), 'When the Tigers Broke Free' (1982), and 'Hey Hey Rise Up' (2022)

- the official albums: *The Piper at the Gates of Dawn* (1967), *A Saucerful of Secrets* (1968), *Ummagumma* (1969), *Atom Heart Mother* (1970), *Meddle* (1971), *The Dark Side of the Moon* (1973), *Wish You Were Here* (1975), *Animals* (1977), *The Wall* (1979), *The Final Cut* (1983), *A Momentary Lapse of Reason* (1987), *The Division Bell* (1994), and *The Endless River* (2014)

- the soundtrack albums: *More* (1969) and *Obscured by Clouds* (1972)

- stray tracks which appeared on official releases: *Zabriskie Point* (1970) and *Picnic: A Breath of Fresh Air* (1970)

This means I have not considered the other official live albums *Delicate Sound of Thunder* (1988), *Pulse* (1995), and *Is There Anybody Out There?* (2000). None of these contain unreleased tracks (with the exception of 'The Last Few Bricks', an instrumental in *The Wall* tour which filled time allowing roadies to almost complete the construction of the wall) or a substantially different version of previously released songs (beyond extended guitar solos, though the *Pulse* version of **COMFORTABLY NUMB** does have dark grungy verses, just as Gilmour always wanted). The four live tracks on *Ummagumma*, however, do present significantly improved versions over the studio releases, demonstrating the band's rapidly developing mastery of dynamics and structure. The re-recordings in *A Collection of Great Dance Songs* (1981) I have likewise left alone, for similar reasons. Nor have I described the demos, live sessions and early alternate versions the Immersion Editions of *Dark Side*, *Wish You Were Here* and *The Wall*, or on the *Early Years* (2016) and *Later Years* (2019) box sets, though I do refer to them when considering the completed studio tracks. There is a great deal of musical and historical interest there, of course, but these remain fragments, sketches, and ephemeral performances. And finally, I have not included the six new tracks composed for the *La Carrera Panamericana* documentary on the eponymous 1991 car race in Mexico, in which David Gilmour, Nick Mason and band manager Steve O'Rourke all participated. These tracks have never been officially released and the video has only ever been released on VHS format. This book is an analysis of the official canon, of all tracks formally recorded and released, and examines how the studio output of Pink Floyd developed, peaked, declined, and returned in lesser if still considerable form. This is a story told in three movements: Explorations (1967–72), Exaltations (1973–79) and Echoes (1982–2022).

Note on the Research

While The Beatles' recording career can be quite precisely mapped, the same is not true for Pink Floyd. Albums recorded in their own Britannia Row studio or on Gilmour's Astoria houseboat were essentially free from label oversight and, while they could record or compose there as they pleased, consequently there aren't records detailing precise dates, who played what, or what production techniques were used. (Engineer Andy Jackson confirmed this by email on 8 November 2023.) Similarly, Château d'Hérouville, where *Obscured By Clouds* was recorded, shut down and was abandoned in 1985, Super Bear studio (where much of *The Wall* was recorded) burned down in 1986, and the group had kicked their EMI producer Norman Smith upstairs by the time of *Atom Heart Mother*.

Hence the recording dates and personnel lists playing on each track are (especially on *A Momentary Lapse of Reason*, which used many session musicians) somewhat proximate and vary according to which source you read. The only people who could really possibly fill in the details are David Gilmour, Nick Mason and Roger Waters, but even then the human memory is highly fallible, as we'll see when it comes to disputes over songwriting and production credits (as with **BREATHE** and **ANOTHER BRICK IN THE WALL PART 2** for example). But perhaps – and this might shock some members of the band – credits aren't that important. The main thing is how Pink Floyd move you as a listener, how they nourish the emotions and the soul, and somehow keep doing so through the decades of being a fan – and this I have always kept in mind when discussing each song.

CHAPTER 1

THE SONGS

I.

EXPLORATIONS (1967–72)

ARNOLD LAYNE (Barrett)
Length: 2.57
Vocals: Syd Barrett **Guitars**: Syd Barrett **Bass**: Roger Waters **Farsifa organ**: Rick Wright
Drums: Nick Mason **Backing vocals**: Rick Wright
Recorded: 29 January 1967, Sound Techniques, London
Producer: Joe Boyd
First released: 11 March 1967 (UK a/side single)
Rating: 8/10

Having signed with EMI in February 1967 after building an audience in the UFO and Marquee clubs throughout 1966, Pink Floyd's choice of first single is a daring excursion in whimsical pop. It is worth noting, too, that the choice was theirs. Unlike most bands, Pink Floyd established a degree of artistic autonomy from their record label from the outset. Built around a descending riff (slightly reminiscent of, if less dramatic than, the introduction to **INTERSTELLAR OVERDRIVE**) in the verse which leaps into a singalong chorus ('*Oh Arnold Layne … it's not the same*'), **ARNOLD LAYNE** is musically notable for the low verse which rises to a peak just as the chorus starts, suggesting excitement at Arnold's butterfly-like transformation.

With the subject matter of the pop single radically expanding in the mid-1960s, rock music was swiftly moving from being an adolescent expression to a genuine artform. The Beatles' *Revolver*, released on 5 August 1966, led the way, with songs less concerned with romance, consumerism or autonomy than with mysticism, spiritual disorientation, community dislocation, and the LSD experience. Though not as startlingly groundbreaking, **ARNOLD LAYNE** similarly advances rock's thematic concerns with its uncensorious take on the eponymous character's '*strange hobby*',* telling a complete story as it does so. Barrett's voice takes on a sneer at the end of the chorus when he sings 'Why can't you see?', condemning the uptight straights for their lack of understanding of this (allegedly) harmless pursuit. Radio stations, as gatekeepers to the nation's musical consumption, were less understanding, with the BBC, Radio Caroline

---

* The song was based on Roger Waters' mother taking in female student lodgers and their undergarments being stolen from the washing line.

and Radio London amongst those banning the song. (Underwear seemed to preoccupy radio managers. The BBC banned The Beatles' 'I am the Walrus', released that November, apparently for its use of the word 'knickers').

While **ARNOLD LAYNE** was cleverly calculated to be a hit single,* it was hardly representative of Pink Floyd's live efforts in early 1967. The song was condensed from its ten-to-fifteen-minute length when played live, being seen as the most likely to be successful when compressed into the regular sub-three-minute pop single. Already, it's worth noting, Pink Floyd's real track lengths were customarily far in excess of the usual pop track.† In early 1967, however, they were fresh and keen to play the pop game (this would change). The shortened time span of the pop single does not, however, mean diminished room for creativity. On the contrary, the most successful singles crammed as much sensation and surprise as they could into their brief spin. **ARNOLD LAYNE** follows this edict with flair if not, as yet, their distinctive genius. That would come.

CANDY AND A CURRANT BUN (Barrett)
Length: 2.38
Vocals: Barrett **Guitars**: Barrett **Bass**: Waters **Farsifa organ**: Wright **Drums**: Mason
Backing vocals: Wright, Waters, Mason
Recorded: 29 January 1967, Sound Techniques, London
Producer: Joe Boyd
First released: 11 March 1967 (UK b/side single)
Rating: 5/10

Seen in retrospect, **CANDY AND A CURRANT BUN** sends out alarming signs of a writer revelling in self-indulgence. Famously rewritten from its initial title 'Let's Roll Another One', the song retains its subject matter of drugs and casual sex, but does so on a nod and a wink ('*Tastes good if you eat it soon*'). Musically it moves on dark waves of sound through the verse, before obscuring Barrett's vocal in the chorus as he half-mutters, half-grimaces his way through the words. This concealment meant that Barrett could sneak in an expletive, no doubt irritated at being censored ('*Oooh, don't talk to me / Please, just fuck with me*'),‡ but the opacity also gives the impression of him losing his identity through greedy self-indulgence. Such murkiness makes **CANDY AND A CURRANT BUN** sinister rather than playful: not for nothing does it also contain the first instance of

---

* Reaching #20 on was highly respectable for a first single. The Beatles only got 'Love Me Do' to #17 in 1962 after some weeks in the chart, and some suspiciously large orders by manager Brian Epstein for his NEMS music store in Liverpool. Pink Floyd's management Blackhill Enterprises allegedly followed suit, spending several hundred pounds to boost its chart performance.

† This was standard practice for jazz groups, which would solo extensively over a main theme (or chorus), but condense when releasing the track as a single. Rick Wright, more than the other members, had a jazz background, which was unusual amongst the UK pop world, most of whom were brought up on showtunes and American R&B.

‡ One of the very first instances of the word in pop music. (The first occasion on British TV had come 18 months earlier, on 13 November 1965, by critic Kenneth Tynan.)

the patented Roger Waters scream.§ The only genuine human note (or perhaps foreshadowing) comes at the end of each verse: *'Please – I'm feeling frail.'*

Using exotic-sounding melisma, cooing backing vocals and a Farsifa organ solo, the track sounds preposterously 1967, and is the only example of lewdness in the entire Pink Floyd canon.¶ It also predates both the Beatles and the Rolling Stones in their own periods of 1967 excess (as exemplified by 'Baby You're a Rich Man' and the entire *Their Satanic Majesties Request* album, respectively). The famous Chelsea-King's Road-Indica bookshop-LSD nexus was clearly in full swing by January of that year (*Sgt. Pepper* was released in June, *Satanic Majesties* in December).

Because **CANDY AND A CURRANT BUN** was left off *Relics* in 1971 (the group likely seeking to move away from their previous drug-oriented image), it developed a mystique and has been absurdly overpraised by some. *Creem* writer Dave Marsh wrote that it 'send chills runnin' up and down your spine, and make you listen time and time again'.** But the truth is more prosaic: **CANDY AND A CURRANT BUN** might perhaps exemplify the drug-oriented culture of the period, but this is not necessarily a good thing; and it's simply not much of a song. The most relevant aspect is its darkness: perhaps even Barrett could tell that self-indulgence was not the road to the palace of wisdom.

SEE EMILY PLAY (Barrett)
Length: 2.53
Vocals: Barrett **Guitars**: Barrett **Bass**: Waters **Farsifa organ**: Wright **Drums**: Mason
Piano: Wright **Electric harpsichord**: Wright **Backing vocals**: Wright, Waters
Recorded: 23 May 1967 at Sound Techniques, London
Producer: Norman Smith
First released: 16 June 1967 (UK a/side single)
Rating: 10/10

Barrett's pop masterpiece **SEE EMILY PLAY** cast a long shadow over both him and the group. It hit #4 in the UK singles charts,†† leading the industry to instantly demand more such masterpieces from him. (None of the other group members were anywhere near ready to offer material of such quality.) While Barrett was the creative force of early Pink Floyd, he was also far more free-spirited (or less disciplined) than Waters, Wright or Mason. Noted by bandmates as having been friendly and approachable in comparison to the fashionable

---

§ As later heard on **POW R. TOC H.**, **CAREFUL WITH THAT AXE, EUGENE**, **SEVERAL SPECIES OF SMALL FURRY ANIMALS**, **COME IN NUMBER 51 YOUR TIME IS UP**, **ANOTHER BRICK IN THE WALL PART 2**, **YOUNG LUST**, **RUN LIKE HELL**, and **TWO SUNS IN THE SUNSET**.
¶ **YOUNG LUST** satirizes it, rather than celebrating it.
** *Creem*, November 1971.
†† At a time of remarkable quality in the pop charts, which in June 1967 included 'A Whiter Shade of Pale', 'Waterloo Sunset', 'Pictures of Lily' and 'Strange Brew'.

insouciance of the time,* Barrett lacked the defences essential for someone who had become instantly famous. This made him highly attractive as a person (Syd always had the best-looking girlfriends), but it augured badly for his ability to handle industry pressures. But all of this still lay ahead.

The remarkable thing is how easy **SEE EMILY PLAY** sounds, gliding on a cloud of sheer beatific euphoria – little wonder then it was the sound of the summer of 1967. As Iain MacDonald has noted, the hippy dream was one of a frictionless takeover 'in which anything involving struggle, conflict or difficulty seemed laughably unenlightened'. Or as Hunter S. Thompson put it in *Fear and Loathing in Las Vegas*, 'Our energy would simply prevail.' The notions of 'play' (also suggested in its original title, 'Games for May') is also highly apposite. The hippy movement rejected both the conservative-authoritarian model (as passed down by the Church, where '*The rich man in his castle, / The poor man at his gate, / God made them, high or lowly, / And ordered their estate*'),† as well as the traditional leftist veneration of work and workers. Tapping into these ideas and concerns gives **SEE EMILY PLAY** a depth of meaning beyond its gaiety and wonder, and reinforce its aptness for the moment.

After headlining, at dawn, the '14 Hour Technicolour Dream' at Alexandra Palace on 29 April 1967, Pink Floyd were the darlings of the moment, their abstract explorations the perfect sound for the acid-dropping attendees. (Their setlist for that show comprised just four tracks: **ASTRONOMY DOMINE**, **ARNOLD LAYNE**, **INTERSTELLAR OVERDRIVE**, and 'Nick's Boogie', which was never officially released by the group).‡ Yet the track remains far from their live sound, refining the example of **ARNOLD LAYNE** to even greater effect. This is a surprising bifurcation for a band just starting out, but it demonstrates how the group strictly adhered to the edicts of what comprised a 7" single. They wanted to be pop stars, although their sense of musical possibility soared far beyond.

Densely packed with hooks and earworm moments, **SEE EMILY PLAY** shows how hard Barrett and the rest of the group (as guided by producer Norman Smith) worked to maximise the song. The obvious model is The Beatles' 'She Loves You' – the supreme exemplar of cramming every moment of a sub-three-minute pop single with surprise and delight. From the off, **SEE EMILY PLAY** pricks the ears: it starts with a plastic ruler being used as a slide up the guitar strings, giving a unique, alien sound, swiftly followed by a short bass pedal point by Waters, then a tom-tom roll and a Farsifa organ comment, thus giving all four members a short showpiece in the first ten seconds. The first line of each verse adds an '*Aah-ooh*' at the end, and the second line, after Mason brings the

---

* Wright later noted how he never knew anyone's name at the time: everyone was too cool to introduce themselves. But Barrett would guilelessly introduce himself as Syd.
† From 'All Things Bright And Beautiful', 1848.
‡ It can be heard on the re-releases (from 1990 onwards) of *Tonite Let's All Make Love in London*, a soundtrack album for the documentary film of the same name about 'swinging London'. It opens with a tom-tom rhythm that anticipates **SET THE CONTROLS FOR THE HEART OF THE SUN**, but descends into about ten minutes of random noodling. You can understand why the group were happy to leave it behind.

track to a halt, springs straight into the delightful singalong chorus. Wright also adds a brief deft comment on piano at the end of each choral line, and each of the three choruses leads to an instrumental break – two bars on the electric harpsichord after the first, the instrumental middle eight after the second, then the fade-out (dominated by Waters' bass) after the third. While the song sticks firmly to the classic pop single formula (Intro–Verse–Chorus–Verse–Chorus–Middle-Eight–Verse–Solo–Chorus–Outro, a pop single methodology perhaps best mastered by UK hitmakers Stock, Aitken and Waterman in the 1980s), there is something fresh happening at almost every moment, and **SEE EMILY PLAY** remains an utter joy more than fifty years after.

The Floyd now being EMI artists as of 28 February, recording was first attempted at EMI Studios in Abbey Road, though, as Mason noted, 'We just could not reproduce the sound of "Arnold Layne", so we all trooped back to Sound Techniques to recreate the magic formula, which gave Joe Boyd a certain wry pleasure.'[§] The legend of EMI Studios rather precedes it: in 1967 it still only had four-track recording facilities, and many studios were more advanced. This was perhaps an unusual amount of leeway[¶] for a new band, though pop and rock acts were gaining more say over their work as sales increased exponentially during the 1960s,[**] and as they came to be considered artists rather than entertainers. The group's interest in sonic experimentation, while here structured within the highly structured format of the 7" single, finds its first expression here. As the band moved from pop singles to rock albums, so their room for experimentation grew and pop discipline declined. But here, **SEE EMILY PLAY** is an astonishingly vivid piece of music making – so merry, so exuberant, so thrillingly alive. It only makes the tragedy of Barrett's subsequent mental collapse ever more poignant.

SCARECROW (Barrett)
Length: 2.11
Vocals: Barrett **Electric guitars**: Barrett **Acoustic guitars**: Barrett **Bass**: Waters
Farsifa organ: Wright **Backing vocals**: Waters, Wright **Flute**: Wright **Cello**: Wright
Slide whistle: Waters **Temple blocks**: Mason **Metal cups**: Mason
Recorded: 22 March 1967, EMI Studios, London
Producer: Norman Smith
First released: 16 June 1967 (UK b/side single)
Rating: 7/10

---

§ Nick Mason, *Inside Out*, p.85.
¶ Then again, The Beatles had spent recently three months recording 'Strawberry Fields Forever', and The Beach Boys had spent a monumental seven months on 'Good Vibrations' – though both had huge leverage over their record companies due to their popularity. But the days of albums being recorded in one day were at an end for major artists (though not for impoverished ones – Black Sabbath's eponymous debut album was recorded over 12 hours, on 16 October 1969).
** A fact of which Roger Waters was well aware. He notes in *Live At Pompeii* that 'the market for rock music is expanding at an extraordinary rate'. No flies on him.

A charming piece of pastoral whimsy, **SCARECROW** is one of the most distinctive Barrett-era songs. Though rock 'n' roll and R&B were mostly regarded as urban music (which essentially meant for black people), the influence of Bob Dylan and British folkies like The Incredible String Band and Donovan brought a rich strain to the English pop (and later rock)[*] scenes. But rather than a stark arrangement with acoustic guitar and little else, **SCARECROW** is a colourful rural evocation, with the multi-tracked temple blocks and metal cups suggesting equine clip-clops, and the Farsifa organ leading the whimsical melody that somehow suggests *Bill and Ben* and sunflowers.

The chorus/refrain '*He stood in a field / Where barley grows*' follows each of the three verses, as though in a nursery rhyme. In the third chorus Barrett elongates the vowels ('*He stoooood in a fieeeeeld / Where baaaarley groooows*'), after which the arrangement thickens and slightly darker tints emerge, as suggested by the cello (played by Wright) and electric guitars. This might suggest the Scarecrow's redundancy when night comes, or could be an acknowledgement that passivity in the face of life's unpredictable fortunes ('*when the wind cut up rough*') isn't always effective. Either way, the darkness lifts a little as the song fades out at about 1.45, leavened with glints of guitar arpeggios. For a short and seemingly simple track, **SCARECROW** is cunningly produced and has more than a hint of sly wit, as with much of Barrett's work. A skein of darkness and unease runs through a good portion of *Piper*, undercutting the whimsy and giving it bite. Flowers can have thorns.

ASTRONOMY DOMINE (Barrett)
Length: 4.12
Vocals: Barrett **Guitars**: Barrett **Bass**: Waters **Farsifa organ**: Wright **Drums**: Mason
Backing vocals: Wright **Vocalisation**: Peter Jenner
Recorded: 11, 12, 17 April 1967, EMI Studios, London
Producer: Norman Smith
First released: 5 August 1967 (*The Piper at the Gates of Dawn* track 1)
Rating: 9/10

The opening song to Pink Floyd's debut album establishes many of the characteristics they would come to be known by – a space theme, musique concrete, a refusal to stick to adolescent love topics, and unusual, sometimes dissonant chords. This was *art* rock, with ambitions far beyond the dancefloor or teenage bedroom. Besides the Floyd's familiar territory, **ASTRONOMY DOMINE** also has some very smart wordplay from Barrett ('*Floating down, the sound resounds / Around the icy waters underground*'), although the lyric as a whole does not mean anything in particular, being instead a string of space-related words and images. (The word 'Domine' in the title has nothing to do with domination,

---

[*] Perhaps first codified in *Led Zeppelin III* (1970)

but is Latin for 'Lord' — Barrett probably put it there because it sort of rhymed with 'Astronomy'.)

The song opens with then-manager Peter Jenner on a megaphone reciting random space-related phrases, though because it fades in and then Barrett's guitar immediately plays over it, it is impossible to hear exactly what's being said.[†] Barrett's guitar is loud, assertive and fantastically resonant, though playing an overture rather than setting up the melody for the rest of the song, while Mason enjoys himself on the introduction, each tom-tom fill unveiling the next section. Then the verse sees Barrett and Wright harmonising excitingly on vocals while Waters, Barrett and Wright play busy notes, keeping the energy high and the tension rising. This peaks at the end of each verse, leading to two descents (originally sung by Barrett, as can be seen on live videos, but here initially played by Wright on the Farsifa organ and then doubled by Barrett on the guitar). The end of every verse couplet has an instrumental fill (the first one brief, the second one longer), keeping the listener's ears constantly at attention — exactly the way **SEE EMILY PLAY** had sustained attention over every moment. (It's odd that Waters or Wright didn't pick up this technique until much later.) This then leads to a rather noodling guitar solo and instrumental section, over which Jenner's megaphoned voice briefly appears, and then we're back for another two repeats of the first verse, as the drums and vocals — but no guitar now — build to a climactic peak.

This is far from the twelve-bar blues and American R&B that inspired so much of the Merseybeat and British Invasion bands, showing both unusual imagination and expert craftsmanship. **ASTRONOMY DOMINE** is also especially well produced, with the tom-toms really resounding, the guitar nice and aggressive, Waters' bass bubbling away manically, and the multiple layers of sound during the instrumental break (such as Barrett on slide guitar) handled superbly. As an opening album track, **ASTRONOMY DOMINE** is a staggering success: bold, authoritative, instantly recognisable, and highly memorable. Here indeed was a completely original and compelling voice in rock music. (It remained in the group's setlist until 1971, then was resuscitated for the group's 1994 *Division Bell* tour and Gilmour's subsequent solo tours.)

LUCIFER SAM (Barrett)
Length: 3.07
Vocals: Barrett **Guitars**: Barrett **Bass**: Waters **Bowed bass**: Waters **Farsifa organ**: Wright **Drums**: Mason **Backing vocals**: Wright **Percussion**: Mason
Recorded: 12, 13, 17, 18 April, 12, 27 June, 1967, EMI Studios, London
Producer: Norman Smith
First released: 5 August 1967 (*The Piper at the Gates of Dawn* track 2)
Rating: 7/10

[†] Some suggestions include: 'Moon in both houses', 'Scorpio, Arabian Skies, Libra', 'Pluto was not discovered until 1930', 'Two seconds to ignition', 'All systems satisfied'. It's probably not important either way – the point was to give a Mission Control sort of atmosphere, and it does that very well.

Opening with a Barrett delay-processed riff complemented by the Farsifa organ by Wright, **LUCIFER SAM** is a song with no great meaning or importance, but it's great fun, and sung and played with great verve. It's simply about Barrett's cat, as the first line makes clear ('*Lucifer Sam, Siam cat*'), though the reference to '*a hip cat*' caused debate on whether it referred to some scene hipster. (The fact that the song was initially titled 'Percy the Rat Catcher' during recording seems to outline its feline character.)

Each verse only has three lines and immediately alternates with the refrain: '*That cat's something I can't explain!*' The repeated assonance ('that', 'cat' and 'can't') gives Mason a great beat to play off, while the elongated 'explain' is strung out with melisma ('*explay-ay-ayn*'). Barrett's ability to create and release tension are remarkably advanced for a first album, making **LUCIFER SAM** (and *Piper* as a whole) rather better than it first appears to be. Similarly, the increase in animation as the song progresses provides a sense of narrative, which is helpful as neither the lyrics nor the song structure do. By the final verse, after a second bridge led by Wright's Farsifa, the melody has disappeared completely, replaced by strummed chords and a manic vocal from Barrett, with the lyrics' excellent syllabics letting him build up the tension through repetition: '*Hiding around on the ground / He'll be found when you're around*'. It all builds to a wonderful peak, even if you're not quite sure what the point is. Musically, **LUCIFER SAM** is most interesting for the group's murky comments on the main musical text, such as is just audible after 'Siam Cat' at 0.32, or indeed the (slightly campy) Hammer Horror-style bowed bass attributed to Waters, though Wright is a more likely contender for this instrument, from 1.31 and throughout the first bridge. With the melody a simplistic four chords, this leaves the group space to comment on and undercut what's being played, by overdubbing Barrett's guitar with large amounts of echo, as well as Wright's various keyboards.[*]

LUCIFER SAM is fundamentally a minor track, but it must count as one of the first rock songs about a pet[†] and is made striking by the dazzling exuberance Barrett brings to his vocals in particular. It's also a remarkable piece of studio trickery and colouring, which no doubt made approximating it live rather difficult (it was never played after 1967). With songs of this quality as album tracks, *Piper* is an astonishingly accomplished debut.

---

[*] The Velvet Underground would do something similar with the astonishing 'Sister Ray' from *White Light/White Heat* (1968) – interjecting abrasive music comments over a brutally elemental garage rock three-chord riff. (The song was highly influential 10 years later: it was covered by Joy Division, was cited in the advert which led to the formation of the Buzzcocks, and was played at the first gig of Siouxsie And The Banshees (with Sid Vicious on drums)).

[†] Cat Stevens released the rather more straightforward 'I Love My Dog' in 1966, which reached number 28 on the singles chart. Songs about dogs were rather more popular in country music. See **SEAMUS**.

MATILDA MOTHER (Barrett)
Length: 3.08
Vocals: Barrett **Guitars**: Barrett **Bass**: Waters **Farsifa organ**: Wright
Hammond organ: Wright **Drums**: Mason **Backing vocals**: Waters, Wright
Recorded: 21 February 1967, EMI Studios, London
Producer: Norman Smith
First released: 5 August 1967 (*The Piper at the Gates of Dawn* track 3)
Rating: 8/10

It is remarkable that at the time when The Beatles were recording their own odes to childhood (John Lennon's 'Strawberry Fields Forever' and Paul McCartney's 'Penny Lane'), Pink Floyd were recording their own tribute to Barrett's wandering spirit of Edenic childhood. There must have been something in the cultural air. This may well have been LSD, a drug which removes adult preconceptions and lets users see the world afresh, recapturing the child's lost perspective. Then again, Barrett's art[‡] had taken childhood as its subject before: in 1965, aged 19, he had created an art project titled, rather childishly, 'Fart Enjoy', which comprised cut-ups taken from sources like the Bible, teen pop and fashion magazines, a wild flower guide, and Beatrix Potter's *The Tale of Mr Jeremy Fisher*, as well as 'two pages of cut-up nursery rhymes'.[§] The conflation of high and popular art,[¶] and radical juxtapositions of childhood, religion, nature and science, seem to have been on Barrett's mind from his earliest days as an artist.

Rock 'n' roll may have started out as teenage music, but the expansion of its language and emotional range during the mid-1960s was remarkable, with an ever-increasing vocabulary, complexity and ambition. Whereas R&B was traditionally pithy and streetwise, adopting the vocabulary of the English nursery allowed pop's lexicon to become florid and whimsical.[**] Instead of tough, spartan Roundheads, pop groups could be Cavaliers – longhaired, sensual, artistic, sensitive, and flowery. (Though, of course, this was adopted by many merely as a fashion. Roger Daltrey was never convincing in a silk cravat.) Through Barrett's songs and fashion sense, Pink Floyd help to create an entire pop sensibility that filtered down through David Bowie, Roxy Music, Marc Bolan, XTC and so on throughout the culture, even to post-millennial bands like Animal Collective. This new style might attest to the rapidly expanding audience for pop music, but it also demonstrates, in the days before professional A&R men and costume designers, a distinct originality and keen sense of marketability. The Beatles and the Rolling Stones had come along and changed fashions completely; now the

---

‡ He studied art at Cambridgeshire College of Arts and Technology (now Anglia Ruskin University) in 1962-4 and then Camberwell College of Arts (now part of the University of the Arts London) in 1964-6. The future Sex Pistols manager Malcolm McLaren attended Camberwell during 1968 and organised a student occupation in support of the demonstrations going on across the Western world.
§ Rob Chapman, *A Very Irregular Head: The Life of Syd Barrett*, p.63.
¶ A staple theme of Pop Art, as popularised by Jasper Johns and Andy Warhol in the early 1960s.
** Taken to its logical conclusion on albums like *Nursery Cryme* (1971) by Genesis.

onus was on new bands to find their own look, their favourite satin shirt, Gohill boots and all.

However, that was still in front of them. In February 1967, **MATILDA MOTHER** was recorded twice: first using a lyric taken from three poems from *Cautionary Tales for Children* by the Edwardian writer Hilaire Belloc, published in 1907. Barrett took a verse from each poem, introducing a new character in each: a boy named Jim, whose '*friends, they were very good to him*'; Henry King, whose '*chief defect*' was '*chewing little bits of string*'; and finally an unnamed character '*who summoned the immediate aid / of London's noble Fire Brigade*'. (This last verse is taken from 'Matilda, Who told lies, and was Burned to Death'.) All of Belloc's poems are in iambic tetrameter, so they all fit snugly into Barrett's lyric. But when permission to use Belloc's words was refused, another version was swiftly put together, Barrett writing a mostly new set of lyrics, changing the verses but keeping the refrains and bridge as they were.

Unusually for *Piper*, Barrett takes a back seat on the vocals, leaving the verses to Richard Wright and only harmonising on the refrains. Wright's singing is as English as Barrett's – no mid-Atlantic accents here – but less nasal and more emotive. Musically, **MATILDA MOTHER** conjures an otherworldly dreamscape, from its opening gently descending bassline and Barrett's elongated vowels, to the sparkling guitar arpeggios during the first verse to the deep-pile harmonies ('*Ohhh, mother*') and falsettos in the bridge, to the exotic strangeness of Wright's Farsifa organ as he takes a solo. There's also judicious amounts of echo and reverb from Norman Smith and engineer Peter Brown to make it sound unique and ethereal. The deeply insular and hallucinogenic combination of nursery-rhyme lyrics and shimmering fantastical music combine to make **MATILDA MOTHER** one of the key songs on the album, and the main track to squarely address the theme of childhood and imagination so prevalent throughout *Piper*.

The alternate version was first made available on the 40th anniversary special edition re-release of *Piper*. This may be down to its greater familiarity, but the second version is superior. This was partly down to a smart arrangement by Norman Smith: the original has a second bridge after the instrumental interlude, with a lyric concerning Matilda's pyromaniacal tendencies – it has a '*Nine-nine-nine!*' shrieked backing vocal (where the remake has '*Waiting!*'), which sounds dreadful to those unfamiliar with it. However, it's fascinating to hear how well the words fit – though Barrett's rewritten piece, with images of '*silver eyes*', '*thousand misty riders*', and '*doll's house, darkness, old perfume*', is remarkable. It's not merely that Barrett is singing about childhood: it feels like he has a direct path to the inchoate consciousness of a child and can take you there with him. This is artistry of the very highest order.

FLAMING (Barrett)
Length: 2.46
Vocals: Barrett **Guitars**: Barrett **Bass**: Waters **Farsifa organ**: Wright **Hammond organ**: Wright **Piano**: Wright **Lowrey organ**: Wright **Drums**: Mason **Finger cymbals**: Mason **Slide whistle**: Waters **Backing vocals**: Waters, Wright
Recorded: 16 March 1967, EMI Studios, London
Producer: Norman Smith
First released: 5 August 1967 (*The Piper at the Gates of Dawn* track 4)
Rating: 7/10

The found and imported sounds that colour Pink Floyd's discography to such great effect find further expression here, in Barrett's ode to both childhood hide-and-seek and (drug-stimulated) imagination. One of the most whimsical tracks on *Piper*, **FLAMING** brilliantly conveys the child's perspective both lyrically and musically, with Barrett's lyric both charmingly guileless and quite openly allusive, while the music uses diverse instrumentation like wind-up toys, slide whistles and a tack piano to effectively convey a dreamy, hallucinogenic innocence.

Opening with a dark cluster on the Lowrey organ augmented by some high-pitched vocalising, the song immediately goes into the first verse with its sing-song Farsifa organ and delicious feather-light bass from Waters. The double-tracked vocal from Barrett is front and centre, conveying a childlike delight at the world, or more precisely the world he has created in this song. His poeticisms and syllabics are wonderful, in phrases like '*Watching buttercups cup the light*' and '*Screaming through the starlit sky*'. After the fourth verse there's an instrumental break, introduced by the winking phrase '*Ever so high …*', at which point the wind-up toys reappear, drifting clouds of Wright's organ playing shimmer, Waters plays a repeated seven-note motif, Wright plays a solo on the tack piano, Barrett strums a twelve-string guitar and it all threatens to drift apart aimlessly – until Waters' bass reintroduces the first verse, this time playing with more urgency (with a more audible guitar from Barrett); after which it does indeed all drift off into the ether, as Barrett's voice elongates with echo and Mason's finger cymbals chiming the song to an end like a thumbs-up from some blissed-out benevolent minor deity.

Though the soundscape of **FLAMING** is highly effective in creating a whimsical soundworld, the song consists of only four verses, with the first repeated. With no middle eight or chorus, the song doesn't develop, and simply exists as its own charming little bubble. This sense of stasis might be a comment on the insularity and solipsism of the young child, or it might be that Barrett was satisfied with a unified ethereal creation. Whatever the reason, **FLAMING** is more of a soundworld than an effective song, thus relegating it behind **MATILDA**

MOTHER and **BIKE** as strong album tracks.* It's both enjoyable and effective, but Barrett's songcraft was remarkably already so much stronger in other songs on *Piper*.

Released as the a-side of a US-only single three months after *Piper* (with **THE GNOME** as the b-side), **FLAMING** was hardly the best song from the album,† and it failed to chart.‡ Yet the band seem to have had some affection for the song, with it staying in their live setlist until around November 1968, and Gilmour taking Barrett's vocal after his departure.§ Perhaps it was more of a spotlight for Wright, who plays some outstanding colourful organ and piano throughout. Although Barrett dominates the song, Wright's musicianship makes **FLAMING** what it is.

POW R. TOC H. (Barrett, Waters, Wright, Mason)
Length: 4.26
Vocals: Barrett **Guitars**: Barrett **Bass**: Waters **Farsifa organ**: Wright **Piano**: Wright
Drums: Mason **Percussion**: Mason **Backing vocals**: Waters, Wright
Recorded: 21 March 1967, EMI Studios, London
Producer: Norman Smith
First released: 5 August 1967 (*The Piper at the Gates of Dawn* track 5)
Rating: 6/10

Perhaps the least consequential song on *Piper*, **POW R. TOC H.** is descended from the atonal freakouts of Frank Zappa, its piano instrumental an echo of The Mothers of Invention's 'It Can't Happen Here' and the screeches at the end suggesting 'Help I'm A Rock'.¶ But rather than simply plagiarising, the group deftly make something of their own through plosive mouth sounds, gull-like squawks, Waters' patented scream, echoing guitar sounds, resounding drums by Mason, and a tea-room orchestra piano solo by Wright. Although the ingredients are unusual, it all hangs together probably through Barrett's sense pop-craft, or on Norman Smith's insistence – there's a sense of arc and trajectory, of opening and closure, which helps guide the listener even when the music feels at its most freeform. However, it is far from matching the synaesthetic majesty of **INTERSTELLAR OVERDRIVE**, feeling far more arbitrary, more of a thrown-together jam than its fellow instrumental. Randomness was in the cultural mix

---

* **ASTRONOMY DOMINE** and **INTERSTELLAR OVERDRIVE** being the obvious stand-outs.
† Surely **ASTRONOMY DOMINE** would have been the best choice on that criterion. **INTERSTELLAR OVERDRIVE** might well be the best song on the album, but at nearly ten minutes long, releasing it as a single would have sent teenagers and radio DJs screaming. (Queen's 'Bohemian Rhapsody', which eight years later was noted for its radio-unfriendly length, is under six minutes).
‡ It was chosen instead of **APPLES AND ORANGES**, which was released in the UK 16 days later, on 18 November 1967, and similarly failed to chart. While that song was clearly inferior to **SEE EMILY PLAY**, it at least would have made chronological sense as a single release, but US record labels tended to treat their customers as suckers.
§ There is footage of the band performing it for French TV on 20 February 1968 on the *Early Years* box set, Gilmour gamely singing Barrett's words and trying not to look embarrassed. Gilmour was never a silk cravat kind of guy.
¶ Both from *Freak Out!*, released in July 1966.

by the mid-1960s** – Ornette Coleman's *Free Jazz* was released in 1961, allowing each member of a double quartet to improvise against the current soloist, while avant-garde composers like Stockhausen introduced aleatory techniques into classical music in an effort to deconstruct†† the underpinnings of the canon. Free jazz and avant-garde classical music however were far more niche, elite music forms, whereas rock music is inherently populist; and marrying structure and randomness into cohesive, marketable four-minute chunks was beyond even Pink Floyd. Like **ASTRONOMY DOMINE** and **FLAMING**, **POW R. TOC H.** shows the band from the outset ready to go far beyond the manual in the search for the sounds to create something new in music – but although it's interesting enough while playing, it doesn't quite add up to anything.‡‡

TAKE UP THY STETHOSCOPE AND WALK (Waters)
Length: 3.05
Vocals: Barrett **Guitars**: Barrett **Bass**: Waters **Farsifa organ**: Wright **Piano**: Wright
Drums: Mason **Timpani**: Mason **Backing vocals**: Waters, Wright
Recorded: 20 March 1967, EMI Studios, London
Producer: Norman Smith
First released: 5 August 1967 (*The Piper at the Gates of Dawn* track 6)
Rating: 6/10

Roger Waters might well be the finest post-war English songwriter after John Lennon,§§ but it took time for his talents to mature. The first recorded track solely written by him is at best embryonic. It does have numerous interesting points: an arresting staccato drum opening, unusual vocal scatting ('*Doctor doctor!*' sung breathily, in the exact manner of **POW R. TOC H.**), a lengthy jammed instrumental section and a lyric concerning a physician, harking all the way to **COMFORTABLY NUMB** – though with none of that track's poetic feeling or verbal ability. None of its components really gel, leaving **TAKE UP THY STETHOSCOPE AND WALK** feeling lumpy and underdeveloped, especially in comparison to the remarkable union of vision and method which Barrett's tracks demonstrate. It's energetic and rather fun, however, and the lyric concerns life and its painful realities (in this case, being bedridden with a cold or the flu), which Waters would make his own as time went by. Here, though, it's little more

---

** In literature there were the contemporaneous cut-ups of William S Burroughs and Brion Gysin.
†† Jacques Derrida's 'Structure, Sign And Play' essay was first given as a lecture in 1966, inaugurating the deconstruction and post-structuralism movements in philosophy and literary studies.
‡‡ The same is true of the title, which has intrigued fans for decades. '**POW R. TOC H.** – what the hell's that about then?' 'It's about nothing, Guy – absolutely nothing ... Why it's called POW R. TOC H.? I have absolutely no idea.' (Rick Wright interviewed by Guy Pratt on Planet Rock, 27 August 2007). The customary suggestion is that it has to do with the army signal's code for Talbot House, a club where soldiers and officers could socialise as equals, but even if that it true, it has absolutely no bearing on the song.
§§ A claim he made himself, in 1992. 'Earlier in this conversation, Waters "pointed out" that he was one of the five best writers of music since the War. So who could possibly rank above him, I wonder? With furrowed brow he ponders the question. "John Lennon," he says. "I'm trying to think," he says. "Er, I can't think of anybody else."' (*Q* magazine, November 1992).

than an acknowledgement that being ill is unpleasant – though the terse three-syllable lines ('*I'm in bed! Aching head! Gold is lead! Choke on bread! Underfed!*') are quite the contrast from Barrett's more florid poeticisms.

TAKE UP THY STETHOSCOPE AND WALK is at least played with considerable vigour. By far the most interesting section is the instrumental break with Barrett yelping enthusiastically and Wright matching him with a highly excited polytonal accompaniment, and Waters' bass also played unusually prominently for the time. The free-jazz stylings effectively suggest the delirium of the patient in bed awaiting healing from the doctor.* The call-and-response style of the verse also hark back to jazz, which often features these *phon-antiphon* structures between the bandleader and backing group. The ending builds up superbly to a musical peak, with the three-times-and-you're-out repetition of '*Realise!*' – though there's no corresponding climax from the lyrics, which just about manage to maintain the rhyme scheme but little more ('*Doctor, kindly tell your wife / That I'm alive / Flowers thrive / Realise*'). But while there's considerable enthusiasm in the performance, the elements do not form a coherent whole. Waters – an extremely tenacious man – would work hard to make amends.

INTERSTELLAR OVERDRIVE (Barrett, Waters, Wright, Mason)
Length: 9.43
Guitars: Barrett **Bass**: Waters **Organ**: Wright **Drums**: Mason **Drum roll**: Norman Smith
Recorded: 16 March, 5, 27 June 1967, EMI Studios, London
Producer: Norman Smith
First released: 5 August 1967 (*The Piper at the Gates of Dawn* track 7)
Rating: 10/10

The centrepiece of *The Piper at the Gates of Dawn*, **INTERSTELLAR OVERDRIVE** is a stunning evocation of the dynamics of outer space, of drifting galaxies and colliding nebulae, cycling from big bang to emptiness and back again. The introductory/closing riff is based on Heart's cover of 'My Little Red Book', which manager Peter Jenner whistled tunelessly to Barrett. Mangled into a simple-to-play theme, and played aggressively by Barrett, it is immediately arresting, and when doubled by Waters' bass, both instantly memorable and muscularly powerful. Though early Pink Floyd could be fey and mannered – a trait that would continue until *Meddle*, in tracks such as **GREEN IS THE COLOUR** and **A PILLOW OF WINDS** – here they show substantial force generating the initial kinetic energy the track spends most of its time unravelling. The track immediately expands to become a freeform exploration of effects suggestive of outer space, with huge amounts of echo, reverb and effects magnificently heightening the atmosphere. (Producer Norman Smith was concurrently engineering *Sgt. Pepper*, for which he won a Grammy.)

---

* Hence the title, which comes from John 5:8 – 'Jesus saith unto him, Rise, take up thy bed, and walk' (in the King James bible).

As all four members spontaneously jam with each other, intermeshing wonderfully, the tempo gradually winds down, giving the impression of drifting galaxies and cooling primordial energies. It's not, of course, just random freeform spontaneity: each musician plays several recurring figures, such as Barrett's recurring 'ping' from 2.20 and Waters' three-note bass motif from 4.43. Eventually (around 6.05), Wright's detached organ-playing (with longer, sustained notes) gives the impression of drifting off into almost empty space, as the bass and guitar settle down into quiet notes rather than brash chords, and Mason moves from the snare and bass drum to shivering around the cymbals. Once it has settled down at 6.58, almost imperceptibly, the tension starts to rise once more. It builds and builds, until the dam bursts with a drum roll,[†] after which the main riff returns, this time disorientated with fierce stereo panning (and a distinctively high run up the fretboard by Waters), and then collapses into itself with huge echo, like a dying star – suggesting the whole thing might repeat again. (Waters would remember this trick.)[‡]

The freeform freak-outs of live 1967 Pink Floyd were key to their early success. The abstract content and unstructured arrangements were memorably described by Waters as:

> totally anarchistic, cooperative anarchy. A complete realisation of aims of psychedelia. If you take LSD, what you experience depends entirely on whom you are. Our music may give you the screaming horrors or throw you into screaming ecstasy. Mostly the latter. We find our audiences stop dancing, standing there totally grooved with mouths open.[§]

This perfectly suited the tripping audience at UFO. As with freeform jazz performed by, say, John Coltrane and Ornette Coleman,[¶] the music appeared released from the confines of normal melody and rhythm to become a sonic wash, waves of pure energy randomly colliding, cohering and falling apart. Combined with an equally innovative light show, which used paint on slides to create random oscillating brightly coloured projections, the live performances were seen as heralding a new wave of British music. EMI's press release on the signing of Pink Floyd boldly stated that the group were 'musical spokesmen for a new movement which involves experimentation in all the arts'. (This implied the synaesthetic effects of psychedelic music.)

The sole representative of their 1966–67 live performances on *Piper*, **INTERSTELLAR OVERDRIVE** uses the sonic imagery of space travel to imply inner exploration. (To 'take a trip', gettit?) LSD associations permeated the early Floyd, sometimes deliberately (as with this song), sometimes

---

[†] Played by Smith. Mason never could do a drum roll.
[‡] See **OUTSIDE THE WALL**.
[§] Hunter Davies, 'Interview with Andrew King and Roger Waters', *Sunday Times*, 30 October 1966.
[¶] In albums like Coleman's *Free Jazz* (1961) and Coltrane's *Ascension* (1966).

unintentionally (*Piper* takes its name from the seventh chapter of *The Wind in the Willows*), and sometimes tragically (through the mental collapse of Syd Barrett). Yet the remaining members of Pink Floyd, while partial to marijuana,[*] were deeply ambivalent about the whole UFO/International Times/Chelsea drug scenes that absorbed the Rolling Stones and the Beatles. Too cynical (or wise) for glib hipness and belief in instant enlightenment, they never assimilated fully into the scene, maintaining a certain crucial distance. Barrett, on the other hand, with his childlike openness, was drawn helplessly into the darker aspects of the drug culture. While Pink Floyd's association with the UFO scene lingered on for several years,[†] by 1968 they had outgrown it. (By that time, too, the social elite had reacted against the Cavalier fripperies of that time anyway, with Roundhead severity becoming fashionable, as exemplified by John Lennon's proletarian denim and heavy blues in the Rolling Stones' *Rock and Roll Circus* film of December '68.)[‡] Their cynical feelings about the scene and distance from it (see **PAINTBOX**) were on the whole wise. In retrospect, that space was crucial in letting them grow and develop.

THE GNOME (Barrett)
Length: 2.13
Vocals: Barrett **Guitars**: Barrett **Bass**: Waters **Celesta**: Wright **Vibraphone**: Wright
Percussion: Mason **Backing vocals**: Waters
Recorded: 20 March 1967, EMI Studios, London
Producer: Norman Smith
First released: 5 August 1967 (*The Piper at the Gates of Dawn* track 8)
Rating: 7/10

THE GNOME is the most whimsical of all the tracks on *Piper*, with its singsong melody and eponymous character[§] straight from L. Frank Baum, Grimm's *Fairy Tales*, or indeed *The Flower Pot Men*, rather than J.R.R. Tolkien.[¶] Coming straight after the intensity of **INTERSTELLAR OVERDRIVE**, its acoustic joviality, clip-clop rhythm (played on a Chinese temple block by Mason) and charming nursery rhyme accompaniment by Wright lightens the atmosphere with its very suburban English folksiness. But where folk music has been traditionally concerned with social realism or the national tradition, Barrett's spin is

---

[*] Engineer John said that Pink Floyd's recording sessions had no record company contact whatsoever, except when their label manager would show up now and again with a couple of bottles of wine and a couple of joints. John Harris, *The Dark Side of the Moon*, p.71.
[†] They were still being asked about it in the *Live At Pompeii* film in 1972. Mason simply says 'We're doing something different now'.
[‡] Lennon's working-class garb was influenced by the revolts of 1968. The Stones likewise went back to Delta blues for *Beggar's Banquet*, released that same December.
[§] Gnomes were first popularized in Romantic literature, particularly Alexander Pope in his *The Rape Of The Lock* (1712):
> The graver Prude sinks downward to a Gnome,
> In search of Mischief still on Earth to roam.
[¶] Tolkien originally called his elves 'gnomes' but changed this in later drafts, though Barrett would not of course have known this.

both imaginative and modern, expanding both the vocabulary and emotional range of rock music. (Whimsy having been more the province of music-hall comedians like Ken Dodd or writers like Lewis Carroll rather than rock 'n' roll, although The Kinks, perhaps the third most popular band in the UK after The Beatles and the Stones, had reintroduced music-hall humour and musical stylings into the British pop lexicon with 'Sunny Afternoon' in June 1966.)

Barrett's vocal is double-tracked and close-miked, giving it a surprising intensity and allowing him to audibly relish the childlike rhymes (*'A blue-green hood / It looked quite good'*). The lyric is no more than a character sketch, introducing the gnome (*'Grimble Grumble'*) eating and sleeping, with his scarlet tunic, big adventure and fresh air. Musically it's the simplest track on *Piper*, mostly consisting of just a strummed acoustic guitar, the pulse of Waters' bass and some clip-clopping percussion by Mason, with some delicate celesta by Wright on the choruses. It's all childlike, playful and whimsical, sounding both entirely natural while being artfully arranged. Yet somehow a skein of unease slips in during the last line of the chorus, as Barrett stretches out *'Oooooh my …'* and adds a shiver of disquiet. There's something not quite as homely and welcoming about the gnome as the rest of the song suggests. As with **SCARECROW**, **THE GNOME** suggests Barrett intuitively understood that such bright gaiety could cast dark shadows, and that fairy tales – from Hansel and Gretel to Bluebeard to Bambi – need a sense of discomfort if not active danger.

CHAPTER 24 (Barrett)
Length: 3.42
Vocals: Barrett **Guitars**: Barrett **Bass**: Waters **Farsifa organ**: Wright **Hohner pianet**: Wright **Cello**: Wright **Harmonium**: Wright **Percussion**: Mason **Gong**: Waters **Backing vocals**: Waters
Recorded: 27 February, 15 March 1967, EMI Studios, London
Producer: Norman Smith
First released: 5 August 1967 (*The Piper at the Gates of Dawn* track 9)
Rating: 7/10

CHAPTER 24 is the most otherworldly track on *Piper*,** an attempt to convey the inscrutable celestial wisdom of the Eastern philosophical tradition. Based, of course, on Chapter 24 of the Chinese *I Ching* ('Book of Changes'),†† the track is unusually stately for Barrett, its limited melody moving ponderously

---

** **INTERSTELLAR OVERDRIVE**, although of course a space exploration, is based on a guitar riff. **CHAPTER 24** is deliberately non-Western in its instrumentation.
†† The first and most significant of the foundational Confucian texts upon which China's imperial examinations were based for nearly two thousand years, the *I Ching* dates back in its current form to around BCE 900, during the Zhou Dynasty. It combines both divination and cosmological texts. The divination was done by scattering bundles of yarrow stalks so as to produce six random numbers, which then corresponded to one of 64 hexagrams. This sounds complicated, but it made understanding the future as easy as scattering sticks and reading a suitably exotic text, which must have delighted the hippy crowd.

and signposted by rather hammy gongs and cymbals. As a song construction, **CHAPTER 24** is a skilful transfer of the ideas and style of the *I Ching* into a rock song,* though less of a direct quotation than an atmospheric summarising,† utilising high-flown, enigmatic but ultimately meaningless phraseology. Barrett deftly corrals his cribbings into two verses (the first being repeated at the end, to give the sense of recurrence) with a repeated refrain – '*Change returns success / Going and coming without error / Action brings good fortune / Sunset … sunrise …*' – at the end of each. Pitched rather high, Barrett's vocal crosses the stereo spectrum, and is deliciously harmonised by Wright during the final line of the refrain. Meanwhile the track begins with Wright's Farsifa organ predominating (though Waters gives it plenty on the gong), then being enriched by a tumbling countermelody. The refrain follows the same style until the '*Sunset … sunrise …*' line, which opens up a dazzling starburst of vocal harmony, being repeated with added echo, as the song fades out rather limply.

This isn't the place to excavate the renewed interest in Eastern philosophy and religion in the 1960s counterculture, but the *I Ching* was obviously in the air, with Bob Dylan lauding its poetry during an interview in 1965 and Allen Ginsberg writing a poem called 'Consulting I Ching Smoking Pot Listening to the Fugs Sing Blake'‡ in 1966. Other modern Western adherents include John Cage, Jorge Luis Borges, Hermann Hesse and Philip K. Dick, and use of it appears in a scene in *Easy Rider* (1969). There is evidently something in the *I Ching* for everyone.

However, as a track, **CHAPTER 24** now feels the most dated from *Piper*. Its high-pitched gongs, vocal and organs make it feel rarefied almost to the point of non-being, a feeling amplified by the studied obscurity of the lyrics ('*The seven is the number of the young light / It forms when darkness is increased by one*'). There's almost nothing earthy or human here,§ which ultimately makes **CHAPTER 24**

---

* John Lennon did something very similar on 'Being For The Benefit Of Mr. Kite!', also recorded during February and March 1967 in Abbey Road Studios, although he took his words from a circus poster rather than a religious text. Both create innovative soundworlds to match their source texts, although the Lennon song has far more direct quotation.

† Chapter 24 of the James Legge translation of 1899, on the character *Fû*, is more bald than you might expect:
Fû indicates that there will be free course and progress (in what it denotes). (The subject of it) finds no one to distress him in his exits and entrances; friends come to him, and no error is committed. He will return and repeat his (proper) course. In seven days comes his return. There will be advantage in whatever direction movement is made.
  1. The first line, undivided, shows its subject returning (from an error) of no great extent, which would not proceed to anything requiring repentance. There will be great good fortune.
  2. The second line, divided, shows the admirable return (of its subject). There will be good fortune.
  3. The third line, divided, shows one who has made repeated returns. The position is perilous, but there will be no error.
  4. The fourth line, divided, shows its subject moving right in the centre (among those represented by the other divided lines), and yet returning alone (to his proper path).
  5. The fifth line, divided, shows the noble return of its subject. There will be no ground for repentance.
  6. The topmost line, divided, shows its subject all astray on the subject of returning. There will be evil. There will be calamities and errors. If with his views he put the hosts in motion, the end will be a great defeat, whose issues will extend to the ruler of the state. Even in ten years he will not be able to repair the disaster.

‡ Published as a pamphlet by Kriya Press in 1967.
§ Beyond a few end-of-line fills from Waters.

feels more like a genre exercise than a track concerning genuine religious feeling or philosophical ideas. Maybe you just had to be there, man.

> **BIKE** (Barrett)
> **Length**: 3.21
> **Vocals**: Barrett **Guitars**: Barrett **Bass**: Waters **Harmonium**: Wright **Celesta**: Wright **Violin**: Wright **Piano**: Wright **Drums**: Mason **Percussion**: Mason **Gong**: Waters **Backing vocals**: Waters
> **Recorded**: 21 May, 5 June 1967, EMI Studios, London
> **Producer**: Norman Smith
> **First released**: 5 August 1967 (*The Piper at the Gates of Dawn* track 11)
> **Rating**: 7/10

The playful whimsy of **THE GNOME** and **SCARECROW** turn here into a plea for understanding and acceptance. It all starts off as tremendous fun, with a rollicking riff and the lyrics not quite matching up to the music, their tumbling rhymes creating a sense of disorder, even as they somehow cohere to end bathetically: '*I've got a bike / You can ride it if you like / It's got a basket / A bell that rings / And things to make it look good / I'd give it to you if I could / But I borrowed it.*' It's a form of talking blues, but very far from Bob Dylan, never mind Woody Guthrie or Pete Seeger, with Wright just about managing to track Barrett's sort-of melody on the harmonium (and playing increasing amounts of tack piano on each verse, lest they become overfamiliar).

But the true note of the song, and the first appearance of distance and absence in the Pink Floyd canon, is the softly sung chorus, the music fading away: '*You're the kind of girl that fits in with my world / I'll give you anything / Everything if you want things.*' Suddenly the game isn't so fun any more: the chaos and nonsense of the preceding verses may have been fun, but they cut you off from humanity, and it's cold, and Syd would like to come inside.¶ With each verse directly followed by a chorus, the sense of bifurcation is clear. This is further gestured by the song's instrumental coda, which begins just over halfway through (at 1.50), sounding like a toybox bursting open just as the proper song's final chord fades out. It contains a bizarre melange of chimes, winding clocks or toys, recordings of the band laughing sped up to sound like seagulls,·· Wright on violin, and various other tape effects. As such it's probably the first example of an album-closing 'hidden track',†† though it obviously is a visible part of *Piper*, and in its chaos and madcap humour does, perhaps, suggest something of schizophrenia. (Although, this is probably reading too much into **BIKE**, which more likely was simply tapping into the Sixties' enthusiasm for 'random' as a method of countering traditional forms, structures and ideas.)

¶   This feeling is often heard on Barrett's solo releases, which flicker between sense and disorder.
·· A technique first used in The Beatles' 'Tomorrow Never Knows' (1966).
†† As seen from bands from Public Enemy to Nirvana, The Stones Roses and many many others.

BIKE was, perhaps rather oddly, chosen for the *Echoes* compilation album, where it has been given the ring of an old-school bicycle's bell at the very start, and has been the final encore for Mason's Saucerful of Secrets touring band during 2022. Unusually for *Piper*, it's a song that's more about the lyrics than the music, up until the coda, at which point it becomes about something other than music. As such, it's a startling conclusion to an astonishing album, but its move towards desiring acceptance rather than flamboyant otherness makes it rather bittersweet, unlike the rest of *Piper* – though perhaps indicative of how Barrett's life would turn out.

The Piper at the Gates of Dawn is a stunning debut, causing Barrett's shadow to hang over the group for years to come. It is unusual for a first album to have both an entirely formed aesthetic and the musical technique to implement it, but *Piper*'s recurring childhood themes, whimsy, and occasional tinges of unease and creeping darkness, made it an entirely new voice in rock music. It is far more pop-oriented than other Pink Floyd albums, with mostly simple verse-chorus-verse compositions and few extended musical excursions (**INTERSTELLAR OVERDRIVE** excepted, of course). Yet it is also bursting with musical invention. Much of the credit for this must go to Wright, who clocks up far more instrumental credits than his bandmates, from the Farsifa, flute and celesta to the violin, vibraphone and cello. Without his remarkable versatility, *Piper* would have been more monochromatic, far less of a technicolour dream. Similar credit must go to producer Norman Smith for facilitating such inventiveness and imagination, particularly for a band making its first album. Many of the releases from 1967 now sound dated to modern ears,[*] but *Piper* very rarely does,[†] which speaks a great deal about Smith's ability to translate ideas into soundworlds. The work on **INTERSTELLAR OVERDRIVE** in particular is astounding. Live versions and demos, such as on *Tonite Let's All Make Love in London*, come nowhere near to realising the uniquely visual otherworldly synaesthesia that the recorded version does.

But, of course, the greatest credit goes to Barrett, whose songwriting is both incredibly imaginative and remarkably professional – focusing entirely on the English whimsy of his writing, rather than the Swinging London glimpsed at in **CANDY AND A CURRANT BUN** and **APPLES AND ORANGES**, or indeed the R&B of their earliest work. This makes *Piper* a highly coherent and consistent work, with a sense of vision that's extraordinary for a first album. And it all sounds so easy and trouble-free – yet producing it, and having to promote it, seem to have crushed Barrett. His voice and vision remain uniquely enthralling, and the most tragic loss in British rock music.[‡]

---

[*] For example, *The Who Sell Out* and the Rolling Stones' *Between The Buttons*.
[†] Though **CHAPTER 24** and **POW R. TOC H.** do sound rather of-their-time now.
[‡] Alongside Ian Curtis of Joy Division.

APPLES AND ORANGES (Barrett)
Length: 3.08
Vocals: Barrett **Guitars**: Barrett **Bass**: Waters **Hammond organ**: Wright **Piano**: Wright
Electric piano: Wright **Drums**: Mason **Tambourine**: Mason **Backing vocals**: Waters, Wright
Recorded: 26/27 October 1967, De Lane Lea Studios, London
Producer: Norman Smith
First released: 18 November 1967 (UK a/side single)
Rating: 4/10

The legend of Syd Barrett gets rather exposed here on the group's third single. Although Waters later attributed the song's failure to its production,[§] which somehow amounted to just two sessions (suggesting either mismanagement, panic, or both),[¶] **APPLES AND ORANGES** is an almost entirely unsuccessful attempt at a single. The sole redeeming feature is the lyric, which features some agreeable wordplay ('*Got a flip-top pack of cigarettes in her pocket / Feeling good at the top / Shopping in sharp shoes*') and is another vignette of a fashionable, sexually charged London (following **CANDY AND A CURRANT BUN**). However, musically it's all over the place, with disjointed rhythms in the verse giving way to a childishly singalong chorus, a pointlessly extended middle section (with ethereal voices repeating the chorus, rather than coming up with an instrumental passage or solo), and ends on a squall of feedback. The production, true, is poor, with the guitar sound repeatedly obscuring Barrett's verse vocal. However, the British public opinion which pushed **SEE EMILY PLAY** to #4 and *The Piper at the Gates of Dawn* to #6 rightly saw little of merit in this song, which failed to chart. The group, with Barrett now visibly declining, were now haunted by the spectre of a short-lived career.

PAINT BOX (Wright)
Length: 3.33
Vocals: Wright **Guitars**: Barrett **Bass**: Waters **Piano**: Wright **Drums**: Mason **Backing vocals**: Waters, Barrett
Recorded: 1 November 1967, De Lane Lea Studios, London
Producer: Norman Smith
First released: 18 November 1967 (UK b/side single)
Rating: 6/10

Just five months after being the darlings of the UFO crowd and the Chelsea demi-monde, **PAINTBOX** reveals an exasperation with the beautiful young

---

[§] '"Apples and Oranges" was a very good song … In spite of mistakes and the production I don't think it was bad. "Apples and Oranges" was destroyed by the production. It's a fucking good song', *Zigzag* magazine, issue 32, 1973.

[¶] Manager Peter Jenner later said, 'If you didn't have a chart record your live money wouldn't go up, and live money was what we all lived on. The records were something that you used to help sell your live gigs.' *Uncut* magazine, 14 March 2017.

things ('*Last night I had too much to drink / Sitting in a club with so many fools / Playing to rules / Trying to impress but feeling rather empty*') and, by extension, a nascent insularity that would come to define mid-period Pink Floyd.*

Wisely omitting specific details lyrically to focus on antisocial dislike (or, perhaps, hungover remembrance) of chatting, drinking and meeting the opposite sex, musically **PAINTBOX** contrasts a minor melancholy atmosphere in the verse and a slight reprieve in the chorus. Without a memorable melody in either, however, **PAINTBOX** only succeeds as a mood piece rather than as an effective song. Stopping and starting each verse with loud strums on the acoustic guitar and chatter on the rims from Mason to indicate ambivalence and uncertainty, the track does effectively convey an atmosphere of weary ennui. Wright's wry attitude is an expansion of the band's emotional palette, which so far had been largely noon-bright and dazzlingly effervescent. It also marks the first lyrical use of the motif of absence ('*I open the door to an empty room / Then I forget*') that would eventually come to dominate the group's output. The effective creation of atmosphere does not necessarily make a song appealing, however, and **PAINTBOX**, though a reasonable effort for Wright's first attempt at songwriting† for the group,‡ and a better track than **APPLES AND ORANGES** (if not a better choice as single), ultimately fails to sustain the listener's interest or sympathies.

IT WOULD BE SO NICE (Wright)
Length: 3.47
Vocals: Wright **Guitars**: Gilmour **Bass**: Waters **Piano**: Wright **Mellotron**: Wright **Farsifa organ**: Wright **Recorder**: Wright **Drums**: Mason **Backing vocals**: Waters, Gilmour
Recorded: 12/13 January 1968, EMI Studios, London
Producer: Norman Smith
First released: 12 April 1968 (UK a/side single)
Rating: 3/10

A facile piece of whimsy, Wright's **IT WOULD BE SO NICE** is his second song for Pink Floyd and first a-side, after Barrett's ejection from the group in February 1968 following his spiralling mental collapse. The tales of Barrett's mental health are many and probably largely apocryphal,§ though it's worth noting that the four remaining members themselves do not agree on the cause of Barrett's

---

* By contrast the Rolling Stones and The Beatles rather relished conquering London society. Lennon later described the mid-60s period as being like 'kings of the jungle' (Jann Wenner, *Lennon Remembers*, p.65).
† There was a suggestion that Wright and Barrett might be taken on as a pair when the band split from their management. Wright said he would have leaped at it, but Barrett was already too unreliable. Wright's early tracks made him the *de facto* frontman during 1968, but his performances on TV recordings at this time clearly demonstrate his discomfort in this role.
‡ Wright had previously sold a song titled 'You're The Reason Why' to the Liverpudlian vocal trio Adam, Mike & Tim, when a student at the Royal College of Music.
§ Interested readers should seek out *Syd Barrett: A Very Irregular Head* by Rob Chapman for the fullest telling of Barrett's life story. The famous Mandrax and hair cream story isn't corroborated by anyone who was there.

mental illness. Wright thinks it was primarily down to LSD,¶ whereas Gilmour has suggested Barrett's psychological issues were more innate.** Regardless of the causes, a bright light had been extinguished, and after famously declining to pick up Barrett when on the way to a gig in Southampton on 26 January 1968, the group were now without their singer, composer and star.††

This left Gilmour, Mason, Waters and Wright to take over from Barrett – or try to, for their efforts to ape him were deeply unconvincing. Nor was there much belief in their abilities, with their management team of Peter Jenner and Andrew King dumping them to continue with Barrett. In place they hired Steve O'Rourke, who had started out selling pet food, subsequently worked at the Bryan Morrison Agency (which looked after contemporaries like The Incredible String Band, Tyrannosaurus Rex and Fairport Convention) and who would manage the band until his death in 2003, although Waters dispensed with his services in 1985.‡‡

IT WOULD BE SO NICE is hence the first of two efforts to write a Barrett-esque single, both of which are unusual as the very few total failures in the Pink Floyd catalogue.§§ (Notably, neither was on the *Relics* early years compilation of 1971, although **CANDY AND A CURRANT BUN** was also absent, meaning while it was somewhat better it became something of an undeserved legend.) It seems strange that the group were still striving for Top 40 success through short jaunty singles, but it must be remembered that album bands didn't really exist before Pink Floyd.¶¶ Singles were what groups did, and the Top 40 was the barometer of the nation's music taste.*** So Wright strived to write something catchy, with music-hall verses and a more forceful, riff-driven chorus. However, neither is memorable, and the urgency on the latter choruses suggest desperation rather than energy. Pop music might look easily compared to classical, jazz or even rock music, but emotion in pop is everything,††† and if it is even slightly contrived the entire song feels laboured or artificial. (Hence why pop is almost

---

¶ 'He had done so much damage, because that's it, that's what it does to you. Too much acid would literally fry your brains.' Wright interview with John Edginton, 2001.

** 'There must be people who are susceptible to this sort of permanent, or if not permanent, then fairly permanent sort of change to their psyche and to the damage that causes them. And I think Syd, must have been one of those.' Gilmour interview with John Edginton, 2001.

†† It was initially suggested that Barrett could become their stay-at-home composer, but on 6 April 1968 it was officially announced that he had left the group.

‡‡ When O'Rourke got into in arguments with Waters, the latter would dismiss his manager's views by saying, 'What do you know? You're only a pet-food salesman!' (Steve O'Rourke obituary, *Daily Telegraph*, 5 November 2003).

§§ **SEAMUS** has often been voted the worst song, but my own candidates are **THE GRAND VIZIER'S GARDEN PARTY** (all three parts) and **SISYPHUS**.

¶¶ And Led Zeppelin, who didn't bother releasing singles at all – not even 'Stairway To Heaven', when it was the most-played song on 70s radio. The idea of a band turning down an easy couple of million pounds for zero work on the basis of artistic integrity nowadays seems almost fantastical.

*** Those days are long gone, but I recall as maybe an 11-year-old listening with my family to the BBC Radio 1 Top 40 countdown every Sunday and keenly discussing the risers and fallers. The music charts were a key part of British popular culture from the mid-1960s until the late-1990s, at which point record company amalgamation gave the industry a renewed stranglehold on a cultural sector that had been relatively vibrant and democratic since The Beatles. It's now amazing to consider radical singles like 'The Model' by Kraftwerk, 'Relax' by Frankie Goes To Hollywood and 'Stay' by Shakespears Sister hitting #1.

††† Compare, for example, Nirvana's 'Smells Like Teen Spirit' and Boston's 'More Than A Feeling', which share chords in their respective choruses yet could not be more different.

always by young people.) **IT WOULD BE SO NICE** is entirely contrived, and never escapes the feeling of being a shoddy jerrymandered construction.

Mason later said: 'At that period we had no direction. We were being hustled about to make hit singles. There's so many people saying it's important, you start to think it is important.'* Fortunately, the group's stubbornness and sense of its own abilities gradually came to the fore, and dismal efforts like this were left behind forever after. It would be their last UK single until **ANOTHER BRICK IN THE WALL PART 2**, eleven years later.† Perhaps the most notable aspect of the song is that they were forced to change the reference to the *Evening Standard* newspaper to 'the *Daily Standard*' – brand names being forbidden on the BBC‡ – but that being the case reinforces the flimsiness of the song. And so ended Wright's very brief opportunity to be the frontman of Pink Floyd.

> **JULIA DREAM** (Waters)
> **Length**: 2.37
> **Vocals**: Wright **Guitars**: Gilmour **Bass**: Waters **Hammond organ**: Wright **Mellotron**: Wright **Percussion**: Mason **Backing vocals**: Waters, Gilmour
> **Recorded**: 12/13 January 1968, EMI Studios, London
> **Producer**: Norman Smith
> **First released**: 12 April 1968 (UK b/side single)
> **Rating**: 6/10

Waters' second individual song is an interesting change of pace for him: his first attempt at a ballad. Sung in a mannered near-falsetto by Gilmour in his first vocal for the group, the track has some nice countermelody by Wright on what sounds like a flute but is actually a mellotron (Lindy Mason was perhaps otherwise engaged).§ There's also no drumming from Mason, who instead plays some woodblocks in the later portion of the track.

The lyric is an early, and rather bold, attempt at an existential examination of sleep, dreams and nightmares. However, the chorus ('*Julia dream / Dreamboat queen / Queen of all my dreams*') might be intended to be circular, with the last word of each phrase starting the next one, but 'dreamboat queen' is an unusually clumsy phrase for Waters. The verses however are nicely suffused with rich imagery and self-questioning, from '*Will she let the weeping willow / Wind his branches around?*' in the first, to '*Will the following footsteps catch me?*' in the third. (The next line, '*Am I really dying?*' would be reused in the re-recorded version of **MOTHER** on *Pink Floyd: The Wall*.) The '*scaly armadillo*' in the second verse, however, is rather overwrought as an image of night fright and fear. Waters was clearly keen to both address psychological issues and to use judicious

---

*   Interview with *Zigzag* magazine, issue 32, 1973.
†   Though their record label kept releasing singles in the USA, none were successful until **MONEY**.
‡   Those were the days of 'sticky-backed plastic' (i.e. Sellotape) on *Blue Peter*.
§   See **THE GRAND VIZIER'S GARDEN PARTY**.

images from the very start, and while **JULIA DREAM** lyrically has an occasional clumsiness, it is evidence of his significant ambitions.

The structure is a simple verse-chorus-verse arrangement, though from the second verse echoing woodblocks (perhaps suggesting an ominous visitor at the door) and electronic sounds start to suffuse the guitar and vocal, as though going from waking to nightmares or from order to chaos. This gives **JULIA DREAM** a greater resonance than its slight melody deserves, and shows how smartly Waters could evoke meaning and poetic connotations through the use of sound rather than through the music itself. This keenness to use outside sounds to freight a song with greater meaning would come to be a hallmark of Pink Floyd. The track then fades out on some pointless electronic sounds from Gilmour on the slide guitar, which might have sounded hip in 1968 but nowadays suggest Waters' then-pervasive inability to come up with a satisfying conclusion.¶

LET THERE BE MORE LIGHT (Waters)
Length: 5.38
Vocals: Gilmour, Wright **Guitars**: Gilmour **Bass**: Waters **Piano**: Wright **Farsifa organ**: Wright **Hammond organ**: Wright **Drums**: Mason **Percussion**: Mason **Backing vocals**: Waters
Recorded: 18 January 1968, EMI Studios, London
Producer: Norman Smith
First released: 29 June 1968 (*A Saucerful of Secrets* track 1)
Rating: 8/10

Released just two months after Waters' tepid **JULIA DREAM**,** here is evidence of the enormous progress he would make as a songwriter. Opening on an arresting and energetic bass figure, the track builds momentum, adding cymbals, multiple organs (which gradually fill the audio spectrum), drums and then guitars in an opening minute of deliciously rising tension.†† From there, via the sizzle of a gong, the sly staccato rhythm emerges ('*Far … Far … Fa-ar … Away-Way*') for just five lines, with some nice melismatic embellishment ('*Something will be doh-eh-oh-eh-un*'), sung in harmony by Waters and Wright in an unusual pairing. From there it explodes onto an incredibly rousing chorus sung by Gilmour, sounding remarkably like Barrett but with far more force and authority. For the first time, Pink Floyd *rock*. There had been nothing of this power or drama on *The Piper at the Gates of Dawn*.

While musically a definite step forward, today **LET THERE BE MORE LIGHT** is most notable lyrically. The sci-fi references and fantastical nature are a first and last for Pink Floyd, telling the tale of some extraterrestrial ship

---

¶ Which is rather odd, given his fixation with John Lennon and the Beatles' skill at going out with a bang.
** Though recorded at the same session.
†† You didn't get such attention to detail in Rolling Stones records. As the musicologist Alan W Pollack has noted, such layering was a patented Beatles recording technique. Queen (especially Brian May) and Roger Waters were evidently right there with their headphones on, taking notes.

'ma[king] contact with the human race' at Gildenhall, a British RAF* base just outside Cambridge. From there it then mentions '*The living soul of Hereward the Wake*'† (a leader of local resistance to the Norman Conquest of England by William the Conqueror) and 'Lucy in the sky'‡ before ending on the most outré image of Waters' Pink Floyd career – '*Summoning his cosmic powers / And glowing slightly from his toes / His psychic emanations flowed*'. You had to be there, man. Structurally the song repeats three shorter choruses and verses, before ending on a rather noodling solo by Gilmour, his first for the band,§ as the song fades out over the last two minutes. The lack of a definite outro indicates again how far Waters had to go yet, but this is a significant step forward in imagination and musical force.¶

> **REMEMBER A DAY** (Wright)
> **Length**: 4.33
> **Vocals**: Wright **Acoustic guitars**: Barrett **Slide guitars**: Barrett **Bass**: Waters **Piano**: Wright **Farsifa organ**: Wright **Drums**: Norman Smith **Backing vocals**: Barrett
> **Recorded**: 9–12 October 1967, De Lane Lea Studios, London
> **Producer**: Norman Smith
> **First released**: 29 June 1968 (*A Saucerful of Secrets* track 2)
> **Rating**: 7/10

Continuing the pensive mood of **PAINTBOX**, **REMEMBER A DAY** moves from the former song's specificities to a more generalised and symbolic meditation on lost innocence. It's a substantial improvement on **PAINTBOX** both musically and lyrically: the resounding tom-toms** at the start of each verse give it an effective kick, and suggest a tumultuous past echoing into the present. Wright sings the verses in a near-falsetto English tone that speaks of reserve, hidden emotion and past pain. The chorus is devastatingly sad ('*Why can't we play today? / Why can't we stay that way?*'), and the lyrics are more image-rich and thematic, talking of the '*evening [that] never comes*' and a time when you could '*dream yourself away*'. This focus on play and the lost country of childhood is of a piece with Barrett's work, albeit from the opposite perspective of mourning at what was lost rather than gleeful play within the strawberry fields of childhood.

REMEMBER A DAY was a holdover from the recording of *Piper at the Gates of Dawn*, and wisely so, its shadowy atmosphere being quite at odds with Barrett's Day-Glo luminousness. It was completed five months later with Barrett adding slide guitar for the outro solo in one of his final sessions with the group.

---

* Royal Air Force.
† 'Wake' simply meaning 'watchful'.
‡ See **MOTHER** for further discussion on the Lennon-Waters connection.
§ Gilmour was then aged just 22. It can feel unfair to critique the efforts of someone so young – who would have thought that their youthful work would sustain attention more than fifty years later? But the role if the critic is to illuminate and illustrate the music, which can sometimes mean decontextualizing it.
¶ Waters was 24 at the time of release.
** Played by Norman Smith, when Mason became frustrated at not getting the right drum part.

While Wright later professed to 'cringe'[††] at **REMEMBER A DAY**, it is one of the most effective and affecting songs on *A Saucerful of Secrets*, and certainly a far better contribution than **SEE-SAW**. Wright's tangible diffidence extended from his personal relations[‡‡] to his opinion of his own writing and playing. This gradually led him to become virtually mute as a musician on *Animals* and *The Wall* until resuscitated by touring *A Momentary Lapse of Reason* and then writing and recording *The Division Bell*. Which is a shame: behind that reserved exterior clearly lay a man of great emotion, who could best express himself on musically, with a great feeling for texture, tone and atmosphere, all the way from here to **CIRRUS MINOR** to **SHEEP**. But here, **REMEMBER A DAY** is a wonderful expression of nostalgia, melancholy and pain, like a bruise you can't stop pressing.

SET THE CONTROLS FOR THE HEART OF THE SUN (Waters)
Length: 5.28
Vocals: Waters **Guitars**: Barrett **Guitars**: Gilmour[§§] **Bass**: Waters **Farsifa organ**: Wright **Celesta**: Wright **Vibraphone**: Wright **Drums**: Mason **Gong**: Waters **Backing vocals**: Waters
Recorded: 7/8 August, 23 October 1967, 11 January 1968, EMI Studios, London
Producer: Norman Smith
First released: 29 June 1968 (*A Saucerful of Secrets* track 3)
Rating: 8/10

SET THE CONTROLS is another great leap forward for Waters (and indeed Mason, whose drumming – with mallets rather than sticks – is terrific). It's the first great Waters composition, and one that helped set the tone for the post-Barrett period. As the failure of **IT WOULD BE SO NICE** indicated, the group as yet struggled to come up with concise, memorable melodies of the kind that Barrett had created with such apparent ease. Thus, the solution was not to try – to instead elongate their song structures and melodies so that they could play with variations of tempo and dynamics within the overarching framework of a basic riff. So **SET THE CONTROLS** is based on minimal harmonic variation, making it feel like a mantra or drone. These are, of course, Eastern imports into rock music and thus made Pink Floyd appear otherworldly and exotic. (Their move away from the camera was a similarly clever move. When it became clear that Wright wasn't up to it, they effectively had no front man, and so let the music come to the fore, letting the audience project whatever they liked onto the music.)

[††] 'I cringe at some of my songs – such as **REMEMBER A DAY**. We were pretty amateurish at the time.' *Q* magazine, August 1996.
[‡‡] Even in the band's earliest days others noted how Waters mistreated him. As band friend Jenny Lesmoir-Gordon recalled, 'It was as if he was using Rick as his punchbag.' (Quoted in Mark Blake, *Comfortably Numb: The Story of Pink Floyd*, 2008).
[§§] This is the only track on which all five members played.

Their label of 'space rock'* would come to irritate the band, particularly Waters, who said: 'Syd had one song that had anything to do with space – Astronomy Domine – that's all. That's the sum total of all Syd's writing about space and yet there's this whole fucking mystique about how he was the father of it all. It's just a load of old bollocks.'† But if we take 'space' in its sense of spaciousness rather than referring to outer space, Pink Floyd did originate many of the techniques that came to refer to space rock:‡ slow tempos, hypnotically repetitive melodies, and open flowing rhythms. There is still, in **SET THE CONTROLS FOR THE HEART OF THE SUN**, a verse-refrain structure, though there is little difference musically. The instrumental break halfway through, however, is little more than Wright adding some light onto the extremely dark-shaded track; there is no change to the beat or melody. (The version on *Ummagumma* is a significant improvement in this area.)

Sometimes cited as one of the great psychedelic song titles,§ **SET THE CONTROLS** is often said to take its name from the Michael Moorcock novel *The Fireclown* (1965),¶ though this is not the case: four times the book mentions 'the heart of the sun' without any reference to setting any controls for that particular location. The lyrics, meanwhile, are cribbed from various poems in a 1965 volume of Chinese poetry from the Tang Dynasty (618–907).** For instance, 'Little by little the night turn around' and 'Under the eaves the swallow is resting' come from poems by Li Shangyin (812–858), and 'Witness the man who raves at the wall / Making the shape of his questions to heaven' comes from Li He (791–817). That Waters cribbed the words from an external source was no matter – Barrett had done something similar from the *I Ching* for **CHAPTER 24**, and of course Waters still had to shape it into a song. But taken altogether, **SET THE CONTROLS**, with its murmured vocals, allusive words, shadowy music and mantra-melody all combine here to something remarkably articulate, coherent, and powerful.†† In its brooding, sinister way it outdoes several of the tracks on *Piper*, and helped the group deliver an outstandingly atmospheric live experience. Waters was now on his way.

---

* See **ASTRONOMY DOMINE**.
† Interviewed for the *Wish You Were Here* song book (1993).
‡ And its progeny, like ambient music – as perhaps best exemplified by The Orb, who took great inspiration from Pink Floyd and later collaborated with Gilmour on an album called *Metallic Spheres* (2010).
§ According to the excellent *The Rock Lists Album* (1982) by John Tobler and Alan Jones.
¶ Also published as *The Winds Of Limbo*.
** A. C. Graham, *Poems of the Late T'ang* (1965). Graham was professor of Classical Chinese at the School of Oriental and African Studies, University of London.
†† It has remained a frequent part of Waters' live setlists, and was the only track from the album to make the *Echoes: The Best Of Pink Floyd* compilation.

CORPORAL CLEGG (Waters)
Length: 4.13
Vocals: Gilmour, Mason, Wright **Guitars**: Gilmour **Bass**: Waters **Farsifa organ**: Wright
Drums: Mason **Percussion**: Mason **Kazoo**: Waters **Backing vocals**: Norman Smith, Waters **Brass**: The Stanley Myers Orchestra‡‡
Recorded: 24 January 1968, EMI Studios, London
Producer: Norman Smith
First released: 29 June 1968 (*A Saucerful of Secrets* track 4)
Rating: 4/10

Most famous now as Waters' first anti-war song, **CORPORAL CLEGG** is a heavy-handed attempt at satire which ultimately grates on the listener. The verses are sung in a deeply sarcastic tone and the kazoo-led choruses come off as equally mordant but even less enjoyable to listen to. The lyric has some fine touches (such as Mrs Clegg's '*another drop of gin*', but its nursery-rhyme simplicity ('*Corporal Clegg had a medal, too / In orange, red and blue / He found it in the zoo*') come across as rather patronising. Given the complex lyricism Waters demonstrated in **SET THE CONTROLS FOR THE HEART OF THE SUN** and **LET THERE BE MORE LIGHT**, this feels like a serious step backwards.

The most notable part of **CORPORAL CLEGG** is perhaps that it's the only song where Mason, Gilmour and Wright combine vocally, the multiple voices and high backing parts perhaps suggestive of Clegg's fractured post-war personality. The sardonic opening guitar riff and high, maddening guitar notes (played throughout the verse) immediately indicate the sourness of the song, though the '*Dear oh dear*' refrain after two verses comes as a swift and welcome contrast. The chorus, with its gentler harmonised singing, suggests a more empathetic understanding of one of the roots of war (Mrs Clegg sending her son off to war while staying in her suburban home enjoying a glass of gin) – before that illusion is shattered by the strident sarcasm of the kazoo, with its ironic singalong tune. **CORPORAL CLEGG** moves swiftly between these sections, demonstrating if nothing else Waters' boldness as a writer and his willingness to tackle important and contemporary themes.§§ It is, however, like most of *Saucerful of Secrets*, embryonic rather than genuinely accomplished.

Satire is not easy to convey in pop and rock music; it either gets played straight, in which case many people miss the point,¶¶ or it feels bludgeoning, as

---

‡‡ Stanley Myers was a composer and conductor who often scored for films. He is probably best known for the theme to *The Deer Hunter* (1978).
§§ In the UK, 1968 was the peak year of protests against the Vietnam War, with a pitched battle outside the US Embassy in Grosvenor Square on 17 March.
¶¶ For example, the Beastie Boys were mocking rock attitudes with '(You Gotta) Fight For Your Right (To Party)', but did so straight-faced and everyone thought they were being serious. Though the inflatable penis probably didn't help. They later became a supreme parody and pastiche band, as in the video for 'Sabotage'. The song is played straight, but the video has plenty of nods and winks.

is the case here. In this instance, Pink Floyd needed a defter touch, in the vein of 'Piggies' or 'Yer Blues' on The Beatles' *White Album*, both of which are pleasant to listen to, with the former a caustic condemnation, the latter a dead-on pastiche.* With both the lyrics and the music in **CORPORAL CLEGG** being aggressive and sarcastic, there's no space for interpretation: it's just aggressively didactic. While *Animals* is frequently, indeed superbly, caustic, it is rarely clumsy and never unenjoyable. **CORPORAL CLEGG** is both.

A SAUCERFUL OF SECRETS (Waters, Wright, Mason, Gilmour)
Length: 11.57
Vocals: Gilmour **Guitars**: Gilmour **Bass**: Waters **Farsifa organ**: Wright **Hammond organ**: Wright **Piano**: Wright **Vibraphone**: Wright **Drums**: Mason **Percussion**: Mason **Cymbals**: Waters
Recorded: April 1968, EMI Studios, London
Producer: Norman Smith
First released: 29 June 1968 (*A Saucerful of Secrets* track 5)
Rating: 8/10

According to Gilmour:

> The band felt we achieved something with the title track of *A Saucerful of Secrets* ... We tried to write the music around the peaks and valleys of the art. My role, I suppose, was to try and make it a bit more musical, and to help create a balance between formlessness and structure, disharmony and harmony.†

This is a fair assessment. It's a substantial leap from the dismal efforts to write a smash-hit single to the avant-garde strategies of this track, requiring full band participation (it's the only fully band-credited track on the album, and thus the first for Gilmour).

Famously, Waters and Mason used architectural symbols to describe what they wanted to do musically. This comes through in the recorded song, which is organised into distinct sections, each with its own atmosphere and tempo. The inspiration, as Gilmour later explained, came when 'Roger and Nick began drawing weird shapes on a piece of paper. We then composed music based on the structure of drawing.'‡ With its inspiration thus being visual and dynamic rather than musical, **A SAUCERFUL OF SECRETS** often strays into the cusp of atonality, but its sense of structural organisation keeps the listener on board. This isn't organised anarchy, as with Ornette Coleman's *Free Jazz* (1961): it's a considered four-piece suite that uses dissonance as part of its sonic palette. As

---

* Although the former was still misread, most famously by Charles Manson.
† *Rock Compact Disc* magazine, Issue 3, September 1992.
‡ *Guitar World*, February 1993.

such it's a stunningly bold venture for a band still feeling its way, though the recorded version would be improved upon subsequently.

The first, named 'Something Else' (0.00–3.57), fades in slowly, with a close-miked cymbal slowed down for extra depth and resonance. Then the organ, slide guitar and guitar feedback (sounding like squeaking mice – the same sound Wright would later use in **SYSYPHUS**). This ominous sound builds and builds in intensity, and remarkably lasts nearly four minutes while still just about retaining the listener's attention.§

The second part, 'Syncopated Pandemonium' (3.57–7.04), is primarily a repeated two-second tape-loop of a syncopated Mason drumming figure (first on the snare and then on the tom-toms), treated with considerable echo. Over this is added atonal piano chords from Wright, cymbal sizzles and some headed-for-outer-space wibbly guitar from Gilmour (created by him sliding a microphone stand leg on the guitar neck). The sum of this pandemonium is a feeling of great energy creating some kind of structured mayhem, though it dissolves into chaos at the end as the drums recede and deep amplifier rumbles take over.

'Storm Signal' (7.04–8.38) is the shortest section, at just over one minute thirty seconds. It's plainly a transitional movement, moving from the chaos of 'Syncopated Pandemonium' through some austere churchy organ chords and some rattling chimes (sounding rather like ticking clocks). It's a movement suggesting time passing, of mundane activity overseen by some greater force. Then the final section, 'Celestial Voices', is itself in two parts – first, the sombre organ sounding like a requiem played in a cathedral, and then halfway through this is joined by the eponymous voices at 10.14, their massed choral voices (a series of overdubs by Gilmour) like a beautiful angelic apparition offering benediction at a scene of immense grief. This section wants to rise to true grandeur, and just about succeeds, though it feels slightly laboured. It is nonetheless an extremely poignant climax to a song that moves from anxiety to mayhem to sad acceptance and then a sombre, heightened mourning. Such emotional tones are not common in rock music and must be unique when put together like this as a suite. It shows the vastness of Pink Floyd's musical imagination and the depth of their humanity to create a sound poem like this.

The version here is a bold effort, considering how new Pink Floyd's approach was, though the live versions on both *Ummagumma* and *Live at Pompeii* are both significantly better. Here they sound constrained by the limits of the studio, and perhaps of Norman Smith (with whose services they would swiftly dispense).¶ Few of the instruments sound like they're in the same room (especially during 'Syncopated Pandemonium'), giving that section a rather sterile, artificial feeling. Gilmour's guitar similarly sounds underpowered and plasticky, rather than

---

§ Compare with the middle section of **PIGS (THREE DIFFERENT ONES)**, by which time the group had mastered building intensity through repetition while retaining the listener's attention.

¶ Wright said, '[Norman Smith] was into the songs, but "Saucerful of Secrets" he just couldn't understand. He said, "I think it's rubbish ... but go ahead and do it if you want."' (Capital Radio, *Pink Floyd Story Part 2*, 24 December 1976).

aggressively turbo-charged. However, these flaws would be worked out in time. In 1968, **A SAUCERFUL OF SECRETS** was a huge step forward for Pink Floyd, pointing directly to future glories.*

SEE-SAW (Wright)
Length: 4.36
Vocals: Wright **Guitars**: Gilmour **Bass**: Waters **Farsifa organ**: Wright **Piano**: Wright **Xylophone**: Wright **Mellotron**: Wright **Drums**: Mason **Percussion**: Mason **Backing vocals**: Gilmour, Norman Smith
Recorded: 24 January 1968, EMI Studios, London
Producer: Norman Smith
First released: 29 June 1968 (*A Saucerful of Secrets* track 6)
Rating: 4/10

The contributions from Waters and Wright sit very uneasily together in 1968 – with Waters' songs often pointing the way towards future glories, and Wright's rather demonstrating why he could not be the group's frontman. It's not that his songs are especially bad: **REMEMBER A DAY** in particular is affecting, and **PAINTBOX** was a deft skewering of fashionable London. But his early tracks tend to be studied, mannered pop, without the boldness or boundary-pushing seen even in Waters' nascent efforts.

SEE-SAW† demonstrates both Wright's virtues and flaws in miniature. It's quite melodic, but weakly sung. It's well-structured and occasionally innovative (for example, lacking a chorus, using instead a refrain: '*She goes up while he goes down*'), but doesn't grab the attention through its own diffidence. It's intelligent but not incisive, and doesn't add up to more than its parts. The constantly ascending and descending melody means it doesn't seem to be one thing or another – neither quite a charming piece of dreamy pop, nor a melancholic rumination on relationships. This in the end makes the song a frustrating experience for the listener.

While its production is thought-out and layered, with Wright taking the piano, then probably overdubbing Farsifa, Mellotron and xylophone, **SEE-SAW** still sounds quite improvisatory and spontaneous. At times the production overwhelms Wright's weak singing, rather muffling his voice behind the instrumentation. The falsetto backing vocals (provided by Wright and producer Norman Smith) are similarly a bit much, and would have been best left to the outro rather than featuring so prominently in the bridge ('*Another time – Ah-ah! Another day – Ah-ah!*').

---

* Or *indirectly*, to be precise. Mason later said, 'A Saucerful of Secrets' had pointed the way ahead, but we studiously ignored the signposts and headed off making *Ummagumma*.' (*Mojo* magazine, March 2013). It remains Mason's favourite album: he named his touring band after it (though perhaps he also astutely noticed a gap in the market for early Floyd, of which neither Waters nor Gilmour play much).

† A typical child's playground ride, often known as a teeter-totter in North America.

The most curious aspect of **SEE-SAW** is its inscrutable lyrics. Perhaps trying to keep up with Waters' more image-rich efforts, Wright uses elliptical phrases which imply meaning, or simply refuse to provide it. The overall story seems to be about a brother and sister, with their relationship taking a turn for the worse ('*She goes up while he goes down*') or perhaps even hinting at incest, though mentions of Marigolds in love, laughing in his sleep and selling plastic flowers may mean something, or nothing. Overall, **SEE-SAW** is an attempt at an ambiguous pop that doesn't succeed because there isn't anything there when examined closely.‡ However, its studied fragility is well placed between the two major statements on side two of the album.

JUGBAND BLUES (Barrett)
Length: 3.00
Vocals: Barrett **Guitars**: Barrett **Bass**: Waters **Keyboards**: Wright **Drums**: Mason
Percussion: Mason **Tin whistle**: Wright **Kazoo**: Mason **Brass section**: The Salvation Army Band
Recorded: 19 October 1967, De Lane Lea Studios, London
Producer: Norman Smith
First released: 29 June 1968 (*A Saucerful of Secrets* track 7)
Rating: 8/10

The last gasp of Syd Barrett in Pink Floyd is an astonishing confessional-turned-cacophony. Its legend has grown over the years, so that it has been described as 'the ultimate self-diagnosis on a state of schizophrenia' (by the band's then-manager Peter Jenner) and 'the sound of someone going mad'.§ But while they do reflect a kind of split personality, the real issue for Barrett in October 1967 was probably more about the vagaries of fame and the requirement to have a persona which could be marketed and sold as a mass product. This is less about schizophrenia than about a rejection of the music industry and the alienating way it feeds on images and personalities for popular consumption. The references to Barrett's clothes (which also appear in 'Vegetable Man',¶ recorded at the same time but unreleased until *The Early Years* compilation in 2016, though it had circulated on bootlegs for decades) suggest this is a matter of image and persona, not a fracturing of personality. Though, of course, it's easy to read it in

---

‡ It was referred to as 'The Most Boring Song I've Ever Heard Bar Two' in the studio, which might have been a dig from Waters, or a self-defensive gesture from Wright, or both. I wonder what the other two were.
§ According to journalist John Harris, in *Seven Ages Of Rock: White Light, White Heat* (2007).
¶ The lyrics to 'Vegetable Man' remind me of 'Public Image' by Public Image Ltd, where in John Lydon discards his persona of Johnny Rotten and reclaims his personality. But where that was driven by Lydon's cold rage, 'Vegetable Man' is more discordant and confused: '*And my turquoise waistcoat is quite out of sight / But oh oh my haircut looks so bad*'.

both ways.* **JUGBAND BLUES** is essentially about the feeling of absence as a performer and the notion of image and reality – exactly the kind of thing Thom Yorke sings about in 'How To Disappear Completely',† but no one ever points to that as proof of schizophrenia. It's also the second time the motif of absence appears in the group's lyrics, following **PAINTBOX**.

JUGBAND BLUES is a song in three parts, with the first Barrett singing on acoustic guitar and accompanied by the band (without Gilmour, of course) on bass, drums and tin whistle, while Barrett sings, *'And I'm grateful that you threw away my old shoes / And brought me here instead dressed in red'*. (This is about image.) It then gives way to a singalong section, though the lyrics don't make much sense beyond Barrett's rejection of material possessions (*'I don't care if nothing is mine'* – quite prophetically, as he lived most of the rest of his life quietly unhindered by such things). And then there's the extraordinary Salvation Army‡ brass band – at first playing a roughly in-tune sort of piece, before turning into a cacophony – all discordant, the brasses bubbling away like tumultuous thoughts, and sounding really quite sinister. It's perhaps an attempt to outdo the ending of The Beatles' 'I am the Walrus', which itself is a demented groove. Either way, it's unlike anything in Pink Floyd and indeed anything outside the most atonal jazz (which Barrett might have picked up from Wright). And then there's the haunting, delicate outro – *'And what exactly is a joke?'*, which is Barrett at his most inscrutable.

Viewed simply as a song, outside of its myth and legend, **JUGBAND BLUES** is actually very good, musically rich and constantly surprising without being overly fragmented. Its lyric is wise and smart, if taken to be about Barrett's rejection of the music industry, and the Salvation Army band is a stroke of genius. Barrett would go on to record two solo albums, *The Madcap Laughs* and *Barrett*, both released in 1970, with the help of his former bandmates. Neither of these is a genuinely worthwhile listen, despite their plethora of fans. Barrett was the brightest of flames, but only for a very short time, for reasons we don't fully understand, and his life is more of a cautionary tale than anything to be venerated.

A Saucerful of Secrets has, according to 2017 data, the lowest sales of any Pink Floyd studio album, at just 1.9 million. This is rather surprising: *More* and *Obscured by Clouds* have the least significant songs in their discography, while *Saucerful* has **LET THERE BE MORE LIGHT**, **SET THE CONTROLS**

---

* I personally suffered from Hallucinogen Persisting Perception Disorder after accidentally over-imbibing some unknown psychedelic drug. I came close to being an acid casualty, being greatly affected for around six months (and suffering symptoms to this day, more than 20 years later). I feel like I have an inkling of what Barrett may have gone through, and I somehow don't feel like **JUGBAND BLUES** (or the other unreleased tracks) genuinely convey the fractured feeling Barrett may have felt. For me, it was as though someone had punched a hole in my skull which was allowing unfiltered reality into my mind. Your consciousness, like your immune system, does a good job of filtering out things that aren't good for you. But what if that filter was suddenly switched off? What if everything felt shatteringly vivid? It is a deeply uncomfortable feeling, one that makes you shut down and hide away from new sensations.

† From *Kid A* (2000).

‡ A proselytizing Christian sect.

FOR THE HEART OF THE SUN, A SAUCERFUL OF SECRETS and **JUGBAND BLUES**. However, recorded in numerous sessions over nearly a year (from 9 May 1967 to 3 May 1968), it has the widest aesthetic approach of any Pink Floyd album, going from propulsive rock to sentimental pop to prog rock to a brooding mantra to heavy-handed satire. However, the parts do not sit well together: on the second half, the shift from the avant-garde to chamber pop to a schizophrenic blues must have been baffling for listeners. It is, unusually for Pink Floyd, an album that is less than the sum of its parts. Nowadays we can see the future greatness in *A Saucerful of Secrets* – but only in embryonic form, for the most part – alongside the band's numerous weaknesses.

POINT ME AT THE SKY (Gilmour, Waters)
Length: 3.35
Vocals: Waters **Guitars**: Gilmour **Bass**: Waters **Hammond organ**: Wright **Piano**: Wright
Glockenspiel: Wright **Percussion**: Mason **Backing vocals**: Waters, Wright
Recorded: 3 November 1968
Producer: Norman Smith
First released: 17 December 1968 (UK a/side single)
Rating: 3/10

Eighteen months after setting the charts alight with **SEE EMILY PLAY**, Pink Floyd were still chasing success in the singles chart, this being how popular success was then judged. Most acts very much played the singles game; The Beatles, the Rolling Stones and The Kinks, dominating mainstream rock in 1968, all shifted huge amounts. But whereas Wright's **IT WOULD BE SO NICE** was at least of a part with his pop-oriented numbers on *A Saucerful of Secrets*, Waters and Gilmour here cynically contrive to scrabble together something vaguely suitable for the pop charts. For perhaps the only time in the Pink Floyd canon their music sounds like derivative hackwork.

POINT ME AT THE SKY is arranged in three distinct sections, none of which leads smoothly to the next. It starts with two gentle verses, sung high by Gilmour, with some Hammond organ backing from Wright. Then a drum roll suddenly jumpstarts the energy and leads to the pre-chorus, which sounds suspiciously like **LET THERE BE MORE LIGHT** sung by Waters, and also includes a 'cosmic' reference, further suggesting a touch of self-plagiarism. And then the chorus is a transparent rip-off of the chorus of 'Lucy in the Sky with Diamonds', with the same line repeated four times by Gilmour, and echoed every time by Wright, at the end lingering before abruptly fading to reintroduce the verse, in a neat but pointless piece of studio trickery. The dynamic shift is the most notable aspect of the song, but it all feels rudimentary: the verse has no real melody, the pre-chorus is passable with its energy and Waters' more passionate singing, and the chorus feels extremely hackneyed. None of the parts sit well with each other, making the dynamics feel unusually amateurish – exactly where the b-side, **CAREFUL WITH THAT AXE, EUGENE**, was so intruguing.

The lyric was probably scrabbled together by both writers, and it's interesting that it has a number of motifs that would be pertinent to both Waters and Gilmour in their mature work: for Waters, a reference to insanity and mention of breathing, and the theme of flying for Gilmour (see **LEARNING TO FLY**). However, it's marred by many of the rhymes feeling forced (*Eugene/McLean/machine, maybe/baby, thin/in, hate/plate*) and a general feeling of not knowing what it's trying to say. The song was released as a single in the UK on 3 November 1968, some five months after *A Saucerful of Secrets*, which according to current industry standards was well behind the time to release more material. No doubt resulting from record label pressure (and perhaps from their own ineptitude at writing a catchy single), a feeling of aimless desperation permeates the track. Like **IT WOULD BE SO NICE** released seven months earlier, it did not chart. Much of Pink Floyd's early work, even when unsuccessful, has a great deal of charm to it. **POINT ME AT THE SKY** does not, and was notably left off the *Relics* compilation of early work.* It's not a complete disaster, but it's as close to one as the group ever came.

CAREFUL WITH THAT AXE, EUGENE (Gilmour, Waters, Wright, Mason)
Length: 5.45
Scat vocals: Gilmour **Scream**: Waters **Guitars**: Gilmour **Bass**: Waters **Hammond organ**: Wright **Vibraphone**: Wright **Drums**: Mason
Recorded: 4 November 1968
Producer: Norman Smith
First released: 17 December 1968 (UK b/side single)
Rating: 7/10

B-sides offer creative bands a chance to experiment, stretch their musical chops, and go beyond their defined formula.† So it was the one of Pink Floyd's best tracks of 1968 was the b-side to a fairly terrible single. As a b-side, it afforded the opportunity to innovate and explore, more even than on an album. Here the group come up with a startlingly effective evocation of mood and atmosphere, building to a crescendo and the spine-chilling Roger Waters scream, before artfully winding it down, in a manner similar to **INTERSTELLAR OVERDIVE**. The Barrett-less group had mastered dynamics, if nothing else.

The Floyd evidently felt they had come up with something special with the tune: it became a live mainstay until 1973 (see Chapter 2), was remade as **COME IN NUMBER 51, YOUR TIME IS UP** on *Zabriskie Point*, and is a highlight on

---

* It wasn't re-released until the 1992 *Shine On* box set.
† B-sides compilations are the best albums by bands as disparate as Anthrax and the Pet Shop Boys: the tracks are more personal, and offer a broader range of music than usual. (Thrash metal band Anthrax cover songs ranging from Kiss to surf band The Chantays).

the live album of *Ummagumma*. And they were right. Starting with a two-note riff from Waters and an exotic sounding Hammond organ from Wright, the atmosphere is dense and tense, artfully raising tempo and tension as Gilmour provides superb ghostly backing vocals. It continues to build as the song title is whispered like some disembodied spectral apparition, shortly after which comes Waters' patented scream at 1.45, at which point a fuzzy Gilmour solo starts to weave in and out. (The name 'Eugene' came from the a-side **POINT ME AT THE SKY**, where the first line states: '*Hey Eugene, this is Henry McClean*' – probably just for the rhyme's sake.) It then slowly winds down, slightly in the manner of **INTERSTELLAR OVERDRIVE**, though always suggesting anxiety and tension rather than anything external. And who needs to come up with a memorable ending when you have dynamics like that?

Although the ingredients are all there, the arrangement doesn't quite make the most of their potential, suggesting a simple lack of time to polish it up in the studio. The tension does not peak with the scream as it should, the scream is delayed for too long after the whispered song title, and the guitar playing is too polite. Live performances would iron all these issues out – **CAREFUL WITH THAT AXE, EUGENE** would be the group's most played song from this point until *Meddle*. Here, the group take the elongated structure and droning melody of **SET THE CONTROLS FOR THE HEART OF THE SUN** and make something entirely original. It's remarkable that their post-Barrett but pre-*Dark Side* career would be set off by a b-side, but it shows again how hard the group worked to improve and how rarely they would issue filler.‡

CIRRUS MINOR (Waters)
Length: 5.18
Vocals: Gilmour **Guitars**: Gilmour **Farsifa organ**: Wright **Hammond organ**: Wright
Recorded: January–February 1969, Pye Studios, London
Producer: Pink Floyd
First released: 13 June 1969 (*More* soundtrack track 1)
Rating: 8/10

Despite their recent failures in releasing singles, the group retained considerable cachet in Europe.§ Something of the exotic perhaps added to their popularity – just as, around this time, European directors such as Antonioni and Godard had huge influence on British and American cinema, which had little idea how to cater to the rock 'n' roll generation.¶ The group made the most of this, touring the Netherlands and Belgium and appearing on local

---

‡ **POINT ME AT THE SKY** wasn't filler. It was a terrible misjudgment.
§ Which then, of course, meant *Western* Europe.
¶ See *Easy Riders, Raging Bulls* (1998) by Peter Biskind for a full account of the cross-fertilisation.

TV shows during 1969* (the only year between 1967 and 1974 in which they did not tour the US).

With *A Saucerful of Secrets* having a more visual and wide-ranging soundscape, recording a film soundtrack was a logical step. There were numerous precedents: the group had already contributed some music to the short film *The Committee* in 1967,† while Miles Davis had released a full soundtrack album for the French film *Ascenseur Pour L'échafaud* in 1957, as had Paul McCartney for *The Family Way* (1967), and Bob Dylan for *Pat Garrett & Billy the Kid* (1967). The opportunity to work with a Nouvelle Vague director‡ was thus a solid career move for a group unsure of its direction.

As a film, *More* is now more of a historical document, showing Ibiza before it became an isle of indulgence in the 1980s. The main characters, Stefan and Estelle,§ meet in Paris but then move to Ibiza and partake in the nascent drug scene there, moving from marijuana to LSD to heroin. Neither is a likeable character so the film never engages the sympathies, but its frank portrayal of subculture behaviour and drugtaking must have made it feel fresh and new. (Reviews were, however, mostly negative.) It now feels highly predictable and primarily of interest because of Pink Floyd's involvement. For the soundtrack, Barbet Shroeder had a novel take: he wanted the group to devise whatever music ought to be incidentally playing, whether from the radio, in a café or Estelle's bedroom. This gave the group an excitingly broad canvas, with Ibiza being relatively exotic in those less-travelled days, but also an agreeably precise setup – Mason later recalled the group watching an early print of the film with a stopwatch so as to record how long their contributions should last.¶ Thus their music goes from party soundtrack to beatific idyll to drug freakout. It must have been much more fun than clowning around for Belgian TV.

For the soundtrack album, the most fleshed-out songs take side one, the atmosphere pieces side two – so, rather oddly, **MAIN THEME** is placed at the start of side two. **CIRRUS MINOR** is perhaps also an odd choice to open the album: it shows the group's growing ability to develop a highly potent atmosphere (as first seen in **CAREFUL WITH AXE, EUGENE**), but also its inability to make more of it. Opening on a full minute of birdsong (taken from the EMI sound effect library), acoustic chords then Wright on the Hammond organ combine to create a strong minor-key atmosphere, evoking a haunted rural twilight atmosphere that is both highly evocative and original. Perhaps only

---

* Some of the promotional appearances can be seen on 1968 *Germin/ation* and 1969 *Dramatis/ation*. They are for the most part cringe-inducing, often featuring the group gamely capering around in the style of the **ARNOLD LAYNE** video, and breaking into embarrassed laughter.
† The movie was re-released as part of the *Early Years* box set, in 2016. The music is mostly illustrative and not particularly interesting.
‡ Barbet Shroeder (1941–) is an Iranian-born Swiss.
§ Played by Klaus Grünberg and Mimsy Farmer, respectively.
¶ 'There was no budget for a dubbing studio with a frame-count facility, so we sat in a viewing theatre, timed the sequences carefully (it's amazing how accurate a stopwatch can be), and then went into Pye Studios in Marble Arch'. Mason, *Inside Out*, p.134.

Nick Drake at the time combined such pastoral atmospheres with such dark shading** – usually British folk music was more upbeat, like Donovan.

Gilmour's double-tracked low voice sounds portentous without being pompous, in that wonderfully understated English way, with the microphone going especially close in the last few lines, perhaps to give it a bit of variety (it couldn't be sung more animatedly). The lyric is another of the group's early pastoral efforts, with the setting evoked by '*Lazing in the haze of midday*' and the theme of time passing ('*Yellow bird,*†† *you are not long / In singing and in flying on*') and life wasting being one of Waters' favourites. The outro by Wright meanwhile recycles the sombre, magisterial chords from the 'Celestial Voices' section of **A SAUCERFUL OF SECRETS**, though about halfway through he overdubs the Farsifa put through a Binson Echorec‡‡ which creates a delicately shimmering sound above the Hammond. It's not quite a climax, but it will do. Overall, **CIRRUS MINOR** is quite close to being a brilliant song and for a soundtrack piece is extraordinary. Little wonder it was re-released on *Relics* two years later.

THE NILE SONG (Waters)
Length: 3.26
Vocals: Gilmour **Guitars**: Gilmour **Bass**: Waters **Drums**: Mason
Recorded: January–February 1969, Pye Studios, London
Producer: Pink Floyd
First released: 13 June 1969 (*More* soundtrack track 2)
Rating: 6/10

Probably the best-known song from *More*, and certainly one of the hardest rocking in the group's entire career, **THE NILE SONG** features Gilmour delivering both a superbly crunching riff and a tremendous roared vocal. Interestingly, there isn't a chorus, though there is a middle-eight ('*Soaring high above the breezes*') after the second verse. Although the words are belted out with real vigour by Gilmour (just at the time when heavy metal was being codified as a genre), the final short line in each verse, with its lingering regret, sounds more authentic. His guitar sound is full of piss and vinegar, grinding away splendidly throughout. Such overdriven sounds were rare in 1969, and the novelty must have been startling. (Hard rock forerunners like Vanilla Fudge and Cream tended to play electrified blues at moderate tempos. The thrilling pace and energy of the genre only really emerged with *Led Zeppelin*, in January 1969, while heavy metal emerged a year later, with Black Sabbath.)

The guitar solo in the instrumental break between the third and fourth verses, however, isn't high enough in the mix so isn't clear enough to hear properly,

---

** In songs like 'River Man' and 'Way To Blue', both from *Five Leaves Left* (1969), which was produced by Joe Boyd (see **ARNOLD LAYNE**).
†† I.e., the sun.
‡‡ This must have been one of their favourite gadgets. See **ONE OF THESE DAYS**.

which is unfortunate because it's another fine example of Gilmour's work. Doing a film soundtrack let the group really stretch their chops – it's impossible to imagine **THE NILE SONG** on *A Saucerful of Secrets* or *Atom Heart Mother* – while allowing Gilmour's superb melodic instincts to come to the fore, even on a song as rocking as this. A soundtrack album might for some bands have been an excuse for lots of filler,* but it's remarkable that both Pink Floyd's examples remain worthwhile listening experiences, though understandably without the unity or conceptual brilliance of their best work.

THE NILE SONG is heard in *More* early in the film during the party where the two main characters meet. It evokes the Dionysian wildness of the late-1960s counterculture about as well as any song could, in a way comparable to The Doors or the Rolling Stones at their most fire-raising. Pink Floyd can be mannered, but it would be foolish to overlook the more agreeably primitive aspect of their canon.

CRYING SONG (Waters)
Length: 3.33
Vocals: Gilmour **Guitars**: Gilmour **Slide guitar**: Gilmour **Bass**: Waters **Vibraphone**: Wright **Drums**: Mason
Recorded: January–February 1969, Pye Studios, London
Producer: Pink Floyd
First released: 13 June 1969 (*More* soundtrack track 3)
Rating: 6/10

The first acoustic ballad by the group also features the first use of the 'stone' image by Waters ('*Help me roll away the stone*'). **CRYING SONG** has a mantra-like drone that gives neither contrast nor relief: Gilmour does use some nice slide guitar and sings the single-note melody in a dreamy distant fashion, but apart from the nice little breaks at the end of each verse there's little more to the song than that. In its slightly sinister dreaminess, Pink Floyd master another atmosphere without developing the progression needed for a satisfying song, making **CRYING SONG** ultimately high-class aural wallpaper – good for a soundtrack album but not much more.

In the film, the song plays as doomed lovers and drug addicts Estelle and Stefan take heroin. The stasis of the song perfectly fits the mental embalming of opiates, which cocoon users in a state of indifference, though we only hear a brief passage of the track. The song thus takes on greater meaning from external sources. Only later would the group's songs convey thematic and expressive significance within themselves.

---

* Even The Beatles gave way to cynicism for their soundtrack to *Yellow Submarine* (1969). 'Only A Northern Song' is basically a fuck-you by George Harrison to the group.

> **UP THE KHYBER** (Mason, Wright)
> **Length**: 2.12
> **Bass**: Waters **Organ**: Wright **Piano**: Wright **Drums**: Mason **Percussion**: Mason
> **Recorded**: January–February 1969, Pye Studios, London
> **Producer**: Pink Floyd
> **First released**: 13 June 1969 (*More* soundtrack track 4)
> **Rating**: 3/10

A kinetic bit of drumming and some plinky-plonky jazz piano from Wright reminiscent of avant-garde jazz pianist Cecil Taylor combine to little substantial effect. This is the only combined writing credit for the two in the Pink Floyd discography, and listening to this we can hear why. It's doesn't offend the ears, but it has no melody or structure. In the film *More*, it does, to be fair, work quite well, as the jarring piano and frenetic drumming suggest Stefan's maddened state as he searches for heroin he desperately hopes has been stashed away. The song's title ('Khyber' = 'Khyber Pass' = 'ass') is meanwhile an inexplicable piece of adolescent immaturity.[†]

> **GREEN IS THE COLOUR** (Waters)
> **Length**: 2.58
> **Vocals**: Gilmour **Guitars**: Gilmour **Bass**: Waters **Piano**: Wright **Farsifa organ**: Wright
> **Percussion**: Mason **Penny whistle**: Lindy Mason
> **Recorded**: January–February 1969, Pye Studios, London
> **Producer**: Pink Floyd
> **First released**: 13 June 1969 (*More* soundtrack track 5)
> **Rating**: 7/10

Floyd at their hippiest. **GREEN IS THE COLOUR** is almost jaunty, with pleasantly folky strummed acoustic chords, childlike penny whistle (from Lindy Mason) and unusually jolly piano from Wright. It features in *More* when Stefan and Estelle dance and make out in Ibizan scenery, complementing their childish drug-fuelled wish to return to nature. It also features one of Gilmour's falsetto vocals – not unusual in early Floyd (also heard in **THE NARROW WAY III** and **FAT OLD SUN**). He sounds astonishingly English and mannered: as far from the roaring dervish of **THE NILE SONG** as possible, and thus displaying his remarkable range. It's genuinely astonishing how the band went from Barrett to Gilmour, one childhood friend to another, in doing so going from an entirely singular writer to one of the best guitar players of the century.

    GREEN IS THE COLOUR was for a time a live mainstay, being played from October 1969 to August 1971, but it has never been played since – Gilmour

---

[†] Maybe it is just to suggest that Stefan is totally fucked.

perhaps struggling to reach those high notes. The live arrangement featured a mostly acoustic opening then a full-band second half played at a lower key, with Gilmour scatting as the song built in intensity towards a climax. As an acoustic showpiece, **FAT OLD SUN** was a far better live track.

CYMBALINE (Waters)
Length: 4.50
Vocals: Gilmour **Guitars**: Gilmour **Bass**: Waters **Piano**: Wright **Farsifa organ**: Wright
Drums: Mason **Bongos**: Mason
Recorded: January–February 1969, Pye Studios, London
Producer: Pink Floyd
First released: 13 June 1969 (*More* soundtrack track 6)
Rating: 7/10

Following Waters' fantasy-oriented efforts in **LET THERE BE MORE LIGHT** and **SET THE CONTROLS FOR THE HEART OF THE SUN**, here is where he first starts to find his voice as a writer: addressing real issues concerning real people. It's also a fine example of the melancholy verse/anthemic chorus dynamic that would be recycled in the future (for example in **STAY, US AND THEM, SHINE ON YOU CRAZY DIAMOND** and **COMFORTABLY NUMB**). It's also the first lyric Waters had written which contains one of his numerous lyrical bullseyes: '*Apprehension creeping / Like a tube-train up your spine*' is his first top-notch simile. More, perhaps, than any other rock composer, Waters can convey genuine existential feeling in his lyrics; this humane empathy and verbal prowess make him surely the greatest lyricist in all of rock music. However, the lines about '*Your manager and agent are both busy on the phone / Selling coloured photographs to magazines back home*' are rather self-absorbed, a tendency that would come into full flower in *The Wall*, though fortunately repressed until then.

Musically, **CYMBALINE** combines Gilmour's portentous lower-register voice in the verses with a spare, skeletal backing (with Mason initially noticeable on the bongos, and Wright subtle and tasteful on the piano rather than organ). Each verse leads immediately to the chorus, which is smart because its soaring melody makes for a wonderful counterpoint, though the musical backing remains essentially the same. Meanwhile, the break after the third verse, with a bit of scatting vocals from Gilmour and then a smidgeon of Farisfa organ from Wright, is understated to the point of inconspicuousness. The organ keeps on during the repeated final chorus, then comes to the fore for a solo, in a satisfying (if not overwhelming) conclusion.

CYMBALINE is one of the first well-structured post-Barrett tunes, with a pleasing dynamic range between the verse and chorus and an excellent Gilmour vocal. It remained in the group's live repertoire until phased out – like almost everything else from their early days – by *Dark Side*. But here, for the first time, Waters finds the subject matter, the method, and the musical setting. In retrospect, taking two years to find his voice was actually quite swift – though it took another four years for that to come to full fruition.

PARTY SEQUENCE (Waters, Wright, Gilmour, Mason)
Length: 1.07
Bongos: Mason **Tin whistle**: Lindy Mason
Recorded: January-February 1969, Pye Studios, London
Producer: Pink Floyd
First released: 13 June 1969 (*More* soundtrack track 7)
Rating: 4/10

A tribal feel comes from Mason beating a rapid tattoo on the bongos and his wife Lindy playing a penny whistle. (Lindy would appear on Mason's next main contribution, **THE GRAND VIZIER'S GARDEN PARTY**, playing flute.)* The music would be used in the film during, appropriately enough, a party scene in Ibiza, when the island was exotically unfamiliar (Spain would still be ruled by Franco for another six years). Like half of the tracks on *More*, it's primarily an atmosphere piece, and here not particularly effective. Perhaps at the time it was suggestive of nearby Morocco, hashish and other exoticisms. Nowadays it feels very ordinary. The world has become much smaller in the fifty years since.

MAIN THEME (Waters, Wright, Gilmour, Mason)
Length: 5.27
Slide Guitars: Gilmour **Bass**: Waters **Farsifa organ**: Wright **Drums**: Mason
Percussion: Mason
Recorded: January-February 1969, Pye Studios, London
Producer: Pink Floyd
First released: 13 June 1969 (*More* soundtrack track 8)
Rating: 6/10

The opening credits of *More* naturally are the time to play **MAIN THEME**. It's a nice, atmospheric piece, with ominous sizzles on the cymbals from Mason and some portentous chords from Wright on the Farsifa creating a general feeling of trepidation. After about a minute of this, Mason and Waters start up a nervy beat, before Wright plays a skittering melody, while Gilmour later adds some slide guitar embellishments. **MAIN THEME** feels both thrown together and superbly atmospheric in the way of the best jammed songs – the sort of thing that takes five minutes if the members of a band know each other inside out (they had played 118 gigs in 1968, 114 of them without Barrett).† **MAIN THEME**

---

* They married in 1968 and would divorce twenty years later.
† Which was quite a reduction from 188 gigs in 1967.

is filmic, atmospheric, and inscrutable – a perfect opener for a film in the days when directors didn't need to signpost everything.

> **IBIZA BAR** (Waters, Wright, Gilmour, Mason)
> **Length**: 3.19
> **Slide Guitars**: Gilmour **Bass**: Waters **Farsifa organ**: Wright **Drums**: Mason
> **Percussion**:Mason
> **Recorded**: January-February 1969, Pye Studios, London
> **Producer**: Pink Floyd
> **First released**: 13 June 1969 (*More* soundtrack track 9)
> **Rating**: 6/10

IBIZA BAR is a re-tread of **THE NILE SONG** except it alternates a loud verse with a quieter chorus, which it repeats three times and then fades out. It also features some great guitar from Gilmour, who must have been one of the first to have the pedals to make the overdriven sound we now universally recognise as hard rock. (The Beatles' 'Revolution', released six months before this was recorded, was probably the first to get that manic exuberant energy by doubling the mic preamp overload by patching two of them together.)*

Like **THE NILE SONG**, while all the parts are there, Floyd at their most rocking aren't quite convincing. The difference between truly successful music is not technique: it is attitude and spirit. The choruses, with their softer vocals, slight diminuendo and pang of gentle regret, feel more authentically Floydian. Still, the group's willingness to venture beyond their comfort zone was key to their development. The boldness seen in **INTERSTELLAR OVERDRIVE** and **A SAUCERFUL OF SECRETS** continued nearly all the way through their career – and for longer than most of their contemporaries.†

The lyrics are unusually thoughtful for a hurried track, suggesting that it conveys themes much on the group's mind. Lines about '*I've aged and aged since the first page / I've lived every that line that you wrote*' and '*The epilogue reads like a sad song / Please pick up your camera / And use me again*' aren't too hard to decipher. Presenting their reflections on the music business as pleas for tolerance for the artist is cleverly meta (and less snivelling than the unfortunate lines about the industry in **CYMBALINE**). This kind of thing would lead in the fullness of time to **HAVE A CIGAR** and **WELCOME TO THE MACHINE**, though here couched with wistfulness instead of bitterness, but without the musical invention that made the later songs rather more memorable.

---

* Engineer Geoff Emerick later said that if he was the studio manager and saw what he was doing, he would fire himself. (*Here, There And Everywhere: My Life Recording The Beatles*, p.253).

† Genesis had moved to Phil Collins-led pop-rock by around 1978. Mike Oldfield's first real pop-rock album *Platinum* was also in 1979. Peter Gabriel followed suit with *So* in 1986. Yes moved to dance-rock with *90125* in 1983. Sustained invention is one of the very hardest things in a creative industry. This is not to say that pop isn't inventive, but simply to note that these acts were no longer setting the boundaries for music.

The only curious thing about **IBIZA BAR,** in fact, is that it doesn't come from any of the scenes from *More* set in Ibiza, but from one at the start of the film, when Stefan arrives in Paris and falls in with a thief and card sharp. Somehow this doesn't seem to have been mentioned more often.

MORE BLUES (Waters, Wright, Gilmour, Mason)
Length: 2.12
Vocals: Gilmour **Guitars**: Gilmour **Bass**: Waters **Organ**: Wright **Drums**: Mason
Recorded: January-February 1969, Pye Studios, London
Producer: Pink Floyd
First released: 13 June 1969 (*More* soundtrack track 10)
Rating: 4/10

A noodling bit of blues jamming, making use of the echo in presumably a large recording space in Pye Studios in London. Gilmour is recorded at the back and Mason at the front, giving the impression of space as their echoes resonate differently. As for the music, it's technically proficient but immediately forgettable, relieved only by its brevity, although it does again demonstrate the band's proficiency in a remarkably broad range of music. But the issue is not competence – after all, many bar bands can play music effectively. It's notable that the post-Barrett Pink Floyd have numerous efforts at blues songs and fail to do anything interesting with any of them, whether this, **WHEN YOU'RE IN** or **SEAMUS**, until they hit the jackpot with **MONEY**. Which might indicate their sheer determination if nothing else.

The band sometimes concluded their gigs with a slow blues doodle similar to this, most famously at Montreal in 1977, in an effort to get the audience to go home – which says much about the interest of this track.

QUICKSILVER (Waters, Wright, Gilmour, Mason)
Length: 7.13
Guitars: Gilmour **Bass**: Waters **Organ**: Wright **Vibraphone**: Wright **Percussion**: Mason
Gong: Waters **Cymbals**: Mason
Recorded: January-February 1969, Pye Studios, London
Producer: Pink Floyd
First released: 13 June 1969 (*More* soundtrack track 11)
Rating: 4/10

Some random atmospherics, in what is by far the longest track on the album. It opens with about a full minute of unclear sounds echoing in some large empty space. Then there's some vaguely eerie organ work from Wright, a gong from Waters (he loved beating that gong, did Roger), then several minutes more of noodling organ work from Wright. It drones on for a bit, then randomly fades out. There's pretty much nothing going on here but the filling of time. Pink Floyd rarely issued filler, but it's hard to think of any other term for this.

During the film, we hear some of the organ work while Estelle and Stefan play with some quicksilver (liquid mercury) on a board, stoned and enjoying seeing it shimmer in the Ibiza sunshine. The track for once doesn't really convey anything in the film.

A SPANISH PIECE (Gilmour)
Length: 1.05
Vocals: Waters, Gilmour **Guitars**: Gilmour **Bass drum**: Gilmour
Recorded: January–February 1969, Pye Studios, London
Producer: Pink Floyd
First released: 13 June 1969 (*More* soundtrack track 12)
Rating: 5/10

Some nice Flamenco guitar by Gilmour, whose musical proficiency clearly rivals that of Wright. The grumbled and spluttered words aren't such a great idea, however. (With Gilmour taking all the vocal duties on *More*, there's a sense of him being put through his paces, rather as, for example, Metallica did with Jason Newsted on *Garage Days Revisited*.)* Either way, Gilmour across the album demonstrates a remarkable versatility and strong melodic instinct. The Beatles would get away with cod-Italian on 'Sun King' a few months later,† but this was helped by their warm humour: the jokey phrases end '*Cake and eat it, parasol*'. Here the cod-Spanish comes off as rather silly, to the detriment of Gilmour's excellent guitar playing (**SEAMUS** would suffer a similar problem). Humour didn't come easily to the Floyd.‡

DRAMATIC THEME (Waters, Wright, Gilmour, Mason)
Length: 2.15
Guitars: Gilmour **Bass**: Waters **Organ**: Wright **Drums**: Mason
Recorded: January–February 1969, Pye Studios, London
Producer: Pink Floyd
First released: 13 June 1969 (*More* soundtrack track 13)
Rating: 6/10

A slight reprise on the main section of **MAIN THEME**, except with a more regular drum beat from Mason, and without any of that song's lengthy intro.

---

* Or perhaps, as Iron Maiden singer Bruce Dickinson said of drummer Nicko McBrain, it was 'like getting a new toy – Can you do *this*? Can you do *this*?' (Iron Maiden, *The Early Days*, 2004).
† *Abbey Road* was released on 26 September 1969.
‡ Waters has long asserted that humour is a strong part of his personality, which might surprise those who only know his material. But consider that Pink Floyd were one of the key financial backers of Monty Python's *The Holy Grail* (1975). Also, it's worth listening to the special edition DVD of *Pink Floyd: The Wall* where Waters and Gerald Scarfe discuss making the film (amongst many other topics) in the commentary. They have a merry old time in each other's company.

Gilmour plays a nice echoey guitar part, but there's no variation – the song just continues in this vein for just over two minutes, and then stops. It's atmospheric and spacey, to be fair – the sort of thing you could immediately imagine being played over the end credits for a film from a hip European director, funnily enough.

More is generally considered the lesser of Pink Floyd's soundtrack albums, with *Obscured by Clouds* now enjoying a heightened reputation. But while *More* has slightly too many atmosphere pieces rather than actual songs, the full tracks are wonderful. **CYMBALINE, CIRRUS MINOR, THE NILE SONG** and **GREEN IS THE COLOUR** are all top-notch tunes, Waters is clearly finding his voice as a songwriter, Gilmour's vocal and guitar efforts are often dazzling, and the range of music is quite remarkable, going from Moroccan souk bar to acid rock freakout to wistful pastoralism. *More* also shows the band hard at work to expand its abilities, though ironically, the band's next album would be a regression on the songwriting front. The enforced limitations of *More* were precisely what allowed the group's creativity to flourish. It would take a few more albums for this lesson to sink in.

ASTRONOMY DOMINE (LIVE) (Barrett)
Length: 8.32
Vocals: Gilmour, Wright **Guitars**: Gilmour **Bass**: Waters **Keyboards**: Wright
Drums: Mason
Recorded: 27 April 1969, Mothers Club, Birmingham
Producer: Pink Floyd
First released: 7 November 1969 (*Ummagumma* disc 1 track 1)
Rating: 8/10

It's remarkable that a band as good live as the Gilmour-Mason-Waters-Wright classic lineup of Pink Floyd only had one official live album while they were together.§ Or maybe it seems remarkable in these days when heritage rock bands release a live album to 'commemorate' every tour. Perhaps as a result, *Ummagumma* was until *Dark Side* the best-selling Floyd album. It's not just that the live album functions as an aide memoire for the nostalgic: each of the four tracks is a notable improvement on their record versions, with greater handling of dynamics (in particular), better soloing, and considerably more aggression, force and power.

ASTRONOMY DOMINE is a case in point. Despite being one of the best tracks on *Piper*, on *Ummagumma* it becomes less of an artificial art-rock construction and more of a gritty space flight on grimy spaceships, such as deeply

---

§ If you exclude the film *Live At Pompeii* (1972), which includes three of the four live songs from *Ummagumma* anyway.

influenced Hawkwind.* It still feels spacebound, but far more organically, with the beautiful interplay of a well-oiled band firing on all pistons. The live track doubles the length of the version on *Piper*, with a longer intro by Wright on the Farsifa and increasing tension from the drums, bass and guitar, before the familiar riff comes in at 0.49, here played with much more swing and power. (Barrett was, of course, a fine and original guitar player, but he's considerably outshone by Gilmour.) The first verse is repeated, after which there's a lengthy instrumental interlude, first with a sky-bound guitar solo from Gilmour† (from 2.52), backed up by some nicely authoritative drumming from Mason, then Wright on the Farsifa (from 4.05), in a cute dynamic shift playing in near-silence apart from some chattering cymbals. Then Waters leads the band in kicking it up several gears until Gilmour leads it to a peak with the familiar riff. Then there's another great near-silence and the third verse (*'Blinding signs flap / Flicker, flicker, flicker blam, pow! pow!'*) and we're into the outro, repeating the first verse again almost a capella, with Gilmour just strumming a chord in each line to see the song home.

As an extended version, **ASTRONOMY DOMINE** makes terrific use of its source material to provide an excellent live experience, turning the original song's echoing riff into a propulsive beast, cleverly shifting from near-silence to thunderous rock several times, and providing Gilmour and Wright the opportunity to show off their soloing chops. Mason pounds and resounds on the bass drum and chatters on the cymbals, with Waters gets several very tasty licks in too. The version here doesn't mean anything different from its studio incarnation, but it certainly demonstrates the cohesion, intelligence and power of a tremendous live band.

CAREFUL WITH THAT AXE, EUGENE (LIVE) (Waters, Wright, Mason, Gilmour)
Length: 8.49
Vocals: Gilmour **Guitars**: Gilmour **Bass**: Waters **Keyboards**: Wright **Drums**: Mason
Scream: Waters
Recorded: 2 May 1969, Manchester College of Commerce
Producer: Pink Floyd
First released: 7 November 1969 (*Ummagumma* disc 1 track 2)
Rating: 10/10

The use of dynamics first utilised in the studio version of this song comes to full fruition here, in a masterful display of control, power and authority. Where the studio version has an ominous atmosphere and builds it through the layering of instruments (starting with the bass, then drums, then ghostly voices, then the patented Waters scream), the live version has all instruments from the start but initially playing quietly and gradually inching up the tension, particularly

---

* For example, 'Brainstorm' on *Doremi Fasol Latido* (1971).
† Parts of it sound like a first draft for the solo in **TIME**.

through the increased volume and insistence of Waters' bass guitar. And where the studio version doesn't really let rip after the utterance of the song's title, the live version most definitely does – and immediately after, with a solid Mason drum fill and Gilmour's guitar being attacked as never before. The Floyd never rocked for the sake of it – aggression was always used to say something, and this approach is never clearer than here.

After the scream at 3.50, the group do some violent high-intensity rock (with some vocal scatting from Gilmour) until about 4.45, at which the tempo and energy levels gradually but perceptibly wind down, the drums moving away from the bass drum to rim taps, and the reintroduction of that sinuous organ from Wright. Gilmour gives it a last ghostly falsetto as Mason sees it out by tapping the cymbals, the song fading to nothing like waking from some grim nightmare. It is an utterly masterful display of power and control, with superb interplay and musicianship from all involved, from the eery exoticisms of Wright's organ to Waters' propulsive bass, Gilmour's exceptional scatting and falsettos, and Mason's superb handling of the various tempi.

The structure of build-up, crescendo and winding-down (or, basically, an ABA pattern) comes indirectly from **INTERSTELLAR OVERDRIVE**, though it had them in a different order. It would be used again, in various ways, in **ECHOES**, **PIGS** and **SHEEP**. By avoiding the verse-chorus-verse cliché but maintaining a sense of unity and cohesion often lacking in prog rock songs with their multiple contrasting sections, Pink Floyd effectively created their own musical forms. This is where technique is less important than taste and expressive ability, with Pink Floyd often bold enough to set their own remarkable standards. 'The only thing that counts,' as Waters says during *Live at Pompeii*, 'is whether it moves you.' Here Pink Floyd's expressive genius finds its first real flowering.

SET THE CONTROLS FOR THE HEART OF THE SUN (LIVE) (Waters)
Length: 9.27
Vocals: Waters **Guitars**: Gilmour **Bass**: Waters **Keyboards**: Wright **Drums**: Mason
Recorded: 2 May 1969, Manchester College of Commerce
Producer: Pink Floyd
First released: 7 November 1969 (*Ummagumma* disc 1 track 3)
Rating: 9/10

As with **ASTRONOMY DOMINE**, this track is considerably expanded (from 5.27 to 9.27), with extended solos from Wright and Gilmour, without fundamentally altering its meaning. Tonally, the verses remain unaltered, with Waters playing the ostinato bassline and singing his poetic lyrics quietly over Wright's exotic Farsifa-playing, but the solos explode with violent energy, shattering the song's earlier sinister and shadowy atmosphere. Where the studio version has similarly dark (and much briefer) solos from Wright after the second verse and another comparable one as the song concludes, the live track contrasts the crepuscular verse with an instrumental section that steadily increases in tempo and energy (Mason doing sterling timekeeping work here). It builds and builds via Gilmour's supercharged guitar, making you feel like you're literally on a rocket to outer space – until it suddenly peaks at 4.46, at which point everything dramatically falls away and Waters' hypnotic bassline returns. It's yet another superb demonstration of the group's dynamic control and eagerness to exploit shifts in mood and feeling. Wright then takes a shimmeringly echoing solo with Gilmour providing spacey high-pitched reverberating guitar, the drums dropping out as the two soloists make you feel like you're floating untethered through the cosmos. From 6.28 the drums gradually return, as the group inch their way back towards the third verse (from 7.52), after which there's a diminuendo to the finish.

SET THE CONTROLS FOR THE HEART OF THE SUN here feels constantly full of energy, coiled menace and intelligent intent, and far more than the initial version takes the listener on a journey. The solos in particular provide marvellous dynamic contrasts to Waters' deliciously sinister verses. The mantra-like construction of the track lets the group do so much with very little melodic material, through repetition, tension and release,[*] and as such provided many lessons for later sonic experiments and glories.

A SAUCERFUL OF SECRETS (LIVE) (Waters, Wright, Mason, Gilmour)
Length: 12.48
Vocals: Gilmour **Guitars**: Gilmour **Bass**: Waters **Keyboards**: Wright **Drums**: Mason
Recorded: 27 April 1969, Mothers Club, Birmingham
Producer: Pink Floyd
First released: 7 November 1969 (*Ummagumma* disc 1 track 4)
Rating: 10/10

The practice from intensive gigging and Gilmour's greater melodic instincts, here combine to greatest effect on the live songs on *Ummagumma*, turning **A SAUCERFUL OF SECRETS** from an interesting experiment to one of the finest and most moving of all Pink Floyd songs. It also marks the first real revelation of Gilmour's astonishing talent,[†] nearly two years after he joined in January 1968. Gilmour's initial period in the group was not easy: he was uncomfortable singing Barrett's pieces or miming them when doing TV appearances, and the group struggled to compose material (see **POINT ME AT THE SKY**). Gilmour slotted in well in their live performances, however, sharing the rest of the group's interest in electronic effects and his versatility facilitated their collective broad-ranging tastes: he could handle blues, folk,

---

[*] As Wright's hero Miles Davis noted regarding *Kind Of Blue*, 'There will be fewer chords but infinite possibilities as to what to do with them.' (Jazz Review, Vol.1, No.2 (Dec. 1958)). A lesson the Floyd certainly grasped.
[†] If you sack your leader, singer and songwriter, it's rather fortuitous to hire his friend from school, who in time turns out to be the 14th greatest guitar player ever (as voted by *Rolling Stone*).

hard rock and country, and his vocals combined wonderfully with Wright's. But never a natural songwriter (instead regularly working as a hired hand when the Floyd were inactive), it took time for his influence on the group to become pronounced. With the material mostly written beforehand, there was little space for Gilmour in *A Saucerful of Secrets*, with only a partial writing credit for the title track, while *More* was a workmanlike endeavour, a job.‡ Live performances were thus the arena in which Gilmour could most influence the band. (He would later be drily mocking about the group in its early days of his membership: 'My initial ambition was just to get the band into some sort of shape. It seems ridiculous now, but I thought the band was awfully bad at the time when I joined. The gigs I'd seen with Syd were incredibly undisciplined. The leader figure was falling apart, and so was the band.')§

A SAUCERFUL OF SECRETS remains divided into four sections ('Something Else', 'Syncopated Pandemonium', 'Storm Signal' and 'Celestial Voices'), with the latter three sections showing the greatest changes. Gilmour's guitar takes far greater prominence in 'Syncopated Pandemonium', where its turbo-charged surging into the atmosphere and beyond make it sound otherworldly yet powerfully muscular. Most significantly, rather than the aloof angelic voices of the studio recording, 'Celestial Voices' now includes magnificent wordless vocalising from Gilmour, alongside a far more dramatic musical figure on his guitar rather than Wright's keyboards. This section is truly astonishing: deeply moving, musically and emotionally satisfying with a sense of climactic catharsis, and intensely articulate. The dynamic shifts handled with superlative skill (Waters' bass-playing is especially good at this), and the climax, as Gilmour sings his lament, is utterly majestic. Here at last Pink Floyd demonstrate more than their potential: here they are for the first time without Barrett a highly articulate and emotionally resonant band. It is just a shame they still struggled to write a great tune as yet. But they would keep trying.

SYSYPHUS – PARTS I-IV (Wright)
Length: 13.28
Piano: Wright **Farsifa organ**: Wright **Drums**: Wright **Cymbals**: Wright
Percussion: Wright **Sound effects**: Wright
Recorded: April–June 1969, EMI Studios, London
Producer: Pink Floyd
First released: 7 November 1969 (*Ummagumma* disc 2 track 1)
Rating: 3/10

With Wright's background in modern jazz, it's slightly surprising that he couldn't come up with freeform pieces in the style of Cecil Taylor or Thelonious Monk.

---
‡   Six out of its 13 tracks are credited to the group, a record high.
§   'Pink Floyd: The Inside Story', *Rolling Stone*, 19 November 1987.

No doubt they are harder than they look, or sound. Here there are four sections of Wright mostly improvising in order to fill his allotted 13 minutes. In sum they go:

Part 1: An ominous, vaguely Arabic sounding overture, with resounding tom-toms and clattering cymbals over a motif repeated four times. It lasts for just over a minute, which feels about thirty seconds too long.

Part 2: Plinky-plonky piano, with a few nice trills and sequences, gradually increasing in tempo and then becoming (at around 1.50) more discordant, as a cymbal enters. The whole thing unravels into pointless dissonance. If you like the monstrous power of John Coltrane at his most avant-garde* you might like this. But probably you won't.

Part 3: Various percussive sounds, plucked piano strings, high-pitched squeaks (sounding like the cartoon characters Pinky and Perky), and more angry-sounding dissonance increasing by the end. It is dreadful.

Part 4: A touch of melody in a pastoral background with birds chirping. The Farsifa playing drifts on, nicely but entirely pointlessly, at one point almost quoting the melody from 'Silent Night'. Wright must have been desperate. Then, just as the listener is beginning to nod off, at 3.15 there's a huge dramatic chord, cymbal-sizzle and resounding tom-toms, which lead to some spacey-sounding keyboards, which increase in intensity, until the motif from Part 1 re-enters. And finally we're done.

Wright clearly has great skill playing the piano and keyboards, but as a composer of musical sequences (never mind actual songs) here his limitations are brutally exposed. Fortunately, both Waters and Gilmour were able to significantly improve their written output while Wright's steadily declined.

GRANTCHESTER MEADOWS (Waters)
Length: 7.26
Vocals: Waters **Guitars**: Waters
Recorded: April–June 1969, EMI Studios, London
Producer: Pink Floyd
First released: 7 November 1969 (*Ummagumma* disc 2 track 2)
Rating: 8/10

A lovely acoustic piece by Waters, enlivened by his rather overwrought lyrics and some musique concrete. It's interesting that when, at this stage, Pink Floyd did pastoral acoustic numbers, they were quite straightforward, very far from the out-there psychedelia of equivalent songs by The Incredible String Band, who would add exotic instruments like the sitar, gimbri, chahanai, dulcimer, pan pipes and water harp, as well as hypnotic drones and exotic melisma to their melodies, in albums like *The Hangman's Beautiful Daughter*

---

* As heard in *Live At The Village Vanguard ... Again!* (1966), for example.

(1968). **GRANTCHESTER MEADOWS** and equivalent songs (like **IF** and **FAT OLD SUN**), however, are far more conventional, belying the group's far-out reputation: their hymns to the English countryside are heartfelt and without artifice. (The song may also allude to the poem 'The Old Vicarage, Grantchester' written in 1912 by Rupert Brooke, which similarly rhapsodises the English countryside.)[†] Folk music traditionally meant authenticity and honesty, emphasising a rootsy realism – hence, for example, the raw untamed voice of early Bob Dylan – which you can hear in Waters' hand moving between the chords.[‡] For a self-consciously beautiful ballad, this adds a touch of grit, without which **GRANTCHESTER MEADOWS** might be slightly cloying. The bee-swatting sound at the end is, similarly, an attempt to deflate the perceived grandiosity of the song. (It's curious that rock musicians get embarrassed when articulating what they love and cherish, but will gladly write about their deepest fears and most pressing neuroses. Or Waters does, anyway.)

The main point of **GRANTCHESTER MEADOWS** is of course the lyric, which focuses on the melodic aspect of the words, and so uses internal rhymes, euphony, assonance and alliteration. It's all very splashy, though not without effect. Meanwhile, there's still plenty of imagery to go around, such as '*golden sun flakes*' and '*a river of green is sliding unseen beneath the trees*'. Waters, however, isn't above a cliché like '*deathly silence*' or an archaic poeticism like '*I lay me down*'. Nonetheless, **GRANTCHESTER MEADOWS** is a remarkable exercise in poeticising Waters' lyrics, and can be very much enjoyed for sheer auditory pleasure in lines like '*the splashing of the kingfisher flashing to the water*'.

Waters also enjoys himself with the production of the track, which features a close-miked vocal and sound effects to generate atmosphere, a trick he would use throughout his career (for example, in **ONE OF THE FEW**). When performed live during 'The Man – The Journey' piece, **GRANTCHESTER MEADOWS** was called 'Daybreak' and featured both Waters and Gilmour, who provided some high harmonies. The rural evocations of Pink Floyd vanished after *Atom Heart Mother*, which is unfortunate. They did them so very well.

[†] It begins:
   Just now the lilac is in bloom,
   All before my little room;
   And in my flower-beds, I think,
   Smile the carnation and the pink;
   And down the borders, well I know,
   The poppy and the pansy blow ...

[‡] A trick done all the way up to Belle And Sebastian's *Fold Your Arms Child, You Walk Like A Peasant* (2000) and beyond.

SEVERAL SPECIES OF SMALL FURRY ANIMALS GATHERED TOGETHER IN A CAVE AND GROOVING WITH A PICT (Waters)
Length: 4.59
Tape effects: Waters **Vocals**: Waters
Recorded: April–June 1969, EMI Studios, London
Producer: Pink Floyd
First released: 7 November 1969 (*Ummagumma* disc 2 track 3)
Rating: 3/10

Tape-loops had been introduced to pop music in The Beatles' revolutionary 'Tomorrow Never Knows' (1966). Utilised there to criss-cross with every greater frequency and so dissolve the listener's sense of time and space, as though when on an acid trip, they had been deployed with great artistry and focus. Here, however, Waters uses them to simulate the sound of, indeed, several small furry animals in a cave with a berserk Scotsman* (who doesn't enter until 3.43, which is probably fortunate). You can almost admire the technique. But the ultimate result is the most absurd sound ever concocted by Pink Floyd. Unlike, say, the atonality of **SYSYPHUS** or the heavy-handed satire of **CORPORAL CLEGG**, one can't even say **SEVERAL SPECIES** is a worthy unsuccessful experiment. It does exactly what it says on the tin – but it's one most shoppers would prefer to leave on the shelf.

This track must, however, count as the group's first effort to integrate animal sounds into their music, as heard later in **SEAMUS**, **ECHOES**, **DOGS**, **PIGS**, **SHEEP**, **THE DOGS OF WAR** and **KEEP TALKING**. Their fondness for this kind of musique concrete – building on their 'The Man – The Journey' live show, which used heartbeats and footsteps to help their music reflect life as it is lived – gives their songs a greater atmosphere, and also a sense of detail that rewards repeated listening.† If a group is to experiment, some efforts will inevitably be unsuccessful. **SEVERAL SPECIES** is, as a song, a failure – but it is the first awkward step on the road to future glories. It's just remarkable to hear a band still sounding so directionless on their fifth studio album.

---

* It's not gibberish but some kind of poem:
  Aye an' a bit of mackerel, settler rack and down
  Ran it down by the home, and I flew
  Well, it slapped me and I flopped it down in the shade
  And I cried, cried, cried
  The tear had fallen down he had taken, never back to raise
  And then cried Mary, and took out wi' your Claymore
  Right outta a' pocket, I ran down, down by the mountain side
  Battlin' the fiery horde that was falling around the feet
  'Never!' he cried, 'Never shall ye get me alive
  Ye rotten hound of the burnie crew!'
  Well I snatched fer the blade and a Claymore cut and thrust
  And I fell down before him round his feet
  Aye, a roar he cried fray the bottom of 'is heart
  That I would nay fall but as dead
  Dead as I can by why' feet, d'ya ken?
  And the wind cried back.

† My own favourite example is the sound of tearing sheets in **ONE OF MY TURNS**.

> **THE NARROW WAY (PARTS 1–3)** (Gilmour)
> **Length**: 12.17
> **Vocals**: Gilmour **Guitars**: Gilmour **Piano**: Gilmour **Organ**: Gilmour **Bass**: Gilmour
> **Drums**: Gilmour **Backing vocals**: Wright (?)
> **Recorded**: 2 May 1969, EMI Studios, Abbey Road, London.
> **Producer**: Pink Floyd
> **First released**: 7 November 1969 (*Ummagumma* disc 2 track 4)
> **Rating**: 6/10

Gilmour's three sections he later described as being thrown together in a panic,[‡] and certainly two of the three pieces articulate nothing much. But Gilmour's guitar playing is so distinctive that it doesn't necessarily matter what he is playing: it's always worth hearing him. The first section was a guitar workout that Gilmour had played on numerous occasions (such as a BBC Radio 1 session for John Peel on 2 December 1968), where it was introduced as 'Baby Blue Shuffle in D Major'.[§] Here he adds some pointless trippy backwards sound effects, to little effect. Gilmour would later cannibalise the piece for **COUNTRY SONG**, a track recorded for the *Zabriskie Point* soundtrack. (Rather as they would remake **CAREFUL WITH THAT AXE, EUGENE** for the same project – the Floyd were usually deft curators of their own material.)

Part II is another guitar workout, but with a completely different atmosphere: dark, sordid, grungy, grim and forbidding, like a desolate overcast volcanic plain. There are some Wright-esque organ flourishes towards the end, and some rudimentary drumming on tom-toms, both apparently by Gilmour (perhaps he borrowed Wright's keyboards). It does effectively create an atmosphere, but then does absolutely nothing with it. It just is for a few minutes, then it goes away.

Part III of **THE NARROW WAY** is by far the best. Opening with a drone carrying over as Part II dissolves, Part III is a memorable mood piece, evoking a dreamily ominous and desolate soundscape. The repeated guitar refrains in the verse sound utterly weary, rising only to collapse as though completely spent. The structure is somewhat unusual, with the chorus twice the length of the chorus, but with there being minimal harmonic variation between the two, this does not immediately stand out. Gilmour's singing does, however, change between a deeper tone in the verse and a near-falsetto in the chorus, which might be backed by Wright or doubled by Gilmour (the two sounding very similar). Gilmour's lyrics describe weary journeys and wrong paths – perhaps a comment on Pink Floyd's relentless gigging, and on their fumbling for inspiration as they toiled in the shadow of Barrett. Famously, Gilmour asked Waters to write the words for this track, but the bassist declined. While the lyrics might

---

[‡] 'It was just desperation really, trying to think of something to do, to write by myself. I'd never written anything before, I just went into a studio and started waffling about, tacking bits and pieces together. I haven't heard it in years. I've no idea what it's like.' *Guitar Heroes*, May 1983.
[§] Gilmour's nickname was Baby Blue, because of his fetching eyes. See also **THE THIN ICE**.

lack Waters' verbal felicity or social and psychological insights, they are perfectly adequate, making it a puzzle why Gilmour was so diffident about his abilities in this area. (See **CHILDHOOD'S END**.)

Part III would be played live as part of 'The Man – The Journey' sequence during 1969. The falsetto section would be pitched lower, enabling Gilmour to belt it out, which rather robs the piece of most of its effect. Gilmour has long since disavowed **THE NARROW WAY**, but if he were to look again, he might be charmed by some of his juvenilia. But only some.

THE GRAND VIZIER'S GARDEN PARTY (PARTS 1–3) (Mason)
Length: 8.46
Percussion: Nick Mason **Flute**: Lindy Mason **Mellotron**: Nick Mason
Xylophone: Nick Mason
Recorded: April–June 1969, EMI Studios, Abbey Road, London
Producer: Pink Floyd
First released: 7 November 1969 (*Ummagumma* disc 2 track 5)
Rating: 2/10

Another three-part tune. In the first part, Lindy Mason plays some pastoral-sounding flute for about forty seconds. In the second, for the first minute Mason flannels about on percussion and cymbals, toying with the resonances of different drums, while punctuating this with cymbals, a xylophone and a snare drum. In the background he uses a Mellotron for atmospheric purposes. Then this all drops out to be replaced by what sounds like underwater echoes of something or other, perhaps like distant whale song, an obscure melody vaguely discernible. Then the sound cuts out here and there. There's more faffing about on the cymbals, drums and xylophone, the sound cutting out randomly and tiresomely – then they all get mixed together for a few minutes before there's a conventional beating about the drum kit. It comes to a climax of sorts when the random drum and xylophone sounds cutting in and out are added for the last ten seconds or so. In the third part, Lindy Mason reprises her flute playing, this time multi-tracked and panned across the stereo spectrum to give the impression of multiple flutes. The melodies are much the same as in Part I. It's pretty enough but utterly pointless. **THE GRAND VIZIER'S GARDEN PARTY** is the sort of thing you only ever need to hear once. There's nothing there.

The use of a frame to organise the contributions from each band member on the studio side of *Ummagumma* might be clever but is meant to conceal their lack of inspiration. Each could noodle for a bit and hope that, in aggregate, it all might come to something worth listening to, rather than actually having something to say. Though the album does have sporadic bursts of enjoyability, it contains several of the weakest moments in Pink Floyd's entire discography.

The live side is, however, exceptional, with each track a significant improvement on its studio version, and displaying mastery of dynamics and emotion. But the studio side shows the band at their most aimless, with only **GRANTCHESTER MEADOWS** and **THE NARROW WAY III** ranking anywhere near their previous material. From this low point,* however,† the band would swiftly integrate their material into stunningly effective and deeply felt statements.

EMBRYO (Waters)
Length: 4.39
Vocals: Gilmour **Guitars**: Gilmour, Waters **Bass**: Waters **Keyboards**: Wright
Piano: Wright **Tape effects**: Waters **Percussion**: Mason
Recorded: November 1968, EMI Studios, London
Producer: Pink Floyd
First released: May 1970 (*Picnic – A Breath of Fresh Air*‡ track 3)
Rating: 6/10

A slow-moving, mostly acoustic song sung by Gilmour, **EMBRYO** is a real Pink Floyd curiosity. Firstly, the lyric takes the perspective of an unborn child ('*All around I hear strange sounds / Come gurgling in my ear / Red the light and dark the night / I feel my dawn is near*'). Secondly, near the end it utilises the chirruping high-pitched sounds later heard in **SEVERAL SMALL SPECIES**, created by Waters' voice being sped up. Third, an early live version used the 'whale song' technique later heard in **ECHOES** and **IS THERE ANYBODY OUT THERE?**, created by Gilmour plugging the leads into his wah-wah pedal the wrong way round. (Ironically, here are many of Pink Floyd's later techniques in embryonic form.) And finally, recorded at the same sessions at **POINT ME AT THE SKY**, **EMBRYO** is a rare instance of a recorded song being essentially unreleased, despite being a mainstay in the group's live setlist during 1970–71.

As a song, **EMBRYO** has minimal melodic movement but some exotic-sounding melisma in the verses ('*All is lo-o-o-ove, is all I a-a-a-am*') and Mason punctuating the rhythm solely by cymbal taps at the end of each line. There's little difference between the verses and choruses, though the final line of the chorus does suddenly ascend to a higher tone in a sudden dazzle of sunlight. The lyric is really rather good, showing Waters' increasing verbal felicity and thematic imagination.§ **EMBRYO** is not a disaster like **POINT ME AT THE**

---

* A low point artistically. Fans were far more enthusiastic about *Ummagumma*. It long remained Pink Floyd's best-selling pre-*Dark Side* album.
† Gilmour in 1995 said the album was 'pretty horrible. Well, the live disc of *Ummagumma* might be all right, but even that isn't recorded well.' (*Der Spiegel*, 5 June 1995).
‡ *Picnic – A Breath of Fresh Air* was a sampler by Pink Floyd's record label Harvest, with other contributions from acts including Deep Purple, Roy Harper and The Pretty Things. The track was later released on the US compilation album *Works*, in 1983, and finally given general release in the *Early Years* box set in 2016.
§ The only similar song I can think of is 'Zombie Eaters' by Faith No More (from 1989's *The Real Thing*), although that's a song from a baby's perspective to its mother. But there's probably more.

SKY, but nor does it ultimately point the way to later glories like the other song recorded at the session – **CAREFUL WITH THAT AXE, EUGENE**. **EMBRYO** ultimately seems not to have been quite one thing or the other, and so fell by the wayside. The group were too smart at shepherding their material to have unheard masterpieces locked in the vault.

BIDING MY TIME (Waters)
Length: 5.18
Vocals: Waters **Guitars**: Gilmour **Piano**: Wright **Organ**: Wright **Drums**: Mason
Trombone: Wright **Backing vocals**: Wright
Recorded: July 1969
Producer: Pink Floyd
First released: 14 May 1971 (*Relics* track 10)
Rating: 6/10

BIDING MY TIME was unreleased prior to the *Relics* album in 1971, and had been heard only when the band performed the 'The Man – The Journey', in which the track appeared as 'Afternoon'. It's another expression of Waters' work-weariness, following **CYMBALINE**, a perspective that would in time mature into a worldly scepticism then sour into splenetic bitterness, but here is a rather elementary lover's plaint of a man having to work too hard and thus be separated from his partner. (Seeds too, perhaps, of the transatlantic phone call discovering a cheating wife in **YOUNG LUST**.)

In any case, **BIDING MY TIME** is a gentle bluesy track, with a structure of just a single verse then a twice-repeated chorus which is barely distinguishable from the verse. Musically it's perhaps the first example of the group doing a late-night cabaret act that would find its best expression in **ST TROPEZ** (see also **LOVE SONG VERSION 6**), testament to the way the group worked so hard to master the idioms of popular music. But what keeps it from banality is the arresting instrumental section, during which the band finally spring to life. First Wright takes a trombone solo from 1.53 (again demonstrating his remarkable versatility), and then Gilmour has a relatively strong guitar solo from 2.18, with Wright interjecting throughout on trombone. Although the instrumental passage is decidedly more energetic and in-your-face than the preceding vocal section, there's no great purpose for it being there. You can imagine Waters saying, 'Then we'll go mad doing solos for a bit, that should fill a few minutes.'* At this stage the group were still exploring their expressive range, rather than using it to say anything specific, which sometimes means songs feel like the group are flying blind. This would continue up until *Meddle*.

---

* Compare with his description of the jamming session that inspired **BREATHE**: 'Let's play E-minor and A for an hour or two. Oh, that sounds alright. That will take up five minutes.' *Classic Albums* 'Pink Floyd – The Dark Side Of The Moon' (2003).

The show-tune brassiness of **BIDING MY TIME** suggests a kinship with 'Make-Up' by Lou Reed, which is quite plausible given that David Bowie (alongside Mick Ronson) produced Reed's *Transformer* album a year after *Relics* was released and was a great Syd Barrett fan.[†]

HEART BEAT, PIG MEAT (Gilmour, Water, Wright, Mason)
Length: 3.12
Vocals: Gilmour **Keyboards**: Wright **Drums**: Mason **Samples**: Gilmour, Mason, Waters, Wright (?) **Tape effects**: Waters (?)
Recorded: 7–12 December, Technicolor Sound Services, Rome
Producer: Pink Floyd
First released: 9 February 1970 (*Zabriskie Point* soundtrack track 1)
Rating: 6/10

Pink Floyd's work with Michael Antonini on *Zabriskie Point* was famously unhappy, the director rejecting every piece the group brought him and continuing to do so when the group had altered the pieces according to his criticisms.[‡] However, the Floyd as always worked hard and came up with pieces of music which in embryonic form demonstrated good ideas that could be expanded for later use. **HEART BEAT, PIG MEAT** is a case in point. With its heartbeat rhythm, random musical and vocal interjections, and dreamy, near-ambient feeling, it is a clear precursor of **SPEAK TO ME**. Here it simply continues for around three minutes then fades out. The title suggests how much 'pigs' was in the culture, thanks to The Beatles and particularly Charles Manson, though Waters would of course make full use of the term in due course.

CRUMBLING LAND (Gilmour, Water, Wright, Mason)
Length: 4.16
Vocals: Gilmour, Wright **Guitars**: Gilmour **Bass**: Waters **Keyboards**: **Drums**: Mason
Backing vocals:
Recorded: 15–22 November, 7–12 December 1969, Technicolor Sound Services, Rome
Producer: Pink Floyd
First released: 9 February 1970 (*Zabriskie Point* soundtrack track 4)
Rating: 6/10

A surprisingly competent Byrds knock-off, **CRUMBLING LAND** sounds especially like 'Wasn't Meant To Follow', a song recorded for The Notorious Byrd Brothers (1968) that featured on the *Easy Rider* (1969) soundtrack.

[†] There's something of Barrett in Ziggy Stardust, as Bowie noted: 'He was the first guy I'd heard to sing pop or rock with a British accent. His impact on my thinking was enormous.' (*Uncut* magazine, 24 January 2014).

[‡] 'Antonioni was there and we did some great stuff, but he'd listen and go – and I remember he had this terrible twitch – "Eet's very beauteeful, but eet's too sad" or "Eets too strroong". It was always wrong consistently. There was always something that stopped it from being perfect. You'd change whatever was wrong and he'd still be unhappy. It was hell.' (*Zigzag* magazine, June 1973).

Gilmour's ventriloquial skills are hugely impressive: though David Bowie has received great plaudits for the range of styles he adopted, Gilmour's range is perhaps only slightly smaller.* **CRUMBLING LAND** hits all the country-rock notes, with acoustic guitar and sweetly harmonised vocals. Lyrically it refers to numerous points in the film, and more than likely to Antonioni himself ('*In his hand a moving picture of the crumbling land / Screaming, dealing, movie man*'). Though David Gilmour would later express puzzlement at Pink Floyd being chosen to create this kind of track,† the group's versatility is remarkable, making them an ideal soundtrack band – if the director knows what they want.

COME IN NUMBER 51, YOUR TIME IS UP (Gilmour, Water, Wright, Mason)
Length: 5.01
Vocals: Waters **Guitars**: Gilmour **Bass**: Waters **Keyboards**: Wright **Drums**: Mason
Backing vocals: Gilmour
Recorded: 15-22 November, 7-12 December 1969, Technicolor Sound Services, Rome
Producer: Pink Floyd
First released: 9 February 1970 (*Zabriskie Point* track 11)
Rating: 7/10

The importance of **CAREFUL WITH THAT AXE, EUGENE** to the post-Barrett era Floyd was considerable, as we've seen. It's re-recorded and renamed here,‡ with greater use of eerie falsetto backing vocals and a more violent explosion at the scream, making it closer to the live version in *Ummagumma*. That said, the shift in dynamics isn't handled as well: the track floats along in vaguely menacing style for a few minutes and then abruptly explodes (at 2.52), rather than gradually ratcheting up and then winding down the tension and violence. This might seem baffling given how successful the *Ummagumma* version was, recorded just six months earlier. However, the track no doubt deliberately parallels the scene in which it appears, near the end of *Zabriskie Point*, where lead character Daria repeatedly imagines a mansion in the Phoenix desert being blown up. The violence of the track perfectly suits the incredible explosions:§ a lesson in how visual rock music can be.

---

* If Bowie did Philly soul, Pink Floyd did disco in **ANOTHER BRICK IN THE WALL PART 2**. Both did ambient electronica – Bowie on *Low*, Gilmour with The Orb (albeit much later). Both did folk, and both did slightly meta rock, in the form of *Ziggy Stardust* and *The Wall*. Perhaps fortunately, however, we are yet to hear any drum n' bass from Gilmour.

† '[A] kind of country & western number which he [Antonioni] could have gotten done better by numerous American groups. But he used ours ... very strange.' (Capital Radio, *Pink Floyd Story Part 3*, 31 December 1976).

‡ Nothing wrong with cannibalizing the b-side of a song that didn't chart. The group were excellent at managing their material. (Unlike, say, Noel Gallagher, who early on gave away strong tracks as b-sides and then could hardly write a decent tune in the later years of Oasis, and Guns N' Roses, whose idea to release two albums *simultaneously* in 1991 was a monumental folly.)

§ The film was a significant flop, taking just $900,000 on production costs of $7m. It is utterly tedious to watch but the cinematography is outstanding.

COUNTRY SONG (Gilmour, Water, Wright, Mason)
Length: 4.37
Vocals: Gilmour **Guitars**: Gilmour **Bass**: Waters **Piano**: Wright **Drums**: Mason
Backing vocals:
Recorded: 15-22 November, 7-12 December 1969, Technicolor Sound Services, Rome
Producer: Pink Floyd
First released: 16 September 1997 (*Zabriskie Point* Bonus Disc track 5)
Rating: 6/10

Making use of the soft-verses-loud-chorus dynamic used in **CYMBALINE**, **COUNTRY SONG** also offers some unusually allusive, metaphorical lyrics. Waters (probably) uses chess metaphors and Lewis Carroll imagery[¶] to describe political tensions, probably relating to Antonioni – '*Run to the treasury and bring me back some gold*' and then at the end, '*the Pink Queen sat / And smiled at the cat who smiled back*', perhaps suggesting the group wanting to have the last laugh. (As indeed they did.)

Musically, Mason meanwhile provides some unusually fussy drumming, with stiff little fills at the end of each line of the verse. Gilmour's crunching guitar from the chorus extends into the outro, though the solo unusually poor for him – technically it's as competent as ever, but it lacks range or emotion, and simply extends the feeling of the chorus as the song fades out. Soundtrack albums seldom offer much time for second thoughts, and here we have Pink Floyd on autopilot. **COUNTRY SONG** wasn't used in *Zabriskie Point*, and only appeared on the bonus disc when the soundtrack album was re-released in 1997, making it a real obscurity. You can hear it point the way towards **US AND THEM** in the way it moves between verse and chorus, but it's no better than average when judged on its own.

UNKNOWN SONG (Gilmour, Water, Wright, Mason)
Length: 6.01
Guitars: Gilmour **Bass**: Waters **Keyboards**: Wright **Drums**: Mason
Recorded: 15-22 November, 7-12 December 1969, Technicolor Sound Services, Rome
Producer: Pink Floyd
First released: 16 September 1997 (*Zabriskie Point* Bonus Disc track 6)
Rating: 6/10

A charming instrumental piece, in two parts – the first, with guitar only, is cribbed from part one of **THE NARROW WAY** (and its earlier incarnation, 'Baby Blue Shuffle in D'). It is countryish, skilfully played, pleasant, and quite forgettable. In art it's possible to be too tasteful, leading to tastelessness. In the second part, kicking in from 1.55, the whole band plays together, retaining the

---

¶ Perhaps cribbed from 'Cry Baby Cry' on The Beatles' *White Album*.

country feel. However, Waters plays the bass line from the 'Funky Dung' section of **ATOM HEART MOTHER**, suggesting that it had been kicking about for a long time and that he was looking for a better place to put it. The group's careful shepherding of its material is seen here once again. **UNKNOWN SONG**, by dint of its two sections, feels slightly more of a song than most of the work on *Zabriskie Point*, though it too was only re-released in 1997 and remains an obscurity for most Pink Floyd fans.

LOVE SCENE VERSION 4 (Wright)
Length: 6.45
Piano: Wright
Recorded: 15–22 November, 7–12 December 1969, Technicolor Sound Services, Rome
Producer: Pink Floyd
First released: 16 September 1997 (*Zabriskie Point* Bonus Disc track 7)
Rating: 6/10

Some lovely delicate piano from Wright evoking melancholy and yearning – the sort of thing he's so very good at. But such competence in only one form brings to mind the marvellous Miles Davis quote, 'You know why I don't play ballads any more? Because I like playing them so much.' Facility can lead to triteness. There are some gorgeous trills here, slightly reminiscent of Herbie Hancock's astonishing piano solo in Miles Davis' 'Circle',* with which Wright was no doubt well acquainted. But the whole thing goes on for maybe three minutes more than it should. It creates and sustains a lovely delicate autumnal atmosphere, but there's no structure – no verse and chorus, no contrast, so it's not quite a proper song. You want some sense of development, but it just goes on, until it ends. It too was first released in 1997.

LOVE SCENE VERSION 6 (Gilmour, Water, Wright, Mason)
Length: 7.26
Guitars: Gilmour **Bass**: Wright **Piano**: Wright **Drums**: Mason
Recorded: 15–22 November, 7–12 December 1969, Technicolor Sound Services, Rome
Producer: Pink Floyd
First released: 16 September 1997 (*Zabriskie Point* Bonus Disc track 8)
Rating: 5/10

A competent slow blues which goes on for more than seven minutes and achieves very little. Gilmour does some decent vamping, and Wright plays some nice piano, but that's about it. It's another showcase of the group's versatility, if nothing else. If you ever wondered what Pink Floyd would sound like as an American cabaret band playing to an empty restaurant and a bar

---
* From *Miles Smiles* (1965).

with some hangdog regulars, this is the tune for you. They're not quite Murph and the Magic Tones,† but they're not too far away. It's remarkable to hear the band who played **INTERSTELLAR OVERDRIVE** and **GRANTCHESTER MEADOWS** playing this. It must be the greatest range in all of rock music.

The *Zabriskie Point* soundtrack is of course shared with other artists, from Jerry Garcia to Patti Page. Pink Floyd's contributions are noticeably more cinematic and atmospheric, and remarkably versatile – going from lounge jazz to sleepy blues to California folk rock. Without the unifying feature of only one band's contributions, *Zabriskie Point* is naturally more bitty and uneven. Working with Antonioni seems to have been an unpleasant, or at least irritating, experience. But it was yet another useful learning curve for the band, who famously had some good leftover musical pieces for subsequent use.‡

ATOM HEART MOTHER (Mason, Gilmour, Waters, Wright, Ron Geesin)
Length: 23.44
Vocals: The John Alldis Choir **Guitars**: Gilmour **Slide guitars**: Gilmour **Bass**: Waters **Hammond organ**: Wright **Farfisa organ**: Wright **Piano**: Wright **Mellotron**: Wright **Drums**: Mason **Percussion**: Mason **Cello**: Haflidi Hallgrimsson **Orchestra** (three trumpets, three horns, three trombones, tuba, two violins, two woodwind): EMI Pops Orchestra **Conductor**: Ron Geesin
Recorded: June 1970
Producer: Pink Floyd
First released: 2 October 1970 (*Atom Heart Mother* track 1)
Rating: 6/10

The period from the late 1960s to the mid-1970s was perhaps unique in the popular music industry where experimentation and being 'far out' were actively encouraged. The long track was a sign of musical ambition and artistic technique, while adding orchestral and symphonic components was seen as pushing the boundaries of rock music, just as The Beatles had done in moving from 'I Want to Hold Your Hand' to 'A Day in the Life'. Some of this initial experimentation led to great long songs, such as 'Sister Ray' by the Velvet Underground (from 1967), whose magnificent black distortion inspired many punk bands. As the progressive arena grew, Genesis,§ Yes,¶ Soft Machine,** King Crimson,††

---

† The cocktail lounge band from *The Blues Brothers* (1980), of course.
‡ See **US AND THEM**, in case you didn't know.
§ For example: 'Supper's Ready', 1972: 22.50.
¶ 'The Revealing Science of God: Dance of the Dawn', 1973: 20.23.
** 'Out-Bloody-Rageous', 1971: 19.37.
†† 'Lizard: Prince Rupert Awakes/Bolero: The Peacock's Tale/The Battle of G', 1970: 23.15.

Rush,* Mike Oldfield,† Tangerine Dream‡ and Van Der Graaf Generator§ all composed numerous lengthy pieces. But as in any trend, some were simply aping the fashion, leading to stitched-together piles of musical waffling. **ATOM HEART MOTHER** isn't quite as bad as that, and retains a certain charm, but in its shapeless noodling it veers close to being merely a relic of its time.¶

Ostensibly comprising six sections, the signposting in **ATOM HEART MOTHER**, however, isn't as clear as, say, in **ECHOES** or **A SAUCERFUL OF SECRETS**. The parts and approximate timings are: 'Father's Shout' (0.00–2.52), 'Breast Milky' (2.52–5.25), 'Mother Fore' (5.25–10.13), 'Funky Dung' (10.13–15.29), 'Mind Your Throats Please' (15.29–19.13) and 'Remergence' (19.13–23.44). The sections were enumerated on the label of the LP, but their rather random designations give no clue to their content. 'Father's Shout' opens with a swelling deep Hammond organ note, then the brass overture fades in from about 0.36 (sounding rather like a 1960s TV station opening theme), and then the main theme or motif of the entire suite is introduced at 1.24. Famously this was described as a 'Theme from an Imaginary Western',** and it does sound suitably grandiose, like watching John Wayne striding along the frontier. Wright described its inception as:

> [T]he idea came about because Dave ... he played it, somewhere or other ... and we all listened to it and thought, 'Oh, that's quite nice', but we all thought the same thing which was that it sounds like a theme from some awful Western; it had that kind of slight pastiche, heroic, plodding quality to it, of horses silhouetted against the sunset. Which is why we thought it'd be a good idea to play on that really and cover it in horns and strings and voices and whatever else.††

In any case, the main theme fades out at 1.55 to be replaced by brass parping away merrily and various found sounds (like motorbikes revving, bombs and explosions), and then we get the main theme again.

'Breast Milky' begins as these sounds all fade away, replaced by recurring motifs by both Waters on bass and Wright on Hammond organ, before a brief cello solo (from 2.59) joins in on top. Mason comes in on drums and then Gilmour adds a lovely, gentle slide guitar solo (from 3.56), in what must be his first excursion

---

* '2112: Overture/The Temples of Syrinx/Discovery', 1976: 20.33.
† His first four albums are all effectively album-length suites. *Ommadawn* (1975) is probably the best of them.
‡ 'Origin of Supernatural Probabilities', 1972: 19.34.
§ 'Plague of Lighthouse Keepers: Eyewitness/Pictures/Lighthouse/Eyewitness', 1971: 23.05.
¶ It's telling that its title was picked from a random newspaper headline. To paraphrase *Seinfeld*, it's a song about *nothing*.
** Music for imaginary films was an idea picked up by Pink Floyd fans The KLF, whose *The White Room* (1991) soundtracks an mostly unseen film, though it's now easily viewable on YouTube. (Their previous album *Chill Out* (1990) had a cover depicting sheep sitting down in a field, in homage to *Atom Heart Mother*.)
†† Capital Radio, *Pink Floyd Story Part 2*, 24 December 1976.

on that instrument. He switches to a regular guitar style at 4.25, soloing more assertively as the brass re-enters, building almost to a crescendo at 5.24.

Everything drops out as 'Mother Fore' begins, with only some drifting Hammond organ work from Wright, until the choir enters at 5.38, singing wordlessly like disembodied angelic apparitions, though gradually adding more bass voices. The atmosphere is rich, spectral and shadowy, like a haunted mansion on a warm summer night. This goes on for far too long before the drums and bass guitar come in at 9.09, giving it a necessary jolt of energy before they all start to drop out at around 10.00.

'Funky Dung' (in other words, 'funky shit') starts with Wright's Hammond organ overlapping the two sections, then we get a recurring bass motif from Waters (recycled from **UNKNOWN SONG**), and Gilmour comes in for another guitar solo at 10.48. It's oddly bluesy and its piercing tone stands out amidst the soft orchestral wash surrounding him. It's not one of his most memorable, however, and like everything else in **ATOM HEART MOTHER** seems to ramble on for a few minutes just because that's the time allotted to him. The backing rhythm is nicely funky, to be fair, but it desperately needs the muscular drive heard in the live tracks of *Ummagumma*. But on it plods until fading away at about 12.40, as the backing rhythm starts to feel more suspenseful from sustained Farsifa organ notes and stop-start drumming. The choir is then reintroduced (at 13.25), this time sounding more like witches and warlocks vengefully casting spells and incantations. The song now artfully builds the tension, with drum beats by Mason stoking the flames and the choir now singing ever higher, until the brass section excitingly re-enters (at 14.45), heralding a grandiose repetition of the main theme (from 14.57).

That completion of the circle would have been a good place to bring it all to an end, but instead we get 'Mind Your Throats Please', the most free-form section (and a precursor of the central section of **ECHOES**, which suggests how much better that song was organised). There are pulsating Mellotron notes, random brass interjections, random electronic sounds, a Leslie-treated announcer's voice (*'Here ... Here ... Here ... Here is a big announcement!'*),[‡‡] then the sound of a passing steam train,[§§] whistle and all, and so on and so on. The sound of a crashing wave seems to bring it all to an end at 17.42, whereat it all hoves back into view, distorted fragments of previous sections (Gilmour solos and all) colliding and merging as the brass re-emerges and takes the listener back to relative normality with the announcer intoning *'Silence in the studio!'* (at 19.11).

The final section, 'Remergence', begins with yet another iteration of the main theme, which then falls away for a repeat of the cello and Hammond organ duet

---

[‡‡] A precursor of the *'Stone ... stone ...'* section of **DOGS**. Though notice how apt it feels in that song, and how arbitrary it is here.

[§§] Redditor _NotJohnLennon_ has pointed out that the Yoko Ono track 'Paper Shoes' (from *Yoko Ono/Plastic Ono Band*, 1970) uses the same train sound effect. The Abbey Road sounds effect library probably wasn't that big.

from 'Breast Milky', then Gilmour again solos on the slide guitar solo and then in a more strident fashion, again in the style of 'Breast Milky', and then the guitars, brass, choir and main theme emerge and combine at 22.15 for a glorious, bombastic, overly lengthy and long-overdue crescendo, choirs and all. And there we are: Pink Floyd's longest individual track, by fifteen seconds over **ECHOES**. But if listening to it sometimes feels a chore, recording it was worse. As Mason notes:

> In order to keep tracks free for the overdubs we had bass and drums on two tracks, and the whole recording had to be done in one pass. Playing the piece without any other instruments meant that getting through it without mistakes demanded the full range of our limited musicianship; matters such as tempo had to be left in abeyance.*

Another issue explains the relative mushiness of the sound: 'We had been forced to supply relatively high levels of backing track to the orchestra on monitor speakers, some of which had been picked up by their microphones. This unerasable spill forever ensured that [the song] lacked the sonic clarity we have always strived for.'† As a production, therefore, **ATOM HEART MOTHER** combines some of the most colourful instrumentation ever recorded by Pink Floyd with some of the poorest recording, with a thinness that makes it feel like a watercolour rather than a bold oil painting.

Yet there's no disputing that **ATOM HEART MOTHER** has arresting stretches of highly imaginative music, and that its symphonic instrumentation and ambition make it a fascinating effort. But without any teleological sense (in other words, any sense of guiding structure or narrative), it remains a hodgepodge, a random agglomeration rather than offering overall coherence. In this sense, its initial name 'The Amazing Pudding' would have been far more apt. It might be thought surprising that a composer like Ron Geesin‡ didn't guide the song towards something more integrated. Geesin's previous work,§ however, wasn't classical but was even more radically freeform than Pink Floyd had attempted, utilising found sounds, poetry, satirical excursions, sound collages, and outright noise, like *The Goon Show* amplified through an aleatory sensibility. As it is, **ATOM HEART MOTHER** is ultimately a charming but failed experiment.

Although the group were proud of it at the time and were filmed playing it live (brass sections, choirs and all), it rapidly fell out of favour, its final performance coming on 22 May 1972. They were smart enough to realise where their true strengths were, taking numerous lessons from it on how to manage lengthy material; and the times were kind enough to ambitious young prog-rockers to

---

*   *Inside Out*, p.146.
†   *Inside Out*, p.147.
‡   Alongside Bob Ezrin for **THE TRIAL**, the only outsider to receive a songwriting credit until *A Momentary Lapse Of Reason*.
§   Such as his 1967 debut album, *A Raise of Eyebrows*.

send the album to #1 in the UK charts (and top ten throughout Western Europe, though only #55 in the USA). Those were really different days.

> **IF** (Waters)
> **Length**: 4.31
> **Vocals**: Waters **Guitars**: Waters **Slide guitar**: Gilmour **Bass**: Waters **Piano**: Wright
> **Hammond organ**: Wright **Drums**: Mason
> **Recorded**: 12 June–21 July 1970
> **Producer**: Pink Floyd
> **First released**: 2 October 1970 (*Atom Heart Mother* track 2)
> **Rating**: 7/10

The most delicate song in the entire Pink Floyd discography is in its own way a typically bold effort by Waters. Its hushed, near-whispered vocals and acoustic guitar both suggest the honesty and lack of artifice of folk music, a move that redoubles the effect of the song's lyrics, which are about self-doubt, weakness, and – as is often remarked – madness.¶ It's a quite radical lyric, neatly reversing the patriotic bombast and public-school derring-do of the Rudyard Kipling poem of the same name** for the recognition (and thus valuing) of fragility and otherness. This reversal of the values of patriarchal, class-bound Britain towards something more inclusive is one of Waters' most enduring strengths as a songwriter, as he would display throughout *Dark Side*, in **WISH YOU WERE HERE** and (rather more implicitly) in 'the bleeding hearts and the artists' in *The Wall*. (Waters would later make great claims about the degree to which empathy was his great theme,†† but it's also very noticeable that his greatest works are often splenetic.)

Besides the acoustic guitar played by Waters, Gilmour adds some slide guitar during the breaks between each verse (there's no chorus, just five verses), and Wright contributes some perfectly judged feather-touch piano. Musically, beyond the acoustic guitar, **IF** is somewhat insubstantial – without a chorus or middle-eight there's no variety of mood or feeling, and the instrumental breaks after the second and fourth verses maintain the same rhythm and so fail to increase tension or momentum. It feels more of a mood piece than a complete song, though after the elephantine multi-movement suite of **ATOM HEART MOTHER**, its slightness comes as something of a relief.

¶ It's the first reference to the subject in Waters' lyrics, though this is the least important aspect of the song, overall.

** The last verse of which runs:
> If you can talk with crowds and keep your virtue,
>   Or walk with Kings—nor lose the common touch,
> If neither foes nor loving friends can hurt you,
>   If all men count with you, but none too much;
> If you can fill the unforgiving minute
>   With sixty seconds' worth of distance run,
> Yours is the Earth and everything that's in it,
>   And—which is more—you'll be a Man, my son!

†† See *Classic Albums: Dark Side of the Moon* episode.

> **SUMMER '68** (Wright)
> **Length**: 5.29
> **Vocals**: Wright **Guitars**: Gilmour **Bass**: Waters **Hammond organ**: Wright **Drums**: Mason
> **Backing vocals**: Gilmour **Percussion**: Mason **Brass**: The Abbey Road Pops Orchestra
> **Recorded**: December 1968–January 1969, 5–20 July 1970
> **Producer**: Pink Floyd
> **First released**: 2 October 1970 (*Atom Heart Mother* track 3)
> **Rating**: 7/10

This song is often rated as Wright's best individual piece,* for its wistfulness and greater melodic invention. It also features an unusually open lyric about a casual fling with a groupie (with absence again a notable motif: '*She left six hours ago*').† Nonetheless, its brass parts are oversaturated, making them really grate on the ears. The group were by now producing their work, with Norman Smith upstairs as 'executive producer' (meaning he was available should they need him: he was rarely summoned). Doing so on just your third album was bold, and to do so with a track like **ATOM HEART MOTHER** was downright foolhardy. Nonetheless, this shows how quickly the group learned, and how keen they were to wrest control.

Opening with a nice piano intro – its confidence and memorability being exactly the sort of thing **SEE-SAW** was lacking – the first verse is then sung by Wright in a typically wistful voice, with only half the band backing him. The song then almost explodes with feeling in the chorus, with its repeated '*How do you feel?*' refrain.

SUMMER '68 is a rare stumble in the group's production – though, as can be seen in the live side of *Ummagumma*, their arrangements could improve significantly. However, in terms of songwriting it demonstrates significant improvement, with a fine intro, arresting chorus, contrasting instrumental section, and pleasantly wistful verse and vocal. Besides the overwhelming brass, however, the real problem is the weakness in Wright's voice, which can't quite carry the verse and needs audible support from Gilmour in the chorus. Excluding the next soundtrack album *Obscured by Clouds*, this was the last solo vocal Wright would have until **WEARING THE INSIDE OUT** twenty-three years later – though he would share the vocals in songs like **ECHOES** and **TIME**, and do a bloody good job of it.

---

* Clare Torry has received a co-writing credit for **THE GREAT GIG IN THE SKY** since 2005. And rightly so.
† The Floyd were rarely seen as ones to enjoy the indulgences enabled by touring, but subsequent references in interviews suggest their own share of prurience. Wright said: 'In the summer of '68, there were groupies everywhere; they'd come and look after you like a personal maid, do your washing, sleep with you and leave with a dose of the clap.' (Q Magazine, November 1994). In the same interview he recalls on the same tour when Gilmour 'drove a motorbike into a restaurant and out again, in a very straight bit of America, and most of the diners pretended it wasn't happening.' Not something which Gilmour brings up now (though he did confirm it to Q Magazine in June 1999: 'Funnily enough, it didn't get any reaction at all. People were so frightened by it that they all stared very hard at their plates.')

FAT OLD SUN (Gilmour)
Length: 5.22
Vocals: Gilmour **Guitars**: Gilmour **Bass**: Gilmour **Farsifa organ**: Wright
Hammond organ: Wright **Drums**: Gilmour **Pedal steel guitars**: Gilmour
Percussion:Gilmour
Recorded: 11-13 June 1970
Producer: Pink Floyd
First released: 2 October 1970 (*Atom Heart Mother* track 4)
Rating: 8/10

Gilmour's first song of note is a lovely pastoral hymn to the Cambridgeshire countryside. Opening with the sound of morning bells,[‡] it's sung beautifully just short of a falsetto, while Gilmour keeps up a lazy strummed shuffle on the acoustic guitar on the verse before shifting to an organ-led hymnal in the chorus. Curiously, Gilmour also plays all the other instruments – even the drums – with the exception of the Farsifa and Hammond organs played by Wright. The others may have been busy working on **ATOM HEART MOTHER**, but it feels slightly neglectful of the new boy – especially a song of this delicacy and charm.

That very delicacy is both the strength and weakness of **FAT OLD SUN**, on which the drums and guitar drop out during the chorus to emphasise its prayer-like quality, particularly the last line: '*Sing to me, sing to me*'. The lyric likewise uses some nice details ('*Distant bells / New-mown grass smells so sweet*', '*Summer evening, birds are calling*') to evoke a gorgeous rural atmosphere of meadows and twilit country lanes. Somehow it doesn't feel hokey but genuinely felt.[§] But while there's something of an uplift at the start of the concluding guitar solo, it meanders on rather inconsequentially and then fades out, while the drums clatter about. A stronger ending – in the manner maybe of **LOST FOR WORDS**, which also fades out but features a more distinctive guitar solo – would move **FAT OLD SUN** into perhaps the group's twenty best songs. As it is, it's a deep cut cherished by many.

Gilmour remains proud of **FAT OLD SUN**, having pushed unsuccessfully for it to be included on the *Echoes* compilation,[¶] and regularly playing it on solo tours. When played live (its run in the live repertoire lasted from September 1970 to November 1971 – see Chapter 3), it was much extended, sometimes lasting over fifteen minutes with a slightly noodling jammed instrumental tacked

---

[‡] Not an allusion to the grim tolling bell opening *John Lennon/Plastic Ono Band*, as that wasn't released until December 1970. They missed each other in the Abbey Road studio by about a month (*Atom Heart Mother* was recorded in various sessions from March to August, while the Lennon album was September-October).

[§] Compare with John Major's evocation of England, which by 1993 was seen as absurd: 'long shadows on county [cricket] grounds, warm beer, invincible green suburbs, dog lovers, and—as George Orwell said—old maids bicycling to Holy Communion through the morning mist.'

[¶] 'I tried to persuade the rest of the Pink Floyd guys that it should go on *Echoes: The Best of Pink Floyd* but they weren't having it.' (*The Sun*, 26 September 2008). Gilmour also notes in the same interview, 'I played the drums on the original recording but the drums are so bad.' He certainly doesn't have Mason's gentle touch.

on. Gilmour also played it during his *On an Island* and *Rattle That Lock* tours, where the studio outro was played with far greater energy and force. But by then he'd had over thirty-five years for second thoughts.

> **ALAN'S PSYCHEDELIC BREAKFAST** (Waters, Mason, Gilmour, Wright)
> **Length**: 13.00
> **Vocals**: Alan Styles **Guitars**: Gilmour **Bass**: Waters **Piano**: Wright
> **Hammond organ**: Wright **Drums**: Mason **Percussion**: Mason
> **Recorded**: 18 June, 10–21 July 1970
> **Producer**: Pink Floyd
> **First released**: 2 October 1970 (*Atom Heart Mother* track 5)
> **Rating**: 6/10

There is a 'Law Of Misnomers': if something has an adjective in its name, you can bet it won't be a good example of it. For example, a 'People's Republic' and a 'Democratic Republic' will actually be dictatorships, while any brand with an adjective (for example 'cool' or 'funky') in its name can be guaranteed not to be so. The law stands true here: the group had never before had to assert the psychedelic nature of their music; there was almost always a broader point to their explorations and experiments. Here, the 'psychedelic' label is a warning that what will unfold will be some directionless noodling. The group's interest in the quotidian and in existential realities (as conveyed through the sound of heartbeats, tick-tocking clocks, footsteps, airport announcements, and so on) here veers into a contentment with the mundane,* as though merely soundtracking aspects of life were enough to dramatise it.†

As with **ATOM HEART MOTHER**, the song is split into a number of sections, though this time less arbitrarily. Here there are three: 'Rise And Shine' (0.00–3.34), 'Sunny Side-Up' (3.35–7.45), and 'Morning Glory' (7.46–13.00). The first begins with just over a minute of background sounds such as a tap dripping, roadie Alan Styles murmuring about breakfasts he has eaten ('*Scrambled eggs, bacon, sausages, tomatoes. Toast, coffee, marmalade, I like marmalade ...*') with some loose double-tracking to create an echoing effect, and matches being struck, presumably to light a gas hob. The music finally enters at 1.02, with a pretty, circular piano riff, on top of which Gilmour first solos rather inconsequentially and then Wright adds a Hammond organ solo from about 2.15. At around 3.14 the music starts to fade out, as the whistling of a kettle is superimposed, then everything fades out for the next section. But as the piano riff remains constant throughout, there's no sense of progress, just a band noodling away over a repeated musical figure. It's pretty and charming but lacks substance.

---

* The same problem sometimes occurs in *Seinfeld* (1989-1998). The greatest episodes are hilarious dissections of life as a series of contingent events; the less successful just obsess about the most trivial details.

† Similarly, Andy Warhol published a novel, *a* (1968), taken directly from two years of tape-recorded conversations from his Factory studio. Not surprisingly, it's unreadable.

'Sunny Side-Up' begins with more contemplation of breakfast from Alan Stiles: '*Breakfast in Los Angeles, macrobiotic stuff*,' which probably seemed terribly hip and progressive at the time. There's more tap drips and match-lighting, the shaking of cereal (or perhaps pulses, the macrobiotic food of choice), and the sound of something frying before a gentle acoustic piece from Gilmour fades in. It's mostly strummed at the beginning, with high notes picked out later on, a slide guitar added on here and there, and Waters keeping a gentle pulse on the bass. It's gentle and delicate and warm and folky and very charming, but essentially rather slight. Gilmour is undoubtedly an exquisite acoustic player, but the band at this stage simply hadn't found a way to integrate that into their repertoire.‡ Sweet and meaningless, 'Sunny Side-Up' fades away from about 7.35.

The final section, 'Morning Glory' (fading in after nearly a minute of murmuring and background noises!), is perhaps more typically Floydian, with a propulsive beat from Mason, opening piano from Wright before he switches to the organ at 10.53, and a forgettable Gilmour solo at 9.52.§ But despite the greater energy, there's little sense of destination: it chunters on amiably, building up steam towards the end thanks to organ playing from Wright and greater force from the band, but without ever suggesting getting anywhere: it starts, builds, then simply ends, as inconsequential as the dripping tap that closes things. And so thirteen minutes are filled.

ALAN'S PSYCHEDELIC BREAKFAST is basically a few band jams stuck together around an inconsequential theme, with a nagging sense that it's there to fill side two of *Atom Heart Mother*, though the three sections are sequenced very well. But for all that it's rather charming, Pink Floyd at their most relaxed and approachable, taking on chamber pop, acoustic folksiness and bluesy rock in a gentle English manner. The band's interest in dramatising existential realities here, however, verges into the banal: there's nothing rock 'n' roll about breakfast. The use of a theme to tie together disparate material would later be done far more successfully on numerous albums, as would the musique concrète and spoken word interjections; while Wright's chamber pop tendencies disappeared altogether after this track.

Atom Heart Mother might be disliked by the band¶ but it is Pink Floyd's most varied album of their post-Barrett incarnations, with moments of great colour, imagination and existential dramatisation. It is also utterly English in a charming way that now feels long gone. But what's less often mentioned is its sly circularity. The opening and closing **ATOM HEART MOTHER** and **ALAN'S PSYCHEDELIC BREAKFAST** mirror each other as multi-part suites; **IF** and

---

§ At this stage of his career, you would not have picked him likely to be one of the best guitarists of all time. But then you would not have imagined at this stage that Waters could go on to write *The Wall*. You can't predict creativity.
¶ Roger Waters: '*Atom Heart Mother* is a really awful and embarrassing record.' (*Rock Compact Disc* magazine, Issue 3, September 1992).

FAT OLD SUN are both delicate acoustic ballads; and then in the middle there's the yearning chamber pop of Wright's **SUMMER '68**. This attention to the structure of an album is, of course, one of Pink Floyd's greatest talents. But *Atom Heart Mother* is also one of the hardest to rate as an album: the title track often feels on the verge of becoming something momentous, though it never quite does, while the short tracks have definite charm without being as consequential as the key tracks on *A Saucerful of Secrets* or *Meddle*. Their main strengths of narrative and structure which the group so emphatically displayed on the live section of *Ummagumma* are nowhere to be found. Consequently, *Atom Heart Mother* feels more like a detour than a forward step* – perhaps akin to the Rolling Stones' *Their Satanic Majesties Request* (1967). Both have moments of unique adventurousness, but they're not what either band does best. Fortunately for Pink Floyd the detour was short-lived.

ONE OF THESE DAYS (Waters, Gilmour, Wright, Mason)
Length: 5.57
Vocals: Mason **Guitars**: Gilmour **Pedal steel guitars**: Gilmour **Bass (right channel)**: Waters **Bass (left channel)**: Gilmour **Piano**: Wright **Hammond organ**: Wright **EMS VCS 3 synthesiser**: Wright **Drums**: Mason **Backwards cymbals**: Mason
Recorded: 19-21, 23-25 July 1971, Morgan Sound Studios, London
Producer: Pink Floyd
First released: 31 October 1971 (*Meddle* track 1)
Rating: 9/10

ONE OF THESE DAYS opens *Meddle* with significantly more aggressive attack, making it a pivotal moment for Pink Floyd. It's as though they're declaring that the random explorations of yesterday have gone – here's something with far more kick (though the group do typically allow themselves forty seconds of atmospheric wind effects before really getting going). The song is a magnificent sonic wash, with the pulsating bass lines (played by both Waters and Gilmour, through the Binson Echorec),† Gilmour's slide guitar, the colourful organ work by Wright and his wonderful spacey *bing!* motif all cohering into wildly exciting waves of sound. There are longueurs – the central breakdown after the song first peaks takes far too long, going from 2.49 to 3.45, though it does peak wonderfully near the end, and there are over thirty seconds of wind noises before the opening bass riffs get going – but the group at this stage had little fear of boring their audience. Indeed, patience was one of their greatest virtues, allowing **ONE OF THESE DAYS** to build its atmosphere and tension to almost unbearable levels, so that when the drums finally kick in at 3.45, there's a wonderful sense

---

* None of its songs are on the *Echoes* compilation.
† 'You can actually hear it if you listen in stereo. The first bass is me. A bar later, Roger joins in on the other side of the stereo picture. We didn't have a spare set of strings for the spare bass guitar, so the second bass is very dull sounding. [laughs] We sent a roadie out to buy some strings, but he wandered off to see his girlfriend instead.' (Gilmour interviewed in *Guitar World*, February 1993).

of release. The stomping rhythm thereafter pulsates with a tremendous physicality: this is a Pink Floyd song you can actually dance to. (The title of the 1981 compilation *A Collection of Great Dance Songs* is, of course, highly ironic.)

The surging rhythm of **ONE OF THESE DAYS** led to some curious avenues. During 1972, the group collaborated with the French ballet director and choreographer Roland Petit in staging a remarkable fusion of music and dance.‡ The group performed **ONE OF THESE DAYS**, **ECHOES**, **CAREFUL WITH THAT AXE, EUGENE** and **OBSCURED BY CLOUDS** on a stage above the dancers giving Petit's interpretation of the songs. The most successful reading was **ONE OF THESE DAYS**, whose calisthenic dance routine was an ideal match for the song's propulsive rhythm. On the other hand, the corporeal nature of ballet means that the most out-there aspects of the track, such as Gilmour's high-pitched slide-guitar solo and Wright's spacey motif, aren't represented in the choreography. However, **ONE OF THESE DAYS**, with its colour and energy, remains best heard simply as abstract music: the title and single vocal utterance (Mason saying '*One of these days I'm going to cut you into little pieces*' in a falsetto, which was then slowed down to sound more like a growl) add nothing to the meaning of the track. Insofar as it has a meaning, **ONE OF THESE DAYS** is simply about the pleasure of sound, and the group's energy, colour and force, and it's one of the group's very best album openers.§ Despite dropping out of the group's live setlist after *Dark Side of the Moon*, when song messages became a key concern, **ONE OF THESE DAYS** was resurrected in 1987 for the Momentary Lapse tour and remains a live Gilmour staple. The live versions on *Delicate Sound of Thunder* and *Pulse* are both absolutely terrific.

A PILLOW OF WINDS (Waters, Gilmour)
Length: 5.10
Vocals: Gilmour **Guitars**: Gilmour **Slide guitars**: Gilmour **Fretless bass**: Gilmour
Piano: Wright **Hammond organ**: Wright **Hi-hat**: Mason
Recorded: July 1971, Morgan Sound Studios, London
Producer: Pink Floyd
First released: 31 October 1971 (*Meddle* track 2)
Rating: 8/10

Expertly cross-fading from **ONE OF THESE DAYS** with the wind blowing, **A PILLOW OF WINDS** is a gorgeous effort to convey the atmosphere of sleep. The group were always keen for their music to dramatise the human condition (from 'The Man–The Journey' onwards), and here the group give a beautiful

---

‡ Ballet was then an artform with a greater appeal to the cultural elite, as Edmund White describes it: 'Whereas intellectuals and artists seldom attended symphonic or orchestral events, back then the ballet attracted the best minds in [New York]... Like rock fans they spoke of the dancers (whom they didn't know) in terms of familiarity: "Karen's put on a few pounds", I'd say, or, "God, Patricia seems more and more neurotic—I think she may be on her way to having a total breakdown one of these days." "Suzanne was sublime tonight in Jerry's boring old Ravel piano concerto."' (*City Boy: My Life in New York in the 1960s and '70s*, pp.175–6).
§ Alongside **ASTRONOMY DOMINE**, **SHINE ON YOU CRAZY DIAMOND**, and **IN THE FLESH?**

evocation of night-time rest and tranquillity. The nylon strings and electric arpeggios sparkle delicately, there is no real tune, giving a droning, slumbering feeling, the delicious fretless bass (played by Gilmour) suggests warm darkness and subdued consciousness, while Gilmour's delicate vocals soothes and consoles without feeling fey or mannered. Mason and Wright meanwhile take a back seat, providing only hi-hat punctuation (only really audible from 2.32 onwards) and subdued piano, respectively. With Gilmour adding a slide guitar solo to bring the song to an end (from 4.05 onwards), **A PILLOW OF WINDS** is a superb atmosphere piece in which the guitar player's contributions loom largest. The track may appear relatively insubstantial, but in comparison to **GREEN IS THE COLOUR**, which also features a droning non-melody, acoustic guitars and a high Gilmour vocal, **A PILLOW OF WINDS** is a far more artful construction, each element in place to create its lush crepuscular atmosphere.

There is some debate over whether Waters played the fretless bass. Gilmour later claimed that 'at least half the bass on all recorded output is me anyway', adding 'Roger playing fretless bass? Please!'* It is well known that Gilmour played the fretless bass on **HEY YOU**, but by the time of *The Wall* recording had become more of an assembly line and both Gilmour and Mason were substituted when necessary. (See **IS THERE ANYBODY OUT THERE?** and **MOTHER**.) If Gilmour did play the bass, then **A PILLOW OF WINDS** would be one of the very few tracks on which Waters does not appear while in the band (most of the others being on *Ummagumma*). This also suggests how pivotal Gilmour had become to the group's recording processes. From being the new boy standing awkwardly and not quite knowing what to do, he had now overtaken Wright in his influence on the band, in both writing and recording.

FEARLESS (Waters, Gilmour, Wright, Mason)
Length: 6.08
Vocals: Gilmour **Guitars**: Gilmour **Bass**: Waters **Piano**: Wright **Drums**: Mason
Percussion: Mason
Recorded: July 1971, Morgan Sound Studios, London
Producer: Pink Floyd
First released: 31 October 1971 (*Meddle* track 3)
Rating: 8/10

The move to sixteen tracks allows **FEARLESS** to enjoy multi-tracked guitars, giving it a rich sheen and multiple simultaneous timbres that tickle the ears delightfully. Which is a good job, because the track itself is rather slight, lacking any great melody or contrasting bridge or chorus. It also features what must be Gilmour's final falsetto vocal, which had marked some of their early work (like **GREEN IS THE COLOUR** and **FAT OLD SUN**) with a slight fey

---

* *Rock Compact Disc* magazine, Issue 3, September 1992.

preciousness: from *Meddle* through to *The Wall*, the group would be increasingly muscular. Opening with some fine ringing chords, **FEARLESS** then ascends stepwise (alongside some brief choral vocals) to a peak from which Gilmour seems to be singing. The chorus, where most of the guitars drop out, are more reflective, contrasting nicely with the elegant climb of the ascending chord sequence in the verses, and showing Gilmour at his more subtle and tasteful. That tastefulness extends to the entire recording: **FEARLESS** is finely textured, with Wright only playing subtle little piano chords at around 3.40 – no distinctive colouring here – and Waters with some very nice touches on bass. It feels as though the whole track has had its edges delicately sanded off. That lack of grit, however, also makes **FEARLESS** slightly too easy to ignore.

Lyrically, it's rather opaque but suggests some kind of optimism and willingness to go it alone, as heard soon after (and rather better) in **CHILDHOOD'S END**. Combining something of the arty mysticism of **SET THE CONTROLS FOR THE HEART OF THE SUN** and the existential concerns of **TIME**, **FEARLESS** is something of a pivot song, albeit less successful than either comparator. It also continues the trick heard in **COUNTRY SONG** of naming characters: in this case '*the idiot*' and '*the magistrate*', while there's a very artful shift from second person in the first verse to first person in the chorus and then third person in the second verse (a trick later used with far greater impact in **DOGS**). The ending – a recording of Liverpool fans singing 'You'll Never Walk Alone' with some whoa-trippy-man spacey effects at the end – suggests both the choral effects of the multi-tracked guitars and the reason for the title, which according to Mason was a 'soccer-inspired equivalent of "awesome" – that had come from Tony Gorvitch, the manager of Family'.[†] Private jokes like this also give early Pink Floyd its insular, self-absorbed character – which was good in letting the group develop as they wanted, but less successful in expanding the group's audience. But rock bands could get away with such things in 1971. Few on their way up would dare try now. Probably because of its multitracking, **FEARLESS** was never played live by Pink Floyd, which is a shame.[‡] But as an album track it works primarily because of its textures, and Gilmour's highly accomplished studio work; yet its lyrical vagueness and placid emotional atmosphere mean **FEARLESS** doesn't feel of any great significance.

SAN TROPEZ (Waters)
Length: 3.43
Vocals: Waters **Guitars**: Waters **Slide guitars**: Gilmour **Bass**: Waters **Piano**: Wright
Drums: Mason **Percussion**: Mason
Recorded: August 1971, Morgan Sound Studios, London
Producer: Pink Floyd
First released: 31 October 1971 (*Meddle* track 4)
Rating: 5/10

[†] Mason, *Inside Out*, p.151.
[‡] Though it has been resurrected by Nick Mason's Saucerful of Secrets band.

Fans of Pink Floyd who start with the classic four albums then work backwards may be surprised to hear **SAN TROPEZ**, even to the point of thinking it sarcastic or simply ironic. But the fact seems to be that it is simply another example of the Floyd in a playful mood, alongside **BIDING MY TIME** and **ALAN'S PSYCHEDELIC BREAKFAST**, for example. Never a frequent aspect of the band's repertoire, after *Meddle* such lively moments disappeared completely. This is rather a shame, although this track's light-hearted feel doesn't mesh with the rest of the album. It's hard to picture Waters in a top hat and cane, singing in front of a tight little cocktail bar band, and yet that's what this track summons up. Nevertheless, the most recognisable, most Floydian aspect of the track is in the recurring refrain (there being no chorus), '*And if you're alone / I'll come home*' – yet another example of the motif of absence, and perhaps a direct precursor of the desperate loneliness of the phonecall in **YOUNG LUST**. Touring might sound glamorous, but being at the mercy of primitive 1970s international calls to sustain relationships must have been very hard, especially at the rate that Pink Floyd toured. Another foreshadowing of later lyrical concerns comes in the lines '*Owning a home / With no silver spoon / I'm drinking champagne / Like a big tycoon*', which obviously predicts **MONEY** and **WELCOME TO THE MACHINE**. Money seems to have been increasingly on Waters' mind, perhaps as a result of four years of toil and the group still being very much a cult, underground band.* Aged 28 when this song was released, he was very likely no longer the naïve young avant-garde artist but someone realising he would have to fight for his slice of the pie.

Slightly reminiscent of the jazz-rock of Steely Dan, though feeling of less significance in the absence of that band's ironic mentality and sardonic lyrics, **SAN TROPEZ** is probably just a fine stylistic excursion on an album needing completed. Musically it features some fine slide guitar from Gilmour, always capable of a genre exercise, from 1.15 to 1.46, and a tearoom orchestra piano solo and outro from Wright at 2.25 until the song fades out. It's all very pastiche and mannered, but exquisitely done. It also shows the Floyd as masters of the creation of atmosphere, as developed from **CAREFUL WITH THAT AXE, EUGENE** onwards. Despite, or due to, its slightness, **SAN TROPEZ** required a great deal of musical and compositional skill. As Kingsley Amis wrote of light verse,† a concert pianist is allowed a certain number of missed notes, but a juggler can't drop a single plate.‡ It is also yet another example of the group creating a complete soundworld, which they by now sound as though they could do at the drop of a hat.

---

* Despite *Atom Heart Mother* reaching #1 in the UK album charts. It didn't even reach the top 50 in the US, where the *real* money was made. The group weren't relentlessly touring America for no good reason.
† In his introduction to the *New Oxford Book of Light Verse* (1978).
‡ Compare with 'I Will' by The Beatles (on the *White Album*) – a light and slight McCartney piece, but highly demanding to play, and requiring 67 takes to get right.

SEAMUS (Waters, Gilmour, Wright, Mason)
Length: 2.16
Vocals: Gilmour **Guitars**: Gilmour **Bass**: Waters **Piano**: Wright **Yowling**: Seamus (dog)
Producer: Pink Floyd
Recorded: May–August 1971, Morgan Studios, London; AIR Studios, London
First released: 31 October 1971 (*Meddle* track 5).
Rating: 4/10

Despite being renowned as Serious Artists (an impression that only grew in the Waters Years), Pink Floyd shared a wry sense of humour (see **SAN TROPEZ**). Here they appropriate the downhome blues style, in a dead-on straight-faced take that's hard to tell whether it's satire or tribute. While The Beatles had many such pastiches on the *White Album* (such as the 1930s dance hall take-off 'Honey Pie' and the Beach Boys send-up 'Back in the USSR'), the Floyd usually lacked a comparable deftness of touch – as with the bludgeoning **CORPORAL CLEGG**, for example. The result is a song that's beautifully played by Gilmour, but lacks any charm (thanks to the canine howling from the eponymous Seamus, owned by Steve Marriot of the Small Faces) or sense (the band not being renowned for excursions into honky-tonk blues). **SEAMUS** is thus an exact approximation of the country blues sound, without the hooks or authenticity of the genre; and, typically, the Floyd can't wring a memorable three-minute tune out of it: it just ends without any sense of closure.

The song was reprised on *Live at Pompeii*, as 'Mademoiselle Nobs'. It's basically the same song, except Gilmour displays a hitherto-unseen skill with the harmonica instead of singing, and a bitch called Nobs replaces Seamus. The most that can be said about **SEAMUS** is that the adventurousness that led them to use animal sounds here would be successfully utilised a few years later in *Animals*, and that they show they can approximate the sound of almost any genre. **SEAMUS** has nonetheless been sometimes voted the worst Pink Floyd song of all time, though Mason's **GRAND VIZIER'S GARDEN PARTY** must surely be a better candidate.

ECHOES (Waters, Gilmour, Wright, Mason)
Length: 23.32
Vocals: Gilmour, Wright **Guitars**: Gilmour **Bass**: Waters **Piano**: Wright **Hammond organ**: Wright **Farsifa organ**: Wright **Drums**: Mason **Percussion**: Mason
Recorded: 7 March–1 May 1971
Producer: Pink Floyd
First released: 31 October 1971 (*Meddle* track 6)
Rating: 10/10

The first masterpiece by the post-Syd Barrett incarnation of Pink Floyd, **ECHOES** was a pivotal moment for the group. After the intriguing but fumbling explorations of their previous two non-soundtrack albums *Ummagumma* and *Atom Heart Mother*, *Meddle* demonstrates a significant leap forward. The reasons for this are not entirely clear, but probably just come from sheer hard work. Certainly by 1971, David Gilmour had been fully integrated into the group, revealing talents on guitar and vocally that far surpass those of Syd Barrett, though Barrett was the far greater writer. The progression to 16-track recording may have helped: certainly, *Meddle* is the first album where textures and timbres are strongly to the fore, in comparison to the previous post-Syd albums which were most successful when creating mood and atmosphere. (Tuneful tracks like **BIDING MY TIME** or **SUMMER '68** seem oddly meaningless in comparison, pleasing in their way but sounding as though they could have been by anyone else. The Floyd's great tracks, from **INTERSTELLAR OVERDRIVE** to **TIME** to **COMFORTABLY NUMB**, could only have been done by them.)

A great deal of touring and studio work had been done, each building on the other: songwriting, performance, dynamics, presentation and self-dramatisation had all improved remarkably. First-person accounts like **PAINT BOX** and **IF** fade away, succeeded by sound-poems and multi-section epics. The first success in the latter vein was, of course, **A SAUCERFUL OF SECRETS**, particularly in its live iteration on *Ummagumma*. But how could that be topped?

ECHOES showed the way (as the group have often said).[*] Coming from a series of experiments and noodlings (whimsically, and now famously, titled 'Nothing, Parts 1–24', then 'The Son of Nothing', then 'The Return of the Son of Nothing'), **ECHOES** was both the culmination and the extension of all Pink Floyd had achieved so far. After Barrett, the group had failed to write a convincing pop single, with a fast-moving melody. So instead, as in their live work, tracks were elongated, driven by rhythm with little melodic variation. After *Atom Heart Mother,* they had a better understanding of structure and architecture, so arrangements became more important. And as Waters gradually came to find his voice lyrically, the words took on more importance. All three elements are significant breakthroughs in **ECHOES**.

The lyrics are literate and poetic without being abstruse, as so often found in prog rock from Yes to Jethro Tull, if the actual meaning is somewhat obscure. Waters described it later as 'The potential that human beings have for recognizing each other's humanity and responding to it, with empathy rather than antipathy,'[†] which seems clear from the third verse – '*Strangers passing in the street / By chance two separate glances meet / And I am you and what I see is me*'[‡] – though the rest remains rather vague. The albatross is a very nice touch, instantly connecting the lyric with Colderidge's *The Rime of the Ancient Mariner*

---

[*] 'I think "Echoes" is the masterwork of the album – the one where we were all discovering what Pink Floyd is about.' Gilmour in *Guitar World*, February 1993.
[†] Roger Waters in *Classic Albums: Dark Side of the Moon*.
[‡] Compare with The Beatles' 'I Am The Walrus' – '*I am he as you are he as you are me / And we are all together*'.

(1798) and giving it a deeper poetic resonance.§ The watery motif likewise is an attempt to move away from the space (cadet) connotations of **INTERSTELLAR OVERDRIVE** and **ASTRONOMY DOMINE**, towards something more earth-bound and concrete. (This is a trend that would continue. As Gilmour later noted, by around this time he had 'started falling out of love with some of that psychedelic noodling stuff'.¶ The direction from here on would be outward, not inward, concrete rather than abstract, and humanist rather than mystical.)

Related to this, song structures begin to simplify. Where **ATOM HEART MOTHER** had (or said it had) six sections without clear divisions or narrative indicators, **ECHOES** signposts its movements clearly, with a long fade-in introduction, a verse-refrain-verse main section, an instrumental jam which fades out to a central abstract noise section, with the sound of wind, rooks, and high-pitched squawks (the famous 'whale' sound, to be reprised in **IS THERE ANYBODY OUT THERE?**), before a fade-in, guitar solo, further verse and climactic fade-out. But essentially it's an ABA pattern – there, and back again. This greater focus made the song easier to digest, even if the melodic pace remained glacial.

But what is so great about **ECHOES** is the sheer mystery and majesty of the track. Wright's opening piano overture has a stately grandeur without ever verging onto self-parody – not a trait the group were given to, perhaps fortunately. It builds unhurriedly, and then dissipates as the tremendous joint vocal by Wright and Gilmour comes in at 2.58, with a musical backing that's similarly unhurried and yet filled with enough incident to keep the ears tuned in, from Mason's velvet-touch drumming to Waters' slinky bass and what sounds like a mosquito trill from a slide guitar just audible in the background. The instrumental break, with its monumental guitar riff by Gilmour** sounding like the impending approach of some enormous doom. There are two verses and two choruses, and then Gilmour's first guitar solo (from 5.26) leads smoothly in from the 'Phantom of the Opera' riff, gliding nicely up and down the fretboard before taking on greater power as the 12/8 riff kicks in again, leading up to a fine crescendo – not shredding but building steadily to a peak at 7.02.

---

§ For example:
>   At length did cross an Albatross,
>   Thorough the fog it came;
>   As if it had been a Christian soul,
>   We hailed it in God's name.
>
>   It ate the food it ne'er had eat,
>   And round and round it flew.
>   The ice did split with a thunder-fit;
>   The helmsman steered us through!
>
>   And a good south wind sprung up behind;
>   The Albatross did follow,
>   And every day, for food or play,
>   Came to the mariner's hollo!

¶ Gilmour in *Classic Albums: Dark Side of the Moon*.

** Stolen, as Waters irately pointed out, by Andrew Lloyd Webber for *The Phantom Of The Opera*: 'I couldn't believe it when I heard it. It's the same time signature – it's 12/8 – and it's the same structure and it's the same notes and it's the same everything. Bastard. It probably is actionable. It really is! But I think that life's too long to bother with suing Andrew fucking Lloyd Webber.' (Q Magazine, June 1992).

And then we get the funk jam. Who knew the Floyd, those nice middle-class boys, could be so groovy? There were intimations of this in the 'Funky Dung' section of **ATOM HEART MOTHER**, but in this sprawling jam led by Waters' bass, they sound both unusually grimy and (thanks to the interplay of Gilmour and Wright) superbly melodic, with each getting to show off their chops against the insistent funk backdrop by Mason and Waters. The contrast between the funk and the high-flown lyrical sentiments and grandeur of the opening is just utterly terrific. Gilmour gets more strident as the jam winds on and slowly fades out, with a high-pitched wail slowly rising in volume and then peaking as the rest of the band drop out and the wind noise comes in (Waters using a slide on his bass strings and sending this through the Binson Echorec).* This brings in the central atonal section, with its wind, crows and alien whale sounds (Gilmour with his wah-wah cables reversed, as in **EMBRYO**). It creates a sense of utter separateness – of being in a cave in Mars, or in a vortex, far, far from everyday human life.

At 14.46 this starts to fade out, as the creeping mossy keyboards from the shore of some prehistoric continent start inching in. Holding the same note for an eternity, the cosmic 'ping' from the start of the song reappears, as the guitar slowly moves towards activity. Holding this droning texture expertly for several minutes, the keyboards, bass and then drums steadily become more active, even starting to sustain a melody – until POW! Everyone else drop outs and Gilmour plays a majestic sparkling arpeggiated guitar solo, like someone suddenly arising over a gloriously sparkling ocean, on top of guitar chords with the greatest sustain ever heard in rock music, each one evoking a feeling of infinity, like they were resonance from the creation of the universe. The group ratchet up the tension, and then beautifully fade away to a final verse and chorus, with the vocal treated through a Leslie cabinet for an extra watery effect. Gilmour then repeats the Phantom riff several times before the songs finally climaxes to a rapturously beautiful choral ascending effect, like you are approaching but never quite reaching heaven or Tolkien's Grey Havens. Magnificent. Utterly magnificent.

If Pink Floyd had done nothing after *Meddle*, **ECHOES** would have assured them of a place in rock's highest echelon. It is the single greatest long-form track in rock music, with a grandeur, scale and imagination that leaves everyone else for dead.† It's also superbly recorded, the group enjoying for the first time the luxury of a 16-track studio – Mason's soft-padded drumming and Gilmour's supercharged guitar being highlights, though what's particularly evident is how smoothly all the parts fit together, as if finely sanded down. (By comparison, **ATOM HEART MOTHER** sounds very lumpy.) Even fifty years later, **ECHOES** never palls – it is always rich with incident, its overarching structure is compelling,

---

* See **ONE OF THESE DAYS** for more on the Binson Echorec.

† Compare for instance to 'Supper's Ready' by Genesis (from *Foxtrot*, 1972). You get the feeling that Genesis were trying to do something similar to **ECHOES**, but while their music attains similar points of grandeur, their lyrical concerns are arcane and abstruse. It builds unsteadily to a climax, but you don't quite know what it's about. **ECHOES** for its length feels far more direct, and far more integrated into a cohesive whole.

its movement towards atonality and then back again is fascinating, and – well, what can you say? **ECHOES** is a stupendous achievement, and yet it's only the beginning of one of the greatest artistic hot streaks in musical history.

Meddle, as reviewers noted at the time, put Pink Floyd right back on track after the charming absurdity of *Atom Heart Mother*. Gilmour's growing influence was key: his guitar work throughout is astonishing, both in range (from the delicate shimmer of **A PILLOW OF WINDS** to the downhome blues of **SEAMUS** to the interstellar propulsive power in **ECHOES**) and expression (his fretless bass on **A PILLOW OF WINDS** is subtly terrific, and his final solo on **ECHOES** leaves the listener in slack-jawed astonishment). What lets *Meddle* down is its tonal inconsistency: it's hard to believe **SAN TROPEZ** is sincere, but it is, and having **SEAMUS** follow it simply expects too much from the average listener. Queen would later get away with perhaps an even greater stylistic range, but their excess was part of their package. Pink Floyd, however, needed something to thread it all together, if they were going to have such a broad musical vision.

But beyond all that is the sense that Pink Floyd's apprenticeship[‡] was approaching completion. They had long mastered atmosphere and dynamics; now, on *Meddle*, they were mastering songs, both short and extended. They had worked exceedingly hard to get to this point, recording six albums in just four years, as well as touring extensively (though they would never match the 188 concerts in 1967 or even the 118 in 1968).[§] Now the door was open for whatever they wanted to do. If only they could think what that might be.

OBSCURED BY CLOUDS (Gilmour, Waters)
Length: 3.03
VCS 3 synthesiser: Gilmour, Waters, Wright **Slide guitars**: Gilmour **Bass**: Waters
Hammond organ: Wright **Drums**: Mason **Electronic drums**: Mason
Recorded: February–April 1972, Strawberry Studios, Ile-de-France, France
Producer: Pink Floyd
First released: 2 June 1972 (*Obscured by Clouds* soundtrack track 1)
Rating: 7/10

During the ten-month recording of *Dark Side of the Moon*, Pink Floyd were extremely busy, touring the UK, Japan, Europe, North America twice, performing at the Roland Petit ballet, and composing and recording their second complete soundtrack album. This was also for Barbet Schroeder, and was done in much the same method as *More*, with stopwatches recording certain cues for which they would compose music. Unlike *More*, the music was not naturally

---

[‡] A term Waters himself used: 'All of that work ... I look upon really as sort of serving our apprenticeship, you know, before we could actually say [adopts hilarious Yorkshire brogue], 'Right, now we're ready. Put on your apron, we're going to make *Dark Side of the Moon*. We've learned how to use our chisels, and we'll do it properly this time." (*The Pink Floyd Story: Which One's Pink?*, 2011).

[§] The nearest they ever came was 111 concerts in 1994. See chapter 2.

being played at the time, but rather was more traditional soundtrack music. This meant it could more easily complement the plot and setting, which concerned a French diplomat's wife and a group of very 1960s hippy explorers searching for a valley in New Guinea marked as 'obscured by clouds' on the only map.*

As with *More*, however, the group had to work quickly and efficiently. However, they had found a new musical toy – synthesisers! – and were keen to try them out. This was not without some resistance from the rock community. Both Waters and Gilmour were asked about their use of synthesisers on *Live at Pompeii* (1972).† The implication that it was somehow less authentic a means of creating music. 'All those things are down to how you control them,' said Gilmour, 'whether you're controlling them, and not the other way round.' While Waters was typically combative: 'It's like saying you give a man a Les Paul guitar and he becomes Eric Clapton! And it's not true. And you give a man an amplifier and a synthesiser and he doesn't become whoever … he doesn't become *us*.'

Synthesisers were still very new in 1972, though The Beatles had utilised a Moog 3-series to great effect on *Abbey Road* (1969) and George Harrison had created an entire, mostly unlistenable album called *Electronic Sound* a few months before that. But with Pink Floyd being restless seekers for new sounds, the only surprise is that they didn't use one sooner. Here in **OBSCURED BY CLOUDS** is their first use of one – a VCS 3 synthesiser played (or programmed) by Gilmour and Waters‡ to open the track. It creates a fine, aggressive, ominous sound, a buzzing drone that is complemented by a steady beat from Mason and then Gilmour's high-pitched slide guitar,§ though nothing else – no middle eight, chorus or any other development of the idea. This works terrifically as an atmosphere piece or even overture, but as a complete song it's somewhat lacking. In the film it is used to fine effect at the opening credits, juxtaposed with nice pictures of the misty and mysterious New Guinea mountains to create an ominous, we're-not-in-Kansas-anymore-Toto feeling.

If you can put yourself back to June 1972, **OBSCURED BY CLOUDS** does, however, sound remarkably modern.¶ Here, in the convergence of synthesisers, electronics and rock music, was the sound of the future.** It would just have to wait until Pink Floyd had actually written some songs, rather than mood pieces like this.††

---

* The film is visually magnificent, but as with *More*, none of the main characters are remotely interesting or sympathetic, making their very 60s exploration of what-it-means-to-be-civilized-in-the-modern-world ultimately very tedious.
† For which the group were also filmed at sessions for *The Dark Side of the Moon*.
‡ Despite the fact that it was Wright who bought it. (Mark Blake, *Comfortably Numb: The Inside Story of Pink Floyd* (2008)).
§ Note how much space Gilmour leaves, though. He never needs to fill each bar.
¶ At a time when the UK Top 40 was filled by songs like 'Vincent' by Don McLean, 'Take Me Back 'Ome' by Slade, 'Metal Guru' by T Rex and 'Rockin' Robin' by Michael Jackson. The forward momentum of pop music had clearly stalled. (See also **SEE EMILY PLAY**).
** So much so that it was stolen by an advertising agency for aftershave brand Denim (produced by Fabergé).
†† The group rather enjoyed freedom from rock structures. Mason later wrote: 'Standard rock song construction was optional: one idea could be spun out for an entire section without worrying about the niceties of choruses and middle eights, and any idea in its shortest, most raw version could work without the need to add solos and frills.' (Mason, *Inside Out*, p.168).

WHEN YOU'RE IN (Gilmour, Waters, Wright, Mason)
Length: 2.18
Guitars: Gilmour **Bass**: Waters **Piano**: Wright **Hammond organ**: Wright **Drums**: Mason
Recorded: February–April 1972, Strawberry Studios, Ile-de-France, France
Producer: Pink Floyd
First released: 2 June 1972 (*Obscured by Clouds* soundtrack track 2)
Rating: 6/10

This track continues straight off where **OBSCURED BY CLOUDS** ends. Starting with three authoritative snaps on the snare drum by Mason, it drops the synthesiser in exchange for piano and organ by Wright, and also has a much more rolling rhythm than the ponderous 4/4 beat of the previous track. There's a pleasing propulsiveness to **WHEN YOU'RE IN**, a bluesy aggression to its playing that feels quite new for Pink Floyd – far from the delicate prissiness of **IF** or **FAT OLD SUN**. There are some tasty Wright fills on the Hammond organ which give it some colour beyond the rather basic (and extensively repeated) guitar riff. As a mood piece, it carries on the ominous tone from **OBSCURED BY CLOUDS** well, though it's one of only three tracks from the album not to be used in the film.‡‡ It's very rare for the rawer side of Pink Floyd to be featured for two songs; note, for instance, how **THE NILE SONG** is followed by **CRYING SONG**, or how **ANOTHER BRICK IN THE WALL PART 3** is followed by **GOODBYE CRUEL WORLD**. This sensitivity to dynamics is a key part of the group's entire musical philosophy, but it does mean there ain't that much rollicking rock 'n' roll.

WHEN YOU'RE IN is also an instrumental, so it simply continues in the same vein for about two minutes then slowly fades out. It's a decent blues piece, though you sense a certain relief at not having to fill it out more comprehensively, and while more successful than **MORE BLUES** it doesn't get much beyond a genre exercise.

BURNING BRIDGES (Wright, Waters)
Length: 3.29
Vocals: Gilmour, Wright **Guitars**: Gilmour **Slide guitars**: Gilmour **Bass**: Waters
Hammond organ: Wright **Drums**: Mason **Percussion**: Mason
Recorded: February–April 1972, Strawberry Studios, Ile-de-France, France
Producer: Pink Floyd
First released: 2 June 1972 (*Obscured by Clouds* soundtrack track 3)
Rating: 6/10

The first sung piece on *Obscured By Clouds* is a rare Wright-Waters collaboration that sees Gilmour and Wright share vocal duties. Gilmour sings alone in the first

---

‡‡ Personally I think it should have been used in the pig-killing scene.

verse in his higher keening voice, adds harmony to an unusually low-toned voice by Wright in the second, then the two of them share the third verse equally. Their voices, as ever, pair together wonderfully well. As with so many Wright-written pieces, **BURNING BRIDGES** is delicately melancholic, with a gently lolloping rhythm filled out by a swelling Hammond organ and sparkling arpeggios from Gilmour. The solo guitar between the second and third verses – there is no chorus – is delicately emotive, played low and with lots of space by Gilmour, and is replicated after the third verse in lieu of an outro, the song simply fading out.

BURNING BRIDGES has a rather vague lyric, suggesting how little time Waters (most likely) had to write it. The first verse is a pretty meaningless collection of images ('*Bridges burning gladly merging with the shadow / Flickering between the lines*'), though it sharpens up as the song progresses. '*Beyond the gilded cage / Beyond the reach of ties / The moment is at hand / She breaks the golden band*' – the final verse conveys how the film's lead character, Vivian, is at a turning point as she encounters the hippy encampment, with a couple sleeping naked in the tent. Cleverly, the vocal ends on an equivocal feeling, with the final word stretched into two syllables and ending on a lower note. The group might have been associated by psychic exploration, but they were too smart to think that enlightenment came automatically to anyone who went 'out there' – to distant lands or via drug ingestion.

THE GOLD IT'S IN THE ...[*] (Gilmour, Waters)
Length: 3.07
Vocals: Gilmour **Guitars**: Gilmour **Bass**: Waters **Drums**: Mason **Percussion**: Mason
Recorded: February–April 1972, Strawberry Studios, Ile-de-France, France
Producer: Pink Floyd
First released: 2 June 1972 (*Obscured by Clouds* soundtrack track 4)
Rating: 7/10

A juicily crunching riff gets **THE GOLD IT'S IN THE ...** off to a great start, and Gilmour's vocal is pleasantly up-tempo (though without ever approaching his belting style). It's initially a very standard verse-chorus-verse construction, with the chugging guitars in the second half of the chorus raising the tension superbly, but the guitar solo after the second chorus carries on in lieu of lyrics for what would be the third and fourth iterations, making over half the song a guitar solo exercise. It's just a shame that Gilmour's playing isn't particularly memorable. It's okay, but you feel like it's the kind of thing he could knock out in his sleep.

The lyric is, however, substantially better, and far more pointed than in **BURNING BRIDGES**, with its opening '*Let's make for the hills / They say there's gold and I'm looking for thrills*' suggesting people searching for enlightenment

---

[*] The song titles are rather proximate. Mason recalled that 'the song titles were hurriedly allocated under pressure to meet the film schedule.' (Mason, p.169).

and finding only fool's gold – as summed up in the closing lines, '*All I want to say / Is count me in on the journey / Don't expect me to stay*'. The group of course understood the flakiness and foolhardiness of people searching for enlightenment through self-indulgence – the example of Barrett was all too obvious, while the deaths of Jimi Hendrix,[†] Janis Joplin and Jim Morrison were still very recent. Yet rock 'n' roll is known, and often revered, for its excesses, which usually means consumption, whether through purchases, or intake of intoxicants. None of this would be particularly associated with the classic Pink Floyd line-up (and would be scathingly satirised in *The Wall* movie,[‡] most specifically during the **YOUNG LUST** sequence with its acerbic evocation of an aftershow party). At this point in time, however, self-possession and hard work rather than indulgence seem to have been their watchwords.

WOT'S ... UH THE DEAL (Gilmour, Waters)
Length: 5.08
Vocals: Gilmour **Guitars**: Gilmour **Lap steel guitars**: Gilmour **Bass**: Waters
Piano: Wright **Hammond organ**: Wright **Drums**: Mason
Recorded: February–April 1972, Strawberry Studios, Ile-de-France, France
Producer: Pink Floyd
First released: 2 June 1972 (*Obscured by Clouds* soundtrack track 5)
Rating: 8/10

A sweet country song, with an outstanding vocal by Gilmour again demonstrating his remarkable range. The rich acoustics and steel guitar are perfectly country-rock, though more like The Byrds than Hank Williams or even Bob Dylan, particularly the vocal melodies (which sound like Gilmour backing himself – another of his great talents). Wright's piano fills and solo after the second chorus, however, for once sound a bit too light-hearted for their own good, like a lounge band instead of a downhome country tune. Wright's background was jazz, not R&B or blues – hence he was inspired by more academic forms of music compared to the working-class origins of the other two genres. This enabled him to play in unusual styles and modes (like the Phrygian mode in **CAREFUL WITH THAT AXE, EUGENE** or the passacaglia in the 'Storm Signal' section of **A SAUCERFUL OF SECRETS**). Gilmour's steel guitar solo is, however, perfectly judged, unfussy, melodic, played with just the right amount of sustain on the notes, and ends perfectly just as the third verse comes in. As a genre exercise, **WOT'S ... UH THE DEAL** is far better than the blues efforts on *Zabriskie Point* and the souk-bar exoticisms on *More*, and is rather a forgotten gem from a band whose stylistic fluency could be astonishing.

[†] With whom Pink Floyd had toured during 1967.
[‡] Despite their later fondness for rich men's toys like expensive cars (Mason), yachts (Wright) and airplanes (Gilmour). Though it should also be pointed out that Gilmour is one of the UK's greatest philanthropists, having given away around £16.6m. (*Sunday Times Giving List 2021*).

MUDMEN (Wright, Gilmour)
Length: 4.20
Guitars: Gilmour **Slide guitars**: Gilmour **Bass**: Waters **Piano**: Wright **Hammond organ**: Wright **VCS 3 synthesiser**: Wright **Vibraphone**: Wright **Electric piano**: Wright
Drums: Mason
Recorded: February–April 1972, Strawberry Studios, Ile-de-France, France
Producer: Pink Floyd
First released: 2 June 1972 (*Obscured by Clouds* soundtrack track 6)
Rating: 6/10

A rather familiar-sounding track opens with Wright's melody on the piano a slightly subdued version of the Hammond organ tune from **BURNING BRIDGES**, shifted to a 4/4 rhythm. That steady beat allows the sound of Mason's placid drumming to come to the fore, and it's apparent (as throughout the album) how straightforward the production and mixing is – quite without the velvet touch heard on **ECHOES** or the deep-pile layering on **FEARLESS**. The same is true of Gilmour's guitar, which (in lieu of any vocals throughout the song) takes a lengthy solo from 1.30 – unusually, his tone is too thin and piercing, particularly when he hits the highest notes on the fretboard around 1.46. Fortunately, the song takes a detour at 2.04 to more placid territory, with some beautifully spacious interplay between Wright and Gilmour. However, that atmosphere is suddenly dispelled at 3.15 when Mason does a small fill and then we're back to Gilmour's shrieking guitar, this time complemented by Wright on the organ, the combination veering unfortunately close to what today we might call sex-jazz music. No doubt at the time this sound was less of a cliché, but it hasn't aged well. Wright's trilling organ does however suggest the heightened rapturous emotion that he was to put to better use in **THE GREAT GIG IN THE SKY**, although funnily enough that would be one of the final songs composed for *Dark Side*. **MUDMEN** was not used in *La Vallée*, perhaps because it strains too hard for effect. It's not without charm, but the rushed production meant there wasn't time to give it the care and attention it needed.

CHILDHOOD'S END (Gilmour)
Length: 4.31
Vocals: Gilmour **Guitars**: Gilmour **Bass**: Waters **Hammond organ**: Wright
VCS 3 synthesiser: Wright **Farsifa organ**: Wright **Drums**: Mason
Recorded: February–April 1972, Strawberry Studios, Ile-de-France, France
Producer: Pink Floyd
First released: 2 June 1972 (*Obscured by Clouds* soundtrack track 7)
Rating: 8/10

Some songs on *Obscured by Clouds* are impaired by their production or the obviously rushed work for their lyrics or structure. But some are strong enough to shine despite any impediments, and **CHILDHOOD'S END** is an excellent example of that. Fading in slowly and opening with a tick-tick groove (just like in **TIME**)* behind an ominous drone, the song is notable for Gilmour's insistent vocal, with its unusual second-person perspective† (also like in **TIME**) making it feel especially pointed and direct. **CHILDHOOD'S END** is unusual in that it has no chorus, just a guitar solo between the second and third verses – again with a slightly unpleasant piercing tone, as with **MUDMEN** – which is reprised as the song ends.

CHILDHOOD'S END is the last lyric solely written by Gilmour for the group until *A Momentary Lapse of Reason*,‡ fifteen years later. Each verse is written as four rhyming couplets, and while there's a sense that he's slightly straining for rhymes at times (*'And then as the sail is hoist / You find your eyes are growing moist'*), it's perfectly serviceable. The themes of ageing, life passing and existential doubt carry across from **CYMBALINE** (and, of course, anticipate songs like **TIME** and **WEARING THE INSIDE OUT**), and like that song includes a reference to the process of songwriting (*'And so all things, time will mend / So this song will end'*). Pink Floyd have never been considered a meta band, making music about music in the same vein as the Beastie Boys or Frank Zappa, no doubt because this tendency in their lyrics ended with this album, just before their stratospheric success, and because there's no satirical or humourous points being made. But this is mostly incidental. **CHILDHOOD'S END** is a quality track, from the sharp grungy groove of the verse to Gilmour's world-weary low-toned singing to the fine details of the lyric, conveying man alone and uncertain (*'Just one man beneath the sky / Just two ears, just two eyes'*). Could Gilmour have improved his writing as Waters had been doing? It's a fine alternative to ponder, but at the time when the guitarist's lyrics were functional, his bandmate's were on the way to becoming the finest in rock music. Letting Waters take over was selfless and all for the betterment of the group's output. A more needy ego than Gilmour's would have resented this.

FREE FOUR (Waters)
Length: 4.15
Vocals: Waters **Guitars**: Gilmour **Bass**: Waters **VCS 3 synthesiser**: Wright **Drums**: Mason
Tambourine: Mason
Recorded: February–April 1972, Strawberry Studios, Ile-de-France, France
Producer: Pink Floyd
First released: 2 June 1972 (*Obscured by Clouds* soundtrack track 8)
Rating: 8/10

---

* And like **TIME** going on unusually long– here it's almost 1.20 before the guitar part comes in. Pink Floyd evidently had very patient fans.
† I.e., addressed to 'You' rather than 'He' or 'She' (third-person) or coming from 'I' (first-person).
‡ Specifically, the tracks, **A NEW MACHINE (PART 1)**, **A NEW MACHINE (PART 2)** and **SORROW**.

Another Waters satirical effort, this time without the grating heavy-handedness of **CORPORAL CLEGG**. The disparity between the jaunty rhythm and singing and the biting, sardonic lyrics make this a perfect example of how to do irony in music: it sets up a dramatic tension or even a kind of dialogue between the two elements, which makes it a far more interesting listen than the earlier effort. The song is most famous, of course, for having the first reference to Waters' father ('*And I am the dead man's son / And he was buried like a mole in a fox hole / And everyone is still on the run*'), though at this stage it's still implicit rather than explicit, with the anti-war theme only half the lyric. The title too is a joke, made explicit with the count in: '*One, two, **free**, four!*' The military-style count and pun on 'free' as 'three' might suggest how the advancing of numbers (and therefore of time and ageing) can be routine and mindless and hence a loss of freedom, or it might just be a pun. Take your pick.

The other part is a further rumination, as with **CHILDHOOD'S END**, on time passing, ageing and regret. At this point, it's these themes which ring most true, with Waters providing a number of absolutely sterling phrases that demonstrate why it was the natural choice for him to become the sole lyricist. The opening verse (reprised at the end, for greater emphasis or perhaps to give the song a circularity)* is a case in point: in short, succinct lines, Waters nails the human condition and the despair of ageing: '*The memories of a man in his old age / Are the deeds of a man in his prime / You shuffle in gloom of the sickroom / And talk to yourself as you die*'. Each verse also contains an internal rhyme in the third line and half-rhymes in the second and fourth lines (*prime/die, rest/less, top/off, begun/drum*). This is less noticeable than in poetry because the vowel sound carries the rhythm, but because of its consistency it must be a deliberate choice by Waters, perhaps to suggest the dislocation and discomfort of ageing. Either way, the entire lyric is masterful. The pace of his development as a writer is staggering. His trajectory throughout his time in Pink Floyd thus sees him go from a novice (see **TAKE UP THY STETHOSCOPE AND WALK**) to someone whose words have echoed in the mind for half a century.

Musically, **FREE FOUR** is most notable for the buzzing tone after every second line – it sounds like a fuzz-boxed bass guitar, like something by Kim Gordon of Sonic Youth or even Steely Dan, but it's actually a lingering note on the VCS 3 synthesiser. It hence splits each verse in two, which might be a comment on the whole life/death duality sorta thing, or might simply be the group using a new toy to add a bit of variety.† **FREE FOUR** was rather remarkably released as a single in the US in July 1972 (suggesting how America might be receptive to a jaunty tune despite the darkness of the lyrics – twelve years before Springsteen's 'Born in the USA'). But though it was the group's first single to

---

* A technique Waters would soon redeploy in *Animals* and *The Wall*.
† As Freud supposedly said on dreams, sometimes a cigar is just a cigar.

garner significant FM radio play in the US, it still failed to chart. Yet **FREE FOUR** isn't just a pebble heralding the avalanche of success that came just ten months later with *Dark Side* – it's one of the group's best deep cuts, and one of the reasons why *Obscured by Clouds* is often the fans' choice as the group's most underrated album.

> **STAY** (Waters, Wright)
> **Length**: 4.05
> **Vocals**: Wright, Gilmour **Guitars**: Gilmour **Bass**: Waters **VCS 3 synthesiser**: Wright
> **Drums**: Mason **Tambourine**: Mason
> **Recorded**: February–April 1972, Strawberry Studios, Ile-de-France, France
> **Producer**: Pink Floyd
> **First released**: 2 June 1972 (*Obscured by Clouds* soundtrack track 9)
> **Rating**: 7/10

Although lust and libidinousness almost never feature in Pink Floyd's lexicon (**YOUNG LUST**, of course, satirising these feelings, and Barrett's **CANDY AND A CURRANT BUN** being five years distant), next-day regret and melancholy were an early theme, also expressed in **SUMMER 68** and **PAINTBOX**. Here, the group put the theme through the gentle verse-urgent chorus formula and came up with a winner. The lyrics are notably more explicit on the theme than Wright's **SUMMER 68**, with the reference to 'the bottle of wine' feeling like a typical Waters touch in its evocation of the everyday and quotidian.‡ It's also more unkind: where **SUMMER 68** agonised over '*How do you feel?*', **STAY** is dismissive: '*Rack my brain and try to remember your name / To find the words to tell you good-bye*'. The chorus meanwhile moves from the immediate to passionate symbolism: '*Midnight blue / Burning gold / A yellow moon / Is growing cold*'. It's a great dynamic.§ The power of the chorus and the impassioned vocal makes **STAY** far more arresting than Wright's previous rather diffident songwriting efforts. It's curious, though, that Wright has twice sung about this topic, while both Gilmour and Waters remain silent on it. (Wright was married from 1964 to 1982 to Juliette Gale; Gilmour married Ginger Hasenbein in 1975, but formed a relationship with her in 1971,¶ while Waters had married Judith Trim in 1969.) Nonetheless, while **STAY** is a striking success, it would, however, very swiftly be far surpassed by the next Waters/Wright composition (and use of the same musical template), **US AND THEM**.

---

‡ Which of course goes back to 'The Man – The Journey', **CYMBALINE**, **ALAN'S PSYCHEDELIC BREAKFAST** and thence to **BREATHE**, **TIME**, and *Dark Side*.
§ The second chorus however alters the lyrics, perhaps in an anticipation of the '*love turns grey*' lyrical bullseye from **ONE OF MY TURNS**: '*Morning dues / Newborn day / Midnight blue / Turned to grey*'.
¶ Her book *The Bright Side of the Moon* (2015) is revealing about Gilmour's style of life during this period.

> **ABSOLUTELY CURTAINS** (Gilmour, Waters, Wright, Mason)
> **Length**: 5.52
> **Hammond organ**: Wright **Farsifa organ**: Wright **VCS 3 synthesiser**: Wright
> **Tack piano**: Wright **Electric piano**: Wright **Percussion**: Mason
> **Recorded**: February–April 1972, Strawberry Studios, Ile-de-France, France
> **Producer**: Pink Floyd
> **First released**: 2 June 1972 (*Obscured by Clouds* soundtrack track 10)
> **Rating**: 6/10

The curtain-closer on *Obscured by Clouds* is a song in two parts, with a magisterial organ piece by Wright succeeded after 3.40 by tribal chants from New Guinea. The opening section is an improvement on the ominous majesty Wright had attempted at the start and closing of **THE GRAND VIZIER'S GARDEN PARTY**. It's big and bold and extremely dramatic, opening on a synthesiser drone (clearly a new favourite toy) and Mason giving it great resonance on the tom-toms and sizzle on the cymbals (or perhaps the gong), while Wright adds a tack piano for some arpeggiated notes. It's all overture but no main course, however – it sets up a magnificent heady atmosphere but simply fades away at 3.40 as the tribal voices take over for the remaining two minutes. This suggests the equivalence of both types of music, which is terrific. They would, however, never attempt this world music style again, though it did suggest avenues other Western groups would explore, from Mike Oldfield to Leftfield on their song 'Afro-Left'. The main consequence of **ABSOLUTELY CURTAINS** is, however, its demonstration of how to set up a highly dramatic opening, which would be further developed on **SHINE ON YOU CRAZY DIAMOND (PARTS I–V)**.

Obscured by Clouds was recorded in just two weeks,* one either side of a Japanese tour in early March 1972, at Strawberry Studios in an eighteenth-century chateau in the village of Hérouville, an hour north-west of Paris. This demanded economy and efficiency, making the song structures the most elementary of Pink Floyd's career. Similarly, the intense workrate meant there was no time to use the studio to create the spacious reverb in which Pink Floyd's sound had so often been bathed. Hence *Obscured by Clouds* is a very bare-bones, back-to-basics listening experience.

But that very same quality reveals the strength of the songwriting and playing on the album. Four tracks are instrumentals, but they are by no means filler padding out the album: **OBSCURED BY CLOUDS** and **ABSOLUTELY CURTAINS** in particular add exciting new avenues to Pink Floyd's rapidly expanding soundworld. Of the other tracks, **WOT'S … UH THE DEAL**,

---

* This was not uncommon for mid-tier bands at the time. Nirvana attempted to turn back the clock with their third album *In Utero* (1993), taking two weeks to record and mix it with producer Steve Albini – though even they required studio enhancements by noted REM producer Scott Litt on two tracks ('Pennyroyal Tea' and 'All Apologies').

CHILDHOOD'S END, **STAY** and **FREE FOUR** are all strong songs in their own right. However, they are all quite traditional verse-chorus-verse sort of tunes, without the breathtaking boldness of **SET THE CONTROLS FOR THE HEART OF THE SUN** or **ECHOES** (which, of course, had far longer gestation periods). Although it has become something of a hardcore fan favourite, *Obscured by Clouds* notably has no songs on the two best-of compilation albums.[†] But recording it was an invaluable lesson: afterwards, it was evident that if Pink Floyd could marry their sonic daring and studio innovations with their newfound songwriting chops, they might be onto a winner.

[†] Neither does *More*.

II.

EXALTATIONS (1973–79)

SPEAK TO ME (Mason)
Length: 1.40
Tape loops: Mason, Waters **Tape effects**: Mason, Waters **Piano**: Wright
Percussion: Mason
Recorded: May 1972–February 1973, EMI Studios, London
Producer: Pink Floyd
First released: 1 March 1973 (*The Dark Side of the Moon* track 1)
Rating: 8/10

The heartbeat first utilised in 'The Man – The Journey' and **HEART BEAT, PIG MEAT**[*] returns, as the overture to the first Pink Floyd album to be written and toured in advance of recording.[†] Put together as a sound collage late in the recording sessions, **SPEAK TO ME** demonstrates how expertly the band by this time could raise suspense without tiring the listener. Whereas **HEART BEAT, PIG MEAT** just sort of ambles on for a period with various random interjections and then ends (rather as bad ambient music does), **SPEAK TO ME** expertly raises tension through the repetition of the pulse-like bass drum beat, as well as careful addition of the various samples from the subsequent tracks. Most significant among these are the '*I've been mad for fucking years*' piece (from 0.36), while there's also the tills and receipts effects from **MONEY** (from 0.40), ominous madcap laughter (from 0.48), a snatch of the synthesiser from **ON THE RUN** (at 0.53) and, ending it all, a chilling scream at 1.09 from **THE GREAT GIG IN THE SKY**. This careful layering[‡] beautifully builds a thick, heady atmosphere, ominous as the moments before a lightning storm, and of course foreshadows all the spectacular aural creations later on in the album. Here is the Floyd now at peak creativity, deftly creating an overture

---

[*] Guns N' Roses did a similar drum pattern for their epic 1991 track 'Coma'. It's one of their best tracks, but at over 10 minutes it helped precipitate the departure of key songwriter Izzy Stradlin, who couldn't remember all the chords.
[†] I'm always reminded of the George Orwell quote on *Animal Farm* (1945): '*Animal Farm* was the first book in which I tried, with full consciousness of what I was doing, to fuse political purpose and artistic purpose into one whole.' (Orwell, *Why I Write*, 1946). For *Animal Farm* read *Dark Side*: after years of apprenticeship, both had finally found a way to fuse ideas and artistry into magnificent works.
[‡] Perhaps inspired by The Beatles' 'Tomorrow Never Knows' from *Revolver* (1966), which introduces a new sound loop every few bars, which then intersect with increasing frequency for the remainder of the song.

that in less than two minutes has as many ideas as any of their songs since the ousting of Barrett.

Often combined with **BREATHE** because of their wonderful segue, **SPEAK TO ME** was one of the final tracks recorded for *Dark Side*, taking elements from songs already completed to form a thumbnail sketch of the album ahead. It's a highly effective piece in its atmospheric charge and brevity – quite the change from the drawn-out nature of **ONE OF THESE DAYS** – though its success led to some absurd band quibbles over credit. Waters, for example, complained in 2003 that he 'really regretted having given away half the writing credits, particularly [Mason's credit for] "Speak to Me". I gave it to him. Nobody else had anything to do with it at all.'§ Though, naturally, Mason remembered it somewhat differently.¶ Whatever the case, the group's bourgeois sense of propriety made them confident enough to label their work Art from the beginning, while also avoiding the excessive desire for artistic self-justification that has scuppered many a once-hungry rock artist.** But this trait also entailed a self-interested approach to song accreditation. While this meant that Waters, for instance, was willing to work hard to write the songs and thereby make more money on publishing, it reduced band solidarity when important areas such as arrangements, instrumentation, vocal harmonies and solos weren't considered composing. Gilmour perhaps suffered the most from this, as his studio work often greatly developed Waters' ideas and demos into fully fledged songs; but prior to *Dark Side*, the rewards hadn't been great enough, or the tax bills large enough, to greatly trouble the band. This happy state of affairs wouldn't last much longer.

BREATHE (Waters, Gilmour, Wright)
Length: 2.43
Vocals: Gilmour **Guitars**: Gilmour **Pedal steel guitars**: Gilmour **Bass**: Waters
Hammond organ: Wright **Electric piano**: Wright **Drums**: Mason **Percussion**: Mason
Recorded: May 1972–February 1973, EMI Studios, London
Producer: Pink Floyd
First released: 1 March 1973 (*The Dark Side of the Moon* track 2)
Rating: 7/10

With a mighty reversed chord, **SPEAK TO ME** moves beautifully into the liquid atmosphere of **BREATHE**. The steel guitar utilised to such great effect in **ONE OF THESE DAYS** (and to lesser effect on **WOT'S … UH THE DEAL**) here is used, through its tuning,†† to suggest the flowing of breath, the entire

---

§ *Uncut* magazine, June 2003.
¶ He says it was 'constructed from cross-fades of all the other pieces on the album, which I put together roughly at home and then finally assembled in the studios' (Mason, *Inside Out*, p.172).
** From Richie Blackmore and his classical pretensions to Sting and his lute to Kanye West's ghastly political positions.
†† So that if you strum the strings, without fingering any frets, it still plays a chord.

process of inhalation and exhalation. It's a wonderful piece of existential imagery, such as the band had been playing with since 'The Man – The Journey' live show in 1969, but where the band would once have been content with one effect to try to conjure their metaphor, now they enrich the track with swelling Hammond organs, delicious ethereal guitars, and on-point lyrics about life and how it is lived. It all feels so much richer than **CYMBALINE** or **CHILDHOOD'S END**. Along with that is the fact that the song is wisely brief, only lasting for two verses and never outstaying its welcome, whereas **SEAMUS** is around the same length but drags its single joke out for far too long. Brevity was a nice and rather overdue trick to acquire. Musically, **BREATHE** is simple enough, but with many fine touches: the gliding waves of slide guitar here suggest dreaminess, whereas in **COMFORTABLY NUMB** they suggest the final vestiges of sanity slipping away; the languid pace, with excellent velvet-touch drumming by Mason, suggests the torpidity of daily life; and the minimal melodic development* suggests the tranquillity the lyrics espouse, in a more effective drone than **GREEN IS THE COLOUR**.

The lyrics – though Waters later mocked them for being typically 'Lower Sixth'† – have a sort of elementary simplicity that contrasts nicely with the album's later verbal profusions like **US AND THEN** and **BRAIN DAMAGE** – and also with the abstruse imagery of **ECHOES**. *'Breathe, breathe in the air / Don't be afraid to care / Leave, but don't leave me / Look around, choose your own ground'* – their minimalism might later discomfit Waters, but their simplicity gives them an unvarnished artlessness that pairs very well with the velvet-rich musical backdrop. **BREATHE** is, in its exhortation to enjoy the simple pleasures of life, a sermon, in the same way that **ECLIPSE** is a litany. The religious overtones of both help give *Dark Side* its particular feeling of near-mystical emotion and significance. This richness of music and meaning, and the dialogue between them, meant that whether consciously or not, the group were now producing world-class work.

ON THE RUN (Waters, Gilmour)
Length: 3.30
Guitars: Gilmour **EMS Synthi AKS**: Gilmour **VCS 3 synthesiser**: Waters
Hammond organ: Wright **Percussion**: Mason
Recorded: May 1972–February 1973, EMI Studios, London
Producer: Pink Floyd
First released: 1 March 1973 (*The Dark Side of the Moon* track 3)
Rating: 9/10

---

* **BREATHE** is mostly two chords: E minor and A. Making great art can look easy (like it took Guns N' Roses just half an hour to write 'Welcome To The Jungle'), but it takes years of very hard work to get there.
† The penultimate year of secondary school, or the first year of A Levels, in the English education system. Waters in *Classic Albums: Dark Side of the Moon*.

Synthesisers were nothing new in rock music by 1973, and *Obscured by Clouds* had occasionally made good use of them. Nothing, though, would have prepared listeners for this: an eight-note synthesiser pattern‡ sped up to 165bpm and treated with a kitchen sink of effects that now sounds like a predictor of techno music. When people famously wanted to test their hi-fi equipment using *Dark Side*, this is one of the key tracks they would play. The busy EMS Synthi loop is adorned by a high-hat (not by Mason but part of the VCS 3's bag of tricks), and never bores the listener through it being panned left and right, and given the Doppler effect to sound higher pitched (and thus coming nearer) or lower pitched (and thus going further away). Then there's a wonderful range of illustrative and emotive sound effects, making **ON THE RUN** one of the densest tracks on *Dark Side*, and the most obvious studio confection. Yet simply as a piece of music it's superbly effective, capturing the feeling of busywork and running to stand still. The numerous audio samples and interjections are exceptional, ranging from the adenoidal airport announcement to the leg of a microphone stand being rubbed against guitar strings to a man panting breathlessly to heartbeats to a synthesised helicopter sound to the sound of someone running in an empty corridor to maniacal laughter.§ **SPEAK TO ME** promised something of this kind, but **ON THE RUN** takes the studio innovations of the Beatles' 'Tomorrow Never Knows' to new levels in evoking aspects of everyday life, while to this day sounding fresh, modern and compelling.

ON THE RUN was one of the last tracks to be recorded for *Dark Side*, having initially been played live and recorded as 'The Travel Sequence', a far more orthodox guitar-based piece, which can be heard on the *Dark Side Immersion* box set (as well as on bootlegs from 1972; see Chapter 2). 'The Travel Sequence' is a very 1970s-style funky jam, clearly descended from the similar section of **ECHOES**, that wouldn't sound out of place in a prime-time cop show or Beastie Boys pastiche thereof, but only the calisthenic top-hat work by Mason suggests the activity and energy the band seem to have been looking for. For all that, it's a fine piece of music, with tremendous guitar playing and spacey sound effects throughout, and enlivened by a breakdown at 1.28, where until recently the band would have been content endlessly playing with the same rhythm. Breaking up what they were doing into digestible chunks seems to have been on their collective minds throughout the recording of *Dark Side*.

‡ E3, G3, A3, G3, D4, C4, D4, E4. The first quartet makes an inverted v-shape, the second a v-shape: the first rises then falls, the second falls then rises. Very clever. The sequence was developed by Waters and then improved by Gilmour. Even credit for this is a matter of honour for them.

§ By road manager Peter Watts. He is the father of actor Naomi Watts (perhaps most famous for the David Lynch film *Mulholland Drive* (2001)), was sacked by Pink Floyd in 1974, and died of a heroin overdose in 1976. He also appears on the back cover of *Ummagumma*. Mason writes: 'Peter Watts […] had become increasingly – and then totally – unreliable. However, since the four of us in the band were not completely in tune with each other, and we had no clear chain of command, our handling of the situation was inept. Peter was fired – at least once – by one band member in the morning, only for another of us to reinstate him the same afternoon […] When the situation with Peter became impossible, we tried to behave with more understanding than we had been able to with Syd, and arranged for Peter to undergo treatment at a clinic, which, though not totally ineffectual, did little to solve the core problem.' (Mason, *Inside Out*, p.199). Might his death have contributed to the darkened vision of *Animals*? Though Waters' saturnine disposition at the time probably required no great stimulus.

Nonetheless, 'The Travel Sequence' doesn't at all convey the themes of travel anxiety* and rat-race mindlessness, and the band's creative processes were not so much in high gear as ferociously turbo-charged. **ON THE RUN** is an astonishing piece of work, brilliantly conceived, superbly engineered, and every bit as artistic as music played with traditional instruments. (Gilmour rightly points out that mixing the track in those days was as much a musical performance as a live show.)† It's the third bullseye in a row on an album whose creativity and expressiveness were now clearly in staggering abundance.

> **TIME** (Waters, Gilmour, Wright, Mason)
> **Length**: 6.53
> **Vocals**: Gilmour, Wright **Guitars**: Gilmour **Bass**: Waters **Farsifa organ**: Wright **VCS 3 synthesiser**: Wright **Electric piano**: Wright **Drums**: Mason **Roto drums**: Mason **Backing vocals**: Doris Troy, Lesley Duncan, Liza Strike, Barry St John
> **Recorded**: May 1972–February 1973, EMI Studios, London
> **Producer**: Pink Floyd
> **First released**: 1 March 1973 (*The Dark Side of the Moon* track 4)
> **Rating**: 10/10

The first sort-of traditional rock song on *Dark Side* features some of Gilmour's finest ever guitar work. But like the rest of the album, it's a rich brew of different musical sources and textures, while Waters' lyric is also prominent for the first time in the album, and is equally outstanding. This heady collective achievement makes **TIME** one of Pink Floyd's best-loved songs. Taking its sweet time in getting going – Mason on the rototoms from 0.50 to 2.26 is slightly absurd, especially just after fifty seconds of chiming clocks‡ – **TIME** is an unconventional rock song with a third taken up by the intro, a verse and refrain structure so there's no chorus, and a diminuendo outro. But with its wonderfully energetic performance, superb gritty verse vocals and magnificent guitar solo by Gilmour, the song teems with vitality and creativity – and it *rocks*. When Mason's drum fill kicks off the main section at 2.28, the tension has been built to such a level that the levee breaks and the song explodes.§

Musically, **TIME** combines a guitar-riff-driven verse with a keyboard-led refrain, giving the song the dynamic range that helps to make it so memorable.

---

* Wright in particular was prey to this: 'For me, one of the pressures of being in the band was this constant fear of dying because of all the travelling we were doing in planes and on the motorways in America and in Europe.' (*Mojo* magazine, March 1998).
† *Classic Albums: Dark Side of The Moon*, 2001.
‡ Is it supposed to symbolise Waters' idea of early life as preparation for the real thing? Possibly. Or maybe they just couldn't let go of their lengthy repetitive passages yet. But thankfully Gilmour's mighty tolling-bell guitar chords and Wright's subtle electric piano add greatly to the atmosphere.
§ The soaring opening Gilmour vocal was a late addition: the initial *Dark Side* shows had the verse as doleful as the refrain. Not surprisingly, **TIME** therefore lacked dynamic and expressive range. It also took time for Gilmour to end the second line 'way-ee-ay'- bootlegs show he was still singing it as one syllable up to 8 March 1973, suggesting that stretching it out was a late studio innovation. I emailed engineer Alan Parsons to ask if it was his idea; on 29 December 2023, he responded, 'No. Happy New Year.' So it was a band idea. I'm only surprised neither Gilmour nor Waters have come out staking a claim on it.

The explosive opening contrasts so well with the elegiac refrain that it's hard to believe that the opening performed by the group was initially almost as melancholic, but the proof is there in the bootlegs. The same is true of the guitar solo, which as played by Gilmour for about a year before release was similar melodically to the final version, but without the soaring passages that now define it. It might just be that greater dynamic shifts were the order of the day (see also **US AND THEM** and **MONEY**). In any case, the guitar solo is both crystalline, with brilliant piercing notes, and melancholic when the band slows down and Gilmour plays some lower notes. Gilmour had never been a guitar hero in the manner of Jimmy Page, Richie Blackmore or even Pete Townshend, but from here on his playing defines the sound of Pink Floyd (*The Final Cut* excepted).

Another key strength of **TIME** is its deft use of the group's singing voices: whereas they once just let the writer sing his song (even when not best suited, as for example in **SEESAW** or **BIDING MY TIME**), now they are allocating singing duties like dramatic roles, rather as Miles Davis organised the solos in *Kind of Blue*: each seems to lead meaningfully on from the last. Wright's doleful voice is perfectly used in the refrain for expressive purposes, though it's also double-tracked to give it more power, which it needs when up against Gilmour's rocking vocals. From here on, this would be one of the group's most brilliant techniques, allowing songs to become dramatic dialogues, as with **DOGS**, **MOTHER**, **COMFORTABLY NUMB** and **NOT NOW JOHN**, with verses and choruses commenting upon each other and layering meaning in each song.¶

Waters' lyric, meanwhile, is tremendous – if not the most original piece compared to mourners of the passing of time like Philip Larkin and Thomas Hardy, it's still brilliantly evocative of human existence. Lines like '*You are young and life is long, and there is time to kill today / And then one day you find ten years have got behind you / No one told you when to run, you missed the starting gun*' and '*Plans that either come to naught or half a page of scribbled lines*' are just magnificent: sentiments to which every bosom return an echo, as Dr Johnson said.** Everyone has felt this (or everyone over 20, anyway). **TIME** is also highly competent poetically – with the refrain for example being in a lilting trochaic tetrameter ('**Tir**ed of **ly**ing **in** the **sun**shine / **Stay**ing **home** to **watch** the **rain**', '**Eve**ry **year** is **get**ting **short**er / **Nev**er **seem** to **find** the **time**').†† The use of the second person is another expert effect, making the listener feel that the group is directly addressing them. From Waters' gauche early attempts at poeticisms like **GRANTCHESTER MEADOWS**, then his indirect attempts to articulate the human condition in songs like **CYMBALINE**, **EMBRYO** and **JULIA DREAM**, he has now donned the mantle of a generational lyricist, alongside

---

¶ Though, almost inevitably, The Beatles were probably the first to do this, on 'We Can Work It Out' in December 1965.

** About Thomas Gray's *Elegy Written in a Country Churchyard* (Johnson, *Lives of the Most Eminent English Poets*, 1781).

†† Though strictly speaking each example has a catalexis in the second line: they're short of one unstressed syllable at the end. If Waters intended that pattern, he's a far greater poet than most people would realise.

John Lennon, Bob Dylan, Lou Reed and Joni Mitchell – and here perhaps even bettering them, since **TIME** often pops up in polls of the greatest song lyrics ever. While his rivals more often tell stories and depict characters, Waters goes right for the jugular by addressing one of the most universal themes and wrapping it in language and metaphors everyone can understand. It's a phenomenal piece of writing.

The combination of music and lyrics are as potent in **TIME** as anything in the entirety of Pink Floyd's work, from **SEE EMILY PLAY** to **ECHOES** to **ANOTHER BRICK IN THE WALL PART 2**. It is simply one of their greatest triumphs – a highly poetic and constantly rewarding evocation of ageing, dawning realisations, and regret, as well as one of their sharpest arrangements thus far (perhaps excepting the excessive rototoms). And it marks the emergence of Gilmour and Waters as the finest in their respective fields. Ironically, a song about wasted opportunities sees Pink Floyd finally making the most of theirs.

THE GREAT GIG IN THE SKY (Wright, Clare Torry)
Length: 4.15
Vocals: Clare Torry **Pedal steel guitars**: Gilmour **Bass**: Waters **Piano**: Wright **Hammond organ**: Wright **Drums**: Mason **Percussion**: Mason
Recorded: May 1972–February 1973, EMI Studios, London
Producer: Pink Floyd
First released: 1 March 1973 (*The Dark Side of the Moon* track 5)
Rating: 7/10

If **BREATHE** is a sermon and **ECLIPSE** a litany, then **THE GREAT GIG IN THE SKY** may well be the elegy – where death itself is addressed. But rather than lamenting the passing of one person in particular, **THE GREAT GIG** is about death itself. Hence why its vocals are wordless, inarticulate – because death is the great unknown. Gilmour has interestingly said that the group 'wanted to put a girl on there, screaming orgasmically'.* Which rather begs the question of what Pink Floyd collectively think about death, but **THE GREAT GIG IN THE SKY** remains inscrutable, for all of its emotiveness and the tremendous vocalisation by Clare Torry running from sensual and intimate to belting raw power to stratospheric spiritualism. It was a very smart move not to have lyrics: nothing verbalised could come close to what Torry conveys.

Musically the song combines one of Wright's finest pieces, with a slightly portentous churchy opening progressing swiftly via some smart slide guitar lines from Gilmour and excellent vocal interjection from Irish doorman Gerry O'Driscoll to establish the theme (*'And I am not frightened of dying. Any time will do, I don't mind. Why should I be frightened of dying? There's no reason for it – you've got to go sometime.'*) A swift drum fill from Mason at 1.06, however, kicks the whole piece

---

* *Rolling Stone*, 'Dark Side At 30: David Gilmour', 12 March 2003. It's surely not a coincidence that in French an orgasm is known as *la petite morte* ('a little death').

into the stratosphere, with Torry's vocal soaring and Wright overdubbing the Hammond organ on top of the piano from 1.23, where it appears as a dazzle-burst of colour and excitement. Torry's vocalising is extremely dramatic but moves expertly with the peaks and troughs of the music, for instance slowing and quieting at 2.32, then moving to a near-whisper as the song fades away at around 4.00 – so much so that it seems remarkable that the addition of a female singer was the third attempt at capturing the necessary otherworldly atmosphere.

In its first configuration, **THE GREAT GIG IN THE SKY** was a solemn, churchy piece with spoken-word interjections from Malcolm Muggeridge[†] (known as a Christian and as a social conservative journalist and commentator), as well as audio recordings of the Bible. Its second iteration was closer to the final recording, but with astronaut dialogue played over it,[‡] in an effort to capture the boundaries of existence. This, though, remained too earth-bound, and it was only in the final weeks of recording *Dark Side* that engineer Alan Parsons suggested Torry to 'wail' over it, noting that 'She had to be told not to sing any words: when she first started, she was doing "Oh yeah baby" and all that kind of stuff, so she had to be restrained on that.'[§] Despite rumours that Torry did it in one take, Gilmour said her contribution was edited together: 'We gave her some dynamic hints: "Maybe you'd like to do this piece quietly, and this piece louder." She did maybe half a dozen takes, and then afterwards we compiled the final performance out of all the bits.'[¶]

Regardless, it's an astonishing performance which turns a solid musical performance into a remarkable tour-de-force. **THE GREAT GIG IN THE SKY**, however, is quite far from the band's repertoire, perhaps because of Torry's vocals, perhaps because of the slight sex-jazz atmosphere of the track, making it feel the least essential track of the album. It's a remarkable feat, but it's not quite as enjoyable a song: something to admire more than something which bears repeated hearings. Sort of like religion itself.

MONEY (Waters)
Length: 6.30
Vocals: Gilmour **Guitars**: Gilmour **Bass**: Waters **Electric piano**: Wright **Drums**: Mason
Tenor saxophone: Dick Parry **Tape loops**: Waters, Mason
Recorded: May 1972–February 1973, EMI Studios, London
Producer: Pink Floyd
First released: 1 March 1973 (*The Dark Side of the Moon* track 6)
Rating: 8/10

[†] He would later make a fool of himself in 1979 fulminating against Monty Python's *Life of Brian*. Pink Floyd had helped to fund Python's previous film, *Monty Python and the Holy Grail* (1975). It's a small world.
[‡] A trick later used by Ian Brown (in 'My Star', 1998) and Lemon Jelly (in 'Space Walk', 2002).
[§] *Rolling Stone*, 'Dark Side At 30: Alan Parsons', 12 March, 2003.
[¶] *Rolling Stone*, 'Dark Side At 30: David Gilmour', 12 March, 2003.

One of the more unlikely US radio hits, **MONEY** is one of the few singles in 7/4 time.[*] It also exemplifies the dichotomies in Pink Floyd's music, being all at once earthy and grandiose, articulate and concise, satirical and empathetic, cerebral and soulful. Not many people think of Pink Floyd as an R&B band, but the blues acts as a base for their more out-there explorations. With that underwiring, Planet Earth was always visible, even if from space, and human concerns (as Waters desired) were always to the fore, even in his psychedelic efforts like **SET THE CONTROLS FOR THE HEART OF THE SUN**, which is essentially a self-portrait of a man seeking inspiration ('*Witness the man who raves at the wall / Making the shape of his question to Heaven / Whether the sun will fall in the evening / Will he remember the lesson of giving?*'). The group had, of course, already recorded tracks like **MORE BLUES**, **WHEN YOU'RE IN** and **SEAMUS**, although none had seemed much more than a genre exercise. Now, however, Waters had come with a genuinely innovative riff[†] with a brilliant lyric that combines utter cynicism with a pithy, streetwise register ('*Do-goody-good bullshit*') and a very smart allusiveness[‡] that expands its meaning beyond a personal protest to a socio-political examination. (He's good at that.)

MONEY is also one of the most studio-confected tracks on *Dark Side*, with its famous introductory tape loop of cash register, coins, paper tearing (to suggest a cheque being ripped from its book), and counting machine, remarkably set to the song's 7/4 rhythm. The provenance of the loop has almost inevitably come to be disputed. Mason, for example, wrote that 'Roger and I constructed the tape loop for "Money" in our home studios and then took it in to Abbey Road.'[§] In 2021, Waters, however, claimed on his Facebook page that 'I made that SFX tape loop for Money in the studio I shared with my wife Judy at the bottom of our garden at 187, New North Road, Islington'[¶] before taking a jab at Gilmour for an interview done nearly forty years earlier in which the guitarist had discussed constructing the tape loop. (Though Gilmour may have been talking about the re-recorded version for *A Collection Of Great Dance Songs* released in 1981). In any case, the way the loop keeps time is just wonderful, and tribute to the imagination and technical deftness of the band.

But alongside that there are numerous studio tricks, with the verses recorded dry, with little reverb (beyond a touch of liquidity from some shimmering guitar parts). The saxophone solo continues in this vein, before the breakdown

---

[*] There's some argument about whether it's in 7/4 or 7/8, with Gilmour for example having said both. But it's in the songbook as 7/4 so we'll just leave it there.
[†] The demo can be heard on *Dark Side* Immersion box set.
[‡] 'I'm alright, Jack' may come from a 1959 film of the same name starring Peter Sellers and satirising British industry and labour relations, although it was a commonly-used phrase long before that.
[§] Adding that 'I had drilled holes in old pennies and then threaded them on to strings; they gave one sound on the loop of seven. Roger had recorded coins swirling around in the mixing bowl Judy used for her pottery, the tearing paper effect was created very simply in front of a microphone and the faithful sound library supplied the cash registers.' (Mason, *Inside Out*, p.174.)
[¶] www.facebook.com/rogerwaters/videos/1473840169633333/

at 3.02 where the song shifts into 4/4 and the sound becomes much more reverberating, creating a larger, choral effect as the guitar solo kicks in. This, however, is contrasted with a short, quieter and very dry section (from 3.48), where the group sound tinny and insubstantial, ending at 4.20 when the drums kick in and the full technicolour sound resumes for the remainder of the solo, but before reverting to the dry sound for the final verse. This shifting dry/wet dynamic is perhaps meant to suggest the group as both penniless beginners and rock star professionals, but unlike **COMFORTABLY NUMB** the shift isn't mirrored by the song itself, so the purpose of it remains obscure.[**] In any case, the aridity of the verses contrasts unfavourably with the gorgeous lushness of the rest of the album, making it one of the group's few ill-judged recording decisions.

Another issue is that the song doesn't really swing. The demo has a terrific Delta blues rhythm to it, a swagger that the group fail (or choose not) to reproduce in the studio version, where the verse may have the same 7/4 beat but feels stiff. However, the saxophone and guitar solos in **MONEY** are both terrific, the former finally bringing out the song's R&B raunch, the latter a soaring rock staple that deconstructs itself in the dry section then triumphantly returns for a piercing climax. Gilmour's vocal is similarly excellent, both gruff and ironic, with his precise intonation making clear the sarcasm of '*goody-good bullshit*' and the fading '*Away ... away ...*' ending suggesting the improbability of dreams of avarice coming true – ironically enough.

MONEY became one of those songs about itself,[††] released as a single and remarkably hitting #13 in the US Billboard Hot 100 on 28 July 1973,[‡‡] after eleven weeks on the chart. Although the group had not released a single in the UK since **POINT ME AT THE SKY**, their US label Capitol were more optimistic and had released **FREE FOUR** in July 1972. It had not charted, making **MONEY** quite the lightning streak in a clear blue sky. It elevated Pink Floyd from contenders to rock royalty, and was still being played by Waters and Gilmour on their most recent tours. Though the track is essentially satirical, there is enough in there to satisfy most rock fans, with the group's various dichotomies now working in harmony rather than against each other to enlarge their capabilities. In **MONEY**, as throughout *Dark Side*, Pink Floyd sound like they can handle anything they cared to try – in marked contrast to the labours of *Ummagumma* and *Atom Heart Mother*. The apprenticeship was over. They were now a truly world-class band.

[**] It was Gilmour's idea, during the solo at least, though he doesn't say to what purpose and the interviewer frustratingly doesn't press him on it: 'It was my idea to break down and become dry and empty for the second chorus of the solo.' *Guitar World*, February 1993.

[††] Alongside, say 'Wannabe' by the Spice Girls, 'Welcome To The Jungle' by Guns N' Roses, and 'The Eternal' by Joy Division.

[‡‡] www.billboard.com/charts/hot-100/1973-07-28/

US AND THEM (Waters, Wright)
Length: 7.51
Vocals: Gilmour, Wright **Guitars**: Gilmour **Bass**: Waters **Hammond organ**: Wright **Piano**: Wright **Drums**: Mason **Tenor saxophone**: Dick Parry **Backing vocals**: Doris Troy, Lesley Duncan, Liza Strike, Barry St John
Recorded: May 1972–February 1973, EMI Studios, London
Producer: Pink Floyd
First released: 1 March 1973 (*The Dark Side of the Moon* track 7)
Rating: 9/10

The final Waters-Wright collaboration (not that there were many) famously sees them reusing a piano sequence from their *Zabriskie Point* soundtrack work for Michelangelo Antonioni. But where 'The Violent Sequence' was a stark, mournful piano piece, **US AND THEM**, like all the tracks on *Dark Side*, is suffused with great riches. It is jazzed up wonderfully by a saxophone (both solo and backing), Gilmour's superlative guitar playing, and excellent female backing vocals. It also has numerous deft studio touches, like the echoing final word on each line of the verse, and the loud-soft dynamic is put to exceptional use here.

But what stands out most is the quality of the music. **US AND THEM** begins with delicate arpeggios from Gilmour and some good complementary basslines from Waters, alongside some more velvet-touch drumming from Mason. Together they create an absorbing, almost hypnotising texture. The tenor saxophone by Dick Parry that comes in at 1.09 is well judged, allowing the song to develop its own atmosphere before adding a new element to it within a reasonable timeframe. Parry's playing is similarly soft and seductive, but adds a rootsy, authentic feeling to the delicate musical framework. On the other hand, the drama and high energy of the choruses create an excellent contrast, with the harmonised vocals of Gilmour and Wright, the female backing singers and Dick Parry all take on a greater urgency – yet notice how skilfully the song moves from the clamour of the chorus to the quiet of the verse, with Gilmour's verse vocal coming in just one beat afterwards ('*Down … and out …*'), as though there were no time to spare. This ability to fill every second with memorable moments hadn't been heard since **SEE EMILY PLAY**. It's the same with the piano solo, which is some rather spare chords over the verse melody, but includes a remarkable vocal interlude by roadie Roger 'The Hat' Manifold: '*Well I mean, they're not gonna kill ya, so like, if you give 'em a quick short, sharp shock, they don't do it again. Dig it? I mean 'e got off light, cos I coulda given 'im a thrashin', but I only hit 'im once. It's only the difference between right and wrong, innit? I mean good manners don't cost nothin' do they, eh?*' Which in its colloquial way illustrates the theme of violence from the side of 'us' rather than 'them', where it concerns respect and ethics, rather than exploitation and militarism.

Waters' fine lyric meanwhile illustrates political divides through many deft bifurcations: '*Us and them*', '*Down and out*', '*Black and blue*', '*With, without*', thus implying poverty, racism and exclusion. While the gentle verses require verbal brevity, the choruses are more urgent and allow for longer lines. The first contains one of his most perfect images: '*The generals sat, while the lines on the map / Moved from side to side*' is a magnificent condemnation of the folly of war – and so much more profound and moving than anything in **CORPORAL CLEGG**. Meanwhile, '*Up and down / And in the end, it's only round and round, and round*' is the best expression of Waters' belief in and use of cycles,* as seen throughout the Pink Floyd canon. Here, it feels aligned to the exhortation of **BREATHE** to appreciate the natural human cycles – breathe in, breathe out; birth, life and death; wax on, wax off.

Overall, **US AND THEM** is one of the key tracks on *Dark Side*, with its superb dynamics, razor-sharp studio work, profound and moving lyrics, tremendous vocals, and wonderful musicianship all combining into a remarkable song. Its pace is sometimes sedate, but here Pink Floyd show how that doesn't necessarily mean an absence of passion or emotion.

ANY COLOUR YOU LIKE (Gilmour, Mason, Wright)
Length: 3.24
Guitars: Gilmour **Bass**: Waters **EMS Synthi A**: Wright **VCS 3 synthesiser**: Wright
Hammond organ: Wright **Minimoog**: Wright **Drums**: Mason **Percussion**: Mason
Recorded: May 1972-February 1973, EMI Studios, London
Producer: Pink Floyd
First released: 1 March 1973 (*The Dark Side of the Moon* track 8)
Rating: 8/10

Sometimes you want to hear a band just playing, like Led Zeppelin on 'The Crunge', Iron Maiden on 'New Strange World' and 'Losfer Words (Big Orra)', or Miles Davis on *Bitches Brew* (producer Teo Marcero's remarkable studio constructions notwithstanding). Pink Floyd were perhaps not the greatest jammers – while jazz musicians are accustomed to listening to each other and playing off of that, rock bands tend to have their own 'bag' and stick to it, making genuine improvisation rare unless you are The Who, the Grateful Dead or Living Colour – but they could definitely noodle away on a theme or atmosphere, as heard from **A SAUCERFUL OF SECRETS** all the way to *The Endless River*. Here, in perhaps Wright's second-most prominent moment on the album after **THE GREAT GIG IN THE SKY**, the group develop a glorious dazzle-wash of colour, Wright's Hammond and Minimoog combining with the EMS and VCS 3 synthesisers to create some very fine timbres. The synthesisers in particular steal the show with starbursts of sizzling colour (from 0.27) and then accompanying Gilmour's solo with trills and shimmering cadences (from around 2.47). These sections are not so much melodic pieces as delightful textural moments that

---

* While also being a rejoinder to The Beatles, whose lines '*And in the end / The love you take / Equals the love you make*' bring their album *Abbey Road* (1969) to its climax.

tickle the ear and give *Dark Side* an even greater feeling of richness, particularly alongside the tremolo-heavy guitar solo and Waters' warm, resonant bass line.

ANY COLOUR YOU LIKE, as the sole instrumental, does not add to the thematic sense of *Dark Side* except in its title, referring to the illusion of consumer choice conveyed by the phrase 'Any customer can have a car painted any color that he wants, as long as it is black', from industrialist Henry Ford. But those were the glory days of staple consumer products and outlets,[*] from Campbell's Soup to Sears Roebuck to Marks and Spencer reaching the developed world. As Andy Warhol said, 'You can be watching TV and see Coca Cola, and you know that the President drinks Coca Cola, Liz Taylor drinks Coca Cola, and just think, you can drink Coca Cola, too.'[†] The glistening tones so artfully played by Wright might therefore suggest the glossy ephemeral consumer images passing by our eyes, particularly those seen in the videos projected onto 'Mr Screen'[‡] for **MONEY** – or maybe he was just busting out some tones that sounded good. Either way, **ANY COLOUR YOU LIKE** sounds wonderful, breaks the tension after the dramatic punch of **US AND THEM**, has marvellous textures, and is skilfully segued between its connecting songs. Gilmour's meandering solo (from 1.19, thus taking up over half the track) meanwhile is pleasantly melodic, though without any particular urgency, making the song feel improvised when compared to the artfully built constructions elsewhere on the album. And though the solo lacks the drama and dynamism of Gilmour's work on **TIME** and **MONEY**, those qualities would be out of place here, demonstrating his concern to suit the song over fretboard onanism. The only thing **ANY COLOUR YOU LIKE** really lacks is a feeling of trajectory, but in an album suffused with meaning, it serves as an excellent cooler between two major statements. Intra-album dynamics now clearly mattered to the group as much as those within individual songs. This is musical mastery.

BRAIN DAMAGE (Waters)
Length: 3.50
Vocals: Waters **Guitars**: Gilmour **Bass**: Waters **Hammond organ**: Wright **VCS 3 synthesiser**: Wright **Drums**: Mason **Bells**: Mason **Backing vocals**: Gilmour, Doris Troy, Lesley Duncan, Liza Strike, Barry St John
Recorded: May 1972–February 1973, EMI Studios, London
Producer: Pink Floyd
First released: 1 March 1973 (*The Dark Side of the Moon* track 9)
Rating: 9/10

---

[*] Products are much more segmented these days, the better to give the illusion of choice when everything is owned by a few companies. For instance, 50 companies had a combined 90% share of US media in 1983, but just six companies controlled the same proportion by 2011 – General Electric, News Corp, Verizon, CBS, Disney and Time-Warner.

[†] Warhol, *The Philosophy of Andy Warhol: From A to B and Back Again*, p.36.

[‡] The circular screen above and behind Mason's drumkit during live shows from 1974 on. It measured about 10m in diameter and pictures and videos could be projected onto it. Some of the animations seen in *Pink Floyd: The Wall* originated from as far back as 1975 (the falling man/leaf one).

Dark Side is a concept album in the truest sense, in that it deals with various themes rather than having a sustained narrative. Only in **BRAIN DAMAGE** and **ECLIPSE** do the group (or rather, Waters) step forward, tie the themes together and say what they truly believe. Initially the concluding track on *Dark Side*, **BRAIN DAMAGE** contains some of Waters' most sustained thoughts on life, the universe and everything, and in view of his later misanthropy it's pleasing to have such warm-heartedness forever associated with him. Not that **BRAIN DAMAGE** is all *'games and daisy chains and laughs'*, of course: its reflections on time, adulthood, madness, and of course Syd Barrett, make it highly poignant and notably personal, for a writer who had avoided writing in the first person since **IF**.

Though the lyrics face up to humanity's mental frailty, throughout it all is a sense of empathy. Waters (and by extension the group) twice declares that *'I'll see you on the dark side of the moon'* – that if life is driving you mad, he knows what it's like; he's with us, he's one of us.§ It's very touching: after exploring the anxieties of mortality, madness, materialism, political divides and the relentless pace of modern life, it is an elegant, humane conclusion to say, 'If you feel that you're the only one, that you seem crazy cause you think everything is crazy – you're not alone.'¶ And it's also, of course, poetically deft: Waters of course knew that the moon was traditionally a symbol of madness, with the words *lunar* and *lunatic* sharing the same root. 'The dark side of the moon' thus symbolises all the outcasts and misfits and heterodox in society, and the group's warm-hearted embrace of them (or us). If this had come at the start of the album it might feel a trite assertion, but here it feels entirely sincere, and fully earned after the journey through the angsts and sorrows of the preceding eight tracks.

The music, meanwhile, is a heady combination of swirling keyboards, guitar arpeggios, piercing guitar notes, female backing vocals and all, which perhaps give the song too bright a sheen. For example, the lines *'And if the dam breaks open many years too soon / And if there is no room upon the hill / And if your head explodes with dark forebodings too'* could be taken from **THE THIN ICE**, one of the most bitterly desolate the group ever recorded. But here, the contrast between the two is highly poetic: the lyrics acknowledge our weaknesses; the rousing music suggests the empathy we need to give to each other. Seen that way, the song is one of Waters' finest compositions. Yet, as throughout *Dark Side*, **BRAIN DAMAGE** is a superb team performance, with Gilmour's emotive leads and rhythmic arpeggiated framework, the surge and colour of Wright's organ, Mason's unhurried, almost magisterial pacing, and the wonderful sighing emotion summoned by the female backing singers** – and, of course, Alan Parson's skill in putting them all together atmospherically. Nonetheless, the

---

§ *'And I am you / And what I see is me'* as he wrote in **ECHOES**.
¶ Waters, *Uncut* Magazine, June 2003.
** For whom this was merely a job. Lesley Duncan later said about the group, 'They weren't very friendly. They were cold, rather clinical. They didn't emanate any kind of warmth ... They just said what they wanted and we did it ... There were no smiles. We were all quite relieved to get out.' (*Classic Rock*, 1 March 2022).

greatest credit must go to Waters, whose exploration of existential concerns has come so very far, and incredibly in just five years.

> **ECLIPSE** (Waters)
> **Length**: 2.03
> **Vocals**: Waters **Guitars**: Gilmour **Bass**: Waters **Hammond organ**: Wright **Drums**: Mason
> **Backing vocals**: Wright, Gilmour, Lesley Duncan, Doris Troy, Barry St John, Liza Strike
> **Recorded**: January 1973, EMI Studios, Abbey Road, London
> **Producer**: Pink Floyd
> **First released**: 1 March 1973 (*The Dark Side of the Moon* track 10)
> **Rating**: 10/10

Added, quite early on to *Dark Side* when it was felt that **BRAIN DAMAGE** lacked sufficient impact,[*] **ECLIPSE** is one of the finest album closers in rock history. The idea is very simple – it's a litany, a list – but with its rising intensity as the band throw everything at it, the song takes on grandeur and magnificence to end the album on a glorious affirmation of empathy and understanding.

Opening with a fabulous twirl of the Hammond organ by Wright, Waters (double-tracked, for greater intensity) then begins his litany with '*All that you touch, all that you see / All that you taste, all you feel*'. This simple structure is repeated, with new additions to the sound mix every four bars – the girls on backing vocals, backing vocals by Gilmour and Wright, increased guitar intensity, increased drum intensity, until it becomes utterly all-encompassing. At the peak, when the entire band (it sounds like) sing, '*And everything under the sun / Is in tune, but the sun is eclipsed by the moon*' it is beyond majestic: it feels like spiritual rapture, a rush of emotional euphoria. The group had displayed some of this emotive ability before – on **ECHOES** and the live version of **A SAUCERFUL OF SECRETS**, for example – but here for the first time recreate their full earth-shattering power in the studio. And the heartbeat on the fade out is another superb touch, a reminder of the endless rhythm of life, and there's the final kicker – '*There's no dark side of the moon really; as a matter of fact, it's all dark*' – from Abbey Road doorman Gerry O'Driscoll.[†]

The use of anaphora, in the repeated '*All that you*' refrain, is a masterful lyrical touch, tying together '*everything under the sun*' in an affirmative pledge.

---

[*] Bootlegs from early in the *Dark Side* tour, such as from January 1972, do include a track called **ECLIPSE**, but initially it was something like the outro to **BIKE**, with slide whistles, slide guitar and manic laughter. The song we recognise as **ECLIPSE** seems to have been first played at Bristol's Colston Hall on 5 February 1972. Waters said: 'We'd started playing everything on the road before we recorded the album. I suggested it all needed an ending. I wrote "Eclipse" and brought it into a gig, at the Colston Hall in Bristol, on a piece of lined paper with the lyrics written out.' (*Uncut* magazine, June 2003). Hence the idea of **ECLIPSE** being a late studio-penned number, akin to **NOBODY HOME**, is quite wrong. The first bootleg I can find containing the proper version of **ECLIPSE** is however on 12 February, at Sheffield City Hall. Naturally it lacks the power of the studio version, but the concept is entirely there.

[†] His recording then went on to say, 'The only thing that makes it look light is the sun', but this wouldn't have fit with Waters' themes.

Though Waters is an atheist, here he produces a Wordsworthian[‡] pantheistic vision, where everything is tied together as part of a greater whole. The imagery is simple but deeply satisfying. Regardless of the poetic allusions and philosophical visions, the musical impact of **ECLIPSE** is colossal, ending *Dark Side* with Pink Floyd's most profound moment yet. **ECLIPSE** also represents the first time the group had ended an album in a satisfying structural or symphonic note. Now they had mastered structure as well as songwriting craft, the studio as instrument, and lyrics that resonate to this day. Having been allowed the space to experiment and develop in the five years since *A Saucerful of Secrets* (and, of course, working ferociously hard in doing so), the Floyd had hit the jackpot. **ECLIPSE** demonstrates the full fruition of the band's singular talents, and ends the group's greatest work to date in a stunning declaration of musical, vocal, technological, recording, and lyrical ability.

The Dark Side of the Moon is justly, alongside *The Wall*, the most famous and most popular of Pink Floyd's albums. Its success became part of its own legend, with its time on the US album chart forever cited.[§] However, simply looked at as a piece of music, the album remains enormously impressive: it is endlessly inventive, deeply emotional, thoughtfully humane, and rousingly empathetic on the trials and troubles of life. Wright had never sounded better (certainly since the departure of Barrett) and his work in **THE GREAT GIG IN THE SKY**, **ANY COLOUR YOU LIKE** and **ECLIPSE** is jaw-dropping, the lyrics had never been more incisive and thought-provoking, Gilmour produces his finest work to date with some especially powerful solos but some exquisite guitar work, for example in **US AND THEM** and **BRAIN DAMAGE**, and the production is stellar. It is not, perhaps, the group's best or most consistent work: there are very minor flaws, such as the overly lengthy introduction to **TIME** and the ill-considered production of **MONEY**, while **ANY COLOUR YOU LIKE**, though a lovely dazzlewash of colour, adds nothing to the thematic sense of the album. But these are minor quibbles. *The Dark Side of the Moon* demonstrates the full flowering and coherence of the group's remarkable talents, and in its expression of human hopes and concerns it is almost miraculously empathetic and hence regarded with almost mystical reverence. It is quite simply an album for the ages.

[‡] As Wordsworth wrote in *Tintern Abbey*:
   A presence that disturbs me with the joy
   Of elevated thoughts; a sense sublime
   Of something far more deeply interfused,
   Whose dwelling is the light of setting suns,
   And the round ocean and the living air,
   And the blue sky, and in the mind of man:
   A motion and a spirit, that impels
   All thinking things, all objects of all thought,
   And rolls through all things.

[§] By June 2024 it had spent a total of 990 weeks on the US Billboard Chart. (The album in second place is the *Legend* compilation for Bob Marley and the Wailers, now sitting at 837 weeks). See www.billboard.com/artist/pink-floyd.

> **SHINE ON YOU CRAZY DIAMOND (PARTS I–V)** (Gilmour, Wright, Waters)
> **Length**: 13.32
> **Vocals**: Waters, Gilmour, Wright **Guitars**: Gilmour **Bass**: Waters **Hammond organ**: Wright **Piano**: Wright **ARP string ensemble**: Wright **Minimoog**: Wright **VCS 3 synthesiser**: Wright **Clavinet**: Wright **EMS Synthi AKS**: Gilmour **Baritone saxophone**: Dick Parry **Tenor saxophone**: Dick Parry **Glass harp**: Waters, Gilmour, Wright **Drums**: Mason **Percussion**: Mason **Backing vocals**: Carlena Williams, Venetta Fielding
> **Recorded**: 13 January–28 July 1975
> **Producer**: Pink Floyd
> **First released**: 12 September 1975 (*Wish You Were Here* track 1)
> **Rating**: 10/10

Pink Floyd toured heavily on the back of *Dark Side*, both to refine it before its release and to follow up on its success. (Rock and pop musicians would never now refine a work live before its release. The machine doesn't let them.) Touring North America, Europe and Japan across 1972–73 and France and Britain in 1974, they racked up 132 performances across cities from Osaka to Akron, Ohio. Concluding the touring on 14 December 1974, they felt, not surprisingly, emotionally spent, but also for once short on ideas for new material.

The group, likewise, were now overnight successes in an industry in which they had been labouring for seven years. *Dark Side* went platinum, though none of their records had even gone gold before, and with that went a considerable increase in media and touring demands: interviews, gigs, presence, pressing the flesh, playing the game. As they were, perhaps, better educated than the usual musician,[*] the Floyd took exception to being treated as industry automatons, and as an asset ripe for exploitation. Though they fairly swiftly returned to the studio in the autumn of 1973, they diverted themselves with the 'Household Objects' project for two months, where (as Mason describes it):

> percussion was created by sawing wood, slamming down hammers of different sizes or thudding axes into tree trunks. For the bass notes we clamped and plucked rubber bands, and then slowed the resulting sounds to lower

---

[*] Apart from Pink Floyd, the contemporary rock group with the greatest academic qualifications would be Queen, with one diploma (Freddy Mercury), two bachelor degrees (Roger Taylor and John Deacon) and one abandoned PhD (Brian May). It's notable that of the best-selling singles in the UK in the 1960s, not one is by a university graduate. (They are by The Beatles, Ken Dodd, Englebert Humperdinck, Elvis Presley, Tom Jones, Acker Bilk, Frank Ifield, Cliff Richard & The Shadows, The Archies, The Tornados, Rolf Harris, The Everly Brothers, The Dave Clark Five, The Searchers, Cilla Black, The Shadows and Frank Sinatra). Pop and rock music was a working-class activity, until groups like Pink Floyd gave it greater cultural resonance (or pretensions, if you prefer). But also, of course, before the university expansions in the 1960s then 1990s, far fewer people went to university: only around 5% of school leavers in 1960. As economist JK Galbraith noted in *The New Industrial State* (1967), the rapidly-expanding service sector required more white-collar skills. Hence, the corollary between the expansion of the university sector and the increased audience for fairly esoteric rock bands.

tape speeds ... [W]e set about breaking light bulbs and stroking wine glasses, and indulged in various forms of water play including stirring bowls of water before pouring them into buckets. We unrolled lengths of adhesive tape, sprayed aerosols, plucked egg slicers and tapped wine bottle tops.[†]

A fun way of spending time, maybe, but an expensive one, given studio costs, and essentially a diversion activity.[‡] It wasn't until January 1975 that the group returned to the studio to get working on the next album, with **SHINE ON YOU CRAZY DIAMOND** having been developed during the 1974 summer tour of France and the winter tour of the UK.

If *Dark Side* was an album of pieces put together with great skill, **SHINE ON YOU CRAZY DIAMOND** follows **ECHOES** in demonstrating the group's mastery of dynamics across a single very long song. Opening on a long static frieze from Wright (utilising the tones from the wine glasses from the Household Objects project) that radiates feelings of sadness and isolation, **SHINE ON** is the keyboardist's greatest moment in the group, his melancholy waves of sound nonetheless suffused with tenderness and humanity.[§] The song, meanwhile, is perhaps the single most intensely emotional song in the Pink Floyd canon, being in essence a prayer of remembrance to Barrett, a hymn to his fallen greatness, and (as with **BRAIN DAMAGE** and **ECLIPSE**) a plea for empathy for the heterodox and minorities in society. With strong contributions from all four members, **SHINE ON** demonstrates Pink Floyd at its collective peak, with majestic playing from Wright, superlative lyrics from Waters, an astonishing series of guitar riffs and solos from Gilmour, and Mason's fine handling of shifts in tempo, as well as his immaculate touch.

Like **ATOM HEART MOTHER** and **A SAUCERFUL OF SECRETS**, **SHINE ON** is divided into several sections: here there are nine, as indicated by the Roman numerals of the two parts, though the shift from one section to the next isn't quite clearly signposted. The idea to split the song into two tracks was an excellent architectural decision, giving the album a journey-and-return feeling as previously evoked on **ECHOES**, and ensuring that the shorter songs, enveloped between the two sections, do not feel minor by comparison. (Whereas **ATOM HEART MOTHER** had overwhelmed delicate songs like **IF** and **FAT OLD SON**. The vigour of **ONE OF THESE DAYS** and **FEARLESS**, however, prevents **ECHOES** from doing similarly on *Meddle*, as does that song's place at the end of the album.) By now the group were masters at organising material to maximise its impact and meaning.

---

† Mason, *Inside Out*, p.194.
‡ Two excerpts from the 'Household Objects' have been released: 'The Hard Way' on the *Dark Side* Immersion Edition, and 'Wine Glasses' on the *Wish You Were Here* Immersion Edition (both released in 2011). The former seems to be mostly rubber bands, but 'Wine Glasses' was of course later put to good use.
§ Although the post-punk movement often emphasised isolation and angst, compare the bleakness of Joy Division or The Cure with this: there's a warmth and empathy in **SHINE ON** lacking in the later bands.

For all of its length, **SHINE ON** melodically largely comes from a four-note motif,* namely B♭, F, G, and E, known as 'Syd's Theme'. Played as a motif from the start of Part II onwards, it really ties the room together. However, from the very start **SHINE ON** is gripping, fading in on the vast static frieze of Part I but diversifying the sound with a Minimoog keyboard solo by Wright from 0.46 and then a guitar solo from Gilmour at 2.10, with a restrained, undistorted and oddly plasticky sound. Part II introduces 'Syd's Theme', played four times with vast echo and authority by Gilmour before the rest of the band finally enter at around 4.27 and the song is properly under way, with yet more soloing of particular excellence, both highly melodic and deeply emotive. Although Wright's various keyboards and synthesisers dominate the overall sound, Gilmour's playing demonstrates astonishing growth from (for example) his fairly undistinguished work on **ATOM HEART MOTHER** just five years earlier.

This takes us to the start of Part III at 6.27, with another Wright Minimoog solo which is (naturally) gentler and more melancholic, taking us up to 7.32 where the band collectively pause for a moment in a wonderful dynamic shift, before resuming with a third Gilmour guitar solo, this time played with a wonderful electric fluidity, building to several peaks before subsiding at 8.38. Part IV begins a few seconds later with the vocals finally coming in at 8.43,† sung with one line by Waters alone, the second line in harmony with Gilmour, and then the refrain '*Shine on, you crazy diamond!*' sung in chorus with backing vocalists Carlena Williams and Venetta Fields. Waters' vocal is initially unusually high-pitched for him, making it sound somewhat like Gilmour, though he sounds far more authoritative in the two choruses (beginning '*You were caught in the crossfire*' and '*Well, you wore out your welcome*' respectively). Part V begins immediately after the second chorus, with Dick Parry taking a baritone saxophone solo, initially in the same 6/8 time and then in an accelerated 12/8 time from 12.01, while Gilmour plays metronomic arpeggios. The saxophone solo peaks and then all the instruments gently fade out, ushered by the arpeggios, then supplanted by the icy pulses of Wright's synthesiser cross-fading from **WELCOME TO THE MACHINE**.

Lyrically, of course, **SHINE ON** is about Syd Barrett, and is perhaps the ultimate expression of the motif of absence in the Pink Floyd canon. If *Dark Side* was a plea for empathy and understanding, and thus implicitly about Barrett, **SHINE ON** is its mirror image: explicitly about Barrett, and by extension anyone who feels at odds with society. (When **SHINE ON** was played live, Waters would most often mention Barrett to the audience, from gigs in 1975 all the way to the Live 8 concert in 2008 and his solo tours beyond. That's

---

* The four-note intro to 'One' by Metallica on *...And Justice For All* (1988) is a clear descendant of 'Syd's Theme'. Metallica aren't noted as being Pink Floyd fans, but that album is certainly their most progressive, most tracks boasting numerous distinct sections and multiple time signatures, played at breath-taking pace and power. By their next album (*Metallica*, 1991) they had unfortunately expunged many of these aspects from their music.

† What balls for a rock band to have a song with an opening instrumental section taking up the first *nine minutes*.

a long time keeping the flame alive. Though the more emotionally buttoned-up Gilmour never followed suit.) It's interesting that the lyrics in **SHINE ON YOU CRAZY DIAMOND I–V** and **VI–IX** are both quite short for such long songs, the former comprising just four short verses of two lines each, four refrains (of '*Shine on you crazy diamond!*') and two choruses at four lines each. But Waters makes the most of his limited space with fantastic images, depicting Barrett in the verses as having a '*look in your eyes / Like black holes in the sky*', and as having '*reached for the secret too soon / You cried for the moon*', the latter combining a mythical sense of Barrett as Daedalus, reaching for the sun but being burned, or as Adam and Eve seeking knowledge and being expelled from Eden, as well as the moon as a symbol of lunacy that harks back to **BRAIN DAMAGE** and far beyond. The choruses, meanwhile, give more detail, saying that Barrett had been '*caught in the crossfire of childhood and stardom*' and having '*wore out your welcome with random precision*' – deftly summarising how he artistically rendered childhood in *Piper* and how his wide-eyed mind left him defenceless for the onslaught of fame, and how he exasperated his bandmates and the music industry with bizarre behaviours that might just have been cryptic gestures of rejection.‡ The second couplet in each chorus, however, shifts as in a prayer to an imperative, calling on Barrett and all who remember him: '*Come on, you raver, you seer of visions / Come on, you painter, you piper, you prisoner, and shine!*' Such heartfelt imagery speaks beautifully of Waters' everlasting admiration of Barrett and all he stood for, and also perhaps his determination to assure his bandmate's legacy (see **WISH YOU WERE HERE**).

SHINE ON may have had a long gestation, but its recorded version is a masterpiece of emotion and musical construction, often voted as Pink Floyd's greatest song, regularly opening concerts, and demonstrating the band at the peak of its collective powers. Wright's playing, with its remarkable colours and textures, was probably never better, Water's lyrics are humane, richly poetic and elegiac, Gilmour's soloing moves beyond even his triumphs in **TIME** and **MONEY** to showcase him as a world-class guitarist, and Mason's commentary on the drums and adroit time-handling across multiple sections are done so skilfully that he seems to never break a sweat. **SHINE ON** is a magnificent tour de force by a group now using all of its gifts for expression.§ If it isn't the best thing they ever did, it isn't far off it.

---

‡ Waters tells stories of the group playing on the Pat Boone show in 1967, Barrett rehearsing perfectly every time, then when the cameras were rolling refusing to participate. Or, famously, trying to teach Waters a song 'Have You Got It Yet?' but continuously changing it. (Interview with John Edginton, 2001).
§ Yet the reviews of *Wish You Were Here* were mixed. The *Rolling Stone* review was particularly scathing, with comments like '[P]assion is everything of which Pink Floyd is devoid.' (*Rolling Stone*, 6 November 1975). You wonder how someone could fail to hear the emotion in every song in this album.

> **WELCOME TO THE MACHINE** (Waters)
> **Length**: 7.32
> **Vocals**: Gilmour **Guitars**: Gilmour **Bass**: Waters **VCS 3 synthesiser**: Waters, Wright **Hammond organ**: Wright **ARP string synthesiser**: Wright **Minimoog**: Wright **Timpani**: Mason **Cymbals**: Mason
> **Recorded**: 13 January–28 July 1975
> **Producer**: Pink Floyd
> **First released**: 12 September 1975 (*Wish You Were Here* track 2)
> **Rating**: 7/10

WELCOME TO THE MACHINE isn't an easy listen, but deliberately so, its discordant synthesisers and Moog-generated sounds intended to create what the German dramatist Bertolt Brecht called 'alienation effects' by drawing attention to the song as an artificial construction. With sounds leaping at the listener from unexpected angles, the track is (as Brecht said) 'stripping the event of its self-evident, familiar, obvious quality and creating a sense of astonishment and curiosity about them'.[*] While many classic songs have the feeling of inevitability to them,[†] alienation effects do precisely the opposite: they demonstrate the artifice of art, the tricks and techniques used to lure the viewer or listener, and show how these are only conventions of modern bourgeois society. Or as Magritte painted in *La Trahison Des Images* (1929), '*Ceci n'est pa une pipe*'.

Lyrically, however, **WELCOME TO THE MACHINE** is more than just an objection to the industry. Waters' acute political sensibility and ability with metaphor ensure he is painting on a broader canvas, allegorising the music business as institutional oppressor. What might initially seem like a rock star's complaint becomes more significant because of its revelation of misguided dreams and how these are used to funnel fresh victims into the capitalist meat-grinder. '*You've been in the pipeline filling in time*' in the first verse, for example, anticipates the view of education as mindless sausage factory in the extraordinary **ANOTHER BRICK IN THE WALL PART 2** sequence from *Pink Floyd: The Wall*, while in the second verse '*What did you dream? / It's all right we told you what to dream*' suggests how the media ensnares those who crave fame through its control of images and narrative. Waters goes on to detail what these were for him: '*You dreamed of a big star / He played a mean guitar / He always ate in the Steak Bar / He loved to drive in his Jaguar*'. Although Waters coveted a Bentley rather than a Jaguar.[‡] Set down so transparently, such thoughts seem rather absurd, but of course personal nirvanas always are ridiculous (hence why **OUTSIDE THE WALL** is so muted). The point is that the machine lures, ensnares and destroys, through whatever you thought

---

[*] Brecht, *Gesammelte Werke*, XV, p. 301.
[†] 'Yesterday' by The Beatles being perhaps the best example. It's almost ludicrous to think of Paul McCartney sitting down and *writing* it. **WISH YOU WERE HERE** is probably Pink Floyd's equivalent, as a chord sequence and musical structure which just flows seamlessly – though of course it too was laboured upon.
[‡] See **PIGS (THREE DIFFERENT ONES)**, note 2.

most dear. The very fact of Pink Floyd having become so successful is what gives **WELCOME TO THE MACHINE** its power. They are no longer outsiders looking hungrily in: they are in the belly of the beast.

All of which is very effective. But the trouble is that **WELCOME TO THE MACHINE**, once you become familiar with the effects, is essentially a drone on acoustic guitar with no development, contrast or resolution. It's only effective as long as you find Wright's synthesiser parts jarring. These are, to be fair, some of Wright's greatest creations, sounding immensely powerful, like huge laser beams from outer space, the string synths like horror movie atmospherics. As an engineering feat, their heft and power are hugely impressive. Yet like all similar art, they only work while the audience is disconcerted. Once assimilated in your mind, they lack effect: as with the squeals and shrieks of late period John Coltrane, the interminable punning allusions of James Joyce in *Finnegans Wake* or the word soups of William S. Burroughs, there's no *there* there, no song or story to sustain the audience's attention. So it is with **WELCOME TO THE MACHINE**: its bitterly sardonic phrasing might be bracing, the discordant synthesisers sound remarkable, the atmosphere is entirely convincing, and Gilmour's singing is as effective as ever, with probably the best use of his rasping tone in the group's discography, but the song's deliberately alienating strategy make them ultimately add up to less than they should. The song is a rejection of audience, both philosophically, which is fine, but also melodically, which is rarely a wise strategy. **WELCOME TO THE MACHINE** wins points for bravery, boldness, vision, imagination, argument, technical competence, and lyrical prowess, but just stumbles when considered as a song.

HAVE A CIGAR (Waters)
Length: 5.24
Vocals: Roy Harper **Guitars**: Gilmour **Bass**: Waters **Electric piano**: Wright **ARP string synthesiser**: Wright **Minimoog**: Wright **Hohner clavinet**: Wright **Drums**: Mason
Recorded: 13 January–28 July 1975
Producer: Pink Floyd
First released: 12 September 1975 (*Wish You Were Here* track 3)
Rating: 7/10

Songs attacking the record industry or media are rarely convincing, whether by Guns N' Roses,[§] The Smiths,[¶] The Stereophonics,[**] or even The Beatles.[††] (Two exceptions: 'Death On Two Legs' by Queen,[‡‡] which is really a character assassination, and 'Complete Control' by The Clash,[§§] which complements

---

[§] 'Get In The Ring' from *Use Your Illusion II* (1991).
[¶] 'Frankly, Mr Shankly' from *The Queen Is Dead* (1985) and 'Paint A Vulgar Picture', from *Strangeways, Here We Come* (1987).
[**] 'Mr Writer', from *Just Enough Education to Perform* (2001).
[††] 'Only A Northern Song' from *Yellow Submarine* (1968).
[‡‡] From *A Night At The Opera* (1975). It's about their former manager Norman Sheffield.
[§§] A non-album single from 1977.

their self-empowerment philosophy.) From the outside they simply appear to be punching down. In reality, of course, multinational corporations have huge power over musicians, with artists having to pay for their own equipment, recording costs, music videos, and touring costs, in exchange for the distribution capabilities and prestige of a major label.* But people want to believe that rock stars are, as Waters put it, 'at the very centre of life',† and them complaining about percentages, marketing budgets or industry parasites seems rather beneath them – even if these grievances are entirely justified. Interestingly, Pink Floyd seem to agree: neither of **WELCOME TO THE MACHINE** or **HAVE A CIGAR** made the *Echoes* compilation.

HAVE A CIGAR recalls **CORPORAL CLEGG** in its heavy-handed satire and unpleasant atmosphere. With a sour but limber guitar, electric piano, bass and drums framework, the track is made vicious by Wright's queasy synthesiser comments, Gilmour's squawking guitar interjections and ferocious but static guitar solos – and, of course, by Roy Harper's vocal, sung with tremendous presence if little subtlety. As Pink Floyd's first genuinely embittered song, **HAVE A CIGAR** marks a turning point in their career away from empathy and towards vitriol, although lyrically it is merely a step along from **CYMBALINE**, **BIDING MY TIME** and **MONEY** in expressing work-weariness and scepticism about capitalism. But where those songs were personal reflections, Waters here personifies his ire through the image of the cigar-chewing industry mogul.‡ Which is quite amusing, especially as Waters' lyrics are a stream of caustic sarcasm (like the famous, '*Oh, by the way, which one's Pink?*'), but ultimately it's rather cheap and undignified compared to the emotional intelligence of *Dark Side*. '*Everybody else is just green, have you seen the chart? / It's a hell of a start, it could be made into a monster / If we all pull together as a team*': sure, such derision is amusing, but the industry mogul is such an absurd figure spouting such self-evident bullshit that he barely deserves a full-scale satirical attack. Judging by the progress from *Wish You Were Here* to *Animals* to *The Wall*, Waters himself agreed, his targets becoming progressively more psychological and internalised.

As a song, however, **HAVE A CIGAR** is artfully constructed, with the group building on its sneering message by creating a complementary soundworld, plastering every moment with sardonic musical phrases. The main ones are Wright's leitmotif synthesisers (first heard at 0.24 and throughout), which create a jarring, queasy feeling, Gilmour's constant guitar interjections after each vocal line, Wright's Hofner clavinet used to create an oscillating, woozy feeling (it

---

* There's an excellent breakdown of the costs for a moderate-selling band by producer Steve Albini. A band could in one year sell 250,000 albums, generate $3m in income, and clear just $4k in profit per band member – less then *$80* a week! See thebaffler.com/salvos/the-problem-with-music. Albini (who died on 7 May 2024) was one of the very few producers not to take royalties on albums he produced.

† The full quote is fascinating: 'Stars – film stars, rock 'n' roll stars – represent, in myth anyway, the life as we'd all like to live it. They seem at the very centre of life. And that's why audiences still spend large sums of money at concerts where they are a long, long way from the stage, where they are often very uncomfortable, and where the sound is often very bad.' (Roger Waters, *Pink Floyd Lyric Book*.)

‡ This was a stock media trope at the time. You can see a similar figure in *Rocky* (1976), with cigar, rose in his buttonhole and all.

can be heard just before the first vocal at 1.02), Gilmour's concluding guitar solo (from 3.17), which starts with piercing high notes, but alternates this with angry mid-range twanging that sounds like the guitar fighting itself and getting nowhere, and Wright's arresting high notes on the ARP string synthesiser. The final studio effect is another alienation effect,[§] a wooshing sound and then the music sounding for the last few seconds as though being played on a tinny radio, reminding the listener that this is an album being listened to, an artistic construct, and thus a commercial property bought and sold and delivered through popular media. Pretty smart.

Meanwhile, Harper's vocal – taken because neither Waters nor Gilmour were satisfied with their attempts to sing it – is commanding, sung with a sneer and an invective that further the song's message. Waters later reflected that he wished he had sung it, because he could have introduced some vulnerability into the vocal. The alternate take available on the *Wish You Were Here Immersion Edition* (2011) has Waters singing lead but harmonised by Gilmour: it's more nuanced, and the lyrics are far easier to parse, but it's too articulate, too precise, whereas Harper could pull off bludgeoning invective, the better to represent the oafishness of the character.[¶] The band made the right choice.[**]

WISH YOU WERE HERE (Waters, Gilmour)
Length: 5.40
Vocals: Gilmour **Guitars**: Gilmour **Pedal steel guitars**: Gilmour **Bass**: Waters **Piano**: Wright **Minimoog**: Wright **Drums**: Mason **Violin**: Stéphane Grappelli
Recorded: 13 January–28 July 1975
Producer: Pink Floyd
First released: 12 September 1975 (*Wish You Were Here* track 4)
Rating: 10/10

One of the most traditional Pink Floyd songs is one of its warmest, most heartfelt and most beloved by its fans. The motif of absence so often used here becomes less a symbol of emptiness or loss than a humane desire for connection, empathy, even what Martin Amis called 'the heat of known beasts'.[††] This is why the folky arrangement is so suitable, and why it initially had a bluesgrassy violin solo by Stéphane Grappelli[‡‡] (later deleted, it started where Gilmour does some 'do-do-do-do' vocal scatting then accompanied the rest of the track), folk music being associated with authenticity and integrity to a degree greater than any genre except

---

§ See **WELCOME TO THE MACHINE**.
¶ Promoter, music publisher, manager, and agent, Bryan Morrison titled his memoirs *Have a Cigar!* He managed Pink Floyd briefly after Peter Jenner and Andrew King decided to stick with Barrett, before Steve O'Rourke took over a year later. In the book he plays into the trope of the oafish, uncomprehending businessman.
** Harper was promised life tickets to Lord's cricket ground, but the group fobbed him off with 'a couple of hundred quid'. How ironic. (Roy Harper interview with John Edginton, 2011).
†† In *Experience* (2000), p.307.
‡‡ Grappelli (1908-1997) was a French jazz violinist and a founder of the Quintette du Hot Club de France, one of the key European jazz groups.

perhaps heavy metal. **WISH YOU WERE HERE** is thus one of the unlikelier Pink Floyd songs, folk being one of the lesser appreciated strands of the band's repertoire, despite songs like **IF, GRANTCHESTER MEADOWS, CRUMBLING LAND** and **A PILLOW OF WINDS** (and later **PIGS ON THE WING** and **MOTHER**). This early earnestness was in due course supplanted by the masks of drama, allowing the band to role-play even when they were being themselves (hence **IN THE FLESH?**). Yet **WISH YOU WERE HERE** isn't just a folksy tune. Its Gilmourish melodicism and structure combines magnificently with its Rogerian imageries and similes and the group's state-of-the-art studiocraft to a degree unparalleled in the group's repertoire until **ANOTHER BRICK IN THE WALL PART 2**. Here the bitterness and discontent that have soured the album so far are reversed, becoming a plea for togetherness – a precursor of **OUTSIDE THE WALL**, but with a great singalong tune. No wonder it's a fan favourite.

Opening with the shifting of radio stations and a brief snatch of the final movement of Tchaikovsky's *Fourth Symphony* following the end of **HAVE A CIGAR** and its alienation-effect radio tinniness, **WISH YOU WERE HERE** unfurls with typically Floydian patience, starting with Gilmour's strummed electric guitar as though through a cheap transistor radio at 0.17, and then the 'real' sound of his acoustic guitar coming in at 0.59.* The distance and contrast between the two are remarkable, an audio representation of absence and misapprehension. After that Gilmour's vocal comes in, with its deliberate grainy quality another attempt to dramatise authenticity. Moving from spartan guitar and vocal to the full band at 2.03 does give the song another lengthy introduction, but the cleverness of the production, with things developing in the layers of sound every ten seconds or so, ensures there's always something stimulating the ears. Once the full song is under way it's essentially an acoustic ballad played with great aplomb, but with numerous excellent hooks, such as the *dur-dum-dum-dum-dum* motif (first foreshadowed at the start of the transistor radio section but not made explicit until the end of the verse 2.39, after which it recurs throughout the guitar solo and outro), and Gilmour's tremendous scat singing which somehow communicates more emotion than words could hope to. Mason's drumming is more evident than usual in pushing the track along, in what feels a great band performance, while Wright restricts himself to some subtle phrasing on the piano, as well as some chunky synthesiser notes during Gilmour's scatting (perhaps lest we forget this is Pink Floyd).

Waters' lyric, meanwhile, is one for the ages, probably his best to that point. '*We're just two lost souls swimming in a fish bowl / Year after year*' – again, sentiments to which every bosom returns an echo. As an expression of existential anxiety it's peerless, the only begetter of countless tattoos and images and internet memes. The first verse, meanwhile, is a series of rhetorical questions, which Waters

---

* After the sound of Gilmour phlegmily coughing at 0.43. There is a rumour that it's there because of Gilmour's addiction to nicotine (and that hearing it made him quit), but it's far more likely there to emphasise the folksy verité of the track. Same with the sound of fingers moving across the strings to the next fret (as also heard on **GRANTCHESTER MEADOWS**).

probably pointed at himself as much as at Barrett, to whom the song is thought to be addressed. Waters' verse deals with reality and deception, self-knowledge and temptation, in a way similar to **WELCOME TO THE MACHINE**. But while that song made these themes explicit, here Waters uses poetic juxtaposition, asking if he can tell apart: *'a green field from a cold steel rail'*, *'hot ashes from trees'* and (most meaningfully) *'a walk-on part in the war for the lead role in a cage'*. The dichotomies prefer the living and the natural over the sterile and manufactured and restricted, like all good English poets. The greater distinction is about *'the walk-on part in the war' as opposed to 'a lead role in a cage'*. Waters clearly already saw his (lead) role in the group as delivering fame and fortune but restricting his actions and mental liberty. But the question he asks is if he will 'go on demanding of myself that I keep auditioning for the walk-on part in the war, 'cause that's where I want to be. I wanna be in the trenches. I don't want to be at headquarters; I don't wanna be sitting in a hotel somewhere. I wanna be engaged.'[†] By 'in the trenches' he means in the thick of any controversy, speaking his truth as he sees it. Hence **WISH YOU WERE HERE** concerns not just loss but the ability to act in the face of a hostile world, opening Waters' activist phase. Syd might have withdrawn from the world but Waters here declares himself as taking over the baton from him to push their worldview forward.

But the greater part of the lyric is where it develops the sense of existential anxiety from **TIME** (*'year after year'*) and empathy from **BRAIN DAMAGE** (*'We're just two lost souls'*), but makes it about us. **WISH YOU WERE HERE** thus combines two of Waters' greatest themes and adds a sense of transcendence that could quite reasonably be called religious. If **ECHOES** did this almost inadvertently, and *Dark Side* did this sporadically, **WISH YOU WERE HERE** is very consciously about connection, empathy, emotional release and consolation – those very human emotions which religion used to succour but nowadays most people find in popular art, especially music and live performances. As such, it's a humanist hymn, and one of the finest, most deeply cherished and most fiercely loved Pink Floyd tracks.

SHINE ON YOU CRAZY DIAMOND (PARTS VI–IX) (Wright, Gilmour, Waters)
Length: 12.29
Vocals: Waters, Gilmour **Guitars**: Gilmour **Steel guitars**: Gilmour **Bass**: Waters, Gilmour **Hammond organ**: Wright **Piano**: Wright **ARP string ensemble**: Wright **Minimoog**: Wright **VCS 3 synthesiser**: Wright **Clavinet**: Wright **EMS Synthi AKS**: Gilmour **Electric piano**: Wright **Drums**: Mason **Percussion**: Mason **Backing vocals**: Wright, Carlena Williams, Venetta Fielding
Recorded: 13 January–28 July 1975
Producer: Pink Floyd
First released: 12 September 1975 (*Wish You Were Here* track 5)
Rating: 10/10

---

† *Pink Floyd: The Story Of Wish You Were Here* (2012).

The second part of **SHINE ON YOU CRAZY DIAMOND** is an extension rather than a reprise, the two parts being clearly bifurcated rather than the second rehashing parts of the first, although there is a call-back between the two parts.* This gives *Wish You Were Here* a tremendous sense of completion, a departure and return as satisfying as the ending of *The Lord of The Rings* or the final movement of Beethoven's *Fifth Symphony*. Building on the sense of return from the reprise of **BREATHE** on *Dark Side* (at the end of **TIME**), **SHINE ON YOU CRAZY DIAMOND (PARTS XI–IX)** is more than a homecoming: it's both an incredible instrumental workout and a glorious climax and catharsis of the emotional charge build up in **PARTS I–V**.

Cross-fading from the (synthesised) wind sounds at the end of **WISH YOU WERE HERE** that create a feeling of desolate isolation, **SHINE ON YOU CRAZY DIAMOND (PARTS VI–IX)** begins with a pulse on the bass guitar before unfolding with some guitar arpeggios and subtle keyboard atmospherics, before Wright comes in with an icy, high-pitched yet colourful synthesiser solo at 0.58. It is (as always with Wright) highly melodic, the sort of thing you could whistle, but its glacial texture redoubles the alienating feeling of the song's opening. With the tension rising throughout Wright's solo, Gilmour then takes a lap steel guitar solo, from 2.24, and it's probably the greatest of his entire career, building beautifully through various sections towards a piercing climax at 4.13–4.24 (when the guitar is artfully doubled up to give it a more choral sound). Meanwhile, Mason keeps a wonderfully swinging tempo backing him, with Gilmour's flowing guitar chords keeping the whole thing moving. It's a majestic piece of music, a piece of high lyricism and enormous emotion. But immediately it finishes at 4.32, Gilmour is back on a traditional guitar, misdirecting the listener by suggesting another solo but then turning to the **SHINE ON** theme and the entire band reprising the opening theme and then (at 4.55) collectively pausing for a moment in a magisterial dynamic shift before Waters resumes singing ('*Nobody knows where you are*'). The control and authority are masterful. Gilmour's guitar commentary during the final verses, meanwhile, is keenly dramatic, another example of the group adding elements to avoid the material feeling stale even when great repetition is building huge tension.

Then there's a final chorus ('*Come on, you boy child, you winner and loser / Come on, you miner for truth and delusion, and shine!*'), at which point tick-tocking twinkling guitar arpeggios seem ready for the song to wind down and fade out (and bring Part VII to a close). But after a signal on the bass from Waters, Wright comes in on the electric piano, and there's something approaching a funk jam. It's not quite the equal of its equivalent on **ECHOES** – it's somewhat

---

* Songs with sequels are usually awful. If an artist has any good ideas for a song, they have usually gone into the original version. Metallica's 'The Unforgiven II' (from *ReLoad*, 1997) and 'The Unforgiven III' (from *Death Magnetic*, 2008) are pointless retreads. U2's 'God Part II' (on *Rattle & Hum*, 1988) tries to answer John Lennon's 'God' (from *John Lennon/Plastic Ono Band*, 1970) and comes up laughably short.

jazzier – but after the intense sentiment and pathos of the previous sections, some warmth and humanity is very welcome. Gilmour plays some very elastic high-toned guitar leads that sound both celestial (aided by some judicious echo towards the end) and compassionate, while Wright enjoys himself with both the Hammond organ and a Hofner clavinet, which allows him to create some groovy electric sounds† which contrast splendidly with the organ and guitar.

Finally these all fade out, the guitar echoes expanding to a cosmic emptiness, for Part IX (from 9.03): a final melancholy funeral march.‡ Softened by the Turkish Delight Farsifa organ, it is nonetheless deeply mournful, its sepulchral pace matched by the sombre tone from Wright (alongside his piano). Yet there's something beautiful about these waves of sound, something tender and humane rather than cold and alienating as on **WELCOME TO THE MACHINE**, a feeling enhanced by the spaciousness of the sound in which Mason has plenty of room to swing. Wright is left to carry the track, and does so extremely admirably, until the final fade-out from the last drum beat at 11.20 when a swirling synthesiser suggests the song circling the drain (or ascending into the universe) as Wright's final Farsifa notes suggest the melody from **SEE EMILY PLAY**. And we're done at 12.29, though the song at no point ever feels padded out or redundant.

SHINE ON YOU CRAZY DIAMOND (PARTS VI–IX) may not be the most skilful musicianship in the prog world, or have the most dramatic transitions, or boast the most philosophical lyrics. What it does have is deep humanity, tremendous soul, and a remarkable sense of melody and sonic architecture. Its rousing climax is deeply satisfying, and the sense of closure from its ending is enormous, like one of the world's greatest journeys finally coming to an end. Considered as a whole alongside **PARTS I–V**, the song displays Pink Floyd's individual talents at perhaps their collective peak, with Wright's contributions perhaps his finest achievement in his entire career, and Gilmour's solos and commentary managing to be majestic, tender and humane, often at the same time. Yet it was also the last gasp for Wright, with Waters dominating the next two albums. It is ironic that the song that was a lament to their former leader ends up being the final chapter of their own coherence as a band. But these things are only apparent in retrospect. Taken as an artistic achievement, **SHINE ON YOU CRAZY DIAMOND** (in both its parts) is a song of the highest order, a magnificent symphonic piece that advances the boundaries of rock music in colour, expression and form.

Wish You Were Here might have been a struggle to make, but it brilliantly builds on the emotional depth and musical range heard on *Dark Side*. Both Gilmour and Wright cite it as their favourite Pink Floyd album, and it's not hard to see

---

† Stevie Wonder plays one on 'Superstition'.
‡ It may have inspired 'The Eternal' by Joy Division (from *Closer*, 1979), which is a straightforward funeral dirge. (Singer Ian Curtis committed suicide shortly before the album was released.)

why: the album is even richer musically than its predecessor, with magnificent soloing from Gilmour throughout, and remarkable tones, textures and colours from Wright. Yet there's something discomfiting about *Wish You Were Here*: a certain coldness, an isolating feeling that runs through **WELCOME TO THE MACHINE, HAVE A CIGAR** and the opening to **SHINE ON YOU CRAZY DIAMOND (PARTS VI–IX)**. The group in retrospect were clearly in transition from the open-hearted humanity of *Dark Side* to the vicious misanthropy of *Animals* and *The Wall*. Like the group's earlier albums, therefore, *Wish You Were Here* lacks a uniform tone, veering from lament to cynicism to tenderness to sarcasm to icy grandeur, but while the range is admirable, it undercuts the compassion for which the album is best known. The more acerbic moments similarly lack the depth of Waters' subsequent political and psychological assaults on *Animals* and *The Wall*, seeming lily-livered by comparison. *Wish You Were Here* ultimately feels like a band craving to escape the treadmill, too honest to do anything other than express its dejection, yet too creative to make something less than superb. But despite containing some of the band's greatest moments, the sneering invective of **HAVE A CIGAR** and the alienating discordance of **WELCOME TO THE MACHINE** mean *Wish You Were Here* doesn't quite satisfy in the same way as *Dark Side*, *Animals* or *The Wall*.* It's very, very, very good, but something of a halfway house between its warm-hearted predecessor and the rage of the subsequent two albums.

PIGS ON THE WING, PT. 1 (Waters)
Length: 1.25
Vocals: Waters **Acoustic guitars**: Waters
Recorded: April–May 1976, Britannia Row, London
Producer: Pink Floyd
First released: 23 January 1977 (*Animals* track 1)
Rating: 7/10

The mid-1970s were a difficult time for the UK. The economy was in the doldrums with three-day weeks, power strikes, and stagflation (until then thought an impossible combination); inflation peaked at 27 per cent in 1975, and nationalised industries repeatedly had to be bailed out. Humiliatingly, the UK had to go to the IMF for an emergency loan in 1976 – the first major economy to do so – which led to the imposition of spending cuts and checks on the health of the economy: not a happy situation for what had recently been a leading world power. Meanwhile, civil war ripped through Northern Ireland, the army killed thirteen innocent bystanders in Londonderry, and IRA bombs repeatedly attacked the mainland. No longer did the beatific hippy dream of frictionless

---

* I feel the same way about Kraftwerk's *Trans Europe Express* (1977) – some of their very greatest moments, but there's something cold and alienating about 'Hall of Mirrors' and 'Showroom Dummies'. *The Man Machine* (1978) and *Computer World* (1981) are far more consistent and satisfying albums.

takeover seem anything other than absurd, while abstract psychedelic explorations and space rock seemed ridiculously out of touch.

The challenge from punk rock was both particular (Johnny Rotten's famous 'I Hate Pink Floyd' T-shirt) and general. The new rock was defiantly in the world, cynical to the point of nihilism, and pointedly abrupt and focused: the first album by The Clash has fourteen songs and eleven last under three minutes; four last less than two. Lengthy jams, gradual accumulations of atmosphere, glacial melodic changes, and ponderous rhythms – in other words, the Floyd's entire schtick – were now unfashionable. The punk drug of choice was speed, inducing a desire for immediate sensation, constant stimulation and a high tempo energy flash. Pink Floyd, of course, had no need to copy any of this. But they were as alert as any of their challengers to the atmosphere of the moment, and filtered it through their sensibility. Thus, *Animals* is as dark, angry and sinister as any punk album, quite comparable to *Rattus Norvegicus* or anything by The Stooges.† Whereas *Dark Side* moves from pressure and anxiety to glorious affirmation and *Wish You Were Here* focuses on sorrow, loss and contempt, *Animals* is a marked progression to a grim, bitter soundscape. Wright's colourful playing is toned down substantially, just as Gilmour's guitar playing becomes both more muscular and piercing. The fey near-falsettos of songs like **FEARLESS** and **GREEN IS THE COLOUR** are replaced by Waters' insistent nasal whine, an expressive nagging sound. (On *More*, Waters had no lead vocals; on *Meddle*, he had only one; but he sings nearly all of *Animals*.)

The band had toured ahead of *Wish You Were Here*, from April to June 1975, but not, oddly, after its release in September. Hence, 1976 was the first year in which the band did not tour. During this time, the band purchased and prepared the Britannia Row studio, in Islington.‡ Though it provided a famously (or notoriously) insular band with their own space in which to write and record, Britannia Row was windowless but especially suited Waters, who still lived nearby. (The others had bought country piles with their recent soaring income, but Waters remained an inner-city socialist until he married for the second time in 1976.)§ The studio, Mason later noted, induced a certain 'workman-like mood'. Perhaps so – *Animals* is certainly the album which efficiently gets the most out of the least melodic material. With its bleak repetitions it builds a

---

† Though The Stooges' droning ten-minute track 'We Will Fall' from their first album does sound sort of Floydian.
‡ Mason says, 'The original deal we had agreed with EMI – where we had taken a cut in our percentage in exchange for unlimited studio time at Abbey Road – had lapsed, and so we were conscious that we might start incurring escalating studio costs. Somehow we convinced ourselves that Britannia Row would be a money-saving move. Indeed, we probably had dreams of a successful commercial studio, despite the substantial capital outlay it entailed.' (Mason, *Inside Out*, p.215). Mason took ownership of it and later converted the building first into serviced offices, then flats. Not an empire, but maybe a small kingdom.
§ Wright was angered by Waters' pretensions of moral superiority. 'I think I was the first of the band to buy a country house. At the time, Roger was an armchair socialist. He told me, "You've really sold out – you've become such a capitalist; you're doing what every other rock star does" ... I said, "Roger, we did it for the kids and you'll be doing the same thing in a few years." It took him, I think, a year and a half to buy his own country seat. I said, "Roger, You're a hypocrite." And he said, "Oh I didn't want it, my wife wanted it."' (*Q Magazine*, November 1994).

uniquely dark, foreboding atmosphere, and it uses musique concrete and sound effects to even better effect than on *Dark Side*.

Yet the first sounds that prick the listener's ears are a delicate acoustic ballad written, performed and sung by Waters. Not since **IF** in 1970 had Waters written something so stark and so personal. But where that song celebrated doubt and uncertainty, in **PIGS ON THE WING (PART 1)** he sings a love song, albeit one couched in irony and bitterness. The acoustic guitar sounds fantastic: deep, rich and resonant,* while Waters' nasal voice is unusually gentle, though less mannered than on **IF**. Over just one verse, Waters sings '*If you didn't care for what happened to me / And I didn't care for you*', couching things in negatives – saying if we didn't care for or love each other, *this* is what would happen. Namely, that: '*We would zig-zag our way, through the boredom and pain / Occasionally taking glances up through the rain / Wondering which of the buggers to blame / And watching for pigs on the wing.*' So life would be just going backwards and forwards, without knowing who or what is troubling us, while seeking some kind of escape – '*pigs on the wing*' meaning when pigs fly, or when something unlikely happens. It's almost a reprise of his themes from **TIME**, but directed to a loved one: without love and connection, life is meaningless – though Waters here emphasises the meaninglessness and pain more than the love. So his trajectory as a songwriter from empathy to bitterness continues.

DOGS (Gilmour, Waters)
Length: 17.03
Vocals: Waters, Gilmour **Guitars**: Gilmour **Bass**: Waters **Hammond organ**: Wright **ARP string ensemble**: Wright **Minimoog**: Wright **Electric piano**: Wright **Farsifa organ**: Wright **Drums**: Mason, Gilmour† **Percussion**: Mason **Whistling**: Brian Humphries
Recorded: April–May 1976, Britannia Row, London
Producer: Pink Floyd
First released: 23 January 1977 (*Animals* track 2)
Rating: 10/10

The forgotten classic of the Pink Floyd catalogue, **DOGS** contains Gilmour's finest guitar work in Pink Floyd, and thus in his entire career (remarkably now totalling nearly sixty years). It is the third-longest song in the group's catalogue,‡ after **ATOM HEART MOTHER** and **ECHOES**, and to some extent follows the template of **ECHOES** and **SHINE ON** – not in the melodies or rhythms but in the prolongation of the tracks through huge repetition and a surprisingly small number of sections or movements. (Musicologist Gilad Cohen points out

---

* Compare, for example, with the acoustic guitar in 'Polly' by Nirvana. It sounds cheap and 'funky' as producer Butch Vig says. (Classic Albums, 'Nirvana – Nevermind', 2005).
† LouderSound, 21 January 2022 (www.loudersound.com/features/raving-and-drooling-how-pink-floyd-made-animals). 'In Dogs, there are some very heavy-duty drum things in the middle eight; that wasn't Nick, that was David. That's not a well-known fact.'
‡ Or fourth, if you combine both parts of **SHINE ON YOU CRAZY DIAMOND**.

that while contemporaries like Jethro Tull and Yes had songs of similar length, they used far greater numbers of distinct sections: 'Close to the Edge' by Jethro Tull comprises twenty sections over 17.40, whereas **DOGS** requires just seven over 17.03.)[§] This may help explain its relative anonymity in the Floyd catalogue, with no appearance in the *Best Of* compilations. It's also noticeable that after the *In the Flesh* tour of 1977, the group have declined to play any of the songs from *Animals* live (whereas **ECHOES** was played in the early dates of the *Momentary Lapse of Reason* tour, and by Gilmour when touring *On An Island*), though Waters plays them quite regularly as a solo artist, especially **PIGS (THREE DIFFERENT ONES)**.

Which is unfortunate, because **DOGS** displays all the great strengths of peak Waters-era Floyd. The playing is muscular but still jaw-droppingly bold and experimental. The solos are some of the best Gilmour ever laid down – his third, brutal one from 5.32 to 6.45 is a masterpiece of phrasing, economy, spacing,[¶] tone and expression. (His second and fourth solos are also superb: the second is almost pastoral, suggesting the salad days of the ambitious businessman, and the fourth is frantic and desperate before suddenly fragmenting into three separate voices at 13.54). The lyric similarly is one of Waters' very finest, with a fine eye for detail ('*A certain look in the eyes with easy smiles*'), a superb dramatic shift from second person ('*You gotta be crazy*') to first person ('*Gotta admit / That I'm a little confused*') and a coda which harks back to *Howl* (1955) by Allen Ginsberg (both starting each long line with '*Who*'),[**] though Waters denies any direct connection.[††]

As is well known, **DOGS** was called 'You Gotta Be Crazy' when it was played during the tours in 1974–75. The changes from the live versions which can be found on bootlegs are significant and vastly to the song's improvement. Though the completed song has long, repetitive sections, these never bore the listener – indeed, **DOGS** remains gripping throughout. Clearly, a great deal of effort went into refining and honing the work, likely making it a genuine group effort. (No songwriting credits were ever given for arrangements, though these were absolutely crucial, especially in longer tracks.) Though the early version contained the initial acoustic riff by Gilmour that seems to have been the foundation for

---

[§] *Expansive Form in Pink Floyd's 'Dogs'*, mtosmt.org/issues/mto.15.21.2/mto.15.21.2.cohen.html

[¶] The inspiration for this must have been Miles Davis – no-one else was brave enough to leave so much of a bar empty, the better to showcase the brilliance of what was played. Gilmour is one of the very few guitar players to have applied this. (After Eddie Van Halen, this idea seemed to disappear completely, as the shredders took over).

[**] ... who were expelled from the academies for crazy & publishing obscene odes on the windows of the skull, who cowered in unshaven rooms in underwear, burning their money in wastebaskets and listening to the Terror through the wall, who got busted in their pubic beards returning through Laredo with a belt of marijuana for New York ...

[††] 'No, no. I didn't make that connection. That's not to say it doesn't exist, of course.' (Roger Waters interviewed in Phil Rose, *Roger Waters and Pink Floyd: The Concept Albums*, p238).

the entire song* and pops up on several occasions throughout, the first section had a similar but far wordier lyric which Gilmour struggled to sing.† The guitar solos are mostly there, but the song keeps returning to the first section with its gobblingly fast lyric. The completed song instead moves clearly from section to section, giving it a feeling of teleological progression entirely absent from the early live versions. (Waters also sings the '*And when you lose control*' section, which Gilmour sounds much better doing.)

DOGS uses these passages very smartly to create distinct atmospheres that complement the ideas in each part of the lyrics. To wit: the opening section, with its bounding energy, recreates the vicious vitality of the youthful businessman (Waters implies it's a man, from details like '*the club tie and the firm handshake*'). The music increases in speed and intensity after the first verse, with Mason drumming more assertively and a bouncing bass line by Waters. But this only leads to the grim realisation that '*In the end you'll pack up, fly down south / Hide your head in the sand / Just another sad old man / All alone and dying of cancer …*' It's a superb, brutal image.

There's then a beautiful instrumental passage in the second section, with a crystalline guitar tone from Gilmour against some wistful backing (with Wright again just audible on the string synthesiser) suggesting the ache of nostalgia, and the wish to have lived a better life. But swiftly this is shooed away by the acoustic guitar chords and the barking of dogs‡ (from 4.48 to 5.31), which clear the space for Gilmour's third guitar solo. This one is perhaps the finest in his entire career, a masterpiece of phrasing, spacing, tone and articulation. It's a savage, bleak cry, played with intense command – from the howling bent notes at the start to the dissonant notes in the middle to the empty spaces throughout, in another superb example of Gilmour's intelligent desire not to overplay, as well as his desire to make the guitar sing. As a musical expression of the isolation and anxiety of the business life, it's simply astonishing.

The third section, also sung by Gilmour, is, however, led by a bassline from Waters. Its low notes and sparse, funereal atmosphere well convey the bleakness of the lyrics: '*And when you lose control, you'll reap the harvest you have sown / And as the fear grows, the bad blood slows and turns to stone*'. And then there's the final condemnation or verdict – '*So have a good drown, as you go down, all alone / Dragged down by the stone*'.

Which leads immediately to the fourth section – a static frieze with the word '*Stone …*' echoing and echoing. It's slightly reminiscent of the middle section

---

* "Dogs' as it was later known was just a simple little chord sequence that I had written and that everyone seemed to like. I liked it because all the chords were very unusual chords and you could play almost any note over the top of them. Like for guitar solos they were great because you could play nearly any note. So you can zoom around anywhere and not worry about what frets you hit or anything because almost anything you do hit if you do it deliberately enough will sound alright.' Interview by Charlie Kendall. *The Source*, NBC, 1984.

† One verse ran: 'You gotta be small to be a big shot / Gotta eat meat to stay at the top / You gotta be trusted, you gotta tell lies / Gotta be able to narrow your eyes.'

‡ The barking sounds are so infinitely better used than in **SEAMUS**, it's almost unbelievable that this is only six years later.

of **ECHOES**, although there are cymbals and a heartbeat[§] bass drum keeping time here. With the string synthesiser notes by Wright lasting for nearly thirty seconds each, there's a feeling of formless drifting, of shapelessness and somnambulance. The echoing barks and '*Stone …*' feel like glimmers of sentience, barely visible amidst the miasma. Here is the moral centre of the businessman's mind. It's empty. Wright plays a notably colourless Minimoog solo to keep things going, then the introductory acoustic riff is played again, which takes us to the next two sections – which, interestingly, reprise the first two sections.

But the lyric – so cleverly – now shifts focus from third person to first person, and from Gilmour to Waters, whose more delicate and nasal voice captures the despair and confusion of which he is singing. '*Sometimes it seems to me / That I'm just being uuuused*' – there's something wonderful about the way he stretches out the last syllable, as though through his nose. Whereas Roy Harper's voice was right for the bludgeoning satire of **HAVE A CIGAR**, Waters' more vulnerable vocal here is exactly right for the poignant realisation of a life wasted. This all builds up to the condemnation (**DOGS** has brilliant last lines in each verse) that '*And you believe at heart, everyone's a killer*' – that the businessman can never trust anyone, that would-be financial assassins are forever lurking.[¶] Which leads to a repeat of the instrumental second section, and Gilmour's fourth solo – the ache, the pain, the longing, but now from the perspective of old age and failure. The reprise is yet another example of how the group could use repetition to add meaning, with each cycle not merely repeating: as with Yeats's gyre, they ascend too. And so it is with **DOGS**: the cycle comes around, but with so much experience between the two, the reprise is a sad-eyed comment on the first.

And so we're into the final coda section, with its '*Who was …*' lines giving a final review of the plutocratic life. Waters is in a condemnatory mood: he audibly growls in the last words of '*Who was fitted with collar and chain*' and ends it with '*Who was found dead on the phone / Who was dragged down by the stone*'. It's a kind of litany, but where **ECLIPSE** develops an increasingly powerful musical background to become a majestic closer, **DOGS** feels slightly anticlimactic – there's no great increase in the instrumentation, although there are more backing vocals and busier drums, with the guitar only repeating and repeating the same sour chords. It's spare and severe, and for once seems to lack musical imagination, as it ends sounding as though it collapses in on itself, exhausted. Which isn't ideal after such a long song: you feel the need for something more authoritative, for the track is utterly mesmerising throughout, both in ideas, musical execution, lyrical concerns and vocal delivery.

Nonetheless, **DOGS** is a great peak of the Waters-era Pink Floyd: it is gripping, inventive, played with great authority, and lyrically both bitter and empathetic. It has, in particular, some of Gilmour's finest work as a musician and as a composer. His guitar solos are all distinct and highly effective.

---

§ Another self-reference, of course.
¶ Waters wasn't wrong. See **IN THE FLESH?** for the group's financial difficulties.

It's astonishing to think that just a few years earlier he was vaguely noodling about on **ATOM HEART MOTHER**. Waters' lyric meanwhile is a fantastic image-rich indictment of both a life lived without a soul and the bitterness of capitalism, and is one of his finest ever. **DOGS** is quite simply one of the greatest songs Pink Floyd ever recorded,[*] and it deserves to be considered in their pantheon of greats alongside, for example, **INTERSTELLAR OVERDRIVE**, **ECHOES**, **WISH YOU WERE HERE** and **COMFORTABLY NUMB**.

PIGS (THREE DIFFERENT ONES) (Waters)
Length: 11.25
Vocals: Waters **Vocoder**: Waters **Talk box**: Gilmour **Guitars**: Gilmour, Waters **Bass**: Gilmour **Hammond organ**: Wright **ARP string synthesiser**: Wright **Piano**: Wright **Clavinet**: Wright **Drums**: Mason **Cowbell**: Mason
Recorded: April–May 1976, Britannia Row, London
Producer: Pink Floyd
First released: 23 January 1977 (*Animals* track 3)
Rating: 9/10

The grim sparseness of **PIGS (THREE DIFFERENT ONES)** is a million miles from the lush soulfulness of *Dark Side* tracks like **THE GREAT GIG IN THE SKY** and **ANY COLOUR YOU LIKE**. It is almost astonishing to hear Waters write and sing with such vitriol and contempt. Nothing in the group's catalogue prior to this had anything like such cynicism and venom. Why? The short answer is that he seems to have found fame an alienating and disappointing experience (whereas he very much liked being wealthy).[†] People want a piece of you because it furthers their ambitions – they want to interview you, or for you to appear on their show, or for you to sign their record so it becomes worth more, or for you to give money to this, that or the other cause, or to sign up this or that incredible investment opportunity. Suddenly, you become a property rather than a person; you become a means to an end, rather than an end in yourself. Waters, raised by a Trotskyite mother, of course knew that this was precisely what Marx meant when discussing alienation: you become a thing rather than a person. It might be a high-class problem compared to someone toiling in a factory, but the spiritual and/or philosophical conflict remained. And so Waters' writing started to explore these darker themes, going from the mourning of innocence in *Wish You Were Here* to a fierce, angry cynicism in *Animals* and *The Wall*.

---

[*] Though I can understand that it did not translate well to a stadium setting. But then many great songs don't, from 'I Feel Love' to 'Smells Like Teen Spirit'. **DOGS** is primarily a brilliant headphones song, like so much by the Floyd, but it would be great to hear in a packed theatre.

[†] 'Money interested me enormously ... I remember coveting a Bentley like crazy. The only way to get something like that was through rock or the football pools. I very much wanted all that material stuff. There's still something wonderful about being able to ring up with a credit card number and being able to buy a plane ticket to anywhere.' (Matthew Gwyther, 'The Dark Side Of Success', *The Observer*, 7 March 1993).

The lyrics to **PIGS (THREE DIFFERENT ONES)** are slightly convoluted, because the first verse (about a '*Big man, pig man*') seems to be about the same kind of plutocratic character as in **DOGS** – '*You well-heeled big wheel*', '*With your head down in the pig bin / Saying "keep on digging"*'. Which is a bit confusing – is he a pig and a dog? The second and third verses are, however, much clearer, being ferocious attacks on Margaret Thatcher and Mary Whitehouse,‡ the leader of the UK Conservative Party (then just Leader of the Opposition),§ and a campaigner seeking to impose what she saw as Christian standards on broadcasting, respectively.¶ Thatcher was then seen as provincial and bourgeois: when competing for the leadership in 1975, 'she was judged to be too narrowly suburban, middle-class and southern in image and appeal'** according to one of her biographers. (She had been nicknamed 'Milk-Snatcher Thatcher' in 1971 for cutting free milk in schools for children aged 7 to 11.) Water's portrait is ferociously venomous, describing her as a '*bus stop rat bag*' and a '*fucked-up old hag*', and saying '*You're hot stuff with a hat pin*' (by this time an archaic bourgeois accessory). Whitehouse, on the other hand, he names directly, labelling her '*a house-proud town mouse*' with '*tight lips and cold feet*' (a brilliant image), then accuses her of '*trying to keep our feelings off the street*'.†† It's sheer invective: there's not much of an argument here beyond labelling as them as Bad People. But, despite more than a sliver of sexism, the verve of the writing and the popularity of the targets lets Waters get away with it.

The best example of Pink Floyd getting the most out of the least melodic material, **PIGS (THREE DIFFERENT ONES)** is also the first song where the lyrics are more important than the music (perhaps excluding **GRANTCHESTER MEADOWS**). Musically it opens with some pig grunts (from the talk box then slowed down), then a circular motif by Wright on the Hammond organ before Gilmour enters on the fretless bass. The organ playing is ominous and slightly eerie. Then Gilmour cuts through with some razor-sharp guitar shards (with Wright adding some string synthesiser), then Mason kicks in, and then the tune is finally off and running – after more than a minute of introductory atmosphere setting. (For comparison, **ONE OF THESE DAYS** takes about thirty seconds to introduce the pulsating bass riff, **TIME** plays with the rototoms until about 2.27 and **SHEEP** has the understated electric piano solo by Wright until about 1.30. The Floyd sure liked to pace themselves.)

This time, however, Waters' voice is front and centre, as the electric guitar is used more rhythmically than as a riff. This means that there's a lot of space in the middle of the mix, with the drums and bass (naturally) taking the lower frequencies and Waters' keening double-tracked voice the higher ones. Which

---

‡ Confirmed by Waters in numerous interviews, such as with *Rolling Stone* on 30 September 2019.
§ She became Prime Minister in 1979. Waters would have more to say about her later in *The Final Cut* (1983) following the Falklands War.
¶ In 1977 she successfully sued *Gay Times* for blasphemy, over its publication of a poem concerning the sexual fantasies of a Roman centurion about the body of Jesus Christ.
** John Campbell, *Margaret Thatcher: The Grocer's Daughter*, p.287.
†† All feelings being *natural* and therefore right, I guess. The 1960s and 1970s were a different time …

means there's the feeling of a lot of space in the sound, an emptiness that Waters' voice thus fills. This is especially true during the '*Ha-ha, charade you are!*' refrain, which fills the spectrum as he adds harmony vocals on the low end. But from this minimalistic setup, the group maintain attention by varying things throughout: halfway through the verse, the guitars audibly increase tension, Mason *thonks* away on a cowbell, and Waters' vocal goes right up next to the mike in a nasal, acidulous, disdainful style. It's fantastically expressive, and brutally articulate.

Similarly, the instrumental break after the second verse (from 4.13) builds and builds a ferocious tension by endless repetition of the same melodic figure. But there's constant variety: the guitars keep ratcheting up the tension every few bars, Gilmour on the talk box starts to add piglike squawks (at 5.14), Wright adds the string synthesiser from 5.43, while the guitars gradually become more dominant in the sound mix. The whole thing feels as tense and dangerous as a lightning storm, with ozone crackling from the electricity. The intensity, power and control are breathtaking. It builds to a peak at about 7.07 and then just dissipates, fading away before Wright's circular organ motif comes back in before we get the third verse, and then an electrifying fadeout with a stellar Gilmour guitar solo.

Though **PIGS (THREE DIFFERENT ONES)** is over eleven minutes long, it never outstays its welcome (unlike **ATOM HEART MOTHER** or **ALAN'S PSYCHEDELIC BREAKFAST** – whatever their charms). It shows how well the group had learned to fill out their sound, and to vary each section enough to keep maintain attention.* The lyrics too are something of a breakthrough: for the first time, they are a vituperative attack,† and they also contain several astonishing images. '*You radiate cold shafts of broken glass*' is probably the single best line in Waters' entire career. **PIGS (THREE DIFFERENT ONES)** shows Pink Floyd in their most bitter and most acerbic mood. It may be uneasy listening, but boy, is it gripping.

SHEEP (Waters)
Length: 10.25
Vocals: Waters **Vocoder**: Waters **Guitars**: Gilmour, Waters **Bass**: Gilmour **Electric piano**: Wright **ARP string synthesiser**: Wright **Hammond organ**: Wright **Minimoog**: Wright
Drums: Mason
Recorded: April-May 1976, Britannia Row, London
Producer: Pink Floyd
First released: 23 January 1977 (*Animals* track 4)
Rating: 9/10

---

* These nuances however would be lost on stadium audiences.
† **DOGS** is more generalised – almost a sociological examination at times – and **CORPORAL CLEGG** is satirical and too clever.

With its propulsive rhythm, ferocious guitar attack, and elementary structure,[‡] **SHEEP** is the most digestible of all the dark, brooding ten-minute slabs on *Animals*. Little wonder then that it was the curtain-jerker, the opening track during the subsequent *In the Flesh* tour of 1977. Yet **SHEEP** also has some of the most sophisticated studio trickery and its lyrics tie the whole concept of the album together in one of the most artistically satisfying, if utterly bleak, cycles the group ever created.

The most obvious studio enhancement is the way that Waters' long vocal note at the end of each line in the verse cross-fades into a synthesiser tone.[§] Waters might not be, as has been often said, the most gifted vocalist, but he certainly gives his all for whatever the song requires, and the sustained notes ('*Harmlessly passing your time in the grassland awaaaaaaaay / Only dimly aware of a certain unease in the aaaaaaair*') merge beautifully with the synthesisers, transforming the human into the mechanical and setting up the guitar and drum smash that punctuate the end of the lines. It's wildly exciting, the Floyd at their most collectively aggressive.[¶] A more subtle studio effect is the reversed drum sounds when Mason enters, so that they are preceded by a slurred echo rather than being followed by a decaying resonance.[**] The point is that it sounds like the rhythm is being dragged into the delirium of the track as the titular sheep run mad and panicking under attack from the dogs. Then there's the '*stone ... stone ...*' motif from **DOGS** (best heard at about 4.08): a reminder of the weight that some still need to throw around. Even sheep. A final significant effect is the Vocoder used for the 'Psalm 23' section in the middle of the track, where Waters just barely audibly recites a version laced with black humour:

> *The Lord is my shepherd, I shall not want*
> *He makes me down to lie, through pastures green*
> *He leadeth me the silent waters by*
> *With bright knives He releaseth my soul*
> *He made me to hang on hooks in high places*
> *He converteth me to lamb cutlets*
> *For lo, He hath great power, and great hunger*
> *When cometh the day we lowly ones*
> *Through quiet reflection, and great dedication*

[‡] ABA – there and back again; just like **INTERSTELLAR OVERDRIVE** and **ECHOES** and **CAREFUL WITH THAT AXE, EUGENE** and *The Wall*. Cycles, innit.

[§] Gilmour: 'Roger was singing a note, and he sort of dragged the note out long, and it just suddenly struck me that we could cross-fade it with a synthesiser note--you know, as his note comes down you just bring up the synthesiser, and you cross-fade them together, and turn the vibrato up on the synthesiser. Just to make a strange effect, and it worked.' 'Shades of Pink – The Definitive Pink Floyd Profile' *From the Source, with host Charlie Kendall* (1984).

[¶] **THE NILE SONG** and **NOT NOW JOHN** are more spotlights for Gilmour.

[**] Mason memorably described it as 'The drums are put on normally, then the tape reversed, and echo put on, so that you just -- as I say, you get that slur, instead of a decay. With something going "CCCHHHHEEEeeeessssshhhhh ...," that's reversed, so you get the thing building up to the actual sound, so it goes "sssshhhhheeeeeEEEEEHHHHHC!".' 'Shades of Pink – The Definitive Pink Floyd Profile' *From the Source, with host Charlie Kendall* (1984).

> Master the art of karate
> Lo, we shall rise up
> And then we'll make the bugger's eyes water

Animals was the first Pink Floyd album to contain lyrics in the LP (as handwritten by Mason), so this section could be read, but making it barely perceptible in the track itself seems an odd choice. Especially because phrases like '*He converteth me to lamb cutlets*' and the sheep '*master[ing] the art of karate*' are brilliantly sardonic.

Musically, **SHEEP** is tremendously exciting. The subtle electric piano solo from Wright (and complementary ovine *baaaing*) builds the tension superbly, the slurred drum sounds (at 1.30) when the rhythm gets under way suggest being sucked into a world of madness, the crunchy guitars from Waters and Gilmour are ferocious, with lots of excellent commentary at the end of the vocal lines, the *bum-de-bum* bassline (played by Gilmour) is straight out of *Doctor Who*[*] and fantastically kinetic, and the concluding guitar solo by Gilmour (from 8.06) injects even greater visceral energy when most bands would be ready to call it a night. **SHEEP** is hence a tour-de-force Pink Floyd performance, in which Waters' sinister vision might dominate but where all four members contribute greatly – especially Gilmour, whose concluding solo (which sounds like a precursor for **RUN LIKE HELL**) and dominating bassline figure are exceptional.

Lyrically, **SHEEP** is another outstanding effort from Waters, the third song in a row to display his gifts for metaphor and his deeply cynical but philosophically coherent world view. Originally titled 'Raving and Drooling' and played during the 1974 summer and winter tours, **SHEEP** was wisely held back during the recording of *Wish You Were Here* (where its aggression would be quite out of place) and its lyrics rewritten. Musically it remains pretty similar, with a galloping rhythm and lengthy vocal notes at the end of each line, although the electric piano introduction, Vocoder middle section and ending guitar solo were later additions. The redrafting process turned **SHEEP** from an ironic attack on the passively subjugated ('*How does it feel to be empty and angry and spaced? / Split up the middle between the illusion of safety in numbers / And the fist in your face*') to a more comprehensive view of the revolutionary process. The sheep, once '*Harmlessly passing your time in the grassland away*', are led by ruthless leaders '*Down well-trodden corridors into the valley of steel*'. But in the Psalm 23 section, the sheep '*Master the art of karate … / And then we'll make the bugger's eyes water*'. Duly empowered, in the final sections the sheep form '*Wave upon wave of demented avengers*' and '*March cheerfully out of obscurity into the dream*' – they have had their revolution and overthrown the dogs. But Waters ends his

---

[*] The show's theme music (debuting in 1963) was one of the first pieces of electronic music in the public consciousness and was highly influential. See **ONE OF THESE DAYS**. Nearly a quarter-century later, in 1987, The Timelords (later known as The KLF) would mash up the *Doctor Who* theme with a Gary Glitter song and achieve a UK #1 single.

fable on a wickedly cautionary note, a grim political cycle: '*Have you heard the news? / The dogs are dead! / You better stay home and do as you're told / Get out of the road if you want to grow old*'. So yesterday's oppressed become tomorrow's tyrants, demanding you keep your head down and '*do as you're told*' if you want to survive their dictates. Meet the new boss, same as the old boss.

Yet while the final guitar solo immediately afterwards (from 8.06) is powerful and scintillating, it doesn't quite capture Waters' point about the grim cycle of oppression and retribution; its brightness and vigour make it seem upbeat, which perhaps gives **SHEEP** a slightly misleading ending. Something more bitter and more despairing, perhaps akin to the final solo in **COMFORTABLY NUMB**, is what was really needed, as **SHEEP** lacks the feeling of a cycle. But this is probably just nitpicking. **SHEEP** is an incredibly potent song, from a writer whose vision, range and depth were now running over, and from a band whose performances and studiocraft were never stronger. **SHEEP** might be ten minutes in hell, but it is enormously invigorating, and demonstrates that Pink Floyd's creativity and vitality were only increasing, ten albums into their recording career.

PIGS ON THE WING (PART 2) (Waters)
Length: 1.23
Vocals: Waters **Acoustic guitars**: Waters
Recorded: April–May 1976, Britannia Row, London
Producer: Pink Floyd
First released: 23 January 1977 (*Animals* track 5)
Rating: 7/10

Fading in from the dying embers of **SHEEP**, **PIGS ON THE WING (PART 2)** completes the heartfelt tune of **PIGS ON THE WING (PART 1)**. Its singer-songwriter feeling of unvarnished honesty from the acoustic guitar and Waters' close-miked nasal voice make the preceding three slabs of mordant satire feel almost a dream, putting them in parenthesis. As Keats wrote, 'Fled is that vision / Do I wake or sleep?'[†] There needs to be a glimmer of hope after the human muck and despair, a denouement to pacify our fears. And it's yet another fine example of the group's expert use of dynamics.

However, the structuring of *Animals*, with the two minutes of the combined **PIGS ON THE WING** tracks bumping up Waters' royalties in disproportion to the musical effort, seems to have caused animosity within the group, or at least from Gilmour. It's fairly absurd that he wrote almost the entirety of the music on side one yet receives only half a writing credit on the whole album. Yet Waters was right to add the two **PIGS ON THE WING** tracks as bookends, justly noting that without them, *Animals* 'would have just been a kind of scream

---

† *Ode To A Nightingale*, 1819.

of rage'.* Their very brevity is effective, making them gentle kisses compared to the seething slabs they counterpoint.

Animals was both strongly promoted and led to the group's first stadium tour† across North America and Europe in 1977, during which all of its tracks were played. Yet, oddly, none of it has ever been played live by Pink Floyd since.‡ Nor were its sales outstanding, only reaching half of those for *Wish You Were Here*: there's a feeling that Pink Floyd were torn between not wanting to play the chart game (by not touring much in 1974 and 1975, and not at all in 1976), yet still wanting to remain successful, if possible, on their own terms.§ Still, *Animals* is often cited as a fan favourite: Gilmour has never sounded better, with his performance on guitar in **DOGS** perhaps the best of his entire career, and Waters' lyrics are ferociously acidic yet enjoyably poetic. (The line '*You radiate cold shafts of broken glass*' is truly one for the ages.) Wright, however, is much less evident, though he does have a solo at the start of **SHEEP**, albeit on an understated electric piano. Shorn of the lush textures of *Dark Side* or *Wish You Were Here*, Pink Floyd here are forbidding, stripped-down and muscular. *Animals* is to all intents and purposes their punk album; it has, with all deference to the Sex Pistols, a huge amount of bollocks. But it is largely undigestible by radio or compilation albums,¶ and so it remains the lost great album of the Pink Floyd canon.**

IN THE FLESH? (Waters)
Length: 3.16
Vocals: Waters **Guitars**: Gilmour **Bass**: Waters **Synthesisers**: Wright **VCS 3**: Waters
Drums: Mason **Backing vocals**: Bruce Johnston, Toni Tennile, Joe Chemay, Stan Farber, Jim Haas, John Joyce, Fred Mandell
Recorded: January–November 1979, Britannia Row, London; Super Bear Studios, Studio Miraval, France; CBS Studios, Cherokee Studios, Producers Workshop and The Village Recorder, USA
Producer: Waters, Gilmour, Bob Ezrin, Jamie Guthrie
First released: 30 November 1979 (*The Wall* disc 1 track 1)
Rating: 8/10

---

* Interview, Capital Radio, 21 January 1977.
† The tour was, of course, called 'In the Flesh'.
‡ *The Wall* tour played only the songs from that album, while **SHEEP** was considered for the *Momentary Lapse* tour but was rejected by Gilmour as its high notes were too hard for him to sing.
§ As Wright noted: 'Everyone never understood, really [...] how we reacted to the business side of it. For example, refusing to do interviews, or being told 'well, if you do an extra week in America you're going to earn this amount of money' and this and this and we'd say 'No, we don't want to do it.' We always went in a way against the accepted business way of doing things, right from the beginning in some ways.' 'Shades of Pink – The Definitive Pink Floyd Profile' *From the Source, with host Charlie Kendall* (1984).
¶ No tracks feature on the latest Pink Floyd best-of, *A Foot In The Door* (2011), though a slightly shortened version of **SHEEP** (9.46 rather than 10.21) features on the double-CD compilation, *Echoes: The Best Of Pink Floyd* (2001).
** Notably, it has the lowest total sales of the groups *Dark Side-Wish You Were Here-Animals-The Wall* hot streak. (In 2017 they were analysed as being: *Animals*, 12.15m, *Wish You Were Here*, 22.3m, *The Wall*, 31.3m, and *Dark Side*, 43.3m. See chartmasters.org/2017/06/cspc-pink-floyd-popularity-analysis/19/).

Following the end of the *In the Flesh* tour on 6 July 1977, Gilmour and Wright busied themselves with solo albums, called *David Gilmour and Wet Dream*, and released in May and September 1978, respectively. With neither Gilmour nor Wright then having much of a public profile, neither album did particularly well, though both are amiably listenable without ever suggesting the magic of the group's combined efforts. Waters, meanwhile, busied himself on composing the demos (or as he called them, drafts) for two conceptual albums. Waters presented both at a meeting and said he would record one as a solo album and one as a Pink Floyd album. One was about the trials of marriage, adulthood and monogamy, while the other was initially called 'Bricks in the Wall' and was about isolation, alienation and madness. The band chose the latter option,†† and so began the most tumultuous period of its existence.

Although the group had made huge amounts of money from their last three albums and the *In the Flesh* tour of 1977,‡‡ with the UK then having a top income tax rate of 83 per cent and 98 per cent on investment income, the group were beguiled by financial advisors Norton Warburg, who invested their money into deeply insecure venture capital enterprises, from fudge manufacturing to children's shoes, a handheld games console, a car hire business and a skateboard manufacturer. However, it turned out that Norton Warburg was a classic Ponzi scheme, with the sums taken in being used for its pay-outs. With each member of the band having created their own investment scheme and invested pre-tax funds, the ramifications were enormous: a potential tax bill of anywhere between £5 million and £12 million.§§ They were effectively bankrupt, after twelve years of hard work and six years of enormous success. As Mason noted, 'The whole experience cast an enormous cloud over us. We had always prided ourselves on being smart enough not to be caught out like this. We saw ourselves as educated, middle class, in control of everything. We had been utterly wrong.' Norton went bust in 1981, and founder Andrew Warburg fled to Spain but was eventually extradited and sentenced to three years at Her Majesty's pleasure in 1987.

This meant the group uprooting to France for a year to avoid the UK's exorbitant tax rates on top earners.¶¶ There was hence a great deal of pressure on

---

†† Though Wright for one disliked it, saying 'Every song was written in the same tempo, same key, same everything.' (*Mojo* magazine, December 1999). Listening to Waters' demo now, Wright has a point, but the conceptual brilliance glued everything together. And Wright could have offered greater musical craft – but he didn't.

‡‡ They were reported to have grossed, for example, $670,000 for one night in Chicago. They were paid $200,000 and 70% of gross receipts over $480,000. The promoter alleged an audience of 65,000, with tickets costing about $10. Hence, they would have made $319,000. The band however claimed that 85,000 people were in attendance that night, and successfully sued the promoter, Celebration/Flip Side productions.

§§ That's £26m-£62m in 2022 money. Big sums. As Gilmour noted, when you get rich, you go from owing people a tenner to owing the tax man millions. 'Ever since then there's not a penny that I haven't signed for. I sign every cheque and examine everything.' (*Observer*, 7 March 1993).

¶¶ In early 1979, the top rate of income tax was 83%, on incomes above £24,000. On 12 June, Chancellor of the Exchequer Geoffrey Howe cut it to 60% (on incomes above £25,000) in his first Budget when Margaret Thatcher became prime minister. Waters' opinions on the tax cut are unknown.

the next album to be successful,* and while they liked France and Mason says they enjoyed 'the opportunity to make a new start on our music without the distractions of lawyers and accountants', the abrupt dislocation doubtless added to their discomfiture and thus to intra-group tensions. But with Gilmour and Wright having recorded solo albums, their wells were now largely empty. And while Waters' demos had to be rewritten and fleshed out instrumentally and in their arrangements, the group had never given any credits for that. The writing was the thing. With the next album being the literal difference between penury and wealth, relations between the band thus began to fracture. It's hard to remain a band of brothers when you think someone might leave you facing a million-pound tax bill.

With Wright and Gilmour both having previously used the Super Bear† studio in Berre-les-Alpes in the south-west of France, about 16 miles from Nice (and two hours up the coast from Saint Tropez), the band relocated there to record in January 1979. The album had been promised by November, which meant a substantial amount of work to complete all the songs on time. The studio thus became more like an assembly line, with sundry outside musicians involved. This substantially changed the holistic soundworld Pink Floyd had so strenuously created over the past nine years, from *A Saucerful of Secrets* to *Animals* – that insular, English universe of anxiety and concern and striving for empathy. *The Wall* would instead be a factory line articulating Waters' deepest fears, and it thus became an ever-more alienating process – particularly for Wright, but also for Waters. (Gilmour and Mason were adept at production and session work, and so seem to have found it all far less traumatic.)

This all no doubt further darkened Waters' already bilious outlook, which by some alchemy matched the spirit of the times in the UK. The year 1979 started with the Winter of Discontent, where mass strike action by trade unions made the country seem ungovernable; unemployment had breached the one million barrier in August 1975 and stayed there; and the new phenomenon of stagflation – rising inflation and contracting economic activity – was puzzling a generation of politicians raised on the certainties of Keynesian economics, where government counter-cyclical spending could solve recessions. Plainly the post-war settlement was falling apart, the UK often being referred to as 'the sick man of Europe'. *The Wall* somehow captures this sense of malady and collapse, of British institutions and culture being under attack, whether education, family, the armed forces, the law, or race-relations and the resurgence of fascism.

The opening track to *The Wall* thus displays a hitherto-unheard aggression, far greater than anything heard on **THE NILE SONG** or even on *Animals*. This is Pink Floyd at its most visceral – creating a fascinating duality with *The Wall*

---

* Also, their last two albums had sold half as much as their predecessor – while *Dark Side* went on to sell 43 million copies, *Wish You Were Here* did 22 million and *Animals* 12 million. Huge amounts still, but perhaps a rather disconcerting trend.

† The studio's name is a pun on the village in which it is located. *Jazz* by Queen, *21 at 33* by Elton John and *Tug of War* by Paul McCartney were also recorded there. It burned down in 1986.

being the group also at its most operatic and conceptual.‡ Opening with the end of final track **OUTSIDE THE WALL** barely audible for seventeen seconds, in yet another of Waters' examples of cycles, **IN THE FLESH?** then shocks with an abrupt pounding on guitars, bass and drums, some viciously aggressive Gilmour riffing, and some excellent jarring stop-and-start rhythms. (The dynamics are yet again masterful.) As the main riff kicks in, Mason sounds extraordinarily animated in his drum fills while the organ plays some high notes above it all, and it's all viciously exciting, in the manner of the best hard rock. The band's previous efforts at really rocking out had been mannered or ironic:§ this is brutally effective, demonstrating their mastery of yet another genre. At 1.32 the sound fades to backing vocals and arpeggios for the single verse, after which the music thunders back in, adding sound effects (very nicely timed for when Waters yells '*Roll the sound effects!*') such as a low-flying Stuka dive bomber, the organs whirring to a crescendo, guitars being thrashed, and then the plane sounding like it is diving in to bomb the listener – and then, when everything drops out, there's the plaintive crying of a child (which, of course, carries across to **THE THIN ICE**). What an opening track.

As a recording, **IN THE FLESH?** hits like a punch to the face with remarkable presence and bottom. New engineer James Guthrie had devised a method to reduce wear and tear from overdubbing, whereby, as Mason writes:

> The drums and bass were initially recorded on an analogue 16-track machine, and mixed down to two tracks on a 24-track machine for the overdubs, retaining the original recording for the final mix. This avoided the inevitable degradation that occurs with the tapes being constantly played for the addition of the other instruments and vocals.¶

This accounts for the tremendous push the band achieve throughout *The Wall*, in songs like this, **THE HAPPIEST DAYS OF OUR LIVES** and **ONE OF MY TURNS**. Also, Gilmour is finally unveiled as a rock guitar hero: the riff is bone-crushing, his soloing is vicious and it all sounds a million miles from the ethereal ambience of **ECHOES** or the dreamy fluidity of *Dark Side*. If **ONE OF THESE DAYS** eight years earlier had inaugurated a new, sharpened, more focused Floyd, **IN THE FLESH?** sees the group at its most brutal.

Yet it's also lyrically extremely deft, with beautiful images like '*the warm thrill of confusion / That space-cadet glow*' and '*If you want to find out what's behind these cold eyes / You'll just have to claw your way through this disguise*'. The performer–audience relationship had never been described with such literate loathing

---

‡ And hence saving it from being another *Tales From Topographical Oceans* or *The Lamb Lies Down On Broadway*.
§ See **THE NILE SONG** and **COME IN NUMBER 51 YOUR TIME IS UP**.
¶ Mason, *Inside Out*, chapter 9.

before.* Implicit is the audience's masochism, a theme that was developed in the storyboarding for *Pink Floyd: The Wall*, where the heads of the adoring fans would explode during the sequence for this song, but this was dropped as too extreme (perhaps wisely). **IN THE FLESH?**, however, inaugurates the final iteration of the classic lineup of Pink Floyd, without the colours and textures hitherto provided by Wright, but with tremendous musical power, lyrical ferocity and conceptual boldness.

THE THIN ICE (Waters)
Length: 2.27
Vocals: Gilmour, Waters **Guitars**: Gilmour **Bass**: Waters **Piano**: Wright **Organ**: Wright
Drums: Mason
Recorded: January–November 1979 , Britannia Row, London; Super Bear Studios, Studio Miraval, France; CBS Studios, Cherokee Studios, Producers Workshop and The Village Recorder, USA
Producer: Waters, Gilmour, Ezrin, Guthrie
First released: 30 November 1979 (*The Wall* disc 1 track 2)
Rating: 8/10

Picking up where **IN THE FLESH?** ended, with the child still crying, we get Gilmour's first vocal of the album (in an album where he has ten vocal credits out of twenty-six tracks yet still feels oddly absent). Ever the professional, Gilmour sings the first verse and refrain beautifully, in his own patented keening style. The main instrument in the first half of the song is the piano, played by Wright in a cold and disconsolate style, while Waters plays some slightly familiar bass ornamentation around the melody.

When Waters enters as a vocalist, however, his tone is terrifying, a viciously bitter† nasal howl like a maddening itch you just can't scratch. It's entirely distinctive and hugely expressive, just as Bob Dylan and Axl Rose and Neil Young are, in their own very separate ways. The piano now playing staccato chords, Waters' brief verse contains further magnificent images ('*The silent reproach / Of a million tear-stained eyes*' and the hugely ominous, '*You'll slip out of your depth and out of your mind*') – already, by the end of the second short track he has outdone the entirety of *Wish You Were Here*, and absolutely everything preceding *Dark Side*. It is the astounding fruition of Waters' literary talent.

After his almost audibly clenched teeth in the final line ('*As you claw the thin ice*'), the drums roll at 1.43 and Gilmour suddenly re-enters with shockingly bold guitar riffs and solos. We are very far away indeed from his fey hippyishness on

---

* John Lydon made clear his contempt for the audience when in the Sex Pistols, but didn't write a song about it while a Pistol (though his later Public Image track 'Fodderstompf' did enact it). W.H. Auden's poem 'On the Circuit' (1965) has some similarities: 'Another morning comes: I see, / Dwindling below me on the plane, / The roofs of one more audience / I shall not see again.'

† *The Wall* is really an album of various kinds of bitterness – from fiercely bitter (**THE THIN ICE**) to angrily bitter (**ANOTHER BRICK IN THE WALL III**) to depressedly bitter (**DON'T LEAVE ME NOW**) to forlornly bitter (**NOBODY HOME**) to violently bitter (**ONE OF MY TUNES**).

GREEN IS THE COLOUR – this is so up-front and in-your-face it's hard to believe this is the same band. Wisely, the group don't overextend themselves, repeating the power-chords-then-solo structure three times then fading out after Gilmour's soloing reaches a peak. Considering the song lasting just over two minutes, **THE THIN ICE** has three distinctive sections, all of which are utterly memorable and successful.‡ Using shorter songs to fit the narrative meant that the group's mastery of dynamics and atmosphere are even more obvious than on their longer tracks like **ECHOES** or **DOGS** – now they have to constantly shift volume, tempo, feeling and style across an entire double album. One of the many remarkable (but unremarked) things about *The Wall* is that they very nearly succeed in doing so over more than eighty minutes of music.§

ANOTHER BRICK IN THE WALL PART 1 (Waters)
Length: 3.21
Vocals: Waters **Guitars**: Gilmour **Bass**: Waters **Piano**: Wright **Minimoog**: Wright
Prophet-5: Wright **Backing vocals**: Gilmour
Recorded: January–November 1979, Britannia Row, London; Super Bear Studios, Studio Miraval, France; CBS Studios, Cherokee Studios, Producers Workshop and The Village Recorder, USA
Producer: Waters, Gilmour, Ezrin, Guthrie
First released: 30 November 1979 (*The Wall* disc 1 track 3)
Rating: 8/10

The third track on *The Wall* is the third exceptional musical partnership between Gilmour and Waters in a row, with Waters' lyrics and artistic conception again beautifully matched by Gilmour's guitar playing. (For a working relationship that was apparently under great strain, the two complement each other increasingly well from *Wish You Were Here* to *The Wall* – perhaps a reflection of the declining influence of Wright.) Gilmour's patient, probing guitar line is a signature creation, one since reprised in many concerts.¶ It builds the tension beautifully, especially after the shrieking guitar crescendo during **THE THIN ICE**. The subtle background playing by Wright on the synthesisers has a similar role in developing atmosphere and tension, though it's very far from the leading role heard just four years earlier in **WELCOME TO THE MACHINE**.

---

‡ Then again, if we're talking acyclical songs, 'Happiness Is A Warm Gun' by The Beatles is just seventeen seconds longer (2.44) and has five sections. 'Bohemian Rhapsody' has five too, but lasts nearly six minutes.

§ There are some longueurs, of course. **DON'T LEAVE ME NOW** is suitably contrasted by **ANOTHER BRICK IN THE WALL III**, but as a song is too samey. **VERA** works thematically but less well as a song, I feel. **EMPTY SPACES** would have been better to have included the 'What Should We Do Now' section later seen in *Pink Floyd: The Wall*. But overall, as a double album *The Wall* sustains the attention better than any other that I know. (I have for example long given up on two-thirds of the songs on Guns N' Roses *Use Your Illusion* albums, I rarely play disc 2 of *Physical Graffiti*, I'm usually yawning by side 4 of *Exile On Main Street*, and even The *White Album* has songs that make me cringe (especially 'Birthday'). Funnily enough, *London Calling* is also from 1979, and shares the ambition and pithiness of *The Wall*, if nothing else.

¶ Such as during *The Division Bell* tour, from which the group would move directly into **ANOTHER BRICK IN THE WALL PART 2**.

The vocal structure sees Waters singing alone in the verse and then harmonised by Gilmour with heavy echo in the refrain. The echo and dark shading create an ominous feeling, of greater powers in control.* Waters' lyric is the first to iterate two of the album's key themes: the loss of the father, and the '*All in all, it was just a brick in the wall*' leitmotif that will recur with variations throughout the album. Here Waters wisely keeps the paternal loss theme non-specific,† singing '*Daddy's flown across the ocean / Leaving just a memory / A snapshot in the family album / Daddy, what else did you leave for me?*' This vagueness allows the theme of loss and be left behind to be universal – everyone can think of a time when they've felt abandoned somehow, and it strikes a very real chord. Yet by the time of *Pink Floyd: The Wall*, Waters no longer bothered with such concerns, with **WHEN THE TIGERS BROKE FREE** making explicit the story of Pink's father being lost during the Second World War. Art is at its best when the listener/viewer/reader can fill in their own stories and emotions to the framework set up by the artist – a lesson well remembered here but later forgotten by Waters, in his later keenness to share his Very Important Ideas.‡

THE HAPPIEST DAYS OF OUR LIVES (Waters)
Length: 1.46
Vocals: Waters **Guitars**: Gilmour **Bass**: Waters **Organ**: Wright **Clavinet**: Wright
Percussion: Mason, James Guthrie **Backing vocals**: Gilmour
Recorded: January-November 1979, Britannia Row, London; Super Bear Studios, Studio Miraval, France; CBS Studios, Cherokee Studios, Producers Workshop and The Village Recorder, USA
Producer: Waters, Gilmour, Ezrin, Guthrie
First released: 30 November 1979 (*The Wall* disc 1 track 4)
Rating: 8/10

The sound effects which *The Wall* brilliantly utilises are used to excellent effect here, with the guitar and synthesiser from **ANOTHER BRICK IN THE WALL PART 1** fading out slowly, and then the buzzing of a helicopter coming in before Waters barks, '*You! Yes, you! Stand still, laddie!*' Authoritarianism, Waters seems to be saying, is all part of the same thing, from abusive teachers to military conflict: each of them has you in their sights. Then the bass guitar

---

* See **IS THERE ANYBODY OUT THERE?**

† As Waters told Radio 1 DJ Tommy Vance during a long interview about *The Wall* on 30 November 1979: '[I]t works on various levels–it doesn't have to be about the war–I mean it *should* work for any generation really. The father is also ... I'm the father as well. You know, people who leave their families to go and work, not that I would leave my family to go and work, but lots of people do and have done, so it's not meant to be a simple story about, you know, somebody's getting killed in the war or growing up and going to school, etc, etc, etc but about being left, more generally.'

‡ During his most recent *This Is Not A Drill* tour, videos of Donald Trump were projected during his rendition of **PIGS (THREE DIFFERENT ONES)**. A reasonable point politically, but I felt it was overly didactic. It reduces art, with all its rich possibilities, to a single political message. Waters felt that his message was the most important thing: 'I was always trying to push the band into more specific areas of subject matter, always trying to be more direct ... I wanted to work with visual material that meant something, where there isn't much left for you to interpret.' (*Rolling Stone*, 19 November 1987).

kicks in with that fantastic riff as the drums punctuate each space. As an intro, it's utterly enthralling, telling you that something BIG and IMPORTANT is coming this way.

The sardonic title perhaps recalls George Orwell, whose essay on his unhappy schooldays was called 'Such, Such Were the Joys' (1948). Unlike Orwell, however, Waters sticks to generalisations of the cruder kind. Though he does note that it is only '*certain teachers*' who '*would hurt the children any way they could*' in the first verse, in the second verse he yells that '*their fat and psychopathic wives / Would thrash them to within inches of their lives*'. He might be right in referring to the way that abuse leads to abuse (in another of the cycles that greatly interest him), but the characterisation is misogynistic and rather juvenile. (The point is made more clearly in the movie, where the teacher is forced to eat a bit of gristle by his unpleasant wife, and then is seen inflicting corporal punishment on a pupil. The point is made more grotesquely in Gerald Scarfe's animation, which has a naked corpulent wife holding the teacher like a puppet on a string, who is then beating the pupil. Subtle, it ain't.)

Beyond the lyrics, the vocal is perhaps the most notable aspect of **THE HAPPIEST DAYS OF OUR LIVES**, with Waters in the first verse singing with almost audibly clenched teeth. The feeling of contempt and disdain is wonderfully palpable. The second verse is sung with more power and urgency, meaning that the sexist sketch of the teacher's wife gets more prominence than perhaps it should. It is hard to consider **THE HAPPIEST DAYS OF OUR LIVES** as a single piece, because more than any other songs on *The Wall*, it is part of a suite, alongside **ANOTHER BRICK IN THE WALL PART 2**. Its creation of a distinct soundworld and its raising of tension are both excellently handled, though for once in *The Wall*, its lyrical insights are handled rather crudely. But as a song it's enormously exciting.

ANOTHER BRICK IN THE WALL PART 2 (Waters)
Length: 3.59
Vocals: Gilmour, Waters, Islington Green School children **Guitars**: Gilmour **Bass**: Waters
Hammond organ: Wright **Prophet-5**: Wright **Drums**: Mason
Recorded: January–November 1979, Britannia Row, London; Super Bear Studios, Studio Miraval, France; CBS Studios, Cherokee Studios, Producers Workshop and The Village Recorder, USA
Producer: Waters, Gilmour, Ezrin, Guthrie
First released: 30 November 1979 (*The Wall* disc 1 track 5)
Rating: 10/10

Pink Floyd do disco – and do it very well. Probably the best known Pink Floyd song around the world, **ANOTHER BRICK IN THE WALL PART 2** is ironically one of the least Floydian-sounding tracks,* with its jaunty rhythm, school choir and sinewy Gilmour solo. Everyone by now knows the story of how producer Bob Ezrin extended the song and added the verse sung by kids from Islington Green School. He said:

> When we played it with the disco drumbeat I said, 'Man, this is a hit! But it's one minute twenty. We need two verses and two choruses.' And they said, 'Well, you're not bloody getting them. We don't do singles, so fuck you.' So ... while they weren't around, we were able to copy the first verse and chorus, take one of the drum fills, put them in between and extend the chorus ... So while we were in America, we sent [engineer] Nick Griffiths to a school near the Floyd studios. I said, 'Give me 24 tracks of kids singing this thing. I want Cockney, I want posh, fill 'em up,' and I put them on the song. I called Roger into the room, and when the kids came in on the second verse there was a total softening of his face, and you just knew that he knew it was going to be an important record.†

Waters was effusive about Ezrin's role, saying 'It was great – exactly the thing I expected from a collaborator,'‡ sniffily implying that Gilmour, Wright and Mason no longer provided such creativity. Gilmour, however, recalls being more involved in the school recording, saying:

> I sent the tape to England and got an engineer to summon some kids. I gave him a whole set of instructions – ten-to-fifteen-year-olds from North London, mostly boys – and I said get them to sing this song in as many ways as you like. And he filled up all the tracks on a 24-track machine with stereo pairs of all the different combinations and ways of singing with all these kids. We got the tape back to L.A., played it, and it was terrific.§

Memory is a funny thing. And success has a thousand fathers.

All of this, of course, took the song a long way from its original form essayed in Waters' demo, though that from the beginning included a buzzing helicopter at the start of the track. That featured Waters in his speak-singing voice and just a sliver of a melody, though most of the lyric (with its clever double-negative '*don't need no*' construction) was there already. Recording an album is, of course, a team effort, and **ANOTHER BRICK IN THE WALL PART 2** is the most composite track on *The Wall*,¶ and remains a startling listen. The scream at the start, Gilmour's magnificent vocal delivery (from the opening dispassionate

---

* Bands like the Beastie Boys, Warren, Blur, Mr Big, and perhaps even Radiohead have suffered a similar indignity of their biggest hit being their least representative song. You don't know where lightning will strike.
† *Mojo* magazine, December 1999.
‡ *Mojo* magazine, December 1999.
§ David Gilmour interview, *Musician* magazine, December 1982.
¶ Lucky Roger, getting all the credit for it.

monotone to the belting, '*Hey! Teacher!*'), his superb strumming guitar, Waters' delicious bass comments (after '*thought control*' for example), the drum fill at 1.01, and then the schoolkids which simply leap out from the speakers – all of these add to Pink Floyd's most tightly focused and incident-rich track since **SEE EMILY PLAY**,** making it a worthy if incredibly unlikely pop single.

Simply considered as a song, **ANOTHER BRICK IN THE WALL PART 2** is a magnificent achievement: its catchy rhythm undercutting the darkness of the song's theme, the irony of its chorus belying the acidulous disdain of the lyric, Waters' quality as a wordsmith on display with the excellent phrase '*dark sarcasm*', and the simplicity of its structure giving it a tight focus. But as one of the key 'message' songs on *The Wall*, it has a force and power that far extends beyond its place as the fifth track on a double album, making it one of Pink Floyd's most renowned songs – played in every concert since (with the exception of the Live 8 gig), and the most streamed song from their entire discography on Spotify. It is also one of their greatest collective achievements and testament to the exceptional craftsmanship of the group and production team. All in all, it's simply one of their greatest moments.

In the film, the song is used for one of the most jaw-dropping scenes, where schoolkids march to the disco beat through Kafkaesque corridors or sit at desks on factory conveyor belts before subsequently plummeting into a sausage grinder – before destroying the school, burning it down and throwing the hated teacher onto the fire. It must have caused millions of adolescent daydreams.

MOTHER (Waters)
Length: 5.32
Vocals: Waters, Gilmour **Guitars**: Gilmour **Bass**: Waters **Keyboards**: Ezrin
Drums: Jeff Picardo **Backing vocals**: Wright
Recorded: January–November 1979, Britannia Row, London; Super Bear Studios, Studio Miraval, France; CBS Studios, Cherokee Studios, Producers Workshop and The Village Recorder, USA
Producer: Waters, Gilmour, Ezrin, Guthrie
First released: 30 November 1979 (*The Wall* disc 1 track 6)
Rating: 8/10

Few rocks songs have the psychological depth of this track, an examination of the neuroses of young men and the harmful effects of overprotective mothering upon them. Built around an acoustic riff, **MOTHER** is musically more complex than it first appears, with ventures into 9/8 and 5/4 during the middle eight and guitar solo respectively. (Mason's inability to handle these time measures necessitated the use of session drummer Jeff Picardo.)†† Its sparse beginning well

---

** It reached #1 across the world, from the US and the UK (where it was Christmas No. 1) to Israel and New Zealand.
†† Picardo had previously played with acts from Steely Dan to Diana Ross, as well as founding Toto.

conveys the simplicity of the child's fears, while the choruses strike deep at your heart, with Gilmour's wonderful keening voice and Waters' tremendous phrases ('*Mamma's gonna keep you right here, under her wing / She won't let you fly, but she might let you sing*' – just magnificent).

Artistically, **MOTHER** is another excursion into acoustic singer-songwriter territory for the band (in the manner of **IF** and **PIGS ON THE WING**), though unlike Bob Dylan's deliberate inscrutability or Bruce Springsteen's novelistic characters, this is a soul-baring of almost unbearable intensity. And yet it's not a cathartic splurge or formless rant: **MOTHER** is extremely artful, from its musical construction to its exceptional lyrics. It thus demonstrates the mastery, by this stage, of Waters' writing. The song is perhaps designed to be compared to the John Lennon song of the same name, the opening track to his first 'real' solo album, *John Lennon/Plastic Ono Band*.* While Lennon's track is painfully autobiographical and bursting with genuine, tormented feeling (to the extent that Lennon repeatedly screams),† **MOTHER** is a more theatrical, measured, and artistic composition. The staging of the conflict between the anxious young man and the fretful mother, as vocalised by Waters' doubt and Gilmour's protectiveness, is highly artful, enabling the listener to read their own fears and anxieties into the song in a way that, for all its gut-wrenching trauma, the Lennon track does not. We feel Lennon's visceral pain in his song; in Pink Floyd's **MOTHER** we recognise our own fears and traumas as human beings. This is a measure of great art.

For the *Pink Floyd: The Wall* soundtrack, **MOTHER** becomes even more haunting, with a soft tingling keyboard introduction (replacing the acoustic guitar) and the vocals in the opening verse further to the fore and with greater reverb, giving the impression of someone alone in a large empty room. (At this point in the film, during Gilmour's searing guitar solo, one can see Roger Waters' brief cameo, as a guest at the wedding of 'Pink'.) Waters' vocal is also considerably sadder, going from understated fear in the LP to a magnificent performance of searing anguish.

GOODBYE BLUE SKY (Waters)
Length: 2.45
Vocals: Gilmour **Guitars**: Gilmour **Bass**: Gilmour **VCS 3 synthesiser**: Waters
EMS synthesiser: Wright **Child's voice**: Harry Waters
Recorded: January–November 1979, Britannia Row, London; Super Bear Studios, Studio Miraval, France; CBS Studios, Cherokee Studios, Producers Workshop and The Village Recorder, USA
Producer: Waters, Gilmour, Ezrin, Guthrie
First released: 30 November 1979 (*The Wall* disc 1 track 7)
Rating: 9/10

---

* The comparison is not fanciful. Pink Floyd had previously referenced The Beatles in **LET THERE BE MORE LIGHT** and in **US AND THEM**.
† The album having been made while Lennon and Ono were undergoing 'primal scream' therapy.

A beautiful acoustic track, **GOODBYE BLUE SKY** is a deeply affecting lament for those affected by the Second World War. It has yet another brilliant Gilmour vocal (double-tracked in the verse, with a slightly longer delay than usual to give a greater choral effect, and tracked by the synthesiser in the outro), his pale voice contrasting nicely with the dark tone of the synthesiser featuring intermittently throughout. His high-pitched '*Oooohs*' are similarly affecting – it's remarkable how much effect Gilmour can have on an album without having written much on it, and testament to his exceptional craftsmanship.

Unlike many songs on *The Wall*, **GOODBYE BLUE SKY** changed very little as a composition between Waters' first demo and the final album. Waters was often proud of his acoustic picking, as heard on **IF** and **GRANTCHESTER MEADOWS**, but wisely yielded the guitar to Gilmour, who plays with both verve and delicacy. Lyrically it feels slightly apart from the rest of the album, being more generally about the war rather than about Pink, and being both empathetic ('*Did-did-did-did you ever wonder why we had to run for shelter when the promise of a brave new world unfurled beneath the clear blue sky?*') and visual ('*Did-did-did-did you see the frightened ones? Did-did-did-did you hear the falling bombs?*') rather than psychological or embittered. The song also gave rise to one of the most memorable images by Gerald Scarfe, an underground creature with a gasmask-like face, scuttling during the bombings of the Second World War.‡ Although Waters gets the writing credit, on the recorded track Gilmour's contribution is enormous, and deserves greater recognition – not that Waters would give that.

With only two verses and a short outro§ (ending on a short descending bass phrase, apparently also played by Gilmour), **GOODBYE BLUE SKY** doesn't outstay its welcome: its delicacy, brevity, and concern for others make it one of the most memorable tracks on *The Wall*, and a pleasing return to a gentle acoustic side of Pink Floyd that seemed to have withered through neglect – though ironically it could be deleted without affecting the album's narrative.

EMPTY SPACES (Waters)
Length: 2.10
Vocals: Waters **Guitars**: Gilmour **Bass**: Waters **Piano**: Wright **VCS 3**: Waters
String synthesiser: Gilmour, James Guthrie **Clavinet**: Gilmour
Recorded: January–November 1979, Britannia Row, London; Super Bear Studios, Studio Miraval, France; CBS Studios, Cherokee Studios, Producers Workshop and The Village Recorder, USA
Producer: Waters, Gilmour, Ezrin, Guthrie
First released: 30 November 1979 (*The Wall* disc 1 track 8)
Rating: 7/10

‡ During the *Pink Floyd: The Wall* talk-through with Waters, Scarfe says that the sequence for **GOODBYE BLUE SKY** is his favourite piece of animation he has done, having lived through that period and having to wear a gas mask.
§ Am I the only person who hears '... Ruby Tuesday' when Gilmour sings the 'Goodbye' before 'blue sky'? It's the same tune!

EMPTY SPACES is a stunning piece of atmospherics. It has a cold majesty, like an ancient abandoned imperial city.* Beginning with some resonating synthesised drum sounds (perhaps later pilfered for **THE DOGS OF WAR**) and an airport or sports stadium tannoy announcement straight out of **ON THE RUN**, Gilmour plays some fine echoey high notes as the synthesisers create a desolate post-apocalyptic soundscape with a sound of crashing thunder. Then suddenly at 0.49 the piano and keyboards come in as everything shifts up a gear (though continuing at the same beat), with Gilmour's guitar shrieking away. At 1.14 the back-masked reversed-vocal hidden message appears,† sounding malevolent and guttural, lasting until Waters' actual vocal starts at 1.29 (heralded by a descending phrase on the bass). Waters' singing is similarly cold and impassive, as he slowly enunciates each syllable: '*What shall ... we use ... to fill ... the final ... spaces? How should I ... complete ... the wall?*' It's a fine vocal performance, unlike anything else he had ever done, and summoning a feeling of pitiless inhumanity.‡

In the movie, of course, **EMPTY SPACES** is replaced by 'What Shall We Do Now?', which lengthens this track by having a longer initial Waters' vocal ('*Shall we set out across this sea of faces? In search of more and more applause?*' being one of the great sardonic takes on stardom) then switching to a more traditional high-tempo rock song, with Gilmour and Waters jointly questioning the ways people seek fulfilment: '*Shall we buy a new guitar? / Shall we drive a more powerful car? / Shall we work straight through the night? / Shall we get into fights? / Leave the lights on? / Drop bombs? / Do tours of the east? Contract diseases?*' The short, pithy lines create a sort of anti-litany,§ a list of excess and a feeling of concomitant revulsion. 'What Shall We Do Now?' however had to be cut from the album for reasons of space, though it rightly returned to the set list in the live performances (where it can be heard on *Is There Anybody Out There?*), and in the movie.

As an evocation of emotional desolation, **EMPTY SPACES** is superb; but *The Wall* has numerous such soundworlds (such as **IS THERE ANYBODY OUT THERE?**, **DON'T LEAVE ME NOW** and the beginning of **ONE OF MY TURNS**) and so they unfortunately do blend in somewhat. This is why the middle section of **ECHOES** is so stunning: nothing on *Meddle* prepared you for it. Pink's isolation might hence better have been dramatised around one central section, rather than evoked in numerous stages. But on the other hand, each track is a gripping enactment of alienation, and **EMPTY SPACES**, with its synthesised mechanical sound, conveys the busy emptiness of modern life¶ as well as anything ever recorded.

---

* It somehow reminds me of the city of Charn from *The Magician's Nephew* by C.S. Lewis.
† The message is one of the only light-hearted moments on the album, a piece of dialogue between Waters and Guthrie: 'Hello, looker. Congratulations. You have just discovered the secret message. Please send your answer to Old Pink, care of the Funny Farm, Chalfont.' 'Roger! Carolyne's on the phone!' 'Okay.'
‡ Although Waters fundamentally regards himself as part of the 'bleeding hearts and the artists', he does seem to enjoy playing the role of the Fascist Dictator during **IN THE FLESH** and **RUN LIKE HELL**.
§ Compare with **ECLIPSE**.
¶ The entire theme of Radiohead's *OK Computer* (1997), let it be noted.

> **YOUNG LUST** (Waters, Gilmour)
> **Length**: 3.25
> **Vocals**: Waters **Guitars**: Gilmour **Bass**: Gilmour **Organ**: Wright **Electric piano**: Wright
> **Drums**: Mason **Backing vocals**: Gilmour
> **Recorded**: January–November 1979, Britannia Row, London; Super Bear Studios, Studio Miraval, France; CBS Studios, Cherokee Studios, Producers Workshop and The Village Recorder, USA
> **Producer**: Waters, Gilmour, Ezrin, Guthrie
> **First released**: 30 November 1979 (*The Wall* disc 1 track 8)
> **Rating**: 7/10

The Floyd do cock-rock – but only to mock, not shock. This crunching number features the raunchiest Gilmour guitar and vocal since **IBIZA BAR**,** but where he provides a solid musical framework, Waters gives it greater meaning by producing a lyric satirising the mindset the music suggests. This poetic ability is another example of what makes him one of the great rock songwriters. Most bands would write words to match the music, but Waters is more interested in the human condition that would lead such a song to be written.

Musically, **YOUNG LUST** is not, however, especially interesting. It comes across rather as 'Sussex Rock' – the music of wealthy musicians now living in Home Counties estates. It does rock, but in a rather skilful, mannered sense – far from the youthful energy and primitivism of genuine rock 'n' roll. (The counter melody on bass, as played by Gilmour, is excellent, though again rather tasteful and clever, instead of dumb or aggressive.)†† But, as with much of *The Wall*, the real interest is in the lyrics, which concern '*a rock 'n' roll refugee*' who needs '*some woman in this desert land*' to '*make me feel like a real man*'. In a perfect miniature of just two verses of four lines each, and a two-line chorus, Waters conveys how Pink has thrown himself into hedonism with groupies and casual sex.

But as the song fades out, there's another excellent counterpoint: a wonderful vignette of a telephone operator trying to connect a collect call to 'Mrs Floyd' from the USA ('*Will you accept the charges?*'). The recipient puts the phone down twice, the operator the second time noting, '*See, he keeps hanging up! And it's a man answering.*' So now that Pink learns that his wife has been having an affair, the world of hedonistic casual sex seems a terrible thing,‡‡ and the self-disgust implicit in such behaviour now comes to the fore.

When **YOUNG LUST** was performed live, Waters and Gilmour sang the chorus at the same microphone (for the only time during the shows), conveying a kinship that had surely almost evaporated and a homosocial bond that reinforces the song's satirising of chauvinism. In the movie, the scene of groupies making

---

** Rather than since **THE NILE SONG**, as so often suggested. **IBIZA BAR** is more aggressive but less heard, since it's deeper into *More*.
†† Compare with John Cale's slab-like bass notes on The Velvet Underground's *White Light/White Heat* (1968), for a prime example of classically-trained primitivism.
‡‡ This might seem rather narcissistic, but sexual politics weren't very advanced in 1979.

their way into the aftershow party is one of its most sardonic moments, in a film replete with many grimly sardonic moments. The brief sight of Bob Hoskins as tour manager chomping on a pineapple and spitting out champagne deftly exemplifies the music industry's excess and vulgarity which no doubt pained four well-educated middle-class Englishmen.

> **ONE OF MY TURNS** (Waters)
> **Length**: 3.41
> **Vocals**: Waters **Guitars**: Gilmour, Lee Ritenour **Bass**: Waters **Piano**: Wright **Organ**: Bob Ezrin **Prophet-5**: Ezrin **Drums**: Mason **Percussion**: Mason **Groupie**: Trudy Young
> **Recorded**: January–November 1979, Britannia Row, London; Super Bear Studios, Studio Miraval, France; CBS Studios, Cherokee Studios, Producers Workshop and The Village Recorder, USA
> **Producer**: Waters, Gilmour, Ezrin, Guthrie
> **First released**: 30 November 1979 (*The Wall* disc 1 track 9)
> **Rating**: 8.5/10

Picking up a groupie, Pink terrorises her and destroys his hotel room in the process. This wasn't such a leap of the imagination for Waters. By the late 1970s, a legendarium of rock star excess had formed, with tales such as Keith Moon driving a Cadillac into a hotel swimming pool, John Bonham motorcycling through the lobby of the Continental Hyatt House Hotel in Hollywood, Queen throwing a party with dwarfs serving bowls of cocaine, everyone destroying hotel rooms and throwing TVs out of the window ... It became a dreadful cliché, a trite formula. Waters had also personally observed singer Roy Harper destroying his dressing room before the Knebworth Festival in 1975.[*] But destructiveness usually comes from self-loathing, and Waters had too much psychological insight not to be aware of that. Hence this song, which reveals the despair and neediness choked up behind such masculine aggression.

Opening with the famous groupie monologue ('*What a fabulous room! Are all these your guitars ...? Wanna take a baaath?*') spoken by the Canadian actor Trudy Young,[†] the song fades in with the Prophet-5 synthesiser played by Ezrin, while we also hear the numbing blanket of a TV muttering in the corner.[‡] The synthesiser's initial droning atonality captures the sense of a mind in a bleak, thoughtless fug, before resolving into a tune as Waters begins his vocal. In a soft, sad voice he sings of the desolate sadness when love turns sour and dies. The lyrics are some of the finest Waters ever composed, with some absolutely sterling similes ('*Like the skin on a dying man*', '*Cold as a razor blade, tight as a tourniquet, dry as a funeral drum*').

---

[*] Although I can't find a direct source for it, the story appears in numerous articles about him in connection with Pink Floyd. Is it one of those rock n' roll legends? There's no mention of it in Mason's book.
[†] Performed by Jerry Hall during *The Wall Live In Berlin*. One wonders what Waters thought of her later marriage to Rupert Murdoch.
[‡] It's playing the long-running US soap opera *Another World* (1964-1999).

But then (at 2.02), the song detonates into a thumping rock track, as Pink explodes from his stupor into a destructive fit. The change is incredible – no edging up towards a peak, as with **CAREFUL WITH THAT AXE, EUGENE**; this is a sudden, shocking violence. You can literally hear him destroying the hotel room, with the sounds of tearing sheets (2.28), glass shattering (2.34–2.38), and the sound of cars zooming past on the 'freeway' (from 2.40 to the end). Meanwhile, Gilmour and session man Lee Ritenour[§] play with vicious concision, with a short solo from Gilmour just before the devastating outro – '*Would you like to call the cops?! / Do you think it's time I stopped?! / Why are you running awaaaaay …?*'

ONE OF MY TURNS was, rather remarkably, chosen as the B-side to **ANOTHER BRICK IN THE WALL PART 2**. Songs with such violence and bleak analysis rarely get into the charts. Its three parts lead smartly from one to the next, the production is stellar (the use of the synthesiser is especially good) and the outro is as bleakly moving (and well sung) as anything Waters ever did. And as an examination of the roots of male violence, **ONE OF MY TURNS** is so far ahead of its time, it is almost embarrassing. It's yet another remarkable track in an album stuffed full of them.

DON'T LEAVE ME NOW (Waters)
Length: 4.08
Vocals: Waters **Guitars**: Waters, Gilmour **Bass**: Gilmour **Organ**: Wright **Piano**: Wright **Synthesiser**: Wright **Bass pedals**: Wright **Drums**: Mason **Backing vocals**: Gilmour
Recorded: January–November 1979, Britannia Row, London; Super Bear Studios, Studio Miraval, France; CBS Studios, Cherokee Studios, Producers Workshop and The Village Recorder, USA
Producer: Waters, Gilmour, Ezrin, Guthrie
First released: 30 November 1979 (*The Wall* disc 1 track 10)
Rating: 6/10

DON'T LEAVE ME NOW is probably the most desolate song on the entirety of *The Wall*, which is saying something. But it comes immediately after **ONE OF MY TURNS**, and rather replicates it, with a similar bleak opening and a concluding turn to more traditional rock music. But where **ONE OF MY TURNS** was musically surprising and a superb dramatisation of male anguish and violence, **DON'T LEAVE ME NOW** feels more static, a wailing complaint rather than fully worked-out song. The lyric is (of course) smart enough to recognise what it is doing, articulating the logic of co-dependence and spousal abuse with brutal clarity: '*I need you, babe / To put through the shredder / In front of my friends*' and '*How could you go? / When you know how I need you? / To beat to a pulp on a Saturday night*' are the two grimmest lines in the entire album. (The

---

§   Usually a jazz-funk guitarist, funnily enough. He was nominated for 16 Grammy awards between 1978 and 1997.

girlfriend-beating theme may have come to Waters from Barrett, who became violent as his mental health declined during 1968.)*

Musically, the song is in two parts, with a static melody, dark synthesisers and a heartbeat rhythm† in the first, played by the band, and then an impassioned coda from 3.05 lasting around a minute with Gilmour again to the fore (though the lyrics here are just a repeated '*Ooooh … babe*'). Three minutes of atmosphere-evocation might have been alright on **ECHOES** or even **ABSOLUTELY CURTAINS**, but coming after similar bleak evocations on **EMPTY SPACES** and the start of **ONE OF MY TURNS** simply feels too much.

Similarly, for once on *The Wall*, the thinness of Waters' voice works against him. The shrillness of the complaint and the pleading nature of the vocal may be intended, or at least hoped to be capitalised upon, but they don't make the track an enjoyable listen. The group were right that an emotional nadir was necessary after the violent outburst of **ONE OF MY TURNS**, but this could easily have been provided by **GOODBYE CRUEL WORLD**, as this track and **ANOTHER BRICK IN THE WALL (PART III)** are essentially redundant. *The Wall* does remarkably well to sustain the listener's interest over the duration of eighty-one minutes, but it's here that it is most at risk of generating boredom. Ultimately, **DON'T LEAVE ME NOW** isn't sufficiently dramatised, and comes across as a morbid complaint, although its lyrics are far more interesting and self-aware than that. It's also astonishing that it was the b-side to **RUN LIKE HELL** – surely **NOBODY HOME** or **MOTHER** would have been better choices.‡

ANOTHER BRICK IN THE WALL (PART III) (Waters)
Length: 1.48
Vocals: Waters **Guitars**: Gilmour, Waters **Bass**: Waters **Prophet-5**: Wright
Synthesiser: Waters, Gilmour **Drums**: Mason
Recorded: January–November 1979, Britannia Row, London; Super Bear Studios, Studio Miraval, France; CBS Studios, Cherokee Studios, Producers Workshop and The Village Recorder, USA
Producer: Waters, Gilmour, Ezrin, Guthrie
First released: 30 November 1979 (*The Wall* disc 1 track 11)
Rating: 6/10

Each iteration of the **ANOTHER BRICK IN THE WALL** trio is more up-tempo than the last, perhaps to suggest the increasing vehemence with which

---

* 'He started to beat [girlfriend] Lindsay up. He did strange things like push her into the toilet and squeeze the toilet door against her, trapping her between door and wall. He would punch her and was also becoming surly … This went on and on. She lacked the capacity to leave an appalling situation.' (Julian Paliacos, *Dark Globe: Syd Barrett & Pink Floyd*, p.331).
† A Floydian trick going back to **HEART BEAT PIG MEAT** and of course **BREATHE**.
‡ The three singles were: **ANOTHER BRICK IN THE WALL PART 2** b/w **ONE OF MY TURNS**, **RUN LIKE HELL** b/w **DON'T LEAVE ME NOW** and **COMFORTABLY NUMB** b/w **HEY YOU**. (**BRING THE BOYS BACK HOME** was the b-side to **WHEN THE TIGERS BROKE FREE** in 1982, ahead of the general release of *Pink Floyd: The Wall*).

Pink is rejecting the outside world, though the song was initially titled 'Drugs', a theme the band were careful to downplay following the collapse of Barrett. The hard-rocking nature of the track also gives the album a necessary jolt of energy between the desolate **DON'T LEAVE ME NOW** and the gentle **GOODBYE CRUEL WORLD**. Much of *The Wall* is architectural, with songs designed both for narrative purposes and for dynamic peaks and troughs. **ANOTHER BRICK IN THE WALL (PART III)** only really makes sense for the latter, as its lyrics don't add anything to the storyline, beyond Pink's final rejection of the world. (Though that is also made explicit in the next track.) Nonetheless, it's played well, with great explosions of sound and shards of guitar flying like shrapnel, though the drumming is oddly placid, while the fluttering keyboards which begin at 0.40 suggest a heartbeat and continue as a remaining symbol of humanity as the song fades out then segue deftly into **GOODBYE CRUEL WORLD**.§ But overall, as an individual track, **ANOTHER BRICK IN THE WALL (PART III)** lacks distinctiveness and feels slightly pointless.¶

GOODBYE CRUEL WORLD (Waters)
Length: 0.48
Vocals: Waters **Bass**: Waters **Prophet-5**: Wright
Recorded: January–November 1979, Britannia Row, London; Super Bear Studios, Studio Miraval, France; CBS Studios, Cherokee Studios, Producers Workshop and The Village Recorder, USA
Producer: Waters, Gilmour, Ezrin, Guthrie
First released: 30 November 1979 (*The Wall* disc 1 track 12)
Rating: 8/10

The third-shortest song in Pink Floyd's catalogue (ahead only of **STOP** and **A NEW MACHINE PART I**), **GOODBYE CRUEL WORLD** packs a remarkably powerful punch considering its brevity. After fading in** with the fluttering keyboards from **ANOTHER BRICK IN THE WALL (PART III)**, Waters gently plays an alternating two-note bass line in front of some excellent subtle atmospherics by Wright, and sings two short verses indicating Pink's complete withdrawal from the outside world. The nursery-rhyme simplicity of the lines ('*Goodbye, goodbye, goodbye*') suggests the finality of the moment: there's no argument, no debate, no complexity – just a simple decision. There is also a typically attentive detail on the final word, as the music drops out completely, and the vocal takes fills the audio spectrum, in a superbly effective illustration of the completeness of Pink's separation from the real world.

---

§ Although there's an odd increase in volume across the segue between the two tracks, in what seems to be one of the very few bad engineering moments on the album. (If it's deliberate I don't see the point of it.)

¶ It's telling that the movie sequence for this track adds nothing to the story either, showing violent clashes between skinheads and police, which while dramatic have no real connection to what has gone before.

** Oddly, there's a notable increase in volume as one track segues to the next. If it's not deliberate (and I can't think why it would be), it is the only instance of poor editing on *The Wall*.

During live shows, **GOODBYE CRUEL WORLD** featured one of the strongest emotional climaxes. The wall having been constructed during the first half of the show (in a superb demonstration of theatrical pacing), all that remained was a single space, at head height. (A filler piece of music called 'The Last Few Bricks' was needed to time it correctly, with snatches from **YOUNG LUST** and **EMPTY SPACES**. It is released on *Is There Anybody Out There?* and can also be seen and heard on Waters' *The Wall Live in Berlin*.) At the final 'Goodbye', the final block is filled. It feels a hugely significant moment, showing a complete mastery of theatre, drama and music. The completed wall sat in front of the audience, huge, Brutalist, Stalinist, completely obscuring the band from view. Here was the theme of absence taken to its logical conclusion. No major group had ever disappeared like that.* The boldness must have been astonishing.†

HEY YOU (Waters)
Length: 4.40
Vocals: Gilmour, Waters **Guitars**: Gilmour **Bass**: Gilmour **Pedal steel**: Gilmour
Organ: Wright **Piano**: Wright **Synthesiser**: Wright **Drums**: Mason **Backing vocals**: Gilmour, Waters
Recorded: January–November 1979, Britannia Row, London; Super Bear Studios, Studio Miraval, France; CBS Studios, Cherokee Studios, Producers Workshop and The Village Recorder, USA
Producer: Waters, Gilmour, Ezrin, Guthrie
First released: 30 November 1979 (*The Wall* disc 2 track 1)
Rating: 8/10

One of the set-piece 'proper songs' on *The Wall*, **HEY YOU** combines two models previously successfully utilised by the group – firstly the nylon strings and fretless bass previously used in **A PILLOW OF WINDS**, and secondly the melancholic verse-rousing chorus form used on **CYMBALINE** and also heard in **US AND THEM**, **SHINE ON YOU CRAZY DIAMOND** and **COMFORTABLY NUMB** (and used incessantly throughout *The Final Cut*). Gilmour sings the first two verses as the nylon strings glitter icily amidst the darkness, and the wonderful suppleness of the fretless bass suggests deep feelings barely held in check. (Whereas in **A PILLOW OF WINDS** the two instruments suggested delicate emotions and slumbering comfort, respectively.) Around this basic platform Wright performs some of his most creative parts on *The Wall*, playing some pretty understated melodies on the electric piano, although this delicate atmosphere is shattered after the second verse as the band surges into hard rock and Gilmour aggressively plays the *We-Don't-Need-No-Education*

---

* Although John Lydon's Public Image Limited performed behind a screen at the New York Ritz in 1981. The audience was enraged by this and bottled them.
† I am too young to have seen *The Wall* performed live by Pink Floyd, though some older friends have (hi Jane!) and assure me it was incredible.

leitmotif on distorted guitar. He builds up to a shrieking guitar solo, with an electric fluidity straight out of Hendrix.

There's then a typical smart dynamic shift as all the instruments drop out, at which point Waters takes up the singing with the middle eight. Unusually, the lyrics – '*But it was only a fantasy / The wall was too high as you can see*' – here are amateurish, the 'as you can see' phrase beloved of beginner poets everywhere needing a hard-e rhyme. Fortunately, this part is only four lines, and the last is truly chilling – '*And the worms ate into his brain*'. Then we're brought back to the isolated atmospherics (as well as the buzzing of flies,‡ lest things not be grim enough) of the start of the song, with final verse sung by Waters with much greater urgency, even desperation. His voice isn't strong enough to carry it, especially in the line, '*Hey you, don't tell me there's no hope at aaaalllll ...*', where he sounds like he's choking on the extended last word. However, he makes amends by powerfully singing the crushing final line, '*Together we stand, divided we fall ...*', which draws things wonderfully to a close.

HEY YOU does, however, feel like a set-piece – it's cleverly thought out, artfully constructed, well dramatised (with the singing moving from Gilmour's restrained despondency to Waters' desperation), and beautifully played. Perhaps consequently, it feels cold and impersonal, even when it's supposed to be impassioned. This coldness is obviously largely intended, through the nylon strings and the dark atmospherics, but somehow **HEY YOU** doesn't make the emotional connection it aims for in its rousing final section. Perhaps rightly, it was left off the movie, though it makes both best-of albums.

IS THERE ANYBODY OUT THERE? (Waters)
Length: 2.44
Vocals: Waters, Gilmour **Guitars**: Joe DiBlasi **Bass**: Waters **Prophet-5**: Wright
Synthesiser: Bob Ezrin
Recorded: January–November 1979, Britannia Row, London; Super Bear Studios, Studio Miraval, France; CBS Studios, Cherokee Studios, Producers Workshop and The Village Recorder, USA
Producer: Waters, Gilmour, Ezrin, Guthrie
First released: 30 November 1979 (*The Wall* disc 2 track 2)
Rating: 8/10

The sound effects utilised so effectively by Pink Floyd in pivotal songs were occasionally used elsewhere, giving them a coherent soundworld. Perhaps the best example of this technique is in **IS THERE ANYBODY OUT THERE?**, where the 'whale sound' from **ECHOES** (and first discovered in **EMBRYO**) is recycled to provide another example of utterly bleak loneliness. But here the isolation is all internal, whereas **ECHOES** conveys '*a distant land*'. The combined

---

‡ A sound created by James Guthrie using a hand-held drill.

voices of Gilmour and Waters (on '*Out there?*') sound like stern wrathful gods, vengefully keeping slighter, helpless beings under their control,* while the atmospherics by Wright and Ezrin similarly establish a soundworld of utter emptiness and desolation.

This is then followed (beginning at 1.25) by an exquisite classical guitar solo, performed by Joe DiBlasi (Gilmour saying he could not do so without a pick). It's beautiful but slightly pointless, though its affectless emotional tone does convey Pink's comfortable numbness. During the film, it illustrates the section where Pink is pathetically making sculptures and arrangements out of the remnants of the hotel room he had earlier destroyed,† and thus, perhaps, a touching comment on the uselessness of art and creativity in the face of destroyed personal relationships. But as an evocation of isolation, **IS THERE ANYBODY OUT THERE?** is peerless. Probably Joy Division and Throbbing Gristle were the only other rock groups anywhere near touching the psychological depths which Pink Floyd were now examining, and their audiences were little more than marginal cults at the time. For Pink Floyd to do so while selling 30 million copies of *The Wall* is a magnificent achievement.

NOBODY HOME (Waters)
Length: 3.26
Vocals: Waters **Bass**: Gilmour **Prophet-5**: Wright **Piano**: Bob Ezrin **Orchestra**: The New York Philharmonic
Recorded: January–November 1979, Britannia Row, London; Super Bear Studios, Studio Miraval, France; CBS Studios, Cherokee Studios, Producers Workshop and The Village Recorder, USA
Producer: Waters, Gilmour, Ezrin, Guthrie
First released: 30 November 1979 (*The Wall* disc 2 track 3)
Rating: 9/10

If *The Wall* is an album of various kinds of bitterness, then **NOBODY HOME** is forlornly, achingly, beautifully bitter. As such it's probably the single most affecting song‡ on the album – although, surprisingly, the last to be written for it. Challenged to write one more song for the album, Waters came back a day later with this.§ Recorded without guitar, this is a piano ballad – something out of the way for *The Wall*, and hence perhaps unusually memorable. Its feeling of emotional desperation and desire for human connection (rather than misery at its absence) also make it feel more heartfelt and openly emotional than usual on the album.

---

* Though maybe it's just me thinking that.
† See **ONE OF MY TUNES**.
‡ Yes, yes, I know, alongside **COMFORTABLY NUMB**.
§ Gilmour remembered, 'Some of the songs – I remember Nobody Home – came along when we well into the thing and he'd gone off in a sulk the night before and come in the next day with something fantastic. It's often good to be geed up into a little state of rage.' (*Mojo* magazine, December 1999). Although you wonder why Gilmour couldn't be geed up a little.

The song opens with some more flickering TV sounds[¶] and then Bob Ezrin on piano, with a touch sounding familiar to anyone who had heard Lou Reed's *Berlin* (1973). There's something oddly European[**] and coldly sophisticated about his style, like someone playing in a hangdog piano bar late at night in Weimar Germany. Waters' vocal has an echo, a trick harking back to **US AND THEM**, though here it perhaps suggests a fragmenting personality, someone who barely knows who they are any more. Sung sadly at the start, the song opens up emotionally as it progresses, with Waters' tone brilliantly conveying acidic disdain ('*Thirteen channels of shit*'), delusion and paranoia ('*I've got amazing powers of observation*'), desolate loneliness ('*There will be nobody home*'), mania ('*I've got wild staring eyes*'), hope ('*A strong urge to fly*'), and the crushing realisation of the pointlessness of it all ('*But I've got nowhere to fly to*'). Waters may not be the world's most talented vocalist,[††] but he can certainly convey emotion, and **NOBODY HOME** displays that with supreme assurance.

The orchestration by Ezrin (performed by the New York Philharmonic, no less) is spare but beautiful, coming in two-thirds of the way through the first verse and on through the chorus, starting as nostalgic-sounding brass, before turning to high-pitched strings at the chorus. The melancholic orchestral flourish that follows, as Waters sings '*The obligatory Hendrix perm*', is one of the most beautifully moving parts in the entire album, and continues alongside the brass and piano to suggest full-spectrum waves of emotion. It's absolutely gorgeous. Everything, however, fades out as Waters sings just two lines for an outro and similarly slips away, in a further suggestion of absence.

It's been widely speculated that the phrases '*a silver spoon on a chain*' and '*a grand piano to prop up my mortal remains*' both refer to Wright, said to have been in the depths of a cocaine addiction at the time (the other source for Water's portrait of a burned-out casualty being, of course, Barrett). Wright denied this, saying:[‡‡]

> It would have been quite easy to say, 'Oh he left because he had a cocaine problem or a drink problem.' I can honestly say that it really was not a drug problem. It was taken without a doubt by him [presumably Waters], me, Dave, Nick, Bob Ezrin, but purely socially, it wasn't lying around in the studio.[§§]

[¶] From the comedy show *Gomer Pyle U.S.M.C.* (1964-69). It ran for 150 episodes and of course inspired the drill sergeant from *Full Metal Jacket* to name one of his recruits.
[**] Though Ezrin was born in Toronto.
[††] During the recording of *The Wall*, Waters struggled to hit the high notes at Super Bear studio (where the altitude apparently made this notoriously difficult), and so decamped to Studio Miraval to record his vocals. Which probably only further reduced the band cohesion during recording.
[‡‡] *Mojo* magazine, December 1999.
[§§] Waters however suggested in the same article that, 'There were people who were doing a lot – some of us had big, big problems. I certainly wasn't doing drugs at that point.'

Whatever the case, **NOBODY HOME** is one of Waters' finest songs, drawing a sad and effective portrait of a someone at the end of their tether desperately seeking human connection and failing to find it. Though it doesn't really sound like the group, it's one of the stand-out tracks on *The Wall*, if somewhat buried behind the guitar pyrotechnics of **RUN LIKE HELL** and the stupendous **COMFORTABLY NUMB**.

> **VERA** (Waters)
> **Length**: 1.35
> **Vocals**: Waters **Guitars**: Gilmour **Bass**: Gilmour **Prophet-5**: Wright **Drums**: Mason
> **Orchestra**: The New York Philharmonic
> **Recorded**: January–November 1979, Britannia Row, London; Super Bear Studios, Studio Miraval, France; CBS Studios, Cherokee Studios, Producers Workshop and The Village Recorder, USA
> **Producer**: Waters, Gilmour, Ezrin, Guthrie
> **First released**: 30 November 1979 (*The Wall* disc 2 track 4)
> **Rating**: 6/10

A lament for the Armed Forces sweetheart Vera Lynn, whose song 'We'll Meet Again' ('*Don't know where, don't know when*') was a moving lament to unstable human connections during the tumults of the Second World War, **VERA** adds little to the narrative, with even Waters seemingly unsure if his point is worth making ('*Does anybody else in here / Feel the way I do?*'). Its sadness and strong vocal* (for Waters) are effective, but not distinct enough from the rest of *The Wall* to make it memorable, though the orchestral arrangement is very fine. 'We'll Meet Again' was used at the start of the demoed version of *The Wall* and before the live shows to set the atmosphere of a lament for those lost in the war (and, by extension, to summon the pain of those who were bereaved). Without this in the album, however, the point is rather lost. **VERA** is ultimately a song more for Waters than for the listener, although it is beautifully sung and has a nice melancholic orchestration. But there's really not much of a song there.

---

* Given the excellence of Waters' singing on *Animals* and *The Wall*, the move towards a near-whispered, half-spoken vocal style on parts of *The Final Cut* and then his solo albums feels rather baffling. Perhaps he wanted listeners to focus on what he was saying, rather than be entranced by the music – as Nietzsche says 'The poet presents his thoughts festively on the carriage of rhythm: usually because they could not walk' (*Human, All Too Human*, 1878). Waters similarly seems to have turned away from musicality to wanting to present his Very Important Ideas. This is unfortunate: he may not have a powerful voice, but his best vocal performances – such as **ECLIPSE**, **SHEEP**, **VERA**, and **ONE OF MY TURNS** – are hugely impressive, with their impassioned feeling and great control. Another reason of course is that he simply isn't nearly as good a musician as Gilmour.

> **BRING THE BOYS BACK HOME** (Waters)
> **Length**: 1.21
> **Vocals**: Waters **Snare drum**: Jeff Pacaro **Drums**: Military drum corps **Strings**: New York Orchestra **Backing vocals**: Choir of New York Opera
> **Recorded**: January–November 1979, Britannia Row, London; Super Bear Studios, Studio Miraval, France; CBS Studios, Cherokee Studios, Producers Workshop and The Village Recorder, USA
> **Producer**: Waters, Gilmour, Ezrin, Guthrie
> **First released**: 30 November 1979 (*The Wall* disc 2 track 5)
> **Rating**: 7/10

One of the many wonderful things about *The Wall* as an album and *Pink Floyd: The Wall* as a film is the way they use details from Waters' early life to build a convincing picture of the life of Baby Boomers, from Pink's Argyle-patterned tank top† to the use of the brass band in this track. The visual and auditory worlds thus created are tremendously coherent, and testament to the efforts of album producers Waters, Gilmour, Ezrin and Guthrie, and film director Alan Parker. As an individual song, **BRING THE BOYS BACK HOME** is straightforward, with its snare drum (played by Jeff Pacaro) and bugling brass, but it's the most naked expression of optimistic feeling in *The Wall*. Waters called it 'the central song on the whole album',‡ though with its soaring trumpets and swirling strings it feels quite unlike anything on *The Wall*. Of course, its grandiose exhortation is placed just before **COMFORTABLY NUMB** to create a typically gripping, dynamic contrast. The short pieces on *The Wall* allowed the group to shift moods and energy levels as they saw fit, without needing to worry about providing contrasting sections within each song: hence the manic fuck-the-lot-of-you! vibe of **ANOTHER BRICK IN THE WALL PART 3** leads to the desolate numbness of **GOODBYE CRUEL WORLD**, or how the massed-chorus ending of **THE TRIAL** leads to the hushed-voice singing on **OUTSIDE THE WALL**. Having mastered moving between different sections by the time of **ECHOES**, at this stage Pink Floyd were supreme craftsmen at holding the listener's attention through varying their music's tempo, energy levels and aggression. But individual tracks matter less than the album as a whole, and some can feel almost redundant. You'd never go, 'Hey, I haven't listened to **BRING THE BOYS BACK HOME** in a while!', in the same way you might for deep album tracks **MATILDA MOTHER** or **CIRRUS MINOR** or **FAT OLD SUN**.

---

† That's a sweater vest to people outside the UK.
‡ '[I]t's partly about not letting people go off and be killed in wars, but it's also partly about not allowing rock and roll, or making cars or selling soap or getting involved in biological research or anything that anybody might do, not letting that become such an important … that it becomes more important than friends, wives, children, other people.' Waters interviewed by Tommy Vance, Radio 1, 30 November 1979.

COMFORTABLY NUMB (Gilmour, Waters)
Length: 6.23
Vocals: Waters, Gilmour **Guitars**: Gilmour **Acoustic guitars**: Lee Ritenour
Bass: Waters, Gilmour **Pedal steel**: Gilmour **Organ**: Wright **Drums**: Mason
Orchestra: New York Philharmonic
Recorded: January–November 1979, Britannia Row, London; Super Bear Studios, Studio Miraval, France; CBS Studios, Cherokee Studios, Producers Workshop and The Village Recorder, USA
Producer: Waters, Gilmour, Ezrin, Guthrie
First released: 30 November 1979 (*The Wall* disc 2 track 6)
Rating: 10/10

The final masterpiece by Pink Floyd,* **COMFORTABLY NUMB** had perhaps the most fraught gestation. The sparring between Gilmour and Waters over this song is legendary; even now, when Gilmour tours he insists on playing it his way (with grungy verses and soaring choruses, to convey the dark/light duality). However, Waters insisted on the antiseptic, clinical verses, and was absolutely right. Gilmour, as the superior craftsman, wanted the more basic dichotomy; Waters, the superior poet, wanted to comment on the state of Pink's mind and where psychosis has taken him. **COMFORTABLY NUMB** also is perhaps the greatest example of the voices of Gilmour and Waters creating a dialogue.† Waters, in the verses, uses a slyly malevolent tone to perform in character as the sleazy doctor ('*Can you show me where it hehrts?*'), Gilmour in the choruses delivering a magnificently uplifting melody in his beautiful high keening voice.

Musically, **COMFORTABLY NUMB** has its roots in an unused demo recorded at the time of Gilmour's 1978 *David Gilmour* solo album.‡ In another example of the group's careful shepherding of its material,§ he kept it for later use and offered it up during *The Wall* sessions. Ezrin was (as you might guess) keener than Waters, but it was demoed by the band under the title 'The Doctor', with lyrics that still needed further work ('*Listen … / I am a physician / And I can help with your condition*'). From the start, however, it combined verses suggesting psychosis with uplifting choruses, as well as a soaring first guitar solo and a darker grungier one at the end, demonstrating that the song's enthralling dialectic was there from conception. In its final recorded state, **COMFORTABLY NUMB** is the group's greatest single example of using Waters' and Gilmour's voices to create a dialogue, with both delivering performances of dramatic skill and intense

---

* It's interesting to note that the post-Barrett classics are concentrated into such a small timeframe – from **ECHOES** in 1971 to **COMFORTABLY NUMB** in 1979. Eight years of greatness in a recording career spanning 55 years (1967-2022) might seem pitifully small – until you remember that most groups never approach anything like this level in their entire career.
† See **MOTHER**.
‡ See **RUN LIKE HELL**.
§ See **US AND THEM**.

feeling. The ironic promises of care from Waters' seedy doctor[¶] are wonderfully illustrated by his glib, nasal phrasing, suggesting the doctor's actual malevolence; while Gilmour's beautiful, earnest, keening singing signifies the genuine emotions of Pink (as of course also shown by the lyrical shift to first person), and his growing distance from them. This contrast is a beautiful piece of theatre, and typical of the late-period Pink Floyd's artfulness. Some may miss the harmonies of Wright and Gilmour, but Waters and Gilmour are able to *mean* so much more.

Musically the song really is in three parts, however: the delirium verses, the soaring choruses (and beautiful first guitar solo from 2.04 to 2.34), and then the second guitar solo (from 4.31 to the fade-out), whose wailing griminess conveys a soul in deep torment. The verses are mostly drums and bass guitar, with rubbery steel-guitar tones sliding by like the last slippery vestiges of sanity floating off into the ether, and a rather subdued orchestral backing introduced halfway through. The chorus, however, has what must be the greatest orchestration in any rock song ever, the gorgeous shimmering strings suggestive of a nirvana that remains just out of reach, yet somehow (perhaps helped by the slightly plodding drums) remaining stately and elegant rather than flashy. There's something just deeply stirring about the orchestral section (for which, of course, Bob Ezrin deserves infinite credit). It can literally make grown men weep. The final guitar solo meanwhile is often lauded as Gilmour's best,[**] and indeed one of the best in all of rock music,[††] with its grime, pain, sustain, and soaring notes.[‡‡] With it lasting over two minutes, Gilmour has a lot of time, but it never feels extraneous: this is an utter master at work, leaving space, repeating and building on licks to give a sense of structure, not overplaying, building to a shrieking climax, and then fading out while leaving the listener wanting more.[§§] It's incredible.

But while the music and performance are magnificent, the lyric might be even better.[¶¶] The verses, with their loaded queries into Pink's mental health and

---

[¶] Waters drew on the experience of being dosed with painkillers when he was ill during the 'In the Flesh' tour of 1977: 'I had one guy once who ... gave me this tranquilizer, it was in Philadelphia, and boy, that was the longest two hours of my life. Trying to do a show when you can hardly lift your arm. If he'd just left me alone, the pain I could have handled. It was no sweat. I could hardly lift my arms or move any of my limbs. God knows what he gave me, but it was some very heavy muscle relaxant.' (Roger Waters interview with Jim Ladd, KLOS Radio, 1980).

[**] Though I personally would vote for the second from **DOGS** as his best – and then maybe the solo from **TIME** and the final solo from **ECHOES**. Though there's no doubt **COMFORTABLY NUMB** is up there with his astonishing best.

[††] *Classic Rock* magazine put it at #2 in 2018, while *Total Guitar* magazine put it at #3 in 2021.

[‡‡] He described the process of making it as: 'I banged out five or six solos. From there I just followed my usual procedure, which is to listen back to each solo and make a chart, noting which bits are good. Then, by following the chart, I create one great composite solo by whipping one fader up, then another fader, jumping from phrase to phrase until everything flows together.' (*Guitar World*, '50 Greatest Guitar Solos', 29 January 2009).

[§§] Ezrin nicely explains the greatness of Gilmour's playing: 'He's incredibly lyrical and melodic, and all his melodic structures are built on a blues foundation. And that makes them really soulful. Aside from that he has a majesty of tone, and that comes from the combination of his slow vibrato and his really precise picking and how strongly he holds the strings, so that the notes ring a long, long time. Add to that an amazing instinct for what's going to work where, and you end up with one of the greatest guitar players of all time ... I've had the privilege of working with some truly great guitar players in my career, but I have to say that David Gilmour is my favorite of all of them, and I'm sure I'm not alone in that.' (*Total Guitar*, 14 June, 2022).

[¶¶] It has my vote for the greatest ever in rock music.

assertions that the doctor can help, are short and deliberately simplistic: '*Come on now / I hear you're feeling down / Well, I can heal your pain / Get you on your feet again*'. The chorus by contrast is longer, more poetic ('*A distant ship-smoke on the horizon*'), and hints at something ineffable, a sense of the numinous that we all yearn for but so rarely admit. '*When I was a child, I had a fleeting glimpse / Out of the corner of my eye / I turned to look but it was gone / I cannot put my finger on it now / The child is grown, the dream is gone*': in four lines Waters does more than some writers do in their whole career. It is an astonishing, unforgettable piece of work, far outsoaring anything by Bob Dylan or Lou Reed or Joni Mitchell or Leonard Cohen or Bruce Springsteen or Billy Joel or anyone else in the rock canon.*

In the movie, **COMFORTABLY NUMB** is one of the horrific peaks, where Pink is found catatonic in his hotel room and dragged to a limo† to perform a show. As madness takes hold he transforms into a revolting blob-like creature, then he rips the putrescent flesh off as he hallucinates himself a fascist dictator. Here Waters is deftly alluding to several things at once: first, the *Triumph of the Will*-level bombast that goes with stadium rock; secondly, the resurgence of street-level fascism in the UK in the form of the National Front, which came fourth in the 1977 Greater London Council election; and thirdly, perhaps, the allure of fascism that grew from the film *Cabaret* (1973) and the swastikas worn by punks in an attempt to beard their elders.‡ Similarly, David Bowie, the litmus-paper of 1970s pop culture, was infamously photographed in May 1976 giving what looked like a fascist salute to his fans (though he denied it fiercely, saying he was caught mid-wave), after flirting with fascism in interviews, such as after a concert in Stockholm, where he said, 'I believe Britain could benefit from a fascist leader. After all, fascism is really nationalism.'§ Great art has resonance: it implies and evokes so much more than its surface level, and here Waters was clearly tapping into something potent in the English cultural and political psyche.

But perhaps the greatest way to experience **COMFORTABLY NUMB** was its live performance during *The Wall* tour. Waters, in his doctor's white coat, sang the verses outside the wall, but the highlight was Gilmour's sudden spotlight reveal on a raised platform on top of the completed wall, in yet another a complete mastery of music and theatre. Even the normally unflappable Gilmour sounded highly proud of it, saying:

> I'm in pitch darkness and no one knows I'm there yet. And Roger's down and he finishes his line, I start mine and … the audience, they're all looking

---

* The only rival could be The Beatles' 'Strawberry Fields Forever', which also addresses mental confusion in a rich poetic lexicon.
† Bob Hoskins is great as the seedy road manager.
‡ For example, by Siouxsie Sioux when accompanying the Sex Pistols on the *Today* show on 1 December 1976 (the famous 'Grundy Incident').
§ David Buckley, *Strange Fascination: David Bowie The Definitive Story*, p.250.

straight ahead and down, and suddenly there's all this light up there and they all sort of – their heads all lift up and there's this thing up there and the sound's coming out and everything. Every night there's this sort of gasp from about 15,000 people. And that's quite something, let me tell you.¶

Although (like much of *The Wall*) not really typical of their sound, **COMFORTABLY NUMB** may be Pink Floyd's greatest song: its smart theatrical structure, astonishing lyrics, stunning orchestration and deeply emotive guitar soloing are all career peaks, or not far off it. Recording it may have been a wounding experience, but it is perhaps the apex of rock music as an artform.** No other song cuts deeper, says so much about the human condition, or hits such moments of beauty and horror. It is a truly stupendous achievement.

THE SHOW MUST GO ON (Waters)
Length: 1.36
Vocals: Gilmour **Guitars**: Gilmour **Bass**: Gilmour **Synthesiser**: Wright, Bob Ezrin
Piano: Ezrin **Drums**: Mason **Backing vocals**: Toni Tenille, Bruce Johnston, Joe Chemay, Stan Farber, Jim Haas, John Joyce
Recorded: January–November 1979, Britannia Row, London; Super Bear Studios, Studio Miraval, France; CBS Studios, Cherokee Studios, Producers Workshop and The Village Recorder, USA
Producer: Waters, Gilmour, Ezrin, Guthrie
First released: 30 November 1979 (*The Wall* disc 2 track 7)
Rating: 5/10

This track must count as the least successful of all on *The Wall*. It may well be that the listener needs some relief after the searing intensity of **COMFORTABLY NUMB**. However, the warm harmonies and cartoonish falsettos (originally intended for the Beach Boys, as ludicrous as that might seem) feel out of place, and rather silly after the searing psychological depths of the preceding tracks. If those aspects are meant to convey Pink now enjoying his psychosis, they do so at the expense of feeling frivolous and out of keeping with the rest of the album. Sounding like a German two-step ('*Oom-pah, oom-pah*') delivered in a warm wash of fine harmonised vocals that sound somewhat like country music (especially in the final a capella line), **THE SHOW MUST GO ON** doesn't overstay its welcome at just over ninety seconds but neither does it really justify its inclusion on the album. If *The Wall* is a theatrical performance, **THE SHOW MUST GO ON** is the piss-break before the main event. Little wonder it was dropped for the movie.

¶ *Shades of Pink – The Definitive Pink Floyd Profile*. From the Source, with host Charlie Kendall (1984).
** There are many other ways to enjoy rock, of course. I enjoy punk for its energy and vitality, The Beatles for their artistry and humanity, Metallica for their power and energy. But as *art*, as a coherent statement, Pink Floyd are leagues ahead.

IN THE FLESH (Waters)
Length: 4.15
Vocals: Waters **Guitars**: Gilmour **Bass**: Waters **VCS 3**: Waters **Synthesiser**: Gilmour, Bob Ezrin **Organ**: Fred Mandell **Drums**: Mason **Backing vocals**: Toni Tenille, Bruce Johnston, Joe Chemay, Stan Farber, Jim Haas, John Joyce
Recorded: January–November 1979, Britannia Row, London; Super Bear Studios, Studio Miraval, France; CBS Studios, Cherokee Studios, Producers Workshop and The Village Recorder, USA
Producer: Waters, Gilmour, Ezrin, Guthrie
First released: 30 November 1979 (*The Wall* disc 2 track 8)
Rating: 8/10

A reprise of the album's opening track, here Pink is in his fascist dictator phase, denouncing gays, blacks, marijuana enthusiasts and those afflicted by acne. Using the same strident riff and martial drumming as **IN THE FLESH?** this version differs in its backing vocals straight out of **THE SHOW MUST GO ON** and more theatrical drumming. Lyrically, this version has longer verses where (after the same introductory lines about the '*space-cadet glow*'), Pink explicitly disavows his identity (saying he '*isn't well / He's back at the hotel*') to become part of '*a surrogate band*'. He's not really there, and it's not even his group: it's like the famous visit of Barrett during the recording of **SHINE ON YOU CRAZY DIAMOND**, and yet another example of the theme of absence, as well as a textbook example of alienation.*

What is there is vituperation and hate, with Waters' sequencing of Pink's targets making clear his irony and the logical absurdity of such odium. Nonetheless, **IN THE FLESH** demonstrates a strong psychological insight. Isolation leads to hate, as the ego needs to find reasons for its distress: it can't be my fault, or that would induce cognitive dissonance,† so it must be the fault of others. So I need scapegoats to explain my pain.‡ It's a form of projection, just as any political scapegoating. The musical bombast and dictator-stance are a reminder that those in power who abuse minorities are often frightened, wounded people, or (even worse) grotesque cynics preying on the anxieties of the powerless. **IN THE FLESH** hence isn't just a reprise, but deepens the themes and meaning of *The Wall* – leading brilliantly to the horrors of **RUN LIKE HELL**.

For *Pink Floyd: The Wall*, **IN THE FLESH** was re-recorded with a Germanic brass band and choir straight out of Nuremberg rallies. With Bob Geldof in excellent form as Pink fomenting the hatred of his audience and backed by the aggressive stares of genuine skinheads, it's a deeply disturbing scene, a terrible

---

* As Thom Yorke sings in Radiohead's 'How To Disappear Completely' from *Kid A* (2000): '*I'm not here / This isn't happening*'.
† A mental process by which we avoid blame.
‡ I have observed this in someone who sank into drug addiction. The worse things got, the more racist he became.

reminder that fascism could arise anywhere and that we are all vulnerable to its grotesque appeal. Unfortunately, it only feels ever more relevant.

> **RUN LIKE HELL** (Waters, Gilmour)
> **Length**: 4.20
> **Vocals**: Waters, Gilmour **Guitars**: Gilmour **Bass**: Gilmour **Prophet-5**: Wright **Drums**: Mason **Percussion**: Bobbye Hall **Backing vocals**: Waters
> **Recorded**: January-November 1979, Britannia Row, London; Super Bear Studios, Studio Miraval, France; CBS Studios, Cherokee Studios, Producers Workshop and The Village Recorder, USA
> **Producer**: Waters, Gilmour, Ezrin, Guthrie
> **First released**: 30 November 1979 (*The Wall* disc 2 track 9)
> **Rating**: 10/10

The second Gilmour co-write within four tracks, **RUN LIKE HELL** helps to significantly increase the tunefulness and potency of the latter parts of *The Wall*, where it's most needed. Its outstanding guitar riff is a rippling surge of energy while the rhythm owes more to disco than Mason's often delicate touch. The riff (as is widely known) is descended from a track on Gilmour's solo album called 'Short And Sweet',[§] which (like most of the album) is pleasant enough but isn't sufficiently fleshed out with either the concepts or dynamic shifts that make Pink Floyd songs so constantly interesting.[¶] Fortunately, it was a far more exciting prospect than Waters' original demo, which didn't feature much of a tune, and so here is one of the final marriage of Gilmour's musicianship and Waters' concepts and lyrics. Bolstered by a pulsating disco beat and fine accompaniment on the bass (played by Gilmour), **RUN LIKE HELL** could almost be a dancefloor track, were it not for the repeated '*Run! Run! Run!*' – halfway between a threat and a warning – the longueurs after the guitar solo, where most of the band drops out to leave the sound of footsteps, breathing, tyres screeching, and someone screaming, and, of course, its grim lyrical content.

Smartly contrasting its enjoyably up-tempo soundscape, **RUN LIKE HELL** lyrically sees an unusual shift to second person, the repeated '*You*' making the song feel specifically pointed, and skilfully evoking someone caught up in the rampage against social scapegoats, or maybe even being victimised as one of them. (It's quite ambiguous, no doubt deliberately to show how quickly in such febrile atmospheres the aggressors can turn on their own.) The evocation of the psychological state in the first verse is brilliant, with images like '*Your favourite disguise*', '*Your empty smile and your hungry heart*', and '*the bile rising from your guilty past*'. The second verse, meanwhile, is a savage psycho-sexual warning: '*Keep your dirty feelings deep inside / And if you're taking your girlfriend out tonight*

[§] Gilmour noted that both songs feature 'a guitar with the bottom string tuned down to a D, and thrashing around on the chord shapes over a D root' (*Musician* magazine, August 1992).

[¶] Gilmour's second solo album *About Face* (1984) isn't much better, but *On An Island* (2006) I find absolutely terrific. *Rattle That Lock* (2015) unfortunately is a reversion to the mean, and has a hideous cover.

/ You'd better park the car well out of sight / 'Cos if they catch you in the back seat trying to pick her locks / They're going to send you back to Mother in a cardboard box'. Waters' voice rises and rises deliriously, coming to a feverish ranting climax in the last line. It's a stunning example of his lyrical and vocal abilities. **RUN LIKE HELL** is one of Waters' very finest lyrics, with an allusion to *Lord of the Flies** (the 'conch shell', which in the novel symbolises order and authority) and perhaps the best image from the entire album, '*Your roller-blind eyes*'. That's worthy of T.S. Eliot, W.H. Auden or any English modernist poet. But it's not just the verbal felicity: it's how Waters visualises this extreme emotional situation and brings it to imaginative life through striking imagery that makes him the greatest of all rock's writers.

The sequence for **RUN LIKE HELL** on *Pink Floyd: The Wall* is the single most chilling moment of the entire film, where the audience for Pink's fascist rally move in a choreographed exhibition of faceless unity and fascist salutes, then his Stormtroopers run amok through the streets, assaulting, vandalising, and raping as they go. The scenes are deeply unsettling,† bringing to mind not just Hitler's Brown Shirts but Oswald Moseley's National Union of Fascists, the National Front‡ and Mao Zedong's Red Guards during the Cultural Revolution.§ This could happen here, the film says, if we're not careful. Don't let it happen again.¶ But overall, the pulsating rhythm, surging riff, vicious poetry and psychological insight of **RUN LIKE HELL** make it one of the greatest moments on *The Wall*, and one that has rarely left the group's live repertoire ever since.**

WAITING FOR THE WORMS (Waters)
Length: 4.04
Vocals: Waters, Gilmour **Guitars**: Gilmour **Bass**: Gilmour **Organ**: Wright **VCS 3**: Waters **Synthesiser**: Gilmour **Piano**: Bob Ezrin **Drums**: Mason **Backing vocals**: Toni Tenille, Bruce Johnston, Joe Chemay, Stan Farber, Jim Haas, John Joyce
Recorded: January–November 1979, Britannia Row, London; Super Bear Studios, Studio Miraval, France; CBS Studios, Cherokee Studios, Producers Workshop and The Village Recorder, USA
Producer: Waters, Gilmour, Ezrin, Guthrie
First released: 30 November 1979 (The Wall disc 2 track 10)
Rating: 8/10

---

* By William Golding, published 1954.
† Although it's obvious that the man attacked by a Rottweiler has padding around his arm.
‡ The Battle of Lewisham on 13 August 1977 saw violent clashes between the National Front and opposition groups, with 111 people injured and riot shields used for the first time on mainland Britain.
§ See *Mao's Last Revolution* (2008) by Roderick Macfarquhar and Michael Schoenhals. The Cultural Revolution (1966-76) resulted in the deaths of untold millions and plunged the country in chaos for a decade.
¶ Although, as with much of *The Wall*, it seems to relish its nightmare visions. Kingsley Amis said 'Nice things are nicer than nasty ones' (in *Lucky Jim*, 1955), which sounds like a syllogism but he has a point: in rock music certainly, we tend to celebrate (self)destructiveness (especially through drugs), chaos and aggression. But these are not nice things. See **OUTSIDE THE WALL**.
** Gilmour has great fun with it on the *Pulse* live album (1995) in particular, teasing the audience with its introductory riff for over a minute and then greatly extending its conclusion to a magnificent all-hands-on-deck ending. That's how you finish a show, kids.

After the fever-pitch intensity of **RUN LIKE HELL**, the listener barely has a moment before the climactic **WAITING FOR THE WORMS**. The song cleverly opens with harmonised falsettos ('*You cannot reach me now / No matter how you try*'), which brighten things for just a moment before the grim power of the 'Waiting' refrain. Waters then takes on the role of a megaphoned megalomaniac, a street rabble-rouser giving instructions to fascists preparing to march through London.†† The tinny electrified sound (created au natural, in the days before digital effects) and Waters' nasal feverish ranting evoke the character perfectly, in another fine example of his underappreciated ventriloquism.‡‡ As the song proceeds his ranting becomes increasingly incomprehensible, instead feeling like a mindless stream of furious screamed invective. It's a terrific theatrical performance. Lyrically, however, it's the only track on *The Wall* to feel dated, through the term '*coloured cousins*' which now feels deeply patronising. But then it is an album that's now forty-three years old, and race relations in the UK are rather more considered.§§

The music in **WAITING FOR THE WORMS** is similarly well thought-out, with the military goose-steps and drums at the start, the harmonised vocals giving the sense of Pink now enjoying his alienation and hallucinations, gentle contrasting verses sung primarily by Gilmour, the '*Waiting*' refrain complemented by the tight aggressive guitar, and then the reappearance of the **ANOTHER BRICK IN THE WALL PART 2** leitmotif, here played in a leaden, brutalist style to a military rhythm. After the second verse, the motif reappears at 2.28 (with cries of '*Hammer! Hammer!*' building from 3.10) as it all builds and builds to a shockingly intense climax. It's reminiscent of the instrumental section from **PIGS (THREE DIFFERENT ONES)**, though here developing tension far more quickly since the rhythm is far simpler.

The movie section is justly famous for the goose-stepping hammers animated sequence by Gerald Scarfe. As a symbol of fascism, it is absolutely tremendous,¶¶ while one of the hammer heads cleverly becomes a megaphone. Not surprisingly, this section is also very dark (the backdrop is a very grey sky), and moves through ever more rapid cuts, interspersed with images of writhing maggots and Bob Geldof as Pink screaming, to an equally powerful climax. It's horrifying and grim, but it takes your breath away.

---

†† Some sentences are discernible, e.g. 'The worms will convene at 1:15 outside Brixton Town Hall where we will be going in force' and 'Now when we get to the other side of Vauxhall Bridge, we're in Westminister Borough area. It's quite possible that we may encounter some Jew boys all the way from 4, 5, and 6 on the way as we go'.
‡‡ See **THE TRIAL**.
§§ This was the time when the word 'coons' was deemed suitable for mainstream TV, as on *Till Death Us Do Part*. Even *Fawlty Towers* uses the words 'wogs' and 'niggers' in one episode ('The Germans', 1975). Fortunately things are much changed.
¶¶ Waters called it 'the most powerful image in the whole film' (*Pink Floyd: The Wall* Deluxe edition, audio commentary).

STOP (Waters)
Length: 0.30
Vocals: Waters **Piano**: Ezrin
Recorded: January–November 1979, Britannia Row, London; Super Bear Studios, Studio Miraval, France; CBS Studios, Cherokee Studios, Producers Workshop and The Village Recorder, USA
Producer: Waters, Gilmour, Ezrin, Guthrie
First released: 30 November 1979 (*The Wall* disc 2 track 11)
Rating: 7/10

As the tension from **WAITING FOR THE WORMS** becomes unbearable, it ends with a sudden cry of '*Stop!*' This leads immediately to **STOP**, where – against a skittering, almost nursery-rhyme piano played by Ezrin – Waters sings a desperate vocal outlining Pink's last grasp of sanity. He sees himself for what he has become, and puts himself on trial – '*I have to know … / Have I been guilty all this time …?*'

In the original screenplay for *Pink Floyd: The Wall*, **STOP** was to be the pivotal moment when Pink realises that the fascism that killed his father is the same that has ensnared him. This realisation would lead to a great denunciation and reaffirmation of his humanity. However, it was perhaps realised that this would remove the doubt and drama of **THE TRIAL**, and so features Pink broken down in an arena bathroom stall, mumbling lines from his poems.* It's one of the most deeply affecting scenes in the film.† The album track, however, is more limited in purpose and effect, though it's still effective.

THE TRIAL (Waters, Ezrin)
Length: 5.13
Vocals: Waters **Guitars**: Gilmour **Bass**: Gilmour **Piano**: Wright **Bass drum**: Mason **Cymbals**: Mason **Backing vocals**: Vicki Brown, Clare Torry **Orchestra**: New York Symphony Orchestra
Recorded: January–November 1979, Britannia Row, London; Super Bear Studios, Studio Miraval, France; CBS Studios, Cherokee Studios, Producers Workshop and The Village Recorder, USA
Producer: Waters, Gilmour, Ezrin, Guthrie
First released: 30 November 1979 (*The Wall* disc 2 track 12)
Rating: 8/10

Where *The Wall* goes from rock opera to penny opera. **THE TRIAL** is one of the great imaginative triumphs of the album, where Waters brilliantly characterises each character as they strut upon the stage for one verse: the obsequious prosecutor,

---

* Including words from **YOUR POSSIBLE PASTS** and '5.11am (The Moment Of Clarity)' from *The Pros and Cons of Hitchhiking*.
† In the background you can hear the 'Master Of Ceremonies' introducing the band, spoken by Gary Yudman, as released in the *Is There Anybody Out There?* live album. It's another smart example of the unified soundworld the group were so adept at creating (see **IS THERE ANYBODY OUT THERE?**).

The Worm, with his florid phrasing and rolled r's; the petty tyrannical barking of The Teacher, who seems to be Scottish; the acidic loathing of The Wife;‡ the Yorkshire homeliness of The Mother;§ and then the grotesque outraged bullying of The Judge.¶ Each, of course, is a caricature, but Waters' talents as a ventriloquist or mimic are rarely if ever mentioned, and here they are on superb display.**

THE TRIAL is, however, more often noted for its music – written by Ezrin, who channels Gilbert and Sullivan, and perhaps Kurt Weil.†† Ezrin rightly received a very unusual (for the time) writing credit: while it's clear from Waters' original demo that the song's psychodrama was outlined from the start, the original melody (or what there was of one) was akin to the **ANOTHER BRICK IN THE WALL PART 2**. By the band demo of the autumn of 1978, on which Ezrin collaborated, the Humpty-Dumpty melody and iambic rhythm had come in, though played on keyboards. The final recording is almost entirely orchestral, with flatulent brass counterpointed by twirling woodwind, until Gilmour's ferocious leitmotif riff gets a final outing backing The Judge's savage declamation. The light opera nature of the verses belies and contrasts beautifully with the complex psychodrama happening vocally and lyrically, making it yet another theatrical bullseye, while the first-person chorus ('*Crazy … / Toys in the attic I am crazy/ Truly gone fishing*') manages to sound unusually humane and is deeply moving. Rather than fetishising Pink's misery and madness, the chorus seems to finally consider him a human being worthy of empathy. The final verdict and subsequent repeated chants to '*Tear down the wall!*' are brilliantly climactic, and a wonderful compositional feat.

Of course, **THE TRIAL** is as far as you can get from Pink Floyd's customary soundworld, even considering the band's astonishing range, but its highly theatrical nature, range of characters, Waters' superb voicing, the deeply moving chorus, and magnificent climax make it an enthralling piece. No other band lay claim to a body of work that goes from Gilbert and Sullivan to pop whimsy to Bob Dylan to freeform spacerock explorations to proto-trance music. **THE TRIAL** is yet another superb feather in the cap for Waters, on an album where his creativity feels boundless.

---

‡ During his *The Wall Live* tour of 2010-2013, he gave The Wife a French accent.
§ Waters' Yorkshire accent is spot on. See note for *Meddle* review on page 99.
¶ Perhaps it's just me, but The Judge's summing up somehow reminds me of that given to Oscar Wilde following his prosecution for gross indecency: 'That you, Wilde, have been the centre of a circle of extensive corruption of the most hideous kind among young men it is impossible to doubt. I shall under such circumstances be expected to pass the severest sentence that the law allows. In my judgment it is totally inadequate for such a case as this. The sentence of the court is that each of you be imprisoned and kept to hard labour for two years.' Richard Ellmann, *Oscar Wilde*, p.448 – I would argue the greatest biography in the English language.
** Some reviewers of *The Wall* complain about Waters' thin voice. For example, The Vulture website says 'Roger Waters is a talented guy, but he has an awful voice. He did what he could with it for a long time, but at a certain point he just decided to go with its screechy essential nature' about **DON'T LEAVE ME NOW**. This is a bit like saying Bob Dylan can be a bit nasal, or that Barry White can be a bit gruff. It's what they *do* with it that counts. (See www.vulture.com/2017/08/all-165-pink-floyd-songs-ranked-from-worst-to-best.html).
†† From whom comes standards 'Mack The Knife' (in *The Threepenny Opera*) and 'What Keeps Mankind Alive?' (covered by The Pet Shop Boys – the b-side to 'Can You Forgive Her?', it can be found on their superb *Alternative* album).

OUTSIDE THE WALL (Waters)
Length: 1.41
Vocals: Waters **Concertina**: Frank Marocco **Clarinet**: Larry Williams **Mandolin**: Trevor Veitch **Backing vocals**: Children's choir from New York
Recorded: January–November 1979, Britannia Row, London; Super Bear Studios, Studio Miraval, France; CBS Studios, Cherokee Studios, Producers Workshop and The Village Recorder, USA
Producer: Waters, Gilmour, Ezrin, Guthrie
First released: 30 November 1979 (*The Wall* disc 2 track 13)
Rating: 7/10

The final track of *The Wall* is where we're supposed to achieve catharsis after the darkness and horror of the preceding eighty minutes – just as after a good drama we are to feel renewed,* or after a horror movie we feel the monster has been bested and balance has been restored. It's the final positive upswing, the restoration of equilibrium. Hence the innocent instrumentation of **OUTSIDE THE WALL** with clarinet and mandolin, and its children's choir, and its lyrics drawing a scene of people holding hands and being nice to each other ('*Some hand in hand / And some gathered together in bands / The bleeding hearts and the artists make their stand*').

But it doesn't really achieve what it sets out to do. It's mixed much too quietly, Waters' voice is barely audible, and it is far too short to counter the preceding bleakness. Also, it cuts off at the end, Waters saying, '*Isn't this where*', resuming at the start of the album (Waters saying '*we came in?*') – so it's all a cycle, and nothing has been altered. The movie version noticeably seeks to rectify these issues, being mixed louder, Waters' vocal being more prominent, and with a bright instrumental outro lasting significantly longer. Yet, as most of it runs during the movie's credits, even then it doesn't achieve the emotional uplift it intends, leaving the viewer emotionally devastated but ultimately unsatisfied.† It was done best when performed live, with the band‡ performing like a group of minstrels, following the astonishing sight of the twenty-foot-high wall having been torn down, which itself would have been hugely cathartic. Each iteration of *The Wall* has its strengths and weaknesses: the fact that it could be transferred from album to stage to film to opera says much about the strength of its central metaphor.§

OUTSIDE THE WALL is hence well-intentioned, but as Waters no doubt found, it's much harder to envision a picture of happiness and unity than to rage against your misery. He was noticeably reluctant to explain it, for example during a 1980 interview saying, 'I can't say anything about the last song … I like

---

* A theory going all the way back to Aristotle's *Poetics* (c. 335BC).
† The final scene, with children clearing up the debris and dismantling Molotov cocktails the morning after a riot, also wants to gesture towards the promise of a peaceful world, that the children are the future, etc etc. But amid so much broken glass and devastation, the point isn't too clear. What stays in the mind is the genuine horror of the **IN THE FLESH** and **RUN LIKE HELL** sequences.
‡ Mason playing acoustic guitar, Wright accordion, Gilmour mandolin, and Waters clarinet.
§ Though dare I note that John Lennon released an album in 1974 titled *Walls And Bridges*?

it as enigmatic. And I like that about it and I wouldn't care to discuss it. I don't even really want to think about it myself.'¶ No doubt he sensed that, as Philip Larkin said quoting French novelist Henry de Montherlant, 'happiness writes white'.** Or it risks seeming absurd, as at the end of *A Christmas Carol* and *It's a Wonderful Life*. Yet by not producing a positive picture, we're simply left with the bitter aftertaste of nihilism, fascism and madness, not the uplift we need after such a traumatic journey.

Rating the individual tracks of *The Wall* is perhaps not the best methodology, as it, like any rock opera, should really be taken as a whole – and *The Wall* is the most operatic of all Pink Floyd albums, with a sustained narrative and an unrelenting psychological exploration of human frailties. Its tracks are to dramatise the story: **BRING THE BOYS BACK HOME**, with its drummer boys and military choir, could never appear in any other Pink Floyd album, for example. Yet its Second World War atmosphere fits well, and its urgent lament and typically skilful crossfade segue artfully into the antiseptic horrors of **COMFORTABLY NUMB**. Similarly, *The Wall* was constructed rather as though on a production line, with outside musicians (as in **IS THERE ANYBODY OUT THERE?**, **THE TRIAL** and **MOTHER**) sometimes to the fore, unlike all of their previous work bar **ATOM HEART MOTHER**. (Though, to be fair, the album had been demoed twice by the band and Bob Ezrin,†† its songs fleshed out and its arrangements put in place.) Even so, the pressures making it seem to have been enormous. It is curious, to say the least, that an album so insistent on the difficulties in human relations should be such an exemplary demonstration of their failure within the group making it. The gods seem to have a great sense of dramatic irony.

All the same, *The Wall*, taken as a whole, is a magnificent triumph. It's certainly not perfect – it lacks the colour of Pink Floyd's previous work, some sections drag, a few of the lyrics are juvenile, and its emotional arc lacks sufficient catharsis – but it is astonishingly bold and frequently hugely moving. Its themes are profound but easily comprehensible (whereas on *Dark Side* they had more often been implied), the musicianship is stellar (Gilmour does magnificent work, from **THE THIN ICE** to **HEY YOU** to **RUN LIKE HELL**, but his solos and vocals on **COMFORTABLY NUMB** are career peaks), the singing is often terrific (Waters produces numerous career-best efforts), the lyrics are among the best in rock music (with timeless images like '*Your button-down lips and your roller-blind eyes*'), and its use of sound effects to create a consistent soundworld is exemplary, from the repeated use of TV samples to screeching wheels and torn sheets. But beyond even all that, *The Wall* is an artistic triumph because it is

---

¶ Interview with Jim Ladd, KMET radio, February 1980.
** Philip Larkin, *Required Writing*, p.47.
†† The bootlegs of this process are excellent listening. *The Wall Immersion Edition* box set from 2012 contains much of this material.

something that no one else could have created and yet which you cannot imagine not existing, thus having what Martin Amis called 'the rarest quality known to any art – that of apparent inevitability'.[*] It is an essential part of the cultural shape of the post-war period – the greatest rock opera of them all,[†] and perhaps the boldest statement by any rock group, ever.[‡] It is the absolute pinnacle of popular music as art,[§] and the final peak of Pink Floyd's career. Their glorious hot streak had lasted four incredible albums in just six years. But the strains of making them, and handling the success they engendered, destroyed intra-band relationships. For the rest of their lives, they will labour in the shadows of their former greatness: wealthy, successful, acclaimed men, but marked and almost haunted by the incredible alchemic achievement of those astonishing years. But you never realise that until it's too late.

---

[*] From 'Iris Murdoch (1919-1999): Age Will Win', reprinted in *The Rub Of Time*, p.76.
[†] It is magnitudes better than The Who's *Tommy* and *Quadrophenia*, for example, never mind *Bat Out Of Hell* or Lou Reed's *Berlin* (also produced by Bob Ezrin).
[‡] Perhaps with the exception of *Metal Machine Music* (1975) by Lou Reed. Except *The Wall* is good to listen to.
[§] Compare with *Thriller* (1982) by Michael Jackson. Nine nearly perfectly sculpted tracks, but little pretension to being more than just a great LP to listen to.

III.

ECHOES (1982–2022)

WHEN THE TIGERS BROKE FREE (Waters)
Length: 3.00
Vocals: Waters **Orchestra**: Michael Kamen **Backing vocals**: Pontarddulais Male Voice Choir
Recorded: November 1981–March 1982
Producer: Pink Floyd
First released: 26 July 1982 (UK a/side single)
Rating: 7/10

After over a year recording *The Wall*, two years performing it live, a year making the film, and with Wright having been fired, the group were subsequently not rudderless but lacking creative drive. The 1980 and 1981 live performances were spectacular and are rightly famous[¶] (if financial loss-leaders), but comprised only eighteen shows in the former year and fourteen in the latter. With various unused tracks having been recorded or demoed during *The Wall* sessions, the initial plan was for a *Spare Bricks* album, in the manner of Radiohead's *Kid A* (2000) and *Amnesiac* (2001), or Metallica's *Load* (1996) and *ReLoad* (1997): companion albums clearly from the same sessions but completed later. The collapse of the group's intra-band democracy is apparent from Gilmour not seeming to offer any material, yet having enough to release a second solo album, *About Face*, in 1984. Regarding this, Waters later said, 'How on earth could I possibly stop Dave Gilmour writing? What would I do? Go round to their house and when they pick up a guitar say, "Put that down"? The idea is absolutely ludicrous.'[**] The fact that he himself might have been impeding bandmates from offering material they had written seems not to have occurred to him.

The issue thus came down to what to do with the leftover material, and here a major breach between Gilmour and Waters emerged. Gilmour felt that the *Spare Bricks* were substandard, which was why they had been rejected, 'so

---

[¶] Sadly yet to receive a proper DVD release. Apparently the wrong lenses were used when recording the 1980 shows, making it look as if they were filmed underwater. The bootleg editions I've seen are barely viewable. You can only hope that the digital software to rectify it will be available at some point. Some better quality footage exists from the 1981 shows in London, but apparently only three tracks were filmed as the plan for the film had moved away from concert performance. ('Pink Floyd – Behind The Wall', *Record Collector*, March 2000).
[**] *Uncut* magazine June 2004.

why are they good enough now?"* Waters, meanwhile, felt that no one else was contributing any material, and he who writes the songs calls the tune, as it were.† Previously the two men had always been able to arrive at a way of working together. Ezrin, who facilitated this during the recording of *The Wall*, had, however, been expelled from the group's inner circle for revealing aspects of the live show.‡ So, following the making of *Pink Floyd: The Wall* (during which Waters fell out with director Alan Parker – you'd think a man so interested in human connection would notice that his working relationships were increasingly dreadful) there was no one left to come between them. It was now *mano é mano* for the musical direction of Pink Floyd. Waters felt that he was the only one contributing material and so had every right to direct things as he saw fit. It's certainly strange that Gilmour had albums worth of material both before and after *The Wall* yet seemed to be empty when it came to Pink Floyd. Something presumably was impeding him. Yet regardless of writing credit, Gilmour had provided outstanding work throughout *Animals* and *The Wall*, putting musical meat on Waters' conceptual bones, demonstrating exceptional talent through the squawk box, fretless bass, best-of-his-generation guitar solos, and vocals ranging from the raucous (**YOUNG LUST**) to desperate nostalgia (**COMFORTABLY NUMB**). It's pointless to place fingers or allocate blame (although the wish to do so still animates many online discussions on Pink Floyd), but clearly the working relationship between Waters and Gilmour was breaking down, and with it perhaps the greatest complementary skill set in rock history.§

WHEN THE TIGERS BROKE FREE illustrates the issues between them. It had been held back from *The Wall* on account of its specificity to the Anzio landings in Italy as part of Operation Shingle, during which Waters' father Eric Fletcher Waters had been killed on 18 February 1944 (when Waters was just five months old). Ezrin and others had felt that *The Wall* would be better to focus less on Waters' own biography and to have Pink as a composite character who would thus represent anyone who had been emotionally damaged in some way. (Hence brilliantly making the audience for *The Wall* pretty much every human being on the planet.) But with the movie due for release in July 1982, a promotional single was needed. Waters wanted to use this song. Gilmour did not. Waters prevailed.

To be fair, **WHEN THE TIGERS BROKE FREE** is deeply moving, with the beautiful, solemn tones of the Pontarddulais Male Voice Choir conveying the

---

* Mark Blake, *Pigs Might Fly*, p.295 – though Blake (like most rock journalists) lazily does not provide a citation. Did he interview Gilmour, or quote him from an interview done elsewhere? But searching the online databases of Pink Floyd interviews comes up blank.

† Waters: 'As anybody in any pop group knows, you live or die by material.' *Uncut* magazine, June 2004. But as a writer, Waters is naturally inclined to emphasise the importance of the role.

‡ Mason recounts, 'A journalist friend (friend no more) had weaselled out of Bob – and published – a full description of the show, including the exclusive revelation of the tumbling wall as the grand finale ... From being one of the inner circle he was suddenly out in the cold. It was made clear to him that he would not even be welcome at the shows. I think now that we just had no idea of how terrifying our combined disapproval could be.' (*Inside Out*, p.265).

§ Lennon and McCartney overlapped greatly, as did Jagger and Richards, but Waters and Gilmour added so much to what the other brought to the table. Perhaps the nearest comparison is Morrissey and Johnny Marr.

social unity Waters saw as increasingly under attack in Thatcher's Britain.[¶] In lieu of Ezrin, Michael Kamen[**] meanwhile provides some understated orchestration. But it's essentially a Waters solo track, about Waters' life and especially Waters' father, and Gilmour is entirely absent from the track, whether at his own choosing or not. As the use of the male voice choir suggests, Waters was highly aware of the connotations of orchestration, and here for the first time he attempts to step out from the shadows and declare himself Pink Floyd. (Though he would do something similar on *Pink Floyd: The Wall*, subtitling it *By Roger Waters*. Never mind Alan Parker, or Gerald Scarfe, or Bob Ezrin, or the band who helped him piece his demos together.)

Unfortunately for Waters, **WHEN THE TIGERS BROKE FREE** is essentially rather slight,[††] with two quietly sung verses and a rousing conclusion (in Waters' patented style) that is brilliantly sung. The orchestration is, however, deeply moving, with its mournful sepia tones and uplifting brass, while the male voice choir conveys the dignity of the common man as beautifully as ever conveyed in song. But more significantly, **WHEN THE TIGERS BROKE FREE** represents the fracturing of the group's unity, as Waters moved to take sole control of its entire output.

THE POST WAR DREAM (Waters)
Length: 3.02
Vocals: Waters **Guitars**: Gilmour **Bass**: Waters **Harmonium**: Michael Kamen
Drums: Mason
Recorded: July–December 1982
Producer: Waters, Michael Kamen, James Guthrie[‡‡]
First released: 21 March 1983 (*The Final Cut* track 1)
Rating: 6/10

The early 1980s feel very far away now,[§§] but they were a time of great political strife, with the Cold War at one of its hottest periods following the Soviet invasion of Afghanistan in 1979, and the splintering of the post-war consensus in the UK, with Margaret Thatcher's monetarist economics rejecting the maintenance of full employment in favour of fighting inflation, and Tony Benn at the peak of his influence in the Labour party.[¶¶] The UK seemed to be in terminal decline: following the humiliations of the IMF loan of 1976 and the Winter of

---

[¶] It's probably no accident that the socialist and rhetorical tradition of south Wales would come under attack in the UK through the person of Neil Kinnock ('the Welsh windbag') from 1983 onwards.
[**] Perhaps best known for his 1999 *S&M* collaboration with Metallica.
[††] It scraped into the UK charts at #39. But it would be included on the *Echoes* compilation.
[‡‡] Gilmour was removed from a production role after constant disagreements with Waters, though he was still paid production royalties. He is a canny lad, or a ruthless bastard, depending on your perspective.
[§§] That period is probably still best captured in *The Secret Diary of Adrian Mole* (1982), but films like *Scum* (1979) also make clear the loss of belief in British institutions at the time. You can feel this disillusion in post-punk albums like *Metal Box* by Public Image Ltd, *Unknown Pleasures* by Joy Division, or *Entertainment!* by Gang Of Four: the sense of a world coming to an end without something to replace it.
[¶¶] *Labour: The Wilderness Years* (1995) is a fine TV documentary on this period of Labour history.

Discontent in 1978–79, under Thatcher unemployment soared, passing 2 million in 1980 and 3 million by 1982; interest rates peaked at 17 per cent; and riots broke out in 1981, most famously in London and Liverpool, but also in Bristol, Manchester and Leeds.

Such was the hour that the Argentinian junta under Leopoldo Galtieri decided to invade the Falkland Islands, a British imperial relic home to around 3,000 inhabitants of mainly British descent, located about 300 miles east of Argentina's southern coast. With Galtieri's economic policies deeply unpopular (GDP shrank 5.2 per cent in 1981 and by 0.7 per cent in 1982),[*] a military win against what seemed to be a terminally declining nation would surely have bolstered support for his rule. Yet the Falklands invasion galvanised the UK politically, with Labour leader Michael Foot[†] aligning his party with the government, and a task force departing the UK in May 1982. Despite the campaign being thought unlikely to deliver victory so far from home, the UK prevailed, with the Argentinian garrison surrendering on 14 June. Victory, after so many imperial retreats and economic failures, was savoured with something like desperate joy, with Thatcher declaring it the rejuvenation of the UK.

Not everyone, of course, agreed. Waters saw it as plain war-mongering, a leader sacrificing men for her own electoral prospects. Likewise, he saw Thatcher's repudiation of the post-war settlement[‡] as despicably callous.[§] Duly inspired, he revised the concept of *Spare Bricks* to become a full anti-war, anti-Thatcher concept album, although Gilmour was dissatisfied with the album's artistic direction. Yet with Waters delivering the material and driving the agenda, all Gilmour could do was acquiesce or leave. Gilmour was thus removed as producer and his work is largely noticeable by its absence in *The Final Cut*, bar a few solos and the blistering guitar and vocals on **NOT NOW JOHN**. Meanwhile, Waters now completely dictated the band's direction[¶] and was able to turn the album into an exploration of the state of the nation as well as an exploration of the psychology and effects of war. (*The Final Cut* is often presented as being highly didactic in its opposition to war, but there's so much more to it than that.) But with the key themes of *The Final Cut* being Waters' outrage at passing geopolitical moments, it is very much an album of its time, and by the 1983 general election (which the Conservatives won in a landslide) just two months later, it already seemed rather outdated, like Michael Foot's donkey jacket.

THE POST WAR DREAM demonstrates all of this in miniature. There is no guitar solo; Waters relies on the soft verse/loud chorus dynamic the band had

---

[*] http://data.worldbank.org/indicator/NY.GDP.MKTP.KD.ZG?locations=AR

[†] A CND member, Foot was easy to portray as weak on defense and the perceived Soviet threat. But he had cut his teeth as an anti-fascist journalist during the Second World War, and opposing Galtieri was a way for him to resume this. See *Michael Foot* by Mervyn Jones (1993).

[‡] The post-war settlement had delivered full employment, healthcare paid for by taxation, nationalised industries, subsidised housing, free education to 15 and an expanding university sector.

[§] '[W]e experienced the beginning of the Welfare State in 1946. The government introduced all that new legislation. At the point where I wrote *The Final Cut*, I'd seen all that chiselled away, and I'd seen a return to an almost Dickensian view of society under Margaret Thatcher.' *Uncut* magazine, June 2004.

[¶] 'I had complete control of *The Final Cut*.' (*Mojo* magazine, 1999).

been playing with since **CYMBALINE**; the lyrics veer from crude caricature to poetic exploration of the British political context; the sound effects are superlative; the vocals range from hushed insidious malevolence to bombastic outrage; and the pace is lumbering. Opening with the sound of traffic and a car radio searching the stations and receiving news stories about the drug trade and the Cold War, it's skilfully evocative of the average person subject to political forces outside their control. Waters' voice when it comes in, however, utilises a sort of speak-singing that emphasises clarity of expression over all other considerations, even musicality. The opening (which, with no chorus, seems more like a spoken-word poem) sets up several recurring themes: the death of Waters' father ('*Was it for this that Daddy died?*'); the working classes sedated by entertainment ('*Did I watch too much TV?*'); resentment at the relative economic decline of the UK, expressed in an ironic racism that Waters seems to associate with blue-collar workers** ('*If it wasn't for the Nips / Being so good at building ships / The yards would still be open on the Clyde*'); and mourning for the post-war settlement ('*Maggie, what have we done? / What have we done to England?*'). The music shifts from yet another sepia-toned opening (harking back to **VERA** and **WHEN THE TIGERS BROKE FREE**) that lasts for over two minutes to a brief bombastic section that wants to be rousing and passionate but doesn't quite achieve it, before fading away to those sepia tones again.

All of these are fine in themselves, but if *The Wall* was stronger on the message than the music, in **THE POST WAR DREAM** the message is paramount. With Wright gone, the absence of the colours and textures so associated with Pink Floyd give Waters a blank slate on which to fulminate. Yet that starkness also diminishes the group lyrically, which now feel blunt and finger-wagging, while emotionally Waters veers from wistfulness to lumbering aggression and back. It's all very reductive, Pink Floyd boiled down to its barest of essentials. Waters may have felt that necessary to complement his lyrics, but others may regret the loss of the warmth and humanity of earlier albums.

YOUR POSSIBLE PASTS (Waters)
Length: 4.22
Vocals: Waters **Guitars**: Gilmour, Waters **Bass**: Waters **Electric piano**: Michael Kamen
Hammond organ: Andy Brown **Drums**: Mason
Recorded: July–December 1982
Producer: Waters, Michael Kamen, James Guthrie
First released: 21 March 1983 (*The Final Cut* track 2)
Rating: 6/10

YOUR POSSIBLE PASTS likewise demonstrates the trouble with *The Final Cut*: the lyrics are exceptionally good, there's a decent melody, but the

---
** See **NOT NOW JOHN**.

instrumentation is deliberately muted and the production is hammer-over-the-head unsubtle. Painting from a limited palette is not necessarily a bad thing, but throughout *The Final Cut* the songs feel diminished, overly reliant on Waters' lyrics and vocals and with very large Gilmour- and Wright-shaped absences, rather than intentionally spare and elemental. In any case, **YOUR POSSIBLE PASTS** has a more wide-ranging melody than most tracks on the album, with its sparse acoustic verses comprising rhyming couplets rising to the end of the first line then falling at the end of the second. These are enlivened by thunderous snare shots in the first two verses, after the third and fifth lines respectively. The chorus, meanwhile, follows each verse and its thunderous sound and aggressive, gritty guitar is a very obvious relation to the chorus in **WAITING FOR THE WORMS**. But here the lyric projects a straightforward wish for connection: ('*Do you remember me? / How we used to be? / Do you think we should be closer?*' Which might be Waters speaking openly and plaintively, but it's also the message of *The Wall* delivered without imagery, metaphor or incisive wit. As with **THE POST WAR DREAM**, it's Pink Floyd *reductio ad absurdum*.

Similarly, the lyrics rehash themes and images from *The Wall*. Waters repeats his feelings on education ('*By the cold and religious we were taken in hand / Shown how to feel good and told to feel bad*') and use of Holocaust imagery ('*In derelict sidings the poppies entwine / With cattle trucks lying in wait for the next time*'). To be fair, each contains exquisite phrasing, but after the huge development in Waters' writing from *Meddle* to *The Wall*, it's odd to hear him four years after the last album still prey to the same obsessions.

But the main problem with **YOUR POSSIBLE PASTS** is that it repeats the quiet/loud shift used just in the previous song, though it will come up again and again in the album. For a band so previously attuned to dynamics this is a remarkable failure. For years they had played **CAREFUL WITH THAT AXE, EUGENE** and **A SAUCERFUL OF SECRETS** and **ECHOES** live, expertly and with huge patience navigating their way through beautiful shifts in tone and atmosphere. Here, Waters seems either deaf to it, or bereft of alternate ideas. Neither view is encouraging. Two decades later, he agreed that he had been too reliant on dynamic shifts in *The Final Cut*, especially **YOUR POSSIBLE PASTS**.* Maybe he'll get around to re-recording it sometime. There's a good song in there somewhere.

---

* 'I would veer away from the over-dramatic use of the drum kit. Some of it I find difficult to listen to. A specific example is "Your Possible Pasts", which is this quite melodic thing and then the drums come in really loud, and I find that slightly irritating now. I'd probably put in some kind of rhythm section that carries you through the song more smoothly. [The sudden outbursts], they'd be toned down. I'd bring the verses up and take the choruses down to the point where you could listen to the song from beginning to end without leaping out of the chair.' *Uncut* magazine, June 2004.

ONE OF THE FEW (Waters)
Length: 1.23
Vocals: Waters **Acoustic Guitars**: Waters **Bass**: Waters **Synthesiser**: Waters
Recorded: July-December 1982
Producer: Waters, Michael Kamen, James Guthrie
First released: 21 March 1983 (*The Final Cut* track 3)
Rating: 7/10

The Final Cut leans into dynamic shifts far too much, but the album does at least contain a satisfying blend of fully fleshed-out and shorter, more tantalising interstitials. Hence, **ONE OF THE FEW** is gripping: a haunting piece expressing the guilt of the survivors of war and reflecting where that trauma subsequently went. Waters' hushed voice, which gets a bit monotonous by **SOUTHAMPTON DOCK**, is here deeply chilling: insidious, tormented, and haunted. The similarly muted acoustic guitar-backing (several times playing a four-note motif reminiscent of 'Syd's Theme' in **SHINE ON YOU CRAZY DIAMOND**) and synthesiser atmosphere are meanwhile vividly foreboding, and thanks to the song's brevity don't require any development. Waters' lyrics don't make it clear, but the '*one of the few*' is The Teacher from *The Wall*,† where they '*land on their feet*' by surviving the war but coming back traumatised and perpetuating a cycle of abuse. This is made clear in the final lines, '*Make 'em laugh, make 'em cry, make 'em lay down and die*'. Though **ONE OF THE FEW** is (quite deliberately) shadowy and musically insubstantial, the depth of Waters' ideas, his sustained world-view, and the song's fine execution make it superbly uneasy listening, and for the first time expands on the ideas from *The Wall* rather than repeating them. There's far more to *The Final Cut* than meets the eye, though it takes a certain stubborn patience to unfold.

THE HERO'S RETURN (Waters)
Length: 2.56
Vocals: Waters **Guitars**: Gilmour, Waters **Bass**: Waters **Synthesiser**: Waters
Electric piano: Andy Brown **Drums**: Mason **Percussion**: Mason
Recorded: July-December 1982
Producer: Waters, Michael Kamen, James Guthrie
First released: 21 March 1983 (*The Final Cut* track 4)
Rating: 6/10

Originally demoed for *The Wall* as 'Teacher, Teacher', **THE HERO'S RETURN** not surprisingly sounds the most like a retread from the previous album on *The Final Cut*. Gilmour's guitar is notably more active than in most songs, there's a chugging rhythm during the refrain that suggests **RUN LIKE HELL**, and

---

† 'We learn a bit more of his past history … So many of the teachers at the Cambridgeshire School for Boys, the school I went to, had gone into teaching after the war. They couldn't think of anything else to do.' Waters in *Uncut* magazine, June 2004.

also the persistent (even dogged) use of dynamic shifts in volume and intensity. As was originally intended, **THE HERO'S RETURN** adds more backstory to the Teacher character first seen in *The Wall*, as with **ONE OF THE FEW** and **PARANOID EYES**. But while those songs add something new to the character, **THE HERO'S RETURN** repeats the trope of the Teacher repeating the cycle of violence by oppressing his pupils, as heard in **THE HAPPIEST DAYS OF OUR LIVES** (and suggested in **ONE OF THE FEW**): '*Trying to clout these little ingrates into shape … / Though they'll never fathom it behind my sarcasm / Desperate memories lie*'. Post-traumatic stress disorder wasn't even codified as a condition until 1978 and only became an official American psychiatric diagnosis in 1980,[*] making Waters' lyric extremely acute psychologically. But intellectual sensitivity does not a good song make. **THE HERO'S RETURN** feels like a re-tread, lacking the vitriol of *The Wall*, and repeating a character when Waters could have, for example, considered a traumatised child or a conscientious objector.

Which is a shame, because melodically **THE HERO'S RETURN** is better than most tracks on *The Final Cut*, with a more active Gilmour guitar (with an opening solo that lays out the song's melody) and an excellent descending chord sequence at the start of the refrain ('*And even now part of me flies / Over Dresden at Angels One Five*')[†] that takes the song emotionally from angry bitterness to resigned anguish. Yet there's also something predictable about the shifts in tone and energy (the drum beats at 1.22 that signal the sudden near-silence except for a whispered Waters vocal, the resurgence at 1.56, and another drop-out at 2.09) – it's a technique that Waters uses almost obsessively on this album, but there's the sense here that the high energy sections are there only to be undercut. They don't feel genuine. Pink Floyd rarely feel contrived or insincere, but there's a flavour of that in **THE HERO'S RETURN**, a very obvious artifice that makes the song less compelling than it ought to be.

THE GUNNER'S DREAM (Waters)
Length: 5.07
Vocals: Waters **Guitars**: Gilmour **Bass**: Waters **Electric piano**: Michael Kamen
Piano: Andy Brown **Drums**: Mason **Saxophone**: Raphael Ravenscroft
Orchestra: National Philharmonic
Recorded: July–December 1982
Producer: Waters, Michael Kamen, James Guthrie
First released: 21 March 1983 (*The Final Cut* track 5)
Rating: 6/10

---

[*] Although the film *First Blood* (1982), starring Sylvester Stallone, is clearly about a Vietnam veteran with PTSD, and was adapted from a novel published in 1972.

[†] 'Angels One Five' is RAF radio code for altitude fifteen thousand feet. There was a 1952 film titled *Angels One Five* starring Jack Hawkins, about the Battle of Britain. Given Waters' vocal enjoyment of *The Dam Busters* (1955) and his use of it in *The Wall* movie, it's fair to assume he took this piece of jargon from the earlier film.

Another exemplary sound effect opens **THE GUNNER'S DREAM**,‡ the rushing air suggesting someone flying at high speed or falling from great altitude. Both are possible in this song, which has the brilliant conceit of a gunner who has ejected from his fighter plane and is falling to his death, but who '*in the space between the heavens / And the corner of some foreign field*' has a dream of a better world. Lyrically **THE GUNNER'S DREAM** is magnificent, with numerous bullseyes: '*foreign field*' obviously refers to the Rupert Brooke poem 'The Soldier',§ where '*If I should die, think only this of me: / That there's some corner of a foreign field / That is for ever England.*' The section where the gunner imagines his funeral is even more emotive, with fantastic phrases such as '*And the silver in her hair shines in the cold November air*' and '*the tear drops rise to meet the comfort of the band*'. Philip Larkin might well envy those lines. The second stanza concerns the gunner's dream and, like all dreams, might easily have been silly put down in words, hence Waters couching them often in negatives: '*no one ever disappears / You never hear their standard issue kicking in your door*' and '*No one kills the children anymore*'. But it's actually, of course, the post-war settlement that the gunner is dreaming of, where there's '*A place to stay / Enough to eat*' – and thus implicitly condemning Thatcher for her opposition to this progressive social order. The loud section lasts just three lines, with Waters raging that '*Night after night / Going round and round my brain / His dream is driving me insane*' – and screaming in the background as though to prove it.

All of which sounds marvellous, until you actually hear **THE GUNNER'S DREAM**, and realise that it's yet another sparsely instrumented mid-tempo track dominated by Waters' voice and lyric, with a brief but lumbering loud section for contrast, with no guitar work worth mentioning and certainly no guitar solo. If you view *The Final Cut* as poetic pieces with slight musical backgrounds you could well find **THE GUNNER'S DREAM** enthralling, for its narrative skill and imagery are as good as anything Bruce Springsteen or Joni Mitchell or Paul Simon could come up with. But if you seek entertainment from music, **THE GUNNER'S DREAM** might be somewhat trying. Here Waters seems almost deliberately to be reducing the auditory pleasure of the tracks, with only the saxophone solo affording any real melody,¶ lest that diminish the significance of his message. This can work – Springsteen's *Nebraska* (1982) is a hugely downbeat and musically minimalist album, yet it captivates because of the unity of vision and method, and his heartfelt empathy for his characters. But Waters isn't as skilled a tunesmith as Springsteen, nor as accomplished with melodies as Gilmour. His gifts for vision, message, lyrics and atmosphere are probably

---

‡ The title is probably a slight joke. Waters supports Arsenal Football Club, whose nickname is the Gunners. Fans are also referred to as Gunners, thus making Waters a gunner and the song largely about his own dream.
§ First published in 1915 in his book *1914 and Other Poems*.
¶ Performed by Raphael Ravenscroft, best known for the stellar saxophone riff on Gerry Rafferty's 'Baker Street'. He would also play on Waters' *The Pros And Cons of Hitchhiking*, and died in 2014.

the greatest in rock music but they need packaging into the rock format, whose elementary pleasures Waters seems to feel are beneath him. Turning the guitars and drums to eleven for half a verse isn't enough to make a song enjoyable to listen to, no matter how skilfully articulate or politically resonant it may be.

PARANOID EYES (Waters)
Length: 3.40
Vocals: Waters **Guitars**: Gilmour, Waters **Bass**: Waters **Organ**: Andy Brown
Drums: Mason **Percussion**: Ray Cooper **Orchestra**: National Philharmonic
Recorded: July–December 1982
Producer: Waters, Michael Kamen, James Guthrie
First released: 21 March 1983 (*The Final Cut* track 6)
Rating: 6/10

Like **SOUTHAMPTON DOCK** a few tracks later on, **PARANOID EYES** is more of a poem than a song. Its three stanzas trace the war trauma of a surviving soldier,[*] from having to don '*a bulletproof mask*' to control his emotional damage, to '*Laughing too loud at the rest of the world / With the boys in the crowd*', before ending '*lost in a haze of alcohol, soft middle age*'. Sung with huge empathy by Waters, the musical background is, however, subtle to the point of barely existing. It's remarkable to think that the same writer composed songs of incredible colour and texture like **ECLIPSE** and **WELCOME TO THE MACHINE** – though, of course, both songs owe an enormous debt to Wright.

PARANOID EYES opens[†] with some delicately fluttering piano in the background, Waters' voice comes in front and centre at 0.13, singing in a measured, half-speaking voice that's still highly emotional and compassionate. There's also some melancholy brass, reminiscent of **NOBODY HOME**, more assertive piano chords (recorded with great echo to suggest the isolation of war survivor), and some very dark-shaded orchestration by Michael Kamen, sounding like it consists primarily of cellos and double bass. All of this is timed to complement Waters' lyrics; for instance, the piano chords coming before and after Waters' lines in the chorus. Between the second and third verses there is something of a musical interlude, with some strummed guitar, piano and organ briefly giving a more upbeat feeling, perhaps suggesting the emotional release of being at the bar with friends – before scything this down by portraying a man needing alcohol to function, hiding '*behind / Brown and mild eyes*' – referencing types of beer. It's very artful, but sympathetic and even tender.

PARANOID EYES is emblematic of people's misapprehension of *The Final Cut*, in that the album's reputation is as an anti-war diatribe, when Waters is more often a humanist demonstrating great empathy with the traumatised and the damaged. **PARANOID EYES** is hence a very fine piece of writing, and an

---

[*] As with **ONE OF THE FEW**, he is The Teacher from *The Wall*.
[†] It's sort of reminiscent of the opening of 'Spread Your Wings' by Queen (from *News Of The World*, 1977).

effective production. Unfortunately, with so little music to it, it doesn't really convince as a Pink Floyd song.

GET YOUR FILTHY HANDS OFF MY DESERT (Waters)
Length: 1.19
Vocals: Waters **Guitars**: Waters **Orchestra**: National Philharmonic
Recorded: July–December 1982
Producer: Waters, Michael Kamen, James Guthrie
First released: 21 March 1983 (*The Final Cut* track 7)
Rating: 6/10

The Final Cut works better when dealing with emotions (as on **ONE OF THE FEW** and **PARANOID EYES**), but geopolitics is a tougher subject to translate effectively to the listener. Either you agree with Waters' perspective, in which case the song doesn't really matter, or you disagree, in which case you'll dislike the song anyway, or the subject leaves you cold, leaving you indifferent to the song (assuming lyrics are important to you). Consequently, **GET YOUR FILTHY HANDS OFF MY DESERT** is more of a time capsule, a reminder of the fraught state of the world in the early 1980s, rather than a piece of music with the power to move or excite.

It begins with probably the most effective sound effect[‡] of the group's career, with the roar of a rocket (or jet plane?) panning from left to right, then an explosion. An ironically jaunty melody on orchestral strings then emerges, following which Waters lays on some invective on world leaders playing at wars for selfish purposes:

> *Brezhnev took Afghanistan*
> *Begin*[§] *took Beirut*
> *Galtieri*[¶] *took the Union Jack.*
> *And Maggie, over lunch one day*
> *Took a cruiser with all hands*
> *Apparently, to make him give it back.*

Over just six lines, Waters enunciates the lyrics with masterful control, with insidious malevolence in the first two lines (and a very deliberate enunciation of the '*t*' in '*Beirut*'), a sudden sarcastic soar at '*Union Jack*', and then a saddened

---

[‡] Worked on by Mason, using a technology called holophonic sound, as created by inventor Hugo Zuccarelli (who is Argentinean, rather than Italian as Mason says). 'We immediately decided to use the system for all the sound effects on the album, and I was volunteered ... to various locations to capture the sound of church bells or footsteps'. He rather sadly adds, 'It was a pity that before I'd even started work on *The Final Cut*, Roger felt it necessary to announce aggressively that since whatever I did 'was drumming', I couldn't claim either extra royalties or credit for any of this work.' (Mason, *Inside Out*, p.271).

[§] Menachem Begin, Israeli Prime Minister 1977–1983. Israel invaded Lebanon (capital: Beirut) on 6 June 1982, following the attempted assassination of the Israeli ambassador to the United Kingdom, three days earlier in London.

[¶] Leopoldo Galtieri, the Argentinean military dictator (1981-1982).

descent thereafter, to a basso-profundo '*give it back*'. There's not much there musically, but it's all just a backdrop for Waters' Important Thing to Say.

The '*cruiser with all hands*' reference is to the British sinking of the *Belgrano* warship during the Falklands War when outside the Maritime Exclusion Zone,* with the loss of '*all hands*' (323 men). This was highly controversial, the two sides of the debate perhaps exemplified by *The Sun* newspaper exulting 'GOTCHA!' while Prime Minister Margaret Thatcher was famously challenged on it by schoolteacher Diana Gould live on BBC TV. Waters obviously disapproved, with the sardonic image of Thatcher at lunch reinforcing the idea of political self-indulgence.

As with **ONE OF THE FEW**, the brevity of **GET YOUR FILTHY HANDS OFF MY DESERT** adds to the sense of variety in *The Final Cut*. Yet although it's essentially a minor piece and notable only for his name-checking the world leaders on his shit list, the song had perhaps the greatest political effect of the group's career, leading to a ban on being played publicly in the USSR from 1985 for 'distortion of Soviet foreign policy ("Soviet aggression in Afghanistan")'.† The group had never played the USSR‡ so this was of no great consequence,§ but it probably tickled Waters and gave him a sense of vindication.

The Final Cut is generally thought of as being very specifically about Waters' father and the Falklands War, but the major songs on it, such as **PARANOID EYES**, **THE HERO'S RETURN** and **THE FINAL CUT**, are far more concerned with war-trauma and cycles of violence. Songs like this however aid the impression of *The Final Cut* being a highly specific (and thus now very dated) protest, rather than speaking about the human condition as Waters had long sought to do. But given the repeated references to Thatcher and the dedication to his father on the album sleeve, you can understand how that impression was formed. It might be misleading, but since *The Final Cut* requires patience, a generosity regarding the sparse melodies, the desire to parse the lyrics, and an understanding of Waters' thematic preoccupations, it generally asks too much of the audience.

---

* The UK having declared a 200 nautical mile exclusion zone around the Falklands, inside of which any Argentinean ship might be attacked, on 12 April 1982.

† Alexei Yurchak, *Everything Was Forever, Until It Was No More*, p.215. Other groups similarly banned perhaps predictably include bands like Black Sabbath, Judas Priest and Iron Maiden, but also Madness (for 'punk' and 'violence'), Julio Iglesias (for 'neo-fascism'), and The Village People (for 'violence'!).

‡ Though they did have a following in the USSR. Yurchak notes that in 1980 the magazine *Krugozor* released 'two "flexi-discs" with the songs "Time," "On the Run," and "Money"' and next year 'released two songs, 'Another Brick in the Wall Part 1' and 'The Trial'. All these songs could be described as perfectly antibourgeois, which made them appropriate for the release.' Though a very wealthy man, Waters would probably accept the 'antibourgeois' designation quite happily.

§ The Gilmour-led band would play five concerts in Moscow in June 1989, following the *glasnost* ('openness') policy initiated by Mikhail Gorbachev. At the time, Soviet roubles were untradeable, so the band were offered payment in barter: 'wood, oil, black caviar … [David Gilmour] shrugged it off and said that they'd perform for free if the expenses for their hotel stay and the transport of their gear from Athens to Moscow and then to Finland were covered. Soviet promoters were ecstatic!' (Alexander Zheleznov, *Pink Floyd – Olimpiyskiy, Moscow, 1989*, www.brain-damage.co.uk/concerts/pink-floyd-olimpiyskiy-moscow-1989.html). Gilmour's take on the story doesn't contradict it: 'When we played there in 1989, the Russian government did provide us with a huge transporter plane to take our equipment from Athens, and they gave us hotel rooms and suchlike. But they could only offer us a small fee in dollars, so there was discussion of them paying in caviar and so on. We were joking! We lost money, that's all. We paid for the event. We thought if we were going to play in Russia, we would rather do it properly.' (*Mojo* magazine, July 1995).

THE FLETCHER MEMORIAL HOME (Waters)
Length: 4.11
Vocals: Waters **Guitars**: Gilmour **Bass**: Waters **Piano**: Michael Kamen **Drums**: Mason
Orchestra: National Philharmonic
Recorded: July–December 1982
Producer: Waters, Michael Kamen, James Guthrie
First released: 21 March 1983 (*The Final Cut* track 8)
Rating: 7/10

The only song from *The Final Cut* to make the *Echoes* compilation, **THE FLETCHER MEMORIAL HOME** is easily one of the album's more melodic tracks, though intensely melancholy, even mournful. Boasting highly impassioned vocals by Waters and a very good (if not especially original) Gilmour guitar solo, the song also features some very typical late-Waters-period attributes. There are frequent dynamic shifts, the insidious speaking voice, dramatic sound effects, a reference to Waters' father, an attack on warmongering leaders, and wonderfully literate lyrics with bullseye metaphors. But what lifts **THE FLETCHER MEMORIAL HOME** above most of *The Final Cut* is the strength of its saturnine melody, which rouses Waters to give his finest vocal of the entire album, and the viciousness of the lyric, which is probably the most venomous Waters ever produced for Pink Floyd.

The track begins with Waters unaccompanied. He is at his most desolate, seeming genuinely close to tears as he opens with '*Take all your overgrown infants away somewhere / And build them a home*', and then sounding utterly desperate at '*A little place of their own*'. The next line is, however, double-tracked and rises rousingly, as he sings the title line '*The Fletcher Memorial Home*' before falling into dejection with '*for incurable tyrants and kings*', with delicious emphasis on the first syllable of **ty**-rants. The second verse (following the same melodic line and emphases as the first) explicates the narcissism Waters sees as fundamental to such people: '*And they can appear to themselves everyday / On closed circuit TV / To make sure they're still real / It's the only connection they feel*'. That's an absolute bullseye, considering that reality TV shows like *Big Brother*, where participants are filmed around the clock, only arrived fifteen years later.

Which leaders does Waters consider '*overgrown infants*'? A near spoken-word interlude extends his enemies list from **GET YOUR FILTHY HANDS OFF MY DESERT**: '*Reagan and Haig*[¶] */ Mr Begin and friend / Mrs Thatcher, and Paisley*[**] */ Mr Brezhnev and party*[††] */ The ghost of McCarthy / And the memories of Nixon / And now, adding colour / A group of anonymous Latin American*

[¶]   Al Haig, Secretary of State under Reagan (1981-1982).
[**] The Reverend Ian Paisley, leader of the Democratic Unionist Party in Northern Ireland from 1971 to 2008.
[††] A nice double meaning, suggesting both the immediate group around Brezhnev, and the Communist Party as a whole.

meat-packing glitterati'.* The final verse is where Waters says what would happen in the *'In the Fletcher Memorial / Home for Colonial / Wasters of Life and Limb'*. He leaves it to the final line: *'Now the Final Solution can be applied'*. This call for political murder is simply brutal – justifiably so, perhaps, but still a shocking line to hear on a mainstream rock album,† and maybe especially so from the band who at the time of *Dark Side* had been so humane and empathetic.

Musically, however, **THE FLETCHER MEMORIAL HOME** isn't quite as memorable. Gilmour's guitar solo from 2.14 hits all the right notes, as it were, with soaring passages, contrasting grungy mid-range snarls, and a typically adept use of space. It just doesn't take flight, sounding overly similar to the guitar solos he had been delivering since **TIME** ten years earlier: Gilmour by numbers. Nor does its high emotion feel particularly suited to this song, which slyly lures the listener in with its air of defeat. But as with **SOUTHAMPTON DOCK** and others on *The Final Cut*, it barely matters. This is a song with a message, to be studied and contemplated, not a rock track to get the spirits moving. It may well be 'the apotheosis of art rock', as the *Rolling Stone* reviewer described it at the time of release, but the emphasis is too strongly on the art.

THE FLETCHER MEMORIAL HOME is nonetheless one of the most arresting tracks on *The Final Cut*, chilling in its demand for lethal restitution, but clear-eyed about the atrocities inflicted by world leaders.‡ It's all the more effective for emotiveness of the music and the way in which Waters so artfully leads up to his demand for execution. It's really quite surprising that so little attention has been paid to this track.§ Rock music had come a long way from *A-wop-bop-a-loo-bop*.

SOUTHAMPTON DOCK (Waters)
Length: 2.13
Vocals: Waters **Guitars**: Waters **Bass**: Waters **Piano**: Michael Kamen
Orchestra: National Philharmonic
Recorded: July–December 1982
Producer: Waters, Michael Kamen, James Guthrie
First released: 21 March 1983 (*The Final Cut* track 9)
Rating: 6/10

---

* A reference to Argentina's meat production industrialists, and to the murder of countless left-wing activists under a period of state terrorism known as the Dirty War (1974-1983).

† Morrissey was questioned by Special Branch (a counter-terrorist police unit) for his song 'Margaret On The Guillotine' (from *Viva Hate*, 1988), which also called for the execution of Thatcher.

‡ The Argentinean Dirty War and similar efforts across South America were backed by the United States. See *Predatory States: Operation Condor and Covert War in Latin America* by J. Patrice McSherry (2005). The US released declassified documents in 1999, making clear its involvement. The U2 song 'Mothers Of The Disappeared' (from *The Joshua Tree*, 1987) also addresses this topic.

§ Given his reputation for smooth diplomacy, it's perhaps also surprising that Gilmour approved of its message, but he voted for its inclusion on the *Echoes* compilation, and declared it 'a great song' in 2001 (*Mojo* magazine, October 2001).

SOUTHAMPTON DOCK is like **PARANOID EYES**: essentially a spoken-word poem rather than a song, its acoustic backing serving as a rhythmic pulse until the final verse when a slight stir of orchestral strings and spare piano chords give it a melancholic sepia tone. As a poem it's touching and heartfelt, but also highly competent, with three six-line stanzas with an AABCCB rhyme scheme, utilising assonance in the AA and CC rhymes (*five/smiled, cenotaph/heart*), their half-rhymes perhaps to reflect the unease of those arriving back or heading out to war from Southampton. The changing perspective in each verse is handled superbly, with the Second World War survivors in the first stanza feeling how '*There were too many spaces in the line*', while in the second a woman (perhaps a soldier's mother) '*bravely waves the boys / Goodbye again*',¶ and in the third there's a bitter resolution, as '*the dark stain spreads between their shoulder blade*s', as Waters suggests soldiers are stabbed in the back by their political leaders. Waters' vocal is meanwhile more subdued than the comparable **GET YOUR FILTHY HANDS OFF MY DESERT**, skilfully conveying some light and shade, but with only a sliver of a melody.

Equally, there's very little music to **SOUTHAMPTON DOCK**, with the barest acoustic and bass guitar accompaniment for two verses (the final two lines with a manic backing vocal by Waters subtly low in the mix), and then a sad hummed interlude. Then from 1.23 some stark piano chords come in, with some sad minor key orchestration barely registering, for the last forty seconds or so. That's all there is. As a poem or spoken-word piece it's superb. As a song it barely registers until you read and re-read the lyrics and take in the significance of Southampton Dock as a departing harbour for British soldiers in the Falklands War. But if you have to study a piece of rock music to enjoy it, it's not really succeeding. Rock music should be immediate, gripping, exciting, moving, able to instantly convey emotion. By the time of *The Final Cut,* such basic pleasures feel as though they are beneath Waters' creative impulses. Which is fine, but in so doing he was dismissing the audience the group had worked so hard to assemble. They had come to see the show, but Waters was no longer interested in being a showman.

In some ways *The Final Cut* feels like Waters' attempt to reproduce John Lennon's *John Lennon/Plastic Ono Band*, a bare-bones scream of an album. But Lennon's songs, though as self-disgusted and embittered as anything by Waters, remain hugely melodic. His vocal on 'Working Class Hero' is superb, there's a gorgeous melody in the stark 'Isolation', and 'Well Well Well' has screams and a fuzzy riff that would make Kurt Cobain proud. **SOUTHAMPTON DOCK** is closer to Leonard Cohen** than John Lennon, but at the cost of dispensing with the musical richness that for many make Pink Floyd what they are.

¶ Although the self-referencing with the mention of her 'quiet desperation' is a bit cheap. See **TIME** (obviously).

** Waters is a big Leonard Cohen fan, choosing his 'Bird on the Wire' for one of his Desert Island Discs in May 2011. See www.bbc.co.uk/sounds/play/b011j39v.

THE FINAL CUT (Waters)
Length: 4.46
Vocals: Waters **Guitars**: Gilmour **Bass**: Waters **Piano**: Michael Kamen
Harmonium: Michael Kamen **Drums**: Mason **Orchestra**: National Philharmonic
Recorded: July–December 1982
Producer: Waters, Michael Kamen, James Guthrie
First released: 21 March 1983 (*The Final Cut* track 10)
Rating: 5/10

The album's title track wants to be the big set piece, with its stirring orchestral chart by Michael Kamen, its big transitions between quiet verses and rousing loud choruses, its brave psychologically penetrating lyrics, its enormously heartfelt vocals, its expert musique concrete effects, and an excellent Gilmour guitar solo. All the ingredients are there. But it feels so forced and so formulaic that **THE FINAL CUT** never takes off as a song. The dynamic shift has been flogged to death throughout the album, the orchestral section is a very obvious inferior knock-off of that from **COMFORTABLY NUMB**, the guitar solo comes out of nowhere since there's no riff and while emotive enough (Gilmour ever the professional) feels somewhat out of place in a piano-led track, the lyrics might be acutely psychoanalytical but seem to be Waters discussing his own head space and thus seem solipsistic, the effects are plainly to disguise the lack of melody in the verses, and Waters' vocals, while clearly impassioned, are bludgeoning and unsubtle, moving from delicate quivering emotiveness to would-be anthemic with the predictability of Coldplay or U2. This formula has been played out in **THE POST WAR DREAM** and **YOUR POSSIBLE PASTS** and **THE GUNNER'S DREAM** already; to replay it for a fourth time is lunacy. In *The Wall*, songs could shift from quiet to loud because of the imaginativeness of the soundworld – as with **THE THIN ICE** or **ONE OF MY TURNS** or **HEY YOU** or even **COMFORTABLY NUMB** – but there's none of that here: just Waters yet again emoting his exquisite lyrics with a hushed musical background then a bludgeoning rock section for a brain-dead contrast. It lacks creativity, imagination, subtlety, and musicianship: in other words, everything that made Pink Floyd such a staggeringly great band.

    Waters may have at last had complete control in *The Final Cut*, but by reducing his bandmates to sessionmen or outcasts, his own limitations as a composer come into brutal relief. It turns out he did need them to '*be closer*'. '*Together they stand, divided they fall.*' The ironies abound. He reflected on this later, noting that 'I was in a pretty sorry state when I was making this record. If I made it now, I'd do things differently. There was so much conflict in my professional life. It wasn't easy making a record in the face of all the goings-on between me and Dave particularly.'[*] That fraught mentality no doubt bleeds into *The Final*

---

[*] *Uncut* magazine, June 2004.

Cut, which is so often the sound of Waters trying to do everything by himself and summoning every ounce of pathos into his songs. But without the artistry of Wright and Gilmour to turn these emotions into soundscapes and digestible rock structures, **THE FINAL CUT** and similar songs lack sufficient musical interest – the melodies, the tunes – for most people. Fleshed out, they could be wonderful. But they're so skeletal, they're '*cold as a razorblade … dry as a funeral drum*'.

> **NOT NOW JOHN** (Waters)
> **Length**: 5.01
> **Vocals**: Gilmour, Waters **Guitars**: Gilmour, Waters **Bass**: Waters **Synthesiser**: Waters
> **Hammond organ**: Andy Brown **Drums**: Mason **Backing vocals**: Doreen Chanter, Irene Chanter
> **Recorded**: July–December 1982
> **Producer**: Waters, Michael Kamen, James Guthrie
> **First released**: 21 March 1983 (*The Final Cut* track 11)
> **Rating**: 8/10

At last, some rock 'n' roll. **NOT NOW JOHN** is the most brutal track in the entire Pink Floyd canon, its thumping guitar riff, roaring vocal and elementary pleasures a bludgeoning satire of the lumpen attitudes of the unenlightened working classes and their attachment to consumer gratification. Like **YOUNG LUST** it satirises its own musical style, but where the older song was a raunchy rock number (and a lampooning of the sexist attitudes associated with the genre), **NOT NOW JOHN** is for the most part a lumbering dinosaur perhaps more reminiscent of Rainbow, Saxon or The Scorpions.[†] But there has to be a dynamic, and Waters sets up two within the song: between Gilmour and the backing singers (who mostly sing '*Fuck all that*' and '*Gotta get on*' in an ironically upbeat, pop style[‡] that seems to be deliberately jarring); and between the roaring verses and the more reflective bridges sung by Waters, recasting the melody from **ONE OF THE FEW**. The dialogue between the two parts is extremely effective, with Gilmour seeming to portray a blue-collar yob[§] whose main thoughts (when not '*Fuck all that*') are '*Come at the end of the shift, we'll go and get pissed*' and '*We showed Argentina, now let's go and show these*'.

Waters, meanwhile, sings in his insidious style: '*Make 'em laugh / Make 'em cry / Make 'em dance in the aisles / Make 'em pay / Make 'em stay / Make 'em feel okay*'. Where the Teacher in **ONE OF THE FEW** perpetuated abuse because

---

[†] Leading hard rock bands of the day, they had all played the Monsters of Rock festival at Castle Donington, Leicestershire, in the first two years since its inception in 1980. The festival promoter was Paul Loasby, who now manages Gilmour.
[‡] This was the time when shiny pop music, often with female backing singers, was starting to dominate the charts. 1983 was the year that Spandau Ballet and Duran Duran had their first #1 singles in the UK.
[§] Quite similar to the character portrayed by Dire Straits in 'Money For Nothing' (from *Brothers In Arms*, 1985).

of his own trauma, now Waters sees the working classes as tranquilised through consumerism and shallow pleasures, and thus stuck in their own cycle of self-defeating victimhood. Which might be true, but it sounds patronising coming from a millionaire rock star, especially when he is simultaneously attacking you for your stupidity and your crass desires.

As a satire, **NOT NOW JOHN** lacks any subtlety, thus hearkening back more to **CORPORAL CLEGG** than **YOUNG LUST**. It's a strange song to come after the empathy of **SOUTHAMPTON DOCK**, for instance, with its scathing portrayal of working-class Thatcherites who chose tax cuts over social solidarity.[*] As a song, however, the ferocity of the attack and the dynamic between the verses and bridges are highly effective, giving *The Final Cut* a long overdue shot of adrenaline, and demonstrating that the meaning of a song is less important than its energy, tone and atmosphere. **NOT NOW JOHN** just comes far too late in the album to redress the balance between the profound and the soporific.

TWO SUNS IN THE SUNSET (Waters)
Length: 5.14
Vocals: Waters **Guitars**: Gilmour, Waters **Bass**: Waters **Piano**: Michael Kamen
Hammond organ: Andy Brown **Saxophone**: Raphael Ravenscroft **Drums**: Andy Newmark
Recorded: July–December 1982
Producer: Waters, Michael Kamen, James Guthrie
First released: 21 March 1983 (*The Final Cut* track 12)
Rating: 6/10

The final Pink Floyd song with Waters as a member of the band takes on the largest geopolitical topic possible, nuclear apocalypse. Some mock Waters for his concerned-liberal take on world affairs, but the early 1980s were a time of heightened Cold War tensions, with the Reagan administration discarding détente to directly challenge the Soviet Union through increased military spending and more aggressive rhetoric. In retrospect, this may have contributed to the collapse of the Soviet Union in 1991, but at the time it felt like the two sides were squaring up for a showdown, heedless of any collateral damage. British popular culture of the time records it: the shattering post-apocalypse film *Threads*, the cartoon *When the Wind Blows* by Raymond Biggs,[†] the Greenham Common Protests, 'Two Tribes' by Frankie Goes to Hollywood, and the re-emergence of CND as an anti-nuclear campaign group. It's perhaps only a surprise that Waters left it so long to pronounce on it.

---

[*] The first Budget under Thatcher in June 1979 cut the basic rate of income tax from 33% to 30%, and the top rate from 83% to 60%. This came at the cost of nearly doubling VAT from 8% to 15%, thus making it a highly regressive Budget – shifting more of the tax burden onto those with lower incomes.
[†] Creator of *The Snowman* (1982) animated film.

TWO SUNS IN THE SUNSET, however, isn't one of the great protest songs, lacking a memorable hook, riff or solo. Basically a skeletal acoustic piece with a predictable shift to an aggressive rock style for a would-be rousing climactic section yielding to a wry, shoulder-shrugging fade-out with a disinterested bluesy saxophone solo, the song almost unbelievably utilises the soft/loud dynamic for the fifth song on the same album.‡ The more aggressive section is, of course, just there for contrast. The lyrics are almost predictably excellent, though by this stage of the album it almost doesn't matter: listeners would be swayed by Waters' artfulness with words, or put off by his aversion to melody, far earlier in the proceedings. Nonetheless, as a take on nuclear apocalypse, it's a touching and intelligent portrayal. If only it was a song.

Following the great *Dark Side–Wish You Were Here–Animals–The Wall* streak, *The Final Cut* cannot help but seem minor, despite its lyrical ambitions. It is, however, the group's weakest album since *Atom Heart Mother*, and without the presence of Wright is musically the thinnest they had ever recorded. Following Waters' superbly impassioned vocals for *The Wall*, it is also depressing to hear him recede into hushed strained semi-singing, and Gilmour is largely notable by his absence. Where songs like **DOGS**, **MOTHER**, **COMFORTABLY NUMB** and **HEY YOU** had brilliantly used the opposing qualities of their voices for dramatic purposes, this is almost completely absent in *The Final Cut*, except in **NOT NOW JOHN**, which comes too late in the album to redress the balance. While the lyrics are superlative, the album also feels overly didactic, with a number of songs (such as **THE POST WAR DREAM** and even **NOT NOW JOHN**) expressing only Waters' ever-more urgent takes on modern life. Perhaps he should have remembered that rock music is based on elementary pleasures rather than intellectual edification, which is why **ANOTHER BRICK IN THE WALL PART 2** needed a disco beat. With Waters' increasing emphasis on lyrics and ideas at the expense of musicality, or even listener enjoyment, little wonder that his audience became increasingly selective. In *The Wall*, the balance had clearly tipped but there was still plenty for the casual listener to enjoy, whilst on *The Final Cut*, it is clearly far out of synch. It is hence the least immediately enjoyable album Pink Floyd ever released. Of course, *Animals* and *The Wall* were challenging, with their saturnine epics and screaming psychodramas, but both albums still had enough rousing rhythms and kick-ass riffs throughout for those who might otherwise be turned off. Some still adore *The Final Cut* for its lyrics, emotion, intellectual coherence, and excellent sound world. Fair enough, if that's what does it for you, but such people are a minority.§

---

‡ Nirvana did something similar on *Nevermind* (1991), but they mixed it up with quiet pieces (like 'Polly' and 'Something In The Way') as well as songs that rocked all the way through ('Breed', 'Territorial Pissings').

§ The album has sold 3.5 million copies as of 2023, one-tenth the sales of *The Wall*. (www.metalcastle.net/the-top-10-best-selling-pink-floyd-albums-until-2023/).

Waters subsequently indulged himself to make a movie (or rather four interlinked music videos) promoting *The Final Cut*, featuring **THE GUNNER'S DREAM, THE FINAL CUT, THE FLETCHER MEMORIAL HOME** and **NOT NOW JOHN**, writing the script and inviting his brother-in-law to direct. It is more humourous, as Waters had wished, than *The Wall* movie, and features Waters and no other member of the band. Starring Alex McAvoy, who had played the Teacher in *The Wall*, as a war veteran disturbed by the state of the nation and by his own war trauma, it is a fairly interesting effort that deserves more attention, even if some of it is very obvious score-settling against Alan Parker. Released in July 1983, it was also the last thing Waters did in the group, with him already recording *The Pros and Cons of Hitchhiking* by this time.

SIGNS OF LIFE (Gilmour, Bob Ezrin)
Length: 4.24
Vocals: Mason **Guitars**: Gilmour **Kurzweil synthesiser**: Wright
Synthesisers: Gilmour, Bob Ezrin, Jon Carin **Sound effects**: Bob Ezrin
Recorded: November 1986–March 1987
Producer: Bob Ezrin, Gilmour
First released: 7 September 1987 (*A Momentary Lapse of Reason* track 1)
Rating: 5/10

All things considered, four years is not a long time for a veteran rock group (as Pink Floyd were by 1987) to go between albums. Fleetwood Mac had seen half a decade between *Mirage* (1982) and *Tango in the Night* (1987), whereas there were just three years between the Rolling Stones' *Undercover* (1983) and their 'comeback' album, *Dirty Work* (1986). More recently, bands like Tool and Boards of Canada spend around five years between albums as a matter of course. But for Pink Floyd, the four-year hiatus was the period of the greatest difficulty in each member's professional life. Perhaps with the exception of Mason, they still all bear the scars of that dreadful period.

Following the release of *The Final Cut*, Gilmour made it politely clear that he had had very little to do with the album (while, ever the professional, still declaring it 'very, very good').* He then recorded and released *About Face* while Waters made *The Pros and Cons of Hitchhiking* with Eric Clapton. Both released in 1984, neither album set the charts alight, and Waters once again found himself falling out with a professional colleague when Clapton left the tour early. (You would think a man with a feeling for rhythm and cycles would notice a recurring pattern.) Famously, Waters then announced his departure from the group, calling it a 'spent force'; Gilmour retorted that he would carry

---

* *Sounds* 'Guitar Heroes' magazine, May 1983.

on with the group;[†] lawyers grew rich on legal posturing and manoeuvres; Mason went in with Gilmour; Bob Ezrin did too, after being pencilled in to produce Waters' second solo album *Radio KAOS*;[‡] Wright was back in, sort of, but not really; a settlement was finally agreed in December 1987[§] (three months *after* the next album was released, meaning it was recorded with legal threats and financial risks[¶] hanging in the air and often arriving over the phone, which cannot have helped creatively). It was all quite unseemly and very much out in the open, whereas the Floyd previously had retained mystique through their distance from the media and disdain for typical rock-star self-aggrandisement. It permanently destroyed the relationship between Gilmour[**] and Waters, and made hope of reconciliation or reformation seem vastly unlikely.[††]

Which all meant that there was a lot riding on the next Pink Floyd album, both professionally and financially. But writing and recording it, however, turned out to be a struggle for Gilmour, who, for example, had not written a Pink Floyd lyric since **CHILDHOOD'S END** in 1972. Using various writing partners, he managed to sketch out enough tracks and got recording. The album, when finally released, is notable for its peak-1980s production, with lots of gated reverb,[‡‡] drum machines, synthesisers and what no doubt felt like cutting-edge studio effects, but which now feel highly dated and synthetic.[§§] Studio problems can mar an album but if the songwriting and performances are strong enough, the quality should still come through.[¶¶] But *A Momentary Lapse of Reason* is by far the least organic sounding of all Pink Floyd albums, and it feels very much

---

[†] Gilmour noted that 'I had an awful lot of time invested in the group ... I was damned if I was going to be forced out. I am an extremely stubborn person, and I will not be forced out of something I consider to be partly mine.' (*Rolling Stone*, 19 November 1987).

[‡] Subsequently receiving a venomous couplet in 'Too Much Rope' from Waters' 1992 album *Amused to Death*: 'Each man has his price Bob / And yours was pretty low'. Waters, like the elephant, does not forget.

[§] Waters received ownership of the copyrights to *The Wall* concept and the inflatable pig from *Animals*. Which meant that when the band later wanted to use the pig, usually appearing during **ONE OF THESE DAYS**, they had to add some obvious porcine testicles to legally distinguish it.

[¶] Mason noted: 'Litigation is a remarkable experience, as you select your gladiators for their fighting skills and then sit back to watch them perform. It is probably the most overpriced form of entertainment I have ever encountered, and also the most nerve-racking.' (Mason, *Inside Out*, p.282).

[**] Gilmour usually downplays conflict, but at the time he was quite upfront: 'In all the interviews he is conducting a vicious wrecking campaign, and I cannot remain friendly with someone like that' (*Creem* magazine, February 1988). Nearly forty years later the two men's bickering continues, as mostly recently seen on a ridiculous squabble over the liner notes for the remastered *Animals* album.

[††] There was an absurd story at this time that Waters had toilet rolls made with Gilmour's face on them. Untrue, but that's how ridiculous things got.

[‡‡] A technique pioneered by Phil Collins and producer Steve Lilywhite (later famous for working with U2), where the reverberations from the snare drum are digitally gated (cut off earlier), so as to make the sound cut off instantly like on knife-edge. This method became synonymous with 80s pop-rock production, being very evident in songs such as (most famously) Collins' 'In The Air Tonight', but also Berlin's 'Take My Breath Away', Kate Bush's 'Running Up The Hill', and Bruce Springsteen's 'Born In The USA'.

[§§] The band seem to agree: the 2019 remaster features re-recorded drum tracks from Mason, while the next album, *The Division Bell*, would very consciously return to band-in-a-room jamming and analogue warmth.

[¶¶] As is most famously heard on Metallica's 1988 album *...And Justice For All*, which is dreadfully tinny but still one of the finest metal albums ever, and also evident on otherwise excellent albums like *White Light/White Heat* by the Velvet Underground or Iron Maiden's eponymous debut. The greatness shines through.

like a band at the limit of its creative abilities. (Three of the eleven tracks are instrumentals, if you include **SIGNS OF LIFE**, while two are slight digitised a capella confections.) Yet it kept the show on the road, it sold by the truckload, the two-year supporting tour was a remarkable success, and it helped to rehabilitate Mason and Wright both as musicians and as key parts of the Pink Floyd story. Sometimes, in the greater perspective, the work is less important than the human relationships it succours. (Though Waters might not agree.)

SIGNS OF LIFE,* however, perhaps reflects the pressures bearing on it. It's an ambient instrumental (with a few indistinguishable words from Mason, perhaps in an echo of **ONE OF THESE DAYS**) acting as an overture before the album proper. In its slow opening and atmospheric build, it feels somewhat dated, in those more immediate times. The group had never worried about testing their audience's patience before (as with **ONE OF THESE DAYS** and **TIME**), but by now it's starting to feel more of a tiresome imposition. What is interesting about **SIGNS OF LIFE** is that by using the sounds of a boat in lapping water,† it initially suggests earlier pastoral evocations such as **ATOM HEART MOTHER** and **FAT OLD SUN**, and thus relocates the group in its salad days before Waters took over, though that chimera evaporates on the introduction of the synthesiser at 0.40. The subsequent computer-esque effect at 1.14 (just when Mason's indecipherable words come in) may have felt cutting-edge in 1987, but it feels almost comically archaic now. The clouds lift at 1.50, in a manner vaguely reminiscent of Wright's glorious chord change during Part I of **SHINE ON YOU CRAZY DIAMOND**, but to no great effect: the circling melody continues on, until Gilmour finally enters at 2.47. He noodles around a bit, sounding wonderfully sharp and bright, leaving space between the phrases, though you never get the sense of any point being made, until everything slowly fades away in the last half-minute or so. Pink Floyd fans are obviously accustomed to lengthy instrumentals, but from **ECHOES** onwards they all felt part of something consequential, with a greater point. This doesn't.

SIGNS OF LIFE is only just enough of a track to justify inclusion. A few previous albums had certainly opened on something relatively slight, such as **SPEAK TO ME** and **PIGS ON THE WING**, but their brevity had served to whet the appetite before something of great contrast and substance. For the most part the group had generally preferred to open an album with a bang, as with **ASTRONOMY DOMINE**, **LET THERE BE MORE LIGHT**, **ONE OF THESE DAYS** and **IN THE FLESH?** Unfortunately, **SIGNS OF LIFE** is neither: it's a shadowy piece of atmospherics that dissipates with the insubstantiality of a dream.

---

* Not a bad title as a rejoinder to a departing member – up there with Rainbow's *Down To Earth* (1978), following the departure of Ronny James Dio. It's also much better than 'Delusions of Maturity', which unbelievably was a potential album title, but rejected for fear of causing Waters to snigger.
† From Gilmour's boatman Langley Iddins, who looks after the Astoria houseboat.

LEARNING TO FLY (Gilmour, Ezrin, Anthony Moore, Jon Carin)
Length: 4.53
Vocals: Gilmour, Mason **Guitars**: Gilmour **Bass**: Tony Levin **Sequencer**: Bob Ezrin
Keyboards: Jon Carin **Drums**: Mason **Percussion**: Steve Forman, Bob Ezrin
Backing vocals: Darlene Koldenhaven, Carmen Twillie, Phyllis St James, Donnie Gerrard
Recorded: November 1986–March 1987
Producer: Bob Ezrin, Gilmour
First released: 7 September 1987 (*A Momentary Lapse of Reason* track 2)
Rating: 7/10

While **LEARNING TO FLY** is an enjoyable song, it's far from the sound you associate with Pink Floyd. This raises the question of what it means to be a Pink Floyd song – are there some inherent qualities? Some style or sound? Does it mean the authorship of one of the group, or one of the two main songwriters? Or the musicianship of Gilmour and Wright? At any rate, this is an upbeat song, with a particularly exciting drum track‡ which originated in a demo by Jon Carin, which from the start had the disjointed rhythm.§ Built up on layers of processed sounds, it is as far away from the organic sounds of 1970s Pink Floyd as you could imagine, but it is nice and catchy – a very 1987 sort of song, down to the backing singers, who could have come from any Top 10 single that year.¶

LEARNING TO FLY starts with a bang, giving the album a jolt of energy exactly when needed after the languor of **SIGNS OF LIFE**, but its pace is only moderate and its lumbering rhythm doesn't quite groove, although the syncopated snare drum BOOSH is a tremendous hook. What does feel authentic, however, is the excellent commentary through the verses from Gilmour,** with its clean lines sounding like a Fender Stratocaster, and the sense of rising excitement that peaks wonderfully in the choruses. This is essentially a pop record, smartly structured with a musical interlude and then a head-in-the-clouds bridge before a final rousing verse and chorus before some nice guitar soloing takes it home. The sound effects are unusually pertinent for *Momentary Lapse*, with recordings of pilot chatter (by Mason, who like Gilmour was taking flying lessons at this time) contributing to the theme and suiting the airborne sound of the chorus. The theme of taking flight, of gaining confidence after arduous difficulties, seems to have had particular meaning for Gilmour and isn't hard to read symbolically ('*A soul in tension that's learning to fly / Condition grounded, but determined to try*') but at the same time does seem to be primarily about, you know, actually gaining one's pilot licence.

---

‡ Perhaps cribbed from 'Raspberry Beret' (1985) by Prince, which has a similar syncopated and synthesised drum beat.
§ Carin said: 'The rhythm pattern is certainly influenced by [David Sylvian's] brother Steve Jansen. Or Yukihiro Takahashi, even. That slightly disjointed, quilt-like rhythmic pattern they do so well. With the parallel 5ths rising and falling in the verses.' (*Brain Damage* interview, August 2007).
¶ That year being the peak of upbeat pop/rock crossovers like Starship's 'Nothing's Gonna Stop Us', Feargal Sharkey's 'A Good Heart', Whitesnake's eponymous album (with 'Here I Go Again'), and Def Leppard's *Hysteria*.
** Reminiscent of 'She Came In Through The Bathroom Window' from The Beatles' *Abbey Road*.

However, beyond Gilmour's contributions **LEARNING TO FLY** sounds very little like Pink Floyd. It's catchy, it's nice, it's fun even, and thus was often played second on the *Momentary Lapse* and *Division Bell* tours, with percussionist Gary Wallis using neon drumsticks to leap about at a standing drum machine (while Mason placidly kept time on a traditional kit). Bassist Guy Pratt points out in his memoir that when played live, 'At my suggestion, at the very end of the song, David and I play the riff from the end of verse two of "Young Lust"',* which is a further example of the unity of the Pink Floyd soundworld. **LEARNING TO FLY** was one of only two tracks from *Momentary Lapse* to be retained on the *Division Bell* tour (the other being **SORROW**), but you can't help but feel like it's really a song for another band.

THE DOGS OF WAR (Gilmour, Moore)
Length: 6.05
Vocals: Gilmour **Guitars**: Gilmour **Bass**: Tony Levin **Keyboards**: Jon Carin
Organ: Bill Payne **Saxophones**: Scott Page. Tom Scott **Drums**: Carmine Appice
Percussion: Carmine Appice **Backing vocals**: Darlene Koldenhaven, Carmen Twillie, Phyllis St James, Donny Gerrard
Recorded: November 1986–March 1987
Producer: Bob Ezrin, Gilmour
First released: 7 September 1987 (*A Momentary Lapse of Reason* track 3)
Rating: 5/10

A synthesised two-note drone makes up most of the music of this track, which if you were being charitable might recall earlier songs with minimal melodic movement, such as **WELCOME TO THE MACHINE**, **SET THE CONTROLS FOR THE HEART OF THE SUN** and **CRYING SONG**, or even the vascular rhythm from **HEART BEAT, PIG MEAT**. If you have a drone, the other parts can go wild, as it anchors the track and gives other instruments something to play off of.† Hence why in **SET THE CONTROLS** Mason could go berserk on the tom-toms and the tempo could shift up and down, because Waters' ostinato baff riff was always there to return to. Here, the drone allows for the sounds of snarling dogs to be played throughout, while Gilmour's fantastic roaring vocal delivery provides a great contrast, and must be one of his most aggressive ever for Pink Floyd. The extended instrumental 4/4 section (from 2.58) kicks in with a superbly vicious drum fill, but the section is an all-too-obvious lift from **MONEY**, saxophone solo and all (from 3.56). The droning section returns at 4.35 for two more verse/chorus iterations, this time with many interjections from saxophone, lead guitar, drum fills and even bass, building to a peak before simply ending after the final '*One world!*' chorus.

---

* *My Bass And Other Animals*, end note #23.
† As Jeff Schwartz notes in his excellent essay 'Sister Ray: Some Pleasures of a Musical Text', published in *The Velvet Underground Companion* (1997).

But somehow the components don't quite combine into something greater. Gilmour's singing is angry and belligerent, and hence matches the lyric, which vociferously condemns political leaders who orchestrate wars for personal gain.‡ The words, while taut and always relevant, still can't escape the desperate search for a rhyme, as with: '*We all have a dark side, to say the least / And dealing in death is the nature of the beast*'. The pointless tag '*to say the least*' coming just after the self-allusion is just horribly, dreadfully clumsy, worsened by the fact that the '*dark side*' reference doesn't make sense, as that album's lyrics used darkness to refer to madness rather than evil. Minor details? Perhaps, but when you're playing in the big leagues these things matter. Overall, **THE DOGS OF WAR** is a good try, but is lacking any difference in purpose between lyrics, music or instrumentation. If they are too consistent, there's no dialogue between the various elements. Pink Floyd had so often excelled in creating art from these interchanges (from **SCARECROW** to **DOGS** and **COMFORTABLY NUMB**), but Gilmour, being a craftsman, is temperamentally conditioned to ensuring things align. This can work well,§ but can also lead to what musicologist Alan W. Pollack calls 'foolish consistency'.¶

ONE SLIP (Gilmour, Phil Manzanera)
Length: 5.10
Vocals: Gilmour **Guitars**: Gilmour, Michael Landau **Sequencer**: Gilmour
Keyboards: Jon Carin, Bob Ezrin **Drums**: Jim Keltner **Percussion**: Mason
Chapman stick: Tony Levin **Backing vocals**: Darlene Koldenhaven, Carmen Twillie, Phyllis St James, Donny Gerrard
Recorded: November 1986–March 1987
Producer: Bob Ezrin, Gilmour
First released: 7 September 1987 (*A Momentary Lapse of Reason* track 4)
Rating: 5/10

Segueing in via some vaguely Latin-sounding synthesisers from **THE DOGS OF WAR**, **ONE SLIP** is the first traditional rock song on *Momentary Lapse*, and the track from which the album's title was taken. If the initial pastoral feel created by sound of lapping water in **SIGNS OF LIFE** suggested the early Floyd, the digital alarms and subsequent drum fills at the start are an even more direct echo, in this instance from the beginning of **TIME**, with its clocks and rototoms.** But it's a self-quotation that makes no particular point as time isn't a theme in this song, which has to do with random encounters and how lives get entangled from fleeting moments – although the alarms might suggest a desire for movement

---

‡ Although 'War Pigs' by Black Sabbath is the definitive example on that theme.
§ It does on Gilmour's solo album *On An Island* (2006), which is almost throughout mature, understated and reflective.
¶ He beautifully analyses every single recorded Beatles track from a musicological perspective at www.icce.rug.nl/~soundscapes/DATABASES/AWP/awp-beatles_canon.shtml. What a great idea.
** The sound comes from the alarm to the Astoria houseboat studio, as engineer Andy Jackson explained: '[T]he alarms on the front, which was me with the alarm system at the studio ... It was me putting the wrong code number in to set it off.' (Andy Jackson interview, *Floydian Slip*, 21 January 2001).

replicated in the urgency of the song's surging riff. The kinetic energy, however, feels forced rather than authentic, although Gilmour's singing is very good. He can always put on a professional performance, if nothing else. The bass solo in the breakdown (from 2.49) is played on a Chapman Stick by Tony Levin, and has a very unfortunate digitised, processed feel. Played live, it sounds fantastic,[*] if not particularly connected to the rest of the track.

The lyric, meanwhile, features perhaps the worst line in the entire Pink Floyd catalogue – '*Or was it the hand of fate, that seemed to fit just like a glove?*' – which isn't so much an infelicity as a gruesome, appalling choice. Why did no one *say* anything? After the remarkable verbal flair of the Waters era, it's grimly fascinating to observe such a slip in standards, which suggests that the problem isn't necessarily in ability but in having the awareness of what is good and what is not.[†] The driving energy of **ONE SLIP** does appeal, particularly after the droning stasis of **THE DOGS OF WAR**, but its melody isn't distinctive, the chorus doesn't provide enough contrast, and the sound effects at the beginning take up over a minute to no great effect. Worst of all, lyrically while at least addressing more adult themes, the verbal clumsiness[‡] is deeply disappointing for a band who had once boasted the finest lyrics in rock music. **ONE SLIP** exemplifies the slip in standards that Pink Floyd now accepted.

ON THE TURNING AWAY (Gilmour, Moore)
Length: 5.42
Vocals: Gilmour **Guitars**: Gilmour **Bass**: Tony Levin **Organ**: Wright **Synthesiser**: Jon Carin **Sequencers**: Gilmour **Drums**: Mason **Percussion**: Mason **Backing vocals**: Wright, Darlene Koldenhoven, Carmen Twillie, Phyllis St James, Donny Gerrard
Recorded: November 1986–March 1987
Producer: Bob Ezrin, Gilmour
First released: 7 September 1987 (*A Momentary Lapse of Reason* track 5)
Rating: 3/10

The two sides of the classic Pink Floyd line-up had, of course, Waters providing the philosophy and vision, Gilmour the musicianship. But without Waters, Gilmour occasionally sounds like he is floundering in a sea of meaninglessness, with musical competence but no artistic point or purpose. In rock music, which requires energy and aggression, that translates to empty bombast, an attempt at scale and grandeur that falls flat on its face.[§] So it is here, in a song which might

---

[*] Though few would know, as the track wasn't included on *Delicate Sound Of Thunder*. However, long-time bassist Guy Pratt demonstrated how to play the part on his YouTube channel, and it sounds hugely superior to the studio version. See www.youtube.com/watch?v=CyckEvPv6lk.

[†] Gilmour's friend Paul McCartney has had the same problem since the break-up of the Beatles. Without John Lennon's contempt for clichés and easy sentimentality, McCartney's albums have so often been trite and unambitious.

[‡] Another example: '*The moment slipped by and soon the seeds were sown / The year grew late and neither one wanted to remain alone*'. The straining for a rhyme is right out of McGonagall.

[§] This is why bad rock music, especially hard rock and heavy metal, is so funny, as with *This is Spinal Tap* (1984) and *The Decline of Civilization Part II: The Metal Years* (1988).

have been performed by Simple Minds or Coldplay or even (good lord) Scottish folk-rock band Runrig. It is every stadium rock cliché bound together in one steaming pile. There are so many cringe-worthy moments that they bear listing:

- The title is pretentious. And is it '*On*' as in 'at the time of' or 'regarding'?
- The opening lines (mostly *a capella*, though there's an atmospheric synthesiser in there) sung by Gilmour, reeking of sincerity and goodwill. It's like lighters-aloft Christian rock.
- The second verse (there's no chorus) begins straight after the first, with some instrumentation coming in, right on cue, especially some sincere and authentic acoustic guitar.
- The third verse follows immediately – still no chorus – and now the drums and bass guitar come in. You could set your watch to it.
- And now the instrumental section, energised by a rousing electric guitar and very Wright-esque organ playing. Pink Floyd by numbers.
- But hush! It falls quiet, there's a brief bass comment, and then – yes! – it all kicks in again for a final verse with numerous backing singers, which just pleads for the audience to hold their arms aloft and sway as one to the music.
- And finally, a soaring guitar solo from 3.27 as the rest of the band plays on. The music finally fades out at 5.41, so nearly 40 per cent of the song is Gilmour indulging himself and hoping it all adds up to something.

Lyrically, **ON THE TURNING AWAY** is clearly heartfelt and sincere, and technically sound: there are no ghastly choices as in **ONE SLIP** or **SORROW**. It might even have inspired others, as The Scorpions may have adapted the line 'the new wind of change' for their 1991 single 'Wind of Change' about the fall of the Berlin Wall. Gilmour clearly retains, even as a very wealthy man, some of his 1960s idealism: in 2021 he was #9 on the *Sunday Times* Giving List 2021, for having given away 12.2 per cent of his income,¶ his website lists fifteen different charities 'that have benefitted in the past' from his philanthropy,** while he famously sold his house in London in 2004 for £3.6 million and gave the proceeds straight to the homeless charity Crisis.†† All of which is extremely commendable, but unfortunately compassion and earnestness are very difficult things to convey in rock music‡‡ without veering into the maudlin.§§

¶ Around £16.6m from a total of £136m, though this is probably educated guesswork as Gilmour doesn't in general publicise his charitable work.
** See www.davidgilmour.com/charity.htm.
†† He was interviewed about it at www.dailymail.co.uk/tvshowbiz/article-182537/Why-David-gave-charity-3-6m.html. 'I'd got to the stage when I realised that Polly and I live here in the countryside and we were not using the house in London. I was also feeling increasingly uncomfortable about our good fortune and others' lack of it.'
‡‡ Creation Records founder Alan McGhee famously called this kind of band, namely Coldplay et al, 'bedwetters'. Folk music is much better at conveying earnestness: think of early Bob Dylan, or Nick Drake. But rock needs energy and verve, not sentimentality.
§§ Although U2 regularly managed it, on standout tracks like 'Bad', 'Faraway (So Close!)' and 'Running To Stand Still'. But great though Gilmour's singing is, it doesn't have that impassioned quality at which Bono specialises.

Although meant to be a transcendent stadium rock moment, **ON THE TURNING AWAY** feels sterile, with even the echoes giving the sense of having been programmed, though Gilmour's singing and guitar playing are, as always, technically strong. For example, he handles the melodic range of the vocals with such ease that you don't notice it. But what is the point of such virtuosity if you are using it on insipid, formulaic banalities like this? It is remarkable to think that this song is on an album that sold over 10 million copies,[*] suggesting the extraordinarily durability of the Pink Floyd brand. **ON THE TURNING AWAY** is so clichéd and witless that it was essentially rewritten for *The Division Bell* as **A GREAT DAY FOR FREEDOM** (with a similar political theme, *a capella* opening and high notes) – but successfully so. Which suggests Gilmour's own thoughts about this track, though he would never say so.

YET ANOTHER MOVIE (Gilmour, Pat Leonard)
Length: 6.28
Vocals: Gilmour **Guitars**: Gilmour **Bass**: Tony Levin **Saxophone**: John Helliwell
Synthesiser: Jon Carin, Patrick Leonard **Sequencers**: Patrick Leonard
Drums: Mason, Jim Keltner **Percussion**: Steve Forman
Recorded: November 1986–March 1987
Producer: Bob Ezrin, Gilmour
First released: 7 September 1987 (*A Momentary Lapse of Reason* track 6)
Rating: 5/10

YET ANOTHER MOVIE is the start of a sequence of shadowy tracks on *Momentary Lapse*, continuing through **ROUND AND AROUND** and **TERMINAL FROST**, the homogeneity of their sound indicative of a quality control that had taken a vacation. The synthesised 'knocking-at-the-door'[†] effect at the start of **YET ANOTHER MOVIE** is at least different, sounding alien or as though you were in the womb, though to no great point or effect – beyond filling forty-five seconds of the album. However, it bears a distinct similarity to the beginning of 'And The Gods Made Love', the first track on *Electric Ladyland* by Jimi Hendrix (1968). There's then a shadowy synthesiser sound,[‡] before the track proper starts at around 1.15 with first some bass and drums at 1.08 (the two sections feeling rather jerry-rigged together). The propulsive

---

[*] Still, there are worse albums that have sold more. Celine Dion has two that have sold more than 20 million each.

[†] Maybe a slight *knocking at the door in Macbeth* effect? Probably not, but art consists of allusions, and it's easy to get carried away sometimes. Check out the film *Room 237* on *The Shining* as an example of a down-the-rabbit-hole overanalysis.

[‡] To which keyboardist Jon Carin stakes a claim, saying, 'I wrote the intro to the song (starting at 45 seconds), the floaty synth pad part that preceded the song, on an Emulator II. That sound then continues through the entire song. It's a similar writing style as the one I employed on **MAROONED** on the next record, my sampled National Resolectric guitar doing the spacey intro with the bends, etc., that sets the mood, then weaves through the rest of the song.' (Carin interviewed at Publius Enigma www.publiusenigma.co.uk/post/a-history-and-anatomy-of-yet-another-movie). Carin played on both *Momentary Lapse* and *Division Bell* but seems to have had a falling out with Gilmour over songwriting credits, and so has been giving his side of the story. Gilmour has not publicly responded.

drumming at the bottom of all the murk keeps things going nicely, and sounds relatively natural, although the prominent bass playing by Tony Levin[§] sounds dreadfully synthetic.

The lyrics present, sadly, yet another string of awkward phrases in desperate search for a rhyme, as with '*The use of force, he was so tough / She'll soon submit, she's had enough*' and '*He's just the same as all the rest / He's not the worst, and he's not the best*'. The shadowy sound and Gilmour's strong but dark-toned delivery help to disguise the words, until repeated listenings make them disappointingly clear. Another issue is that for once on the album the lyrics are rather cryptic: they feel like a series of unconnected images, possibly drawn from various films. This reading is given credence by the barely distinguishable audio clips from two films, the Marlon Brando Western *One-Eyed Jacks* (1961) and *Casablanca* (1942), audible from 1.12 and 5.18 respectively. Hence, the opacity of the sound would for once on the album heighten the meaning of the song, suggesting the tedium of hotel rooms and TVs flickering with inane movies during never-ending tours. Though, of course, *The Wall* explored this theme (and used similar techniques) some eight years earlier. However, Gilmour seems to have said[¶] that 'It's a more surrealistic effort than anything I've attempted before. I don't even know what all of it means myself.' The ambiguity of **YET ANOTHER MOVIE** gives it a certain enigmatic charm, though there's ultimately less to it than you first think.

ROUND AND AROUND (Gilmour)
Length: 1.02
Guitars: Gilmour **Bass**: Tony Levin **Sequencer**: Gilmour **Keyboards**: Jon Carin
Recorded: November 1986–March 1987
Producer: Bob Ezrin, Gilmour
First released: 7 September 1987 (*A Momentary Lapse of Reason* track 7)
Rating: 2/10

ROUND AND AROUND is a piece of mildly atmospheric filler, and little more. It segues in from **YET ANOTHER MOVIE** and was initially considered part of the same track, in the fashion of **SPEAK TO ME** and **BREATHE**. It sounds like music introducing the companies behind bad 1980s action films. You can just about see Chuck Norris or Jean-Claude Van Damme out there in the Vietnamese jungle, ready to whoop ass on some evil Commie ninjas. **ROUND AND AROUND** is a piece of synthetic nothingness, with the slightest synthesised shadowy atmosphere lit up by occasional flashing skeins of electrified guitar. It fills just over a minute, or 2 per cent of the entire album. Gilmour must really have been struggling. There's literally no reason for the track to be there.

---

§ Perhaps best known as a long-serving member of Peter Gabriel's band.
¶ Allegedly for *Only Music* magazine in December 1987, but I cannot find a full source for it.

A NEW MACHINE (PART 1) (Gilmour)
Length: 1.46
Vocals: Gilmour **Synthesiser**: Gilmour, Patrick Leonard **Vocoder**: Gilmour
Programming: Gilmour
Recorded: November 1986–March 1987
Producer: Bob Ezrin, Gilmour
First released: 7 September 1987 (*A Momentary Lapse of Reason* track 8)
Rating: 5/10

David Gilmour is known as someone who represses his feelings,* in the best English manner† (see **WHAT DO YOU WANT FROM ME?**). Yet this brief digitised vocal exercise is a howl of anguish from him, even an audible unburdening. It's interesting from biographical and technological perspectives (the digitisation is, like so much of *Momentary Lapse*, futuristic in a highly dated sense), but it's barely a song. Brief interludes are alright in small doses, as *The Wall* so consistently proved, so this just about gets a pass. The trouble is that an interlude needs to feel rich with ideas or atmosphere, as with **IS THERE ANYBODY OUT THERE?** or **GOODBYE CRUEL WORLD**, so as to make the listener wish that they could keep hearing more. Unfortunately, **A NEW MACHINE (PART 1)** is sufficiently enamoured with its production techniques‡ that it is prepared to forgo any real artistic point. It sounds like the equipment has taken over.§

TERMINAL FROST (Gilmour)
Length: 6.17
Guitars: Gilmour **Keyboards**: Jon Carin, Bob Ezrin **Piano**: Wright
Kurtweil synthesiser: Wright **Bass**: Tony Levin **Saxophone**: Tom Scott, John Helliwell
Drum machine: Mason **Percussion**: Bob Ezrin **Backing vocals**: Darlene Koldenhoven, Carmen Twillie, Phyllis St James, Donny Gerrard
Recorded: November 1986–March 1987
Producer: Bob Ezrin, Gilmour
First released: 7 September 1987 (*A Momentary Lapse of Reason* track 9)
Rating: 5/10

---

* Though he recalled his conflict with Waters: 'Sometimes I drove home from the recording studio and screamed and swore, although I was alone in the car.' (*Der Spiegel*, 5 June 1995). It could be that he sought to make that into art in this track.

† Bob Ezrin described the intra-band conflict from the time of *The Wall*: 'It was all done under that English smiling, left-handed, adversarial stance they take, with the smiles on their faces and soft voices. But basically they were saying, "I hate you, and I'm going to kill you."' (*Rolling Stone*, 19 November 1987).

‡ '"A New Machine" has a sound I've never heard anyone do. The noise gates, the Vocoders, opened up something new which to me seemed like a wonderful sound effect that no one had done before; it's innovation of a sort.' (Gilmour interviewed in *Musician* magazine, August 1992).

§ 'There's a danger that we could become slaves to all our equipment, and in the past we have. But what we're trying to do is sort it all out, so that we're not. But I agree, I mean it worries me sometimes that we have this much equipment, and you can hide behind it.' (Wright interviewed during *Live At Pompeii* in 1972. Very wise. *Momentary Lapse* feels like the only time the group were burdened by, or hiding behind, technology rather than using it to express themselves).

Yet another instrumental. This meandering piece is, to be fair, nicely atmospheric and visual, if never quite feeling worthy of your time: it's a noodling piece straight out of 1980s TV drama soundtracks occasionally enlivened by the excellence of Gilmour's guitar, which just about makes it worthwhile. (Yes, he's always worth hearing, but you'd still prefer it if there was an actual song attached.) **TERMINAL FROST** has an ABA structure, with a shadowy, somnolent opening much too similar to **YET ANOTHER MOVIE** for comfort, a slightly sunnier middle section with soprano saxophones, a return to the first section and slow fade-out.

Musically, **TERMINAL FROST** does have parts that prick the ears, although they don't add up to anything coherent. The once-every-bar authoritative thump on the snare drum (or the digitised equivalent thereof) keeps the entire track from collapsing into cloudy nothingness. The repeated guitar lick is artful, if lacking development, but unlike on **PIGS (THREE DIFFERENT ONES)** it doesn't build tension, and unlike **SHINE ON YOU CRAZY DIAMOND** it isn't memorable enough to be a motif. Like so much of *Momentary Lapse*, it is just there, until it isn't. The same is true of the entire track, which exists not so much in the crepuscular state it portrays but in a liminal zone between being and non-being. It's not quite a song, but it's a track on an album, so we have to treat it as one. All it really does is fill six minutes and seventeen seconds.

A NEW MACHINE (PART 2) (Gilmour)
Length: 0.38
Vocals: Gilmour **Synthesiser**: Gilmour, Patrick Leonard **Vocoder**: Gilmour
Programming: Gilmour
Recorded: November 1986–March 1987
Producer: Bob Ezrin, Gilmour
First released: 7 September 1987 (*A Momentary Lapse of Reason* track 10)
Rating: 3/10

Gilmour just about got a pass for **A NEW MACHINE (PART 1)**, but adding a second part, at less than forty seconds, with no difference in style or technique, is either self-indulgence or straining to fill out an album. The sole benefit may be that it gave Gilmour another songwriting credit and so a higher proportion of the royalties on the album,¶ but listeners don't care about that. Whereas the first part at least pricks the ears of the listener and shows a more personal side of Gilmour, here the track is essentially without any merit or artistic point.

¶ See **PIGS ON THE WING PART 2**. But Waters had valid artistic and structural reasons for splitting **PIGS ON THE WING**. There are no such justifications for **A NEW MACHINE (PART 2)**.

> **SORROW** (Gilmour)
> **Length**: 8.46
> **Vocals**: Gilmour **Guitar**: Gilmour **Bass**: Tony Levin **Keyboards**: Gilmour, Bob Ezrin
> **Kurtweil synthesiser**: Wright **Synthesiser**: Gilmour **Drum machine**: Gilmour
> **Backing vocals**: Darlene Koldenhaven, Carmen Twillie, Phyllis St James, Donny Gerrard
> **Recorded**: November 1986–March 1987
> **Producer**: Bob Ezrin, Gilmour
> **First released**: 7 September 1987 (*A Momentary Lapse of Reason* track 11)
> **Rating**: 6.5/10

A mighty, mighty Gilmour guitar sound opens **SORROW**, which is probably the best track on the album. Its immensity might be intended to show how much life and vitality there was in Pink Floyd, or might be down to the bombastic influence of cocaine,[*] or maybe somewhere in the capacious territory between both. The vastness of the sound comes from it having been recorded inside the Los Angeles Memorial Sports Arena[†] when played through its PA system, with the band having relocated to the city in February–March 1987 to complete recording and mastering with Ezrin. (Their willingness to move was what Ezrin says induced him to work with Gilmour and Mason rather than Waters, as Ezrin wanted to be close to his children during the school year.) The guitar sound is terrific, undoubtedly, but does it really need to last 1 minute 46 seconds? That's longer than some songs from the first album by The Clash![‡]

As a song, then, **SORROW** is a rather portentous set piece that isn't quite as inspired as it thinks it is. Gilmour, for instance, was proud of the lyric which came from a poem he wrote and is unusually florid ('*Plumes of smoke rise and merge into the leaden sky*') but still has painfully gauche efforts at rhyming ('*He's haunted by the memory of a lost paradise / In his youth or a dream, he can't be precise*'). For the most part **SORROW** gets away with it thanks to the strength of the music, which nicely marries a lumbering rhythm to murky, downbeat

---

[*] 'I became too fond of the coke. I think it happened because I got divorced and decided to go on the razzle and it all coincided with the Floyd coming back.' (Quoted in Mark Blake, *Pigs Might Fly: The Story of Pink Floyd*, p.365. Though again no citation). The *Momentary Lapse* tour was something of a party tour. But following Gilmour's relationship with Polly Samson, he swore off cocaine and *The Division Bell* tour became much more sober, to the resentment of the younger members of the touring band. Bassist Guy Pratt is admirably honest about this in his memoir *My Bass and Other Animals*, and revealing about the resentment and misogyny which Samson encountered. She has rather admirably never spoken about this. (I invited her to be interviewed about her *Division Bell* lyric writing for this book, but she maintained her dignified silence).

[†] An indoor sports arena primarily used for basketball, it seems to have been something of a favourite for the group, who played there for five consecutive nights during the *Wish You Were Here* tour (23–27 April, 1975), seven nights during *The Wall* tour (7–13 February 1980) and then four nights during the subsequent *Momentary Lapse* tour (26-8 & 30 November 1987). They give the city a miss when touring *Animals*, after police harassment of fans during the 1975 shows (which helped inspire the **IN THE FLESH?** sequence in *Pink Floyd: The Wall*), playing nearby Anaheim instead.

[‡] 'What's My Name?' – 1.41. '48 Hours' – 1.36. Since the punk era, only The Smiths have dared to have songs lasting just two minutes: 'William It Was Really Nothing' is 2.09 and 'Panic' is 2.19. More often singles last around four minutes, ponderously moving through the same old verse-chorus-verse structure. See *The Manual* by Bill Drummond and Jimmy Cauty for more on classic pop structure and methods. Unfortunately, copies are like gold dust, but you can read it online, if you look. (Drummond writes, in his later book *45* (1999), about calling a bookseller trying to find a copy and feeling like J.R Hartley.)

verses which may lack melodic interest but have a fine chord change every eighth bar. The real problem comes in the bridge, which doesn't segue smoothly from the verse and (as with **ON THE TURNING AWAY**) utilises hokey stadium rock clichés. With its near-falsetto, reverb-rich vocals, it might be intended to sound like a prayer, but it comes across as a vapid piece of Californian positive thinking:§ '*One world, one soul / Time pass, the river roll*'. The '*one world*' motif had been done by Queen a few years earlier, and rather better,¶ while the river symbol would be used in a vastly superior way a few years later, in **HIGH HOPES**. Here it just feels banal and trite.

Similarly, as with so many of the group's early songs, it sounds like they couldn't come up with a good ending, so it simply fades out while Gilmour's guitar solo drags on from 6.02 onwards and hence lasts over two and a half minutes. The playing is, as always, technically impressive but isn't distinctive, lacking (for example) the space and economy of the solo from **DOGS** or the soaring lines from **TIME**. Similarly, with **SORROW** not having a chorus, only a bridge, there's not enough variety to the song as a whole as the fretboard wibbling drags on endlessly over the exact same riff. Live versions, with extended solos and an outro, are even longer, at 9.28 for *Delicate Sound of Thunder* and 10.49 on *Pulse*, and fall on the wrong side of tedium. Despite these complaints, however, **SORROW** is still, alongside **LEARNING TO FLY**, about the best track on *Momentary Lapse*, with the sound in the opening solo truly impressive and the track boasting a notably higher musical ambition. The guitar sound likewise is one of the most impressive ever laid down by Gilmour.

The remastered version, with Mason adding skins to replace Gilmour's drum machine, sounds marginally less synthetic, removing the gating on the drums and thus letting them resound somewhat. But the problem with **SORROW**, as with *Momentary Lapse* as a whole, is not the production. Or not primarily. The main problem is the material, which is simply weak, both lyrically and musically.** Coming at a time of enormous stress for Gilmour, and when his own songwriting had not really been tested for over a decade, **SORROW** unfortunately demonstrates how musical proficiency and cutting-edge production (as it was) just aren't enough. Art needs a sense of vision, of direction, not just of craft. Gilmour is certainly a greatly superior musician to Waters, but without Roger's dominating direction, the guitarist flounders, unable to distinguish between what is adroit and what is emotive. **SORROW** is the great set piece

---

§ If you have the stomach for it, check out the book by Gilmour's first wife Ginger, *Memoirs of the Bright Side of the Moon* (2015). It contains gems such as (on p.30) 'After one outing, upon returning to the Chateau wearing our new fluffy imitation furry platform boots, Nick Mason commented, 'You girls should get in a bit of Culture'. It was the first time that I had ever heard that word ... Admittedly and perhaps indignantly, we didn't do it at the time. Since then I have become a serious Culture buff. I have become a messenger for the need of Culture and Beauty and its importance for maintaining World Peace.'

¶ There's a great video of Queen demoing the song, with the lyric 'One dump, one turd, two tits John Deacon.'

** By comparison, *Hysteria* by Def Leppard is another achingly 1987 album with lots of gating and processed sounds, but it has superb songcraft.

of the album, but it is cold, synthetic, and tries too hard to convince you of its own greatness. It's a *cocaine* song.

There's no doubt that the recording of *Momentary Lapse* was difficult. Quite apart from the stresses of ruptured relationships, lawsuits and financial manoeuvres, Gilmour's songwriting and the recording process were both strewn with difficulties. Neither Mason nor Wright were in good form, while the cast of studio hands could only take direction rather than providing the vision which *Momentary Lapse* so glaringly needs. Gilmour's role in taking it all upon himself might have been artistically foolhardy, but in another sense it's almost heroic. There was no need for him to do so, besides the feeling that he was a major part of Pink Floyd and that only he would decide whether to call it a day. Mason says 'I think David and I felt that we had to get it right, or we would be slaughtered. As a result it is a very "careful" album with very few risks taken.'* In a sense this is true: the album is far from a pop reinvention, as with Genesis or Yes; it continues the themes of madness, absence, ruefulness and regret; Gilmour's guitar playing and soloing are distinctive and in fine fettle; his singing (as in **THE DOGS OF WAR**) is often excellent. But *Momentary Lapse* lacks not just vision but basic creativity: for the first time in the group's output, there are clichés, platitudes, banality, outright filler and dreadful lapses in standards, from a band which had exemplified inventiveness and technical mastery. As critic Robert Christgau says of Eric Clapton, 'like many other guys whose hand-ear coordination is off the curve, he's a casual tunesmith and a corny lyricist'.† This is all too evident here. *The Final Cut* certainly has its weaknesses, but its ambition has never been in doubt, and its production and lyrics are both excellent, leaving *Momentary Lapse* as easily the weakest official album in the group's discography. Yet it was a major commercial success, and so enabled Pink Floyd to continue; it revitalised Mason and Wright both as musicians and as members of the band; it confirmed Gilmour's captaincy of the group; and the subsequent tour played to perhaps 10 million people around the world.‡ It also ensured the next album would be made in far more propitious circumstances.

CLUSTER ONE (Gilmour, Wright)
Length: 5.56
Guitars: Gilmour **Piano**: Wright **Kurtweil synthesiser**: Wright **Drums**: Mason
Percussion: Mason
Recorded: January–December 1993
Producer: Bob Ezrin, Gilmour
First released: 28 March 1994 (*The Division Bell* track 1)
Rating: 7/10

---

* Mason, *Inside Out*, p.289.
† Robert Christgau, *Grown Up All Wrong*, p.87.
‡ There is only attendance data for 88 shows out of 200. The average attendance for the 88 shows is 55,000. Extrapolating from that to 200 shows gives a total of 11,014,000. So let's call it around 10 million.

The *Momentary Lapse* tour of 1987–89, as its length suggests, was remarkably successful. The touring group assembled numerous high-calibre musicians, such as Guy Pratt (who had done session work for Madonna, Michael Jackson and Peter Gabriel), Gary Wallis (whose hyper-kinetic performances on percussion gave the usually static group an unusual visual interest), and Tim Renwick (a low-key but much travelled guitarist, who had even played with Waters on his *Pros and Cons of Hitchhiking* tour). After ten years without a 'proper' Floyd tour, the band's highly resilient fanbase were desperate to go to the show. And what a show it was, with lasers, pyrotechnics, inflatable pigs, crashing overhead dive bombers and glittering mirror balls, with Wright back in the saddle, and with the group donning some achingly 1980s baggy suits.§ The group played 200 shows¶ in ninety-eight cities, and visited new countries such as the USSR, New Zealand, Finland and Norway. The tour seems to have been great fun for all concerned;** bassist Guy Pratt tells many great stories in his memoir *My Bass and Other Animals*. (His tale of the blind bowling team in Pittsburgh is priceless.)†† Coming at a time when kitchen-sink indie was dying out (The Smiths, for instance, split in 1987), and interest in psychedelia was returning as the drug ecstasy (MDMA) started to filter into the UK, the tour was perfectly timed for a time when people wanted their minds blown by spectacle again. Guy Pratt estimates that the group's Maine Road show on 8 August 1988 was when the crossover between football casuals,‡‡ rock and psychedelia began in earnest, heralding the Madchester movement and the popularity of groups like the Happy Mondays and the Stone Roses.§§

Another slight instrumental, in the manner of **SIGNS OF LIFE**, **CLUSTER ONE**, however, gives immediate notice that *The Division Bell* will be different from *Momentary Lapse*. The earlier song's dark opening synthesisers are replaced by an opening cloudiness¶¶ that lifts like the dawning sun, whereupon Gilmour's tender guitar notes and Wright's delicate piano intermingle wonderfully. Alongside some delicate commentary on the drums from Mason, this finally sounds like a band listening to each other, playing with and for each other, and feeling a subtle sense of joy just from being in a room together. The

---

§ During the *Division Bell* tour it was mercifully back to jeans and sensible haircuts.
¶ A total of 200, if you include the 1990 Knebworth gig.
** If rather drug-heavy. See **SORROW** note 1.
†† 'When we arrived in Pittsburgh ... the hotel was also playing host to the contestants in the World Blind Bowling Championship finals! I kid you not ... Just as David was about to sing, 'Think I'll buy me a football team,' he happened to look at me, and I mouthed, 'Think I'll buy me a blind bowling team. It's the only time I've ever known David lose it; he was laughing so much he couldn't sing the line.'' You can hear this all quite audibly in the bootleg of the show on 30 May 1988. See Chapter 3.
‡‡ A term denoting not casual fans but those interested in hooliganism and the clean look of Italian designer labels. In an interesting feedback loop, they took their style from Italian fans who themselves were inspired by the violence of English fans.
§§ *The Rockonteurs*, Series 1 Episode 41, with Noel Gallagher. Pratt's podcast with Gary Kemp has them interviewing many musical greats and is an excellent listen.
¶¶ Actually, it's the sound of space, as engineer Andy Jackson explained: '[I]t is the sound of electromagnetic noise from the solar wind. I mean, it just sounds like a lot of crackles to me and you. But that's what it is. It's electromagnetic noise from the solar wind. So it's a genuine piece of space noise. As near as you can get.' (Andy Jackson interview, *Floydian Slip*, 21 January 2001).

interplay is understated but wonderful, from the slight echo of 'Syd's Theme' from **SHINE ON YOUR CRAZY DIAMOND** from Wright at 3.48 onwards (though playing only the first three notes) to Gilmour's wonderful responses on the guitar, delicate but melodic and with just enough variety to keep the ears pricked. There's a delicious shift in atmosphere at 3.45, feeling like the sun is finally coming up, as well as a sedate rhythm from Mason at 4.27 and finally a thumping bit of low-end guitar twanging at 5.06, all preventing things from becoming too repetitive.

At last, you feel, here is Pink Floyd back as a band. The sense of them listening to each other, and being inspired by each other as they play, is beautifully tangible, hanging in the air like something about to be born. **CLUSTER ONE** is also the first Gilmour-Wright shared credit since **MUDMEN** from *Obscured by Clouds*, twenty-one years earlier. It may not be musically more than a lovely, warm bit of jamming by a band that knows its limitations, but its soulfulness and subtle joy foreshadow all that is good about *The Division Bell*.

WHAT DO YOU WANT FROM ME? (Gilmour, Wright, Polly Samson)
Length: 4.21
Vocals: Gilmour, Wright **Guitars**: Gilmour **Bass**: Guy Pratt **Hammond organ**: Wright
Synthesisers: Jon Carin **Electric piano**: Wright **Keyboards**: Jon Carin **Drums**: Mason
Percussion: Mason **Backing vocals**: Sam Brown, Durga McBroom, Carol Kenyon, Jackie Sheridan, Rebecca Leigh-White
Recorded: January–December 1993
Producer: Bob Ezrin, Gilmour
First released: 28 March 1994 (*The Division Bell* track 2)
Rating: 6.5/10

But first we get some outright aggression from Gilmour. Not quite bursting out of the box as **LEARNING TO FLY** did at a comparative place on *Momentary Lapse*, **WHAT DO YOU WANT FROM ME?** nonetheless has (after a short jamming introduction, with a tasty bit of bass fretwork from Guy Pratt) an enjoyably vicious kick once it gets going, a feeling redoubled by some remarkable soloing from Gilmour, with soaring lines suggestive of his comparative from **TIME**, albeit with a far more bluesy, saturnine feel. Gilmour's voice meanwhile feels very much front and centre, and his singing conveys just the right blend of weary resignation and defensive antagonism that signals a declining relationship.

WHAT DO YOU WANT FROM ME? is hence, in terms of tone at least, as it's hardly a raging rocker, one of Gilmour's angriest and bitterest songs. The way his guitar sounds both bluesy and crystalline can hardly be better exemplified than here, and the way his guitar lines melodically play off the end of each line gives the verses so much to tickle the ear, in the manner of The Beatles' 'She Came in Through the Bathroom Window' or even Dire Straits' 'Sultans of

Swing'. Each line of the slightly droning verse ends with some short terrifically phrased guitar part from Gilmour, perhaps symbolising the conflict between impassivity and articulation, or maybe just him seeking to liven up a song lacking great melodic interest. In either case, his playing is excellent: distinctive, melodic, and expressive in just the right measures.

But while the guitar lines sounds fantastic, the verses don't manage to maintain this level of creativity: the chorus isn't distinct enough from the verses to really register, and the gentler bridge ('*You can have anything you want / You can drift, you can dream, even walk on water / Anything you want*') feels like just the same melody sung at the same pace with less venom and quieter instrumentation. Also, the backing vocals sound somewhat hackneyed – the late 1980s having been the prime era of the female backing vocalists,[*] sometimes essentially as eye candy,[†] sometimes for a bit of soul,[‡] and sometimes to hit the high notes, but it felt like a stadium rock cliché by the early 1990s, after Nirvana had come along sniggering at such artifices. *The Division Bell* on the whole does very well to avoid the contemporary clichés into which *Momentary Lapse* quite often stumbled, but it doesn't always succeed.

Although **WHAT DO YOU WANT FROM ME?** succeeds on numerous levels, especially as a band performance and as a showcase for Gilmour's extraordinary guitar playing, there's just something lacking: a fresh riff or hook or inventive structure. Gilmour has vast gifts as a musician, singer, writer and producer, but his sense of craft, of knowing which chords lead to which chords, sometimes makes for music that is homogenous, or in other words predictable, even bland. **WHAT DO YOU WANT FROM ME?** spills over with genuine emotion and has Gilmour's finest soloing since *The Wall*, but while he has done a great job dressing up the material here, the fact that it required such ornamentation in the first place is what's most revealing.

POLES APART (Gilmour, Samson, Nick Laird-Clowes)
Length: 7.03
Vocals: Gilmour **Guitars**: Gilmour, Tim Renwick **Bass**: Gilmour **Keyboards**: Wright, Jon Carin **Programming**: Jon Carin **Drums**: Mason **Percussion**: Mason
Recorded: January–December 1993
Producer: Bob Ezrin, Gilmour
First released: 28 March 1994 (*The Division Bell* track 3)
Rating: 8/10

---

[*] Did Robert Palmer inaugurate this with his 'Addicted To Love' video? Or was it Bob Marley with the I-Threes?
[†] See Guns N' Roses playing at the Freddie Mercury Tribute concert in 1992. The cameraman filming the backing singers from behind so as to capture their posteriors knew *exactly* what he was doing.
[‡] The Black Crowes did this very well.

Musically **POLES APART** is a hugely admirable track, with exquisite acoustic guitar playing in particular,* and also some superbly fluid bass and authoritative singing. Yet there's something vicious and uniquely petulant about the lyrics,† making the song feel less worthy than it should. Acknowledged by Polly Samson as being about Barrett and Waters,‡ her words are uncharitable to both of them, making **POLES APART** feel exceedingly partial (whereas Gilmour has repeatedly credited Waters' lyrical efforts and his shouldering the leadership of the band).§ Judged this way, **POLES APART** is quite vindictive, and undermines the entire 'Keep talking' ethos of the album.

Which is unfortunate, because musically **POLES APART** is excellent, the ringing acoustic notes so rich and warm, the overall sound beautifully organic, the atmosphere so expressive with sadness, nostalgia, affection and compassion. There's a wonderful mature feeling: of discontent and discord transcended, all those absurd youthful squabbles long gone. The opening ringing guitar is so clean and melodic, the supple bass tone (from 0.06) warm and fluid, the keyboards gently melodic, that **POLES APART** feels like a vision of middle age as a kind of serenity. Gilmour's voice when it comes in at 0.37 is likewise pleasantly warm and expressive, suggesting regret and empathy. The lurch downwards ('*Why did we tell you ...*') in the second two lines wisely keep the song's melodic line from getting repetitive, while their lower tone suggests a move from simple nostalgia to something more complex or unpleasant. The second verse (there being no chorus or even refrain) follows immediately after, this time varied by the addition of Mason (from 1.28 onwards, just as the '*Hey you*' line starts).

Then there's a rather lengthy (unless you're Pink Floyd) instrumental section from 2.18 onwards, beginning with a lovely whirring keyboard solo from Wright that suggests light spreading through the sky, which fades out at around 2.50 alongside all the other instruments except the ringing guitar motif. At this point the mood darkens, with sombre orchestral atmospherics, circus sounds like a steam-organ, church bells (a foreshadowing of **HIGH HOPES**) and the mewling of a child. The circus sounds in particular give the impression of childishness, but their shadowiness suggest that all this has been left behind – a sense reinforced when the drums come galloping back in at 4.10 (alongside the guitar motif), dispersing all the clouds in a superb resurgence that evokes the band's renewed self-confidence, or perhaps Gilmour's own faith in himself as bandleader. Either

---

* The guitar tuning is DADGAD (rather than the natural tuning of EADGBE). 'One day, I was on holiday in Greece and I had an acoustic guitar with me. I just decided to tune the bottom string down to D, and continued to experiment until I arrived at that tuning. Then I mucked around a bit and 'Poles Apart' fell out of it a few minutes later.' *Guitar World*, September 1994. DADGAD tuning is actually pretty common: Led Zeppelin's 'Kashmir' uses it.

† This aspect of it reminds me of 'Make Me Smile (Come Up And See Me)' by Steve Harley and Cockney Rebel, a catchy, popular tune (it hit #1 in the UK in 1974). Until you listen to the verses and realise that he's sneering nastily at his old band mates.

‡ Samson: 'It's about Syd in the first verse and Roger in the second'. ('Here We Go, Here We Go, Here We Go', Q magazine, November 1994).

§ For example: 'The lyrics came from Roger – as did a lot of the motivation and a lot of great stuff. I wouldn't for a minute try to play down Roger's importance in our career, 'cause that would be unfair.' 'The Color Of Floyd', *Interview* magazine, July 1994.

way, it's a majestic moment, redoubled with a final verse that emphasises this rekindling, when '*the years and all the sadness fell away from me*'.

The lyrics, then, consist mainly of a number of pointed rhetorical questions in the first two verses, before drawing a kind of conclusion in the third. The verse concerning Barrett seems bizarrely uncharitable. Singing '*Did you know it was all going to go so wrong for you? / And did you see it was all going to be so right for me?*', Gilmour thus appears to belittle a man with schizophrenia and congratulate himself on the commercial success of an album that had more to do with brand name than artistic success. In the second verse, meanwhile, the '*Hey you*' callback immediately brings Waters to mind. The words are as vindictive, asking, '*Did you ever realise what you'd become?*', and as self-congratulatory, saying that Waters had been '*Leading the blind while I stared out the steel in your eyes*'. The discord between the warm mature music and spiteful lyrics creates quite a sense of dissonance. Of course, popular music often works better when lyrics contrast with or form a dialogue with the musical feeling.¶ But that works when there's an artistic point to it, some conflict being dramatised. Here, it simply suggests that Samson was inspired by stories from her partner** on the group's early days, and that Gilmour either was indifferent to her unkind lyric or agreed with it. This mars **POLES APART**, where it should be the cornerstone of the first side of *Division Bell*, because it is musically quite beautiful.

MAROONED (Gilmour, Wright)
Length: 5.29
Guitars: Gilmour **Bass**: Gilmour **Piano**: Wright **Kurtweil synthesiser**: Wright
Keyboards: Wright, Jon Carin **Drums**: Mason
Recorded: January–December 1993
Producer: Bob Ezrin, Gilmour
First released: 28 March 1994 (*The Division Bell* track 4)
Rating: 7/10

It's curious that Pink Floyd's instrumentals after Barrett are mostly minor pieces. While the Waters-dominated era laid great influence on the lyrics, their earlier work (from **CAREFUL WITH THAT AXE, EUGENE** to **ECHOES**) had often emphasised atmosphere over almost every other musical consideration. Some of the soundtrack work, to be fair, was rushed hackwork, but even then it demonstrated the group's astonishing versatility.†† So, following **CLUSTER ONE**, which was really a musical starter, here is a great example of the interplay and melodic sense of Gilmour, Wright and Mason (alongside long-time touring band members Guy Pratt and Jon Carin). Opening with the

---

¶ As Jeff Schwartz also points out in 'Sister Ray: Some Pleasures of the Musical Text'.
** They married in 1994 during the *Division Bell* tour.
†† For example, **MORE BLUES** and **A SPANISH PIECE**.

sound of waves and seagulls* and then a brief rising melody on the keyboards, Gilmour's electric guitar cuts through nicely with a bittersweet piercing tone, with lots of space and reverb – you feel like those notes could go on forever.† As the song gets under way, with Wright on the piano, Gilmour's soloing continues, with a lyrical, singing feel to his playing. (He bends notes more than an octave by using a DigiTech whammy pedal.)‡ This is far from psychedelic noodling: this is mature, expressive, sophisticated rock music. Wright's accompaniment is similarly excellent, unflashily providing wistful ballast to Gilmour's elevated notes. The voting panel on the Grammys felt similarly and awarded Pink Floyd 'Best Rock Instrumental Performance' in 1995 – the only one they would ever receive from that august committee. **MAROONED** may not have great originality or forceful things to say, but in its subdued power and subtle expressiveness, it is a very fine latter-day track. It is also recorded superbly, with a warm, band-in-a-room feeling – far from the sterile digitised horrors of *A Momentary Lapse of Reason*.

A GREAT DAY FOR FREEDOM (Gilmour, Samson)
Length: 4.17
Vocals: Gilmour **Guitars**: Gilmour **Bass**: Gilmour **Piano**: Jon Carin **Synthesiser**: Jon Carin
Drums: Mason **Percussion**: Mason **Orchestral arrangement**: Michael Kamen
Recorded: January–December 1993
Producer: Bob Ezrin, Gilmour
First released: 28 March 1994 (*The Division Bell* track 5)
Rating: 8/10

Though Gilmour is, of course, known primarily as a guitar player, he says 'I love singing. I have spent as much of my life trying to improve my singing as I have practising guitar.'§ *The Division Bell*, far more than *Momentary Lapse*, gives Gilmour a chance to shine as a vocalist. Here, during the verses he sings almost entirely *a cappella* (besides some piano accompaniment and subtle synthesiser atmospherics), and it's wonderful. In a relatively high key (though far from the near falsetto he could produce in the group's early days, as heard on **GREEN IS THE COLOUR** and **FAT OLD SUN**), Gilmour's voice has probably never been as prominent – previous songs that demanded great vocals from him, such as **THE DOGS OF WAR** and **YOUNG LUST**, had an equally strong musical component (or tried to). On **A GREAT DAY FOR FREEDOM** his voice has to carry the song – but succeeds masterfully.

---

* Perhaps a callback to **ECHOES**.
† As is Gilmour's normal methodology, the guitar solo was pieced together from several efforts. 'I probably took three or four passes at [Marooned] and took the best bits out of each.' *Guitar World*, September 1994.
‡ 'It's a great little unit, but I haven't even begun to explore half the things it does. The fact that it allows you to bend a note a full octave is quite shocking.' *Ibid*.
§ *Daily Telegraph*, 19 September 2015 www.telegraph.co.uk/music/artists/david-gilmour-interview-ahead-of-uk-tour/

Opening with a verse about the hopefulness following the collapse of the Berlin Wall and the collapse of Soviet control over Eastern Europe ('*And with glasses high, we raised a cry / For freedom had arrived*'), with terrific control and sustained notes, this is immediately followed by a chorus, which artfully turns from the political to the personal, with a beautifully warm, glowing musical background and lush vocal harmonies, itself skilfully contrasted by some resigned lyrics ('*I dreamed you had left my side / No warmth, not even pride remained*') that seem to link personal dissatisfaction and political strife. A second verse then returns to the political theme, this time from the present perspective and its disappointments ('*Now frontiers shift like desert sands / While nations wash their bloodied hands / Of loyalty, of history / In shades of grey*'). A second chorus has a different lyric, and then from 2.23 there's an extended guitar solo – superbly melodic, with terrific clean lines as the rich orchestral backdrop continues, if perhaps overlong at almost two minutes and thus close to half of the song. But you can't tell the boss to cut the solos. It would be like telling Lemmy from Motorhead to turn his bass down a bit.

Though the lyric is commonly thought to refer to Waters, due to the opening line '*on the day the wall came down*', Gilmour insisted the song was about the 'wonderful moment of optimism when the Wall came down – the release of Eastern Europe from the non-democratic side of the socialist system' and how 'what they have now doesn't seem to be much better'.[¶] In another interview to promote *The Division Bell* he said, '[M]aybe a note of caution should be sounded because you can read too much into it. "A Great Day for Freedom", for example, has got nothing to do with Roger or his "wall". It just doesn't.'[**] Given the moves in recent years towards authoritarianism in Central and Eastern Europe,[††] **A GREAT DAY FOR FREEDOM** is thus remarkably perceptive, and proof that Waters wasn't the only political thinker in the band.[‡‡]

To some extent, **A GREAT DAY FOR FREEDOM** also feels like a Gilmour response to the 'spoken word' tracks from *The Final Cut*, such as **PARANOID EYES** and **SOUTHAMPTON DOCK**. Both primarily feature a singer on their own, albeit with some subtle musical background and atmospherics. But Gilmour shows how to make a song out of it: the vocal melody is strong, the piano forms an effective counterpoint, and the chorus creates an excellent dynamic shift, by changing the perspective, atmosphere, emotion and melody. **A GREAT DAY FOR FREEDOM** is hence another very fine track on *The Division Bell*, demonstrating very strong craftsmanship, musicianship and songwriting. Quite the turnaround from *Momentary Lapse*.

¶   *Guitar World*, September 1994.
**   *Interview* magazine, July 1994.
††   See Anne Applebaum, *Twilight of Democracy: The Seductive Lure of Authoritarianism* (2020).
‡‡   See **ON THE TURNING AWAY** for more on Gilmour's political conscience and charitable work.

WEARING THE INSIDE OUT (Wright, Moore)
Length: 6.49
Vocals: Wright, Gilmour **Guitars**: Gilmour **Bass**: Guy Pratt **Piano**: Wright
Synthesiser: Wright **Farsifa organ**: Wright **Saxophone**: Dick Parry **Drums**: Mason
Backing vocals: Sam Brown, Durga McBroom, Carol Kenyon, Jackie Seridan, Rebecca Leigh-White
Recorded: January–December 1993
Producer: Bob Ezrin, Gilmour
First released: 28 March 1994 (*The Division Bell* track 6)
Rating: 7/10

Ennui and world-weariness are the other side of the middle-age sophistication, experience, acceptance and regret found elsewhere on *The Division Bell*. Here these two emotions have their apotheosis, with Wright's melancholy voice and mournful chords deftly complemented by a late-night saxophone and backing singers that could belong to Sade or any night-time wine bar jazz band. Which is not to dismiss **WEARING THE INSIDE OUT**: its overall effect might feel somewhat self-pitying, but the emotional charge is high, and a characteristic organ solo from Wright (from 2.37) gives a beautiful burst of uplifting emotion, and links it back to his former glories from up until *Wish You Were Here*. There's something deliciously melancholy, like a film noir, about the opening instrumental section, and while Wright's soft-timbred singing might lack range, it has a beautiful vulnerability – the sort of thing at which Pink Floyd once excelled, for example in **GREEN IS THE COLOUR** or **REMEMBER A DAY**, before they started to put on muscle and aggression under Waters' leadership.

Lyrically, **WEARING THE INSIDE OUT** deftly articulates the feelings of failure and loss of vitality that are associated with a mid-life crisis. It's very tempting to try to read into the words some aspects of Floydian history, specifically regarding Wright's ejection from the band, but things are wisely kept very non-specific and symbolic: '*Extinguished by light, I turn on the night / Wear its darkness with an empty smile*'. There is rather a sense of the lyrics being too wordy and florid, such as '*in a word – overrun*' or '*My nervous system all awry*' but as an expression of depression, '*no more than alive / I'd barely survive*' and '*This bleeding heart's / Not beating much*' are superbly bleak (and the latter a nice call back to '*the bleeding hearts and the artists*' from **OUTSIDE THE WALL**). It might all seem a bit self-pitying – this is all very far from the spleen of *Animals* – but it does feel like a genuine portrayal of despair. The backing singers (Sam Brown, Durga McBroom, Carol Kenyon, Jackie Sheridan and Rebecca Leigh-White), meanwhile, in the refrains dramatise the personal conflict of the terminally depressed, knowing what they want but seeing life as a passing cavalcade, or seeing themselves from outside: '*Won't hear a sound* (He's curled into the corner) / *From my mouth* (But still the screen is flickering) / *I've spent too long* (With an endless stream of garbage to) / *On the inside out* (Curse the place)'. While the ending holds out some hope: '*Now we can hear* (Waiting for the flames to break) / *Ourselves again*', a feeling redoubled by Gilmour's subsequent concluding guitar solo, which is typically emotional and authoritative. With such impassioned feeling lurking within him, it seems to say, there's hope for our man yet.

Although the melancholy atmosphere is effective, the doggedness of the song's structure means it starts to feel a little oppressive, with multiple soundalike verses (four of them) and choruses inducing the sense of weariness that the song ought to be dramatising. Taking nearly seven minutes in a song with such little harmonic variety is similarly what civil servants call 'a brave decision'. The title, meanwhile, is another lame pun to which Wright seems to have been partial.[*] **WEARING THE INSIDE OUT** is the most thorough expression of Wright's melancholy, but lacking Water's boldness and insight or Gilmour's craftsmanship and sense of proportion, it feels something of a trudge.[†] It's a worthy effort, and was keenly welcomed as Wright's first lead vocal since *Obscured by Clouds*, but ultimately it drags on the listener just slightly too much for comfort.

TAKE IT BACK (Gilmour, Samson, Laird-Clowes, Ezrin)
Length: 6.12
Vocals: Gilmour **Guitars**: Gilmour, Tim Renwick **Bass**: Gilmour **Keyboards**: Wright
Organ: Wright **Programming**: Jon Carin **Drums**: Mason **Percussion**: Gary Wallis
Backing vocals: Sam Brown, Durga McBroom, Carol Kenyon, Jackie Sheridan, Rebecca Leigh-White
Recorded: January–December 1993
Producer: Bob Ezrin, Gilmour
First released: 28 March 1994 (*The Division Bell* track 7)
Rating: 6/10

There are powerful Gilmour vocals all the way through the Pink Floyd canon, from **SAUCERFUL OF SECRETS** (the live version) to **WELCOME TO THE MACHINE** to **YOUNG LUST** to **THE DOGS OF WAR**. But here, while Gilmour's voice is tremendous, for once you feel it's trying to disguise the weakness of the material. The repeated rising intonation at the start of every second line ('*Her love rains down on me / **Easy** as the breeze / I listen to her breathing / It **sounds** like the waves on the sea*') is exciting, but is the only thing of interest melodically in the entire song, and so eventually becomes grating. **TAKE IT BACK** is hence something of a one-trick pony of a song, desperately requiring propping up through Gilmour's admittedly superb vocal. Musically **TAKE IT BACK** utilises an EBow[‡] unit to good effect, with a superb rippling sound

---

[*] His solo album mostly about his life sailing? *Wet Dream*. Yuck. And **UP THE KHYBER**? Jesus man.
[†] Guy Pratt says the idea for the song came from him: 'The only Pink Floyd song ever that came from an idea of mine ... I came up with this idea of by using a delay creating a bass pad and then playing chords over the top then doing it as one piece.' See www.youtube.com/watch?v=CyckEvPv6lk.
[‡] This 'small battery-powered unit replaces the pick in the right hand letting the guitarist mimic strings, horns, and woodwinds with unbelievable sensitivity.' From www.ebow.com. See **KEEP TALKING**.

from Gilmour's guitar halfway between **RUN LIKE HELL** and the sparkling arpeggios in **ECHOES**, but there's not enough variety so it all feels slightly monotonous. Similarly, the instrumental break from 2.26 feels very similar structurally to the one in **POLES APART**, with a drop-out, gathering and resurgence, and while the guitar solo does build to a satisfying peak at 2.54, it all feels too homogenous. The repeated outro choruses, meanwhile, just bludgeon the song to death during an unnecessary and ultimately tedious final two minutes.

Lyrically, **TAKE IT BACK** is one of those songs that has two parallel meanings:[*] on the one hand it could be about a female partner ('*I was thinking all about her / Burning with rage and desire*') and on the other it could be about Mother Earth resuming control of the planet following an environmental apocalypse ('*Now I have seen the warnings / Screaming from all sides / It's easy to ignore them / God knows I've tried*'). The fact that the video accompanying the single showed various ecological scenes, from icebergs to volcanic lava to deserts, suggests the latter was the main intention.

TAKE IT BACK ultimately feels like it wants to be an Adult Contemporary Top 40 track,[†] with its female backing singers and moderately chugging pace, but while the song's sound and initial impression are good, there's just not enough going on in there for it to merit sustained listening. For once Pink Floyd feel rather hollow.

COMING BACK TO LIFE (Gilmour)
Length: 6.19
Vocals: Gilmour **Guitars**: Gilmour **Bass**: Guy Pratt **Hammond organ**: Wright **Kurtweil synthesiser**: Wright **Keyboards**: Jon Carin **Drums**: Mason
Recorded: January–December 1993
Producer: Bob Ezrin, Gilmour
First released: 28 March 1994 (*The Division Bell* track 8)
Rating: 6.5/10

After some great but overlengthy guitar noodling, another virtuoso *a cappella* singing performance (from 1.30) from Gilmour gets this track going. As with **A GREAT DAY FOR FREEDOM**, his voice sounds superb: mature and sophisticated, yet powerful and confident. If far from the vigour of **YOUNG LUST** or **NOT NOW JOHN**, Gilmour's tone is wonderfully clean and expressive, and he handles some pretty high notes with what feels like ease. (And here the spotlight is much more directly on him as the band leader than in the group's early days.) Unfortunately, the music isn't as inspired, with a mid-paced riff kicking in at 2.35 and never changing pace in the remaining four minutes. There are only two and

---

[*]   Some others being 'Golden Brown' by The Stranglers (about a girl with golden-brown skin, and heroin), and of course 'Every Breath She Takes' by The Police.
[†]   It was released as a single in May 1994, making it to #23 in the UK. The US was less charitable, only sending it to #73.

a half verses, and with neither chorus nor refrain, **COMING BACK TO LIFE** lacks the contrasts or dynamics to retain interest, with the last minute and a half taken up by another overlong Gilmour solo on top of the same clomping riff. It's not that Gilmour's playing is tedious – far from it: the final solo is highly lyrical, and with its warm contented atmosphere you can almost sense Gilmour smiling at the rest of the band as he plays. But with solos topping and tailing the song, and another after the second verse, they comprise well over half the body of the track, which is disproportionate given the thinness of the other musical elements. Like **TAKE IT BACK**, Gilmour's singing and soloing are absolutely terrific, but you feel are designed to conceal the thinness of the material.

Lyrically, **COMING BACK TO LIFE** is the clearest iteration of the rebirth motif present throughout *Division Bell* (see also **POLES APART**, **WEARING THE INSIDE OUT** and **TAKE IT BACK**). The words (solely written by Gilmour) are pleasantly literate and competent,‡ and clearly a loving tribute to his relationship with Samson, and a reflection of his mid–late 1980s personal slump (fighting for control of the band, struggling to complete the album, divorcing his first wife Ginger,§ and by all accounts partying too much during the *Momentary Lapse* tour):

> *Where were you*
> *When I was burned and broken …*
> *And where were you*
> *When I was hurt and I was helpless?*
> *'Cause the things you say*
> *And the things you do surround me*

Good, direct, emotional stuff, but the second verse is more metaphorical, with slightly hackneyed images like '*the seeds of life / And the seeds of change were planted*'.¶ The final image of being '*headed straight / Into the shining sun*' is, however, effective, when placed alongside the warm inviting music. Gilmour may never write an image as effective as '*your roller-blind eyes*' or capture the human condition like on **TIME**, but when he opens up and writes about his feelings he can do so very effectively. It's just a shame that he seems to prefer not to.

But how much did Gilmour have to do with its composition? Floyd contributor and session man Jon Carin has disputed Gilmour's authorship of this song. Carin said on his Facebook page:

---

‡ Such competence is pleasant after *Momentary Lapse*. I still can't get over the line '*Or was it the hand of fate, that seemed to fit just like a glove?*' on **ONE SLIP**. Is there an equivalent of the Razzies for bad lyrics? There ought to be.

§ They were married from 1975 to 1990 and had four children together. He also has four children with Samson, making him one of the most fecund people in rock music. (Although Mick Jagger, Willie Nelson, Flavor Flav and Rod Stewart also have eight children, while Bob Marley had eleven (acknowledged) and Ray Charles had twelve).

¶ The line 'This dangerous but irresistible pastime' refers to sex: '"Oh it's sex, obviously," Gilmour grudgingly tells me, "sex and procreation"'. (*Q* magazine, November 1994).

I laid down a demo by myself of the song on multitrack including the intro synths, drums, piano, harmonium, B3 organ, the distorted sampled electric guitar sustained sound in the middle sanction [sic] etc. Then on top, the lead vocals & acoustic guitars were done, then the bass, then real drums, all superimposed on my demo.[*]

Though Carin obviously can't be counted as a neutral observer.[†] Regardless, **COMING BACK TO LIFE** is one of the weaker songs on *Division Bell*, with its outstanding musicianship and emotional weight unable to conceal its weakness as a composition.

KEEP TALKING (Gilmour, Wright, Samson)
Length: 6.10
Vocals: Gilmour **Talk box**: Gilmour **Guitars**: Gilmour, Tim Renwick **Bass**: Guy Pratt
Hammond organ: Wright **Synthesiser**: Wright **Keyboards**: Jon Carin
Programming: Jon Carin **Drums**: Mason **Backing vocals**: Sam Brown, Durga McBroom, Carol Kenyon, Jackie Sheridan, Rebecca Leigh-White
Recorded: January–December 1993
Producer: Bob Ezrin, Gilmour
First released: 28 March 1994 (*The Division Bell* track 9)
Rating: 8/10

The fourth track in a row to last for between six and seven minutes suggests a certain lack of care about album dynamics on *The Division Bell*, a lapse of the remarkable architectural sense of the Hot Streak albums. Certainly side two[‡] (from **TAKE IT BACK** onwards) isn't as strong as the first. However, the album picks up towards the end, with **KEEP TALKING** the first upturn. Dark, intriguing, richly recorded with frequent earworms and hooks, **KEEP TALKING** is the perhaps the best expression of late-period Floydian studiocraft, alongside a memorably oscillating central motif[§] that maintains interest throughout. The oscillation is no doubt meant to represent vacillation or emotional turbulence, with its on-the-one-hand-but-on-the-other movement deftly conveying uncertainty or incoherence. This is superb songcraft, where the writer not only recognises the metaphorical implications of the music but also builds on them, so that the song is a superbly integrated whole. Similarly, the numerous little earworm moments are extremely enjoyable, such

---

[*] www.facebook.com/joncarinofficial/posts/473441917489318
[†] After going public with his dissatisfaction over the writing credits for *Momentary Lapse* and *Division Bell*, Carin was cast out of the Pink Floyd inner circle, though he continues to perform with Waters. Sidemen are expected to bring ideas, but under the aegis of the bandleader. How that translates to ownership is essentially about power. But it has always been this way: there were arguments about Miles Davis taking credit for songs on *Kind Of Blue*, 40 years earlier, and there doubtless have been ever since someone put his name to a composition and made money from it.
[‡] If it makes sense to think about albums from the CD era as having Side 1 and Side 2. But old habits die hard.
[§] Also played with an EBow – see **TAKE IT BACK**.

as the subtle twinkling synthesisers at 0.46, and the fantastic slide down the bass frets by Guy Pratt at 1.29, just before Gilmour's vocal finally kicks in: superb studiocraft.

Lyrically, **KEEP TALKING** is one of the key tracks on *Division Bell*, its theme of communication going far beyond the romantic to suggest that it is an essential part of our humanity, though not without its difficulties. The mantra by Hawking ('*It doesn't have to be like this / All we need to do is make sure / We keep talking*'), with its impersonal computerised voice, suggests how much easier communication is without emotion, and thus our weakness as humans subject to these passions. And yet while the refrain isn't above a touch of lyrical triteness, the relentless power of the riff as it slams back in to the verse gives **KEEP TALKING** a very sizable kick.

Structurally, **KEEP TALKING** establishes numerous potent binary oppositions: between the verse vocal by Gilmour and the refrain's computerised voice (by physicist Stephen Hawking,¶ but taken from an advert for British Telecom, rather than being performed for the song); between the masculine inarticulacy of the verses and the feminine pleading of the backing singers ('*Why won't you talk to me?! You never talk to me! What are you thinking?! What are you feeling?!*');** between the insistent oscillating riff, and the soaring guitar and synthesiser solos that lift off from 2.48 and 3.25 respectively; and between the refrain and Gilmour's superbly fluid, quavering guitar responses. Just to rub things in even more, Gilmour even ends the song vocalising into a talk box. (Gettit?) Yet the instrument isn't just a metaphor: the talk box gives the ending a further dark shading and replaces Gilmour's vocals, and reinforces the idea of inarticulacy. **KEEP TALKING** is a terrific example of how to take an idea, tease out its connotations and develop them, so as to give the song as much meaning as possible. The only minor flaw is that structurally perhaps it's a little too predictable, with two verses and two refrains, with the two solos coming in the middle, though this does give yet another nice evocation of a fractured pairing. **KEEP TALKING** is hence easily one of the best tracks on *Division Bell*, and a very powerful demonstration of later-day songwriting, craftsmanship and performance. There was some gas in the tank yet.

¶ Author of the best-selling 1988 book *A Brief History of Time* (an explainer on cosmology and theories on time, relativity and black holes), Hawking was Lucasian Professor of Mathematics at the University of Cambridge. He suffered Motor Neuron Disease from the age of 21 and lost his voice in 1985 following pneumonia *(Stephen Hawking: A Life in Science* by Michael White and John Gribbin, 2002). He died in 2018, having been the most famous scientist of his era.

** This might be a ludicrous reading, but there's a hint of *The Waste Land* (1922) by T.S. Eliot in there:
'My nerves are bad tonight. Yes, bad. Stay with me.
Speak to me. Why do you never speak. Speak.
What are you thinking of? What thinking? What?
I never know what you are thinking. Think.'
Maybe male callousness and female pleading in the face of it is just a long-standing theme.

LOST FOR WORDS (Gilmour, Samson)
Length: 5.13
Vocals: Gilmour **Guitars**: Gilmour **Bass**: Gilmour **Piano**: Jon Carin **Keyboards**: Wright, Jon Carin **Synthesiser**: Jon Carin **Drums**: Mason
Recorded: January–December 1993
Producer: Bob Ezrin, Gilmour
First released: 28 March 1994 (*The Division Bell* track 10)
Rating: 6/10

One of the less inventive tracks on *Division Bell*, **LOST FOR WORDS** increases the incidence of the non-communication theme but ironically says nothing more about it. Like **WEARING THE INSIDE OUT**, the narrator is paralysed by feelings of failure; as with **KEEP TALKING** and **WHAT DO YOU WANT FROM ME?**, this renders him near mute while still articulately discussing his feelings; like **POLES APART** there's vindictiveness towards an unnamed other, and self-congratulations as signalled by the snippet from the end of a boxing match where the announcer cries '*Ladies and gentlemen, the winner by a knockout ...!*'; and also like **POLES APART**, a biographical reading is irresistible. Is it Waters that Gilmour is singing about and that Samson wrote about, as '*wasting your time on your enemies / Engulfed in a fever of spite / Beyond your tunnel vision reality fades / Like shadows into the night*'? Who else but Waters could Gilmour be referring to in the second verse when, with greater urgency, he sings, '*So I open my door to my enemies / And I ask 'Could we wipe the slate clean?' / But they tell me to please go fuck myself / You know you just can't win*'? (Unless Gilmour has a lot of enemies that we don't know about.)* The expletive sounds shocking when sung in Gilmour's clean expressive vocal style, and for only the fourth time in the entire Pink Floyd canon – the others being **NOT NOW JOHN**, **PIGS (THREE DIFFERENT ONES)** and **CANDY AND A CURRANT BUN** back in 1967, where it was slurred and murky. Here it's very deliberate, in a rare instance of Gilmour's anger boiling over.

The only interview where Gilmour directly discusses this song only asks what he would do if someone told him to fuck himself. Ever-skilled at evading personal revelations, Gilmour merely lays out the hypotheticals: 'Well, the options are immediate [laughs]. You can simply become a good contortionist – there's one option. Or just deck him. Or talk the matter out.'† Which is bizarrely uninformative – didn't the interviewer wonder who the song referred to? In any case, the reputation of *The Division Bell* and of Gilmour himself of emotional maturity and contentment‡ are belied by this track, whose childish self-congratulation

---

* Although Gilmour can appear aloof, he also seems to be a good and loyal friend. When Paul McCartney's wife Linda died in 1998, he went on tour playing 1950s oldies, just to cheer himself up and get himself out of the house. Who was unobtrusively playing rhythm guitar? A certain David Jon Gilmour.
† *Guitar World*, September 1994.
‡ If you want to hear these qualities, Gilmour's later solo album *On An Island* (2006) is far better at conveying them.

and spite§ make it rather off-putting, despite Gilmour's excellent singing (particularly the urgency of the second verse), his fine clean guitar tone, the supple warmth of the music, and the fine contribution from Wright (or Jon Carin, or both) on keyboards in enhancing that atmosphere.

> **HIGH HOPES** (Gilmour, Samson)
> **Length**: 8.34
> **Vocals**: Gilmour **Guitars**: Gilmour **Lap steel guitar**: Gilmour **Bass**: Gilmour **Kurtweil synthesiser**: Wright **Piano**: Jon Carin **Drums**: Mason **Church bell**: Mason
> **Orchestral arrangement**: Michael Kamen **Voices**: Charlie Gilmour, Steve O'Rourke
> **Recorded**: January–December 1993
> **Producer**: Bob Ezrin, Gilmour
> **First released**: 28 March 1994 (*The Division Bell* track 11)
> **Rating**: 9.5/10

The first song written for *Division Bell*¶ is also its best, and the finest by the group since *The Wall* a quarter-century earlier. Taking the same final place on the album as **SORROW** but doing a hugely superior job as a curtain-closer, **HIGH HOPES** was for twenty years also the final act of the group's entire career, and did this magnificently. Stately, reflective, deeply emotive, and superbly inventive, **HIGH HOPES** is the sound of experience looking back on youth without illusions, seeing life in all its gnarled and untidy glory. It asks if it was all worth it, and – rather like **ECLIPSE** – ends on a litany of beautiful images, poetically suggesting that it was indeed.

Opening with the sound of rural church bells (perhaps hearkening back to **FAT OLD SUN**, another pastoral take on Gilmour's Cambridge youth), and bees humming,** the bells turn to a stately pulse from 0.11, which is then counterpointed by a staccato piano hook (played by Jon Carin), which feels like pin-pricks of nostalgia or memory. Gilmour's deep-toned vocal enters at 0.49 (after a lovely rising note on the bass, while the piano switches to chords), with a slight breathy quality to it, yet sounding stately, dignified, world-weary, reflective, poignant – and above all, utterly assured. The drums, guitar, bass and backing vocals enter for a refrain at 1.12 (just after the key line '*The ringing of the division bell had begun*'), as the song builds intensity and drama, though this is only for two lines. **HIGH HOPES** is prepared, like the best of Pink Floyd, to

---

§   Though the lyrics are by Samson, who appears to be notably more vindictive about Waters than Gilmour usually does. Her February 2023 tweet calling Waters 'antisemitic to your rotten core. Also a Putin apologist and a lying, thieving, hypocritical, tax-avoiding, lip-synching, misogynistic, sick-with-envy, megalomaniac' suggests that old wounds may not be healing (twitter.com/PollySamson/status/1622513762602205184). Gilmour retweeted her, saying 'Every word demonstrably true' (twitter.com/davidgilmour/status/1622735222562226176), in a fine example of English understatement.

¶   'High Hopes, my first composition for the album. The song originated from a phrase that my girlfriend suggested, about how time brings you down … So, if you like, the first thing that got written for the album was much more personal than I've tended to be. And I suppose it set the scene for what was to follow.' *Guitar World*, September 1994.

** A call-back to Waters' **GRANTCHESTER MEADOWS**? Maybe. There's a superb coherence to Pink Floyd's soundworld.

make you wait for the emotional pay-off. Resuming the piano and church bell orchestration, a second verse follows in the same style, but moves to the chorus ('*The grass was greener*') instead of the refrain, with Gilmour's voice rising in tone and becoming more overtly emotional, conveying nostalgia, longing and self-doubt. If not quite up there with Waters' astonishing characterisations in **THE TRIAL**, it's still a remarkable display of vocal authority and control.

But this too is cut short, lasting just four lines, leading to another verse and refrain with the same musical structure, which then brings a musical interlude (from 2.56). With its drummer-boy snares, plucked acoustic strings, and atmospheric synthesiser by Wright, its bold cinematic atmosphere suggests emotional scenes from life, and adds to the track's intensity, if without suggesting anything climactic. Yet it too is cut short for the piano and church bells to resume, and then a final verse and a second chorus that extends the meaning of the first through its concluding litany of poignant images ('*The dawn mist glowing / The water flowing / The endless river / For ever and ever*'). And then from 5.16 there's that lap steel guitar solo: the finest ever by Gilmour on that instrument (even better than on **ONE OF THESE DAYS**), with a majesty and emotion that are simply incomparable. With the track's walking pace and open feel, Gilmour has a lot of space to work in, and makes the most of it, going from relatively low notes to build to a dramatic peak at 6.08 but not finishing there, developing the melodic theme of the solo (a four-note pattern that hits feelings of sadness and nostalgia just like 'Syd's Theme' from **SHINE ON YOU CRAZY DIAMOND**) and peaking again before fading out to the exquisite sound of church bells tolling away in a steady pulse.

All told, **HIGH HOPES** is Pink Floyd's best song since **COMFORTABLY NUMB**, combining intense emotion with a universal theme, excellent musicianship (Gilmour's lap steel solo is absolutely masterful) with an unhurried but unpredictable structure, and poetic lyrical flair with superb vocals. It gives *The Division Bell* a real emotional heft, and retains its sense of nostalgia, reflection and world-weariness by never sounding forced or unearned. The track also keeps the listener on their toes by constantly shifting from section to section earlier than expected, which might symbolise the way life throws random uppercuts at you. Fading out with the church bells still ringing, like a pulse echoing down the years, **HIGH HOPES** demonstrates all that is good about Gilmour-led Pink Floyd, from his very fine singing to his deeply affecting soloing to the more direct and personal lyrics. Going from the youthful exuberance of **ARNOLD LANE** to the undeceived malcontent of age and experience* in **HIGH HOPES**

---

* Something about **HIGH HOPES** reminds me of Philip Larkin's evocation of his readers in *All What Jazz* (1970): 'Sometimes I imagine them, sullen fleshy inarticulate men, stockbrokers, sellers of goods, living in thirty-year-old detached houses among the golf courses of Outer London, husbands of ageing and bitter wives they first seduced to Artie Shaw's 'Begin the Beguine' or the Squadronaires' 'The Nearness of You'; [...] men in whom a pile of scratched coverless 78s in the attic can awaken memories of vomiting blindly from small Tudor windows to Muggsy Spanier's 'Sister Kate', or winding up a gramophone in a punt to play Armstrong's 'Body and Soul'; men whose first coronary is coming like Christmas; who drift, loaded helplessly with commitments and obligations and necessary observances, into the darkening avenues of age and incapacity, deserted by everything that once made life sweet.' Larkin of course is the doyen of undeception.

was a perfect journey, an artistic trajectory of such coherence that nothing more needed to be said. (Though the temptation is always to keep feeding the monster. Welcome to the machine.)

With a far more organic feel than *Momentary Lapse*, *The Division Bell* is also by far the better album, if perhaps only once reaching the group's former glories. Its theme of non-communication registers without deflecting from the music, and its warm 'band in a room' atmosphere is a huge improvement over the previous album's ghastly 1980s production. There are, however, marked slips in some of the songwriting, particularly **TAKE IT BACK**. Yet songs like **HIGH HOPES**, **KEEP TALKING** and **MAROONED** are inventive, intelligent and touching, and many would place **HIGH HOPES** on the group's all-time greats. Gilmour and Samson's lyrics are also generally far better than those on *Momentary Lapse*, with some of them more revealing than any songs released by the group since **STAY** from 1972, while also avoiding stinkers that sullied tracks like **ONE SLIP**. *The Division Bell* may not stake out new musical ground – not many rock artists succeed in doing so when aged 48, as Gilmour was at the time of release – but it re-established Pink Floyd as a respectable creative force in a way that *Momentary Lapse* failed to, that album's chart success notwithstanding. Gilmour's voice, meanwhile, has never sounded better, and takes centre stage on songs like **COMING BACK TO LIFE**, **WHAT DO YOU WANT FROM ME?** and **A GREAT DAY FOR FREEDOM**. His guitar playing is likewise tremendous: clean, uncluttered, lyrical, affecting, and utterly authoritative. Wright, meanwhile, does not get many traditional Farsifa or Hammond moments, but his piano playing is often urbanely melancholy and superbly judged, and his moment in the spotlight in **WEARING THE INSIDE OUT** is very welcome. All of which means *The Division Bell* is not a veritable classic, but its mature, understated pleasures are always worth hearing, and it's really the only solid original album the band have released following the end of their hot streak in 1979. Without it their legacy would look very different.

THINGS LEFT UNSAID (Gilmour, Wright)
Length: 4.26
Guitar: Gilmour **EBow guitar**: Gilmour **Keyboards**: Wright **Percussion**: Mason, Bob Ezrin
Recorded: January–December 1993, November 2013–January 2014
Producer: Gilmour, Phil Manzanera, Youth, Andy Jackson
First released: 7 November 2014 (*The Endless River* track 1)
Rating: 5/10

Various references and rumours of what would become *The Endless River* had long circulated. The *Division Bell* sessions had apparently also yielded numerous ambient tracks, usually referred to as 'The Big Spliff'. Pink Floyd doing ambient music required no great leap of the imagination: in fact, they were godfathers of the genre, with later innovators like The KLF* and The Orb† keen to assert their debt to the Floyd while anonymously created ambient versions of *Dark Side* and various other tracks such as **ECHOES** and **SHEEP** already exist.‡ But it wasn't until after Wright's death in 2008 that Gilmour decided to make something of the tapes. With further work by Gilmour, Mason, co-producers Phil Manzanera, Youth, and Andy Jackson, Bob Ezrin, Guy Pratt and various session men, the album was completed and released in 2014.

Gilmour described *The Endless River* as 'a continuous flow of music that builds gradually over four separate pieces over the 55-odd minutes'.§ With each track segueing artfully to the next, the loud/quiet fast/slow dynamics and resolutions typical of pop and rock were abandoned, in favour of a steady stream of atmospheric music. Without any real vocals except in one track, *The Endless River* also immediately cuts out half of what made Pink Floyd. This isn't to say there aren't pleasant surprises, but musically *The Endless River* largely takes its cue from the repetitiveness of ambient music, without achieving the style or cumulative effect of that genre.

THINGS LEFT UNSAID exemplifies this tension – or lack of it – perfectly. Fading in slowly, with some dialogue from Wright from 0.14 ('There's certainly an unspoken understanding … But there's a lot of things unsaid as well') and then less distinguishable criss-crossing lines from what sounds like Wright and others (perhaps Gilmour?), until 0.49, when there's a thump like a computer game loading screen. The music – or soundscape – goes from nebulous to atmospherically cloudy, with shifting notes suggesting moving clouds and silvery veins of crystalline Gilmour guitar hinting at a melody but never quite getting there, either. After a much slighter thump at 3.48, Gilmour starts playing a higher-pitched EBow guitar,¶ to create sounds rather like whale songs. **THINGS LEFT UNSAID** is typically Floydian in its unhurried nature, but unlike former glories never once suggests it is going anywhere. It just drifts by like one of the many YouTube space ambient videos: pleasant, but unmemorable. It isn't the case that ambient music doesn't create proper songs: 'Little Fluffy Clouds' by The Orb and the entire *Sakura* and *Grinning Cat* albums by Japanese artist Susumu Yokota do so brilliantly. But you need some kind of hook to hang onto, and *The Endless River* almost defiantly refuses to supply any. It was all very well patiently developing soundscapes in **ECHOES** or **SHINE ON YOU CRAZY DIAMOND** or even **CAREFUL WITH THAT AXE, EUGENE**, but these always ultimately lead somewhere.

---

* Their album *Chill Out* (1990) has a cover featuring sheep in a field, in a sly take on *Atom Heart Mother*, and samples **ON THE RUN**.

† They made the *Metallic Spheres* album with Gilmour in 2010. It's quite good, if not a patch on The Orb's glory days. Orb member Youth is a co-producer on *The Endless River*.

‡ They are widely but incorrectly attributed to The Orb.

§ BBC Radio 6 Music interview, 6 October 2014.

¶ See **TAKE IT BACK** and **KEEP TALKING** for more on the EBow. Guitarists like to say that every new guitar produces a song. The same seems true for devices like the EBow.

IT'S WHAT WE DO (Gilmour, Wright)
Length: 6.17
Guitars: Gilmour **Keyboards**: Wright **Percussion**: Mason
Recorded: January–December 1993, November 2013–January 2014
Producer: Gilmour, Phil Manzanera, Youth, Andy Jackson
First released: 7 November 2014 (*The Endless River* track 2)
Rating: 6/10

As the atmosphere dissolves at the end of **THINGS LEFT UNSAID** and into the next track **IT'S WHAT WE DO**, a touch of keyboards from Wright opens the latter song, though it too fades for some resounding chords by Gilmour and then Wright takes on the Farsifa for a bit of noodling from 0.13 to 1.00, while Gilmour repeats the guitar parts and there's some nice atmospheric background. This fades away, then Wright's Farsifa comes in again, this time with Mason adding a placid, unhurried rhythm and some very resonant drum fills, Gilmour playing some lead guitar wibbles and Wright thickening the brew with more keyboards of various textures. Wright drops out at 2.29 and Gilmour then has a long, meandering but entirely distinctive guitar solo, with fine bent notes, lots of spaces and that quintessential bluesy-yet-spacey vibe. He's a much better craftsman than at the time of, say, **MEDDLE**,** so here he sounds authoritative, even magisterial – but it still lacks vision. In other words, he's a world-class guitarist doodling away. The backing atmosphere alters while Gilmour plays, perhaps suggesting the sunlight shimmering on a shifting sea, or to obscure the fact that his solo just goes on and on to no real point. **IT'S WHAT WE DO** has rather a traditional Pink Floyd rhythm to it so isn't an ambient track, and could almost have come from the *Dark Side* rehearsals or maybe been a *Wish You Were Here* reject. The shifting atmospheres around the soloists is actually a nice touch, like a man standing still while the world around him changes. Which is probably what life feels like when you're in your sixties. But at over six minutes, **IT'S WHAT WE DO** is a few musical ideas spread very thinly and only propped up by the fact that it's almost always enjoyable to hear a Gilmour guitar solo.

EBB AND FLOW (Gilmour, Wright)
Length: 1.55
Guitars: Gilmour **Keyboards**: Wright **Percussion**: Mason
Recorded: January–December 1993, November 2013–January 2014
Producer: Gilmour, Phil Manzanera, Youth, Andy Jackson
First released: 7 November 2014 (*The Endless River* track 3)
Rating: 6/10

** Well, you would hope so, after 43 more years as a professional musician.

The final resounding chord of **IT'S WHAT WE DO** crossfades deftly into **EBB AND FLOW**, fading away to be replaced by what sounds like universe static or dolphin chatter – though only for four seconds, as a brief cymbal-sizzle wipes the aural slate clean for Wright to play a tasteful, typically subdued electric piano solo, interspersed with some Gilmour guitar flourishes that repeat as motifs throughout the album. These are shiny, metallic and high-pitched, giving a tingling sensation, or the sense that the guitar strings themselves are singing. It sounds superb. **EBB AND FLOW** has no drumming, but there's a very nice cymbal *tiss* at 1.23 as Gilmour plays an open chord and Wright continues on the electric piano, all three elements marvellously combining to suggest a new dawn breaking. But these all just fade out, leaving only the faint sounds of (perhaps) woodland animals at night for the last twenty seconds. And that's side one finished. **EBB AND FLOW** sounds pretty good over its ninety seconds of music: in fact, it's much superior to the rather similar **ROUND AND AROUND** from *Momentary Lapse*. It's just that these things work best as interstitials between actual songs.

SUM (Gilmour, Wright, Mason)
Length: 4.48
Guitars: Gilmour **Keyboards**: Wright, Damon Iddins **Percussion**: Mason
Recorded: January–December 1993, November 2013–January 2014
Producer: Gilmour, Phil Manzanera, Youth, Andy Jackson
First released: 7 November 2014 (*The Endless River* track 4)
Rating: 6/10

Opening with swirling womb-like sounds,* and a hint of the beginning of **CLUSTER ONE**, **SUM** starts to coalesce into keyboard chords at around 0.45 that hearken back to the opening of **ASTRONOMY DOMINE** from *Ummagumma*. These, however, continue on uninterrupted for over thirty seconds, until a powerful guitar chord rips apart the ethereal atmosphere at 1.22. Then, as the keyboards carry on, a solid drumbeat from Mason gives it all a sense of power and drive, while Gilmour plays some guitar licks. And so it carries on, Mason's drum fills promising to take the song somewhere but never settling into anything other than this holding pattern. Finally, as the guitar fades into the sky at around 4.06, an electric piano emerges and offers a mid-range doodling for twenty seconds as the soundworld starts to disintegrate into shimmering skies and bird song. In its energetic phase **SUM** is reminiscent of the opening of **TIME** with its rototoms and mighty guitar chords – but that built up a huge amount of tension before kicking into its magnificent verses and choruses, whereas this track has moments that sound promising but never amount to anything. It's not that traditional forms are essential to enjoy music, but rather that **SUM** builds tension almost expertly and then fails to deliver.

---

* Slightly reminiscent of the opening to 'Caramel' by Blur, from their *13* album (1999).

SKINS (Gilmour, Wright, Mason)
Length: 2.37
Guitars: Gilmour **Bass**: Andy Jackson **Keyboards**: Wright **Percussion**: Mason
Recorded: January–December 1993, November 2013–January 2014
Producer: Gilmour, Phil Manzanera, Youth, Andy Jackson
First released: 7 November 2014 (*The Endless River* track 5)
Rating: 6/10

As the shimmer continues from **SUM**, the sound of Mason beating various drum skins gradually fades in, offering Mason a rare chance to step into the limelight. (It must be his first since being the sole focus during **ONE OF THESE DAYS** from *Live at Pompeii* in 1972.) Meanwhile, the atmosphere swirls manically around, giving the impression of Mason alone and spotlighted while everything moves chaotically around him. Mason's tattoo is a pretty basic figure, but the tones are skilfully varied between tom-toms, snares and metallic rim-taps (or something like it), and the dynamic between repetition and chaos maintains the listener's attention for the two minutes allotted. This is no **GRAND VIZIER'S GARDEN PARTY**: it's quite good, in fact, until you remember that the group had done the repeated-drum-figure-while-chaos-spirals-out-of-control thing much more successfully in **A SAUCERFUL OF SECRETS**, a mere forty-six years earlier. **SKINS** smartly doesn't outstay its welcome, the drums fading away alongside an electrified guitar shard from Gilmour at 1.46, but leaving an overgenerous forty-five seconds of echoes, electronic burbling and spacey atmospherics.

UNSUNG (Wright)
Length: 1.07
Guitars: Gilmour **Keyboards**: Wright **Percussion**: Mason
Recorded: January–December 1993, November 2013–January 2014
Producer: Gilmour, Phil Manzanera, Youth, Andy Jackson
First released: 7 November 2014 (*The Endless River* track 6)
Rating: 5/10

Some shimmering keyboards by Wright (slightly reminiscent of 'Sex Object' by Kraftwerk),† some searching, piercing wah-wah-pedalled guitar from Gilmour (reminiscent of the start of **MAROONED**), punctuated by some drums and expensive-sounding piano, before pretty quickly fading out. That's really all there is. It's high-class doodling, expertly produced – but doodling is really all that it is. It isn't atmospheric, because there's no atmosphere being suggested, and it isn't ambient music, which usually means a slowly building effect through repetition. Here you feel simple aimlessness, a wish simply to play rather than to have to write. Pink Floyd may be fine doodlers, but you can't call the songs

---

† From their 1986 album *Electric Café*.

improvisations; there's no sense of each musician listening to each other and that affecting what they play. It's just aural wallpaper. High quality wallpaper, for sure, but wallpaper all the same.

ANISINA (Gilmour)
Length: 3.16
Guitars: Gilmour **Keyboards**: Wright **Percussion**: Mason **Tenor saxophone**: Gilad Atzmon **Clarinet**: Gilad Atzmon
Recorded: January-December 1993, November 2013-January 2014
Producer: Gilmour, Phil Manzanera, Youth, Andy Jackson
First released: 7 November 2014 (*The Endless River* track 7)
Rating: 6/10

Ending side two, **ANISINA** is the first to feel like an actual song, with a sprightly walking rhythm, a melody and an identifiable structure, with verses and successive choruses over which we have clarinet, saxophone and guitar solos. For once the atmosphere is upbeat and sustained rather than shadowy and fragmentary; yet it still feels insubstantial, probably because the melody is rather too close to that in the chorus of 'I'm Going Home', the torch song sung by Frank N' Furter in *The Rocky Horror Picture Show* (1975). The soaring clarinet line is pretty but clichéd, though the piano by Wright has a very welcome stateliness, giving **ANISINA** much-needed heft when combined with a misjudged country-style steel guitar (from 0.39) and the trite would-be transcendent chorus melody. Further echoing themselves, the group add a very sneaky and entirely unnecessary glimmer/echo of the strings from **COMFORTABLY NUMB** at around 0.26: perhaps an attempt at crowd-pleasing, but surely the last thing Pink Floyd should be doing. Later on, the lush backing vocals from **A GREAT DAY FOR FREEDOM** reappear, or are evoked at least, at around 1.16. These efforts to evoke themselves might be conceptually coherent: *The Endless River* is rather like a Joycean stream of flickering memories and song fragments, sometimes cohering, sometimes not, perhaps symbolising memory in old age. However, as with *The Final Cut*, a compelling concept does not necessarily lead to a good album. You've got to have tunes, man. But judged simply as an individual track, **ANISINA** does at least bring side two to a fairly effective end, featuring one of the stronger melodies on *The Endless River*. But that's a low bar.

THE LOST ART OF CONVERSATION (Wright)
Length: 1.42
Piano: Wright **Synthesiser**: Wright **Percussion**: Gilmour **Guitar**: Gilmour
Recorded: January-December 1993, November 2013-January 2014
Producer: Gilmour, Phil Manzanera, Youth, Andy Jackson
First released: 7 November 2014 (*The Endless River* track 8)
Rating: 5/10

Side three begins with three tracks with the same running time: a triptych of sorts? Floating in first is **THE LOST ART OF CONVERSATION**, which begins with ethereal atmospherics and a slightest tinge of guitar from 0.14 to 0.29. A doodling bit of piano from Wright then fades in, in a rather ghostly way, the echoing resonance suggestive of the perennial Floydian motif of absence, but here very specifically recalling Wright's own death. It's a nice, typically melancholic piece of piano from Wright, and played with his impeccable touch, but it really is just him aimlessly noodling about on the piano. A few liquid Gilmour chords (reminiscent of **BREATHE**) add a subtle colouring, and there's a brief deep resonance from a bass drum briefly darkening the atmosphere off at 1.23. *The Endless River* was marketed as a tribute to Wright and as his 'swansong,'* but getting past the emotion, songs like **THE LOST ART OF CONVERSATION** are just tarted-up snippets of doodlings. The engineering might be great, the painterly touches by Gilmour are those of a master craftsman in developing atmosphere, but it just doesn't add up to anything much. Vain echoes, desist.

ON NOODLE STREET (Gilmour, Wright)
Length: 1.42
Guitars: Gilmour **Keyboards**: Wright, Jon Carin **Percussion**: Mason **Bass**: Guy Pratt
Recorded: January–December 1993, November 2013–January 2014
Producer: Gilmour, Phil Manzanera, Youth, Andy Jackson
First released: 7 November 2014 (*The Endless River* track 9)
Rating: 6/10

Segueing in from **THE LOST ART OF CONVERSATION**, **ON NOODLE STREET** quickly moves into slinky late-night jazz† territory, thanks to a warm refined pulse from long-time bassist Guy Pratt.‡ It's all very twilight, with electric piano from Wright or perhaps Jon Carin, an unhurried beat from Mason and atmospheric keyboards shimmering past. **ON NOODLE STREET** builds a highly elegant if entirely familiar atmosphere for its duration, but doesn't extend it or develop it. It's just there for a period and then it ends. Though it is interesting to hear the group playing adult contemporary music that you might sooner expect to hear from Sade or late-period George Michael,§ **ON NOODLE STREET** isn't a pastiche: like the stylistic diversions on *Obscured by Clouds*, it illustrates the group's remarkably catholic taste and abilities. But unlike *Obscured by Clouds*, the group haven't made a song of it – even considering its part in side three of *The Endless River*.

---

* 'Btw Pink Floyd album out in October is called "The Endless River". Based on 1994 sessions is Rick Wright's swansong and very beautiful.' Tweet from Polly Samson on 5 July 2014. twitter.com/PollySamson/status/485411029573439488.
† Fortunately nothing like the sex-jazz music of **MUDMEN**.
‡ If you take his term in the group as 1987 to 2022, that's 35 years. Waters had 19 years, 1966 to 1985.
§ Especially his album *Older* (1996), which I adore.

NIGHT LIGHT (Gilmour, Wright)
Length: 1.42
Guitars: Gilmour **Keyboards**: Wright **Percussion**: Mason
Recorded: January–December 1993, November 2013–January 2014
Producer: Gilmour, Phil Manzanera, Youth, Andy Jackson
First released: 7 November 2014 (*The Endless River* track 10)
Rating: 4/10

NIGHT LIGHT drifts along with occasional glints of the silvery Gilmour guitar first heard in **THINGS LEFT UNSAID**, alongside nebulous, drifting keyboards. The guitar isn't quite a musical motif (as with the guitar figure heard repeatedly in *The Wall*), but rather a recurring ingredient or musical fragment, ultimately adding to very little. It's just there. Several classic Pink Floyd songs feature asynchronous, drifting sections, such as **DOGS** and **ECHOES**, but these always had some artistic point to them. **NIGHT LIGHT**, on the other hand, is vaguely nebulous and sounds sort of nice enough, but is plainly intended simply as a dynamic shift before **ALLONS-Y (1)**.

ALLONS-Y (1) (Gilmour)
Length: 1.57
Guitars: Gilmour **Keyboards**: Wright, Jon Carin **Percussion**: Mason **Bass**: Bob Ezrin
Percussion loop: Jon Carin
Recorded: January–December 1993, November 2013–January 2014
Producer: Gilmour, Phil Manzanera, Youth, Andy Jackson
First released: 7 November 2014 (*The Endless River* track 11)
Rating: 6/10

Wherein Gilmour does a bit of that chugging, driving guitar from **RUN LIKE HELL**, and there's exactly the same drum beat. After the longueurs of **ON NOODLE STREET** and **NIGHT LIGHT**, **ALLONS-Y (1)** does provide a welcome touch of drive and energy, but there's a very unfortunate feeling of fan service, of Gilmour pandering to the fan base by giving us a taste of his most loved guitar pieces. **ALLONS-Y (1)**[*] has an enjoyable surging chord change every eight bars and some adequate soloing on top of the **RUN LIKE HELL** riff, but ultimately feels like less than its constituent parts because of their familiarity. Its dynamic shift from **NIGHT LIGHT** might be welcome but it's hardly the kind of masterful tonal shift the band once displayed, as on the move from **ONE OF MY TURNS** to **DON'T LEAVE ME NOW** or on the numerous sections in **ECHOES**. There is craft, to be fair, but with inferior materials.

---

[*] That's 'let's go' in French, of course: a reminder of the group's Francophilia, and Gilmour's linguistic skills – see **SAINT TROPEZ**.

AUTUMN '68 (Wright)
Length: 1.35
Royal Albert Hall Organ: Wright **Keyboards**: Damon Iddins
Recorded: 26 June 1969, November 2013–January 2014
Producer: Gilmour, Phil Manzanera, Youth, Andy Jackson
First released: 7 November 2014 (*The Endless River* track 12)
Rating: 7/10

Sandwiched between **ALLONS-Y (1)** and **ALLONS-Y (2)** is **AUTUMN '68**, which features Wright playing on the famed[†] organ in the Royal Albert Hall, taking from a recording of the group's concert there on 26 June 1969. Why then the '68 title? It must be an allusion to **SUMMER '68**, perhaps a reflection of the more sophisticated sound of this track. Wright's organ playing is typically elegant and stately, and also a reminder that rock once had to knock down the doors of high culture to gain acceptance as a valid artform. Now, when rock music is no longer a living cultural force in Western countries,[‡] its force and danger have also disappeared, and legacy bands release box sets costing hundreds of pounds, and you can have a Sex Pistols credit card. But nothing lasts forever. As a track, **AUTUMN '68** is basically Wright warming up on the organ, with some atmospheric touches added to enrichen the texture, such as a shimmering gong and cymbal-sizzles at various points, and a Mike Oldfield-esque piece of guitar from 1.10. But the track starts to dissolve in the last twenty seconds, and giving just over a minute of Wright playing, which makes **AUTUMN '68** one of the few tracks on *The Endless River* where you wished it carried on for longer.

ALLONS-Y (2) (Gilmour)
Length: 1.32
Guitars: Gilmour **Keyboards**: Wright, Jon Carin **Percussion**: Mason **Bass**: Bob Ezrin
Percussion loop: Jon Carin
Recorded: January–December 1993, November 2013–January 2014
Producer: Gilmour, Phil Manzanera, Youth, Andy Jackson
First released: 7 November 2014 (*The Endless River* track 13)
Rating: 6/10

Reprising **ALLONS-Y (1)**, with more guitar soloing on top of the **RUN LIKE HELL**-esque riff, **ALLONS-Y (2)** has a satisfying sense of drive, but only for

---

[†] It has its own website (www.royalalberthallorgan.com), a Wikipedia page and a Twitter account. That's fame.

[‡] The total revenue of the recorded music industry was US$31.2 billion in 2022 (www.ifpi.org/ifpi-global-music-report-global-recorded-music-revenues-grew-9-in-2022/). Whereas video games were expected to hit revenues of US$334 billion in 2023 (www.statista.com/outlook/dmo/digital-media/video-games/worldwide). That's where the energy of young people is. Popular music once was an essential part of the British national identity and discourse, but no longer. There's a great Facebook page which posts Ceefax pages of the Top 10 singles from bygone years. I saw one from 1987, when I was eight years old, and I could instantly remember nine of them. See www.facebook.com/classiccharts. If you don't know what Ceefax was, ask your dad. Or maybe your grandad.

about a minute, given the fade-in and fade-out, and it hence ultimately feels unnecessary. Did Gilmour partition the tracks to give himself a greater share of royalties, as he suggested Waters did with **PIGS ON THE WING (PART 1)** and **PIGS ON THE WING (PART 2)**?* As it is, there's no feeling of return or development from **ALLONS-Y (2)**, no artistic point at all. Pink Floyd were once the great musical architects, using artful song placement to create meaning throughout their hot streak from *Dark Side* to *The Wall*. Gilmour is, of course, an exceptional craftsman as a musician, but that ear for detail does mean he sometimes fails to see the broader picture. A reprise should be a comment on what has happened in the period between the two tracks – think about how the reprise of **BREATHE** at the end of **TIME** feels like a homecoming after a tiring journey, or how the acoustic tenderness of **PIGS ON THE WING (PART 2)** chases away the horror, paranoia and disgust of **DOGS**, **PIGS (THREE DIFFERENT ONES)** and **SHEEP**. Whereas **ALLONS-Y (2)** is just a slight variation on its predecessor.

TALKIN' HAWKIN' (Gilmour, Wright)
Length: 3.29
Guitars: Gilmour **Keyboards**: Wright **Percussion**: Mason **Bass**: Guy Pratt **Backing vocals**: Durga McBroom
Recorded: January–December 1993, November 2013–January 2014
Producer: Gilmour, Phil Manzanera, Youth, Andy Jackson
First released: 7 November 2014 (*The Endless River* track 14)
Rating: 6/10

The final track of side three is the most substantial, both artistically and in terms of its duration. After six tracks lasting less than two minutes, **TALKIN' HAWKIN'** is the first to go beyond three minutes. But of far greater import is that it feels much richer than its predecessors on side three, with gorgeous melancholic (if somewhat repetitive) piano, some wonderful soloing from Gilmour, and excellent backing vocals† from backing mainstay Durga McBroom, who had toured with the group on the *Momentary Lapse* and *Division Bell* tours. But there's another sense of fan service in the use of words from Stephen Hawking, which of course recalls **KEEP TALKING**. That song felt original, creative, thoughtful, and Floydian in the best sense of the word. **TALKIN' HAWKIN'** by comparison feels a rather pointless and certainly less effective retread. Some might think it enough to hear the band's off-cuts, but when compared to the gargantuan achievements throughout the group's career, from **SEE EMILY PLAY** to **HIGH HOPES**, tracks like **TALKIN' HAWKIN'** can't help but appear pedestrian. It's not bad, but it ain't boss, and boy, Pink Floyd can do boss.

---

* And as he himself probably did on **A NEW MACHINE PART 1** and **A NEW MACHINE PART 2**.
† Though they do seem to hearken back to the backing vocals on **BRAIN DAMAGE**.

CALLING (Gilmour, Anthony Moore)
Length: 3.37
Guitars: Gilmour **Keyboards**: Wright, Anthony Moore **Percussion**: Mason
Recorded: January–December 1993, November 2013–January 2014
Producer: Gilmour, Phil Manzanera, Youth, Andy Jackson
First released: 7 November 2014 (*The Endless River* track 15)
Rating: 5/10

Side four opens with **CALLING**, which itself opens with what sounds like the dark dystopian introductory music to an RPG video game from the mid-2000s: our overly polygonised hero finds himself in an alien landscape far in the future, and you have to help him find his way back to Earth. Joking aside, **CALLING** does sound rather like a sci-fi soundscape, with shards of electricity and ominous atmospherics, before taking shape at 1.21 with a keyboard melody of three notes repeated in successively lower tones, alongside more ominous piano chords. Then after a drifting section (with pulsing womb sounds right at the end), a guitar comes in at 2.13: Gilmour playing some desolate, keening, searching notes, albeit in a very 1980s, thin-toned fuzz-box sort of way.‡ After a computer loading-screen thump at 2.46, the tone shifts: there's a sense of light and warmth coming through the shadowiness, of moving towards recognisable landscapes and humanity, before drifting to nowhere specific (or to **EYES TO PEARLS**, at least). **CALLING** barely sounds Floydian: it feels more like Gilmour trying to find space to interject a guitar solo over some rather hackneyed atmospherics devised by people who haven't played a video game in a decade. It certainly creates and sustains an atmosphere, but it's still slightly like your grandad wandering into a teenage online gaming session, or Stan Marsh explaining why rock music was the real thing to the *South Park* kids playing *Guitar Hero*. At best one can applaud Gilmour for trying something new so far into his career, but his talents are surely best suited to actual songs.

EYES TO PEARLS (Gilmour)
Length: 1.51
Guitars: Gilmour **Keyboards**: Wright **Percussion**: Mason **Bass**: Andy Jackson
Recorded: January–December 1993, November 2013–January 2014
Producer: Gilmour, Phil Manzanera, Youth, Andy Jackson
First released: 7 November 2014 (*The Endless River* track 16)
Rating: 5/10

A tick-tocking Gilmour guitar lead opens this, creating a modicum of drama and tension, especially on top of the vibrating gongs, sizzling cymbals, energetic bass-playing by producer Andy Jackson, and deep-echoed drums, all of which

---

‡ If you've ever seen the TV show *Garth Merenghi's Darkplace* (2004), you'll know *exactly* the kind of sound.

float spaciously around the background. Good stuff – except, like everything on *The Endless River*, it doesn't go anywhere. There's increased drama and atmosphere once the keyboards enter at 1.01, alongside a few instances of what vaguely sounds like the 'bing!' motif from **ONE OF THESE DAYS**, which keep the whole thing ticking over until at around 1.30, when the atmospherics and keyboards drop out, leaving the guitar figure, bass and drums there to slowly fade out. **EYES TO PEARLS** could be a pretty decent introduction to a song, but what's the point in developing the tension and atmosphere if you're going to immediately segue to something different or fail to capitalise on them? If this is Gilmour's understanding of ambient music – and this is a guy who had just recently recorded an album with The Orb,* titled *Metallic Spheres* (2010) – it's only apparent how little he appreciates the genre.

SURFACING (Gilmour)
Length: 2.46
Guitars: Gilmour **Keyboards**: Wright **Percussion**: Mason **Backing vocals**: Durga McBroom
Recorded: January–December 1993, November 2013–January 2014
Producer: Gilmour, Phil Manzanera, Youth, Andy Jackson
First released: 7 November 2014 (*The Endless River* track 17)
Rating: 6/10

Sparkling guitar arpeggios open **SURFACING**, recalling the delicious opening to **POLES APART**. But here they lead to some superb Gilmour soloing from 0.28, high and crystalline and as utterly distinctive as ever, firstly over the sparkling intro guitar riff and a few drum fills, then on top of a rather plodding mid-tempo rhythm that kicks off from 0.57 (alongside a rather ill-fitting wordless Durga McBroom backing vocal). Gilmour continues soloing with emotion and intensity throughout, but there's never the sense in **SURFACING** of it meaning anything, the tempo unchanging, the atmosphere and emotional tone unvarying. The song fades away in the last fifteen seconds, adding the sound of tolling church bells at the last moment in a very unnecessary hearkening-back to **HIGH HOPES**. That song had enormous gravitas and emotion. **SURFACING** by comparison is tasteful – a dread word when it comes to rock music, which is at its best when it's transgressive – and consequently inconsequential, never achieving the emotional response merited by the quality of Gilmour's playing. But it takes more than that to have an enjoyable song.†

---

* Their album *The Orb's Adventures Beyond The Ultraworld* (1991) is probably the single greatest in the entire ambient genre, alongside Aphex Twin's *Selected Ambient Works Vol II* (1994).
† Think about those instrumental albums by guitar maestros like Steve Vai, Joe Satriani or even Yngwie Malsteem, where the lead guitar basically replaces the vocals. Musical onanism.

LOUDER THAN WORDS (Gilmour, Polly Samson)
Length: 4.40 (single) 6.36 (album)
Guitars: Gilmour **Keyboards**: Wright **Piano**: Wright **Rhodes piano**: Wright **Percussion**: Mason **Bass**: Bob Ezrin **Viola**: Chantal Leverton **Violins**: Victoria Lyon, Honor Watson **Cello**: Helen Nash **Backing vocals**: Durga McBroom, Louise Marshall, Sarah Brown
Recorded: January–December 1993, November 2013–January 2014
Producer: Gilmour, Phil Manzanera, Youth, Andy Jackson
First released: 14 October 2014 (single)
Rating: 6.5/10

Some songs become difficult to consider dispassionately because of their circumstances or the legend that grew up around them. The Beatles' 'Let It Be' is one of their lesser songs, but its message of endurance gives it an undue prominence.[‡] Similarly, The Eagles' 'Hotel California' and Fleetwood Mac's 'Dreams' have taken on a legend greater than the tracks deserve, but perhaps this is the nature of popular music, freighted with cultural resonances as well as memories of the time. 'Extraordinary how potent cheap music is,' Noel Coward rather snobbishly wrote,[§] but it's a wonderful psychological trick that allows popular music to take on a greater significance. And so it is here with **LOUDER THAN WORDS**, a slight yet overlong song, given greater import because it is the first to squarely address the internal conflicts within Pink Floyd[¶] – and as the sole track on *The Endless River* to have lyrics, its words have a far greater significance. Pink Floyd were always skilled at handling these thematic significances, but the material almost always stood up to the meaning burdened upon them. **LOUDER THAN WORDS**, however, doesn't quite justify that.

Opening with church bells, linking it to **FAT OLD SUN**[**] and **HIGH HOPES**, **LOUDER THAN WORDS** unfurls via sparkling guitar arpeggios and delicate piano, before sliding (via a minor Mason drum fill) into a plodding-tempo pop-rock song with half a tune and no great difference between verse and chorus melodically. At least during the verse there is some fine guitar commentary from Gilmour, and his voice (sounding slightly thin but increasingly characterful) is front and centre. But during the chorus the band disguise the lack of melodic variety by layering on the backing singers and the keyboards (though they don't sound anything like Wright). But this diminishes the presence of Gilmour, turning **LOUDER THAN WORDS** into something of a generic Adult Contemporary[††] song. Which is the last thing you want from Pink Floyd, who have managed to sound thoroughly distinctive all the way from *The Piper at the Gates of Dawn* to (most of) *The Division Bell*.

[‡] And the fact that it's a perennial choice of music teachers. Imagine if they taught schoolchildren about 'I Am The Walrus' or 'Tomorrow Never Knows'!
[§] In *Private Lives* (1930).
[¶] In **POLES APART** the theme might be similar but the lyrics are more circumlocutory.
[**] Always a favourite of Gilmour's. He tried to get it on the *Echoes* compilation but the others weren't having it.
[††] Gilmour's solo work isn't above such triteness. The title track from his *Rattle That Lock* album (2015) is remarkably bland.

While Polly Samson is undoubtedly a skilled writer, and her work on *The Division Bell* for the most part helps to raise it several notches above *Momentary Lapse*, there's a certain gaucheness here to the lyrics. 'Diss' for example is surely out of place as a word sung by a man approaching the age of 70. The song wants to be a major statement, you feel, a summary of the relationships in the band and a reflection on the magic of interlocking creative impulses, but Samson can only summarise it as 'This thing that we do'. It's just trite. The music similarly feels undistinguished, and can't help but suffer in comparison to the stately grandeur of **HIGH HOPES** as an album closer and career-ender for Pink Floyd. It's a real shame, but then very few artists know when to call it a day, and ending is usually messy and painful.*

TBS9 (Gilmour, Wright)
Length: 2.27
Guitar: Gilmour **Bass**: Guy Pratt **Keyboards**: Wright **Piano**: Wright **Drums**: Mason
Percussion: Mason
Recorded: January–December 1993, November 2013–January 2014
Producer: Gilmour, Phil Manzanera, Youth, Andy Jackson
First released: 7 November 2014 (*The Endless River* track 19)
Rating: 7/10

The long-rumoured title of the leftover *Division Bell* material was 'The Big Spliff',† here coyly hinted at in an acronym. This piece was presumably one of the original pieces compiled by engineer Andy Jackson before Wright's death caused Gilmour to go back into the tapes to revisit the sessions. **TBS9** sounds more authentic than most of the other pieces on *The Endless River*, less of a studio construct and more of a jam session. Fading in slowly with delicate shimmering keyboards and low-pitched guitar vibrato for a full minute, some elegant piano then ascends into the mix amidst some nice cymbal shimmers from Mason and fretless bass trills, continuing in this vein for a further minute or so before fading out. It's gorgeously ethereal, delicately atmospheric and rich with possibility. As a fragment, **TBS9** is one of the best on the album because it feels like a band in a room, listening to each other, developing a sound and an emotion. It doesn't get much beyond that, but here it really does feel like Pink Floyd in the raw, a song-acorn of the kind which grew into **ECHOES** and all of the material on *The Division Bell*. Would it be worth developing into a complete song? Sometimes

---

* Rock music usually involves the sense of a group as a band of brothers, a collective bonded by sweat rather than blood. Losing original musicians is almost always seen as a diminution. Public Image Ltd reacted against this ethos by initially styling itself as a communications company. Check out their 1980 interview on *The Tom Snyder Show* on YouTube.

† The title came from producer Andy Jackson: 'I took it upon myself to make "The Big Spliff",' admits Jackson, on his early attempts at compiling an ambient companion LP, 'which was just a comical title I came up with. It never got thought about again, really.' *Uncut* magazine, 4 March 2015.

the fragment, with its tantalising suggestion of what might have been, can be even more enjoyable than something fleshed out.‡

TBS14 (Gilmour, Wright)
Length: 4.11
Guitars: Gilmour **Keyboards**: Wright **Synthesiser**: Wright **Drums**: Mason **Bass**: Guy Pratt
Recorded: January–December 1993, November 2013–January 2014
Producer: Gilmour, Phil Manzanera, Youth, Andy Jackson
First released: 7 November 2014 (*The Endless River* track 20)
Rating: 7/10

Another track that feels jammed in real time, **TBS14** is mellow and nostalgic and crepuscular. Feeling very much like Gilmour, Mason and Wright (as well as long-time bassman Guy Pratt) in a room, this track doesn't particularly go anywhere, but again there's something particularly authentic about it. Wright's keyboard swirls and adds emotion, Gilmour plays a marvellous-sounding tremolo-rich solo§ before moving on to strummed guitar licks at 2.24, while Mason keeps a none-more-steady beat throughout. **TBS14** has the jamming feeling of inchoate creativity, of directions being mapped out while remaining uncertain. There's a lovely feeling to it, a certain tenderness in the guitars (aided by the considerable tremolo), and a sense of genuine creativity – here is something being ushered into the world, almost there, inchoate but genuine. A tantalising taste, but a heady one. If only more of *The Endless River* had been like this.

NERVANA (Gilmour)
Length: 5.32
Guitars: Gilmour **Bass**: Guy Pratt (?) **Keyboards**: Wright **Drums**: Mason
Recorded: January–December 1993, November 2013–January 2014
Producer: Gilmour, Phil Manzanera, Youth, Andy Jackson
First released: 7 November 2014 (*The Endless River* track 21)
Rating: 6/10

---

‡ Just like *Ozymandias* (1818).
§ I might be wrong but it somehow recalls the guitar solo in 'Blind Curve' from Marillion's exceptional *Misplaced Childhood* album (1985). There's a rather poignant mention of Gilmour in an interview with Marillion guitar player Steve Rothery: 'Really, my guitar playing is a mix of [Camel's] Andy Latimer, Steve Hackett and David Gilmour […] It's funny, because I know Andy Latimer and Steve Hackett really well now. David Gilmour, though … ummm … Yeah, he's up there in the stratosphere.' Interview, *loudersound.com*, 22 March 2017.

David Gilmour does like a bit of loud abrasive guitar.* With almost the same opening as **CANDY AND A CURRANT BUN**, **NERVANA** swiftly goes into abrasive guitar mode, with a great punchy sound and suitable complementary playing from Mason (sounding about as inspired as he gets) and Wright (giving some subtle atmospherics but not much more – this is far from his melancholy style). The title is presumably a reference to Nirvana,† who of course were huge in the early 1990s, and perhaps to the nerve required to rock without self-consciousness (Gilmour being 68 years old at the time *The Endless River* was released). **NERVANA** is probably the hardest rocking Pink Floyd track since **NOT NOW JOHN**, and is agreeably hard-driving and energetic. But it never breaks out of its own parameters: it has a fine chord sequence and some excellent soloing, and Mason, Wright and Pratt match Gilmour all the way, yet it never feels like something new or distinctive. **NERVANA** might be some damn good jamming but compared to **TBS9** and **TBS14** there's a greater sense of post-facto studio manipulation (the chord sequence follows the opening guitar abrasion rather too neatly). **NERVANA** ultimately comes across as less of a song and more of a wish to have something suitable to contrast with the previous tracks. There's no doubt that the fierce guitar playing is authentically Gilmour, but its placement in *The Endless River* (despite being a bonus track, alongside **TBS9** and **TBS14**) is more architectural than artistic.

It's hard to rate *The Endless River* as an album. It's clearly something of a eulogy, and feels heartfelt. Gilmour as a guitarist is always worth hearing; his tone and touch are incomparable. The return of Wright will delight many Floydies, and **AUTUMN '68** is a brief but unexpected delight, showcasing his superlative playing. Hearing the band at their most relaxed and most basic since **ALAN'S PSYCHEDELIC BREAKFAST** is a pleasure, and numerous tracks consciously suggest earlier glories. Removing emotion and narrative from the actual music is therefore difficult. Similarly, it's hard to rate each track individually when they are clearly meant to flow into each other. Perhaps this is the wrong analytical framework to judge songs which are not meant to be heard individually. But, simply judged as music and without considering the intra-band and band-fan relationships to which it sometimes alludes, *The Endless River* is Pink Floyd playing within their parameters, and padded out to disguise the absence of songs. For the most part, it lacks the creativity or surprise that comes from genuine jamming, though with Gilmour, Mason and Wright having played around

---

* 'You know, once you've had that guitar up so loud on the stage, where you can lean back and volume will stop you from falling backward, that's a hard drug to kick.' *Rolling Stone*, 'Pink Floyd: Journey to the Dark Side', 13 October 2011. But this isn't just a personal preference, there are good artistic reasons for high volume. Richard Perks aptly describes it: 'Using highly powered valve amplification dramatically affects the responsiveness of the instrument, directly informing the player's touch, which in turn impacts the aesthetic character and tone generated.' (Chris Hart and Simon A. Morrison (eds.), *The Routledge Handbook of Pink Floyd*, 2023).

† *The Division Bell* tracks were recorded January–December 1993, some time before Kurt Cobain's suicide in April 1994.

1,000 concerts together (see Chapter 2), it's no surprise that they have their bag, as the jazz musicians say, and stick to it. They needed some young hotshots to challenge them, as, for instance, Miles Davis repeatedly did throughout his career (and so bringing to prominence incredible talents like John Coltrane, Cannonball Adderley, Herbie Hancock, Wayne Shorter and Tony Williams).‡ But who's going to challenge David Gilmour? It would be like arguing with Paul McCartney about what makes a good tune, or Bob Dylan about a good lyric. You just don't do that.

What is surprising is that, despite earlier rumours, this is really not an ambient album: it's just some mostly studio-confected noodling of various moods and flavours, occasionally hinting at ambient tones and textures (as with **THINGS LEFT UNSAID** and **NIGHT LIGHT**), but more often just sedate rock rhythms and atmospheric artificial flavourings. Because it's Gilmour, Mason and Wright playing, *The Endless River* repeatedly invokes Pink Floyd's earlier achievements, but it never comes anywhere close to matching them. As an idea, and from a marketing perspective, *The Endless River* is a triumph. But artistically it has little to say: it's three very successful musicians doodling away, without urgency, without vision and only themselves in mind. If *The Division Bell* was something of an echo of the classic Pink Floyd sound, *The Endless River* is song fragments flickering past like memories in old age; an endless river, indeed, but one going nowhere. It's an echo of an echo. But for many people that was enough.§

HEY, HEY, RISE UP! (Gilmour, Andriy Khlyvnyuk, Stepan Charnetskii)
Length: 3.27
Vocals: Andriy Khlyvnyuk **Guitars**: Gilmour **Bass**: Guy Pratt **Keyboards**: Nitin Sawhney
Drums: Mason **Choir**: Veryovka Ukrainian Folk Choir
Recorded: February–March 2022
Producer: Gilmour
Released: 8 April 2022
Rating: 2/10

The final, final coda from Pink Floyd is a charity single for Ukrainian humanitarian causes following the Russian invasion in February 2022. With Gilmour having a personal connection to Ukraine (his son Charlie is married to the Ukrainian artist Janina Pedan), he felt compelled to act, saying, 'It's a really difficult and frustrating thing to see this extraordinarily crazy, unjust attack by a major power on an independent, peaceful, democratic nation. The frustration of seeing that and thinking "what the fuck can I do?" is sort of unbearable.'¶ As a song it opens with a folk choir (slightly reminiscent of **WHEN THE TIGERS**

---

‡ See *Miles Davis: The Definitive Biography* by Ian Carr. There's a brilliant quote from Miles Davis: 'Do you know why I don't play ballads anymore. Because I love ballads so much.'
§ *The Endless River* has sold over 10 million copies.
¶ *The Guardian*, 7 April 2022. www.theguardian.com/music/2022/apr/07/pink-floyd-reform-to-support-ukraine

BROKE FREE) then combines irritatingly bombastic singing by Khlyvnyuk, right out of any Eastern European nightclub, with virtuoso but heavy-handed soloing by Gilmour. The sense of two musical cultures not really meeting is apt, as Gilmour took the vocal by Khlyvnyuk (singing a Ukrainian anthem 'Oh, the Red Viburnum in the Meadow' a capella) from an Instagram post, and then built the backing around it. He told *Rolling Stone*:

> I took his voice and put it into my recorder and played it back in time with a click track and then played along with it on my guitar. When the vocal finished, I just kept going and let my guitar lead me into some new guitar chords and parts for the rest of the song. [Those chords] sounded like they could be part of the same song but that part of a new sequence.*

As a charity single, **HEY, HEY, RISE UP!** sits in the lengthy line of worthy efforts that stink musically. 'Do They Know It's Christmas?',† 'We Are the World', 'Let's Stonk', 'Ferry Cross the Mersey', Wet Wet Wet's version of 'With a Little Help from My Friends' … **HEY, HEY, RISE UP!** at least has some exalted company, though it's really not worthy of the Pink Floyd name. But David Gilmour is an old, wealthy and successful man who does as he likes, whatever armchair critics might say, and from what are plainly the best of intentions. Fair enough. Though it still would have been wiser to end the group on **HIGH HOPES**, artists live in the here and now, not in an ideal world that allows for a flawless trajectory, unspoiled by compromise or regret. Only Syd Barrett had that luxury. Gilmour at least now has put the band to bed. But what a band it was.

---

* *Rolling Stone*, 8 April 2022 www.rollingstone.com/music/music-features/pink-floyd-david-gilmour-ukraine-interview-1334514/
† Actually I have a sneaking fondness for this song. The bells at the start immediately take me back to childhood Christmases.

CHRONOLOGY

Concerts and Record Releases

I have included only confirmed gigs which had paying customers. Curiosities like the group playing at an end-of-film party for Vanessa Redgrave (on 4 March 1968) have therefore been excluded. I have not noted the dates of cancelled gigs either. This makes their early European tours seem somewhat paltry, but you can read between the lines: taking a group abroad is expensive, and you need to cram in as many gigs as possible to make it pay.

What is immediately evident is the enormous efforts the group made in search of success, particularly to conquer America. Eight North American tours were undertaken before *Dark Side* was released, with a total of 341 gigs played across the US during their career, from the tiniest of clubs to the biggest stadiums. It's also noticeable that after *Dark Side*, the group significantly reduced the number of shows they played: going from eighty-five in 1972 to twenty-seven in 1974 and thirty in 1975. This is rather surprising – you would have thought they would be keen to capitalise on the overwhelming success of *Dark Side*. Perhaps, like Miles Davis, they used success to allow them to work on their own terms, rather than following standard industry protocol of an album-tour every two years. If so, this may help explain the remarkable flowering of their creativity during their *Dark Side–The Wall* hot streak. Under Gilmour's leadership, however, the importance of live performances rebounded, and they played 200 shows in the *Momentary Lapse* tours (1987–89) and 111 in the *Division Bell* tour (1994). (This might also be down to the economics of the music industry: gigs brought in much more money by the 1980s.)

	Year	Address	Country	World Events	Music
	1966				
1	Sunday 9 January	The Goings On Club, Archer Street, London	UK		*Love* released by Love.
2	Friday 11 March	Rag Ball, Concourse Area, University of Essex, Colchester	UK	French President Charles de Gaulle says French troops will be removed from NATO and that all French NATO bases will close within a year.	
3	Saturday 12 March	Rag Ball, Concourse Area, University of Essex, Colchester	UK		
4	Sunday 13 March	The Marquee, Wardour Street, London	UK		
5	Sunday 27 March	The Marquee, Wardour Street, London	UK		
6	Sunday 3 April	The Marquee, Wardour Street, London	UK	Soviet spacecraft Luna 10 becomes the first man-made lunar satellite.	
7	Sunday 14 April	The Marquee, Wardour Street, London	UK		
8	Sunday 1 May	The Marquee, Wardour Street, London	UK		The Beatles, The Rolling Stones and The Who perform at the NME's poll winners' show at the Empire Pool in London. It is The Beatles' last conventional live concert in Britain.
9	Sunday 8 May	The Marquee, Wardour Street, London	UK		
10	Sunday 15 May	The Marquee, Wardour Street, London	UK	The South Vietnamese army besieges Da Nang.	
11	Sunday 5 June	The Marquee, Wardour Street, London	UK	Gene Cernan completes the second US spacewalk.	
12	Sunday 12 June	The Marquee, Wardour Street, London	UK		
13	Friday 30 September	London Free School, All Saints Church Hall, Powis Gardens, London	UK	Bechuanaland Protectorate gains independence from the UK, renamed as Botswana.	
14	Saturday 15 October	International Times All Night Rave, The Roundhouse, Chalk Farm, London	UK		*Complete & Unbelievable: The Otis Redding Dictionary of Soul* released by Otis Redding.
15	Wednesday 19 October	Top Rank Suite, Brighton	UK		
16	Friday 21 October	London Free School, All Saints Church Hall, Powis Gardens, London	UK	Aberfan disaster occurs in South Wales, killing 116 children and 28 adults.	
17	Friday 28 October	London Free School, All Saints Church Hall, Powis Gardens, London	UK		*Face To Face* released by The Kinks.
18	Friday 4 November	London Free School, All Saints Church Hall, Powis Gardens, London	UK	Flooding of the Arno River collapses the embankment in Florence, destroying countless works of art and killing over one hundred people.	
19	Saturday 5 November	Wilton Hall, Bletchley	UK		
20	Saturday 5 November	The Clubhouse, Five Acres Country Club, Bricket Wood, nr. Watford	UK		
21	Tuesday 8 November	London Free School, All Saints Church Hall, Powis Gardens, London	UK	Ronald Reagan elected Governor of California.	
22	Friday 11 November	London Free School, All Saints Church Hall, Powis Gardens, London	UK		'Ready Steady Who' EP released by The Who.
23	Saturday 12 November	Corn Exchange, Bedford	UK		
24	Sunday 13 November	Starlite Ballroom, Greenford	UK		
25	Tuesday 15 November	London Free School, All Saints Church Hall, Powis Gardens, London	UK	Gemini XII returns to Earth, with Jim Lovell and Buzz Aldrin.	
26	Friday 18 November	Hornsey College of Art, Hornsey, London	UK	US Roman Catholic bishops end the rule against eating meat on Fridays.	
27	Saturday 19 November	Main Hall, Technical College, Canterbury	UK		*That's Life* released by Frank Sinatra.
28	Tuesday 22 November	London Free School, All Saints Church Hall, Powis Gardens, London	UK		
29	Tuesday 29 November	London Free School, All Saints Church Hall, Powis Gardens, London	UK		

257

	Year	Address	Country	World Events	Music
30	Saturday 3 December	*Psychodelphia Versus Ian Smith*, The Roundhouse, Chalk Farm, London	UK		*Got Live If You Want It!* released by The Rolling Stones.
31	Monday 12 December	*You're Joking – A Benefit Concert For Oxfam*, Royal Albert Hall, London	UK		
32	Friday 16 December	The Architects Association, Bedford Square, London	UK		The Jimi Hendrix Experience release their first single in the UK, 'Hey Joe'.
33	Tuesday 20 December	Art School Psychedelic Freak Out, Cambridgeshire College of Art and Technology, Cambridge	UK		
34	Thursday 22 December	The Marquee, Wardour Street, London	UK		
35	Friday 23 December	*UFO Presents Night Tripper*, The Blarney Club, Tottenham Court Road, London	UK	Last episode of British rock TV programme *Ready Steady Go!* (1963-66) after 178 episodes.	UFO Club opens in London.
36	Thursday 29 December	The Marquee, Wardour Street, London	UK		
37	Friday 30 December	*UFO Presents Night Tripper*, The Blarney Club, Tottenham Court Road, London	UK		
38	Saturday 31 December	The Roundhouse, Chalk Farm, London	UK	East German Premier Walter Ulbricht discusses negotiations on German reunification.	
	1967				
1	Thursday 5 January	The Marquee, Wardour Street, London	UK		
2	Friday 6 January	*Freak Out Ethel*, Seymour Hall, Paddington, London	UK		
3	Sunday 8 January	The Upper Cut, Forest Gate, London	UK	Operation Cedar Falls starts during Vietnam War.	
4	Friday 13 January	UFO, The Blarney Club, Tottenham Court Road, London	UK		
5	Saturday 14 January	The Great Hall, University of Reading, Whiteknights, Reading	UK	The Human Be-In takes place at Golden Gate Park, San Francisco, USA.	
6	Monday 16 January	The Clubroom, Institute of Contemporary Arts, Mayfair, London	UK		
7	Tuesday 17 January	*Music In Colour by The Pink Floyd*, Commonwealth Institute, Kensington, London	UK		
8	Thursday 19 January	The Marquee, Wardour Street, London	UK		*Between the Buttons* released by The Rolling Stones.
9	Friday 20 January	UFO, The Blarney Club, Tottenham Court Road, London	UK	Governor Reagan fires Clark Kerr, president of California's university system, for being too soft on student protests.	
10	Saturday 21 January	The Birdcage Club, Eastney, Portsmouth	UK		
11	Friday 27 January	UFO, The Blarney Club, Tottenham Court Road, London	UK		
12	Saturday 28 January	Student Union Common Room, University of Essex, Wivenhoe Park, Colchester	UK		
13	Thursday 2 February	The Stoke Hotel, Guildford	UK		
14	Friday 3 February	*All Nite Rave*, Queen's Hall, Leeds	UK	Ronald Ryan the last man hanged in Australia.	
15	Thursday 9 February	New Addington Hotel, New Addington, Croydon	UK		
16	Friday 10 February	Leicester College of Art and Technology, Leicester	UK	Ratification of 25th Amendment to the United States Constitution (concerning presidential succession and disability).	*Trogglodynamite* released by The Troggs.
17	Saturday 11 February	Old Refectory, Falmer House, University of Sussex, Falmer, Brighton	UK		
18	Friday 17 February	*St. Catherine's College Valentine Ball*, Dorothy Ballroom, Cambridge	UK		
19	Saturday 18 February	California Ballroom, Dunstable	UK	China sends three divisions to Tibet, to contain fighting during the Cultural Revolution (1966-1976).	
20	Monday 20 February	Adelphi Ballroom, West Bromwich	UK		

	Year	Address	Country	World Events	Music
21	Friday 24 February	Ricky Tick Club, Thames Hotel, Windsor	UK	The Soviet Union forbids Warsaw Pact nations from forming diplomatic relations with West Germany.	
22	Friday 24 February	UFO, The Blarney Club, Tottenham Court Road, London	UK		
23	Saturday 25 February	Ricky Tick Club, Hounslow	UK		
24	Tuesday 28 February	Blaises Club, Imperial Hotel, Knightsbridge, London	UK		
25	Wednesday 1 March	The Dance Hall, Eel Pie Island Hotel, Twickenham	UK	Red Guards return to schools in China during the Cultural Revolution.	
26	Thursday 2 March	Assembly Hall, Worthing	UK		
27	Friday 3 March	Market Hall, St. Albans	UK		The Animals refuse to perform a show in Ottawa unless they are paid in advance. The audience riots, causing $5000 in damages.
28	Friday 3 March	UFO, The Blarney Club, Tottenham Court Road, London	UK		
29	Saturday 4 March	Poly Rag Ball, The Large Hall, Regent Street Polytechnic, London	UK	First British North Sea gas pumped ashore at Easington, East Riding of Yorkshire.	
30	Sunday 5 March	Saville Theatre, Shaftesbury Avenue, London	UK		
31	Tuesday 7 March	Malvern Big Beat Sessions, Winter Gardens, Malvern	UK	Suspected mobster Jimmy Hoffa begins 8-year prison sentence for attempting to bribe a jury. He would disappear on 30 July 1975.	
32	Thursday 9 March	The Marquee, Wardour Street, London	UK	Stalin's daughter, Svetlana Alliluyeva, defects to the USA.	
	Friday 10 March	RECORD RELEASE – ARNOLD LAYNE SINGLE			
33	Friday 10 March	UFO, The Blarney Club, Tottenham Court Road, London	UK		
34	Saturday 11 March	Main Hall, Canterbury Technical College, Canterbury	UK		The Velvet Underground & Nico released by The Velvet Underground.
35	Sunday 12 March	Agincourt Ballroom, Camberley	UK		
36	Friday 17 March	Kingston Technical College, Kingston-upon-Thames	UK	General election in Sierra Leone, followed by a military coup against the new government on 22nd March.	'The Grateful Dead' released by Grateful Dead.
37	Saturday 18 March	Enfield College of Technology, Enfield	UK		
38	Thursday 23 March	Rotherham College of Technology Dance, Clifton Hall, Rotherham	UK		
39	Friday 24 March	Ricky Tick Club, Hounslow	UK		
40	Saturday 25 March	Ricky Tick Club, Thames Hotel, Windsor	UK	USSR performs nuclear test at Semipalatinsk Test Site, Kazakhstan.	The Who perform their first concert in the United States, in New York.
41	Saturday 25 March	New Yorker Discotheque, Swindon	UK		
42	Saturday 25 March	Shoreline Club, Caribbean Hotel, Bognor Regis	UK		
43	Tuesday 28 March	Chinese R&B Jazz Club, Corn Exchange, Bristol	UK	Pope Paul VI issues the encyclical Populorum Progressio.	
44	Wednesday 29 March	The Dance Hall, Eel Pie Island Hotel, Twickenham	UK		
45	Friday 31 March	Top Spot Ballroom, Ross-on-Wye	UK		Jimi Hendrix sets fire to his guitar on stage for the first time.
46	Saturday 1 April	The Birdcage Club, Eastney, Portsmouth	UK	The United States Department of Transportation begins operations.	Don't Stop Me Now! released by Cliff Richard.
47	Thursday 6 April	City Hall, Salisbury	UK		
48	Friday 7 April	Floral Hall, Belfast	UK	Israeli-Syrian border clashes.	
49	Saturday 8 April	Rhodes Centre, Bishops Stortford	UK		The UK wins the Eurovision Song Contest for the first time with Sandie Shaw singing 'Puppet on a String'.
50	Saturday 8 April	The Roundhouse, Chalk Farm, London	UK		
51	Sunday 9 April	Brittania Rowing Club, Nottingham	UK		
52	Monday 10 April	The Pavilion, Bath	UK	The first Boeing 737 takes its maiden flight.	

	Year	Address	Country	World Events	Music
53	Thursday 13 April	Tilbury Railway Club, Tilbury	UK	France wins its fourth Five Nations Rugby Championship.	
54	Saturday 15 April	Kinetic Arena – K4 Discoteque, Main Ballroom, West Pier, Brighton	UK		The Beatles sign a contract with EMI, agreeing to stay together for 10 years.
55	Wednesday 19 April	Bromel Club, Court Hotel, Downham, Bromley	UK		
56	Thursday 20 April	Queen's Hall, Barnstaple	UK		
57	Friday 21 April	Starlite Ballroom, Greenford	UK	Military coup in Greece.	
58	Friday 21 April	UFO, The Blarney Club, Tottenham Court Road, London	UK		
59	Saturday 22 April	Benn Memorial Hall, Rugby	UK		
60	Sunday 23 April	Starlite Ballroom, Greenford	UK		
61	Monday 24 April	Blue Opera Club, The Feathers, Ealing Broadway, London	UK		
62	Tuesday 25 April	The Stage Club, Clarendon Restaurant, Oxford	UK	Muhammad Ali refuses military service. He is stripped of his boxing title and barred from professional boxing for three years.	
63	Friday 28 April	The Tabernacle Club, Hillgate, Stockport	UK		
64	Saturday 29 April	14-Hour Technicolour Dream, Alexandra Palace, Muswell Hill, London	UK	Fidel Castro announces that all intellectual property belongs to the people and that Cuba intends to translate and publish technical literature without compensation.	
65	Sunday 30 April	Plaza Teen Club, Thornton Lodge Hall, Huddersfield	UK		
66	Wednesday 3 May	The Moulin Rouge, Ainsdale, Southport	UK		
67	Thursday 4 May	Locarno Ballroom, Coventry	UK		
68	Saturday 6 May	Kitson College, Leeds	UK	Dr. Zakir Hussain becomes the first Muslim president of India.	
69	Sunday 7 May	King & Queen Mojo A Go-Go, Mojo Club, Tollbar, Sheffield	UK		The Beach Boys win the most popular group award at the NME Poll-Winners Concert.
70	Friday 12 May	Games For May, Queen Elizabeth Hall, South Bank, London	UK		Are You Experienced? is released by the Jimi Hendrix Experience in the UK.
71	Saturday 13 May	St. George's Ballroom, Hinckley	UK	The USSR ratifies a treaty with the UK and the USA banning nuclear weapons in space.	
72	Friday 19 May	Club A Go-Go, Newcastle	UK		
73	Saturday 20 May	Floral Hall, Southport	UK		
74	Tuesday 23 May	Town Hall, High Wycombe	UK		
75	Wednesday 24 May	Bromel Club, Court Hotel, Downham, Bromley	UK	Glasgow Celtic beat Internazionale of Milan 2-1 to win the European Cup, the first British team to win the trophy.	
76	Thursday 25 May	Grosmont Wood Farm, Cross Ash, nr. Abergavenny	UK		
77	Friday 26 May	Empress Ballroom, Winter Gardens, Blackpool	UK		Sgt. Pepper's Lonely Hearts Club Band by The Beatles is rush released in the UK ahead of the scheduled June 1 release date.
78	Saturday 27 May	Civic Hall, Nantwich	UK	Australian referendum removes two discriminatory sentences referring to Indigenous Australians from the Constitution.	
79	Monday 29 May	Barbecue 67, Tulip Bulb Auction Hall, Spalding	UK		
80	Friday 2 June	UFO, The Blarney Club, Tottenham Court Road, London	UK	Race riots in Boston.	
81	Friday 9 June	College of Commerce, Queen's Gardens, Hull	UK		From The Beginning released by Small Faces.
82	Friday 9 June	UFO, The Blarney Club, Tottenham Court Road, London	UK		
83	Saturday 10 June	The Nautilus Club, South Pier, Lowestoft	UK		

	Year	Address	Country	World Events	Music
84	Sunday 11 June	*Immage*, Patronaatgebouw, Terneuzen, Netherlands	UK	Race riot in Tampa, Florida after the shooting death of Martin Chambers by police while allegedly robbing a camera store.	
85	Sunday 11 June	Concertgebouw, Vlissingen, Netherlands	UK		
86	Tuesday 13 June	Blue Opera Club, The Feathers, Ealing Broadway, London	UK		
	Friday 16 June	**RECORD RELEASE – SEE EMILY PLAY SINGLE**			The Monterey Pop Festival, one of the world's first outdoor rock music festivals, opens in Monterey, California.
86	Friday 16 June	Tiles, Oxford Street, London	UK		
87	Saturday 17 June	The Ballroom, Dreamland Amusement Park, Margate	UK	China tests its first hydrogen bomb.	
88	Tuesday 20 June	Commemoration Ball, Magdalen College, Oxford	UK		
89	Wednesday 21 June	Bolton College of Art Midsummer Ball, Rivington Hall Barn, Bolton	UK		
90	Friday 23 June	Rolls Royce Apprentices Ball, Locarno Ballroom, Derby	UK		*Small Faces* released by Small Faces.
91	Friday 23 June	The 8-Hour Psycho-Chromatic Fantasy, Bradford University, Bradford	UK		'Flowers' released by The Rolling Stones.
92	Monday 26 June	Warwick University, Coventry	UK		
93	Wednesday 28 June	The Dance Hall, Eel Pie Island Hotel, Twickenham	UK	Israel annexes East Jerusalem.	The Supremes perform for the first time as Diana Ross & the Supremes.
94	Saturday 1 July	The Swan, Yardley, Birmingham	UK	First British colour TV broadcast, on BBC2.	*The Times* publishes the 'Who breaks a butterfly upon a wheel?' editorial, criticising the prison sentences given to Mick Jagger and Keith Richard two days earlier.
95	Sunday 2 July	Midnight City, Digbeth, Birmingham	UK		
96	Monday 3 July	The Pavilion, Bath	UK	*News At Ten* premieres on ITV.	
97	Wednesday 5 July	The Dance Hall, Eel Pie Island Hotel, Twickenham	UK		
98	Friday 7 July	The Birdcage Club, Eastney, Portsmouth	UK		
99	Saturday 8 July	The Roundhouse, Chalk Farm, London	UK		
100	Saturday 15 July	Stowmarket Carnival, The Cricket Meadow, Stowmarket	UK		
101	Sunday 16 July	Redcar Jazz Club, Coatham Hotel, Redcar	UK	UK announces closure of its military bases in Malaysia and Singapore ("east of Suez").	
102	Tuesday 18 July	The Palace Ballroom, Douglas, Isle of Man	UK	Race riots in Durham, North Carolina.	
103	Wednesday 19 July	Floral Hall, Gorleston	UK		
	SCOTLAND AND NORTH ENGLAND TOUR				
104	Thursday 20 July	Two Red Shoes Ballroom, Elgin	UK	Race riots in Memphis, Tennessee.	
105	Friday 21 July	Ballerina Ballroom, Nairn	UK		
106	Saturday 22 July	Beach Ballroom, Aberdeen	UK		
107	Sunday 23 July	Cosmopolitan Ballroom, Carlisle	UK	One of the worst riots in US history begins in Detroit: 43 killed, 342 injured and 1,400 buildings burned.	
108	Monday 24 July	The Maryland Ballroom, Glasgow, Scotland	UK	The Beatles and other eminent members of British society sign a petition in *The Times* to legalise marijuana.	*Best Of The Beach Boys Vol. 2* released by The Beach Boys.
109	Tuesday 25 July	The Palladium Ballroom, Greenock, Scotland	UK		
110	Friday 28 July	UFO, The Blarney Club, Tottenham Court Road, London	UK		
111	Saturday 29 July	The Dereham Exchange, East Dereham	UK	Fire on USS Forrestal in Gulf of Tonkin kills 134.	
	Friday 4 August	**RECORD RELEASE – *THE PIPER AT THE GATES OF DAWN***			*Aretha Arrives* released by Aretha Franklin.

(Concerts during August cancelled owing to Syd's declining mental health)

	Year	Address	Country	World Events	Music
112	Friday 1 September	UFO Festival, The Roundhouse, Chalk Farm, London	UK	Ilse Koch, known as the 'Witch of Buchenwald', commits suicide in Aichach women's prison.	*Crusade* released by John Mayall & the Bluesbreakers.
113	Saturday 2 September	UFO Festival, The Roundhouse, Chalk Farm, London	UK		
	SCANDINAVIAN TOUR				
114	Saturday 9 September	Boom, Aarhus, Denmark	Denmark		
115	Sunday 10 September	Gyllene Cirkeln, Stockholm, Sweden	Sweden	Gibraltar votes to remain British in sovereignty referendum.	
116	Monday 11 September	Starclub, Copenhagen, Denmark	Denmark		
117	Tuesday 12 September	Starclub, Copenhagen, Denmark	Denmark		
118	Wednesday 13 September	Starclub, Copenhagen, Denmark	Denmark		
	IRISH TOUR				
119	Friday 15 September	The Starlite Ballroom, Belfast	UK		'Something Else By The Kinks' released by The Kinks.
120	Saturday 16 September	Flamingo Ballroom, Ballymena	Ireland	Anni Pede breaks women's marathon world record time (3:07:26).	
121	Sunday 17 September	The Arcadia Ballroom, Cork, Republic of Ireland	Ireland		The Doors appear on *The Ed Sullivan Show* and perform 'Light My Fire'. Jim Morrison reneges on agreement that the line 'Girl, we couldn't get much higher' be changed for the show.
122	Tuesday 19 September	The Speakeasy Club, Margaret Street, London	UK		
123	Thursday 21 September	Assembly Hall, Worthing	UK		
124	Friday 22 September	Tiles, Oxford Street, London	UK		
125	Saturday 23 September	Corn Exchange, Chelmsford	UK		
126	Wednesday 27 September	Fifth Dimension, Leicester	UK		
127	Thursday 28 September	Skyline Ballroom, Hull	UK		
128	Friday 30 September	The Imperial Ballroom, Nelson, Lancashire	UK		The BBC restructures its radio services, renaming its national stations Radio 1, Radio 2, Radio 3 and Radio 4.
129	Sunday 1 October	Saville Theatre, Shaftesbury Avenue, London	UK		
130	Friday 6 October	Top Rank Suite, Brighton	UK		
131	Saturday 7 October	University of Bristol, Clifton, Bristol	UK		
132	Friday 13 October	The Pavilion, Weymouth	UK		
133	Saturday 14 October	César's Club, Bedford	UK		
134	Saturday 21 October	University of York, Hesslington, York	UK	Approximately 70,000 Vietnam War protesters march in Washington, D.C. and rally at the Lincoln Memorial.	
135	Monday 23 October	The Pavilion, Bath	UK		*Sorcerer* released by Miles Davis.
136	Saturday 28 October	Dunelm House, University of Durham, Durham	UK		
	NORTH AMERICAN TOUR				
137	Saturday 4 November	Winterland Auditorium, San Francisco, USA	USA		
138	Sunday 5 November	Cheetah Club, Santa Monica, Los Angeles, USA	USA	Yemeni president Abdullah al-Sallal flees the country following a coup.	
139	Thursday 9 November	Fillmore Auditorium, San Francisco, USA	USA		*Disraeli Gears* released by Cream.
140	Friday 10 November	Winterland Auditorium, San Francisco, USA	USA		

	Year	Address	Country	World Events	Music
141	Saturday 11 November	Winterland Auditorium, San Francisco, USA	USA	Carl Stokes sworn-in as first black mayor of a major US city in Cleveland, Ohio.	
142	Monday 13 November	*Hippy Happy Fair*, De Oude Ahoy Hallen, Ahoy Heliport, Rotterdam, Netherlands	Netherlands		
	JIMI HENDRIX UK PACKAGE TOUR				
143	Tuesday 14 November	*The Alchemical Wedding*, Royal Albert Hall, Kensington, London	UK		
144	Wednesday 15 November	Winter Gardens, Bournemouth	UK		
	RECORD RELEASE APPLES AND ORANGES SINGLE				
145	Friday 17 November	City Hall, Sheffield	UK		
146	Friday 17 November	City Hall, Sheffield	UK		
147	Friday 17 November	*All Night Garden Party*, Queen's Hall, Leeds	UK		
148	Saturday 18 November	Empire Theatre, Liverpool	UK	The British pound is devalued from US$2.80 to US$2.40. Prime Minister Harold Wilson makes disastrous 'pound in your pocket' broadcast.	
149	Saturday 18 November	Empire Theatre, Liverpool	UK		
150	Sunday 19 November	Coventry Theatre, Coventry	UK		
151	Sunday 19 November	Coventry Theatre, Coventry	UK		
152	Wednesday 22 November	Guildhall, Portsmouth	UK	UN Security Council passes Resolution 242 saying Israel must return occupied land.	Otis Redding records '(Sittin' On) The Dock Of The Bay' at Stax Records' studio in Memphis, Tennessee.
153	Wednesday 22 November	Guildhall, Portsmouth	UK		
154	Thursday 23 November	Sophia Gardens Pavilion, Cardiff	UK		
155	Thursday 23 November	Sophia Gardens Pavilion, Cardiff	UK		
156	Friday 24 November	Colston Hall, Bristol	UK		
157	Friday 24 November	Colston Hall, Bristol	UK		
158	Saturday 25 November	Opera House, Blackpool	UK		
159	Saturday 25 November	Opera House, Blackpool	UK		
160	Sunday 26 November	Palace Theatre, Manchester	UK		
161	Sunday 26 November	Palace Theatre, Manchester	UK		
162	Monday 27 November	Whitla Hall, Queen's College, Belfast	UK	French President Charles de Gaulle rejects British application to join the EEC for the second time.	'Magical Mystery Tour' EP released by The Beatles.
163	Monday 27 November	Whitla Hall, Queen's College, Belfast	UK		
164	Friday 1 December	Central Hall, Catham	UK		*Axis: Bold As Love* released by The Jimi Hendrix Experience.
165	Friday 1 December	Central Hall, Catham	UK		
166	Saturday 2 December	The Dome, Brighton	UK		
167	Saturday 2 December	The Dome, Brighton	UK		
168	Sunday 3 December	Theatre Royal, Nottingham	UK	Former Indonesian president Sukarno placed under house arrest.	
169	Sunday 3 December	Theatre Royal, Nottingham	UK		
170	Monday 4 December	City Hall, Newcastle	UK		
171	Monday 4 December	City Hall, Newcastle	UK		
172	Tuesday 5 December	Green's Playhouse, Glasgow, Scotland	UK	Christiaan Barnard carries out the world's first heart transplant at Groote Schuur Hospital in Cape Town, South Africa.	George Harrison begins recording *Wonderwall Music*.
173	Tuesday 5 December	Green's Playhouse, Glasgow, Scotland	UK		

	Year	Address	Country	World Events	Music
174	Wednesday 6 December	Royal College of Art, Kensington, London	UK		*Their Satanic Majesties Request* released by The Rolling Stones.
175	Friday 8 December	Chiselhurst Caves, Chiselhurst	UK		
176	Sunday 10 December	The Birdcage, Harlow	UK	Guatemalan author Miguel Ángel Asturias awarded the Nobel Prize for Literature.	Otis Redding dies in plane crash with four others.
177	Wednesday 13 December	Flamingo Ballroom, Redruth	UK	Unsuccessful coup against Greek King Constantine II.	
178	Thursday 14 December	The Pavilion Ballroom, Bournemouth	UK		
179	Friday 15 December	Middle Earth, Covent Garden, London	UK		*The Who Sell Out* released by The Who.
180	Saturday 16 December	Ritz Ballroom, King's Heath, Birmingham	UK		
181	Saturday 16 December	The Penthouse, Constitution Hill, Birmingham	UK		
182	Thursday 21 December	The Speakeasy Club, Margaret Street, London	UK		
183	Friday 22 December	Olympia Exhibition Halls, Olympia, London	UK		
	1968				
1	Friday 12 January	Guild Of Students, University of Aston, Birmingham	UK		
2	Saturday 13 January	Winter Gardens Pavilion, Weston-super-Mare	UK		Johnny Cash records *At Folsom Prison*.
3	Friday 19 January	Town Hall, Lewes	UK	Northern Ireland's Prime Minister Terence O'Neill calls for 'a new endeavour by organisations in Northern Ireland to cross denominational barriers'.	
4	Saturday 20 January	The Pavilion Ballroom, Hastings	UK		
5	Friday 26 January	Old Refectory, Student's Union, Southampton University, Southampton	UK		
6	Saturday 27 January	Leicester College of Art and Technology, Leicester	UK		
7	Saturday 10 February	The Imperial Ballroom, Nelson	UK		
8	Friday 16 February	ICI Fibres Club, Pontypool	UK		The Beatles, Mike Love, Mia Farrow, Donovan and others travel to India to visit Maharishi Mahesh Yogi at Rishikesh.
	EUROPEAN TOUR				
9	Saturday 17 February	*Imaage*, Patronaatsgebouw, Terneuzen, Netherlands	Netherlands	Soviet Union wins its third Olympic ice hockey gold medal at Winter Olympics in Grenoble, France.	
10	Saturday 17 February	Concertgebouw, Vlissingen, Netherlands	Netherlands		
11	Thursday 22 February	Rijschool, Leuven, Belgium	Belgium		
12	Friday 23 February	Pannenhuis, Antwerp, Belgium	Belgium	Wilt Chamberlain becomes first NBA player to score 25,000 points.	'(Sittin' On) The Dock Of The Bay' released by Otis Redding.
13	Saturday 24 February	Cheetah Club, Brussels, Belgium	Belgium		
14	Sunday 25 February	*'t Smurf*, De Engh, Bussum, Netherlands	Netherlands		*Fleetwood Mac* released by Fleetwood Mac.
15	Monday 26 February	*Domino Club*, Lion Hotel, Cambridge	UK		
16	Saturday 9 March	Faculty of Technology Union, Manchester Technical College, Manchester	UK		
17	Thursday 14 March	Whitla Hall, Belfast	UK		
18	Thursday 14 March	Whitla Hall, Belfast	UK		
19	Friday 15 March	*The Stage Club*, Clarendon Restaurant, Oxford	UK	British Foreign Secretary George Brown resigns.	
20	Saturday 16 March	Crawdaddy, The Ballroom, Casino Hotel, Taggs Island, Hampton	UK	My Lai Massacre in Vietnam.	
21	Wednesday 20 March	New Grafton Rooms, Liverpool	UK		

	Year	Address	Country	World Events	Music
22	Friday 22 March	Main Hall, Woolwich Polytechnic, London	UK		
23	Thursday 18 April	Piper Club, Rome, Italy	Italy	London Bridge sold to American oil tycoon Robert P McCulloch for $2,460,000.	
	Friday 19 April	RECORD RELEASE 'IT WOULD BE SO NICE' (US 3 JUNE)			Odessey And Oracle released by The Zombies.
24	Friday 19 April	Piper Club, Rome, Italy	Italy		
25	Saturday 20 April	Raven Club, RAF Waddington, Waddington	UK	Pierre Trudeau becomes the 15th Prime Minister of Canada.	
26	Friday 3 May	Westfield College, Hampstead, London	UK		
27	Saturday 4 May	Theatre 140, Brussels, Belgium	Belgium		Just Because I'm A Woman released by Dolly Parton.
28	Sunday 5 May	Theatre 140, Brussels, Belgium	Belgium		Buffalo Springfield perform together for the last time in Long Beach, California.
29	Monday 6 May	First European International Pop Festival, Palazzo Dello Sport, Rome, Italy	Italy	Street battles between students and troops in Paris.	At Folsom Prison released by Johnny Cash.
30	Saturday 11 May	Brighton Arts Festival - The Gentle Sound of Light, University of Sussex, Falmer, Brighton	UK		
31	Friday 17 May	Middle Earth, Covent Garden, London	UK		
32	Thursday 23 May	Whisky A Go Go, RK Verenigingsgebouw, Zaandam, Netherlands	Netherlands		
33	Thursday 23 May	Paradiso, Amsterdam, Netherlands	Netherlands		
34	Friday 24 May	The Punch Bowl, Lapworth, nr. Birmingham	UK	French President Charles de Gaulle proposes constitutional referendum, and promises to resign if his proposals are rejected.	Ogdens' Nut Gone Flake released by Small Faces.
35	Saturday 25 May	Mayfair Suite, The Belfry Hotel, Wishaw, Sutton Coldfield	UK		
36	Sunday 26 May	OZ Magazine Benefit, Middle Earth, Covent Garden, London	UK		Little Willie John dies in prison after being convicted of manslaughter.
	BELGIUM AND NETHERLANDS TOUR				
37	Thursday 30 May	Hotel Billard Place, Antwerp, Belgium	Belgium	West German Parliament passes German Emergency Acts, in constitutional amendment.	The Beatles begin recording The White Album.
38	Friday 31 May	Fantasio, Amsterdam, Netherlands	Netherlands		
39	Friday 31 May	Lijn 3, Amsterdam, Netherlands	Netherlands		
40	Saturday 1 June	Lijn 3, Amsterdam, Netherlands	Netherlands		
41	Saturday 1 June	't Smurf, De Engh, Bussum, Netherlands	Netherlands		
42	Saturday 1 June	Eurobeurs, Apeldoorn, Netherlands	Netherlands		
43	Sunday 2 June	Concertgebouw, Vlissingen, Netherlands	Netherlands		
44	Monday 3 June	De Pas, Heesch, Netherlands	Netherlands	Valerie Solanas shoots pop artist Andy Warhol, near-fatally wounding him.	
45	Monday 3 June	Parochieel Ontspannings Centrum, Weesp, Netherlands	Netherlands		
46	Saturday 8 June	Market Hall, Haverfordwest	UK	James Earl Ray is arrested for the assassination of Martin Luther King Jr.	
47	Wednesday 12 June	May Ball, King's College, Cambridge	UK	US premiere of horror film Rosemary's Baby, directed by Roman Polansky.	
48	Friday 14 June	Midsummer Ball, University College London, London	UK		In-A-Gadda-Da-Vida released by Iron Butterfly.
49	Saturday 15 June	Magic Village, Manchester	UK		

	Year	Address	Country	World Events	Music
50	Friday 21 June	Commemoration Ball, Balliol College, Oxford	UK	US Supreme Court Chief Justice Earl Warren announces he will resign.	Bare Wires released by John Mayall's Bluesbreakers.
51	Friday 21 June	Middle Earth, Covent Garden, London	UK		
52	Saturday 22 June	The First Holiness Kitschgarden For The Liberation of Love & Peace in Colours, Den Haag, Netherlands	Netherlands		
53	Saturday 22 June	Lower Common Room, University of East Anglia, Norwich	UK		
54	Wednesday 26 June	Sheffield Arts Festival, Lower Refectory, Sheffield University, Sheffield	UK	Iwo Jima and Bonin Islands returned to Japan.	
	Friday 28 June	RECORD RELEASE *A SAUCERFUL OF SECRETS* (US 27 JULY)			
55	Friday 28 June	Students Celebration Dance – The End Of It All Ball, Music Hall, Shrewsbury	UK		
56	Saturday 29 June	*Midsummer High Weekend*, The Cockpit, Hyde Park, London	UK		First Hyde Park free concert, at which Pink Floyd perform alongside Tyrannosaurus Rex, Roy Harper, and Jethro Tull.
57	Saturday 29 June	Town Hall, Torquay	UK		
	NORTH AMERICAN TOUR				
58	Monday 8 July	Kinetic Playground, Chicago, Illinois, USA	USA		
59	Friday 12 July	Grande Ballroom, Detroit, Michigan, USA	USA		*Delilah* released by Tom Jones.
60	Saturday 13 July	Fifth Dimension, Ann Arbor, Michigan, USA	USA		
61	Monday 15 July	Steve Paul's, The Scene, New York City, New York, USA	USA	Commercial air travel begins between the US and the USSR.	
62	Tuesday 16 July	Steve Paul's, The Scene, New York City, New York, USA	USA		
63	Wednesday 17 July	Steve Paul's, The Scene, New York City, New York, USA	USA	Saddam Hussein becomes Vice Chairman of the Revolutionary Council in Iraq after a coup d'état.	*Shades Of Deep Purple* released by Deep Purple.
64	Thursday 18 July	The Boston Tea Party, Boston, Massachusetts, USA	USA		
	Friday 19 July	RECORD RELEASE *TONITE LET'S ALL MAKE LOVE*			
65	Friday 19 July	The Boston Tea Party, Boston, Massachusetts, USA	USA		*Music In A Doll's House* released by Family.
66	Saturday 20 July	The Boston Tea Party, Boston, Massachusetts, USA	USA		
67	Wednesday 24 July	*Philadelphia Music Festival*, John F. Kennedy Stadium, Philadelphia, Pennsylvania, USA	USA	The first International Special Olympics Summer Games are held at Soldier Field in Chicago, Illinois.	
68	Friday 26 July	Shrine Exposition Hall, Exposition Park, Los Angeles, California, USA	USA		*In Search Of The Lost Chord* released by The Moody Blues.
69	Saturday 27 July	Shrine Exposition Hall, Exposition Park, Los Angeles, California, USA	USA	Race riot in Gary, Indiana.	
70	Friday 2 August	Avalon Ballroom, San Francisco, California, USA	USA		
71	Saturday 3 August	Avalon Ballroom, San Francisco, California, USA	USA		Yes perform live for the first time.
72	Sunday 4 August	Avalon Ballroom, San Francisco, California, USA	USA		*Wheels Of Fire* released by Cream.
73	Friday 9 August	Eagles Auditorium, Seattle, Washington, USA	USA		
74	Saturday 10 August	Eagles Auditorium, Seattle, Washington, USA	USA	Race riots in Miami, Chicago and Little Rock, Arkansas.	
75	Sunday 11 August	Eagles Auditorium, Seattle, Washington, USA	USA		
76	Friday 16 August	Sounds Factory, Sacramento, California, USA	USA		
77	Saturday 17 August	Sounds Factory, Sacramento, California, USA	USA		
	Monday 19 August	RECORD RELEASE '*LET THERE BE MORE LIGHT*' (USA)			*The Best of The Beach Boys Vol. 3* released by The Beach Boys.

	Year	Address	Country	World Events	Music
78	Friday 23 August	The Bank, Torrance, Los Angeles, California, USA	USA		*Mr. Wonderful* released by Fleetwood Mac.
79	Saturday 24 August	The Bank, Torrance, Los Angeles, California, USA	USA	France explodes its first hydrogen bomb.	'Stoned Soul Picnic' released by The 5th Dimension.
80	Saturday 31 August	*Kastival '68 Festival*, Kasterlee, Belgium	Belgium		
81	Wednesday 4 September	*Middle Earth*, The Club House, Richmond Athletic Club, Richmond, Surrey	UK		
82	Friday 13 September	Mothers, Erdington, Birmingham	UK	Albania officially withdraws from the Warsaw Pact upon the Soviet Union-led invasion of Czechoslovakia.	
83	Friday 20 September	Victoria Rooms, University of Bristol, Clifton, Bristol	UK		
84	Thursday 26 September	Mayfair Ballroom, Newcastle	UK	Theatre censorship ends in Britain.	
85	Friday 27 September	Queen's Hall, Dunoon	UK		*Picturesque Matchstickable Messages from the Status Quo* released by Status Quo.
86	Tuesday 1 October	The Maryland Ballroom, Glasgow	UK	*Night of the Living Dead*, directed by George A. Romero, premieres in Pittsburgh.	*In Person at the Whisky a Go Go* released by Otis Redding.
87	Friday 4 October	Mothers, Erdington, Birmingham	UK		
88	Sunday 6 October	The Country Club, Belsize Park, London	UK		
89	Wednesday 16 October	Theatre du Huitieme, Lyon, France	France	African-American athletes Tommie Smith and John Carlos raise their fists in a black power salute after winning gold and bronze medals in the Olympic men's 200 metres.	*Electric Ladyland* released by The Jimi Hendrix Experience.
90	Friday 18 October	Industrial Club, Norwich	UK	Police find 219 grains of cannabis resin in John Lennon and Yoko Ono's apartment in London. They are subsequently fined £150.	
91	Saturday 19 October	Theatre 140, Brussels, Belgium	Belgium		
92	Sunday 20 October	Theatre 140, Brussels, Belgium	Belgium		
93	Friday 25 October	The Boat House, Kew, London	UK		*This Was* released by Jethro Tull.
94	Saturday 26 October	Union Hall, Imperial College, Kensington, London	UK		
95	Saturday 26 October	*Middle Earth*, The Roundhouse, Chalk Farm, London	UK		
96	Friday 1 November	The Sound of Colours, Highbury Technical College, Portsmouth	UK	Motion Picture Association of America introduces rating system (G, M, R, and X).	*Wonderwall Music* released by George Harrison.
97	Saturday 2 November	Main Hall, Watford Technical College, Watford	UK	A banned march in Derry, North Ireland, is joined by thousands with the Royal Ulster Constabulary unable to prevent it going ahead.	
98	Thursday 7 November	Porchester Hall, Queensway, London	UK		
99	Friday 8 November	Fishmonger's Arms, Wood Green, London	UK		John and Cynthia Lennon are granted a divorce.
	WEST GERMAN AND SWISS TOUR				
100	Friday 15 November	Blow Up Club, Munich, West Germany	Germany		
101	Saturday 16 November	Restaurant Olten-Hammer, Olten, Switzerland	Switzerland		
102	Saturday 16 November	*Grosse Tanzparty*, Coca-Cola Halle, Abtwil, Switzerland	Switzerland		
103	Sunday 17 November	*2nd Pop & Rhythm And Blues Festival*, Hazyland, Kongresshaus, Zurich, Switzerland	Switzerland	Alexandros Panagoulis sentenced to death for attempting to assassinate Greek dictator George Papadopoulos.	
104	Friday 22 November	*Crawdaddy*, The Club House, Richmond Athletic Club, Richmond, Surrey	UK	Northern Ireland Prime Minister Terence O'Neill announces a package of reforms granting concessions to the Catholic minority.	*The Beatles* (better known as *The White Album*) released by The Beatles.
105	Saturday 23 November	The Large Hall, Regent Street Polytechnic, London	UK		
106	Sunday 24 November	The Country Club, Belsize Park, London	UK		

	Year	Address	Country	World Events	Music
107	Wednesday 27 November	Keele University, Newcastle-under-Lyme	UK		
108	Friday 29 November	Hanover Lodge, Bedford College, Regents Park, London	UK		*Astral Weeks* released by Van Morrison.
109	Thursday 5 December	Bournemouth College Students Union Christmas Dance, Royal Arcade Ballrooms, Bournemouth	UK		
	Friday 6 December	RECORD RELEASE 'POINT ME AT THE SKY'			*Beggars Banquet* released by The Rolling Stones.
110	Saturday 7 December	Kaleidoscope '68, Liverpool Stadium, Liverpool	UK	Orbiting Astronomical Observatory 2 launched into orbit from Cape Canaveral.	
111	Wednesday 11 December	Students Union, St. Andrews University, St. Andrews	UK		The Rolling Stones' Rock and Roll Circus is filmed, with the last appearance of Brian Jones as a member of the Stones.
112	Thursday 12 December	*Christmas Revels Ball*, College of Art, Dundee	UK	Arthur Ashe becomes the first black player ranked World #1 in tennis.	
113	Friday 13 December	The New Marquee, Leeds	UK		
114	Sunday 15 December	City Hall, Newcastle	UK		
115	Friday 27 December	Grote Zaal, De Doelen, Rotterdam, Netherlands	Netherlands		
116	Saturday 28 December	*Flights To Lowlands Paradise II*, Margriethal-Jaarbeurs, Utrecht, Netherlands	Netherlands	Israeli armed forces attack airport in Beirut, destroying more than a dozen aircraft.	
1969					
1	Friday 10 January	Fishmonger's Arms, Wood Green, London	UK	Soviet Union launches Venera 6 toward Venus.	*Led Zeppelin* released in the US by Led Zeppelin.
2	Sunday 12 January	Mothers, Erdington, Birmingham	UK		*Led Zeppelin* released in the UK by Led Zeppelin.
3	Saturday 18 January	Homerton College, Cambridge	UK	Four-party Vietnam peace talks began in Paris.	*Dusty In Memphis* released by Dusty Springfield.
4	Saturday 18 January	London College of Printing, Elephant and Castle, London	UK		
5	Saturday 18 January	Middle Earth, The Roundhouse, Chalk Farm, London	UK		
6	Saturday 25 January	Sixty Nine Club, Royal York Hotel, Ryde, Isle of Wight	UK		
7	Friday 14 February	*Valentine's Ball*, Edward Herbert Building, Loughborough University of Technology, Loughborough	UK		
8	Monday 17 February	The Ballroom, Bay Hotel, Whitburn, Sunderland	UK		Johnny Cash and Bob Dylan record together in Nashville, Tennessee.
9	Tuesday 18 February	*Manchester & Salford Students' Shrove Rag Ball*, Main Debating Hall, Manchester University, Manchester	UK		Lulu and Maurice Gibb are married in the UK.
10	Friday 21 February	Alhambra Theatre, Bordeaux, France	UK		
11	Monday 24 February	The Dome, Brighton	UK	Stormont parliamentary elections held in Northern Ireland.	Johnny Cash performs 'A Boy Named Sue' at San Quentin State Prison.
12	Tuesday 25 February	Marlowe Theatre, Canterbury	UK	West Germany gives $5 million to an Arab terrorist as ransom for passengers and crew of a hijacked jumbo jet.	
13	Wednesday 26 February	New Cavendish Ballroom, Edinburgh, Scotland	UK		
14	Thursday 27 February	*Glasgow Arts Lab Benefit*, The Maryland Ballroom, Glasgow, Scotland	UK		
15	Friday 28 February	Commemoration Ball, Queen Elizabeth College, Kensington, London	UK		
16	Saturday 1 March	University College, Bloomsbury, London	UK		Jim Morrison of The Doors is arrested in Miami for allegedly exposing himself during a performance.

	Year	Address	Country	World Events	Music
17	Monday 3 March	*Vic Rooms Dance*, Victoria Rooms, University of Bristol, Clifton, Bristol	UK	United States Navy establishes the Navy Fighter Weapons School (also known as Top Gun) at Miramar, California.	
18	Saturday 8 March	Reading University Rag Ball, New Union, University of Reading, Whiteknights, Reading	UK		
19	Tuesday 11 March	Lawns Centre, Cottingham	UK		*Tons Of Sobs* released by Free.
20	Friday 14 March	Van Dike Club, Devonport, Plymouth	UK		
21	Saturday 15 March	Kee Club, Bridgend, Glamorgan, Wales	UK		Judy Garland marries Mickey Deans in London.
22	Wednesday 19 March	*Going Down Ball*, The Refectory, University College, Singleton Park, Swansea, Wales	UK	Sino-Russian border skirmish kills hundreds.	
23	Friday 21 March	Blackpool Technical College & School of Art and St. Anne's College of Further Education Arts Ball, Empress Ballroom, Winter Gardens, Blackpool	UK	Chicago 8 indicted in aftermath of disturbances at Chicago Democratic convention.	
24	Saturday 22 March	*Easter Endsville*, Refectory Hall, University Union, Leeds University, Leeds	UK		
25	Thursday 27 March	St. James' Church Hall, Chesterfield	UK		
26	Monday 14 April	Royal Festival Hall, South Bank, London	UK		
27	Saturday 26 April	Light & Sound Concert, Main Hall, Bromley Technical College, Bromley	UK		*It's Our Thing* released by The Isley Brothers.
28	Sunday 27 April	Mothers, Erdington, Birmingham	UK		
29	Friday 2 May	Student Union Building, College of Commerce, Manchester	UK	British liner Queen Elizabeth II leaves Southampton on maiden voyage to New York.	
30	Saturday 3 May	The Sports Hall, Queen Mary College, Mile End, London	UK		*Stand!* released by Sly & the Family Stone.
31	Friday 9 May	Camden Fringe Festival Free Concert, Parliament Hill Fields, Hampstead Heath, London	UK		*Beginnings* released by Ambrose Slade (later known as Slade).
32	Friday 9 May	Old Refectory, Student's Union, Southampton University, Highfield, Southampton	UK		
33	Saturday 10 May	*Nottingham Pop & Blues Festival*, Notts County Football Ground, Nottingham	UK	The Battle of Dong Ap Bia (Hamburger Hill), begins during the Vietnam War.	
34	Thursday 15 May	*It's A Drag – City of Coventry College of Art May Ball*, Locarno Ballroom, Coventry	UK	An American teenager dies in St. Louis, Missouri, of an unknown condition later identified as the first confirmed case of HIV/AIDS in North America.	
	UK TOUR				
35	Friday 16 May	Town Hall, Leeds	UK		*Unicorn* released by Tyrannosaurus Rex.
36	Saturday 24 May	City (Oval) Hall, Sheffield	UK		
37	Sunday 25 May	*Benefit for The Fairport Convention*, The Roundhouse, Chalk Farm, London	UK		
38	Friday 30 May	Fairfield Halls, Croydon	UK	Riots in Curaçao mark the start of an Afro-Caribbean civil rights movement on the island.	
39	Sunday 1 June	*Eight Weeks Ball*, Main Marquee, Pembroke College, Oxford	UK		
40	Sunday 8 June	Rex Ballroom, Cambridge	UK	US President Richard Nixon and South Vietnamese President Nguyễn Văn Thiệu meet at Midway Island.	
41	Tuesday 10 June	Ulster Hall, Belfast, Northern Ireland	UK		
	Friday 13 June	**RECORD RELEASE *MORE* (US RELEASE 9 AUGUST)**			Mick Taylor joins The Rolling Stones.
42	Friday 13 June	*Students Dance*, Great Hall, Devonshire House, University of Exeter, Exeter	UK		

	Year	Address	Country	World Events	Music
43	Saturday 14 June	Colston Hall, Bristol	UK		
44	Sunday 15 June	Guildhall, Portsmouth	UK	The Campaign for Social Justice publish second edition of 'Northern Ireland The Plain Truth', setting out set out allegations of discrimination against Catholics by Unionists.	
45	Monday 16 June	The Dome, Brighton	UK		*Trout Mask Replica* released by Captain Beefheart.
46	Friday 20 June	Town Hall, Birmingham	UK	Georges Pompidou elected President of France.	*Aoxomoxoa* released by Grateful Dead.
47	Saturday 21 June	Royal Philharmonic, Liverpool	UK		*Deep Purple* released by Deep Purple in the US.
48	Sunday 22 June	Free Trade Hall, Manchester	UK		Judy Garland dies aged 47.
49	Tuesday 24 June	Commemoration Ball, Main Marquee, Queen's College, Oxford	UK		
50	Thursday 26 June	*The Final Lunacy!*, Royal Albert Hall, Kensington, London	UK		
51	Friday 27 June	Van Dike Club, Devonport, Plymouth	UK	Honduras and El Salvador break diplomatic relations following rioting at a football match.	
52	Saturday 28 June	Saturday Dance Date, Winter Gardens Pavilion, Weston-super-Mare	UK	Stonewall riots in New York City mark the start of the modern gay rights movement in the US	
53	Monday 30 June	President's Ball, Top Rank Suite, Cardiff, Wales	UK		
54	Friday 4 July	Selby Arts Festival, St. James Street Recreation Ground, Selby	UK		
55	Friday 1 August	Van Dike Club, Devonport, Plymouth	UK		*Stand Up* released by Jethro Tull.
56	Friday 8 August	9th National Jazz Pop Ballads & Blues Festival, Plumpton Race Track, Streat	UK		The Beatles have their photo taken on a zebra crossing at Abbey Road, London.
57	Saturday 9 August	Paradiso, Amsterdam, Netherlands	Netherlands	Members of the Manson Family invade the home of actress Sharon Tate and her husband Roman Polanski in Los Angeles, killing Tate and four others.	
58	Saturday 13 September	*The Sam Cutler Stage Show – Rugby Rag's Blues Festival*, Rainsbrook, Ashlawn Road, Rugby	UK		John Lennon and Plastic Ono Band perform at the Toronto Rock and Roll Revival.
	NETHERLAND AND BELGIUM TOUR				
59	Wednesday 17 September	Concertgebouw, Amsterdam, Netherlands	Netherlands		
60	Friday 19 September	Grote Zaal, De Doelen, Rotterdam, Netherlands	Netherlands		*Then Play On* released by Fleetwood Mac.
61	Saturday 20 September	Concertzaal, Groningen, Netherlands	Netherlands		
62	Sunday 21 September	Het Holpinghuis, Nijmegen, Netherlands	Netherlands		
63	Wednesday 24 September	Stadtsgehoorzal, Leiden, Netherlands	Netherlands	Tôn Đức Thắng elected president of North Vietnam.	Deep Purple and the Royal Philharmonic Orchestra perform the Concerto for Group and Orchestra at the Royal Albert Hall.
64	Thursday 25 September	Staargebouw, Maastricht, Netherlands	Netherlands		
65	Friday 26 September	Theatre 140, Brussels, Belgium	Belgium		*Abbey Road* released by The Beatles.
66	Saturday 27 September	Theatre 140, Brussels, Belgium	Belgium		
67	Sunday 28 September	Theatre 140, Brussels, Belgium	Belgium		
68	Friday 3 October	Debating Hall, Birmingham University, Edgbaston, Birmingham	UK		
69	Saturday 4 October	New Union, Reading University, Whiteknights Park, Reading	UK		
70	Friday 10 October	Edward Herbert Building, Loughborough University of Technology, Loughborough	UK		*In The Court Of The Crimson King* released by King Crimson.

	Year	Address	Country	World Events	Music
71	Saturday 11 October	*International Essener Pop & Blues Festival '69*, Grughalle, Essen, West Germany	Germany	Second Synod of Bishops begins in Rome.	
72	Saturday 18 October	University College London, Bloomsbury, London	UK		*Live at Yankee Stadium* released by the Isley Brothers.
73	Friday 24 October	Fillmore North, Locarno Ballroom, Sunderland	UK		
74	Saturday 25 October	*Actuel Festival*, Mont de l'Enclus, Amougies, Belgium	Belgium		*Second Winter* released by Johnny Winter.
75	Monday 27 October	Electric Garden, Glasgow, Scotland	UK	Nobel Prize in Economics awarded to John Tinbergen.	
76	Saturday 1 November	Main Debating Hall, Manchester University, Manchester	UK		Elvis Presley hits #1 on the *Billboard* chart for the first time in eight years with 'Suspicious Minds'.
	Friday 7 November	**RECORD RELEASE *UMMAGUMMA* (US 8 NOVEMBER)**			*Manfred Mann Chapter Three* released by Manfred Mann Chapter Three.
77	Friday 7 November	Main Hall, Waltham Forest Technical College, Walthamstow, London	UK		
78	Saturday 8 November	Refectory Hall, University Union, Leeds University, Leeds	UK		
79	Wednesday 26 November	Friars Club, Queensway Hall, Civic Centre, Dunstable	UK	Draft Lottery bill signed by President Nixon.	
80	Thursday 27 November	Mountford Hall, Liverpool University, Liverpool	UK		
81	Friday 28 November	Brunel University Arts Festival Weekend, Refectory Hall, Brunel University, Uxbridge	UK		
82	Sunday 30 November	The Lyceum, Strand, London	UK		Simon & Garfunkel's TV special 'Songs of America' aired.
83	Saturday 6 December	Afan Festival Of Progressive Music, Afan Lido, Indoor Sports Centre, Port Talbot, Wales	UK		Altamont Free Concert is held in northern California. Attendee Hunter Meredith is killed by a Hell's Angel acting as security after pulling out a gun.
	1970				
1	Saturday 10 January	The Ballroom, University of Nottingham, Beeston, Nottingham	UK		
2	Saturday 17 January	Lawns Centre, Cottingham, Hull	UK		
3	Sunday 18 January	Fairfield Halls, Croydon, London	UK		
4	Monday 19 January	The Dome, Brighton	UK		*Hello, I'm Johnny Cash* released by Johnny Cash.
5	Friday 23 January	Theatre des Champs-Elysees, Paris, France	France	UCLA fires Angela Davis for being a communist.	*A Song For Me* released by Family.
6	Saturday 24 January	Theatre des Champs-Elysees, Paris, France	France		James 'Shep' Sheppard, of The Heartbeats and Shep and the Limelites, is found murdered in his car.
7	Monday 2 February	Palais de Sports, Lyon, France	France		
8	Thursday 5 February	Sophia Gardens Pavilion, Cardiff	UK		
9	Saturday 7 February	Royal Albert Hall, Kensington, London	UK		
10	Sunday 8 February	Opera House, Manchester	UK		
11	Wednesday 11 February	Town Hall, Birmingham	UK	John Lennon pays fines of £1,344 given to 96 people protesting the South African rugby tour of Scotland.	The film *The Magic Christian*, starring Peter Sellers and Ringo Starr, premiers in New York City.
12	Saturday 14 February	King's Hall, Town Hall, Stoke-on-Trent	UK		The Who record *Live at Leeds*.
13	Sunday 15 February	Empire Theatre, Liverpool	UK		
14	Tuesday 17 February	City Hall, Newcastle	UK		Joni Mitchell announces that she is retiring from live performances. (The retirement lasts less than a year.)
15	Sunday 22 February	Electric Garden, Glasgow, Scotland	UK		
16	Monday 23 February	McEwan Hall, University of Edinburgh, Edinburgh, Scotland	UK	Guyana becomes a republic.	

	Year	Address	Country	World Events	Music
17	Saturday 28 February	University Union, Leeds University, Leeds	UK		Led Zeppelin perform in Copenhagen under the pseudonym The Nobs, to avoid a lawsuit by Count Eva von Zeppelin, descendant of airship designer Ferdinand von Zeppelin.
18	Friday 6 March	Great Hall, Imperial College, London	UK		Stevie Wonder Live released by Stevie Wonder.
19	Saturday 7 March	Colston Hall, Bristol	UK		
20	Sunday 8 March	Mothers, Erdington, Birmingham	UK		
21	Monday 9 March	City (Oval) Hall, Sheffield	UK		
	EUROPEAN TOUR				
22	Wednesday 11 March	Stadthalle, Offenbach, West Germany	Germany		Déjà Vu released by Crosby, Stills, Nash & Young.
23	Thursday 12 March	Auditorium Maximum, Hamburg Universitat, Hamburg, West Germany	Germany	US voting age lowered from 21 to 18.	
24	Friday 13 March	Technische Universitat, West Berlin, West Germany	Germany		A Beard Of Stars released by Tyrannosaurus Rex.
25	Saturday 14 March	Meistersinger Halle, Nurnberg, West Germany	Germany	The 1970 World's Fair opens in Suita, Osaka, Japan.	
26	Sunday 15 March	Niedersachsenhalle, Hannover, West Germany	Germany		David Bowie marries Angela Barnett.
27	Thursday 19 March	Konserthuset, Stockholm, Sweden	Sweden		
28	Friday 20 March	Akademiska Foreningens Stora Sal, Lund, Sweden	Sweden		
29	Saturday 21 March	Tivolis Koncertsal, Copenhagen, Denmark	Denmark	The first Earth Day proclamation is issued by San Francisco Mayor Joseph Alioto.	
30	Monday 30 March	Le Festival Musique Evolution, Le Bourget (Aeroport de Paris), Siene St Denis, France	France		Bitches Brew released by Miles Davis.
	NORTH AMERICAN TOUR				
31	Thursday 9 April	Filmore East, New York City, New York, USA	USA		Remedies released by Dr. John.
32	Friday 10 April	Aragon Ballroom, Chicago, Illinois, USA	USA		Paul McCartney announces that he has left The Beatles.
33	Saturday 11 April	The Gymnasium, State University of New York, Long Island, New York, USA	USA	Apollo 13 launched toward the Moon.	
34	Sunday 12 April	Boston Tea Party, Boston, Massachusetts	USA		
35	Thursday 16 April	Filmore East, New York City, New York, USA	USA	Rev. Ian Paisley wins a by-election for the Northern Ireland Parliament.	
36	Friday 17 April	Electric Factory, Philadelphia, Pennsylvania, USA	USA		Johnny Cash performs at the White House at the invitation of President Richard Nixon.
37	Saturday 18 April	Electric Factory, Philadelphia, Pennsylvania, USA	USA		
38	Wednesday 22 April	Capitol Theatre, Port Chester, New York, USA	USA	The first Earth Day is celebrated in the US.	Live released by Iron Butterfly.
39	Friday 24 April	Eastown Theatre, Detroit, Michigan, USA	USA	Gambia becomes a republic.	Grace Slick of Jefferson Airplane is invited to a tea party at the White House by Tricia Nixon, daughter of Richard Nixon. Slick arrives with Abbie Hoffman, who is on trial for conspiring to riot at the 1968 Democratic National Convention. The pair planned to spike Nixon's tea cup with an LSD. Slick is recognised (although Hoffman is not) and told to leave because she is on the FBI list.
40	Saturday 25 April	Eastown Theatre, Detroit, Michigan, USA	USA		
41	Wednesday 29 April	Filmore West, San Francisco, California, USA	USA	The US and South Vietnam launch an incursion into Cambodia, expanding the Vietnam War.	
42	Friday 1 May	Civic Auditorium, Santa Monica, California, USA	USA		
43	Thursday 7 May	Pauley Pavilion, UCLA, Los Angeles, California, USA	USA		
44	Saturday 9 May	Terrace Ballroom, Salt Lake City, Utah, USA	USA		

	Year	Address	Country	World Events	Music
45	Tuesday 12 May	Municipal Auditorium, Atlanta, Georgia, USA	USA	Race riots in Augusta, Georgia.	
46	Thursday 15 May	The Warehouse, New Orleans, Louisiana, USA	USA	1976 Winter Olympics are awarded to Denver, Colorado (later rejected).	
47	Friday 16 May	The Warehouse, New Orleans, Louisiana, USA	USA		*Live At Leeds* released by The Who.
	Friday 29 May	**RECORD RELEASE *ZABRISKIE POINT* SOUNDTRACK (US RELEASE 11 APRIL)**			
48	Saturday 27 June	Bath Festival of Blues & Progressive Music '70, Bath & West Showground, Shepton Mallet	UK		
49	Sunday 28 June	The Holland Pop Festival '70, Kralinge Bos, Rotterdam, Netherlands	Netherlands	US ground troops withdraw from Cambodia.	
50	Sunday 12 July	1st Open Air Pop Festival, Reiterstadion Soers, Aachen, West Germany	Germany		
51	Saturday 18 July	Hyde Park Free Concert, London	UK		
52	Sunday 26 July	XI Festival International de Jazz, Pinede Gould, Antibes Juan-le-Pins, France	France		
53	Saturday 8 August	Festival de St. Tropez, Les Caves du Roy, St. Tropez, France	France		*Runt* released by Todd Rundgren.
54	Wednesday 12 August	Fete de St. Raphael, L'Amphitheatre Romain, St Raphael, France	France	Thor Heyerdahl crosses the Atlantic Ocean after 57 days on the raft Ra II.	
55	Monday 31 August	Charlton Park, Bishopsbourne, nr. Canterbury	UK		*Sunflower* released by The Beach Boys.
56	Saturday 12 September	Fete de L'Humanite, Grand Scene, Bois de Vincennes, Paris, France	France	Timothy Leary escapes from jail in California.	
	NORTH AMERICAN TOUR				
57	Saturday 26 September	Electric Factory, Philadelphia, Pennsylvania, USA	USA		
58	Sunday 27 September	Filimore East, New York City, New York, USA	USA	Pope Paul VI names Saint Teresa of Avila as the first female Doctor of the Church.	
59	Thursday 1 October	Memorial Coliseum, Portland, Oregon, USA	USA		
	Friday 2 October	**RECORD RELEASE *ATOM HEART MOTHER***			
60	Friday 2 October	Moore Theater, Seattle, Washington, USA	USA		
61	Saturday 3 October	Moore Theater, Seattle, Washington, USA	USA		Janis Joplin dies from a heroin overdose, at the age of 27.
62	Sunday 4 October	The Gymnasium, Gonzaga University, Spokane, Washington, USA	USA		
63	Tuesday 6 October	Central Washington University, Ellensburg, Washington, USA	USA		
64	Wednesday 7 October	Gardens Arena, Vancouver, British Columbia, Canada	Canada		
65	Thursday 8 October	Jubilee Auditorium, Calgary, Alberta, Canada	Canada	Aleksandr Solzhenitsyn is awarded the Nobel Prize in Literature.	
66	Friday 9 October	Sales Pavilion Annex, Edmonton, Alberta, Canada	Canada	Khmer Republic is proclaimed in Cambodia which begins the civil war with the Khmer Rouge.	
67	Saturday 10 October	Centennial Auditorium, Saskatoon, Saskatchewan, Canada	Canada	Fiji gains independence from the UK.	
68	Sunday 11 October	Centre of the Arts, Regina, Saskatchewan, Canada	Canada		
69	Tuesday 13 October	Centennial Concert Hall, Winnipeg, Manitoba, Canada	Canada		

	Year	Address	Country	World Events	Music
70	Thursday 15 October	Terrace Ballroom, Salt Lake City, Utah, USA	USA		*Jackson 5 Christmas Album* released by The Jackson 5.
71	Friday 16 October	Pepperland Auditorium, San Rafael, California, USA	USA		
72	Saturday 17 October	Pepperland Auditorium, San Rafael, California, USA	USA	Anwar Sadat sworn in as 3rd President of Egypt.	
73	Sunday 18 October	University College of San Diego, San Diego, California, USA	USA		
74	Wednesday 21 October	Filimore West, San Francisco, California, USA	USA	Nobel Peace Prize awarded to Norman E Borlaugh.	
75	Friday 23 October	Civic Auditorium, Santa Monica, California, USA	USA		*Trespass* released by Genesis.
76	Sunday 25 October	Boston Tea Party, Boston, Massachusetts, USA	USA		
	EUROPEAN TOUR				
77	Friday 6 November	Concertgebouw, Amsterdam, Netherlands	Netherlands		
78	Saturday 7 November	Grote Zaal, De Doelen, Rotterdam, Netherlands	Netherlands	Race riots in Daytona Beach, Florida.	
79	Wednesday 11 November	Konserthuset, Gothenburg, Sweden	Sweden		*That's The Way It Is* released by Elvis Presley.
80	Thursday 12 November	Falkoner, Centret, Copenhagen, Denmark	Denmark		
81	Friday 13 November	Vejlby-Risskov Hallen, Aarhus, Denmark	Denmark	Hafez al-Assad comes to power in Syria, following a military coup.	
82	Saturday 14 November	Ernst-Merck-Halle, Hamburg, West Germany	Germany		*Barrett* released by Syd Barrett.
83	Saturday 21 November	*Super Pop 70 VII*, Casino de Montreux, Montreux, Switzerland	Switzerland		*Greatest Hits* released by Sly & The Family Stone.
84	Sunday 22 November	*Super Pop 70 VII*, Casino de Montreux, Montreux, Switzerland	Switzerland		
85	Wednesday 25 November	Friedrich Ebert Halle, Ebertpark, Ludwigshafen, West Germany	Germany	Japanese author Yukio Mishima commits ritual suicide after an unsuccessful coup attempt.	
86	Thursday 26 November	Killesberg Halle 14, Stuttgart, West Germany	Germany		*All Things Must Pass* released by George Harrison.
87	Friday 27 November	Niedersachsenhalle, Hannover, West Germany	Germany		*Play It Loud* released by Slade.
88	Saturday 28 November	Saarlandhalle, Saarbrucken, West Germany	Germany		
89	Sunday 29 November	Circus Krone, Munich, West Germany	Germany		
	UK TOUR				
90	Friday 11 December	Regent Theatre, Brighton	UK		*John Lennon/Plastic Ono Band* released by John Lennon.
91	Saturday 12 December	The Roundhouse, Dagenham, London	UK		The Doors play their final concert with Jim Morrison at The Warehouse in New Orleans, Louisiana.
92	Friday 18 December	Town Hall, Birmingham	UK	Polish uprising in Gdynia fails.	*T. Rex* released by T. Rex.
93	Sunday 20 December	Colston Hall, Bristol	UK		*H To He, Who Am the Only One* released by Van der Graaf Generator.
94	Monday 21 December	Free Trade Hall, Manchester	UK	Elvis Presley meets Richard Nixon in the White House.	
95	Tuesday 22 December	City Hall, Sheffield	UK		
	1971				
1	Saturday 17 January	The Roundhouse, Chalk Farm, London	UK	Sinn Féin end their 65-year abstentionist policy and agree that elected representatives will take their seats at the Dáil.	*Linda Ronstadt* released by Linda Ronstadt.
2	Saturday 23 January	University Union, Leeds University, Leeds	UK	Riots break out in the Shankill Road area of Belfast, North Ireland.	
3	Wednesday 3 February	Great Hall, University of Exeter, Exeter	UK	House searches by the British army in Catholic areas of Belfast result in serious rioting.	Davy Jones announces he is leaving the Monkees.
4	Friday 12 February	Lecture Theatre Block 6 & 7, University of Essex, Wivenhoe Park, Colchester	UK		*Eat A Peach* released by The Allman Brothers.

	Year	Address	Country	World Events	Music
5	Saturday 13 February	Student Union Bar, Farnborough Technical College, Farnborough	UK	Backed by American air and artillery support, South Vietnamese troops invade Laos.	
6	Saturday 20 February	Student Union, Queen Mary College, Twickenham	UK		*Elvis Now* released by Elvis Presley.
	EUROPEAN TOUR				
7	Wednesday 24 February	Halle Munsterland, Munster, West Germany	Germany	Algeria nationalises 51 percent of French oil concessions.	*Jack Johnson* released by Miles Davis.
8	Thursday 25 February	Grosser Saal, Musikhalle, Hamburg, West Germany	Germany		*Pink Moon* released by Nick Drake.
9	Friday 26 February	Stadthalle, Offenbach, West Germany	Germany	Two Royal Ulster Constabulary officers shot and killed by the Irish Republican Army.	
10	Saturday 3 April	Sportpaleis Ahoy, Rotterdam, Netherlands	Netherlands		
11	Friday 16 April	Top Rank Suite, Doncaster	UK		
12	Thursday 22 April	Norwich Lads Club, Norwich	UK	The USSR's Soyuz 10 launches as the world's first mission to the first space station.	*Sky's The Limit* released by The Temptations.
13	Friday 7 May	Central Hall, University of Lancaster, Bailrigg, Lancaster	UK		
	Friday 14 May	**RECORD RELEASE *RELICS* (US RELEASE 17 JULY)**			*Carpenters* released by The Carpenters.
14	Saturday 15 May	Garden Party, Crystal Palace Bowl, Crystal Palace, London	UK		
15	Tuesday 18 May	University of Stirling, Stirling, Scotland	UK	Bulgarian constitution goes into effect.	
16	Wednesday 19 May	Caledonian Cinema, Edinburgh, Scotland	UK	*Mars 2* is launched by the Soviet Union.	*Honky Château* released by Elton John.
17	Thursday 20 May	The Ballroom, University of Strathclyde, Glasgow, Scotland	UK		
18	Friday 21 May	Students Union, Trent Polytechnic, Nottingham	UK	Chelsea beat Real Madrid 2-1 in Athens to win European Cup Winner's Cup.	*What's Going On* released by Marvin Gaye.
19	Wednesday 2 June	Student Health Centre Refectory, University of Edinburgh, Edinburgh, Scotland	UK		
	EUROPEAN TOUR				
20	Friday 4 June	Philipshalle, Dusseldorf, West Germany	Germany	Joseph Luns appointed Secretary-General of NATO.	*Budgie* released by Budgie.
21	Saturday 5 June	Berliner Sportspalast, West Berlin, West Germany	Germany		
22	Saturday 12 June	Palais de Sports, Lyon, France	France		*Some Time In New York City* released by John Lennon and Yoko Ono.
23	Tuesday 15 June	Abbaye de Royaumont, Royaumont, France	France		
24	Saturday 19 June	Palazzo Delle Manifesazioni Artistiche, Brescia, Italy	Italy	State of emergency in Columbus, Georgia, due to racial disturbances.	*Homemade* released by The Osmonds.
25	Sunday 20 June	Palazzo Dello Sport, Rome, Italy	Italy		The first Glastonbury Festival to take place at the summer solstice opens.
26	Wednesday 23 June	Hatfield Polytechnic, Hatfield	UK		*Byrdmaniax* released by The Byrds.
27	Saturday 26 June	Free Concert, Amsterdamse Bos, Amsterdam, Netherlands	Netherlands		
28	Thursday 1 July	*Internationale Musikforum Ossiachersee*, Congress Center Villach, Stiftshoff, Ossiach, Austria	Austria	UK and Argentina sign accord on Falkland Islands.	*Push Push* released by Herbie Mann.
	JAPANESE TOUR				
29	Friday 6 August	*Hakone Aphrodite '71*, Seikei Gakuen Jofundai, nr. Lake Ashi, Hakone, Japan	Japan		

	Year	Address	Country	World Events	Music
30	Saturday 7 August	*Hakone Aphrodite '71*, Seikei Gakuen Jofundai, nr. Lake Ashi, Hakone, Japan	Japan	Apollo 15 returns to Earth.	
31	Monday 9 August	Festival Hall, Osaka, Japan	Japan	With internment permitted in Northern Ireland, British security forces arrest hundreds of nationalists and detain them without trial; 20 people die in the riots that follow.	
	AUSTRALIAN TOUR				
32	Friday 13 August	Festival Hall, Melbourne, Australia	Australia		King Curtis is murdered aged 37.
33	Sunday 15 August	St. Leger Stand, Randwick Racecourse, Sydney, Australia	Australia	Nixon announces that the United States will no longer convert dollars to gold at a fixed value, ending the Bretton Woods monetary system.	*Rock Of Ages* released by The Band.
34	Saturday 18 September	*Festival de Musique Classique*, Pavilion de Montreux, Montreux, Switzerland	Switzerland		
35	Wednesday 22 September	Kungliga Tennishallen, Stockholm, Sweden	Sweden		
36	Thursday 23 September	KB Hallen, Copenhagen, Denmark	Denmark		
37	Sunday 10 October	Great Hall, Bradford University, Bradford	UK		
38	Monday 11 October	Town Hall, Birmingham	UK		*On The Corner* released by Miles Davis.
	NORTH AMERICAN TOUR				
39	Friday 15 October	Winterland Auditorium, San Francisco, California, USA	USA		
40	Saturday 16 October	Civic Auditorium, Santa Monica, California, USA	USA		
41	Sunday 17 October	Convention Hall, San Diego, California, USA	USA		
42	Tuesday 19 October	National Guard Armory, Eugene, Oregon, USA	USA	A group of Northern Ireland MPs begin 48-hour hunger strike against internment.	
43	Thursday 21 October	Willamette University, Salem, Oregon, USA	USA		
44	Friday 22 October	Paramount Theatre, Seattle, Washington, USA	USA		*I'm Still In Love With You* released by Al Green.
45	Saturday 23 October	Gardens Arena, Vancouver, British Columbia, Canada	Canada		*My Favorite Songwriter: Porter Wagoner* released by Dolly Parton.
46	Tuesday 26 October	Eastown Theater, Detroit, Michigan, USA	USA		
47	Wednesday 27 October	Auditorium Theatre, Chicago, Illinois, USA	USA	The Democratic Republic of the Congo is renamed Zaire.	
48	Thursday 28 October	Hill Auditorium, University of Michigan, Ann Arbor, Michigan, USA	USA	UK Parliament votes 356-244 in favour of joining the European Economic Community.	
49	Sunday 31 October	Fieldhouse, University of Toledo, Toledo, Ohio, USA	USA		
50	Tuesday 2 November	McCarter Theatre, Princeton University, Princeton, New Jersey, USA	USA		
51	Wednesday 3 November	Central Theatre, Passaic, New Jersey, USA	USA	The UNIX Programmer's Manual is published.	*The Inner Mounting Flame* released by Mahavishnu Orchestra.
52	Thursday 4 November	Lowes Theatre, Providence, Rhode Island, USA	USA		
		RECORD RELEASE *MEDDLE* (US RELEASE 30 OCTOBER)			
53	Friday 5 November	Assembly Hall, Columbia University, New York City, New York, USA	USA	Bolivia passes death penalty for political kidnapping.	*Madman Across the Water* released by Elton John.
54	Monday 8 November	Peace Bridge Exhibition Center, Buffalo, New York, USA	USA		*Led Zeppelin IV* released by Led Zeppelin.

	Year	Address	Country	World Events	Music
55	Tuesday 9 November	Centre Sportif, Universite de Montreal, Montreal, Quebec, Canada	Canada	US table tennis team arrives in China, starting 'ping-pong diplomacy'.	
56	Wednesday 10 November	Pavilion de la Jeunesse, Quebec City, Quebec, Canada	Canada		
57	Thursday 11 November	Music Hall, Boston, Massachusetts, USA	USA		
58	Friday 12 November	Irvine Auditorium, University of Pennsylvania, Philadelphia, Pennsylvania, USA	USA		*Nursery Cryme* released by Genesis.
59	Saturday 13 November	Convention Hall, Asbury Park, New Jersey, USA	USA		
60	Sunday 14 November	The Gymnasium, State University of New York, Long Island, New York, USA	USA		
61	Monday 15 November	Main Hall, Carnegie Hall, New York City, New York, USA	USA	Intel releases the world's first microprocessor, the Intel 4004.	*Homecoming* released by America.
62	Tuesday 16 November	Lisner Auditorium, George Washington University, Washington D.C., USA	USA		
63	Friday 19 November	Syria Mosque Theater, Pittsburgh, Pennsylvania, USA	USA		
64	Saturday 20 November	Taft Auditorium, Cincinnati, Ohio, USA	USA		*There's A Riot Goin' On* released by Sly & The Family Stone.
	1972				
1	Thursday 20 January	The Dome, Brighton	UK	Unemployment in UK passes 1 million.	Live debut of *Dark Side of the Moon*, halted by technical difficulties.
2	Friday 21 January	Guildhall, Portsmouth	UK		Keith Richards jumps on stage to jam with Chuck Berry at the Hollywood Palladium, but is ordered off for playing too loud.
3	Saturday 22 January	Winter Gardens, Bournemouth	UK		
4	Sunday 23 January	Guildhall, Southampton	UK	UK Prime Minister Ted Heath signs accession treaty for British membership of the EEC.	
5	Thursday 27 January	City Hall, Newcastle	UK	Two New York City Police Department officers assassinated by members of the Black Liberation Army (BLA).	
6	Friday 28 January	Town Hall, Leeds	UK		
7	Thursday 3 February	Locarno Ballroom, Coventry	UK	US airlines begin mandatory inspection of passengers and baggage.	
8	Saturday 5 February	Colston Hall, Bristol	UK		
9	Thursday 10 February	De Montfort Hall, Leicester	UK		David Bowie starts touring *Ziggy Stardust* in Tolworth, Surrey.
10	Friday 11 February	Free Trade Hall, Manchester	UK		
11	Saturday 12 February	City Hall, Sheffield	UK		
12	Sunday 13 February	Empire Theatre, Liverpool	UK		A Led Zeppelin concert in Singapore is cancelled when officials refuse to let them off the airplane because of their long hair.
13	Thursday 17 February	Rainbow Theatre, Finsbury Park, London	UK		
14	Friday 18 February	Rainbow Theatre, Finsbury Park, London	UK	California abolishes the death penalty.	
15	Saturday 19 February	Rainbow Theatre, Finsbury Park, London	UK		Paul McCartney's single 'Give Ireland Back To The Irish' is banned by the BBC.
16	Sunday 20 February	Rainbow Theatre, Finsbury Park, London	UK		
	JAPANESE TOUR				
17	Monday 6 March	Tokyo-To Taiikukan, Tokyo, Japan	Japan		

	Year	Address	Country	World Events	Music
18	Tuesday 7 March	Tokyo-To Taiikukan, Tokyo, Japan	Japan		
19	Wednesday 8 March	Festival Hall, Osaka, Japan	Japan		
20	Thursday 9 March	Festival Hall, Osaka, Japan	Japan		*Shades Of A Blue Orphanage* released by Thin Lizzy.
21	Friday 10 March	Dai-Sho-Gun Furitsu Taiikukan, Kyoto, Japan	Japan		
22	Monday 13 March	Nakajima Sports Center, Sapporo, Japan	Japan	The UK and the People's Republic of China resume diplomatic ties after 22 years.	
23	Thursday 29 March	Free Trade Hall, Manchester	UK		
24	Friday 30 March	Free Trade Hall, Manchester	UK	The Parliament of Northern Ireland is suspended amidst increasing strife.	
	NORTH AMERICAN TOUR				
25	Friday 14 April	Fort Homer Hesterly Armory Auditorium, Tampa, Florida, USA	USA	The IRA explodes twenty-four bombs across Northern Ireland.	*Three Friends* released by Gentle Giant.
26	Saturday 15 April	The Sportatorium, Pembroke Pines, Florida, USA	USA		
27	Tuesday 18 April	Symphony Hall, Atlanta Memorial Arts Center, Atlanta, Georgia, USA	USA		
28	Thursday 20 April	Syria Mosque Theater, Pittsburgh, Pennsylvania, USA	USA		*Dr. John's Gumbo* released by Dr. John.
29	Friday 21 April	The Lyric Theatre, Baltimore, Maryland, USA	USA		
30	Saturday 22 April	Civic Theatre, Akron, Ohio, USA	USA	An 11-year-old boy dies from a rubber bullet fired by the British Army in Belfast.	
31	Sunday 23 April	Music Hall, Cincinnati, Ohio, USA	USA		
32	Monday 24 April	Allen Theatre, Cleveland, Ohio, USA	USA		
33	Wednesday 26 April	Ford Auditorium, Detroit, Michigan, USA	USA		
34	Thursday 27 April	Ford Auditorium, Detroit, Michigan, USA	USA	The Burundian Genocide begins; more than 500,000 Hutus die.	
35	Friday 28 April	Auditorium Theatre, Chicago, Illinois, USA	USA		
36	Saturday 29 April	Spectrum Theater, Philadelphia, Pennsylvania, USA	USA		New York mayor John Lindsay announces that he is supporting John Lennon and Yoko Ono in their battle for a green card.
37	Monday 1 May	Carnegie Hall, New York City, New York, USA	USA	North Vietnamese soldiers occupy Quang Tri Activities Committee.	
38	Tuesday 2 May	Carnegie Hall, New York City, New York, USA	USA		
39	Wednesday 3 May	Concert Hall, John F. Kennedy Center for Performing Arts, Washington D.C. USA	USA		
40	Thursday 4 May	Music Hall, Boston, Massachusetts, USA	USA		
41	Thursday 18 May	Deutschlandhalle, West Berlin, West Germany	Germany		
42	Sunday 21 May	2nd British Rock Meeting, Germersheim, West Germany	Germany		*America Eats Its Young* released by Funkadelic.
43	Monday 22 May	*The Amsterdam Rock Circus*, Olympisch Stadion, Amsterdam, Netherlands	Netherlands	The Dominion of Ceylon becomes the Republic of Sri Lanka.	
44	Wednesday 28 June	The Dome, Brighton	UK	US President Richard Nixon scraps the Vietnam draft.	
45	Thursday 29 June	The Dome, Brighton	UK		
	NORTH AMERICAN TOUR				
46	Friday 8 September	Municipal Auditorium, Austin, Texas, USA	USA		*All The Young Dudes* released by Mott The Hoople.
47	Saturday 9 September	Music Hall, Houston, Texas, USA	USA	Soviet Union beats the United States 51-50 at basketball in highly contentious game.	

	Year	Address	Country	World Events	Music
48	Sunday 10 September	McFarlin Auditorium, Southern Methodist University, Dallas, Texas, USA	USA	Brazilian Emerson Fittipaldi becomes the youngest Formula One champion aged 25.	
49	Monday 11 September	Memorial Hall, Kansas City, Missouri, USA	USA		
50	Tuesday 12 September	Civic Center Music Hall, Oklahoma City, Oklahoma, USA	USA		
51	Wednesday 13 September	Henry Levitt Arena, Wichita, Kansas, USA	USA		
52	Friday 15 September	Community Center Arena, Tuscon, Arizona, USA	USA		*Foxtrot* released by Genesis.
53	Saturday 16 September	Golden Hall, San Diego, California, USA	USA		
54	Sunday 17 September	Big Surf, Tempe, Arizona, USA	USA	Uganda announces that there are Tanzanian troops in its territory.	
55	Tuesday 19 September	University of Denver Arena, Denver, Colorado, USA	USA		
56	Friday 22 September	Hollywood Bowl, Los Angeles, California, USA	USA		
57	Saturday 23 September	Winterland Auditorium, San Francisco, California, USA	USA	Philippine president Ferdinand Marcos place the country under martial law.	
58	Sunday 24 September	Winterland Auditorium, San Francisco, California, USA	USA		
59	Wednesday 27 September	Gardens Arena, Vancouver, British Columbia, Canada	Canada		
60	Thursday 28 September	Memorial Coliseum, Portland, Oregon, USA	USA		Rory Storm dies aged 33 from appendicitis.
61	Friday 29 September	Hec Edmundson Pavilion, University of Washington, Seattle, Washington, USA	USA		Miles Davis unveils his new nine-piece band at the Lincoln Center Philharmonic Hall.
62	Saturday 30 September	Gardens Arena, Vancouver, British Columbia, Canada	Canada		
63	Saturday 21 October	Empire Pool, Wembley, London	UK		
	EUROPEAN TOUR				
64	Friday 10 November	KB Hallen, Copenhagen, Denmark	Denmark		*See All Her Faces* released by Dusty Springfield.
65	Saturday 11 November	KB Hallen, Copenhagen, Denmark	Denmark		
66	Sunday 12 November	Ernst-Merck-Halle, Hamburg, West Germany	Germany		*Doremi Fasol Latido* released by Hawkwind.
67	Tuesday 14 November	Philipshalle, Dusseldorf, West Germany	Germany	The Dow Jones closes above 1,000 for the first time.	
68	Wednesday 15 November	Sporthalle, Boblingen, West Germany	Germany		
69	Thursday 16 November	Festhalle, Frankfurt, West Germany	Germany		*Seventh Sojourn* released by The Moody Blues.
70	Friday 17 November	Festhalle, Frankfurt, West Germany	Germany		
	ROLAND PETIT BALLET SHOWS				
71	Wednesday 22 November	Salle Valliers, Marseille, France	France	USA ends 22-year travel ban to China.	
72	Thursday 23 November	Salle Valliers, Marseille, France	France		
73	Friday 24 November	Salle Valliers, Marseille, France	France		
74	Saturday 25 November	Salle Valliers, Marseille, France	France		
75	Sunday 26 November	Salle Valliers, Marseille, France	France		
	EUROPEAN TOUR (Resumed)				
76	Tuesday 28 November	Palais de Sports, Toulouse, France	France	Roger Bontems and Claude Buffet are guillotined at La Santé Prison, in the last executions in France.	
77	Wednesday 29 November	Les Arenas, Parc des Expositions, Poitiers, France	France	Atari release the arcade version of *Pong*.	

	Year	Address	Country	World Events	Music
78	Friday 1 December	Centre Sportif, Ile Des Vannes, Paris, France	France		*Octopus* released by Gentle Giant.
79	Saturday 2 December	Centre Sportif, Ile Des Vannes, Paris, France	France		
80	Sunday 3 December	Parc des Expositions, Caen, France	France		
81	Tuesday 5 December	Sport Palais, Vorst Nationaal, Brussels, Belgium	Belgium		
82	Thursday 7 December	Palais de Sports, Lille, France	France	The last manned Moon mission, Apollo 17 is launched. The crew take the *Blue Marble* photograph of Earth.	
83	Friday 8 December	Parc des Expositions, Nancy, France	France		*Live In Japan* released by Deep Purple.
84	Saturday 9 December	Hallenstadion, Zurich, Switzerland	Switzerland		
85	Sunday 10 December	Palais de Sports, Lyon, France	France		
	1973				
	ROLAND PETIT BALLET SHOWS				
1	Saturday 13 January	Palais de Sports de la Porte de Versailles, Paris, France	France		*Who Do We Think We Are* released by Deep Purple.
2	Saturday 13 January	Palais de Sports de la Porte de Versailles, Paris, France	France		
3	Sunday 14 January	Palais de Sports de la Porte de Versailles, Paris, France	France	Two Royal Ulster Constabulary officers killed in Derry by car bomb.	Elvis Presley's *Aloha From Hawaii Via Satellite* television special is broadcast in over 40 countries.
4	Sunday 14 January	Palais de Sports de la Porte de Versailles, Paris, France	France		
5	Saturday 3 February	Palais de Sports de la Porte de Versailles, Paris, France	France		
6	Saturday 3 February	Palais de Sports de la Porte de Versailles, Paris, France	France		
7	Sunday 4 February	Palais de Sports de la Porte de Versailles, Paris, France	France	International inspection team sent to Vietnam to observe progress on Paris truce agreement.	*Aloha From Hawaii Via Satellite* released by Elvis Presley.
8	Sunday 4 February	Palais de Sports de la Porte de Versailles, Paris, France	France		
	NORTH AMERICAN TOUR				
9	Sunday 4 March	Dane County Memorial Coliseum, Madison, Wisconsin, USA	USA		
10	Monday 5 March	Cobo Arena, Detroit, Michigan, USA	USA		
11	Tuesday 6 March	Kiel Opera House, St. Louis, Missouri, USA	USA		The New York Office of the US Immigration Department cancels John Lennon's visa extension five days after granting it.
12	Wednesday 7 March	International Ampitheatre, Chicago, Illinois, USA	USA	US Senate creates Select Committee on Presidential Campaign Activities, investigating Watergate scandal.	*Byrds* released by The Byrds.
13	Thursday 8 March	University of Cincinnati Fieldhouse, Cincinnati, Ohio, USA	USA		Paul McCartney is fined £100 after pleading guilty to growing marijuana at his Scottish farm.
14	Saturday 10 March	Memorial Gymnasium, Kent State University, Kent, Ohio, USA	USA	Governor of Bermuda Sir Richard Sharples assassinated in Government House.	
15	Sunday 11 March	Maple Leaf Gardens, Toronto, Ontario, Canada	Canada		
16	Monday 12 March	The Forum, Montreal, Quebec, Canada	Canada		
17	Wednesday 14 March	Music Hall, Boston, Massachusetts, USA	USA		
18	Thursday 15 March	Spectrum Theater, Philadelphia, Pennsylvania, USA	USA	USSR launches Prognoz 3.	
	Friday 16 March	**RECORD RELEASE *DARK SIDE OF THE MOON* (US RELEASE 1 MARCH)**			
19	Saturday 17 March	Radio City Music Hall, New York City, New York, USA	USA	US National Security Adviser Henry Kissinger meets Chinese leader Mao Zedong.	*Tanx* released by T. Rex.
20	Sunday 18 March	Palace Theatre, Waterbury, Connecticut, USA	USA		
21	Monday 19 March	Providence Civic Center, Providence, Rhode Island, USA	USA		

	Year	Address	Country	World Events	Music
22	Thursday 22 March	Hampton Coliseum, Hampton, Virginia, USA	USA		*For Your Pleasure* released by Roxy Music.
23	Friday 23 March	Charlotte Park Center, Charlotte, North Carolina, USA	USA	Gold goes up $10 overnight to $95/oz in London.	Lou Reed is bitten on the buttocks by a fan during a concert in Buffalo, New York.
24	Saturday 24 March	Municipal Auditorium, Atlanta, Georgia, USA	USA		
25	Friday 18 May	Earl's Court Exhibition Hall, Earl's Court, London	UK	Cod War: Britain announces that the Royal Navy will protect British trawlers fishing in the disputed 80 km (50 mi) limit around Iceland.	
26	Saturday 19 May	Earl's Court Exhibition Hall, Earl's Court, London	UK		*Yessongs* released by Yes.
NORTH AMERICAN TOUR					
27	Sunday 17 June	Saratoga Performing Arts Center, Saratoga Springs, New York, USA	USA		
28	Monday 18 June	Roosevelt Stadium, Union City, New Jersey, USA	USA	US President Richard Nixon begins talks with Soviet leader Leonid Brezhnev.	
29	Tuesday 19 June	Civic Center Arena, Pittsburgh, Pennsylvania, USA	USA		*Smokey* released by Smokey Robinson.
30	Wednesday 20 June	Merriweather Post Pavilion, Columbia, Maryland, USA	USA		
31	Thursday 21 June	Merriweather Post Pavilion, Columbia, Maryland, USA	USA		
32	Friday 22 June	Buffalo Memorial Auditorium, Buffalo, New York, USA	USA		*Touch Me in the Morning* released by Diana Ross.
33	Saturday 23 June	Olympia Stadium, Detroit, Michigan, USA	USA		
34	Sunday 24 June	Blossom Music Center, Cuyahoga Falls, Ohio, USA	USA	Leonid Brezhnev addresses the American people on television, the first Soviet leader to do so.	
35	Monday 25 June	Convention Center, Louisville, Kentucky, USA	USA	Erskine Hamilton Childers elected the President of Ireland.	*Hey Now Hey (The Other Side Of The Sky)* released by Aretha Franklin.
36	Tuesday 26 June	Lake Spivey Park, Jonesboro, Georgia, USA	USA		
37	Wednesday 27 June	Jacksonville Coliseum, Jacksonville, Florida, USA	USA		
38	Thursday 28 June	The Sportatorium, Pembroke Pines, Florida, USA	USA	Elections held for the Northern Ireland Assembly, which will lead to power-sharing between unionists and nationalists in for the first time.	
39	Friday 29 June	Tampa Stadium, Tampa, Florida, USA	USA		The Scorpions play their first gig with Uli Roth.
40	Friday 12 October	Munchener Olympiahalle, Munich, West Germany	Germany	Richard Nixon nominates Gerald Ford to replace Spiro Agnew as Vice President, following Agnew's resignation.	
41	Saturday 13 October	Stadthalle, Vienna, Austria	Austria		*Selling England By The Pound* released by Genesis.
42	Saturday 4 November	A Benefit for Robert Wyatt, Rainbow Theatre, Finsbury Park, London	UK		
1974					
1974 FRENCH TOUR					
1	Tuesday 18 June	Hall 1, Parc des Expositions, Toulouse, France	France		
2	Wednesday 19 June	Les Arénas, Parc des Expositions, Poitiers, France	France	North Yemen suspends its constitution.	Ozark Music Festival opens in Sedalia, Missouri.
3	Friday 21 June	Hall 1, Palais des Expositions, Dijon, France	France		
4	Saturday 22 June	Théâtre de Plein Air, Parc des Expositions, Colmar, France	France		
5	Monday 24 June	Palais de Sports de la Porte de Versailles, Paris, France	France		*Endless Summer* released by The Beach Boys.
6	Tuesday 25 June	Palais de Sports de la Porte de Versailles, Paris, France	France		
7	Wednesday 26 June	Palais de Sports de la Porte de Versailles, Paris, France	France	A bar code is scanned for the first time, at the Marsh Supermarket in Troy, Ohio.	*Bad Company* released by Bad Company.

	Year	Address	Country	World Events	Music
	BRITISH WINTER TOUR 1974				
8	Monday 4 November	Usher Hall, Edinburgh, Scotland	UK		
9	Tuesday 5 November	Usher Hall, Edinburgh, Scotland	UK	Walter E Washington becomes first elected mayor of Washington, D.C.	
10	Friday 8 November	Odeon, Newcastle	UK	Lord Lucan disappears and is never seen again after his nanny is found murdered in London.	*Sheer Heart Attack* released by Queen.
11	Saturday 9 November	Odeon, Newcastle	UK		
12	Thursday 14 November	Empire Pool, Wembley, London	UK		*Country Life* released by Roxy Music.
13	Friday 15 November	Empire Pool, Wembley, London	UK	International Energy Agency formed in Paris.	
14	Saturday 16 November	Empire Pool, Wembley, London	UK		
15	Sunday 17 November	Empire Pool, Wembley, London	UK	First Greek election since the fall of the junta of 1967-1974 is held.	
16	Tuesday 19 November	Trentham Gardens, Stoke-on-Trent	UK		*Get Up With It* released by Miles Davis.
17	Friday 22 November	Sophia Gardens Pavilion, Cardiff	UK	UN General Assembly recognises Palestine's right to sovereignty.	
18	Thursday 28 November	Empire Theatre, Liverpool	UK		In his final public performance, John Lennon joins Elton John on stage at Madison Square Garden.
19	Friday 29 November	Empire Theatre, Liverpool	UK		*Slade in Flame* released by Slade.
20	Saturday 30 November	Empire Theatre, Liverpool	UK		
21	Tuesday 3 December	The Hippodrome, Birmingham	UK		
22	Wednesday 5 December	The Hippodrome, Birmingham	UK	Final episode of *Monty Python's Flying Circus* broadcast by the BBC.	
23	Thursday 6 December	The Hippodrome, Birmingham	UK		
24	Monday 9 December	Palace Theatre, Manchester	UK		
25	Tuesday 10 December	Palace Theatre, Manchester	UK		
26	Friday 13 December	The Hippodrome, Bristol	UK	Malta becomes a republic.	
27	Saturday 14 December	The Hippodrome, Bristol	UK		*So What* released by Joe Walsh.
	1975				
	NORTH AMERICAN TOUR				
1	Tuesday 8 April	Pacific National Exhibition Coliseum, Vancouver, British Columbia, Canada	Canada		*Toys In The Attic* released by Aerosmith.
2	Thursday 10 April	Seattle Center Coliseum, Seattle, Washington, USA	USA		
3	Saturday 12 April	Cow Palace, San Francisco, California, USA	USA		*Straight Shooter* released by Bad Company.
4	Sunday 13 April	Cow Palace, San Francisco, California, USA	USA	The Kataeb militia kills 27 Palestinians in Ain El Remmeneh, Lebanon, triggering the Lebanese Civil War (1975-1990).	
5	Thursday 17 April	Denver Coliseum, Denver, Colorado, USA	USA	Khmer Rouge forces capture Phnom Penh, ending the Cambodian Civil War, renaming the country Democratic Campuchea, with mass evacuation of American troops and Cambodian civilians.	
6	Saturday 19 April	Tuscon Community Center Arena, Tuscon, Arizona, USA	USA		
7	Sunday 20 April	Arizona State University, Tempe, Arizona, USA	USA		
8	Monday 21 April	Sports Arena, San Diego, California, USA	USA	South Vietnam's last president Nguyễn Văn Thiệu resigns.	*Playing Possum* released by Carly Simon.
9	Tuesday 22 April	Los Angeles Memorial Sports Arena, Los Angeles, California, USA	USA		*Fly By Night* released by Rush.
10	Wednesday 23 April	Los Angeles Memorial Sports Arena, Los Angeles, California, USA	USA		

	Year	Address	Country	World Events	Music
11	Thursday 24 April	Los Angeles Memorial Sports Arena, Los Angeles, California, USA	USA	Red Army Faction terrorists take over the West German embassy in Stockholm, take 11 hostages and demand the release of the group's jailed members.	Pete Ham of the group Badfinger dies from suicide.
12	Friday 25 April	Los Angeles Memorial Sports Arena, Los Angeles, California, USA	USA		
13	Saturday 26 April	Los Angeles Memorial Sports Arena, Los Angeles, California, USA	USA		
14	Sunday 27 April	Los Angeles Memorial Sports Arena, Los Angeles, California, USA	USA		
15	Saturday 7 June	Atlanta Stadium, Atlanta, Georgia, USA	USA	Start of first Cricket World Cup in England.	
16	Monday 9 June	Capital Center, Landover, Maryland, USA	USA	Live radio broadcasts from the UK House of Commons begin.	
17	Tuesday 10 June	Capital Center, Landover, Maryland, USA	USA		That's *The Way (I Like It)* released by KC And The Sunshine Band.
18	Thursday 12 June	Spectrum Theater, Philadelphia, Pennsylvania, USA	USA		
19	Friday 13 June	Spectrum Theater, Philadelphia, Pennsylvania, USA	USA		*Red Octopus* released by Jefferson Starship.
20	Sunday 15 June	Roosevelt Stadium, Union City, New Jersey, USA	USA		
21	Monday 16 June	Nassau Veterans Memorial Coliseum, Long Island, New York, USA	USA		
22	Tuesday 17 June	Nassau Veterans Memorial Coliseum, Long Island, New York, USA	USA		*The Last Concert* released by The Modern Jazz Quartet.
23	Wednesday 18 June	Boston Gardens, Boston, Massachusetts, USA	USA		Talking Heads play their first show at CBGBs in New York.
24	Friday 20 June	Three Rivers Stadium, Pittsburgh, Pennsylvania, USA	USA	*Jaws* is released and becomes a popular summer hit, setting the standard for Hollywood blockbusters.	
25	Sunday 22 June	County Stadium, Milwaukee, Wisconsin, USA	USA		Performing in Vancouver, Alice Cooper falls off the stage, breaking six ribs.
26	Monday 23 June	Olympia Stadium, Detroit, Michigan, USA	USA		
27	Tuesday 24 June	Olympia Stadium, Detroit, Michigan, USA	USA		*The Basement Tapes* released by Bob Dylan.
28	Thursday 26 June	Autostade, Montreal, Quebec, Canada	Canada	Indian Prime Minister Indira Gandhi declares a state of emergency.	
29	Saturday 28 June	Ivor Wynne Stadium, Hamilton, Ontario, Canada	Canada	Cape Verde Islands gain independence from Portugal.	*In The City* released by Tavares.
30	Saturday 5 July	Knebworth Park, Stevenage, Hertfordshire	UK		
	Friday 12 September	RECORD RELEASE *WISH YOU WERE HERE*			
	1977				
	Friday 21 January	RECORD RELEASE *ANIMALS* (US RELEASE 12 FEB)		US President Jimmy Carter pardons almost all Vietnam War draft dodgers.	
	EUROPEAN TOUR				
1	Sunday 23 January	Westfalenhalle, Dortmund, West Germany	Germany		
2	Monday 24 January	Westfalenhalle, Dortmund, West Germany	Germany	Massacre of Atocha occurs in Madrid, with five labour leaders assassinated, during Spain's transition to democracy.	
3	Wednesday 26 January	Festhalle, Frankfurt, West Germany	Germany		Patti Smith falls off the stage in Tampa, Florida, and receives 22 stitches to head lacerations.
4	Thursday 27 January	Festhalle, Frankfurt, West Germany	Germany		
5	Saturday 29 January	Deutschlandhalle, West Berlin, West Germany	Germany		'Spiral Scratch' EP released by The Buzzcocks.

	Year	Address	Country	World Events	Music
6	Sunday 30 January	Deutschlandhalle, West Berlin, West Germany	Germany		
7	Tuesday 1 February	Stadthalle, Vienna, Austria	Austria		
8	Thursday 3 February	Hallenstadion, Zurich, Switzerland	Switzerland		*Cheap Trick* released by Cheap Trick.
9	Friday 4 February	Hallenstadion, Zurich, Switzerland	Switzerland	Eleven commuters killed when an elevated train derails from the Loop in Chicago.	*Rumours* released by Fleetwood Mac.
10	Thursday 17 February	Sportpaleis Ahoy, Rotterdam, Netherlands	Netherlands	Kalakuta Republic (a commune created by Nigerian musician and activist Fela Kuti) burnt to the ground by troops in Lagos.	
11	Friday 18 February	Sportpaleis Ahoy, Rotterdam, Netherlands	Netherlands		*Damned! Damned! Damned!* released by The Damned.
12	Saturday 19 February	Sportpaleis Ahoy, Rotterdam, Netherlands	Netherlands	France performs nuclear test at Mururoa Atoll.	
13	Sunday 20 February	Sportpaleis, Antwerp, Belgium	Belgium		*Unpredictable* released by Natalie Cole.
14	Tuesday 22 February	Pavillon de Paris, Porte de Pantin, Paris, France	France		
15	Wednesday 23 February	Pavillon de Paris, Porte de Pantin, Paris, France	France		
16	Thursday 24 February	Pavillon de Paris, Porte de Pantin, Paris, France	France	US President Jimmy Carter announces US foreign policy will consider human rights.	
17	Friday 25 February	Pavillon de Paris, Porte de Pantin, Paris, France	France	Oil tanker explosion near Honolulu, Hawaii, spills 31 million gallons of crude oil.	*Peter Gabriel* released by Peter Gabriel.
18	Sunday 27 February	Olympiahalle, Munich, West Germany	Germany		
19	Monday 28 February	Olympiahalle, Munich, West Germany	Germany		
	BRITISH TOUR				
20	Tuesday 15 March	Empire Pool, Wembley, London	UK	US House of Representatives begins 90-day test of televising its sessions.	*Islands* released by The Band.
21	Wednesday 16 March	Empire Pool, Wembley, London	UK		*Works Volume 1* released by Emerson, Lake & Palmer.
22	Thursday 17 March	Empire Pool, Wembley, London	UK	US restricts citizens from visiting Cuba, Vietnam, Cambodia and North Korea.	*The Idiot* released by Iggy Pop.
23	Friday 18 March	Empire Pool, Wembley, London	UK		
24	Saturday 19 March	Empire Pool, Wembley, London	UK		
25	Monday 28 March	New Bingley Hall, Staffordshire County Showground, Stafford	UK	Morarji Desai forms a government in India.	
26	Tuesday 29 March	New Bingley Hall, Staffordshire County Showground, Stafford	UK		*Commodores* released by The Commodores.
27	Wednesday 30 March	New Bingley Hall, Staffordshire County Showground, Stafford	UK		
28	Thursday 31 March	New Bingley Hall, Staffordshire County Showground, Stafford	UK		
	IN THE FLESH – NORTH AMERICAN TOUR (PART 1)				
29	Friday 22 April	Miami Baseball Stadium, Miami, Florida, USA	USA	Optical fibre is first used to carry live telephone signals.	
30	Sunday 24 April	Tampa Stadium, Tampa, Florida, USA	USA		
31	Tuesday 26 April	The Omni Coliseum, Atlanta, Georgia, USA	USA	Famed New York nightclub Studio 54 opens.	
32	Thursday 28 April	Assembly Center, Louisiana State University, Baton Rouge, Louisiana, USA	USA	Baader-Meinhof Gang jailed for life in West Germany.	
33	Saturday 30 April	Jeppensen Stadium, Houston, Texas, USA	USA		Led Zeppelin sets a new world record attendance for an indoor solo attraction when 76,229 people attend a concert at the Pontiac Silverdome, Michigan.
34	Sunday 1 May	Tarrant County Convention Center Arena, Fort Worth, Texas, USA	USA	Taksim Square massacre occurs in Istanbul, resulting in 34 deaths and hundreds of injuries.	
35	Wednesday 4 May	Veterans Memorial Coliseum, Phoenix, Arizona, USA	USA		
36	Friday 6 May	Anaheim Stadium, Anaheim, California, USA	USA		*Holly Days* released by Denny Laine.

	Year	Address	Country	World Events	Music
37	Saturday 7 May	Anaheim Stadium, Anaheim, California, USA	USA		
38	Monday 9 May	Oakland Coliseum Arena, Oakland, California, USA	USA	Patty Hearst released from prison.	
39	Tuesday 10 May	Oakland Coliseum Arena, Oakland, California, USA	USA		
40	Thursday 12 May	Memorial Coliseum, Portland, Oregon, USA	USA		
	IN THE FLESH – NORTH AMERICAN TOUR (PART 2)				
41	Wednesday 15 June	County Stadium, Milwaukee, Wisconsin, USA	USA	Spain has its first democratic elections in 41 years.	
42	Friday 17 June	Freedom Hall, Louisville, Kentucky, USA	USA		*Quark, Strangeness and Charm* released by Hawkwind.
43	Sunday 19 June	Soldier Field, Chicago, Illinois, USA	USA		
44	Tuesday 21 June	Kemper Area, Kansas City, Missouri, USA	USA	Former Nixon Chief of Staff H. R. Haldeman imprisoned.	
45	Thursday 23 June	Riverfront Coliseum, Cincinnati, Ohio, USA	USA		
46	Saturday 25 June	Municipal Stadium, Cleveland, Ohio, USA	USA		
47	Monday 27 June	Boston Gardens, Boston, Massachusetts, USA	USA	Djibouti gains independence from France.	
48	Wednesday 29 June	Spectrum Theater, Philadelphia, Pennsylvania, USA	USA		*Feel the Fire* released by Jermaine Jackson.
49	Friday 1 July	Madison Square Garden, New York City, New York, USA	USA	Virginia Wade wins the women's singles title at Wimbledon, the last British woman to do so.	
50	Saturday 2 July	Madison Square Garden, New York City, New York, USA	USA		
51	Sunday 3 July	Madison Square Garden, New York City, New York, USA	USA		
52	Monday 4 July	Madison Square Garden, New York City, New York, USA	USA		
53	Wednesday 6 July	Stade Du Parc Olympique, Montreal, Quebec, Canada	Canada	France performs nuclear test at Mururoa Atoll.	
	1980				
	THE WALL IN CONCERT				
1	Thursday 7 February	Los Angeles Memorial Sports Arena, Los Angeles, California, USA	USA		*Sugarhill Gang* released by The Sugarhill Gang.
2	Friday 8 February	Los Angeles Memorial Sports Arena, Los Angeles, California, USA	USA		David Bowie and his wife Angie file for divorce.
3	Saturday 9 February	Los Angeles Memorial Sports Arena, Los Angeles, California, USA	USA		
4	Sunday 10 February	Los Angeles Memorial Sports Arena, Los Angeles, California, USA	USA		
5	Monday 11 February	Los Angeles Memorial Sports Arena, Los Angeles, California, USA	USA		
6	Tuesday 12 February	Los Angeles Memorial Sports Arena, Los Angeles, California, USA	USA		*Bryan Adams* released by Bryan Adams.
7	Wednesday 13 February	Los Angeles Memorial Sports Arena, Los Angeles, California, USA	USA	The 1980 Winter Olympics open in Lake Placid, New York.	
8	Sunday 24 February	Nassau Veterans Memorial Coliseum, Long Island, New York, USA	USA		
9	Monday 25 February	Nassau Veterans Memorial Coliseum, Long Island, New York, USA	USA		*Warm Thoughts* released by Smokey Robinson.
10	Tuesday 26 February	Nassau Veterans Memorial Coliseum, Long Island, New York, USA	USA	Military coup under Desi Bouterse in Suriname.	
11	Wednesday 27 February	Nassau Veterans Memorial Coliseum, Long Island, New York, USA	USA	Guerrillas begin Dominican embassy siege in Colombia, holding 60 people hostage, including 14 ambassadors.	

	Year	Address	Country	World Events	Music
12	Thursday 28 February	Nassau Veterans Memorial Coliseum, Long Island, New York, USA	USA		John Lennon and Yoko Ono begin recording the *Double Fantasy* album.
13	Monday 4 August	Earl's Court Exhibition Hall, Earl's Court, London	UK		*Crimes of Passion* released by Pat Benatar.
14	Tuesday 5 August	Earl's Court Exhibition Hall, Earl's Court, London	UK		
15	Wednesday 6 August	Earl's Court Exhibition Hall, Earl's Court, London	UK		
16	Thursday 7 August	Earl's Court Exhibition Hall, Earl's Court, London	UK	Lech Wałęsa leads the first strike at the Gdańsk Shipyard in Poland.	
17	Friday 8 August	Earl's Court Exhibition Hall, Earl's Court, London	UK		*Give Me the Night* released by George Benson.
18	Saturday 9 August	Earl's Court Exhibition Hall, Earl's Court, London	UK		
	1981				
1	Friday 13 February	Westfalenhalle, Dortmund, West Germany	Germany		
2	Saturday 14 February	Westfalenhalle, Dortmund, West Germany	Germany	Fire in a Dublin nightclub Stardust kills 48 people and injured 214.	Ultravox reach #2 on the UK Singles Chart with 'Vienna', but are kept off #1 by 'Shaddap You Face' by Joe Dolce.
3	Sunday 15 February	Westfalenhalle, Dortmund, West Germany	Germany		
4	Monday 16 February	Westfalenhalle, Dortmund, West Germany	Germany		*Another Ticket* released by Eric Clapton.
5	Tuesday 17 February	Westfalenhalle, Dortmund, West Germany	Germany	Pope John Paul II starts visit to the Philippines.	
6	Wednesday 18 February	Westfalenhalle, Dortmund, West Germany	Germany		
7	Thursday 19 February	Westfalenhalle, Dortmund, West Germany	Germany		George Harrison ordered to pay $587,000 for 'subconscious plagiarism' of his song 'My Sweet Lord'.
8	Friday 20 February	Westfalenhalle, Dortmund, West Germany	Germany		*Duran Duran* released by Duran Duran.
9	Saturday 13 June	Earl's Court Exhibition Hall, Earl's Court, London	UK	Marcus Sarjeant fires six blanks at Queen Elizabeth II at the Trooping the Colour ceremony in London.	
10	Sunday 14 June	Earl's Court Exhibition Hall, Earl's Court, London	UK		
11	Monday 15 June	Earl's Court Exhibition Hall, Earl's Court, London	UK		
12	Tuesday 16 June	Earl's Court Exhibition Hall, Earl's Court, London	UK		*Made in America* released by The Carpenters.
13	Wednesday 17 June	Earl's Court Exhibition Hall, Earl's Court, London	UK	Fighting between Muslims and Christians in Cairo kills 14.	
14	Thursday 18 June	Earl's Court Exhibition Hall, Earl's Court, London	UK	AIDS formally recognised by medical professionals in San Francisco, California.	
	1987				
	A MOMENTARY LAPSE OF REASON NORTH AMERICAN TOUR				
	Monday 7 September	**RECORD RELEASE *A MOMENTARY LAPSE OF REASON***			*Actually* released by Pet Shop Boys.
1	Wednesday 9 September	Lansdowne Park Stadium, Ottawa, Ontario, Canada	Canada	US presidential candidate Gary Hart admits to adultery.	
2	Saturday 12 September	Forum de Montreal, Montreal, Quebec, Canada	Canada		Michael Jackson's *Bad* World Tour begins in Tokyo.
3	Sunday 13 September	Forum de Montreal, Montreal, Quebec, Canada	Canada	Metal scrappers open an abandoned radiation source in a hospital in Goiânia, Brazil, causing the worst-ever radiation incident in an urban area and resulting in four deaths.	
4	Monday 14 September	Forum de Montreal, Montreal, Quebec, Canada	Canada		*Primitive Cool* released by Mick Jagger.
5	Wednesday 16 September	Municipal Stadium, Cleveland, Ohio, USA	USA		
6	Thursday 17 September	Municipal Stadium, Cleveland, Ohio, USA	USA	Pope John Paul II arrives for his first visit to San Francisco, and embraces several AIDS sufferers.	

	Year	Address	Country	World Events	Music
7	Saturday 19 September	John F. Kennedy Stadium, Philadelphia, Pennsylvania, USA	USA	Farm Aid III held in Lincoln, Nebraska.	
8	Monday 21 September	Canadian National Exhibition Stadium, Toronto, Ontario, Canada	Canada		
9	Tuesday 22 September	Canadian National Exhibition Stadium, Toronto, Ontario, Canada	Canada		*E.S.P.* released by Bee Gees.
10	Wednesday 23 September	Canadian National Exhibition Stadium, Toronto, Ontario, Canada	Canada		
11	Friday 25 September	Rosemont Horizon, Rosemont, Chicago, Illinois, USA	USA	Military coup in Fiji.	
12	Saturday 26 September	Rosemont Horizon, Rosemont, Chicago, Illinois, USA	USA		
13	Sunday 27 September	Rosemont Horizon, Rosemont, Chicago, Illinois, USA	USA	*Star Trek: The Next Generation* debuts on TV.	
14	Monday 28 September	Rosemont Horizon, Rosemont, Chicago, Illinois, USA	USA		*Come On Pilgrim* released by Pixies.
15	Wednesday 30 September	County Stadium, Milwaukee, Wisconsin, USA	USA		
16	Saturday 3 October	Carrier Dome, Syracuse University, Syracuse, New York, USA	USA	The Canada–United States Free Trade Agreement is reached.	
17	Monday 5 October	Madison Square Garden, New York City, New York, USA	USA		*Heaven On Earth* released by Belinda Carlisle.
18	Tuesday 6 October	Madison Square Garden, New York City, New York, USA	USA	Major-General Sitiveni Rabuka (leader of the military coup) declares Fiji a republic.	
19	Wednesday 7 October	Madison Square Garden, New York City, New York, USA	USA		
20	Saturday 10 October	Brendan Byrne Meadowlands Arena, East Rutherford, New Jersey, USA	USA		
21	Sunday 11 October	Brendan Byrne Meadowlands Arena, East Rutherford, New Jersey, USA	USA	LGB civil rights march in Washington, D.C. draws estimated 200,000.	
22	Monday 12 October	Brendan Byrne Meadowlands Arena, East Rutherford, New Jersey, USA	USA		*Alphabet City* released by ABC.
23	Wednesday 14 October	Hartford Civic Center, Hartford, Connecticut, USA	USA		*Surfing With The Alien* released by Joe Satriani.
24	Thursday 15 October	Hartford Civic Center, Hartford, Connecticut, USA	USA	'Great Storm of 1987' as hurricanes hit southern England, killing 23 people.	
25	Friday 16 October	Providence Civic Center, Providence, Rhode Island, USA	USA		
26	Saturday 17 October	Providence Civic Center, Providence, Rhode Island, USA	USA		
27	Monday 19 October	Capital Centre, Landover, Maryland, USA	USA	Black Monday: Stock markets fall sharply around the world, with the Dow Jones falling 508 points (22.6%).	*Kick* released by INXS.
28	Tuesday 20 October	Capital Centre, Landover, Maryland, USA	USA		
29	Wednesday 21 October	Capital Centre, Landover, Maryland, USA	USA		*Abigail* released by King Diamond.
30	Thursday 22 October	Capital Centre, Landover, Maryland, USA	USA	Nobel prize for literature awarded to Joseph Brodsky.	
31	Sunday 25 October	Dean E. Smith Student Activities Center, University of North Carolina, Chapel Hill, North Carolina, USA	USA		
32	Monday 26 October	Dean E. Smith Student Activities Center, University of North Carolina, Chapel Hill, North Carolina, USA	USA	Head of Salvadoran Human Rights Commission Herbert Ernesto Anaya Sanabria assassinated.	*Live At Wembley* released by Meat Loaf.
33	Friday 30 October	Tampa Stadium, Tampa, Florida, USA	USA		*Faith* released by George Michael.
34	Sunday 1 November	Orange Bowl, Miami, Florida, USA	USA		
35	Tuesday 3 November	The Omni Coliseum, Atlanta, Georgia, USA	USA		
36	Wednesday 4 November	The Omni Coliseum, Atlanta, Georgia, USA	USA		*Rhyme Pays* released by Ice-T.
37	Thursday 5 November	The Omni Coliseum, Atlanta, Georgia, USA	USA	South African ANC-leader Govan Mbeki freed.	

	Year	Address	Country	World Events	Music
38	Saturday 7 November	Rupp Arena, Lexington, Kentucky, USA	USA		
39	Sunday 8 November	Rupp Arena, Lexington, Kentucky, USA	USA	Twelve people are killed by an IRA bomb at a Remembrance Day service at Enniskillen, Northern Ireland.	Cher released by Cher.
40	Tuesday 10 November	Pontiac Silverdome, Pontiac, Detroit, Michigan, USA	USA		
41	Thursday 12 November	Hoosier Dome, Indianapolis, Indiana, USA	USA	Workers rebel against Nicolae Ceaușescu's communist rule in Brașov, Romania.	
42	Sunday 15 November	St. Louis Arena, St. Louis, Missouri, USA	USA		
43	Monday 16 November	St. Louis Arena, St. Louis, Missouri, USA	USA		
44	Wednesday 18 November	Astrodome, Houston, Texas, USA	USA	King's Cross fire on the London Underground kills 31 people.	Sony buys CBS Records for about $2 billion.
45	Thursday 19 November	Frank Erwin Center, University of Texas, Austin, Texas, USA	USA		
46	Friday 20 November	Frank Erwin Center, University of Texas, Austin, Texas, USA	USA		
47	Saturday 21 November	Reunion Arena, Reunion Park, Dallas, Texas, USA	USA	Two Chicago television stations are hijacked by unknown pirate dressed as Max Headroom.	
48	Sunday 22 November	Reunion Arena, Reunion Park, Dallas, Texas, USA	USA		
49	Monday 23 November	Reunion Arena, Reunion Park, Dallas, Texas, USA	USA		The Eternal Idol released by Black Sabbath.
50	Thursday 26 November	Los Angeles Memorial Sports Arena, Los Angeles, California, USA	USA		
51	Friday 27 November	Los Angeles Memorial Sports Arena, Los Angeles, California, USA	USA		Live ... In The Raw released by W.A.S.P.
52	Saturday 28 November	Los Angeles Memorial Sports Arena, Los Angeles, California, USA	USA		
53	Sunday 29 November	Los Angeles Memorial Sports Arena, Los Angeles, California, USA	USA	Korean Air Flight 858 is blown up on the way to Bangkok, killing 115 crew and passengers, on orders of North Korean government.	
54	Monday 30 November	Los Angeles Memorial Sports Arena, Los Angeles, California, USA	USA		
55	Tuesday 1 December	Los Angeles Memorial Sports Arena, Los Angeles, California, USA	USA	Digging begins for Channel Tunnel between England and France.	
56	Thursday 3 December	Oakland Coliseum Arena, Oakland, California, USA	USA		
57	Friday 4 December	Oakland Coliseum Arena, Oakland, California, USA	USA		
58	Saturday 5 December	Oakland Coliseum Arena, Oakland, California, USA	USA		
59	Sunday 6 December	Oakland Coliseum Arena, Oakland, California, USA	USA		
60	Tuesday 8 December	Kingdome, Seattle, Washington, USA	USA	First Intifada begins in the Gaza Strip and West Bank.	Inside Information released by Foreigner.
61	Thursday 10 December	Pacific National Exhibition Coliseum, Vancouver, British Columbia, Canada	Canada		
62	Friday 11 December	Pacific National Exhibition Coliseum, Vancouver, British Columbia, Canada	Canada		
	Monday 14 December	RECORD RELEASE 'ON THE TURNING AWAY' (US RELEASE 24 NOVEMBER)			You're Living All Over Me released by Dinosaur Jr.

1988

A MOMENTARY LAPSE OF REASON NEW ZEALAND AND AUSTRALIA TOUR

1	Friday 22 January	Western Springs Stadium, Auckland, New Zealand	New Zealand		
2	Wednesday 27 January	Sydney Entertainment Centre, Sydney, Australia	Australia		

#	Year	Address	Country	World Events	Music
3	Thursday 28 January	Sydney Entertainment Centre, Sydney, Australia	Australia	Supreme Court in Canada declares anti-abortion law unconstitutional.	Matthew John Trippe files a a lawsuit claiming that he was secretly hired to pose as Nikki Sixx of Mötley Crüe during 1983 and 1984.
4	Friday 29 January	Sydney Entertainment Centre, Sydney, Australia	Australia		
5	Saturday 30 January	Sydney Entertainment Centre, Sydney, Australia	Australia	Ship sinks near Anacortes, Washington, spilling 70,000 gallons of oil.	
6	Sunday 31 January	Sydney Entertainment Centre, Sydney, Australia	Australia		
7	Monday 1 February	Sydney Entertainment Centre, Sydney, Australia	Australia		
8	Tuesday 2 February	Sydney Entertainment Centre, Sydney, Australia	Australia		*I'm Your Man* released by Leonard Cohen.
9	Wednesday 3 February	Sydney Entertainment Centre, Sydney, Australia	Australia		
10	Thursday 4 February	Sydney Entertainment Centre, Sydney, Australia	Australia		
11	Friday 5 February	Sydney Entertainment Centre, Sydney, Australia	Australia		
12	Sunday 7 February	Entertainment Centre, Brisbane, Australia	Australia		
13	Monday 8 February	Entertainment Centre, Brisbane, Australia	Australia		*Who Killed The JAMS?* released by The Justified Ancients of Mu Mu (also known as The KLF).
14	Thursday 11 February	Thebarton Oval, Adelaide, Australia	Australia		
15	Saturday 13 February	National Tennis Centre, Melbourne, Australia	Australia	1988 Winter Olympics open in Calgary, Canada.	
16	Sunday 14 February	National Tennis Centre, Melbourne, Australia	Australia		
17	Monday 15 February	National Tennis Centre, Melbourne, Australia	Australia		
18	Tuesday 16 February	National Tennis Centre, Melbourne, Australia	Australia		*Nada Como El Sol* released by Sting.
19	Wednesday 17 February	National Tennis Centre, Melbourne, Australia	Australia		
20	Thursday 18 February	National Tennis Centre, Melbourne, Australia	Australia		
21	Friday 19 February	National Tennis Centre, Melbourne, Australia	Australia		
22	Saturday 20 February	National Tennis Centre, Melbourne, Australia	Australia	Nagorno-Karabakh Autonomous Oblast votes to secede from the Azerbaijani Soviet Socialist Republic and join the Armenian SSR, triggering the First Nagorno-Karabakh War.	
23	Wednesday 24 February	Fremantle Oval, Perth, Australia	Australia	South African government bans the United Democratic Front.	Memphis Slim dies aged 72.
	A MOMENTARY LAPSE OF REASON JAPANESE TOUR				
24	Wednesday 2 March	Budokan Grand Hall, Tokyo, Japan	Japan		The 30th Annual Grammy Awards are held in New York.
25	Thursday 3 March	Budokan Grand Hall, Tokyo, Japan	Japan		
26	Friday 4 March	Yoyogi Olympic Pool, Tokyo, Japan	Japan		
27	Saturday 5 March	Yoyogi Olympic Pool, Tokyo, Japan	Japan		
28	Sunday 6 March	Yoyogi Olympic Pool, Tokyo, Japan	Japan	A British Army SAS team shoot dead three unarmed members of the IRA in Gibraltar.	
29	Tuesday 8 March	Joh Hall, Osaka, Japan	Japan		*Racing After Midnight* released by Honeymoon Suite.
30	Wednesday 9 March	Joh Hall, Osaka, Japan	Japan		
31	Friday 11 March	Rainbow Hall, Nagoya, Japan	Japan	English pound note ceases to be legal tender, replaced by one pound coin.	
	A MOMENTARY LAPSE OF REASON NORTH AMERICAN TOUR				
32	Friday 15 April	Memorial Coliseum, Los Angeles, California, USA	USA	Meteorite explodes over Indonesia.	
33	Monday 18 April	Mile High Stadium, Denver, Colorado, USA	USA		*Barbed Wire Kisses* released by The Jesus And Mary Chain.
34	Wednesday 20 April	Hughes University, California State University at Sacramento, California, USA	USA	The remaining passengers of Kuwait Airways Flight 422 are released by Lebanese guerillas, bringing an end to the world's longest skyjacking.	

	Year	Address	Country	World Events	Music
35	Friday 22 April	Oakland Coliseum Arena, Oakland, California, USA	USA		
36	Saturday 23 April	Oakland Coliseum Arena, Oakland, California, USA	USA		Whitney Houston has a 7th consecutive Billboard #1 single with 'Where Do Broken Hearts Go', breaking the record of The Beatles and Bee Gees.
37	Monday 25 April	Municipal Stadium, Phoenix, Arizona, USA	USA		Rock manager Doc McGhee is sentenced to five years probation following a 1982 seizure of nearly 40,000 pounds of marijuana.
38	Tuesday 26 April	Municipal Stadium, Phoenix, Arizona, USA	USA		Guitar released by Frank Zappa.
39	Thursday 28 April	Texas Stadium, Dallas, Texas, USA	USA		
40	Saturday 30 April	Citrus Bowl, Orlando, Florida, USA	USA	World Expo 88 opens in Brisbane, Australia.	The Eurovision Song Contest is won by singer Celine Dion representing Switzerland.
41	Wednesday 4 May	Carter-Finchley Stadium, North Carolina State University, Raleigh, North Carolina, USA	USA		
42	Friday 6 May	Foxboro Stadium, Foxboro, Boston, Massachusetts, USA	USA		
43	Sunday 8 May	Foxboro Stadium, Foxboro, Boston, Massachusetts, USA	USA		
44	Wednesday 11 May	Stade du Parc Olympique, Montreal, Quebec, Canada	Canada		
45	Friday 13 May	Canadian National Exhibition Stadium, Toronto, Ontario, Canada	Canada		Chet Baker died aged 58.
46	Sunday 15 May	Veterans Stadium, Philadelphia, Pennsylvania, USA	USA	The Soviet Army begins its withdrawal from Afghanistan.	
47	Monday 16 May	Veterans Stadium, Philadelphia, Pennsylvania, USA	USA	US Surgeon-General C Everett Koop reports that nicotine is as addictive as heroin.	You Can't Do That On Stage Anymore, Vol. 1 released by Frank Zappa.
48	Wednesday 18 May	University of Northern Iowa Dome, Cedar Falls, Iowa, USA	USA		
49	Friday 20 May	Camp Randall Stadium, University of Madison-Wisconsin, Madison, Wisconsin, USA	USA		
50	Saturday 21 May	Rosemont Horizon, Rosemont, Chicago, Illinois, USA	USA		Long Cold Winter released by Cinderella.
51	Sunday 22 May	Rosemont Horizon, Rosemont, Chicago, Illinois, USA	USA		
52	Tuesday 24 May	Metrodome, Minneapolis, Minnesota, USA	USA	UK Parliament passes Section 28, prohibiting the promotion of homosexuality by local government.	OU812 released by Van Halen.
53	Thursday 26 May	Arrowhead Stadium, Kansas City, Missouri, USA	USA		
54	Saturday 28 May	Ohio State University Stadium, Columbus, Ohio, USA	USA	Somali National Movement launches major offensive against Somali government forces.	
55	Monday 30 May	Three Rivers Stadium, Pittsburgh, Pennsylvania, USA	USA		Down In The Groove released by Bob Dylan.
56	Wednesday 1 June	Robert F. Kennedy Stadium, Washington D.C, USA	USA		Close released by Kim Wilde.
57	Friday 3 June	Giants Stadium, East Rutherford, New Jersey, USA	USA		
58	Saturday 4 June	Giants Stadium, East Rutherford, New Jersey, USA	USA		
59	Sunday 5 June	Giants Stadium, East Rutherford, New Jersey, USA	USA	Russian Orthodox Church celebrates its 1000th anniversary.	
	A MOMENTARY LAPSE OF REASON EUROPEAN TOUR				
60	Friday 10 June	Stade de la Beaujoire, Nantes, France	France	Spontaneous 100,000 strong mass night-singing demonstrations in Estonian Soviet Socialist Republic (leading to the Singing Revolution).	
	Monday 13 June	**RECORD RELEASE 'ONE SLIP' SINGLE**			
61	Monday 13 June	Stadion Feyenoord, Rotterdam, Netherlands	Netherlands		Forever Your Girl released by Paula Abdul.

	Year	Address	Country	World Events	Music
62	Tuesday 14 June	Stadion Feyenoord, Rotterdam, Netherlands	Netherlands	Marilyn O'Brian Boteler sues Chuck Berry for $5,000,000, alleging he assaulted her.	
63	Thursday 16 June	Reichstagsgelande, West Berlin, West Germany	Germany		
64	Saturday 18 June	Maimarktgelande, Mannheim, West Germany	Germany		*Roll With It* released by Steve Winwood.
65	Tuesday 21 June	Place d'Armes, Chateau de Versailles, France	France		
66	Wednesday 22 June	Place d'Armes, Chateau de Versailles, France	France		Red Hot Chili Peppers guitarist Hillel Slovak dies aged 26 from a heroin overdose.
67	Saturday 25 June	Niedersachsenstadion, Hannover, West Germany	Germany		Motown Records is sold to MCA and an investment firm for $61 million.
68	Monday 27 June	Westfalenhalle, Dortmund, West Germany	Germany	Gare de Lyon rail accident in Paris, France, as an incoming train crashes into an outbound train, killing 56.	
69	Tuesday 28 June	Westfalenhalle, Dortmund, West Germany	Germany		*It Takes A Nation of Millions To Hold Us Back* released by Public Enemy.
70	Wednesday 29 June	Westfalenhalle, Dortmund, West Germany	Germany		
71	Friday 1 July	Praterstadion, Vienna, Austria	Austria	Soviet Union votes to end the Communist Party's monopoly on economic and other non-political power.	
72	Sunday 3 July	Olympiastadion, Munich, West Germany	Germany		
73	Wednesday 6 July	Stadio Comunale, Turin, Italy	Italy	The Piper Alpha platform in the North Sea is destroyed by explosions and fires, killing 165 oil workers.	
74	Friday 8 July	Stadio Comunale Braglia, Modena, Italy	Italy		
75	Saturday 9 July	Stadio Comunale Braglia, Modena, Italy	Italy		*Substance* released by Joy Division.
76	Monday 11 July	Stadio Flaminio, Rome, Italy	Italy		*Brian Wilson* released by Brian Wilson.
77	Tuesday 12 July	Stadio Flaminio, Rome, Italy	Italy		
78	Friday 15 July	Stade du Municipa Charles Berty, Grenoble, France	France		
79	Sunday 17 July	Stade de l'Ouest, Nice, France	France	Four billion viewers watch Nelson Mandela's 70th Birthday Tribute.	
80	Wednesday 20 July	Estadio de Sarria, Barcelona, Spain	Spain		
81	Friday 22 July	Estadio Vicente Calderon, Madrid, Spain	Spain		
82	Sunday 24 July	Espace Richter, Montpellier, France	France		
83	Tuesday 26 July	Fussballstadion, Basel, Switzerland	Switzerland		
84	Thursday 28 July	Stadium du Nord, Lille, France	France	Winnie Mandela's home in Soweto, South Africa, destroyed by arson.	
85	Sunday 31 July	Gentofte Stadion, Copenhagen, Denmark	Denmark		
86	Tuesday 2 August	Valle Hovin Stadion, Oslo, Norway	Norway		*Back To Avalon* released by Kenny Loggins.
87	Friday 5 August	Wembley Stadium, London	UK		
88	Saturday 6 August	Wembley Stadium, London	UK	Tompkins Square Park Police Riot occurs in New York City.	
89	Monday 8 August	Maine Road Stadium, Manchester	UK	Thousands of protesters in Burma (now Myanmar) killed during anti-government demonstrations.	*Straight Outta Compton* released by N.W.A.
	A MOMENTARY LAPSE OF REASON NORTH AMERICAN TOUR				
89	Friday 12 August	The Coliseum, Cleveland, Ohio, USA	USA		Public Enemy stage a concert at Riker's Island prison.
90	Saturday 13 August	The Coliseum, Cleveland, Ohio, USA	USA		
91	Sunday 14 August	The Coliseum, Cleveland, Ohio, USA	USA		
92	Tuesday 16 August	Palace of Auburn Hills, Detroit, Michigan, USA	USA		
93	Wednesday 17 August	Palace of Auburn Hills, Detroit, Michigan, USA	USA	US Republican convention nominates George H. W. Bush as presidential candidate.	
94	Friday 19 August	Nassau Veterans Memorial Coliseum, Long Island, New York, USA	USA		

	Year	Address	Country	World Events	Music
95	Saturday 20 August	Nassau Veterans Memorial Coliseum, Long Island, New York, USA	USA	A ceasefire brings an end to the Iran-Iraq War (1980-1988).	
96	Sunday 21 August	Nassau Veterans Memorial Coliseum, Long Island, New York, USA	USA		
97	Monday 22 August	Nassau Veterans Memorial Coliseum, Long Island, New York, USA	USA	Australia unveils the Platinum Koala, its first platinum coin.	
98	Tuesday 23 August	Nassau Veterans Memorial Coliseum, Long Island, New York, USA	USA		*Nothing's Shocking* released by Jane's Addiction.
	Monday 21 November	RECORD RELEASE *DELICATE SOUND OF THUNDER*			

1989

ANOTHER LAPSE EUROPEAN TOUR

	Year	Address	Country	World Events	Music
1	Saturday 13 May	Festivalweise, Werchter, Belgium	Belgium	Around 2,000 students begin hunger strike in Tiananmen Square, Beijing.	
2	Tuesday 16 May	Arena di Verona, Verona, Italy	Italy		*Slowly We Rot* released by Obituary.
3	Wednesday 17 May	Arena di Verona, Verona, Italy	Italy	More than 1,000,000 Chinese protesters march through Beijing demanding greater democratic rights.	
4	Thursday 18 May	Arena di Verona, Verona, Italy	Italy		*Nearly Human* released by Todd Rundgren.
5	Saturday 20 May	Arena Concerti, Monza, Italy	Italy	Chinese government declares martial law in Beijing.	
6	Monday 22 May	Stadio Comunale Ardenza, Livorno, Italy	Italy		*The Miracle* released by Queen.
7	Tuesday 23 May	Stadio Comunale Ardenza, Livorno, Italy	Italy		
8	Thursday 25 May	Stadio Simonetta Lamberti, Cava De' Tirreni, Italy	Italy		*Broadway the Hard Way* released by Frank Zappa.
9	Friday 26 May	Stadio Simonetta Lamberti, Cava De' Tirreni, Italy	Italy	Danish parliament legalises same-sex marriage.	
10	Wednesday 31 May	Olympic Stadium Spiridon Spiros Louis, Athens, Greece	Greece		
11	Saturday 3 June	Olympic Stadium, Moscow, Russia	USSR		
12	Sunday 4 June	Olympic Stadium, Moscow, Russia	USSR	A violent military crackdown takes place on pro-democracy protesters in Tiananmen Square, Beijing, killing hundreds.	
13	Tuesday 6 June	Olympic Stadium, Moscow, Russia	USSR		
14	Wednesday 7 June	Olympic Stadium, Moscow, Russia	USSR		
15	Thursday 8 June	Olympic Stadium, Moscow, Russia	USSR		
16	Saturday 10 June	Lahden Surhali, Lahti, Finland	Finland		
	Monday 12 June	VIDEO RELEASE *DELICATE SOUND OF THUNDER*		Canadian Olympian Ben Johnson (winner of 1988 100m race) admits using steroids.	*Big Tyme* released by Heavy D & The Boyz.
17	Monday 12 June	Globe Arena, Stockholm, Sweden	Sweden		
18	Tuesday 13 June	Globe Arena, Stockholm, Sweden	Sweden		
19	Wednesday 14 June	Globe Arena, Stockholm, Sweden	Sweden	Ronald Reagan given honorary knighthood by Queen Elizabeth II.	
20	Friday 16 June	Festwiesse Im Stadtpark, Hamburg, West Germany	Germany	A crowd of 250,000 gathers in Budapest for the reburial of Imre Nagy, the former Hungarian Prime Minister who had been executed in 1958.	
21	Sunday 18 June	Mungersdorfer Stadion, Cologne, West Germany	Germany		
22	Tuesday 20 June	Festhalle, Frankfurt, West Germany	Germany		*Batman* released by Prince.
23	Wednesday 21 June	Festhalle, Frankfurt, West Germany	Germany		

	Year	Address	Country	World Events	Music
24	Thursday 22 June	Festhalle, Frankfurt, West Germany	Germany	British police arrest 260 people celebrating the summer solstice at Stonehenge.	
25	Friday 23 June	Linzer Stadion, Linz, Austria	Austria		
26	Sunday 25 June	Neckarstadion, Stuttgart, West Germany	Germany		*Cosmic Thing* released by The B-52s.
27	Tuesday 27 June	Palais Omnisports de Paris-Bercy, Paris, France	France		*One Night of Sin* released by Joe Cocker.
28	Wednesday 28 June	Palais Omnisports de Paris-Bercy, Paris, France	France		
29	Thursday 29 June	Palais Omnisports de Paris-Bercy, Paris, France	France	South Africa's National Party adopts five year programme, including plan for Black majority rule in national and local government.	
30	Friday 30 June	Palais Omnisports de Paris-Bercy, Paris, France	France		
31	Saturday 1 July	Palais Omnisports de Paris-Bercy, Paris, France	France		*Bulletproof Heart* released by Grace Jones.
32	Tuesday 4 July	London Arena, Isle of Dogs, London	UK		
33	Wednesday 5 July	London Arena, Isle of Dogs, London	UK	South African President P. W. Botha meets the imprisoned Nelson Mandela for the first time	
34	Thursday 6 July	London Arena, Isle of Dogs, London	UK		
35	Friday 7 July	London Arena, Isle of Dogs, London	UK		
36	Saturday 8 July	London Arena, Isle of Dogs, London	UK	Carlos Saul Menem becomes President of Argentina.	
37	Sunday 9 July	London Arena, Isle of Dogs, London	UK		The Monkees reunite for a concert in Los Angeles and are inducted into the Hollywood Walk of Fame the next day.
38	Monday 10 July	Goffertpark, Nijmegen, Netherlands	Netherlands	Approximately 300,000 coal miners go on strike in Siberia, demanding better living conditions.	*Earth Moving* released by Mike Oldfield.
39	Wednesday 12 July	Stade Olympique de la Pontaise, Lausanne, Switzerland	Switzerland		
40	Saturday 15 July	Canale di San Marco, Piazza San Marco, Venice, Italy	Italy		*UHF – Original Motion Picture Soundtrack And Other Stuff* released by Weird Al Yankovic.
41	Tuesday 18 July	Stade Velodrome, Marseille, France	France		
	1994				
	Monday 28 March	**RECORD RELEASE *THE DIVISION BELL* (US RELEASE 4 APRIL)**			
	THE DIVISION BELL – NORTH AND SOUTH AMERICAN TOUR				
1	Wednesday 30 March	Joe Robbie Stadium, Miami, Florida, USA	USA		
2	Sunday 3 April	Alamo Dome, San Antonio, Texas, USA	USA		
3	Tuesday 5 April	Rice University Stadium, Houston, Texas, USA	USA		Kurt Cobain dies aged 27 from suicide.
4	Saturday 9 April	Autodromo Hermanos Rodriguez, Mexico City, Mexico	Mexico	STS-59 (Endeavour) launches into orbit.	*Crash! Boom! Bang!* released by Roxette.
5	Sunday 10 April	Autodromo Hermanos Rodriguez, Mexico City, Mexico	Mexico		
6	Thursday 14 April	Jack Murphy Stadium, San Diego, California, USA	USA		
7	Saturday 16 April	The Rose Bowl, Los Angeles, California, USA	USA	Voters in Finland decide to join the European Union in a referendum.	
8	Sunday 17 April	The Rose Bowl, Los Angeles, California, USA	USA		
9	Wednesday 20 April	Oakland Coliseum, Oakland, California, USA	USA	New national flag adopted by South Africa.	
10	Thursday 21 April	Oakland Coliseum, Oakland, California, USA	USA	The Red Cross says hundreds of thousands of Tutsi have been killed in the Rwandan Genocide.	*Illmatic* released by Nas.
11	Friday 22 April	Oakland Coliseum, Oakland, California, USA	USA		
12	Sunday 24 April	Sun Devil Stadium, Arizona State University, Phoenix, Arizona, USA	USA		*Full Moon Fever* released by Tom Petty.
13	Tuesday 26 April	Sun Bowl Stadium, University of Texas at El Paso, El Paso, Texas, USA	USA	First ever multi-racial elections in South Africa.	*American Recordings* released by Johnny Cash.
14	Thursday 28 April	Texas Stadium, Dallas, Texas, USA	USA		

	Year	Address	Country	World Events	Music
15	Friday 29 April	Texas Stadium, Dallas, Texas, USA	USA		
16	Sunday 1 May	Legion Field, University of Alabama, Birmingham, Alabama, USA	USA	Formula 1 driver Ayrton Senna killed whilst leading the San Marino Grand Prix.	
17	Tuesday 3 May	Bobbie Dodd Stadium, Georgia Institute of Technology, Atlanta, Georgia, USA	USA		*Middle Class Revolt* released by The Fall.
18	Wednesday 4 May	Bobbie Dodd Stadium, Georgia Institute of Technology, Atlanta, Georgia, USA	USA		
19	Friday 6 May	Tampa Stadium, Tampa, Florida, USA	USA	The Channel Tunnel opens between England and France.	Pearl Jam files a complaint with the US Justice Department against Ticketmaster, charging that the company has a monopoly on the concert ticket business.
20	Sunday 8 May	Vanderbilt University Stadium, Nashville, Tennessee, USA	USA		
21	Tuesday 10 May	Carter-Finchley Stadium, North Carolina State University, Raleigh, North Carolina, USA	USA	Nelson Mandela is inaugurated as South Africa's first black president.	Tupac Shakur starts a 15-day sentence for attacking director Allen Hughes on the set of a video shoot.
22	Thursday 12 May	Death Valley Stadium, Clemson University, Clemson, South Carolina, USA	USA		
23	Saturday 14 May	Louisiana Superdrome, New Orleans, Louisiana, USA	USA		
	Monday 16 May	RECORD RELEASE 'TAKE IT BACK' SINGLE (US 31 MAY)		Tennis star Jennifer Capriati arrested on possession of marijuana.	
24	Wednesday 18 May	Foxboro Stadium, Foxboro, Boston, Massachusetts, USA	USA	A genetically modified tomato is deemed safe for human consumption by the FDA.	
25	Thursday 19 May	Foxboro Stadium, Foxboro, Boston, Massachusetts, USA	USA		
26	Friday 20 May	Foxboro Stadium, Foxboro, Boston, Massachusetts, USA	USA		
27	Sunday 22 May	Stade du Parc Olympique, Montreal, Quebec, Canada	Canada		
28	Monday 23 May	Stade du Parc Olympique, Montreal, Quebec, Canada	Canada	Roman Herzog elected President of Germany.	*Seal* released by Seal.
29	Tuesday 24 May	Stade du Parc Olympique, Montreal, Quebec, Canada	Canada		*David Byrne* released by David Byrne.
30	Thursday 26 May	Municipal Stadium, Cleveland, Ohio, USA	USA	Michael Jackson marries Lisa Marie Presley.	
31	Friday 27 May	Municipal Stadium, Cleveland, Ohio, USA	USA		The Eagles launch their 'Hell Freezes Over' tour in Burbank, California.
32	Sunday 29 May	Ohio State University Stadium, Columbus, Ohio, USA	USA		
33	Tuesday 31 May	Three Rivers Stadium, Pittsburgh, Pennsylvania, USA	USA		*Ill Communication* released by Beastie Boys.
34	Thursday 2 June	Veterans Stadium, Philadelphia, Pennsylvania, USA	USA	Chinook military helicopter crashes in northern Scotland, killing 29.	
35	Friday 3 June	Veterans Stadium, Philadelphia, Pennsylvania, USA	USA		*Balls to Picasso* released by Bruce Dickinson.
36	Saturday 4 June	Veterans Stadium, Philadelphia, Pennsylvania, USA	USA		
37	Monday 6 June	Carrier Dome, Syracuse, New York, USA	USA	Ceasefire negotiations for the Yugoslav War begin in Geneva.	
38	Friday 10 June	Yankee Stadium, New York City, New York, USA	USA		
39	Saturday 11 June	Yankee Stadium, New York City, New York, USA	USA		
40	Tuesday 14 June	Hoosier Dome, Indianapolis, Indiana, USA	USA		*Suicidal for Life* released by Suicidal Tendencies.
41	Thursday 16 June	Cyclone Stadium, Iowa State University, Ames, Iowa, USA	USA		Kristen Pfaff (bass guitarist for Hole) dies aged 27.
42	Saturday 18 June	Mile High Stadium, Denver, Colorado, USA	USA	Gay Games open in New York City.	
43	Monday 20 June	Arrowhead Stadium, Kansas City, Missouri, USA	USA		*Bee Thousand* released by Guided by Voices.

	Year	Address	Country	World Events	Music
44	Wednesday 22 June	Hubert H. Humphrey Metrodome, Minneapolis, Minnesota, USA	USA		
45	Saturday 25 June	British Columbia Place Stadium, Vancouver, British Columbia, Canada	Canada	The last Russian troops leave Germany.	
46	Sunday 26 June	British Columbia Place Stadium, Vancouver, British Columbia, Canada	Canada		
47	Tuesday 28 June	Commonwealth Stadium, Edmonton, Alberta, Canada	Canada	The Aum Shinrikyo cult carry out a gas attack at Matsumoto, Japan, killing eight people.	*Tiger Bay* released by Saint Etienne.
48	Friday 1 July	Winnipeg Stadium, Winnipeg, Manitoba, Canada	Canada		*Year of the Dog* released by Wolfstone.
49	Sunday 3 July	Camp Randall Stadium, University of Madison-Wisconsin, Madison, Wisconsin, USA	USA		
50	Tuesday 5 July	Canadian National Exhibition Stadium, Toronto, Ontario, Canada	Canada	Jeff Bezos founds Amazon in Seattle.	*I Ain't Movin'* released by Des'ree.
51	Wednesday 6 July	Canadian National Exhibition Stadium, Toronto, Ontario, Canada	Canada		
52	Thursday 7 July	Canadian National Exhibition Stadium, Toronto, Ontario, Canada	Canada		
53	Saturday 9 July	Robert F. Kennedy Stadium, Washington D.C., USA	USA		
54	Sunday 10 July	Robert F. Kennedy Stadium, Washington D.C., USA	USA		
55	Tuesday 12 July	Soldier Field, Chicago, Illinois, USA	USA	Allied occupation of Berlin ends with a ceremony attended by US President Bill Clinton.	*Dewdrops in the Garden* released by Deee-Lite.
56	Thursday 14 July	Pontiac Silverdome, Detroit, Michigan, USA	USA		
57	Friday 15 July	Pontiac Silverdome, Detroit, Michigan, USA	USA		
58	Sunday 17 July	Giants Stadium, East Rutherford, New Jersey, USA	USA		
59	Monday 18 July	Giants Stadium, East Rutherford, New Jersey, USA	USA	Rwandan Patriotic Front troops capture city of Gisenyi, forcing the interim government to flee to Zaire and ending the Rwandan genocide.	*The Space Age Playboys* released by Warrior Soul.
	THE DIVISION BELL – EUROPEAN TOUR				
60	Friday 22 July	Estadio de Alavalade, Lisbon, Portugal	Portugal	Military coup in Gambia.	
61	Saturday 23 July	Estadio de Alavalade, Lisbon, Portugal	Portugal		
62	Monday 25 July	Estadio Anoeta, San Sebastian, Spain	Spain		*Whaler* released by Sophie B. Hawkins.
63	Wednesday 27 July	Estadi Olimpic, Barcelona, Spain	Spain		
64	Saturday 30 July	Chateau de Chantilly, Chantilly, France	France	Suede announce that guitarist Bernard Butler has left the band.	
65	Sunday 31 July	Chateau de Chantilly, Chantilly, France	France		
66	Tuesday 2 August	Mungersdorfer Stadion, Cologne, Germany	Germany	Whitewater hearings begin in US Congress.	*Creep Wit' Me* released by Ill Al Skratch.
67	Thursday 4 August	Olympiastadion, Munich, Germany	Germany		
68	Saturday 6 August	Fussballstadion, Basel, Switzerland	Switzerland		
69	Sunday 7 August	Fussballstadion, Basel, Switzerland	Switzerland	Ernesto Samper sworn in as president of Colombia.	
70	Tuesday 9 August	Ampmitheatre du Chateau de Grammont, Montpellier, France	France		*Burn My Eyes* released by Machine Head.
71	Thursday 11 August	Esplanade des Quinconces, Bordeaux, France	France		The Moscow Music Peace Festival opens. Headline acts include Bon Jovi, Ozzy Osbourne, Mötley Crüe, Skid Row, Cinderella, and the Scorpions
72	Saturday 13 August	Hockenheimring, Hockenheim, Germany	Germany		
73	Tuesday 16 August	Niedersachsenstadion, Hannover, Germany	Germany	IBM Simon smartphone released – the first ever commercially available smartphone.	*Come* released by Prince.
74	Wednesday 17 August	Niedersachsenstadion, Hannover, Germany	Germany		

	Year	Address	Country	World Events	Music
75	Friday 19 August	Lufthafen Wiener Neustadt, Vienna, Austria	Austria		
76	Sunday 21 August	Maifeld am Olympiastadion, Berlin, Germany	Germany	Ernesto Zedillo wins Mexican presidential election.	
77	Tuesday 23 August	Parkstadion, Gelsenkirchen, Germany	Germany		Grace released by Jeff Buckley.
78	Thursday 25 August	Parken, Copenhagen, Denmark	Denmark		
79	Saturday 27 August	Ullevi Stadion, Gothenburg, Sweden	Sweden		
80	Monday 29 August	Valle Hovin Stadion, Oslo, Norway	Norway		Definitely Maybe released by Oasis.
81	Tuesday 30 August	Valle Hovin Stadion, Oslo, Norway	Norway		II released by Boyz II Men.
82	Thursday 2 September	Festivalweise, Werchter, Belgium	Belgium		
83	Friday 3 September	Stadion Feyenoord, Rotterdam, Netherlands	Netherlands	Russia and the People's Republic of China agree to stop targeting their nuclear weapons towards each other.	
84	Saturday 4 September	Stadion Feyenoord, Rotterdam, Netherlands	Netherlands		
85	Sunday 5 September	Stadion Feyenoord, Rotterdam, Netherlands	Netherlands		Change Giver released by Shed Seven.
86	Tuesday 7 September	Strahov Stadion, Prague, Czech Republic	Czech Republic		
87	Thursday 9 September	Stade de la Meinau, Strasbourg, France	France		
88	Saturday 11 September	Stade du Gerland, Lyon	France		
89	Monday 13 September	Stadio Delle Alpi, Turin, Italy	Italy	President Bill Clinton signs the Federal Assault Weapons Ban.	Ready To Die released by The Notorious B.I.G.
90	Wednesday 15 September	Stadio Fruili, Udine, Italy	Italy	Islamic fundamentalists kidnap and behead 16 people in Algeria.	A 1957 audio tape of John Lennon performing with The Quarrymen on the day he met Paul McCartney is auctioned for £78,500.
91	Friday 17 September	Festa Nazionale Dell' Unita, Modena, Italy	Italy		
92	Sunday 19 September	Studi Di Cinecitta, Rome, Italy	Italy	US troops invade Haiti to restore President Jean-Bertrand Aristide to power, following the 1991 military coup.	Kylie Minogue released by Kylie Minogue.
93	Monday 20 September	Studi Di Cinecitta, Rome, Italy	Italy		Whip-Smart released by Liz Phair.
94	Tuesday 21 September	Studi Di Cinecitta, Rome, Italy	Italy		
95	Thursday 23 September	Stade du Gerland, Lyon, France	France		
96	Saturday 25 September	Stade de la Pontaise, Lausanne, Switzerland	Switzerland		
	THE DIVISION BELL – UK SHOWS				
97	Wednesday 12 October	Earl's Court Exhibition Hall, Earl's Court, London	UK		Jimmy Page and Robert Plant: No Quarter (Unledded) premieres on MTV.
98	Thursday 13 October	Earl's Court Exhibition Hall, Earl's Court, London	UK	Nobel Prize for Literature awarded to Japanese writer Kenzaburo Oe.	The Cult released by The Cult.
99	Friday 14 October	Earl's Court Exhibition Hall, Earl's Court, London	UK		
100	Saturday 15 October	Earl's Court Exhibition Hall, Earl's Court, London	UK	After three years of exile, Haitian president Aristide returns to his country.	
101	Sunday 16 October	Earl's Court Exhibition Hall, Earl's Court, London	UK		
	Monday 17 October	**RECORD RELEASE 'HIGH HOPES'**			The Return Of The Space Cowboy released by Jamiroquai.
102	Monday 17 October	Earl's Court Exhibition Hall, Earl's Court, London	UK		
103	Wednesday 19 October	Earl's Court Exhibition Hall, Earl's Court, London	UK	160 killed in fighting during Second Chechen War.	Sly released by Massive Attack.
104	Thursday 20 October	Earl's Court Exhibition Hall, Earl's Court, London	UK		
105	Friday 21 October	Earl's Court Exhibition Hall, Earl's Court, London	UK	North Korea signs pact pledging to end its nuclear ambitions.	

	Year	Address	Country	World Events	Music
106	Saturday 22 October	Earl's Court Exhibition Hall, Earl's Court, London	UK		*Orange* released by The Jon Spencer Blues Explosion.
107	Sunday 23 October	Earl's Court Exhibition Hall, Earl's Court, London	UK		*The Special Collectors Edition* released by Blur.
108	Wednesday 26 October	Earl's Court Exhibition Hall, Earl's Court, London	UK	Jordan and Israel sign peace accord.	
109	Thursday 27 October	Earl's Court Exhibition Hall, Earl's Court, London	UK		
110	Friday 28 October	Earl's Court Exhibition Hall, Earl's Court, London	UK		
111	Saturday 29 October	Earl's Court Exhibition Hall, Earl's Court, London	UK		
2005					
1	Saturday 2 July	Live 8, Hyde Park, London	UK	Venus Williams beats Lindsay Davenport for her third Wimbledon singles title.	
2022					
	8 April 2022	RECORD RELEASE 'HEY HEY RISE UP!'			

BOOTLEG GUIDE

Bootlegs are commonly labelled 'ROIO' – records of indeterminate/independent origin. They are not official releases and being caught with recording equipment at a concert could lead to ejection. (Or Axl leaping off the stage to take it from you, if you were at a Guns N' Roses concert.) On the other hand, the ubiquity of camera phones means many people nowadays spend the concert recording it from a terrible angle and with even worse audio, just to prove they were there. (There's a dreadful photo somewhere of Bono giving it the full impassioned singing schtick with camera-phone-holding fans all around him, and no one is actually in the moment, they're all recording him.) So the legal issue of recordings has essentially become moot. However, back in the day, vinyl and CD bootlegs could be found in the dodgier record shops, satisfying the demand for live performances from the hardcore fan base, and demonstrating to record companies whether the appetite for live albums (which are essentially cheap cash-grabs) existed. Very few live albums genuinely enhance a musical reputation,* usually because so little effort is put into them, or because acts just aren't great live.

For Pink Floyd, it's remarkable that bootlegs going back to 1967 even exist. We should be glad that they do, for capturing historical and evolutionary moments in the band's career. Until the *In the Flesh* tour of 1977, when set lists became more rigid owing to the requirements of the stage props, the band could improvise and stretch out as they wished, making for fascinating listening. Bootlegs from subsequent tours, supporting *Animals*, *The Wall*, *Momentary Lapse* and *Division Bell*, are hence far more homogenous, but aren't entirely lacking in interest. Waters' comments to the audience can be captivating, especially when he is angry, while Gilmour's polite but distant remarks demonstrate his use of words as bricks in his own wall. Musically, the later performances are also far more consistent (with the last three tours having substantial backing groups), but soloing is very much about being in the moment, with Gilmour, Wright, Dick Parry and others having variable inspiration. The setlist for the *Momentary Lapse* tour was particularly inflexible, running exactly the same for

---

* Yeah, I know: *Live At Leeds, Kiss Alive!, At Folsom Prison, If You Want Blood You've Got It, Get Yer Ya-Ya's Out!, No Sleep Til Hammersmith, Stop Making Sense, Nirvana Unplugged,* and *Decade of Aggression* by Slayer. But compare that to the number released!

almost two years less a few exceptions, which must have been mentally draining. The *Division Bell* tour therefore had two setlists which could be alternated as the band wished, while also allowing for songs to be added on occasion.

However, the sense of intimacy and veracity from bootlegs is unsurpassable, making them great listening for anyone wanting to go beyond the official releases. Most gigs from the later tours have multiple recordings available, hence the selection here is what seemed to be the best choice for each available concert, based on a) completeness of the set list; and b) the audio quality. I have also only included live performances, thus excluding the audio from early TV appearances, radio sessions (although some recordings are from radio broadcasts of live performances) and so on. This is an effort to document the career of Pink Floyd as a performing band. Perhaps in time there can be a book devoted to the band's media appearances, akin to *The Complete Beatles Chronicle* by Mark Lewisohn, but this is not it.

There are hence a remarkable 500+ bootlegs out there from the 1,200 shows performed by Pink Floyd. I do not claim the recordings covered here to be definitive – there may well be others yet to come to light, or superior or more complete versions. This is quite likely, as Pink Floyd have in recent years uploaded live performances from 1970 to 71 onto Spotify, probably so as to establish legal ownership of them (as copyrights expire after fifty years). But before they dole out live albums to keep the machine going, this is Pink Floyd captured in the flesh, raw and vital, by those who were there. Go see what you can find.

1967

Date: 10-09-1967
Location: Gyllene Cirklen, Stockholm, Sweden
Track Listing: Matilda Mother, Pow R Toc H, Scream Thy Last Scream, Set The Controls For The Heart Of The Sun, See Emily Play, Interstellar Overdrive
Audio Rating: ★★★★
Miscellaneous: The group sound in excellent fettle, and very powerful. **SET THE CONTROLS FOR THE HEART OF THE SUN** has been played by both Waters and Mason in recent tours, making it by far the longest surviving Floyd live track. But **SEE EMILY PLAY** fails to convert to a live version.

Date: 13-09-1967
Location: Star Club, Copenhagen, Denmark
Track Listing: Reaction In G, Arnold Layne, One In A Million, Matilda Mother, Scream Thy Last Scream, Astronomy Domine
Audio Rating:
Miscellaneous: 'One in a Million' is a rather droning jam lasting over six minutes. It is wisely unreleased. 'Reaction in G' and 'Scream Thy Last Scream' have been widely bootlegged, but they were officially released in the *Early Years* boxset.

Date: 13-11-1967
Location: Hippy Happy Fair, De Oude Ahoy Hallen, Ahoy Heliport, Rotterdam, Netherlands
Track Listing: Audience/Tuning, Reaction In G, Pow R Toc H, Scream Thy Last Scream, Set The Controls For The Heart Of The Sun, Interstellar Overdrive
Audio Rating: ★★★♪
Miscellaneous: The last bootleg with Barrett. His departure was officially announced on 6 April 1968. The performance sounds very good but the audio keeps cutting out. Last recorded versions of **POW R TOC H**, 'Reaction in G', and 'Scream Thy Last Scream'.

1968

Date: 06-05-1968
Location: First European International Pop Festival, Palazzo Dello Sport, Rome, Italy
Track Listing: Intro/Astronomy Domine, Interview With Roger Waters, Intro/Set The Controls For The Heart Of The Sun
Audio Rating: ★★★★
Miscellaneous: The first bootleg with Gilmour in the band. Introductions come from Dutch radio.

Date: 31-05-1968
Location: Paradiso, Amsterdam, Netherlands
Track Listing: Early Show: Tuning, Let There Be More Light, Interstellar Overdrive, Set The Controls For The Heart Of The Sun, A Saucerful Of Secrets. Late Show: Keep Smiling People, Let There Be More Light, Set The Controls For The Heart Of The Sun, Flaming, A Saucerful Of Secrets
Audio Rating: ★★♪
Miscellaneous: 'Keep Smiling People' is an instrumental improvisation that is clearly an early version of 'Careful With That Axe, Eugene' (released in November). The band sound immensely powerful (playing in what sounds like a small club) but the audio is not great, especially in the late show. Last recorded performances of **LET THERE BE MORE LIGHT** and **FLAMING**.

Date: 26/27(?)-07-1968
Location: Shrine Exposition Hall, Los Angeles, California, USA
Track Listing: Interstellar Overdrive, A Saucerful Of Secrets
Audio Rating: ★★♪
Miscellaneous: The tracks are probably from different performances (the band playing The Shrine Exposition Hall on 26 and 27 July), as the audio sounds different.

Date: 28-12-1968
Location: Flight To Lowlands Paradise II, Margriethal-Jaarbeurs, Utrecht, Netherlands
Track Listing: Astronomy Domine, Careful With That Axe, Eugene, Interstellar Overdrive, Set The Controls For The Heart Of The Sun, A Saucerful Of Secrets
Audio Rating: ★★
Miscellaneous: Great to hear an enthusiastic audience. The band sound energised, despite the poor audio. The Netherlands was a great location for their early post-Syd tours.

1969

Date: 27-3-1969
Location: St James Hall, Chesterfield, England
Track Listing: Astronomy Domine, Careful With That Axe, Eugene, Interstellar Overdrive,

Set The Controls For The Heart Of The Sun, A Saucerful Of Secrets
Audio Rating: ★★
Miscellaneous: Sound is extremely muffled, very little high-end. The version of **A SAUCERFUL OF SECRETS** goes on for seventeen minutes.

Date: 14-04-1969
Location: Royal Festival Hall, London, England
Track Listing: Daybreak, Part 1, Work, Doing It, Afternoon, Sleep, Nightmare, Daybreak, Part 2, The Beginning, Beset By The Creatures Of The Deep, The Narrow Way, The Pink Jungle, The Labyrinths Of Auximines, Behold The Temple Of Light, The End Of The Beginning, Interstellar Overdrive
Audio Rating: ★★♪
Miscellaneous: First performance of 'The Man – The Journey' suite. Not the greatest rendition by the sound of it.

Date: 09-05-1969
Location: University of Southampton, Southampton, England
Track Listing: Astronomy Domine, Careful With That Axe, Eugene, Interstellar Overdrive, The Beginning, Beset By The Creatures Of The Deep, A Saucerful Of Secrets
Audio Rating: ★★★♪
Miscellaneous: Curious to contain both **CAREFUL WITH THAT AXE, EUGENE** and 'Beset by the Creatures of the Deep', the latter being an early version of the former, albeit with no scream.

Date: 22-06-1969
Location: Free Trade Hall, Manchester, England
Track Listing: Daybreak (Part 1), Work, Afternoon, Doing It!, Sleeping, Nightmare, Daybreak (Part 2), The Beginning, Beset By The Creatures Of The Deep, The Narrow Way, Behold The Temple Of Light, The End Of The Beginning, Set The Controls For The Heart Of The Sun
Audio Rating: ★★★
Miscellaneous: 'Afternoon' is better known as **BIDING MY TIME**, and is rarely heard as a live version. Sounds like Wright playing a trombone on it.

Date: 26-06-1969
Location: Royal Albert Hall, South Kensington, London, England
Track Listing: Afternoon, Doing It, Sleeping, Nightmare, Daybreak, The Beginning, Beset By The Creatures Of The Deep, The Narrow Way, The Pink Jungle, The Labyrinths Of Auximine, Behold The Temple Of Light, The End Of The Beginning, Set The Controls For The Heart Of The Sun
Audio Rating: ★★♪
Miscellaneous: The Royal Albert Hall, where at one time performing there meant you were Art. The performance doesn't, however, gel. Little wonder that 'The Man – The Journey' was essentially an abortive idea.

Date: 08-08-1969
Location: 9th National Jazz & Blues Festival, Plumpton Racecourse, Plumpton, Sussex, England
Track Listing: Set The Controls For The Heart Of The Sun, Cymbaline, The Beginning, Beset By The Creatures Of The Deep, The Narrow Way, The Pink Jungle, The Labyrinths Of Auximenes, Behold The Temple Of Light, The End Of The Beginning, Interstellar Overdrive
Audio Rating: ★★★♪
Miscellaneous: Playing the material as 'The Man – The Journey' maybe seemed a good idea at the time, but the band don't especially enthused by it.

Date: 09-08-1969
Location: Paradiso, Amsterdam, Netherlands
Track Listing: Interstellar Overdrive, Set The Controls For The Heart Of The Sun, Careful With That Axe, Eugene, A Saucerful Of Secrets
Audio Rating: ★★★★
Miscellaneous: Not much caught of **INTERSTELLAR OVERDRIVE** (only 4.16). A nice crisp recording.

Date: 17-09-1969
Location: Concertgebouw, Amsterdam, Netherlands
Track Listing: Introduction, Daybreak, Work, Teatime, Afternoon, Doing It, Sleep, Nightmare, Daybreak Reprise, The Beginning, Beset By The Creatures Of The Deep, The Narrow Way, The Pink Jungle, The Labyrinths Of Auximenes, Behold The Temple Of Light, The End Of The Beginning
Audio Rating: ★★★★♪
Miscellaneous: Very clear audio. During **THE NARROW WAY** you can hear Gilmour struggle with the chorus (especially the 'A little bit'

phrase) that is in falsetto in *Ummagumma*. This was its last recorded performance.

Date: 11-10-1969
Location: Song Days Festival, Essen, West Germany
Track Listing: Introduction And Tuneups, Astronomy Domine, Green Is The Colour, Careful With That Axe, Eugene, Interstellar Overdrive (Cut)
Audio Rating: ★★
Miscellaneous: Festivals not surprisingly have worse audio than the intimate clubs and theatres of the group's early days, but surely playing a delicate acoustic number like **GREEN IS THE COLOUR** wasn't a good idea.

Date: 25-10-1969
Location: Amougies Pop & Jazz Festival, Belgium
Track Listing: Astronomy Domine, Green Is The Colour, Careful With That Axe, Eugene, Tuning Up With Frank Zappa, Interstellar Overdrive, Set The Controls For The Heart Of The Sun, A Saucerful Of Secrets
Audio Rating: ★★★
Miscellaneous: Big audience cheers. The band sound on fire, unfortunately the audio is pretty poor.

Date: 06-12-1969
Location: Afan Indoor Sports Centre, Port Talbot, Wales
Track Listing: Green Is The Colour, Careful With That Axe, Eugene, Interstellar Overdrive (Cuts), Set The Controls For The Heart Of The Sun
Audio Rating: ★★
Miscellaneous: Hard to judge the performance because the audio is so poor.

1970

Date: 18-01-1970
Location: Fairfield Hall, Croydon, England
Track Listing: Careful With That Axe, Eugene, Embryo, Main Theme From More, Biding My Time, A Saucerful Of Secrets, Astronomy Domine, Heart Beat, Pig Meat, The Violent Sequence, Set The Controls For The Heart Of The Sun, The Amazing Pudding
Audio Rating: ★★
Miscellaneous: 'The Amazing Pudding' is of course the initial name for **ATOM HEART MOTHER**, and the rendition here lasts for nearly twenty-eight minutes.

Date: 23-01-1970
Location: Théâtre Des Champs Elysées, Paris, France
Track Listing: Daybreak Part 1, Work, Tea Time, Afternoon, Doing It!, Sleep, Nightmare, A Saucerful Of Secrets, Audience, Astronomy Domine, Green Is The Colour, Careful With That Axe, Eugene, The Violent Sequence, Main Theme (From 'More'), Set The Controls For The Heart Of The Sun, The Violent Sequence, The Amazing Pudding
Audio Rating: ★★✦
Miscellaneous: This version of 'The Amazing Pudding' lasts a mere twenty-four minutes.

Date: 11-02-1970
Location: Town Hall, Birmingham, England
Track Listing: Embryo, Main Theme From More, Careful With That Axe, Eugene, Sysyphus, Heart Beat, Pig Meat, Oenone, Moonhead, The Violent Sequence, Set The Controls For The Heart Of The Sun, The Amazing Pudding
Audio Rating: ★★
Miscellaneous: 'Oenone' is a Wright-led instrumental that with its undulating keyboards sounds quite like **QUICKSILVER**. 'Moonhead' was played live during the 1969 moon landing BBC TV show.

Date: 28-02-1970
Location: Refectory Hall, Leeds University, Leeds, England
Track Listing: Embryo, Careful With That Axe, Eugene, Set The Controls For The Heart Of The Sun, Atom Heart Mother, A Saucerful Of Secrets, Interstellar Overdrive
Audio Rating: ★★
Miscellaneous: **ATOM HEART MOTHER** is barely distinguishable.

Date: 12-03-1970
Location: Auditorium Maximum, Hamburg University, Hamburg, West Germany
Track Listing: Embryo, Interstellar Overdrive, The Amazing Pudding
Audio Rating: ★★✦
Miscellaneous: **EMBRYO**, rather oddly, has a bit of a funk jam in the middle.

Date: 13-03-1970
Location: Konzert Saal, West German Technische Universitat, West Berlin, West Germany

Track Listing: Astronomy Domine, Careful With That Axe, Eugene, Cymbaline, A Saucerful Of Secrets, Embryo, Interstellar Overdrive, Set The Controls For The Heart Of The Sun, Atom Heart Mother, Blues
Audio Rating: ★★★
Miscellaneous: Band sound on excellent form amidst the audio murk.

Date: 14-03-1970
Location: Meistersinger Halle, Nuremberg, West Germany
Track Listing: Astronomy Domine, Careful With That Axe, Eugene, Cymbaline, A Saucerful Of Secrets, Embryo, Interstellar Overdrive, Set The Controls For The Heart Of The Sun, The Amazing Pudding
Audio Rating: ★★★↲
Miscellaneous: Sound initially wavery, but it settles down. Some occasional muffling and buffeting though.

Date: 15-03-1970
Location: Niedersachsenhalle, Hannover, West Germany
Track Listing: Careful With That Axe, Eugene, Cymbaline, A Saucerful Of Secrets, Embryo, Interstellar Overdrive, Set The Controls For The Heart Of The Sun, Consequently, Set The Controls For The Heart Of The Sun (No Eq Version), Consequently (No Eq Version)
Audio Rating: ★★★
Miscellaneous: 'Consequently' is another early name for **ATOM HEART MOTHER**. It goes on for nearly nineteen minutes, and feels like it. The song versions without EQ are naturally rawer but have greater presence.

Date: 20-03-1970
Location: Akademsika Foreningens Stora Sal, Lund, Sweden
Track Listing: Astronomy Domine, Careful With That Axe, Eugene, Cymbaline, A Saucerful Of Secrets, Embryo, Interstellar Overdrive, Set The Controls For The Heart Of The Sun, Atom Heart Mother
Audio Rating: ★★★
Miscellaneous: Wright's keyboards more distinct than other instruments, which can be muddy, but an excellent performance.

Date: 11-04-1970
Location: Stony Brook, New York City, New York, USA
Track Listing: Audience/Tuning Up, Astronomy Domine, Careful With That Axe, Eugene, Cymbaline, The Amazing Pudding, Set The Controls For The Heart Of The Sun, A Saucerful Of Secrets (Cuts)
Audio Rating: ★★★
Miscellaneous: Very audible comments from what seem to be the bootlegger and his woman friend. Waters introduces **CAREFUL WITH THAT AXE, EUGENE** as 'an X-rated instrumental'.

Date: 22-04-1970
Location: Port Chester, New York City, New Yorkl, USA
Track Listing: Grantchester Meadows, Astronomy Domine, Cymbaline, Atom Heart Mother, Intro & Rant, Embryo, Green Is The Colour, Careful With That Axe, Eugene, Set The Controls For The Heart Of The Sun, A Saucerful Of Secrets (Cuts)
Audio Rating: ★★★↲
Miscellaneous: Very clear sound – until the band gets loud. The version of **SET THE CONTROLS FOR THE HEART OF THE SUN** is a very tasty seventeen minutes long.

Date: 29-04-1970
Location: Fillmore West, San Francisco, California, USA
Track Listing: Grantchester Meadows, Astronomy Domine, Cymbaline, Atom Heart Mother, Embryo, Green Is The Colour, Careful With That Axe, Eugene, Set The Controls For The Heart Of The Sun, A Saucerful Of Secrets, Interstellar Overdrive
Audio Rating: ★★★★↲
Miscellaneous: One of the best-sounding bootlegs, though the sound oscillates a bit (making it sound like Gilmour's pitching is off during **GREEN IS THE COLOUR**).

Date: 01-05-1970
Location: Civic Auditorium, Santa Monica, California, USA
Track Listing: Grantchester Meadows/Astronomy Domine (Drops), Cymbaline (Tape Flip), Atom Heart Mother (Tape Flip), Tuning, Embryo, Green Is The Colour/Careful With That Axe (Tape Flip), Eugene, Set The Controls For The Heart Of The Sun (Tape Flip), Interstellar Overdrive, A Saucerful Of Secrets (Tape Flip)
Audio Rating: ★★★↲
Miscellaneous: Quite clear for the most part but

volume drops and tape flips mar the recording. Prior to **INTERSTELLAR OVERDRIVE**, Waters announces, 'Right, we've been doing this one since we were teenagers, which is a long time, and it's called Interstellar Overdrive.'

Date: 27-06-1970
Location: Bath Festival, Bath, England
Track Listing: The Amazing Pudding
Audio Rating: ★★
Miscellaneous: Festivals were not Pink Floyd's forte, and they stopped playing them as soon as they could. They really needed their own PA system, as evidenced by the rotten sound here.

Date: 28-06-1970
Location: Kralingen Pop Festival, Rotterdam, Netherlands
Track Listing: Astronomy Domine, Green Is The Colour, Careful With That Axe, Eugene, The Amazing Pudding, Set The Controls For The Heart Of The Sun, A Saucerful Of Secrets, Interstellar Overdrive
Audio Rating: ★★↗
Miscellaneous: More bad sound. The band do at least sound enthused.

Date: 12-07-1970
Location: Soersfestival 3-Day Open Air Festival, Aachen Soerser Stadium, Aachen, West Germany
Track Listing: Astronomy Domine, Green Is The Colour, Careful With That Axe, Eugene, Atom Heart Mother, Set The Controls For The Heart Of The Sun, A Saucerful Of Secrets, Interstellar Overdrive
Audio Rating: ★★
Miscellaneous: More bad festival sound.

Date: 18-07-1970
Location: Hyde Park, London, England
Track Listing: Blues, Embryo, Green Is The Colour, Careful With That Axe, Eugene, Set The Controls For The Heart Of The Sun
Audio Rating: ★★★↗
Miscellaneous: Audible conversations from those nearby the recorder.

Date: 08-08-1970
Location: Saint-Tropez Music Festival, Saint-Tropez, France
Track Listing: Soundcheck/Cymbaline, Atom Heart Mother, Embryo, Green Is The Colour, Careful With That Axe, Eugene, Set The Controls For The Heart Of The Sun
Audio Rating: ★★★
Miscellaneous: Quite a good version of **ATOM HEART MOTHER**.

Date: 12-09-1970
Location: Fête De L'humanité, Paris, France
Track Listing: Astronomy Domine, Green Is The Colour, Careful With That Axe, Eugene, Set The Controls For The Heart Of The Sun
Audio Rating: ★★★
Miscellaneous: An energetic performance.

Date: 26-09-1970
Location: Electric Factory, Philadelphia, Pennsylvania, USA
Track Listing: Astronomy Domine, Cymbaline, A Saucerful Of Secrets, Interstellar Overdrive, Fat Old Sun, Green Is The Colour, Careful With That Axe, Eugene
Audio Rating: ★★★★
Miscellaneous: The first performance of **FAT OLD SUN**, much extended (to 13.46) with an instrumental section at times replicating **CAREFUL WITH THAT AXE, EUGENE**.

Date: 29-09-1970
Location: Fillmore East, San Francisco, California, USA
Track Listing: Astronomy Domine, Green Is The Colour, Careful With That Axe, Eugene, One Of These Days, Atom Heart Mother, Set The Controls, Fat Old Sun
Audio Rating: ★★★↗
Miscellaneous: **ONE OF THESE DAYS** and **ATOM HEART MOTHER** are from Carnegie Hall 15-11-1971, so naturally sound different. For the 27-09-1970 tracks, they don't sound too inspired.

Date: 16-10-1970
Location: Pepperland Auditorium, San Rafael, California, USA
Track Listing: Astronomy Domine (1st Attempt), Astronomy Domine (2nd Attempt), Astronomy Domine (3rd Attempt), Astronomy Domine (4th Attempt), Tune Up, Fat Old Sun, Tune Up, Cymbaline, Tune Up, Atom Heart Mother, Tune Up, Embryo, Announcement/Tune Up, Green Is The Colour, Careful With That Axe, Eugene, Tune Up, Set The Controls For The Heart Of The Sun, Tune Up, A Saucerful Of Secrets
Audio Rating: ★★★★

Miscellaneous: Numerous outages due to the club being unable to handle the power requirements of the band's sound system. Roger handles it with good humour and English politeness. *Atom Heart Mother* had just been released (2 October in the UK and 10 October in the US). Both sound and performance are very good.

Date: 23-10-1970
Location: Civic Center, Santa Monica, California, USA
Track Listing: Fat Old Sun, Cymbaline, A Saucerful Of Secrets, Atom Heart Mother (With Orchestra And Choir)
Audio Rating: ★★★★
Miscellaneous: ATOM HEART MOTHER performed here in all its elephantine majesty with orchestra and choir, to great applause. One of the best sounding bootlegs.

Date: 06-11-1970
Location: Concertgebouw, Amsterdam, Netherlands
Track Listing: Astronomy Domine, Fat Old Sun, Cymbaline, Atom Heart Mother, Embryo, Green Is The Colour, Careful With That Axe, Eugene, Set The Controls, A Saucerful Of Secrets
Audio Rating: ★★
Miscellaneous: Hard to rate the performance, sound is so bad.

Date: 07-11-1970
Location: Grote Zaal De Doelen, Rotterdam, Netherlands
Track Listing: Announcer And Tunings, Astronomy Domine, Fat Old Sun, Cymbaline, Atom Heart Mother, Embryo, Green Is The Colour, Careful With That Axe, Eugene, Set The Controls For The Heart Of The Sun, A Saucerful Of Secrets (Tape Flip), Blues
Audio Rating: ★★★
Miscellaneous: Overloaded at louder moments, but generally clear.

Date: 11-11-1970
Location: Göteborg, Konserthuset, Sweden
Track Listing: Astronomy Domine, Fat Old Sun, Cymbaline, Atom Heart Mother, Embryo (Fade Out), Green Is The Colour (Cut), Careful With That Axe, Eugene, Set The Controls For The Heart Of The Sun, A Saucerful Of Secrets (Cut)
Audio Rating: ★★★
Miscellaneous: A little blurry sounding, but enormously powerful at times. Quieter songs can be murky.

Date: 12-11-1970
Location: Falkoner Centret, Copenhagen, Denmark
Track Listing: Astronomy Domine, Fat Old Sun, Cymbaline, Atom Heart Mother, Green Is The Colour, Careful With That Axe, Eugene, Set The Controls For The Heart Of The Sun, A Saucerful Of Secrets, Embryo
Audio Rating: ★★★
Miscellaneous: Sound oscillates at times, but is otherwise very clear.

Date: 13-11-1970
Location: Vejby Risskov Hallen, Aarhus, Denmark
Track Listing: Cymbaline, Atom Heart Mother, Embryo (Cut), Green Is The Colour (Fades In), Careful With That Axe, Eugene, Set The Controls For The Heart Of The Sun, A Saucerful Of Secrets, Blues.
Audio Rating: ★★
Miscellaneous: Very indistinct.

Date: 14-11-1970
Location: Ernst-Merck Halle, Hamburg, West Germany
Track Listing: Astronomy Domine, Fat Old Sun (Cut)
Audio Rating: ★★★
Miscellaneous: Truncated recording – shame, because the sound is good.

Date: 21-11-1970
Location: Altes Casino, Montreux, Switzerland
Track Listing: Astronomy Domine, Fat Old Sun, Cymbaline, Atom Heart Mother, Embryo, Green Is The Colour, Careful With That Axe, Eugene, Set The Controls For The Heart Of The Sun, A Saucerful Of Secrets, Just Another Twelve Bar, More Blues
Audio Rating: ★★★★
Miscellaneous: Yes, the casino from Deep Purple's 'Smoke On The Water'. The fire occurred a year later, on 4 December 1971. Two blues encores, the first of which is nice and lively, the second more sedate. Great show and audio recording.

Date: 22-11-1970
Location: Altes Casino, Montreux, Switzerland

Track Listing: Astronomy Domine, Fat Old Sun, Cymbaline, Atom Heart Mother, Embryo, Green Is The Colour, Careful With That Axe, Eugene, Set The Controls For The Heart Of The Sun, A Saucerful Of Secrets, Interstellar Overdrive
Audio Rating: ★★★♪
Miscellaneous: The last live outing of **INTERSTELLAR OVERDRIVE**.

Date: 25-11-1970
Location: Friedrich Ebert Halle, Ludwigshafen, West Germany
Track Listing: Astronomy Domine, Fat Old Sun, Cymbaline, Atom Heart Mother, Embryo, Audience/Tuning, Green Is The Colour, Careful With That Axe, Eugene, Set The Controls For The Heart Of The Sun, Saucerful Of Secrets
Audio Rating: ★★★
Miscellaneous: Audience very spirited and the band rise to the occasion.

Date: 26-11-1970
Location: Killesberghalle, Stuttgart, West Germany
Track Listing: Fat Old Sun, Green Is The Colour, Cymbaline, Atom Heart Mother, Embryo
Audio Rating: ★★★
Miscellaneous: Another truncated recording, although the five tracks last almost an hour.

Date: 27-11-1970
Location: Niedersachsenhalle, Hannover, West Germany
Track Listing: Astronomy Domine, Fat Old Sun, Cymbaline, Corrosion, Embryo, Atom Heart Mother, Green Is The Colour, Careful With That Axe, Eugene, Set The Controls For The Heart Of The Sun, A Saucerful Of Secrets
Audio Rating: ★★★♪
Miscellaneous: 'Corrosion' has also been referred to as 'Corrosion in the Pink Room'. It's an improvised piece that was never released, with a pulsating bass riff and whirring keyboards.

Date: 29-11-1970
Location: Circus Crone, Munich, West Germany
Track Listing: Astronomy Domine, Fat Old Sun, Cymbaline, Atom Heart Mother, Embryo, Green Is The Colour, Careful With That Axe, Eugene, Set The Controls For The Heart Of The Sun, Audience/Tuning, A Saucerful Of Secrets (Cuts)
Audio Rating: ★★★
Miscellaneous: Band deliver an excellent performance.

Date: 22-12-1970
Location: City Hall, Sheffield, England
Track Listing: Alan's Psychedelic Breakfast, Embryo, Fat Old Sun, Careful With That Axe, Eugene, Set The Controls For The Heart Of The Sun, A Saucerful Of Secrets, Celestial Power Loss, Celestial Voices, Atom Heart Mother, Atom Heart Mother Reprise
Audio Rating: ★★★
Miscellaneous: The only recorded performance of **ALAN'S PSYCHEDELIC BREAKFAST**. It includes the sound of a boiling kettle and what must be the radio transmission of a BBC comedy show, to audience laughter. The power cuts out during the 'Celestial Voices' section of **A SAUCERFUL OF SECRETS**, just when Gilmour's vocal comes in, but they manage to resume.

1971

Date: 17-01-1971
Location: 'Implosion at the Roundhouse', The Roundhouse, Camden Town, London, England
Track Listing: Astronomy Domine, Embryo, Fat Old Sun
Audio Rating: ★★★♪
Miscellaneous: Only a fragmentary recording, the full set list apparently comprising **EMBRYO, ASTRONOMY DOMINÉ, FAT OLD SUN, CAREFUL WITH THAT AXE, EUGENE, CYMBALINE, SET THE CONTROLS FOR THE HEART OF THE SUN, A SAUCERFUL OF SECRETS**, and **ATOM HEART MOTHER**. Sound is clear except for the vocals.

Date: 23-01-1971
Location: Refectory Hall, Leeds University, Leeds, England
Track Listing: A Saucerful Of Secrets, Tunings, Blues
Audio Rating: ★★★
Miscellaneous: Another fragment as the group begin a tour of British universities. The Who's *Live at Leeds* was recorded in the same location eleven months earlier.

Date: 12-02-1971
Location: Lecture Theatre, University of Essex, Colchester, England

Track Listing: Atom Heart Mother, Embryo, Careful With That Axe, Eugene, Astronomy Domine, Cymbaline, Set The Controls For The Heart Of The Sun, A Saucerful Of Secrets
Audio Rating: ★★★
Miscellaneous: This version of **ATOM HEART MOTHER** lasts 18.30.

Date: 13-02-1971
Location: Students Union Bar, Technical College, Farnborough, Hampshire, England
Track Listing: Atom Heart Mother, Tuning, Embryo, Tuning, Careful With That Axe, Eugene, Cymbaline, Tuning, Astronomy Domine, Tuning, Set The Controls For The Heart Of The Sun, Tuning, A Saucerful Of Secrets (Cut)
Audio Rating: ★★★★
Miscellaneous: Lovely clear audio. Doesn't sound there were many people there. **A SAUCERFUL OF SECRETS** cuts out at 14.15, just before Gilmour starts singing in the 'Celestial Voices' section.

Date: 24-02-1971
Location: Halle Munsterland, Münster, West Germany
Track Listing: Embryo, Green Is The Colour, Careful With That Axe, Eugene (Cuts), Fat Old Sun, Cymbaline
Audio Rating: ★★★★↵
Miscellaneous: **CAREFUL WITH THAT AXE, EUGENE** cuts out at 3.37, only resuming with the subsequent applause. **FAT OLD SUN** lasts 14.13, with a high-tempo section kicking in at 7.02. Another very good audio recording.

Date: 25-02-1971
Location: Grosser Saal Musikhalle, Hamburg, West Germany
Track Listing: Green Is The Colour, Careful With That Axe, Eugene, Cymbaline, Embryo, Set The Controls For The Heart Of The Sun, A Saucerful Of Secrets, Atom Heart Mother
Audio Rating: ★★★↵
Miscellaneous: **ATOM HEART MOTHER** is performed with an orchestra and choir. Sound is very clear during quieter moments but overloaded when the band turn it up to eleven.

Date: 26-02-1971
Location: Grosser Stadthalle, Offenbach am Main, West Germany

Track Listing: Astronomy Domine, Green Is The Colour, Careful With That Axe, Eugene, Embryo, Set The Controls For The Heart Of The Sun, Cymbaline, A Saucerful Of Secrets, Atom Heart Mother, Audience, Atom Heart Mother (Reprise), Pink Blues
Audio Rating: ★★★
Miscellaneous: **ATOM HEART MOTHER** again performed with an orchestra and choir. There's a reprise, mostly of Gilmour's slide guitar solo, just afterwards. 'Pink Blues' is just their jamming blues encore.

Date: 03-04-1971
Location: Oude Ahoy Hallen, Rotterdam, Netherlands
Track Listing: Astronomy Domine, Careful With That Axe, Eugene, Fat Old Sun, Tuning Up, Set The Controls For The Heart Of The Sun, Cymbaline, Tuning Up And Announcement, A Saucerful Of Secrets, Atom Heart Mother, Embryo
Audio Rating: ★★↵
Miscellaneous: Quite hissy and indistinct. **FAT OLD SUN** lasts over fifteen minutes. Waters does some of the 'Pictish rant' from **SEVERAL SPECIES** during **A SAUCERFUL OF SECRETS**, in between 'Syncopated Pandemonium' and 'Storm Signal'.

Date: 15-05-1971
Location: Garden Party, Crystal Palace Bowl, London, England
Track Listing: Atom Heart Mother, Rain-Tapers-Tuneups, Careful With That Axe, Eugene, Fat Old Sun, Tapers-Audience-Tuneups, The Return Of The Son Of Nothing, Set The Controls For The Heart Of The Sun, Audience-Tuneups, Embryo
Audio Rating: ★★
Miscellaneous: Very faint and indistinct. The taper and the people around are far more audible. Just before **CAREFUL WITH THAT AXE, EUGENE**: 'I don't wanna go, I'm staying here. Well, I wanna tape this.' 'Well, have you switched that off?' 'No, it's still going.' 'Look, you're going to get soaking wet.' 'Well where we gonna go then?' You can hear the rain. First recorded performance of 'The Return of the Son of Nothing' as far as I know. The lyrics are different to **ECHOES** but the music is mostly there.

Date: 18-05-1971
Location: Pathfoot Building Refectory, Stirling University, Stirling, Scotland
Track Listing: Atom Heart Mother, Set The Controls For The Heart Of The Sun, Fat Old Sun, Careful With That Axe, Eugene, The Return Of The Son Of Nothing, A Saucerful Of Secrets (Incomplete)
Audio Rating: ★★
Miscellaneous: This recording seems to have previously been labelled as coming from the concert at the University of Strathclyde, played two days later. The audio unfortunately is poor, with substantial hiss and a wavering sound.

Date: 04-06-1971
Location: Philips Veranstal Tungshalle, Dusseldorf, West Germany
Track Listing: Atom Heart Mother, Careful With That Axe, Eugene, Fat Old Sun, Embryo, The Return Of The Son Of Nothing, Set The Controls For The Heart Of The Sun, Cymbaline, Audience/Tuning, A Saucerful Of Secrets (Cuts)
Audio Rating: ★★♪
Miscellaneous: **FAT OLD SUN** stops dead at 11.32, during the energetic jamming section. **A SAUCERFUL OF SECRETS** cuts out at 3.17, during the 'Something Else' section, so not even reaching Mason's syncopated drum pattern.

Date: 05-06-1971
Location: Sportpalast, West Berlin, West Germany
Track Listing: Careful With That Axe, Eugene, Fat Old Sun, Embryo, Tuning And Announcement, Set The Controls For The Heart Of The Sun, The Return Of The Son Of Nothing, Audience, Cymbaline, A Saucerful Of Secrets, Astronomy Domine, Blues
Audio Rating: ★★★
Miscellaneous: Audience start to clap along during the funky section of 'The Return of the Son of Nothing'.

Date: 12-06-1971
Location: Palais Des Sports, Lyon, France
Track Listing: Dj Introduction, Set The Controls For The Heart Of The Sun, Cymbaline, Atom Heart Mother
Audio Rating: ★★♪
Miscellaneous: A recording of the radio broadcast on Europe 1's *Musicorama* programme. **ATOM HEART MOTHER** is performed with orchestra and choir.

Date: 19-06-1971
Location: Palazzo Delle Manifestazioni Artistiche, Brescia, Italy
Track Listing: Atom Heart Mother, Careful With That Axe, Eugene, Tuning Up, Fat Old Sun, Embryo, The Return Of The Son Of Nothing, Set The Controls For The Heart Of The Sun, Cymbaline, A Saucerful Of Secrets
Audio Rating: ★★★
Miscellaneous: **ATOM HEART MOTHER** lasts just 15.44.

Date: 20-06-1971
Location: Palazzo Dello Sport, Rome, Italy
Track Listing: Announcements, Atom Heart Mother, Careful With That Axe, Eugene, Fat Old Sun, Embryo, The Return Of The Son Of Nothing, Set The Controls For The Heart Of The Sun, Cymbaline, A Saucerful Of Secrets, Announcements, Astronomy Domine, Announcements
Audio Rating: ★★★♪
Miscellaneous: The last performance of **ASTRONOMY DOMINE** until 1994.

Date: 26-06-1971
Location: Amstel Free Concert, Amsterdamse Bos, Amsterdam, Netherlands
Track Listing: Careful With That Axe, Eugene, Cymbaline, Set The Controls For The Heart Of The Sun, A Saucerful Of Secrets, Embryo
Audio Rating: ★★★
Miscellaneous: The summer festival season begins, and with it a loss of audio quality.

Date: 01-07-1971
Location: Internationale Musikforum, Ossiachersee, Congress Center Villach, Ossiach, Austria
Track Listing: Tuning Up, The Return Of The Son Of Nothing, Careful With That Axe, Eugene, Set The Controls For The Heart Of The Sun, Atom Heart Mother
Audio Rating: ★★★
Miscellaneous: **ATOM HEART MOTHER** performed with an orchestra and choir, and takes over twenty-eight minutes.

Date: 06-08-1971
Location: Hakone Aphrodite Open Air Festival, Hakone, Kanagawa, Japan

Track Listing: Opening Announcement, Atom Heart Mother, Careful With That Axe, Eugene, Set The Controls For The Heart Of The Sun, Echoes, A Saucerful Of Secrets, Closing Announcement
Audio Rating: ★★★♪
Miscellaneous: Sound clearer than usual for festivals, but distant-sounding. Audience rather more audible. No song introduction recorded, so it's not clear why **ECHOES** now has its proper name – the lyrics are still an early draft.

Date: 09-08-1971
Location: Festival Hall, Osaka, Japan
Track Listing: Green Is The Colour, Careful With That Axe, Eugene, Fat Old Sun, Atom Heart Mother, Echoes, Set The Controls For The Heart Of The Sun, Cymbaline, A Saucerful Of Secrets
Audio Rating: ★★♪
Miscellaneous: **ATOM HEART MOTHER** performance a mere nineteen minutes.

Date: 13-08-1971
Location: Festival Hall, Melbourne, Australia
Track Listing: Atom Heart Mother, Green Is The Colour, Careful With That Axe, Eugene, Echoes, Set The Controls For The Heart Of The Sun, Cymbaline, A Saucerful Of Secrets (Cuts)
Audio Rating: ★★★♪
Miscellaneous: The group's first time playing in Australia. **A SAUCERFUL OF SECRETS** cuts out after 5.44. Last performance of **GREEN IS THE COLOUR**.

Date: 18-09-1971
Location: Festival de Musique Classique, Pavillon De Montreux, Montreux, Switzerland
Track Listing: Echoes, Careful With That Axe, Eugene, Set The Controls For The Heart Of The Sun, Cymbaline, Atom Heart Mother, A Saucerful Of Secrets
Audio Rating: ★★★★
Miscellaneous: 'Overhead, the albatross hangs motionless upon the air …' And now **ECHOES** is approaching its final form, give or take a few guitar lines.

Date: 23-09-1971
Location: KB Hallen, Copenhagen, Denmark
Track Listing: Careful With That Axe, Eugene, Fat Old Sun, Set The Controls For The Heart Of The Sun, Atom Heart Mother, Echoes, Cymbaline, A Saucerful Of Secrets, Blues
Audio Rating: ★★★
Miscellaneous: The first wind-down blues in a while, after the audience noisily demand an encore.

Date: 16-10-1971
Location: Civic Auditorium, Santa Monica, California, USA
Track Listing: Careful With That Axe, Eugene, Fat Old Sun, Set The Controls For The Heart Of The Sun, Atom Heart Mother, Embryo, Cymbaline, Blues, Echoes, A Saucerful Of Secrets
Audio Rating: ★★★♪
Miscellaneous: Unusually good bottom end.

Date: 17-10-1971
Location: Convention Hall, San Diego, California, USA
Track Listing: Careful With That Axe, Eugene, Fat Old Sun, Atom Heart Mother, Embryo, Set The Controls For The Heart Of The Sun, Cymbaline, Blues
Audio Rating: ★★★♪
Miscellaneous: No **ECHOES** for some reason.

Date: 27-10-1971
Location: Auditorium Theater, Chicago, Illinois, USA
Track Listing: Embryo, Fat Old Sun, Set The Controls For The Heart Of The Sun, Tuning Up And Atom Heart Mother Excerpt, Tuning Up And Atom Heart Mother, One Of These Days, Careful With That Axe, Eugene, Cymbaline Excerpt, Cymbaline, Tuning Up, Echoes, A Saucerful Of Secrets
Audio Rating: ★★★
Miscellaneous: First performance of **ONE OF THESE DAYS**. (*Meddle* was released 30 October 1971.)

Date: 28-10-1971
Location: Hill Auditorium, Ann Arbor, Michigan, USA
Track Listing: Embryo, Fat Old Sun, Set The Controls For The Heart Of The Sun, Atom Heart Mother, One Of These Days, Cymbaline, Echoes, Blues
Audio Rating: ★★♪
Miscellaneous: Noisy but very enthusiastic audience.

Date: 31-10-1971
Location: Fieldhouse, University of Toledo, Toledo, Ohio, USA
Track Listing: Tuning, Set The Controls For The Heart Of The Sun, Atom Heart Mother, One Of These Days, Careful With That Axe, Eugene, Cymbaline, Echoes, Blues
Audio Rating: ★★★♪
Miscellaneous: Pretty good but lacks clarity/definition in the higher frequencies.

Date: 05-11-1971
Location: Hunter College, City University of New York, New York City, New York, USA
Track Listing: Embryo, Fat Old Sun, Set The Controls For The Heart Of The Sun, Atom Heart Mother, One Of These Days, Careful With That Axe, Eugene, Cymbaline, Echoes, A Saucerful Of Secrets
Audio Rating: ★★★
Miscellaneous: **EMBRYO** lasts nearly twenty minutes.

Date: 06-11-1971
Location: Emerson Gym, Case Western Reserve University, Cleveland, Ohio, USA
Track Listing: Embryo, Fat Old Sun, Set The Controls For The Heart Of The Sun, Atom Heart Mother, One Of These Days, Careful With That Axe, Eugene, Cymbaline, Echoes, Blues
Audio Rating: ★★★★♪
Miscellaneous: One of the best from 1971, in terms of audio at least. Terrific clarity.

Date: 10-11-1971
Location: Pavillon De La Jeunesse, Quebec, Canada
Track Listing: Introduction, Embryo, Fat Old Sun, Set The Controls For The Heart Of The Sun, One Of These Days, Atom Heart Mother (Cuts), Cymbaline, Careful With That Axe, Eugene, Echoes, A Saucerful Of Secrets
Audio Rating: ★★★♪
Miscellaneous: **ATOM HEART MOTHER** cuts out after fourteen minutes, skipping to the introduction to **CYMBALINE**.

Date: 12-11-1971
Location: Irvine Auditorium, Pennsylvania State University, Philadelphia, Pennsylvania, USA
Track Listing: Tuning, Embryo, Fat Old Sun, Set The Controls For The Heart Of The Sun (Cuts), Echoes

Audio Rating: ★★★
Miscellaneous: Another truncated recording. **SET THE CONTROLS FOR THE HEART OF THE SUN** cuts out after 13.17, just as Wright's spacey solo is starting to wind down.

Date: 15-11-1971
Location: Carnegie Hall, New York City, New York, USA
Track Listing: One Of These Days, Atom Heart Mother (Cuts)
Audio Rating: ★★★★
Miscellaneous: Yet another truncated recording. Maybe security staff were more alert. Enthusiastic audience, lots of whooping and clapping for **ONE OF THESE DAYS**. Meanwhile **ATOM HEART MOTHER** starts during Gilmour's electric guitar solo and ends about five minutes later.

Date: 16-11-1971
Location: Lisner Auditorium, George Washington University, Washington DC, USA
Track Listing: Embryo, Fat Old Sun, Set The Controls For The Heart Of The Sun, Atom Heart Mother, One Of These Days, Careful With That Axe, Eugene, Cymbaline, Echoes
Audio Rating: ★★★★
Miscellaneous: The *Washington Post* review of this concert: 'The band sounded sometimes like a screaming saw, sometimes like a fleet of intergalactic jets. A guitar with this group, became a screeching bird. Drums were explosions.'

Date: 20-11-1971
Location: Taft Auditorium, Cincinnati, Ohio, USA
Track Listing: Embryo, Fat Old Sun, Set The Controls For The Heart Of The Sun, Atom Heart Mother, Careful With That Axe, Eugene, Cymbaline, Echoes, Blues
Audio Rating: ★★★♪
Miscellaneous: **EMBRYO** lasts an incredible twenty-eight minutes – even longer than **ECHOES** as performed here – with a fairly interminable jam/Gilmour solo at the end. Last performances of **EMBRYO, FAT OLD SUN** and **CYMBALINE**. Was that a big sigh of relief?

1972

Date: 20-01-1972
Location: The Dome, Brighton, England
Track Listing: Breathe (Fades In), The Travel Sequence, Time, Breathe (Reprise), The Mortality Sequence, Money, Technical Problems And Tuning, Atom Heart Mother, Tuning, Careful With That Axe, Eugene
Audio Rating: ★★
Miscellaneous: The *Dark Side* material captured for the first time, though obviously still in embryonic form, and in a very raw recording. The excerpt from **BREATHE** only last nine seconds. The gig was also struck by technical problems: they get only two minutes-odd into **MONEY** before something breaks down, though the audience politely claps when Waters says something (it's barely audible). They then crank out a fifteen-minute version of **ATOM HEART MOTHER** and a **CAREFUL WITH THAT AXE, EUGENE** lasting eleven.

Date: 21-01-1972
Location: The Guildhall, Portsmouth, England
Track Listing: Speak To Me, Breathe, Travel Sequence, Time, Breathe (Reprise), The Mortality Sequence, Money, Us And Them, Any Colour You Like, Brain Damage, Eclipse, Tuning Up, More Tuning Up, One Of These Days, Set The Controls For The Heart Of The Sun, Echoes (Cuts), Echoes
Audio Rating: ★★★
Miscellaneous: A complete early version of *Dark Side*, though the lyrics in some cases are still first drafts. 'The Mortality Sequence' has long drawn-out organ notes from Wright, reminiscent of his pieces in **CIRRUS MINOR** or the 'Celestial Voices' section of **A SAUCERFUL OF SECRETS**, and spoken-word pieces from the Bible and Malcolm Muggeridge. Floyd circa 1969 might have been happy enough with that. **ANY COLOUR YOU LIKE** lasts only eighty seconds and features Gilmour doing high-pitched vocal scatting, while **ECLIPSE** is a hodge-podge aural freakout, probably most similar to the end of **BIKE**.

Date: 22-01-1972
Location: Winter Gardens, Bournemouth, England
Track Listing: Breathe, The Travel Sequence, Time, Breathe (Reprise), The Mortality Sequence, Money, Us And Them, Any Colour You Like, Brain Damage, Eclipse
Audio Rating: ★★★✓
Miscellaneous: No **SPEAK TO ME**. What was recorded is just as the previous gig, unsurprisingly.

Date: 23-01-1972
Location: The Guildhall, Southampton, England
Track Listing: Speak To Me, Breathe, The Travel Sequence, Time, Breathe (Reprise), The Mortality Sequence, Money, Us And Them, Any Colour You Like, Brain Damage, One Of These Days, Careful With That Axe, Eugene, Echoes, A Saucerful Of Secrets
Audio Rating: ★★
Miscellaneous: Very hissy, rather distant-sounding. **ONE OF THESE DAYS** has three full minutes of wind effects before the bass riff kicks in.

Date: 27-01-1972
Location: City Hall, Newcastle Upon Tyne, England
Track Listing: Breathe, The Travel Sequence, Time, Breathe (Reprise), The Mortality Sequence, Money, Us And Them, Any Colour You Like, Brain Damage, One Of These Days, Careful With That Axe, Eugene, Echoes, A Saucerful Of Secrets
Audio Rating: ★★✓
Miscellaneous: No **SPEAK TO ME**. Quieter moments barely audible, but when the band rocks (as on **MONEY** or **CAREFUL WITH THAT AXE, EUGENE**), it sounds decent.

Date: 28-01-1972
Location: Leeds University, Leeds, England
Track Listing: Speak To Me, Breathe, The Travel Sequence, Time, Breathe (Reprise), The Mortality Sequence, Money, Us And Them, Any Colour You Like, Brain Damage, Eclipse, One Of These Days, Careful With That Axe, Eugene, Echoes (Fade In), Set The Controls For The Heart Of The Sun, Blues
Audio Rating: ★★
Miscellaneous: **BRAIN DAMAGE** and **ECLIPSE** suffer from significant wobbliness, probably from dying batteries. **ECHOES** comes at the start of the vocals, and still lasts another thirty-one minutes.

Date: 12-02-1972
Location: City Hall, Sheffield, England
Track Listing: One Of These Days, Careful With That Axe, Eugene, Speak To Me, Breathe, The Travel Sequence, Time, Breathe (Reprise), The Mortality Sequence, Money, Us And Them, Any Colour You Like, Brain Damage, Eclipse, Set The Controls For The Heart Of The Sun, Echoes
Audio Rating: ★★↓
Miscellaneous: **US AND THEM** is listed on the bootleg notes as coming after 'The Mortality Sequence' and being split due to a tape flip, but it's just some Wright keyboards that sound like the intro to **US AND THEM** as 'The Mortality Sequence' fades out. **US AND THEM** actually comes after **MONEY**, as always in the *Dark Side* setlist. This show features the first performance of **ECLIPSE** as we know it from the album. It's a huge improvement over the earlier version.

Date: 17-02-1972
Location: Rainbow Theatre, London, England
Track Listing: Speak To Me, Breathe, Travel Sequence, Time, Breathe (Reprise), The Mortality Sequence, Money, Us And Them, Any Colour You Like, Brain Damage, Eclipse, Tuning Up, One Of These Days, Careful With That Axe, Eugene, Echoes, Tuning Up, Set The Controls For The Heart Of The Sun
Audio Rating: ★★★↓
Miscellaneous: Still slightly hissy but a significant improvement in audio clarity over previous *Dark Side* performances. **ANY COLOUR YOU LIKE** by now is over three minutes.

Date: 18-02-1972
Location: Rainbow Theatre, London, England
Track Listing: Speak To Me, Breathe, Travel Sequence, Time, Home Again, Mortality Sequence, Money, Us And Them, Any Colour You Like, Brain Damage, Eclipse, Tuning Up, One Of These Days, Tuning Up, Careful With That Axe, Eugene, Echoes
Audio Rating: ★★★
Miscellaneous: Much more hiss than the previous night, but there's still a good presence to the music.

Date: 19-02-1972
Location: Rainbow Theatre, London, England
Track Listing: Breathe (Fades In), On The Run, Time, Breathe (Reprise), The Mortality Sequence, Money, Us And Them, Any Colour You Like, Brain Damage, Eclipse, One Of These Days, Careful With That Axe, Eugene, Echoes, A Saucerful Of Secrets, Second Cud (Blues), Set The Controls For The Heart Of The Sun
Audio Rating: ★★★
Miscellaneous: Starts out murkier than the previous two nights, though it gets more crisp as it goes on. Includes their rather pointless blues encore.

Date: 20-02-1972
Location: Rainbow Theatre, London, England
Track Listing: Speak To Me (Cuts In), Breathe, Travel Sequence, Time, Breathe (Reprise), The Mortality Sequence, Money, Us And Them, Any Colour You Like, Brain Damage, Eclipse, One Of These Days, Careful With That Axe, Eugene, Echoes, A Saucerful Of Secrets, Blues, Set The Controls For The Heart Of The Sun
Audio Rating: ★★★★
Miscellaneous: A fourth night at the Rainbow in London. They must have thought they'd made it. Sound is very good, audio significantly more detailed – you can hear Mason's top-hat for example.

Date: 06-03-1972
Location: Tokyo Tallkukan, Tokyo, Japan
Track Listing: Speak To Me, Breathe, On The Run, Time, Breathe (Reprise), The Mortality Sequence, Money, Us And Them, Any Colour You Like, Brain Damage, Eclipse, Japanese Announcer, Tuning, One Of These Days, Careful With That Axe, Eugene, Echoes, A Saucerful Of Secrets
Audio Rating: ★★★
Miscellaneous: Murky sounding. **ECHOES** lasts a full half hour.

Date: 07-03-1972
Location: Tokyo Tallkukan, Tokyo, Japan
Track Listing: Speak To Me, Breathe, On The Run, Time, Breathe (Reprise), The Mortality Sequence, Money, Us And Them, Any Colour You Like, Brain Damage, Eclipse, One Of These Days, Careful With That Axe, Eugene, Echoes, Set The Controls For The Heart Of The Sun
Audio Rating: ★★↓
Miscellaneous: Murky, echoey and distant.

Date: 08-03-1972
Location: Festival Hall, Osaka, Japan

Track Listing: Speak To Me, Breathe, On The Run, Time, Breathe (Reprise), The Mortality Sequence, Money, Us And Them, Any Colour You Like, Brain Damage, Eclipse, Echoes
Audio Rating: ★★✦
Miscellaneous: Just the one track from the second set, for whatever reason.

Date: 09-03-1972
Location: Festival Hall, Osaka, Japan
Track Listing: Speak To Me, Breathe, The Travel Sequence, Time, Breathe (Reprise), The Mortality Sequence, Money, Us And Them, Any Colour You Like, Brain Damage, Eclipse, Tunings, One Of These Days, Tunings, Careful With That Axe, Eugene, Tunings, Echoes
Audio Rating: ★★
Miscellaneous: Quiet and murky. Only Gilmour's solos and Waters' scream in **CAREFUL WITH THAT AXE, EUGENE** cut through.

Date: 10-03-1972
Location: Tallkukan Hall, Kyoto, Japan
Track Listing: Speak To Me, Breathe, On The Run, Time, Breathe (Reprise), The Great Gig In The Sky, Money, Us And Them, Any Colour You Like, Brain Damage, Eclipse, One Of These Days, Careful With That Axe, Eugene, Echoes
Audio Rating: ★★✦
Miscellaneous: Still murky and distant-sounding, but little hiss.

Date: 13-03-1972
Location: Nakajima Sports Center, Sapporo, Hokkaido, Japan
Track Listing: Speak To Me, Breathe, On The Run, Time, Breathe (Reprise), The Great Gig In The Sky, Money, Us And Them, Any Colour You Like, Brain Damage, Eclipse, One Of These Days, Careful With That Axe, Eugene, Echoes, Atom Heart Mother
Audio Rating: ★★★✦
Miscellaneous: Much greater audio clarity. A now-rare outing for **ATOM HEART MOTHER**.

Date: 30-03-1972
Location: Free Trade Hall, Manchester, UK
Track Listing: Speak To Me, Breathe, The Travel Sequence, Time, Breathe (Reprise), The Mortality Sequence, Money, Us And Them, Any Colour You Like, Brain Damage, Eclipse (Cuts Off), One Of These Days, Careful With That Axe, Eugene, Echoes, Set The Controls For The Heart Of The Sun
Audio Rating: ★★★
Miscellaneous: **ECLIPSE** is cut off just at 'Everything under the sun is in tune'.

Date: 15-04-1972
Location: Sportatorium, Hollywood, Florida, USA
Track Listing: Us And Them, Any Colour You Like, Brain Damage, Eclipse, One Of These Days, Careful With That Axe, Eugene, Tuning Up, Echoes, Set The Controls For The Heart Of The Sun
Audio Rating: ★✦
Miscellaneous: Misses the first half of *Dark Side*. Sound is very wobbly. **US AND THEM** lasts just sixteen seconds, during the 'For want of a price' lyric.

Date: 16-04-1972
Location: Township Auditorium, Columbia, South Carolina, USA
Track Listing: Breathe, Travel Sequence, Time, Breathe (Reprise), The Mortality Sequence, Money, Us And Them, Any Colour You Like, Brain Damage (Cut), One Of These Days, Careful With That Axe, Eugene, Echoes, Atom Heart Mother
Audio Rating: ★★★✦
Miscellaneous: Missing **SPEAK TO ME** and **ECLIPSE**, while **BRAIN DAMAGE** cuts towards the end.

Date: 20-04-1972
Location: Syria Mosque Theatre, Pittsburgh, Pennsylvania, USA
Track Listing: Speak To Me, Breathe, The Travel Sequence, Time, Breathe (Reprise), The Mortality Sequence, Money, Us And Them, Any Colour You Like, Brain Damage, Eclipse, One Of These Days, Careful With That Axe, Eugene, Echoes
Audio Rating: ★★★
Miscellaneous: **ECHOES** lasts a mere eighteen minutes and thirty seconds.

Date: 23-04-1972
Location: Music Hall, Cincinnati, Ohio, USA
Track Listing: Speak To Me, Breathe, The Travel Sequence, Time, Breathe (Reprise), The Mortality Sequence, Money, Us And Them, Any Colour You Like, Brain Damage (Cut), Eclipse, One Of These Days (Cut),

Careful With That Axe, Eugene, Echoes (Cut), Saucerful Of Secrets
Audio Rating: ★★★
Miscellaneous: **BRAIN DAMAGE** has a faded cut at 3.10, **ONE OF THESE DAYS** one at 1.38, and **ECHOES** two – the first at 15.23, then it cuts off entirely at 20.09. Sound is a little hissy but generally clear enough.

Date: 27-04-1972
Location: Ford Auditorium, Detroit, Michigan, USA
Track Listing: Breathe, The Travel Sequence, Time, Breathe (Reprise), The Mortality Sequence, Money, Us And Them, Any Colour You Like, Brain Damage, Eclipse, One Of These Days, Careful With That Axe, Eugene, Echoes, Set The Controls For The Heart Of The Sun, Blues
Audio Rating: ★★♩
Miscellaneous: Fades in at the start of **BREATHE**. Their blues jam gets an outing here, and serves as a reminder of why bands need proper songs.

Date: 28-04-1972
Location: Auditorium Theater, Chicago, Illinois, USA
Track Listing: Speak To Me, Breathe, The Travel Sequence, Time, Breathe (Reprise), The Mortality Sequence, Money, Us And Them, Any Colour You Like, Brain Damage, Eclipse, One Of These Days, Careful With That Axe, Eugene, Echoes, Set The Controls For The Heart Of The Sun
Audio Rating: ★★★★
Miscellaneous: Lovely crisp sound, only problem is it sometimes gets overloaded when the band is at its loudest.

Date: 02-05-1972
Location: Carnegie Hall, New York City, New York, USA
Track Listing: One Of These Days, Careful With That Axe, Eugene, Echoes, A Saucerful Of Secrets
Audio Rating: ★★★
Miscellaneous: Setlist seems very short, but apparently this is the entire concert. Still, they had got to Carnegie Hall – this was the second of two nights there. There's the sound of a big flare or pyrotechnic at Waters' first scream during **CAREFUL WITH THAT AXE, EUGENE**, which you can imagine as being very impressive.

Date: 04-05-1972
Location: Boston Music Hall, Boston, Massachusetts, USA
Track Listing: Speak To Me, Breathe, The Travel Sequence, Time, Breathe (Reprise), The Mortality Sequence, Money, Us And Them, Any Colour You Like, Brain Damage (Tape Flip), Eclipse, Tune Ups, One Of These Days, Careful With That Axe, Eugene, Echoes (Tape Flip)
Audio Rating: ★★♩
Miscellaneous: Muffled and indistinct. There are two tape flip gaps: at 2.51 during **BRAIN DAMAGE**, and at 14.17 during **ECHOES**.

Date: 18-05-1972
Location: Deutschlandhalle, West Berlin, West Germany
Track Listing: Speak To Me, Breathe, The Travel Sequence, Time, Breathe (Reprise), The Mortality Sequence, Money, Us And Them, Any Colour You Like, Brain Damage, Eclipse, One Of These Days, Careful With That Axe, Eugene, Echoes, Set The Controls For The Heart Of The Sun
Audio Rating: ★★★★
Miscellaneous: Fine recording of a very good performance. The atmosphere during **CAREFUL WITH THAT AXE, EUGENE** is beautifully worked.

Date: 21-05-1972
Location: British Rock Meeting, Insel Grun, Germersheim, West Germany
Track Listing: Atom Heart Mother, Set The Controls For The Heart Of The Sun, One Of These Days, Careful With That Axe, Eugene, Echoes, A Saucerful Of Secrets
Audio Rating: ★★★★
Miscellaneous: Performance at a German music festival (despite the name), hence the shorter setlist. Sound is unusually clear for this kind of event.

Date: 22-05-1972
Location: Amsterdam Rock Circus, Olympic Stadium, Amsterdam, Netherlands
Track Listing: Atom Heart Mother, One Of These Days, Echoes, Careful With That Axe, Eugene, A Saucerful Of Secrets
Audio Rating: ★★♩
Miscellaneous: Another European festival, with the group headlining. The last time **ATOM HEART MOTHER** was played. Audio very murky.

Date: 28-06-1972
Location: The Dome, Brighton, England
Track Listing: Speak To Me, Breathe, The Travel Sequence, Time, Breathe (Reprise), The Mortality Sequence, Money, Us And Them, Any Colour You Like, Brain Damage, Eclipse, One Of These Days, Careful With That Axe, Eugene, Echoes, Set The Controls For The Heart Of The Sun
Audio Rating: ★★★↙
Miscellaneous: Back at The Dome to replace the shortened gig there from January. **TIME** now has the familiar clocks and alarms opening.

Date: 10-09-1972
Location: McFarlin Auditorium, Dallas, Texas, USA
Track Listing: The Mortality Sequence (Fade In), Money, Us And Them, Any Colour You Like, Brain Damage, Eclipse, One Of These Days, Careful With That Axe, Eugene (Cut), Careful With That Axe, Eugene (Continued), Set The Controls For The Heart Of The Sun, Echoes
Audio Rating: ★★★
Miscellaneous: After a near-three month break, 'The Mortality Sequence' now sounds closer to **THE GREAT GIG IN THE SKY**, at least in terms of Wright's piano work, though it still has the spoken word pieces. The rest is as you were. It's noticeable though how silent the audience is at quieter musical moments.

Date: 22-09-1972
Location: Hollywood Bowl, Los Angeles, California, USA
Track Listing: Breathe, The Travel Sequence, Time, Breathe (Reprise), The Mortality Sequence, Money, Us And Them, Any Colour You Like, Brain Damage, Eclipse, One Of These Days, Careful With That Axe, Eugene, Echoes, A Saucerful Of Secrets, Set The Controls For The Heart Of The Sun
Audio Rating: ★★★↙
Miscellaneous: No **SPEAK TO ME**. The last time **A SAUCERFUL OF SECRETS** was played. Audio almost very good except for the vocals sounding unclear.

Date: 23-09-1972
Location: Winterland Auditorium, San Francisco, California, USA
Track Listing: Speak To Me, Breathe, The Travel Section, Time, Breathe (Reprise), The Mortality Sequence, Money, Us And Them, Any Colour You Like, Brain Damage, Eclipse, One Of These Days, Careful With That Axe, Eugene
Audio Rating: ★★↙
Miscellaneous: Sounds like it was being played in a room down the hall. By now, a very standard setlist.

Date: 24-09-1972
Location: Winterland Auditorium, San Francisco, California, USA
Track Listing: Speak To Me, Breathe, The Travel Section, Time, Breathe (Reprise), The Mortality Sequence, Money, Us And Them, Any Colour You Like, Brain Damage, Eclipse, One Of These Days, Careful With That Axe, Eugene, Echoes
Audio Rating: ★★★
Miscellaneous: Somewhat more present and detailed than the previous night in San Francisco, but not by much.

Date: 21-10-1972
Location: Wembley Empire Pool, London, England
Track Listing: Speak To Me, Breathe, The Travel Section, Time, Breathe (Reprise), The Mortality Sequence, Money, Us And Them, Any Colour You Like, Brain Damage, Eclipse (Cut), Intermission And Announcer, One Of These Days, Tuneups, Careful With That Axe, Eugene, Echoes (Fade), Echoes (Continued), Set The Controls For The Heart Of The Sun, Tuneups And Audience, Blues
Audio Rating: ★★★↙
Miscellaneous: **ECLIPSE** cuts right at 'Everything under the sun' and **ECHOES** cuts at 19.32 then continues on another track for another nearly six minutes (just when Gilmour's arpeggio guitar solo comes in).

Date: 10-11-1972
Location: K.B. Hallen, Copenhagen, Denmark
Track Listing: Speak To Me, Breathe, The Travel Section, Time, Breathe (Reprise), The Mortality Sequence, Money, Us And Them, Any Colour You Like, Brain Damage, Eclipse, One Of These Days, Careful With That Axe, Eugene, Echoes
Audio Rating: ★★★↙
Miscellaneous: A final European tour to end the year. They really worked very, very hard. Audio is somewhat muffled but pretty clear and detailed.

Date: 12-11-1972
Location: Ernst Merck Halle, Hamburg, West Germany
Track Listing: Speak To Me, Breathe, The Travel Section, Time, Breathe (Reprise), The Mortality Sequence, Money, Us And Them, Any Colour You Like, Brain Damage, Eclipse, One Of These Days, Careful With That Axe, Eugene, Echoes, Set The Controls For The Heart Of The Sun
Audio Rating: ★★★
Miscellaneous: Sound varies, becoming more muffled and more clear at various points, but generally better in the higher frequencies. (Mason's bass drum is an indistinct thwomp, but Wright's keyboard and Gilmour's solo are generally detailed.)

Date: 14-11-1972
Location: Phillips Halle, Düsseldorf, West Germany
Track Listing: Speak To Me, Breathe, The Travel Section, Time, Breathe (Reprise), The Mortality Sequence, Money, Us And Them, Any Colour You Like, Brain Damage, Eclipse, One Of These Days, Careful With That Axe, Eugene, Echoes, Set The Controls For The Heart Of The Sun
Audio Rating: ★★★★
Miscellaneous: Excellent sound. The band sound hugely authoritative – viciously powerful when they want to be, but also capable of great delicacy.

Date: 16-11-1972
Location: Festhalle, Frankfurt, West Germany
Track Listing: Speak To Me, Breathe, The Travel Section, Time, Breathe (Reprise), The Mortality Sequence, Money, Us And Them, Any Colour You Like, Brain Damage, Eclipse, One Of These Days, Careful With That Axe, Eugene, Echoes, Set The Controls For The Heart Of The Sun
Audio Rating: ★★★♩
Miscellaneous: Not quite as good audio as the previous night in West Germany, but pretty good nonetheless. **SET THE CONTROLS FOR THE HEART OF THE SUN** staggers on, its other-worldly atmosphere quite at odds with the warmth and humanity of the *Dark Side* songs – but also demonstrating the group's remarkable range.

Date: 17-11-1972
Location: Festhalle, Frankfurt, West Germany
Track Listing: Speak To Me, Breathe, The Travel Section, Time, Breathe (Reprise), The Mortality Sequence, Money, Us And Them, Any Colour You Like, Brain Damage, Eclipse, One Of These Days, Careful With That Axe, Eugene, Echoes, Set The Controls For The Heart Of The Sun
Audio Rating: ★★★★
Miscellaneous: **ANY COLOUR YOU LIKE** is by now closer to its final, studio version, with Gilmour's lead and Wright's keyboards, rather than Gilmour's vocal scatting. It's exciting to hear the album coming together. The sound here is very good.

Date: 29-11-1972
Location: Palais Des Sports, Poitiers, France
Track Listing: Speak To Me, Breathe, The Travel Section, Time, Breathe (Reprise), The Mortality Sequence, Money, Us And Them, Any Colour You Like, Brain Damage, Eclipse, One Of These Days, Careful With That Axe, Eugene, Echoes
Audio Rating: ★★★♩
Miscellaneous: A noisier audience than has been usual up until now. Some entertaining dialogue from those around the taper: 'Il y a encore du rouge?' ('Is there any more red wine?') and 'Assis, bande de cons!' ('Sit down, you idiots!').

Date: 01-12-1972
Location: Palais Des Sports De Saint-Ouen, Paris, France
Track Listing: The Travel Section (Incomplete), Time, Breathe (Reprise), The Mortality Sequence, Money, Us And Them, Any Colour You Like, Brain Damage, Eclipse, One Of These Days, Careful With That Axe, Eugene, Blues, Echoes, Childhood's End
Audio Rating: ★★★★
Miscellaneous: Missing **SPEAK TO ME** and **BREATHE,** comes in maybe halfway through 'The Travel Sequence'. A first outing for **CHILDHOOD'S END**. *Obscured by Clouds* had been released in the UK on 2 June 1972 – odd that none of its songs had been played live previously.

Date: 05-12-1972
Location: Sport Paleis Vorst National, Brussels, Belgium
Track Listing: Speak To Me, Breathe, The Travel Section, Time, Breathe (Reprise), The Mortality Sequence, Money, Us And Them, Any Colour

You Like, Brain Damage, Eclipse, One Of Those Days, Careful With That Axe, Eugene, Echoes, Childhood's End
Audio Rating: ★↙
Miscellaneous: Wobbly and distant-sounding.

Date: 07-12-1972
Location: Palais Des Sports, Lille, France
Track Listing: Speak To Me, Breathe, The Travel Section, Time, The Mortality Sequence, Money, Us And Them, Any Colour You Like, Brain Damage, Eclipse, One Of These Days, Careful With That Axe, Eugene, Echoes
Audio Rating: ★★★↙
Miscellaneous: Some 'Pictish' scatting from Waters during **CAREFUL WITH THAT AXE, EUGENE**. A rather shorter gig than from the rest of the year: only three encores, not really a second set any more. **ECHOES** doesn't even last twenty minutes. Guess they were feeling tired after an extremely busy year.

Date: 09-12-1972
Location: Hallenstadion, Zurich, Switzerland
Track Listing: Speak To Me, Breathe, The Travel Section, Time, The Mortality Sequence, Money, Us And Them, Any Colour You Like, Brain Damage, Eclipse, One Of These Days, Careful With That Axe, Eugene, Echoes
Audio Rating: ★★★↙
Miscellaneous: **MONEY** cuts near the end (at 5.02, during 'Share it fairly, but don't take a slice of my pie') due to a tape flip.

Date: 10-12-1972
Location: Palais Des Sports, Lyon, France
Track Listing: Speak To Me, Breathe, The Travel Section, Time, Breathe (Reprise), The Mortality Sequence, Money, Us And Them, Any Colour You Like, Brain Damage, Eclipse, Tuneup, One Of These Days, Tuneup, Careful With That Axe, Eugene, Tuneup, Echoes
Audio Rating: ★★★
Miscellaneous: Band do sound tired (Gilmour's voice sounds a bit flat), though Waters does his Pictish ranting bit on **CAREFUL WITH THAT AXE, EUGENE** (from around 4.42). The audience chant something before **ECHOES** that sounds something like 'Heartbeat! Heartbeat! Heartbeat!' but it's hard to make out.

1973
Date: 13-01-1973
Location: Palais Des Sports De La Porte De Versailles, Paris, France
Track Listing: One Of These Days, Obscured By Clouds, When You're In, Careful With That Axe, Eugene, Echoes
Audio Rating: ★★
Miscellaneous: One of the Roland Petit Ballet nights. Audio unfortunately sounds like it was being recorded with a hand-held cassette recorder: very amateurish.

Date: 06-03-1973
Location: Kiel Auditorium, St Louis, Missouri, USA
Track Listing: Echoes, Obscured By Clouds, When You're In, Childhood's End (Cut), Childhood's End (Continued), Careful With That Axe, Eugene, Speak To Me, Us And Them (Cut), Us And Them (Continued), Any Colour You Like, Brain Damage, Eclipse, One Of These Days
Audio Rating: ★★★
Miscellaneous: As played during 1973, **OBSCURED BY CLOUDS** has a long introduction by Wright, lasting around two minutes. **CHILDHOOD'S END** cuts after seven minutes, being elongated by numerous solos. The opening bass notes to **CAREFUL WITH THAT AXE, EUGENE** are greeted by someone yelling 'Oh WOW!' **US AND THEM** cuts during the 'Down … and out' verse.

Date: 07-03-1973
Location: International Amphitheatre, Chicago, Illinois, USA
Track Listing: Echoes, Obscured By Clouds, When You're In, Childhood's End, Careful With That Axe, Eugene, Speak To Me, Breathe, On The Run, Time, Breathe (Reprise), The Great Gig In The Sky, Money, Us And Them, Any Colour You Like, Brain Damage, Eclipse, One Of These Days
Audio Rating: ★★★
Miscellaneous: Quieter moments work better, but loud sections overload the recorder.

Date: 08-03-1973
Location: The Fieldhouse, University of Cincinnati, Cincinnati, Ohio, USA
Track Listing: Echoes, Obscured By Clouds, When You're In, Childhood's End, Careful With That Axe, Eugene, Speak To Me, Breathe, On The Run, Time, Breathe (Reprise), The Great

Gig In The Sky, Money, Us And Them, Any Colour You Like, Brain Damage (Cut)
Audio Rating: ★★★✓
Miscellaneous: Missing **ECLIPSE** and the usual encore **ONE OF THESE DAYS**.

Date: 10-03-1973
Location: Memorial Gymnasium, Kent State University, Kent, Ohio, USA
Track Listing: Echoes, Obscured By Clouds, When You're In, Childhood's End, Careful With That Axe, Eugene, Speak To Me, Breathe, On The Run, Time, Breathe (Reprise), The Great Gig In The Sky, Money, Us And Them, Any Colour You Like, Brain Damage, Eclipse
Audio Rating: ★★✓
Miscellaneous: The audio isn't great, which is a shame because the screams on **CAREFUL WITH THAT AXE, EUGENE** are amazing.

Date: 11-03-1973
Location: Maple Leaf Gardens, Toronto, Ontario, Canada
Track Listing: Echoes, Obscured By Clouds, When You're In, Set The Controls For The Heart Of The Sun, Careful With That Axe, Eugene, Speak To Me, Breathe, On The Run, Time, Breathe (Reprise), The Great Gig In The Sky, Money, Us And Them, Any Colour You Like, Brain Damage, Eclipse, Crowd, One Of These Days
Audio Rating: ★★★✓
Miscellaneous: **SET THE CONTROLS FOR THE HEART OF THE SUN** really sounds very archaic in the setlist compared to the *Dark Side* material, but the audience greet it very warmly.

Date: 14-03-1973
Location: Boston Music Hall, Boston, Massachusetts, USA
Track Listing: Careful With That Axe, Eugene, Obscured By Clouds, When You're In, Set The Controls For The Heart Of The Sun (Tape Flip), Echoes, Speak To Me, Breathe, On The Run, Time, Breathe (Reprise), The Great Gig in the Sky, Money, (Tape Flip), Us And Them, Any Colour You Like, Brain Damage, Eclipse (Tape Flip), Tune Ups, One Of These Days
Audio Rating: ★★★★
Miscellaneous: For some reason the bootleg has **ATOM HEART MOTHER** listed in place of **OBSCURED BY CLOUDS** and **WHEN YOU'RE IN**, but the last time that song was played was on 22 May 1972. The audio is occasionally overloaded but during quieter moments is terrific.

Date: 17-03-1973
Location: Radio City Music Hall, New York City, New York, USA
Track Listing: Obscured By Clouds, When You're In, Audience/Tuning, Set The Controls For The Heart Of The Sun, Audience/Tuning, Careful With That Axe, Eugene, Audience/Tuning, Echoes, Speak To Me, Breathe, On The Run, Time, Breathe (Reprise), The Great Gig In The Sky, Money, Us And Them (Cut), Any Colour You Like, Brain Damage, Eclipse, One Of These Days
Audio Rating: ★★★✓
Miscellaneous: **US AND THEM** only lasts two minutes forty-one seconds.

Date: 18-05-1973
Location: Earl's Court Exhibition Hall, London, England
Track Listing: Obscured By Clouds, Set The Controls For The Heart Of The Sun, Careful With That Axe, Eugene, Echoes, Speak To Me, Breathe, On The Run, Time, Breathe (Reprise), The Great Gig In The Sky, Money, Us And Them, Any Colour You Like, Brain Damage, Eclipse, One Of These Days
Audio Rating: ★★★✓
Miscellaneous: Lengthy versions of **OBSCURED BY CLOUDS** with extended solos. The bootleg has **WHEN YOU'RE IN** listed in place of **SET THE CONTROLS FOR THE HEART OF THE SUN**.

Date: 19-05-1973
Location: Earl's Court Exhibition Hall, London, England
Track Listing: Obscured By Clouds, When You're In, Tuning, Set The Controls For The Heart Of The Sun, Tuning, Careful With That Axe, Eugene, Echoes, Speak To Me, Breathe, On The Run, Time, Breathe (Reprise), The Great Gig In The Sky, Money, Us And Them, Any Colour You Like, Brain Damage, Eclipse, Tuning, One Of These Days
Audio Rating: ★★★✓
Miscellaneous: **OBSCURED BY CLOUDS** lasts just six minutes. Lots of clapping along to **ONE OF THESE DAYS**, audience hitherto respectfully quiet.

Date: 17-06-1973
Location: Performing Arts Center, Saratoga, New York, USA
Track Listing: Obscured By Clouds, When You're In, Set The Controls For The Heart Of The Sun, Careful With That Axe, Eugene, Echoes, Speak To Me, Breathe, On The Run, Time, Breathe (Reprise), The Great Gig In The Sky, Money, Us And Them, Any Colour You Like, Brain Damage, Eclipse, One Of These Days
Audio Rating: ★★★★
Miscellaneous: Some excellent bottom-end on this recording, though the higher frequencies can be a bit piercing.

Date: 18-06-1973
Location: Roosevelt Stadium, Jersey City, New Jersey, USA
Track Listing: Obscured By Clouds, When You're In, Set The Controls For The Heart Of The Sun, Careful With That Axe, Eugene, Echoes, Speak To Me, Breathe, On The Run, Time, Breathe (Reprise), The Great Gig In The Sky, Money, Us And Them, Any Colour You Like, Brain Damage, Eclipse, One Of These Days
Audio Rating: ★★★♪
Miscellaneous: Overly echoey, which is unfortunate because otherwise the audio is quite crisp.

Date: 20-06-1973
Location: Merriweather Post Pavilion, Columbia, Maryland, USA
Track Listing: Obscured By Clouds, When You're In, Set The Controls For The Heart Of The Sun, Careful With That Axe, Eugene, Echoes, Speak To Me, Breathe, On The Run, Time, Breathe (Reprise), The Great Gig in the Sky, Money, Us And Them, Any Colour You Like, Brain Damage, Eclipse, One Of These Days
Audio Rating: ★★★
Miscellaneous: Vocals occasionally sound a little flat, which is unusual.

Date: 24-06-1973
Location: Blossom Music Center, Cuyahoga Falls, Ohio, USA
Track Listing: Obscured By Clouds, When You're In, Speak To Me, Breathe, On The Run, Time, Breathe (Reprise), The Great Gig In The Sky
Audio Rating: ★♪
Miscellaneous: A very incomplete recording, and awful sound.

Date: 28-06-1973
Location: Sportatorium, Hollywood, Florida, USA
Track Listing: Obscured By Clouds, When You're In, Set The Controls For The Heart Of The Sun, Careful With That Axe, Eugene (Cuts), Echoes, Speak To Me, Breathe, On The Run, Time, Breathe (Reprise), The Great Gig In The Sky, Money, Us And Them, Any Colour You Like, Brain Damage, Eclipse, One Of These Days
Audio Rating: ★★★★♪
Miscellaneous: The cuts in **CAREFUL WITH THAT AXE, EUGENE** occur at the beginning, with the full electric tempest and screams coming at about 0.20. Audio is very good, clear and well balanced.

Date: 29-06-1973
Location: Tampa Stadium, Tampa, Florida, USA
Track Listing: Obscured By Clouds, When You're In, Set The Controls For The Heart Of The Sun, Careful With That Axe, Eugene, Echoes, Speak To Me, Breathe, On The Run, Time, The Great Gig in the Sky, Money, Us And Them, Any Colour You Like, Brain Damage, Eclipse, One Of These Days
Audio Rating: ★★★
Miscellaneous: Quite a lot of nearby audience chatter, which might appeal as testimony to the event to some, or deter as distraction from the music to others. In any case, there's quite a lot of it, with about two minutes before **SET THE CONTROLS FOR THE HEART OF THE SUN** gets going, for example.

Date: 12-10-1973
Location: Olympiahalle, Munich, West Germany
Track Listing: Obscured By Clouds, When You're In, Set The Controls For The Heart Of The Sun, Careful With That Axe, Eugene, Echoes, Speak To Me, Breathe, On The Run, Time, Breathe (Reprise), The Great Gig In The Sky, Money, Us And Them, Any Colour You Like, Brain Damage (Cut), Eclipse, One Of These Days
Audio Rating: ★★♪
Miscellaneous: There's a cut at the start of **BRAIN DAMAGE**, but it's before the lyrics and the intro is repetitive in a hypnotic kind of way,

so you don't really notice. You can hear a shift in audience ambience, though.

Date: 13-10-1973
Location: Stadthalle, Vienna, Austria
Track Listing: Obscured By Clouds, When You're In, Set The Controls For The Heart Of The Sun, Careful With That Axe, Eugene, Echoes, Speak To Me, Breathe, On The Run, Time, Breathe (Reprise), The Great Gig In The Sky, Money, Us And Them, Any Colour You Like, Brain Damage, Eclipse, One Of These Days
Audio Rating: ★★★⸍
Miscellaneous: The last time **SET THE CONTROLS FOR THE HEART OF THE SUN** was played by Pink Floyd. Performance is very good. Sound is quite variable, for some reason. It is generally better during the first set.

Date: 04-11-1973
Location: Rainbow Theatre, London, England (Early Show)
Track Listing: Speak To Me, Breathe, On The Run, Time, Breathe (Reprise), The Great Gig In The Sky, Money, Us And Them, Any Colour You Like, Brain Damage, Eclipse, Obscured By Clouds, When You're In
Audio Rating: ★★★⸍
Miscellaneous: The last time **OBSCURED BY CLOUDS** and **WHEN YOU'RE IN** were played. Shame the Gilmour-led band didn't play more deep cuts. The Rainbow shows were benefits for Robert Wyatt of Soft Machine, who had become paralysed from the waist down after falling out of a fourth-floor window. (He had drummed on two tracks from Syd Barrett's *The Madcap Laughs* in 1970.) The seating capacity in those days was just 3,040.

1974

Date: 22-06-1974
Location: Parc Des Expositions, Colmar, France
Track Listing: Shine On You Crazy Diamond, Raving And Drooling, Echoes, Speak To Me, Breathe, On The Run, Time, Breathe (Reprise), The Great Gig In The Sky, Money, Us And Them, Any Colour You Like, Brain Damage, Eclipse
Audio Rating: ★★★⸍
Miscellaneous: The first gig in seven months took place in Toulouse on 18 June. This concert, in Colmar (a town numbering just 64,771 in 1975, near the German and Swiss borders) was four days later. Instruments sometimes superb, sometimes muffled, while the vocals occasionally sound a bit flat (**THE GREAT GIG IN THE SKY** sounds quite laboured). As throughout the 1974 tours, **ON THE RUN** is 50 per cent longer than its studio version, taking some ninety seconds before the synthesiser pattern kicks in, and **SHINE ON YOU CRAZY DIAMOND** starts with a reedy organ solo before the 'Syd's Theme' motif, rather than the familiar static-frieze fade-in.

Date: 24-06-1974
Location: Palais De Sports, Paris, France
Track Listing: Shine On You Crazy Diamond, Raving And Drooling, Echoes (Cut), Speak To Me, Breathe, On The Run, Time, Breathe (Reprise), The Great Gig In The Sky, Money, Us And Them, Any Colour You Like, Brain Damage, Eclipse, One Of These Days
Audio Rating: ★★⸍
Miscellaneous: Gilmour's stratospheric guitar leads during **ECHOES** sound amazing, despite the bad audio.

Date: 04-11-1974
Location: Usher Hall, Edinburgh, Scotland
Track Listing: You Gotta Be Crazy
Audio Rating: ★★★
Miscellaneous: You can hear why 'You Gotta Be Crazy' had to be revised to become **DOGS**. Too many words, the structure doesn't feel coherent, and it's all lacking colour or variety.

Date: 05-11-1974
Location: Usher Hall, Edinburgh, Scotland
Track Listing: Shine On You Crazy Diamond, Raving And Drooling, Echoes, Speak To Me, The Great Gig In The Sky (Cut), The Great Gig In The Sky (Restart), Money, Us And Them, Any Colour You Like, Brain Damage, Eclipse
Audio Rating: ★★★
Miscellaneous: Quite a lot of hiss, though the instruments are pretty clear.

Date: 09-11-1974
Location: The Odeon, Newcastle Upon Tyne, England
Track Listing: Shine On You Crazy Diamond, Raving And Drooling, Gotta Be Crazy, Speak To Me, Breathe, On The Run, Time, Breathe (Reprise), The Great Gig In The Sky, Money, Us And Them, Any Colour You Like, Brain Damage, Eclipse (Fades), Echoes

Audio Rating: ★★★
Miscellaneous: A bit of sarcastic clapping before they start. Bet it's been a while since that happened. Vocals sound particularly bad – a few tones deeper, as though slurred. Which is strange because the instrumentation is fine.

Date: 15-11-1974
Location: Empire Pool, Wembley, London, England
Track Listing: Shine On You Crazy Diamond, Jimmy Young Intro, Raving And Drooling, You Gotta Be Crazy, Speak To Me, Breathe, On The Run, Time, Breathe (Reprise), The Great Gig In The Sky, Money, Us And Them, Any Colour You Like, Brain Damage, Eclipse
Audio Rating: ★★★
Miscellaneous: Recorded for BBC radio, hence the Jimmy Young intro.

Date: 16-11-1974
Location: Empire Pool, Wembley, London, England
Track Listing: Intro, Shine On You Crazy Diamond, Tuneups, Intro, Raving And Drooling, Tuneups, You Gotta Be Crazy, Speak To Me, Breathe, On The Run, Time, Breathe (Reprise), The Great Gig In The Sky, Money, Us And Them, Any Colour You Like, Brain Damage, Eclipse
Audio Rating: ★★★♪
Miscellaneous: Both 'Raving and Drooling' and 'You Gotta Be Crazy' are performed well, though their subsequent superior incarnations do demonstrate the wisdom of Waters in holding them from *Wish You Were Here* and reworking them into **SHEEP** and **DOGS**. 'Raving and Drooling', for example, has an **ECHOES**-like patience in working through the gradations of its sound, which is nice but demands a certain forbearance, while during 'Gotta Be Crazy' Gilmour quite clearly struggles with the vocal section, and the Waters-sung climax doesn't achieve anything like the cumulative force it wants to.

Date: 17-11-1974
Location: Empire Pool, Wembley, London, England
Track Listing: Raving And Drooling, You Gotta Be Crazy (Cut), Shine On You Crazy Diamond, Speak To Me, Breathe, On The Run, Time, Breathe (Reprise), The Great Gig In The Sky (Cut), Money, Us And Them, Any Colour You Like, Brain Damage, Eclipse
Audio Rating: ★★★♪
Miscellaneous: The cut in 'You Gotta Be Crazy' comes in the first few seconds and is barely noticeable. The cut in **THE GREAT GIG IN THE SKY**, meanwhile, comes near the end and is just a brief fade. The performance of **ECHOES** is very good instrumentally but sounds a bit flat vocally.

Date: 19-11-1974
Location: Trentham Gardens, Stoke-On-Trent, England
Track Listing: Speak To Me, Breathe, On The Run, Time, Breathe (Reprise), The Great Gig In The Sky, Money, Us And Them, Any Colour You Like, Brain Damage, Eclipse, Echoes
Audio Rating: ★★★
Miscellaneous: Only the *Dark Side* set available from this bootleg. Band sound like they're struggling to generate momentum.

Date: 29-11-1974
Location: Empire Theatre, Liverpool, England
Track Listing: Raving And Drooling, You've Gotta Be Crazy, Shine On You Crazy Diamond (Tape Flip), Speak To Me, Breathe, On The Run, Time, Breathe (Reprise), The Great Gig In The Sky, Money, Us And Them (Cut/Tape Flip), Any Colour You Like, Brain Damage, Eclipse
Audio Rating: ★★♪
Miscellaneous: Band sound quite energetic, audience also sounding enthusiastic, but audio is poor and inconsistent. Waters: 'This is a song about Syd Barrett. It's called Shine On You Crazy Diamond.'

Date: 09-12-1974
Location: The Palace Theatre, Manchester, England
Track Listing: Raving And Drooling, You've Gotta Be Crazy, Shine On You Crazy Diamond, Speak To Me, Breathe, On The Run, Time, Breathe (Reprise), The Great Gig In The Sky, Money, Us And Them, Any Colour You Like, Brain Damage, Eclipse, Echoes
Audio Rating: ★★★♪
Miscellaneous: Whatever speaker the keyboards are coming out of, the recorder seems to be standing right next to it at the beginning of the concert, but fortunately the sound becomes more centred later on.

Date: 13-12-1974
Location: Hippodrome, Bristol, England
Track Listing: Raving And Drooling, You Gotta Be Crazy, Shine On You Crazy Diamond, Speak To Me, Breathe, On The Run, Time, Breathe (Reprise), The Great Gig In The Sky, Money, Us And Them, Any Colour You Like, Brain Damage, Eclipse, Echoes
Audio Rating: ★★
Miscellaneous: Awful audio, but the band sound on good form.

Date: 14-12-1974
Location: Hippodrome, Bristol, England
Track Listing: Introduction, Raving And Drooling, Gotta Be Crazy, Shine On You Crazy Diamond, Speak To Me, Breathe, On The Run, Time, Breathe (Reprise), The Great Gig In The Sky, Money, Us And Them, Any Colour You Like, Brain Damage, Eclipse, Echoes
Audio Rating: ★★★♪
Miscellaneous: A second night in Bristol. The introduction has a rare Gilmour vocal interjection, with him shouting 'Hello!' before Waters takes over. The performance of **SHINE ON** is particularly outstanding, with excellent soloing from Gilmour and Wright. The rest of the gig is very, very good.

1975

Date: 04-08-1975
Location: Pacific National Exhibition Park, Vancouver, British Columbia, Canada
Track Listing: Raving And Drooling, You Gotta Be Crazy, Shine On You Crazy Diamond I-V, Have A Cigar, Shine On You Crazy Diamond VI-IX, Speak To Me, Breathe, On The Run, Time, Breathe (Reprise), The Great Gig In The Sky, Money, Us And Them (Tape Flip), Any Colour You Like, Brain Damage, Eclipse
Audio Rating: ★★★♪
Miscellaneous: Quite clear sounding, but very subdued audio.

Date: 10-04-1975
Location: Seattle Center Coliseum, Seattle, Washington, USA
Track Listing: Raving And Drooling, Audience & Tunings, You've Gotta Be Crazy, Audience & Tunings, Shine On You Crazy Diamond Parts I-V, Have A Cigar, Shine On You Crazy Diamond Parts VI-IX, Speak To Me, Breathe, On The Run, Time, Breathe (Reprise), The Great Gig In The Sky, Money, Us And Them, Any Colour You Like, Brain Damage, Eclipse, Echoes
Audio Rating: ★★★★
Miscellaneous: *Wish You Were Here* was not released until 12 September 1975, but the tracks from it here are close to their studio versions, which might say something about how methodically the group worked on its material. The intro for **SHINE ON YOU CRAZY DIAMOND**, for example, has changed to become close to its final version. 'Raving and Drooling' and 'You Gotta Be Crazy', however, haven't changed from their previous live incarnations. **HAVE A CIGAR** has a slightly lengthier introduction.

Date: 13-04-1975
Location: Cow Palace, Daly City, California, USA
Track Listing: Raving And Drooling, Shine On You Crazy Diamond Parts I-V, Have A Cigar, Shine On You Crazy Diamond Parts VI-IX, Speak To Me, Breathe, On The Run, Time, Breathe (Reprise), The Great Gig In The Sky, Money, Us And Them, Any Colour You Like, Brain Damage, Eclipse, Echoes
Audio Rating: ★★★♪
Miscellaneous: Daly City is just south of San Francisco, and part of the same peninsula. Cow Palace is only about 4 miles from the more famous Candlestick Park.

Date: 20-04-1975
Location: Activity Center, Arizona State University, Tempe, Arizona, USA
Track Listing: Announcements And Audience, Raving And Drooling, You've Gotta Be Crazy, Speak To Me, Breathe, On The Run, Time, Breathe (Reprise), The Great Gig In The Sky, Money, Us And Them, Any Colour You Like, Brain Damage, Eclipse, Echoes (Excerpts)
Audio Rating: ★★♪
Miscellaneous: **ECHOES** cuts out at about 8.01. The audience sound hugely excited, shame the audio is poor.

Date: 21-04-1975
Location: Sports Arena, San Diego, California, USA
Track Listing: Speak To Me, Breathe, On The Run, Time, Breathe (Reprise), The Great Gig In The Sky, Money, Us And Them, Shine On You Crazy Diamond VI-IX, Echoes

Audio Rating: ★★★★
Miscellaneous: Audience also highly enthusiastic. The band no longer have to work the crowd but can bask in the shadows of yesterday's triumphs.

Date: 26-04-1975
Location: Los Angeles Memorial Sports Arena, Los Angeles, California, USA
Track Listing: Mike Test, Audience & Tuning, Raving And Drooling, Audience And Tuning, You Gotta Be Crazy, Audience And Tuning, Shine On You Crazy Diamond Parts I-V, Have A Cigar, Shine On You Crazy Diamond Parts VI-IX, Speak To Me, Breathe, On The Run, Time, Breathe (Reprise), The Great Gig In The Sky, Money, Us And Them, Any Colour You Like, Brain Damage, Eclipse, Audience And Tuning, Echoes
Audio Rating: ★★★★★
Miscellaneous: This is one of the concerts Waters spoke about in *Pink Floyd: The Wall Deluxe*, where he discusses the inspiration for the **IN THE FLESH?** sequence with Gerald Scarfe. Waters says that the Police Chief Edward M. Davis indulged in incredibly heavy-handed policing of mostly young fans. (There were 511 arrests during the group's five-night run there, though more than half didn't face any charges, and 181 were juveniles.)* Waters misremembers it as being during the *Animals* tour, but the band gave Los Angeles a miss during 1977, instead playing nearby Anaheim. The audio is one of the best in existence.

Date: 09-06-1975
Location: Capitol Center, Landover, Maryland, USA
Track Listing: Raving And Drooling, You Gotta Be Crazy, Shine On You Crazy Diamond I-V, Have A Cigar, Shine On You Crazy Diamond VI-IX, Speak To Me, Breathe, On The Run, Time, Breathe (Reprise), The Great Gig In The Sky, Money, Us And Them (Tape Flip), Any Colour You Like, Brain Damage, Eclipse
Audio Rating: ★★★★✦
Miscellaneous: Great audio for the most part. Landover is a small suburb, but the Capitol Center was home to the Washington Bullets NBA team, and could hold nearly 20,000 people. The film *Heavy Metal Parking Lot* (1986) was shot outside the arena.

Date: 10-06-1975
Location: Capitol Center, Landover, Maryland, USA
Track Listing: Raving And Drooling, Audience & Tuning, You've Gotta Be Crazy, Shine On You Crazy Diamond Parts I-V, Have A Cigar, Shine On You Crazy Diamond Parts VI-IX
Audio Rating: ★★★★
Miscellaneous: A truncated recording.

Date: 12-06-1975
Location: The Spectrum, Philadelphia, Pennsylvania, USA
Track Listing: Raving And Drooling, Gotta Be Crazy, Shine On You Crazy Diamond Parts I-V, Have A Cigar, Shine On You Crazy Diamond Parts VI-IX, Speak To Me, Breathe, On The Run, Time, Breathe (Reprise), The Great Gig In The Sky, Money, Us And Them, Any Colour You Like, Brain Damage, Eclipse
Audio Rating: ★★✦
Miscellaneous: Very murky.

Date: 15-06-1975
Location: Roosevelt Stadium, Jersey City, New Jersey, USA
Track Listing: Intro, Raving And Drooling, You Gotta Be Crazy, Shine On You Crazy Diamond Parts I-V, Have A Cigar, Shine On You Crazy Diamond Parts VI-IX, Speak To Me, Breathe, On The Run, Time, Breathe (Reprise), The Great Gig In The Sky, Money, Us And Them, Any Colour You Like, Brain Damage, Eclipse, Intermission, Echoes
Audio Rating: ★★★
Miscellaneous: A nice intimate atmosphere, but audio is too quiet.

Date: 16-06-1975
Location: Nassau Coliseum, Uniondale, New York, USA
Track Listing: Raving And Drooling, Gotta Be Crazy, Shine On You Crazy Diamond Parts I-V, Have A Cigar, Shine On You Crazy Diamond Parts VI-IX, Speak To Me, Breathe, On The Run, Time, The Great Gig In The Sky, Money, Us And Them, Any Colour You Like, Brain Damage, Eclipse, Echoes
Audio Rating: ★★★★✦
Miscellaneous: Gilmour's guitar in particular

---

* www.latimes.com/entertainment/music/posts/la-et-ms-1975-rock-concert-511-arrested-19760425-story.html

sounds terrific, but Wright's keyboard parts are also unusually clear.

Date: 17-06-1975
Location: Nassau Coliseum, Uniondale, New York, USA
Track Listing: Tuning, Raving And Drooling, You Gotta Be Crazy, Shine On You Crazy Diamond I-V, Have A Cigar, Shine On You Crazy Diamond VI-IX, Speak To Me, Breathe, On The Run, Time, Breathe (Reprise), The Great Gig In The Sky, Money, Us And Them, Any Colour You Like, Brain Damage, Eclipse, Encore Call & Tuning, Echoes
Audio Rating: ★★★★
Miscellaneous: Not quite as clear as the previous concert, though Wright remains more distinguishable than usual.

Date: 18-06-1975
Location: Boston Garden, Boston, Massachusetts, USA
Track Listing: Raving And Drooling, You've Gotta Be Crazy, Shine On You Crazy Diamond I-V (Spliced), Have A Cigar, Shine On You Crazy Diamond VI-IX (Spliced), Speak To Me, Breathe, On The Run, Time, Breathe (Reprise), The Great Gig In The Sky, Money, Us And Them (Spliced), Any Colour You Like, Brain Damage, Eclipse, Echoes
Audio Rating: ★★★★
Miscellaneous: 'This one [bizarre retching noises] ... this is called **SHINE ON YOU CRAZY DIAMOND**.' What was going on there, Roger?

Date: 20-06-1975
Location: Three Rivers Stadium, Pittsburgh, Pennsylvania, USA
Track Listing: Audience And Tuning Up, Raving And Drooling, You Gotta Be Crazy, Shine On You Crazy Diamond Parts I-V, Have A Cigar, Shine On You Crazy Diamond Parts VI-IX, Speak To Me, Breathe, On The Run, Time, Breathe (Reprise), The Great Gig In The Sky, Money, Us And Them, Any Colour You Like, Brain Damage, Eclipse, Echoes
Audio Rating: ★★↙
Miscellaneous: Very thin-sounding.

Date: 22-06-1975
Location: Milwaukee Stadium, Milwaukee, Wisconsin, USA
Track Listing: Speak To Me, Breathe, On The Run, Time, Breathe (Reprise), The Great Gig In The Sky, Money, Us And Them, Any Colour You Like, Brain Damage, Eclipse, Echoes
Audio Rating: ★↙
Miscellaneous: Concert cut short due to heavy rainfall and blighted by stoppages throughout.

Date: 24-06-1975
Location: Olympia Stadium, Detroit, Michigan, USA
Track Listing: Raving And Drooling, You've Gotta Be Crazy, Shine On You Crazy Diamond Parts I-V, Have A Cigar, Shine On You Crazy Diamond Parts VI-IX, Speak To Me, Breathe, On The Run, Time, The Great Gig in the Sky, Money, Us And Them, Any Colour You Like, Brain Damage, Eclipse, Encore Break, Echoes
Audio Rating: ★★★
Miscellaneous: Very distant-sounding but fairly clear.

Date: 28-06-1975
Location: Ivor Wynne Stadium, Hamilton, Ontario, Canada
Track Listing: Raving And Drooling, You've Gotta Be Crazy, Shine On You Crazy Diamond Parts I-V, Have A Cigar, Shine On You Crazy Diamond Parts VI-IX, Speak To Me, Breathe, On The Run, Time, Breathe (Reprise), The Great Gig In The Sky, Money, Us And Them, Any Colour You Like, Brain Damage, Eclipse, Crowd, Echoes
Audio Rating: ★★★★↙
Miscellaneous: Just a touch overloaded at moments of peak volume, otherwise the audio is tremendous.

Date: 05-07-1975
Location: Knebworth Park, Hertfordshire, England
Track Listing: Raving And Drooling, You Gotta Be Crazy, Shine On You Crazy Diamond Parts I-V, Have A Cigar, Shine On You Crazy Diamond Parts VI-IX, Speak To Me, Breathe, On The Run, Time, Breathe (Reprise), The Great Gig In The Sky, Money, Us And Them, Any Colour You Like, Brain Damage, Eclipse, Echoes
Audio Rating: ★★★
Miscellaneous: The second Knebworth festival, but the last festival the group would play for fifteen years (when they returned to this venue). The poor sound is probably an indication why. The audience don't sound enthused at all, chatting away during guitar

and saxophone solos, despite Pink Floyd being the headliner.

1977

Date: 23-01-1977
Location: Westfallenhalle, Dortmund, West Germany
Track Listing: Sheep, Pigs On The Wing (Part I), Dogs, Pigs On The Wing (Part Ii), Pigs, Shine On You Crazy Diamond Parts I-V, Welcome To The Machine, Have A Cigar, Wish You Were Here, Shine On You Crazy Diamond Parts VI-IX, Money, Us And Them
Audio Rating: ★★★♪
Miscellaneous: Gilmour sounds gruffer than before, perhaps deliberately in light of the more aggressive material. **PIGS (THREE DIFFERENT ONES)** has lengthier solos, stretching it to 17.26.

Date: 24-01-1977
Location: Westfallenhalle, Dortmund, West Germany
Track Listing: Sheep, Pigs On The Wing (Part I), Dogs, Pigs On The Wing (Part Ii), Pigs (Three Different Ones), Shine On You Crazy Diamond Parts I-V, Welcome To The Machine, Have A Cigar, Wish You Were Here, Shine On You Crazy Diamond Parts VI-IX, Money
Audio Rating: ★★
Miscellaneous: No **US AND THEM**, maybe the recorder got busted. Audio very faint.

Date: 27-01-1977
Location: Festhalle, Frankfurt, West Germany
Track Listing: Sheep, Pigs On The Wing (Part 1), Dogs, Pigs On The Wing (Part 2), Pigs (Three Different Ones), Shine On You Crazy Diamond I-V, Welcome To The Machine, Have A Cigar, Wish You Were Here, Shine On You Crazy Diamond VI-IX, Money
Audio Rating: ★★★♪
Miscellaneous: No **US AND THEM** here either. Sound is good. **MONEY** has a nice R&B swing to it.

Date: 29-01-1977
Location: Deutschlandhalle, West Berlin, West Germany
Track Listing: Sheep, Pigs On The Wing (Part 1), Dogs, Pigs On The Wing (Part 2), Pigs (Three Different Ones), Shine On You Crazy Diamond I-V, Welcome To The Machine, Have A Cigar, Wish You Were Here, Shine On You Crazy Diamond VI-IX, Money
Audio Rating: ★★♪
Miscellaneous: Audience clap their way through **MONEY** and band deliver a rocking version.

Date: 30-01-1977
Location: Deutschlandhalle, West Berlin, West Germany
Track Listing: Sheep, Pigs On The Wing (Part 1), Dogs, Pigs On The Wing (Part 2), Pigs (Three Different Ones), Shine On You Crazy Diamond I-V, Welcome To The Machine, Have A Cigar, Wish You Were Here, Shine On You Crazy Diamond VI-IX, Money
Audio Rating: ★★★
Miscellaneous: Gilmour's second solo in **DOGS** (from 5.22 here) has more shredding than usual, at the start at least. During **MONEY** Gilmour adds 'Yes I do!' after singing 'And I need a Lear Jet.'

Date: 01-02-1977
Location: Stadthalle, Vienna, Austria
Track Listing: Sheep, Pigs On The Wing (Part 1), Dogs, Pigs On The Wing (Part 2), Pigs (Three Different Ones), Shine On You Crazy Diamond I-V, Welcome To The Machine, Have A Cigar, Wish You Were Here, Shine On You Crazy Diamond VI-IX, Money, Us And Them
Audio Rating: ★★★♪
Miscellaneous: Audience sound fervent.

Date: 03-02-1977
Location: Hallenstadion, Zürich, Switzerland
Track Listing: Intro, Sheep, Pigs On The Wing (Part 1), Dogs, Pigs On The Wing (Part 2), Pigs (Three Different Ones), Shine On You Crazy Diamond I-V False Start, Shine On You Crazy Diamond I-V, Welcome To The Machine, Have A Cigar, Wish You Were Here, Shine On You Crazy Diamond VI-IX, Money
Audio Rating: ★★★★
Miscellaneous: Band sound on excellent form, for example giving a ferocious guitar solo in **HAVE A CIGAR**, and the audience are audibly appreciative. The false start to **SHINE ON** only lasts about ten seconds.

Date: 04-02-1977
Location: Hallenstadion, Zürich, Switzerland
Track Listing: Sheep, Pigs On The Wing (Part 1), Dogs, Pigs On The Wing (Part 2), Pigs

(Three Different Ones), Shine On You Crazy Diamond I-V, Welcome To The Machine, Have A Cigar, Wish You Were Here, Shine On You Crazy Diamond VI-IX, Money
Audio Rating: ★★★
Miscellaneous: Did the band get drunk after the first night? Gilmour's vocal sometimes sounds disinterested, though his guitar is always expressive.

Date: 17-02-1977
Location: Ahoy, Rotterdam, Netherlands
Track Listing: Sheep, Pigs On The Wing (Part 1), Dogs, Pigs On The Wing (Part 2), Pigs (Three Different Ones), Shine On You Crazy Diamond I-V, Welcome To The Machine, Have A Cigar, Wish You Were Here, Shine On You Crazy Diamond VI-IX, Money
Audio Rating: ★★✶
Miscellaneous: Very murky, though the band sounds energetic and aggressive.

Date: 18-02-1977
Location: Ahoy, Rotterdam, Netherlands
Track Listing: Sheep, Pigs On The Wing (Part 1), Dogs, Pigs On The Wing (Part 2), Pigs (Three Different Ones), Shine On You Crazy Diamond I-V, Welcome To The Machine, Shine On You Crazy Diamond VI-IX, Money (Cut)
Audio Rating: ★★★
Miscellaneous: Slightly better than the previous night in Rotterdam, but still not great sounding. **MONEY** cuts out halfway through, during the quiet section of the guitar solo.

Date: 19-02-1977
Location: Ahoy, Rotterdam, Netherlands
Track Listing: Sheep, Pigs On The Wing (Part 1), Dogs, Pigs On The Wing (Part 2), Pigs (Three Different Ones), Shine On You Crazy Diamond I-V, Welcome To The Machine, Have A Cigar, Wish You Were Here, Shine On You Crazy Diamond VI-IX, Money
Audio Rating: ★★★
Miscellaneous: A third night in Rotterdam, without any improvement to audio. (Maybe locals were averse to using Philips recording equipment.)

Date: 20-02-1977
Location: Sportpaleis, Antwerp, Belgium
Track Listing: Sheep, Pigs On The Wing (Part 1), Dogs, Pigs On The Wing (Part 2), Pigs (Three Different Ones), Shine On You Crazy Diamond I-V, Welcome To The Machine, Have A Cigar, Wish You Were Here, Shine On You Crazy Diamond VI-IX, Money
Audio Rating: ★★★★
Miscellaneous: **SHEEP** is missing most of Wright's introductory solo. **SHINE ON YOU CRAZY DIAMOND (PARTS I-V)** is also missing the beginning, opening with Gilmour already playing his first solo.

Date: 22-02-1977
Location: Pavillon De Paris, Paris, France
Track Listing: Sheep, Pigs On The Wing (Part 1), Dogs, Pigs On The Wing (Part 2), Pigs (Three Different Ones), Shine On You Crazy Diamond I-V, Welcome To The Machine, Have A Cigar, Wish You Were Here, Shine On You Crazy Diamond VI-IX, Money
Audio Rating: ★★★✶
Miscellaneous: Band sound on very good form. Pavillon De Paris was a former slaughterhouse, and was nicknamed 'Les Abbatoirs'. This wasn't just a joke choice of location by the band: the list of acts who played there during 1977 is impressive, from Donna Summer to AC/DC to Chuck Berry to Joan Baez to Fleetwood Mac.

Date: 23-02-1977
Location: Pavillon De Paris, Paris, France
Track Listing: Sheep, Pigs On The Wing (Part 1), Dogs, Pigs On The Wing (Part 2), Pigs (Three Different Ones), Shine On You Crazy Diamond I-V, Welcome To The Machine, Have A Cigar, Wish You Were Here, Shine On You Crazy Diamond VI-IX
Audio Rating: ★★✶
Miscellaneous: Very hissy, and a truncated recording with no encore.

Date: 24-02-1977
Location: Pavillon De Paris, Paris, France
Track Listing: Sheep, Pigs On The Wing (Part 1), Dogs, Pigs On The Wing (Part 2), Pigs (Three Different Ones), Shine On You Crazy Diamond I-V, Welcome To The Machine, Have A Cigar, Wish You Were Here, Shine On You Crazy Diamond VI-IX, Money
Audio Rating: ★★✶
Miscellaneous: Recorded from a radio transmission, therefore has DJs speaking over it in parts. **SHEEP** is missing its ending.

Date: 25-02-1977
Location: Pavillon De Paris, Paris, France
Track Listing: Sheep, Pigs On The Wing (Part 1), Dogs, Pigs On The Wing (Part 2), Pigs (Three Different Ones), Shine On You Crazy Diamond I–V, Welcome To The Machine, Have A Cigar, Wish You Were Here, Shine On You Crazy Diamond VI–IX, Money
Audio Rating: ★★★★
Miscellaneous: Finally some good audio, and a great band performance too.

Date: 27-02-1977
Location: Olympiahalle, Munich, West Germany
Track Listing: Sheep, Pigs On The Wing (Part 1), Dogs, Pigs On The Wing (Part 2), Pigs (Three Different Ones), Shine On You Crazy Diamond I–V, Welcome To The Machine, Have A Cigar, Wish You Were Here, Shine On You Crazy Diamond VI–IX, Money
Audio Rating: ★★★⯪
Miscellaneous: Vocals notably clearer than the instruments, which lack definition, though the performance has great energy.

Date: 28-02-1977
Location: Olympiahalle, Munich, West Germany
Track Listing: Sheep, Pigs On The Wing (Part 1), Dogs, Pigs On The Wing (Part 2), Pigs (Three Different Ones), Shine On You Crazy Diamond I–V, Welcome To The Machine, Have A Cigar, Wish You Were Here, Shine On You Crazy Diamond VI–IX, Money
Audio Rating: ★★★⯪
Miscellaneous: The two nights in Munich sound very similar, and are shared on the same bootleg so very probably come from the same recorder. Both sound somewhat muddy, but some instruments are clearer than others, for example the saxophone during **MONEY**. Quieter songs like **PIGS ON THE WING** don't translate well.

Date: 15-03-1977
Location: Empire Pool, Wembley, London, England
Track Listing: Sheep, Pigs On The Wing (Part 1), Dogs, Pigs On The Wing (Part 2), Pigs (Three Different Ones), Shine On You Crazy Diamond I–V, Welcome To The Machine, Have A Cigar, Wish You Were Here, Shine On You Crazy Diamond VI–IX, Money
Audio Rating: ★★★⯪
Miscellaneous: The UK leg of the *In the Flesh* tour only comprised two venues, in London and Staffordshire. The audio here is fairly clear but muffled, thus favouring quieter moments. (You can hear Mason tapping a tambourine during the 'Stone …' section of **DOGS**, for example.)

Date: 18-03-1977
Location: Empire Pool, Wembley, London, England
Track Listing: Sheep, Pigs On The Wing (Part 1), Dogs, Pigs On The Wing (Part 2), Pigs (Three Different Ones), Shine On You Crazy Diamond I–V, Welcome To The Machine, Have A Cigar, Wish You Were Here, Shine On You Crazy Diamond VI–IX, Us And Them
Audio Rating: ★★⯪
Miscellaneous: Some hiss and quite murky. **US AND THEM** is the encore, rather than **MONEY**.

Date: 19-03-1977
Location: Empire Pool, Wembley, London, England
Track Listing: Sheep, Pigs On The Wing (Part 1), Dogs, Pigs On The Wing (Part 2), Pigs (Three Different Ones), Shine On You Crazy Diamond I–V, Welcome To The Machine, Have A Cigar, Wish You Were Here, Shine On You Crazy Diamond VI–IX (Cut)
Audio Rating: ★⯪
Miscellaneous: Very bad audio. **PIGS ON THE WING** is barely decipherable. **SHINE ON YOU CRAZY DIAMOND VI–IX** cuts out just before the line 'Nobody knows where you are'.

Date: 31-03-1977
Location: New Bingley Hall, Stafford, England
Track Listing: Sheep, Pigs On The Wing (Part 1), Dogs, Pigs On The Wing (Part 2), Pigs (Three Different Ones), Shine On You Crazy Diamond I–V, Welcome To The Machine, Have A Cigar, Wish You Were Here, Shine On You Crazy Diamond VI–IX, Money
Audio Rating: ★★★⯪
Miscellaneous: New Bingley Hall was noted for both audience enthusiasm and poor acoustics, both of which are evident here.

Date: 22-04-1977
Location: Miami Baseball Stadium, Miami, Florida, USA
Track Listing: Intro, Sheep, Pigs On The Wing (Part 1), Dogs, Pigs On The Wing (Part 2), Pigs (Three Different Ones), Shine On You Crazy Diamond I-V, Welcome To The Machine, Have A Cigar, Wish You Were Here, Shine On You Crazy Diamond VI-IX, Money, Us And Them
Audio Rating: ★★★
Miscellaneous: First date of the North American tour. An enthusiastic audience is chastised by someone yelling 'Sit down! You dumb motherfuckers!' during **SHEEP**. (He has another go during the first part of **SHINE ON YOU CRAZY DIAMOND I-V** - 'Sit down! Sit down! You motherfucker!') Quieter moments – indicating how the tour would go – are almost drowned out with whistles and shouts.

Date: 24-04-1977
Location: Tampa Stadium, Tampa, Florida, USA
Track Listing: Intro, Sheep, Pigs On The Wing (Part 1), Dogs, Pigs On The Wing (Part 2), Pigs (Three Different Ones), Shine On You Crazy Diamond I-V, Welcome To The Machine, Have A Cigar, Wish You Were Here, Shine On You Crazy Diamond VI-IX, Money
Audio Rating: ★★★★
Miscellaneous: Another rowdy crowd, but the audio is good.

Date: 26-04-1977
Location: The Omni, Atlanta, Georgia, USA
Track Listing: Intro, Sheep, Pigs On The Wing (Part 1), Dogs, Pigs On The Wing (Part 2), Pigs (Three Different Ones), Shine On You Crazy Diamond I-V, Welcome To The Machine, Have A Cigar, Wish You Were Here, Shine On You Crazy Diamond VI-IX (Cuts)
Audio Rating: ★★★★♪
Miscellaneous: Excellent sound, could just be a little louder.

Date: 28-04-1977
Location: Assembly Center, Louisiana State University, Baton Rouge, Louisiana, USA
Track Listing: Sheep, Pigs On The Wing (Part 1), Dogs, Pigs On The Wing (Part 2), Pigs (Three Different Ones), Shine On You Crazy Diamond I-V, Welcome To The Machine, Have A Cigar, Wish You Were Here, Shine On You Crazy Diamond VI-IX, Money
Audio Rating: ★★★
Miscellaneous: Quieter moments sound drowned out, audio murky elsewhere.

Date: 30-04-1977
Location: Jeppeson Stadium, Houston, Texas, USA
Track Listing: Sheep, Pigs On The Wing (Part 1), Dogs, Pigs On The Wing (Part 2), Pigs (Three Different Ones), Shine On You Crazy Diamond I-V, Welcome To The Machine, Have A Cigar, Wish You Were Here, Shine On You Crazy Diamond VI-IX, Money, Us And Them
Audio Rating: ★★★♪
Miscellaneous: **SHEEP** comes in halfway through the first verse. One of the few gigs to have both **MONEY** and **US AND THEM** as encores. Endless whistling from the audience, especially at quiet moments.

Date: 01-05-1977
Location: Tarrant County Convention Center, Fort Worth, Texas, USA
Track Listing: Sheep, Pigs On The Wing (Part 1), Dogs, Pigs On The Wing (Part 2), Pigs (Three Different Ones), Shine On You Crazy Diamond I-V, Welcome To The Machine, Have A Cigar, Wish You Were Here, Shine On You Crazy Diamond VI-IX, Money, Us And Them
Audio Rating: ★★★★
Miscellaneous: Occasionally distant-sounding, but nice and clear.

Date: 06-05-1977
Location: Anaheim Stadium, Anaheim, California, USA
Track Listing: Pigs On The Wing (Part 1), Dogs, Pigs On The Wing (Part 2), Pigs (Three Different Ones), Shine On You Crazy Diamond I-V, Welcome To The Machine, Have A Cigar, Wish You Were Here, Shine On You Crazy Diamond VI-IX
Audio Rating: ★★★♪
Miscellaneous: Missing both **SHEEP** and encore.

Date: 07-05-1977
Location: Anaheim Stadium, Anaheim, California, USA
Track Listing: Sheep, Pigs On The Wing (Part 1), Dogs, Pigs On The Wing (Part 2), Pigs (Three Different Ones), Shine On You Crazy Diamond I-V, Welcome To The Machine, Have

A Cigar, Wish You Were Here, Shine On You Crazy Diamond VI-IX
Audio Rating: ★★★♪
Miscellaneous: Raucous audience constantly shouting out. Audio has some sibilance.

Date: 09-05-1977
Location: Alameda Coliseum, Oakland, California, USA
Track Listing: Sheep, Pigs On The Wing (Part 1), Dogs, Pigs On The Wing (Part 2), Pigs (Three Different Ones), Shine On You Crazy Diamond I-V, Welcome To The Machine, Have A Cigar, Wish You Were Here, Shine On You Crazy Diamond VI-IX, Money, Us And Them, Careful With That Axe, Eugene
Audio Rating: ★★★★♪
Miscellaneous: The last performance of **CAREFUL WITH THAT AXE, EUGENE** (and the first since 1973), which gets a big cheer – but then it is an unexpected third encore. Audio is superb. Gilmour's slide guitar solo during **SHINE ON YOU CRAZY DIAMOND VI-IX** sounds especially good.

Date: 10-05-1977
Location: Alameda Coliseum, Oakland, California, USA
Track Listing: Sheep, Pigs On The Wing (Part 1), Dogs, Pigs On The Wing (Part 2), Pigs (Three Different Ones), Shine On You Crazy Diamond I-V, Welcome To The Machine, Have A Cigar, Wish You Were Here, Shine On You Crazy Diamond VI-IX, Money, Us And Them
Audio Rating: ★★★♪
Miscellaneous: The vociferous crowd seem determined to interject themselves into any quiet moment, which prevents the slow accumulation of tension on which the group so often relied. During **SHINE ON YOU CRAZY DIAMOND I-V** it's particularly egregious.

Date: 15-06-1977
Location: Milwaukee Stadium, Milwaukee, Wisconsin, USA
Track Listing: Sheep, Pigs On The Wing (Part 1), Dogs, Pigs On The Wing (Part 2), Pigs (Three Different Ones), Shine On You Crazy Diamond I-V, Welcome To The Machine, Have A Cigar, Wish You Were Here, Shine On You Crazy Diamond VI-IX
Audio Rating: ★★♪
Miscellaneous: The second leg of the North American tour gets under way after a month off. Recording has several cuts throughout. No encores recorded.

Date: 17-06-1977
Location: Freedom Hall, Kentucky Fair and Exposition Center, Louisville, Kentucky, USA
Track Listing: Shine On You Crazy Diamond I-V, Welcome To The Machine, Have A Cigar, Wish You Were Here, Shine On You Crazy Diamond VI-IX, Money
Audio Rating: ★★♪
Miscellaneous: Only the second set available. The opening to the guitar solo by Snowy White during **SHINE ON YOU CRAZY DIAMOND I-V** (just before the lyrics finally enter, at around 7.49) is badly fluffed.

Date: 19-06-1977
Location: Soldier Field, Chicago, Illinois, USA
Track Listing: Sheep, Pigs On The Wing (Part 1), Dogs, Pigs On The Wing (Part 2), Pigs (Three Different Ones), Shine On You Crazy Diamond I-V, Welcome To The Machine, Have A Cigar, Wish You Were Here, Shine On You Crazy Diamond VI-IX, Money
Audio Rating: ★★★♪
Miscellaneous: Everyone clapping along during **MONEY**. Hard to tell if they're in on the joke or not.

Date: 25-06-1977
Location: Municipal Stadium, Cleveland, Ohio, USA
Track Listing: Sheep, Pigs On The Wing (Part 1), Dogs, Pigs On The Wing (Part 2), Pigs (Three Different Ones), Shine On You Crazy Diamond I-V, Welcome To The Machine, Have A Cigar, Wish You Were Here, Shine On You Crazy Diamond VI-IX, Us And Them, Money
Audio Rating: ★★★★
Miscellaneous: Firecrackers going off, audience very audible, but the audio clarity is very good.

Date: 27-06-1977
Location: Boston Garden, Boston, Massachusetts, USA
Track Listing: Sheep, Pigs On The Wing (Part 1), Dogs, Pigs On The Wing (Part 2), Pigs (Three Different Ones), Shine On You Crazy Diamond I-V, Welcome To The Machine, Have A Cigar, Wish You Were Here, Shine On You Crazy Diamond VI-IX, Money, Us And Them

Audio Rating: ★★★★
Miscellaneous: Firecrackers set off at the start of **SHINE ON YOU CRAZY DIAMOND I-V**, though Waters doesn't remonstrate. Sound is lovely and clear. The extended guitar solo in **MONEY** is fantastic.

Date: 29-06-1977
Location: Spectrum Theater, Philadelphia, Pennsylvania, USA
Track Listing: Sheep, Pigs On The Wing (Part 1), Dogs, Pigs On The Wing (Part 2), Pigs (Three Different Ones), Shine On You Crazy Diamond I-V, Welcome To The Machine, Have A Cigar, Wish You Were Here, Shine On You Crazy Diamond VI-IX, Money, Us And Them
Audio Rating: ★✦
Miscellaneous: Vocals barely distinguishable in parts. Higher frequencies, such as guitar solos and keyboards, come through most clearly, but this is often a tough listen. This is reputedly the concert where Waters was injected with a tranquilliser to enable him to play after being stricken with hepatitis, producing feelings of dissociation that he would articulate in **COMFORTABLY NUMB**.

Date: 01-07-1977
Location: Madison Square Garden, New York City, New York, USA
Track Listing: Sheep, Pigs On The Wing (Part 1), Dogs, Pigs On The Wing (Part 2), Pigs (Three Different Ones), Shine On You Crazy Diamond I-V, Welcome To The Machine, Have A Cigar, Wish You Were Here, Shine On You Crazy Diamond VI-IX, Money
Audio Rating: ★★
Miscellaneous: Not much better than the previous show.

Date: 02-07-1977
Location: Madison Square Garden, New York City, New York, USA
Track Listing: Sheep, Pigs On The Wing (Part 1), Dogs, Pigs On The Wing (Part 2), Pigs (Three Different Ones), Shine On You Crazy Diamond I-V, Welcome To The Machine, Have A Cigar, Wish You Were Here, Shine On You Crazy Diamond VI-IX, Money, Us And Them
Audio Rating: ★★★★
Miscellaneous: Excellent sound. Firecrackers going off at various points, getting boos during the intro for **SHEEP** for example. Two loud volleys of them going off during the intro to **SHINE ON YOU CRAZY DIAMOND I-V** earn even audience resentment.

Date: 03-07-1977
Location: Madison Square Garden, New York City, New York, USA
Track Listing: Sheep, Pigs On The Wing (Part 1), Dogs, Pigs On The Wing (Part 2), Pigs (Three Different Ones), Shine On You Crazy Diamond I-V, Welcome To The Machine, Have A Cigar, Wish You Were Here, Shine On You Crazy Diamond VI-IX, Money, Us And Them
Audio Rating: ★★★✦
Miscellaneous: Waters loses his rag with the firecracker crews at several moments. He says 'You cunt!' during **PIGS ON THE WING (PART 1)**. After **DOGS** he says (to loud cheers) 'You stupid motherfucker ...! Why doesn't anybody else in here with fireworks just fuck off and let the rest of us get on it with it!' In **PIGS ON THE WING (PART 2)** (during which he sings the lyrics from **PART 1**): 'I'll start that again, because that's the wrong verse. Having words with that stupid motherfucker sort of put me off.' After **PIGS (THREE DIFFERENT ONES)** he says: 'Thank you, we're gonna take a break – twenty minutes and then we'll come back with another set. And don't throw any more fucking fireworks – alright?' His request doesn't work: more fireworks go off during the rest of the concert.

Date: 04-07-1977
Location: Madison Square Garden, New York City, New York, USA
Track Listing: Sheep, Pigs On The Wing (Part 1), Dogs, Pigs On The Wing (Part 2), Pigs (Three Different Ones), Shine On You Crazy Diamond I-V, Welcome To The Machine, Have A Cigar, Wish You Were Here, Shine On You Crazy Diamond VI-IX, Money, Us And Them
Audio Rating: ★★★★
Miscellaneous: A national holiday, which could be predicted to bring the firecrackers. During **PIGS ON THE WING (PART 2)**, fireworks go off and Waters substitutes a venomous 'You shit-bag!' for 'And I know that you care.' The beginning of **MONEY** is missing. The band's performance is outstanding.

Date: 06-07-1977
Location: Stade Du Parc Olympique, Montreal, Quebec, Canada
Track Listing: Sheep, Pigs On The Wing (Part 1), Dogs, Pigs On The Wing (Part 2), Pigs (Three Different Ones), Shine On You Crazy Diamond I-V, Welcome To The Machine, Have A Cigar, Wish You Were Here, Shine On You Crazy Diamond VI-IX, Money, Us And Them, Blues
Audio Rating: ★★★♪
Miscellaneous: Probably the most famous and most consequential concert never released as a live album. At the start of **PIGS ON THE WING (PART 2)**, someone lets off a firecracker which makes Waters livid: 'Oh for fuck's sake, stop letting off fireworks and shouting and screaming, I'm trying to sing a song! I mean I don't care, if you don't want to hear it, you know, fuck it – I'm sure there's a lot of people here who *do* want to hear it. So why don't you just be quiet, and if you want to let your fireworks off go outside and let them off out there, and if you want to shout and scream and holler go and do it out there! But I'm trying to sing a song that some people want to listen to. *I* want to listen to it.'

The spitting incident occurs at the end of **PIGS (THREE DIFFERENT ONES)**, during a quieter instrumental section (not on the studio version). During it Waters seems to go berserk, shouting, 'Wow! Hey! Come back pig! Come back! All is forgiven! Come on boy! Closer! Closer!' It sounds like he's literally losing his mind. The band respond with an increase in tempo and viciousness, which makes it all quite remarkable to hear.

During the show the audience are extremely noisy, for sure, and incessantly yell for 'More!' after **US AND THEM**. The band (minus Gilmour) play their wind-down blues track as a final encore, Waters saying: 'Listen, we can't play any other songs, so we're just going to play some music to go home to [indecipherable]. We're just going to play a slow blues so everybody can just calm down a bit.'

Perhaps not surprisingly, the Olympic Stadium, especially the Montreal Tower and its 45° incline, is caricatured on the inside cover of *The Wall*, where it looks nightmarishly alienating.

1980

Date: 01-02-1980
Location: Paramount Studios, Los Angeles, California (Rehearsals)
Track Listing: The Thin Ice, Another Brick In The Wall Part, The Happiest Days Of Our Lives, Another Brick In The Wall Part, Mother, Goodbye Blue Sky, A Few More Bricks, What Shall We Do Now?, Young Lust, One Of My Turns, Stop Building The Wall, The Last Few Bricks, Goodbye Cruel World, Hey You, Don't Start The Tape, Is There Anybody Out There?, Nobody Home, What's On TV?, Vera, Bring The Boys Back Home, Comfortably Numb, The Show Must Go On
Audio Rating: ★★★★★
Miscellaneous: If you want to hear what it's like to work for Roger Waters (or what it was like in 1980), here it is. He can be best heard in the tracks 'Stop Building the Wall' and 'Don't Start the Tape' which are mostly his comments to James Guthrie (working as sound mixer). His comments are exacting ('We don't have any click track or count in the cans, James, which makes it difficult! Go back to the top of that breathing tape and sort it out. Stop! Stop building the wall!') and border on the sadistic. The audio is very probably from the sound desk and is excellent.

Date: 07-02-1980
Location: L.A. Sports Arena, Los Angeles, California, USA
Track Listing: Pre Show, Radio Blurb, In The Flesh?, The Thin Ice, Another Brick In The Wall Part 1, The Happiest Days Of Our Lives, Another Brick In The Wall Part 2, Mother, Goodbye Blue Sky, Empty Spaces, A Break To Put The Fire Out, Empty Spaces (Continued), What Shall We Do Now?, Young Lust, One Of My Turns, Don't Leave Me Now, Another Brick In The Wall Part 3, Goodbye Cruel World, Hey You, Is There Anybody Out There?, Nobody Home, Vera, Bring The Boys Back Home, Comfortably Numb, The Show Must Go On, Radio Blurb 2, In The Flesh, Run Like Hell, Waiting For The Worms, Stop, The Trial, Outside The Wall, Good Night
Audio Rating: ★★★♪
Miscellaneous: The first live performance. Waters misses a cue in **THE TRIAL** but otherwise as a performance it's pretty good. A firework let off causes curtains in the ceiling to smoulder – you can hear the extinguishers

trying to put them out during **MOTHER** – then go up in flames during **EMPTY SPACES**, at which point Waters halts the proceedings and gets it taken care of. Good man.

Date: 08-02-1980
Location: L.A. Sports Arena, Los Angeles, California, USA
Track Listing: In The Flesh?, The Thin Ice, Another Brick In The Wall Part 1, The Happiest Days Of Our Lives, Another Brick In The Wall Part 2, Mother, Goodbye Blue Sky, Empty Spaces, What Shall We Do Now?, Young Lust, One Of My Turns, Don't Leave Me Now, Another Brick In The Wall Part 3, The Last Few Bricks, Goodbye Cruel World, Hey You, Is There Anybody Out There?, Nobody Home, Vera, Bring The Boys Back Home, Comfortably Numb, The Show Must Go On, In The Flesh, Run Like Hell, Waiting For The Worms, Stop, The Trial, Outside The Wall
Audio Rating: ★★★★
Miscellaneous: A storming performance and very good audio.

Date: 09-02-1980
Location: L.A. Sports Arena, Los Angeles, California, USA
Track Listing: Intro/In The Flesh?, The Thin Ice, Another Brick In The Wall Part 1, The Happiest Days Of Our Lives, Another Brick In The Wall Part 2, Mother, Goodbye Blue Sky, Empty Spaces, What Shall We Do Now?, Young Lust, One Of My Turns, Don't Leave Me Now, Another Brick In The Wall Part 3, The Last Few Bricks, Goodbye Cruel World, Hey You, Is There Anybody Out There?, Nobody Home, Vera, Bring The Boys Back Home, Comfortably Numb, The Show Must Go On, In The Flesh, Run Like Hell, Waiting For The Worms, Stop, The Trial, Outside The Wall
Audio Rating: ★★★
Miscellaneous: Waters introduces **RUN LIKE HELL**: 'Do you like my pig?! Go home pig, go on, off you go. This next tune is one for all the paranoids in the audience – I'm sure there's a few out there! It's called "Run Like Hell".'

Date: 10-02-1980
Location: L.A. Sports Arena, Los Angeles, California, USA
Track Listing: Intro/In The Flesh?, The Thin Ice, Another Brick In The Wall Part 1, The Happiest Days Of Our Lives, Another Brick In The Wall Part 2, Mother, Goodbye Blue Sky, Empty Spaces, What Shall We Do Now?, Young Lust, One Of My Turns, Don't Leave Me Now, Another Brick In The Wall Part 3, The Last Few Bricks, Goodbye Cruel World, Hey You, Is There Anybody Out There?, Nobody Home, Vera, Bring The Boys Back Home, Comfortably Numb, The Show Must Go On, In The Flesh, Run Like Hell, Waiting For The Worms, Stop, The Trial, Outside The Wall
Audio Rating: ★★★↓
Miscellaneous: The recorder caught just the end of the MC's speech, with him saying 'There's going to be an incredible amount of rock 'n' roll tonight, so ...' before **IN THE FLESH?** cuts him off. The audience sound very enthusiastic.

Date: 12-02-1980
Location: L.A. Sports Arena, Los Angeles, California, USA
Track Listing: Intro/In The Flesh?, The Thin Ice, Another Brick In The Wall Part 1, The Happiest Days Of Our Lives, Another Brick In The Wall Part 2, Mother, Goodbye Blue Sky, Empty Spaces, What Shall We Do Now?, Young Lust, One Of My Turns, Don't Leave Me Now, Another Brick In The Wall Part 3, The Last Few Bricks, Goodbye Cruel World, Hey You, Is There Anybody Out There?, Nobody Home, Vera, Bring The Boys Back Home, Comfortably Numb, The Show Must Go On, In The Flesh, Run Like Hell, Waiting For The Worms, Stop, The Trial, Outside The Wall
Audio Rating: ★★↓
Miscellaneous: Audience are remarkably enthusiastic. The band sound energised by this, for example during the funk jam part of **ANOTHER BRICK IN THE WALL PART 2**, which is one of the few points where they can stretch out, while **RUN LIKE HELL** sounds vicious.

Date: 13-02-1980
Location: L.A. Sports Arena, Los Angeles, California, USA
Track Listing: In The Flesh?, The Thin Ice, Another Brick In The Wall Part 1, The Happiest Days Of Our Lives, Another Brick In The Wall Part 2, Mother, Goodbye Blue Sky, Empty Spaces, What Shall We Do Now?, Young Lust, One Of My Turns, Don't Leave Me Now, Another Brick In The Wall Part 3, The Last Few Bricks, Goodbye Cruel World, Hey You,

Is There Anybody Out There?, Nobody Home, Vera, Bring The Boys Back Home, Comfortably Numb, The Show Must Go On, In The Flesh, Run Like Hell, Waiting For The Worms, Stop, The Trial, Outside The Wall
Audio Rating: ★★★✩
Miscellaneous: Audio improves after first few minutes.

Date: 24-02-1980
Location: Nassau Veterans Memorial Coliseum, Long Island, New York, USA
Track Listing: The Thin Ice, Another Brick In The Wall Part 1, The Happiest Days Of Our Lives, Another Brick In The Wall Part 2, Mother, Goodbye Blue Sky, Empty Spaces, What Shall We Do Now?, Young Lust, One Of My Turns, Don't Leave Me Now, Another Brick In The Wall Part 3, The Last Few Bricks, Goodbye Cruel World, Hey You, Is There Anybody Out There?, Nobody Home, Vera, Bring The Boys Back Home, Comfortably Numb, The Show Must Go On, In The Flesh, Run Like Hell, Waiting For The Worms
Audio Rating: ★★
Miscellaneous: Poor audio and quite a lot of noise and conversation from spectators around the recorder. Band are remarkably consistent.

Date: 25-02-1980
Location: Nassau Veterans Memorial Coliseum, Long Island, New York, USA
Track Listing: In The Flesh?, The Thin Ice, Another Brick In The Wall Part 1, The Happiest Days Of Our Lives, Another Brick In The Wall Part 2, Mother, Goodbye Blue Sky, Empty Spaces, What Shall We Do Now?, Young Lust, One Of My Turns, Don't Leave Me Now, Another Brick In The Wall Part 3, The Last Few Bricks, Goodbye Cruel World, Hey You, Is There Anybody Out There?, Nobody Home, Vera, Bring The Boys Back Home, Comfortably Numb, The Show Must Go On, In The Flesh, Run Like Hell, Waiting For The Worms, Stop, The Trial, Outside The Wall
Audio Rating: ★★★
Miscellaneous: At 2:28 into **NOBODY HOME**, a female venue employee asks the recorder, 'Is that a pipe you've got there? Is that a pipe you've got there?' He casually says, 'No, it's a microphone.' And she just lets him be. Remember the scene in *The Song Remains The Same* when the police let some ticketless fans in? There was a time when not everyone was busting their ass for The Man. Band sound on top form.

Date: 26-02-1980
Location: Nassau Veterans Memorial Coliseum, Long Island, New York, USA
Track Listing: Intro, In The Flesh?, The Thin Ice, Another Brick In The Wall Part 1, The Happiest Days Of Our Lives, Another Brick In The Wall Part 2, Mother, Goodbye Blue Sky, Empty Spaces, What Shall We Do Now?, Young Lust, One Of My Turns, Don't Leave Me Now, Another Brick In The Wall Part 3, The Last Few Bricks, Goodbye Cruel World, Hey You, Is There Anybody Out There?, Nobody Home, Vera, Bring The Boys Back Home, Comfortably Numb, The Show Must Go On, In The Flesh, Run Like Hell, Waiting For The Worms, Stop, The Trial, Outside The Wall
Audio Rating: ★★★✩
Miscellaneous: Clarity improves after initially sounding quite muffled.

Date: 27-02-1980
Location: Nassau Veterans Memorial Coliseum, Long Island, New York, USA
Track Listing: In The Flesh?, The Thin Ice, Another Brick In The Wall Part 1, The Happiest Days Of Our Lives, Another Brick In The Wall Part 2, Mother, Goodbye Blue Sky, Empty Spaces, What Shall We Do Now?, Young Lust, One Of My Turns, Don't Leave Me Now, Another Brick In The Wall Part 3, The Last Few Bricks, Goodbye Cruel World, Hey You, Is There Anybody Out There?, Nobody Home, Vera, Bring The Boys Back Home, Comfortably Numb, The Show Must Go On, In The Flesh, Run Like Hell, Waiting For The Worms, Stop, The Trial, Outside The Wall, Post Show
Audio Rating: ★★★✩
Miscellaneous: A boisterous audience, which as before seems to push the band to deliver.

Date: 28-02-1980
Location: Nassau Veterans Memorial Coliseum, Long Island, New York, USA
Track Listing: Intro, In The Flesh?, The Thin Ice, Another Brick In The Wall Part 1, The Happiest Days Of Our Lives, Another Brick In The Wall Part 2, Mother, Goodbye Blue Sky, Empty Spaces, What Shall We Do Now?, Young Lust, One Of My Turns, Don't Leave Me Now,

Another Brick In The Wall Part 3, The Last Few Bricks, Goodbye Cruel World, Hey You, Is There Anybody Out There?, Nobody Home, Vera, Bring The Boys Back Home, Comfortably Numb, The Show Must Go On, In The Flesh, Run Like Hell, Waiting For The Worms, Stop, The Trial, Outside The Wall
Audio Rating: ★★★★★
Miscellaneous: One of the best bootlegs of *The Wall*, easily comparable to *Is There Anybody Out There?* (which was compiled from the August 1980 and June 1981 performances at Earl's Court). Maybe the group were demob happy: after this gig they had a six-month break before the first London shows.

Date: 04-08-1980
Location: Earl's Court Exhibition Hall, London, England
Track Listing: Intro, In The Flesh?, The Thin Ice, Another Brick In The Wall Part 1, The Happiest Days Of Our Lives, Another Brick In The Wall Part 2, Mother, Goodbye Blue Sky, Empty Spaces, What Shall We Do Now?, Young Lust, One Of My Turns, Don't Leave Me Now, Another Brick In The Wall Part 3, The Last Few Bricks, Goodbye Cruel World, Hey You, Is There Anybody Out There?, Nobody Home, Vera, Bring The Boys Back Home, Comfortably Numb, The Show Must Go On, In The Flesh, Run Like Hell, Waiting For The Worms, Stop, The Trial, Outside The Wall
Audio Rating: ★★★
Miscellaneous: Too many mid-frequencies make it quite boxy sounding.

Date: 05-08-1980
Location: Earl's Court Exhibition Hall, London, England
Track Listing: Intro, In The Flesh?, The Thin Ice, Another Brick In The Wall Part 1, The Happiest Days Of Our Lives, Another Brick In The Wall Part 2, Mother, Goodbye Blue Sky, Empty Spaces, What Shall We Do Now?, Young Lust, One Of My Turns, Don't Leave Me Now, Another Brick In The Wall Part 3, The Last Few Bricks, Goodbye Cruel World, Hey You, Is There Anybody Out There?, Nobody Home, Vera, Bring The Boys Back Home, Comfortably Numb, The Show Must Go On, In The Flesh, Run Like Hell, Waiting For The Worms, Stop, The Trial, Outside The Wall
Audio Rating: ★★★★
Miscellaneous: Clear and crisp audio, though some songs (for example **COMFORTABLY NUMB**) fade in a bit, and you have to turn up the speakers quite high. Waters introduces **RUN LIKE HELL**: 'This next one's for all you disco fans. There's a nice bouncy beat.'

Date: 06-08-1980
Location: Earl's Court Exhibition Hall, London, England
Track Listing: Intro, In The Flesh?, The Thin Ice, Another Brick In The Wall Part 1, The Happiest Days Of Our Lives, Another Brick In The Wall Part 2, Mother, Goodbye Blue Sky, Empty Spaces, What Shall We Do Now?, Young Lust, One Of My Turns, Don't Leave Me Now, Another Brick In The Wall Part 3, The Last Few Bricks, Goodbye Cruel World, Hey You, Is There Anybody Out There?, Nobody Home, Vera, Bring The Boys Back Home, Comfortably Numb, The Show Must Go On, In The Flesh, Run Like Hell, Waiting For The Worms, Stop, The Trial, Outside The Wall
Audio Rating: ★★★★*
Miscellaneous: Excellent sounding, but just feels a touch less inspired than other nights.

Date: 07-08-1980
Location: Earl's Court Exhibition Hall, London, England
Track Listing: Intro, In The Flesh?, The Thin Ice, Another Brick In The Wall Part 1, The Happiest Days Of Our Lives, Another Brick In The Wall Part 2, Mother, Goodbye Blue Sky, Empty Spaces, What Shall We Do Now?, Young Lust, One Of My Turns, Don't Leave Me Now, Another Brick In The Wall Part 3, The Last Few Bricks, Goodbye Cruel World, Hey You, Is There Anybody Out There?, Nobody Home, Vera, Bring The Boys Back Home, Comfortably Numb, The Show Must Go On, In The Flesh, Run Like Hell, Waiting For The Worms, Stop, The Trial, Outside The Wall
Audio Rating: ★★★
Miscellaneous: One of the weaker bootlegs of *The Wall*. The band's own recording must have been better, as ten songs were used for *Is There Anybody Out There?*

Date: 09-08-1980
Location: Earl's Court Exhibition Hall, London, England
Track Listing: Intro, In The Flesh?, The Thin Ice, Another Brick In The Wall Part 1, The Happiest

Days Of Our Lives, Another Brick In The Wall Part 2, Mother, Goodbye Blue Sky, Empty Spaces, What Shall We Do Now?, Young Lust, One Of My Turns, Don't Leave Me Now, Another Brick In The Wall Part 3, The Last Few Bricks, Goodbye Cruel World, Hey You, Is There Anybody Out There?, Nobody Home, Vera, Bring The Boys Back Home, Comfortably Numb, The Show Must Go On, In The Flesh, Run Like Hell, Waiting For The Worms, Stop, The Trial, Outside The Wall
Audio Rating: ★★★↙
Miscellaneous: The source of the 'Master of Ceremonies' introduction heard on *Is There Anybody Out There?* The selections from 1980 come from only three nights (7–9 August) but it's unclear if those were the only ones recorded by the band. (The initial purpose was that filmed footage would be part of a movie of *The Wall*, but this idea was discarded after Alan Parker took over as director.) Allegedly this is the only 'soundboard' bootleg of *The Wall*. The audio is very clear but lacks body and there's a degree of hiss.

1981
Date: 13-02-1981
Location: Westfallenhalle, Dortmund, West Germany
Track Listing: Intro, In The Flesh?, The Thin Ice, Another Brick In The Wall Part 1, The Happiest Days Of Our Lives, Another Brick In The Wall Part 2, Mother, Goodbye Blue Sky, Empty Spaces, What Shall We Do Now?, Young Lust, One Of My Turns, Don't Leave Me Now, Another Brick In The Wall Part 3, The Last Few Bricks, Goodbye Cruel World, Hey You, Is There Anybody Out There?, Nobody Home, Vera, Bring The Boys Back Home, Comfortably Numb, The Show Must Go On, In The Flesh, Run Like Hell, Waiting For The Worms, Stop, The Trial, Outside The Wall
Audio Rating: ★★★
Miscellaneous: Audio initially very poor but improves as the show goes on.

Date: 14-02-1981
Location: Westfallenhalle, Dortmund, West Germany
Track Listing: Intro/In The Flesh?, The Thin Ice, Another Brick In The Wall Part 1, The Happiest Days Of Our Lives, Another Brick In The Wall Part 2, Mother, Goodbye Blue Sky, Empty Spaces, What Shall We Do Now?, Young Lust, One Of My Turns, Don't Leave Me Now, Another Brick In The Wall Part 3, The Last Few Bricks, Goodbye Cruel World, Hey You, Is There Anybody Out There?, Nobody Home, Vera, Bring The Boys Back Home, Comfortably Numb, The Show Must Go On, In The Flesh, Run Like Hell, Waiting For The Worms, Stop, The Trial, Outside The Wall
Audio Rating: ★★★↙
Miscellaneous: Audience audibly enthusiastic.

Date: 15-02-1981
Location: Westfallenhalle, Dortmund, West Germany
Track Listing: Intro, In The Flesh?, The Thin Ice, Another Brick In The Wall Part 1, The Happiest Days Of Our Lives, Another Brick In The Wall Part 2, Mother, Goodbye Blue Sky, Empty Spaces, What Shall We Do Now?, Young Lust, One Of My Turns, Don't Leave Me Now, Another Brick In The Wall Part 3, The Last Few Bricks, Goodbye Cruel World, Hey You, Is There Anybody Out There?, Nobody Home, Vera, Bring The Boys Back Home, Comfortably Numb, The Show Must Go On, In The Flesh, Run Like Hell, Waiting For The Worms, Stop, The Trial, Outside The Wall (Cut)
Audio Rating: ★★★↙
Miscellaneous: Very enthusiastic crowd, for example clapping to the beat during **ANOTHER BRICK IN THE WALL PART 2** and **RUN LIKE HELL**.

Date: 16-02-1981
Location: Westfallenhalle, Dortmund, West Germany
Track Listing: Intro, In The Flesh?, The Thin Ice, Another Brick In The Wall Part 1, The Happiest Days Of Our Lives, Another Brick In The Wall Part 2, Mother, Goodbye Blue Sky, Empty Spaces, What Shall We Do Now?, Young Lust, One Of My Turns, Don't Leave Me Now, Another Brick In The Wall Part 3, The Last Few Bricks, Goodbye Cruel World, Hey You, Is There Anybody Out There?, Nobody Home, Vera, Bring The Boys Back Home, Comfortably Numb, The Show Must Go On, In The Flesh, Run Like Hell, Waiting For The Worms, Stop, The Trial, Outside The Wall
Audio Rating: ★★★
Miscellaneous: Clear but a bit murky, like it's being played around a corner.

Date: 17-02-1981
Location: Westfallenhalle, Dortmund, West Germany
Track Listing: Intro, In The Flesh?, The Thin Ice, Another Brick In The Wall Part 1, The Happiest Days Of Our Lives, Another Brick In The Wall Part 2, Mother, Goodbye Blue Sky, Empty Spaces, What Shall We Do Now?, Young Lust, One Of My Turns, Don't Leave Me Now, Another Brick In The Wall Part 3, The Last Few Bricks, Goodbye Cruel World, Hey You, Is There Anybody Out There?, Nobody Home, Vera, Bring The Boys Back Home, Comfortably Numb, The Show Must Go On, In The Flesh, Run Like Hell, Waiting For The Worms, Stop, The Trial, Outside The Wall
Audio Rating: ★★★★★♪
Miscellaneous: A bit more audience conversation than usual.

Date: 18-02-1981
Location: Westfallenhalle, Dortmund, West Germany
Track Listing: Intro/In The Flesh?, The Thin Ice, Another Brick In The Wall Part 1, The Happiest Days Of Our Lives, Another Brick In The Wall Part 2, Mother, Goodbye Blue Sky, Empty Spaces, What Shall We Do Now?, Young Lust, One Of My Turns, Don't Leave Me Now, Another Brick In The Wall Part 3, The Last Few Bricks, Goodbye Cruel World, Hey You, Is There Anybody Out There?, Nobody Home, Vera, Bring The Boys Back Home, Comfortably Numb, The Show Must Go On, In The Flesh, Run Like Hell, Waiting For The Worms, Stop, The Trial, Outside The Wall
Audio Rating: ★★★
Miscellaneous: Sound is rather subdued. Audio levels move quite significantly during **IN THE FLESH?**, no doubt the recording device adapting to the sheer volume from the band.

Date: 20-02-1981
Location: Westfallenhalle, Dortmund, West Germany
Track Listing: Intro, In The Flesh?, The Thin Ice, Another Brick In The Wall Part 1, The Happiest Days Of Our Lives, Another Brick In The Wall Part 2, Mother, Goodbye Blue Sky, Empty Spaces, What Shall We Do Now?, Young Lust, One Of My Turns, Don't Leave Me Now, Another Brick In The Wall Part 3, The Last Few Bricks, Goodbye Cruel World, Hey You, Is There Anybody Out There?, Nobody Home, Vera, Bring The Boys Back Home, Comfortably Numb, The Show Must Go On, In The Flesh, Run Like Hell, Waiting For The Worms, Stop, The Trial, Outside The Wall
Audio Rating: ★★★
Miscellaneous: Rather murky at louder parts, such as **YOUNG LUST**.

Date: 13-06-1981
Location: Earl's Court Exhibition Hall, London, England
Track Listing: Intro, In The Flesh?, The Thin Ice, Another Brick In The Wall Part 1, The Happiest Days Of Our Lives, Another Brick In The Wall Part 2, Mother, Goodbye Blue Sky, Empty Spaces, What Shall We Do Now?, Young Lust, One Of My Turns, Don't Leave Me Now, Another Brick In The Wall Part 3, The Last Few Bricks, Goodbye Cruel World, Hey You, Is There Anybody Out There?, Nobody Home, Vera, Bring The Boys Back Home, Comfortably Numb, The Show Must Go On, In The Flesh, Run Like Hell, Waiting For The Worms, Stop, The Trial, Outside The Wall
Audio Rating: ★★♪
Miscellaneous: A four-month break after West Germany, five London shows on consecutive days. Gilmour's solo in **ANOTHER BRICK IN THE WALL PART 2** is very unlike the album, and he sounds a bit flat during **COMFORTABLY NUMB** (though this may be down to the poor audio).

Date: 14-06-1981
Location: Earl's Court Exhibition Hall, London, England
Track Listing: Intro, In The Flesh?, The Thin Ice, Another Brick In The Wall Part 1, The Happiest Days Of Our Lives, Another Brick In The Wall Part 2, Mother, Goodbye Blue Sky, Empty Spaces, What Shall We Do Now?, Young Lust, One Of My Turns, Don't Leave Me Now, Another Brick In The Wall Part 3, The Last Few Bricks, Goodbye Cruel World, Hey You, Is There Anybody Out There?, Nobody Home, Vera, Bring The Boys Back Home, Comfortably Numb, The Show Must Go On, In The Flesh, Run Like Hell, Waiting For The Worms, Stop, The Trial, Outside The Wall
Audio Rating: ★★★★
Miscellaneous: An enthusiastic audience seems to gee up the band.

Date: 15-06-1981
Location: Earl's Court Exhibition Hall, London, England
Track Listing: Intro/In The Flesh?, The Thin Ice, Another Brick In The Wall Part 1, The Happiest Days Of Our Lives, Another Brick In The Wall Part 2, Mother, Goodbye Blue Sky, Empty Spaces, What Shall We Do Now?, Young Lust, One Of My Turns, Don't Leave Me Now, Another Brick In The Wall Part 3, The Last Few Bricks, Goodbye Cruel World, Hey You, Is There Anybody Out There?, Nobody Home, Vera, Bring The Boys Back Home, Comfortably Numb, The Show Must Go On, In The Flesh, Run Like Hell, Waiting For The Worms, Stop, The Trial, Outside The Wall
Audio Rating: ★★★★
Miscellaneous: Lovely and crisp sounding, if lacking bottom end.

Date: 16-06-1981
Location: Earl's Court Exhibition Hall, London, England
Track Listing: Intro/In The Flesh?, The Thin Ice, Another Brick In The Wall Part 1, The Happiest Days Of Our Lives, Another Brick In The Wall Part 2, Mother, Goodbye Blue Sky, Empty Spaces, What Shall We Do Now?, Young Lust, One Of My Turns, Don't Leave Me Now, Another Brick In The Wall Part 3, The Last Few Bricks, Goodbye Cruel World, Hey You, Is There Anybody Out There?, Nobody Home, Vera, Bring The Boys Back Home, Comfortably Numb, The Show Must Go On, In The Flesh, Run Like Hell, Waiting For The Worms, Stop, The Trial, Outside The Wall
Audio Rating: ★★★★*
Miscellaneous: Absolutely terrific sounding, crisp, with both low end and trebles captured. Gilmour's nylon strings at the start of **GOODBYE BLUE SKY** resonate beautifully, and there's a great raw edge to his guitar during **YOUNG LUST**. Waters' introduction to **RUN LIKE HELL** has to be heard to be believed. With a lot of whistling going on between songs he says, 'This next song's for all the whistlers in the audience. Are there any whistlers in the audience? Let's all have a fucking good whistle! [attempts to whistle] Pffffft! Christ, I must learn to do that, it sounds like such fun! This is called "Run Like Hell". I'd like to see you all getting your hands together and having a good time! Mmmm! Disco! Get down!'

Date: 17-06-1981
Location: Earl's Court Exhibition Hall, London, England
Track Listing: Intro, In The Flesh?, The Thin Ice, Another Brick In The Wall Part 1, The Happiest Days Of Our Lives, Another Brick In The Wall Part 2, Mother, Goodbye Blue Sky, Empty Spaces, What Shall We Do Now?, Young Lust, One Of My Turns, Don't Leave Me Now, Another Brick In The Wall Part 3, The Last Few Bricks, Goodbye Cruel World, Hey You, Is There Anybody Out There?, Nobody Home, Vera, Bring The Boys Back Home, Comfortably Numb, The Show Must Go On, In The Flesh, Run Like Hell, Waiting For The Worms, Stop, The Trial, Outside The Wall
Audio Rating: ★★★★
Miscellaneous: The final show of the Gilmour-Mason-Waters-Wright lineup until 2005. They don't sound like a band falling apart. Like the rest of *The Wall* tour, the performance is highly professional, if without any spontaneity, the band sound potent and Waters' vocal performance is (given his limitations) quite remarkable. But falling apart it was.

1987

Date: 07-08-1987
Location: Pearson Airport, Toronto, Ontario, Canada
Track Listing: Tunings, Echoes, Signs Of Life, Learning To Fly, A New Machine Part 1, Terminal Frost, A New Machine Part 2, Sorrow, The Dogs Of War, On The Turning Away, One Of These Days, Time, Wish You Were Here, Welcome To The Machine, Us And Them, Money, Another Brick In The Wall Part 2, Comfortably Numb, One Slip, Run Like Hell
Audio Rating: ★★★★★
Miscellaneous: A rehearsal for the world tour, which was filmed and thus concerned more with appearance than performance, with numerous songs being incomplete or cutting out. The audio, however, comes from the soundboard, and without any fans or other distractions is of practically studio fidelity – you can hear exactly how the live rendition of the studio song would sound. However, Gilmour seems to be holding back vocally for the tour's opening night.

Date: 09-09-1987
Location: Lansdowne Park Stadium, Ottawa, Ontario, Canada

Track Listing: Echoes, Signs Of Life, Learning To Fly, A New Machine Part 1, Terminal Frost, A New Machine Part 2, Sorrow (Cut), The Dogs Of War, Yet Another Movie, On The Turning Away, One Of These Days, Time, On The Run, Wish You Were Here, Welcome To The Machine, Us And Them, Money, Another Brick In The Wall Part 2, Comfortably Numb, One Slip, Run Like Hell
Audio Rating: ★★★★
Miscellaneous: Absolutely rapturous audience, which is quite amazing considering *Momentary Lapse* had only just been released. The vocals to **SORROW** cut out briefly at the start of the third verse.

Date: 12-09-1987
Location: Forum De Montreal, Montreal, Quebec, Canada
Track Listing: Echoes, Signs Of Life, Learning To Fly, A New Machine Part 1, Terminal Frost, A New Machine Part 2, Sorrow, The Dogs Of War, Yet Another Movie, On The Turning Away, One Of These Days, Time, On The Run, Wish You Were Here, Welcome To The Machine, Us And Them, Money, Another Brick In The Wall Part 2, Comfortably Numb, One Slip, Run Like Hell, Shine On You Crazy Diamond
Audio Rating: ★★★♪
Miscellaneous: **SHINE ON YOU CRAZY DIAMOND** is played as an unusual encore. Gilmour slightly exasperatedly announces it: 'Okay, you'll have to quieten down a little bit for this one, because otherwise we won't hear a thing and neither will you. So en fois de silence ... A bit of quiet please, thank you ... Shut up!' At which a fan screams 'PINK FLOYD NUMBER ONE ... YEAH!!!!' Montreal Pink Floyd fans seem to be particularly rabid. The performance of **SHINE ON YOU CRAZY DIAMOND** is rather rough, the band apparently not being able to hear themselves play.

Date: 13-09-1987
Location: Forum De Montreal, Montreal, Quebec, Canada
Track Listing: Echoes, Signs Of Life, Learning To Fly, Yet Another Movie, A New Machine Part 1, Terminal Frost, A New Machine Part 2, Sorrow, The Dogs Of War, On The Turning Away, One Of These Days, Time, On The Run, Wish You Were Here, Welcome To The Machine, Us And Them, Money, Another Brick In The Wall Part 2, Comfortably Numb, Audience, One Slip, Run Like Hell, Shine On You Crazy Diamond
Audio Rating: ★★★♪
Miscellaneous: Second night in Montreal, not quite as rabid but still utterly fervent.

Date: 14-09-1987
Location: Forum De Montreal, Montreal, Quebec, Canada
Track Listing: Echoes (Fade In), Signs Of Life, Learning To Fly, Yet Another Movie, A New Machine Part 1, Terminal Frost, A New Machine Part 2, Sorrow (Incomplete), The Dogs Of War, On The Turning Away, One Of These Days, Time, On The Run, Wish You Were Here, Welcome To The Machine, Us And Them, Money, Another Brick In The Wall Part 2, Comfortably Numb, Audience, One Slip, Run Like Hell, Shine On You Crazy Diamond
Audio Rating: ★★♪
Miscellaneous: **ECHOES** starts about one-third of the way through, during the funk jam.

Date: 16-09-1987
Location: Municipal Stadium, Cleveland, Ohio, USA
Track Listing: Echoes, Signs Of Life, Learning To Fly, Yet Another Movie, Round And Around, A New Machine Part I, Terminal Frost, A New Machine Part Ii, Sorrow, Dogs Of War, On The Turning Away, One Of These Days, Time, On The Run, Wish You Were Here, Welcome To The Machine, Us And Them, Money, Another Brick In The Wall Part 2, Comfortably Numb, One Slip, Run Like Hell, Shine On You Crazy Diamond
Audio Rating: ★★★
Miscellaneous: After **ANOTHER BRICK IN THE WALL PART 2**, Gilmour says, 'Thank you! Wow, what fun, eh? That's it, do it. There is always a way ... All right, thank you very much for coming, all you people. This is a big place isn't it? We haven't been here in a few years. Anyway, one more, and then it will be time to go, so thank you again for coming, I hope you've all had a good time.'

Date: 17-09-1987
Location: Municipal Stadium, Cleveland, Ohio, USA
Track Listing: Echoes, Signs Of Life, Learning To Fly, Yet Another Movie, A New Machine Part 1, Terminal Frost, A New Machine Part 2,

Sorrow, The Dogs Of War, On The Turning Away, One Of These Days, Time, On The Run, Wish You Were Here, Welcome To The Machine, Us And Them, Money, Another Brick In The Wall Part 2, Comfortably Numb, Run Like Hell, Shine On You Crazy Diamond
Audio Rating: ★★★✦
Miscellaneous: **ONE SLIP** gets benched for a few gigs. A bit ambitious having it as an encore – and notable that it didn't make the *Division Bell* tour.

Date: 19-09-1987
Location: John F. Kennedy Stadium, Philadelphia, Pennsylvania, USA
Track Listing: Echoes, Signs Of Life, Learning To Fly, Yet Another Movie, Round And Around, A New Machine I, Terminal Frost, A New Machine Ii, Sorrow, Dogs Of War, On The Turning Away, One Of These Days, Time, On The Run, Wish You Were Here, Welcome To The Machine, Us And Them, Money, Another Brick In The Wall Part 2, Comfortably Numb, Run Like Hell, Shine On You Crazy Diamond
Audio Rating: ★★★★
Miscellaneous: Audio very clear, but the bass is louder than the other guitars.

Date: 21-09-1987
Location: Canadian National Exhibition Stadium, Toronto, Ontario, Canada
Track Listing: Echoes, Signs Of Life, Learning To Fly, Yet Another Movie, A New Machine Part 1, Terminal Frost, A New Machine Part 2, Sorrow, The Dogs Of War, On The Turning Away, One Of These Days, Time, On The Run, Wish You Were Here, Welcome To The Machine, Us And Them, Money, Another Brick In The Wall Part 2, Comfortably Numb, One Slip, Run Like Hell
Audio Rating: ★★★★
Miscellaneous: **ONE SLIP** returns, **SHINE ON YOU CRAZY DIAMOND** departs as an encore.

Date: 22-09-1987
Location: Canadian National Exhibition Stadium, Toronto, Ontario, Canada
Track Listing: Echoes, Signs Of Life, Learning To Fly, Yet Another Movie, Round & Round, A New Machine Part 1, Terminal Frost, A New Machine Part 2, Sorrow, Dogs Of War, Intro/On The Turning Away, One Of These Days, Time, On The Run, Wish You Were Here, Welcome To The Machine, Us And Them, Money, Another Brick In The Wall Part 2, Intro/Comfortably Numb, One Slip, Run Like Hell
Audio Rating: ★★★✦
Miscellaneous: Audience very audible skirling and whooping, making Gilmour's occasional comments indecipherable (not that he says much of great note).

Date: 23-09-1987
Location: Canadian National Exhibition Stadium, Toronto, Ontario, Canada
Track Listing: Echoes, Signs Of Life, Learning To Fly, Yet Another Movie, A New Machine Part 1, Terminal Frost, A New Machine Part 2, Sorrow, Dogs Of War, On The Turning Away, One Of These Days, Time, On The Run, Wish You Were Here, Welcome To The Machine, Us And Them, Money, Another Brick In The Wall Part 2, Comfortably Numb, One Slip, Run Like Hell
Audio Rating: ★★★
Miscellaneous: Sound somewhat wobbly.

Date: 25-09-1987
Location: Rosemont Horizon, Rosemont, Chicago, Illinois, USA
Track Listing: Echoes, Signs Of Life, Learning To Fly, Yet Another Movie, Round And Around, A New Machine Part 1, Terminal Frost, Sorrow, Dogs Of War, On The Turning Away, One Of These Days, Time, On The Run, Wish You Were Here, Welcome To The Machine, Us And Them, Money, Another Brick In The Wall Part 2, Comfortably Numb, One Slip, Run Like Hell
Audio Rating: ★★★★
Miscellaneous: The last time **ECHOES** was played. Mason: 'David now observes that one of the reasons we couldn't quite recapture the feel of the original was that the younger musicians we were now working with were so technically proficient they were not able to unlearn their technique and just noodle around as we had in the early Seventies." They must be talking about Guy Pratt or Jon Carin.

Date: 26-09-1987
Location: Rosemont Horizon, Rosemont, Chicago, Illinois, USA
Track Listing: Shine On You Crazy Diamond, Signs Of Life, Learning To Fly, Yet Another Movie, A New Machine Part 1, Terminal Frost, A

---

* Mason, *Inside Out*, p.290.

New Machine Part 2, Sorrow, Dogs Of War, On The Turning Away, One Of These Days, Time, On The Run, Wish You Were Here, Welcome To The Machine, Us And Them, Money, Another Brick In The Wall Part 2, Comfortably Numb, One Slip, Run Like Hell
Audio Rating: ★★★
Miscellaneous: SHINE ON YOU CRAZY DIAMOND takes its place as the opening track, a position it kept throughout the next tour. It is received absolutely rapturously – no wonder the tour improved the morale of Wright and Mason.

Date: 27-09-1987
Location: Rosemont Horizon, Rosemont, Chicago, Illinois, USA
Track Listing: Shine On You Crazy Diamond, Signs Of Life, Learning To Fly, Yet Another Movie, A New Machine Part 1, Terminal Frost, A New Machine Part 2, Sorrow, Dogs Of War, On The Turning Away, One Of These Days, Time, On The Run, Wish You Were Here, Welcome To The Machine, Us And Them, Money, Another Brick In The Wall Part 2, Comfortably Numb, One Slip, Run Like Hell
Audio Rating: ★★
Miscellaneous: Very muddy and muffled sounding.

Date: 28-09-1987
Location: Rosemont Horizon, Rosemont, Chicago, Illinois, USA
Track Listing: Shine On You Crazy Diamond, Signs Of Life, Learning To Fly, Yet Another Movie, Round And Around, A New Machine Part 1, Terminal Frost, Sorrow, Dogs Of War, On The Turning Away, One Of These Days, Time, On The Run, Wish You Were Here, Welcome To The Machine, Us And Them, Money, Another Brick In The Wall Part 2, Comfortably Numb, One Slip, Run Like Hell
Audio Rating: ★★★✦
Miscellaneous: A fourth night in Chicago.

Date: 30-09-1987
Location: County Stadium, Milwaukee, Wisconsin, USA
Track Listing: Shine On You Crazy Diamond, Signs Of Life, Learning To Fly, Yet Another Movie, Round And Around, A New Machine Part 1, Terminal Frost, Sorrow, Dogs Of War, On The Turning Away, One Of These Days, Time, On The Run, Wish You Were Here, Welcome To The Machine, Us And Them, Money, Another Brick In The Wall Part 2, Comfortably Numb, One Slip, Run Like Hell
Audio Rating: ★★★★
Miscellaneous: A NEW MACHINE PART 2 absent for whatever reason.

Date: 03-10-1987
Location: Carrier Dome, Syracuse University, Syracuse, New York, USA
Track Listing: Shine On You Crazy Diamond, Signs Of Life, Learning To Fly, Yet Another Movie, A New Machine Part 1, Terminal Frost, A New Machine Part 2, Sorrow, The Dogs Of War, On The Turning Away, One Of These Days, Time, On The Run, Wish You Were Here, Welcome To The Machine, Us And Them, Money, Another Brick In The Wall Part 2, Comfortably Numb, One Slip, Run Like Hell
Audio Rating: ★★★★
Miscellaneous: Vocals notably less clear than the instruments (especially Gilmour's guitar, which sounds amazing).

Date: 05-10-1987
Location: Madison Square Garden, New York City, New York, USA
Track Listing: Shine On You Crazy Diamond, Signs Of Life, Learning To Fly, Yet Another Movie, Round And Around, A New Machine I, Terminal Frost, A New Machine Ii, Sorrow, The Dogs Of War, On The Turning Away, One Of These Days, Time, On The Run, Wish You Were Here, Welcome To The Machine, Us And Them, Money, Another Brick In The Wall Part 2, Comfortably Numb, One Slip, Run Like Hell
Audio Rating: ★★★★
Miscellaneous: The group's first time playing in Madison Square Garden since July 1977, when Waters lost his temper at the fireworks being let off.

Date: 06-10-1987
Location: Madison Square Garden, New York City, New York, USA
Track Listing: Shine On You Crazy Diamond, Signs Of Life, Learning To Fly, Yet Another Movie, A New Machine Part 1, Terminal Frost, A New Machine Part 2, Sorrow, The Dogs Of War, On The Turning Away, One Of These Days, Time, On The Run, Wish You Were Here, Welcome To The Machine, Us And Them, Money, Another Brick In The Wall Part 2, Comfortably Numb, One Slip, Run Like Hell

Audio Rating: ★★★↙
Miscellaneous: The very end of **SORROW** and the first seconds of **THE DOGS OF WAR** are missing, presumably for a tape change. Some of the second solo in **COMFORTABLY NUMB** is also missing.

Date: 07-10-1987
Location: Madison Square Garden, New York City, New York, USA
Track Listing: Shine On You Crazy Diamond, Signs Of Life, Learning To Fly, Yet Another Movie, A New Machine Part 1, Terminal Frost, A New Machine Part 2, Sorrow, The Dogs Of War, On The Turning Away, One Of These Days, Time, On The Run, Wish You Were Here, Welcome To The Machine, Us And Them, Money, Another Brick In The Wall Part 2, Comfortably Numb, One Slip, Run Like Hell
Audio Rating: ★★★↙
Miscellaneous: A third night at MSG.

Date: 10-10-1987
Location: Brendan Byrne Meadowlands Arena, East Rutherford, New Jersey, USA
Track Listing: Shine On You Crazy Diamond, Signs Of Life, Learning To Fly, Yet Another Movie, A New Machine Part 1, Terminal Frost, A New Machine Part 2, Sorrow, The Dogs Of War, On The Turning Away, One Of These Days, Time, On The Run, Wish You Were Here, Welcome To The Machine, Us And Them, Money, Another Brick In The Wall Part 2, Comfortably Numb, One Slip, Run Like Hell
Audio Rating: ★★★↙
Miscellaneous: Brendan Byrne Meadowlands Arena closed in 2015 and has since been used to film TV series, including *The Equalizer*, *Tales of the Walking Dead* and *The Walking Dead: Dead City*.

Date: 11-10-1987
Location: Brendan Byrne Meadowlands Arena, East Rutherford, New Jersey, USA
Track Listing: Shine On You Crazy Diamond, Signs Of Life, Learning To Fly, Yet Another Movie, A New Machine Part 1, Terminal Frost, A New Machine Part 2, Sorrow, The Dogs Of War, On The Turning Away, One Of These Days, Time, On The Run, Wish You Were Here, Welcome To The Machine, Us And Them, Money, Another Brick In The Wall Part 2, Comfortably Numb, One Slip, Run Like Hell
Audio Rating: ★★★↙
Miscellaneous: Very standard gig, but they got to have fun afterwards.

Date: 11-10-1987
Location: The World nightclub, Manhattan, New York
Track Listing: Instrumental, I Know My Baby Loves Me, Respect, Born Under A Bad Sign, Instrumental, I Heard It Through The Grapevine, Hideaway
Audio Rating: ★★★
Miscellaneous: An impromptu show in a New York nightclub playing R&B standards, with backing singers Rachel Fury and Margaret Taylor getting a chance to shine. You can almost see Gilmour wearing a pair of blues musician's sunglasses and having a boozy laugh.

Date: 12-10-1987
Location: Brendan Byrne Meadowlands Arena, East Rutherford, New Jersey, USA
Track Listing: Shine On You Crazy Diamond, Signs Of Life, Learning To Fly, Yet Another Movie, A New Machine Part 1, Terminal Frost, A New Machine Part 2, Sorrow, The Dogs Of War, On The Turning Away, One Of These Days, Time, On The Run, Wish You Were Here, Welcome To The Machine, Us And Them, Money, Another Brick In The Wall Part 2, Comfortably Numb, One Slip, Run Like Hell
Audio Rating: ★★★↙
Miscellaneous: 'Thank you! Thank you very much! Good night! Thank you very much for coming out.' Gilmour will never be one of the stage raconteurs.

Date: 14-10-1987
Location: Hartford Civic Center, Hartford, Connecticut, USA
Track Listing: Shine On You Crazy Diamond, Signs Of Life, Learning To Fly, Yet Another Movie, A New Machine Part 1, Terminal Frost, A New Machine Part 2, Sorrow, The Dogs Of War, On The Turning Away, One Of These Days, Time, On The Run, Wish You Were Here, Welcome To The Machine, Us And Them, Money, Another Brick In The Wall Part 2, Comfortably Numb, One Slip, Run Like Hell
Audio Rating: ★★★★
Miscellaneous: Sounds excellent, the vocals being particularly clear.

Date: 15-10-1987
Location: Hartford Civic Center, Hartford, Connecticut, USA
Track Listing: Shine On You Crazy Diamond, Signs Of Life, Learning To Fly, Yet Another Movie, A New Machine Part 1, Terminal Frost, A New Machine Part 2, Sorrow, The Dogs Of War, On The Turning Away, One Of These Days, Time, On The Run, Wish You Were Here, Welcome To The Machine, Us And Them, Money, Another Brick In The Wall Part 2, Comfortably Numb, One Slip, Run Like Hell
Audio Rating: ★★★★✦
Miscellaneous: Also excellent audio, perhaps helped by the Hartford Civic Center being an indoors venue.

Date: 16-10-1987
Location: Providence Civic Center, Providence, Rhode Island, USA
Track Listing: Shine On You Crazy Diamond, Signs Of Life, Learning To Fly, Yet Another Movie, A New Machine Part 1, Terminal Frost, A New Machine Part 2, Sorrow, The Dogs Of War, On The Turning Away, One Of These Days, Time, On The Run, Wish You Were Here, Welcome To The Machine, Us And Them, Money, Another Brick In The Wall Part 2, Comfortably Numb, One Slip, Run Like Hell
Audio Rating: ★★✦
Miscellaneous: Very distant sounding.

Date: 17-10-1987
Location: Providence Civic Center, Providence, Rhode Island, USA
Track Listing: Shine On You Crazy Diamond, Signs Of Life, Learning To Fly, Yet Another Movie, A New Machine Part 1, Terminal Frost, A New Machine Part 2, Sorrow, The Dogs Of War, On The Turning Away, One Of These Days, Time, On The Run, Wish You Were Here, Welcome To The Machine, Us And Them, Money, Another Brick In The Wall Part 2, Comfortably Numb, One Slip, Run Like Hell
Audio Rating: ★★★★★✦
Miscellaneous: A touch murky, but clear enough.

Date: 19-10-1987
Location: Capital Centre, Landover, Maryland, USA
Track Listing: Shine On You Crazy Diamond, Signs Of Life, Learning To Fly, Yet Another Movie, A New Machine Part 1, Terminal Frost, A New Machine Part 2, Sorrow, The Dogs Of War, On The Turning Away, One Of These Days, Time, On The Run, Wish You Were Here, Welcome To The Machine, Us And Them, Money, Another Brick In The Wall Part 2, Comfortably Numb, One Slip, Run Like Hell
Audio Rating: ★★★✦
Miscellaneous: During **MONEY**, Gilmour says something sotte voce after 'I think I'll buy myself a football team' – can anyone make out what he's saying? Previously he has said things like 'Yes I do!' but this sounds different.

Date: 20-10-1987
Location: Capital Centre, Landover, Maryland, USA
Track Listing: Shine On You Crazy Diamond, Signs Of Life, Learning To Fly, Yet Another Movie, A New Machine Part 1, Terminal Frost, A New Machine Part 2, Sorrow, The Dogs Of War, On The Turning Away, One Of These Days, Time, On The Run, Wish You Were Here, Welcome To The Machine, Us And Them, Money, Another Brick In The Wall Part 2, Comfortably Numb, One Slip, Run Like Hell
Audio Rating: ★★★
Miscellaneous: Distant-sounding but clear.

Date: 21-10-1987
Location: Capital Centre, Landover, Maryland, USA
Track Listing: Shine On You Crazy Diamond, Signs Of Life, Learning To Fly, Yet Another Movie, A New Machine Part 1, Terminal Frost, A New Machine Part 2, Sorrow, The Dogs Of War, On The Turning Away, One Of These Days, Time, On The Run, Wish You Were Here, Welcome To The Machine, Us And Them, Money, Another Brick In The Wall Part 2, Comfortably Numb, One Slip, Run Like Hell
Audio Rating: ★★✦
Miscellaneous: Quite hissy and distant-sounding.

Date: 22-10-1987
Location: Capital Centre, Landover, Maryland, USA
Track Listing: Shine On You Crazy Diamond, Signs Of Life, Learning To Fly, Yet Another Movie, A New Machine Part 1, Terminal Frost, A New Machine Part 2, Sorrow, The Dogs Of War, On The Turning Away, One Of These Days, Time, On The Run, Wish You Were Here, Welcome To The Machine, Us And Them,

Money, Another Brick In The Wall Part 2, Comfortably Numb, One Slip, Run Like Hell
Audio Rating: ★★★
Miscellaneous: A fourth night in Maryland. It must have been obvious by now that the tour was going extremely well.

Date: 25-10-1987
Location: Dean E. Smith Student Activities Center, University of North Carolina, Chapel Hill, North Carolina, USA
Track Listing: Shine On You Crazy Diamond, Signs Of Life, Learning To Fly, Yet Another Movie, A New Machine Part 1, Terminal Frost, A New Machine Part 2, Sorrow, The Dogs Of War, On The Turning Away, One Of These Days, Time, On The Run, Wish You Were Here, Welcome To The Machine, Us And Them, Money, Another Brick In The Wall Part 2, Comfortably Numb, One Slip, Run Like Hell
Audio Rating: ★★♪
Miscellaneous: Sounds like the taper put the microphone into a bag for the first set after **SHINE ON YOU CRAZY DIAMOND**. The audio improves for the second set, but it's still rather muffled and distant.

Date: 26-10-1987
Location: Dean E. Smith Student Activities Center, University of North Carolina, Chapel Hill, North Carolina, USA
Track Listing: Shine On You Crazy Diamond, Signs Of Life, Learning To Fly, Yet Another Movie, A New Machine Part 1, Terminal Frost, A New Machine Part 2, Sorrow, The Dogs Of War, On The Turning Away, One Of These Days, Time, On The Run, Wish You Were Here, Welcome To The Machine, Us And Them, Money, Another Brick In The Wall Part 2, Comfortably Numb, One Slip, Run Like Hell
Audio Rating: ★★★
Miscellaneous: Audio improves as it goes on. The second set is really quite good.

Date: 30-10-1987
Location: Tampa Stadium, Tampa, Florida, USA
Track Listing: Shine On You Crazy Diamond, Signs Of Life, Learning To Fly, Yet Another Movie, A New Machine Part 1, Terminal Frost, A New Machine Part 2, Sorrow, The Dogs Of War, On The Turning Away, One Of These Days, Time, On The Run, Wish You Were Here, Welcome To The Machine, Us And Them, Money, Another Brick In The Wall Part 2, Comfortably Numb, One Slip, Run Like Hell
Audio Rating: ★★♪
Miscellaneous: Awfully hissy. Sounds like all in attendance had a good time, though.

Date: 01-11-1987
Location: Orange Bowl, Miami, Florida, USA
Track Listing: Shine On You Crazy Diamond, Signs Of Life, Learning To Fly, Yet Another Movie, A New Machine Part 1, Terminal Frost, A New Machine Part 2, Sorrow, The Dogs Of War, On The Turning Away, One Of These Days, Time, On The Run, Wish You Were Here, Welcome To The Machine, Us And Them, Money, Another Brick In The Wall Part 2, Comfortably Numb, One Slip, Run Like Hell
Audio Rating: ★★★♪
Miscellaneous: The concluding guitar solo in **RUN LIKE HELL** sounds magnificent.

Date: 03-11-1987
Location: The Omni Coliseum, Atlanta, Georgia, USA
Track Listing: Shine On You Crazy Diamond, Signs Of Life, Learning To Fly, Yet Another Movie, A New Machine Part 1, Terminal Frost, A New Machine Part 2, Sorrow, The Dogs Of War, On The Turning Away, One Of These Days, Time, On The Run, Wish You Were Here, Welcome To The Machine, Us And Them, Money, Another Brick In The Wall Part 2, Comfortably Numb, One Slip, Run Like Hell
Audio Rating: ★★★♪
Miscellaneous: Audience go absolutely bat-shit during the second set – one of the strongest audience responses captured, sheer delirium. The guitars sound superb but everything else a bit echoey.

Date: 04-11-1987
Location: The Omni Coliseum, Atlanta, Georgia, USA
Track Listing: Shine On You Crazy Diamond, Signs Of Life, Learning To Fly, Yet Another Movie, A New Machine Part 1, Terminal Frost, A New Machine Part 2, Sorrow, The Dogs Of War, On The Turning Away, One Of These Days, Time, On The Run, Wish You Were Here, Welcome To The Machine, Us And Them, Money, Another Brick In The Wall Part 2, Comfortably Numb, One Slip, Run Like Hell
Audio Rating: ★★★
Miscellaneous: The last verse of **MONEY** and very beginning of **ANOTHER BRICK IN THE**

WALL PART 2 are missing. The audience reaction to Gilmour's entry in **SHINE ON YOU CRAZY DIAMOND** is breathtaking.

Date: 10-11-1987
Location: Pontiac Silverdome, Pontiac, Detroit, Michigan, USA
Track Listing: Shine On You Crazy Diamond, Signs Of Life, Learning To Fly, Yet Another Movie, A New Machine Part 1, Terminal Frost, A New Machine Part 2, Sorrow, The Dogs Of War, On The Turning Away, One Of These Days, Time, On The Run, Wish You Were Here, Welcome To The Machine, Us And Them, Money, Another Brick In The Wall Part 2, Comfortably Numb, One Slip, Run Like Hell
Audio Rating: ★★★↙
Miscellaneous: The Silverdome was one of the biggest stadiums in the US (it hosted a record-breaking claimed attendance of 93,173 for WrestleMania III eight months earlier, on 29 March 1987). The attendance for Pink Floyd was reputedly a sold-out 46,192.

Date: 12-11-1987
Location: Hoosier Dome, Indianapolis, Indiana, USA
Track Listing: Shine On You Crazy Diamond, Signs Of Life, Learning To Fly, Yet Another Movie, A New Machine Part 1, Terminal Frost, A New Machine Part 2, Sorrow, The Dogs Of War, On The Turning Away, One Of These Days, Time, On The Run, Wish You Were Here, Welcome To The Machine, Us And Them, Money, Another Brick In The Wall Part 2, Comfortably Numb, One Slip, Run Like Hell
Audio Rating: ★★
Miscellaneous: **SORROW** cuts during the guitar solo but picks it up for the concluding iteration of the main riff.

Date: 15-11-1987
Location: St Louis Arena, St Louis, Missouri, USA
Track Listing: Shine On You Crazy Diamond, Signs Of Life, Learning To Fly, Yet Another Movie, A New Machine Part 1, Terminal Frost, A New Machine Part 2, Sorrow, The Dogs Of War, On The Turning Away, One Of These Days, Time, On The Run, Wish You Were Here, Welcome To The Machine, Us And Them, Money, Another Brick In The Wall Part 2, Comfortably Numb, One Slip, Run Like Hell
Audio Rating: ★★★

Miscellaneous: Another extremely loud crowd. There's a fade-out/fade-in at around 8.16 in **SORROW**, presumably for a tape change.

Date: 16-11-1987
Location: St Louis Arena, St Louis, Missouri, USA
Track Listing: Yet Another Movie (Fade In), A New Machine Part 1, Terminal Frost, A New Machine Part 2, Sorrow, The Dogs Of War, On The Turning Away, One Of These Days (Fade In), Time, On The Run, Wish You Were Here, Welcome To The Machine, Us And Them, Money, Another Brick In The Wall Part 2, Comfortably Numb, One Slip, Run Like Hell
Audio Rating: ★★★
Miscellaneous: Comes in one-third through **YET ANOTHER MOVIE**, thus missing **SHINE ON YOU CRAZY DIAMOND**, **SIGNS OF LIFE**, and **LEARNING TO FLY**. **ONE OF THESE DAYS** similarly fades in about halfway through.

Date: 18-11-1987
Location: Astrodome, Houston, Texas, USA
Track Listing: Shine On You Crazy Diamond, Signs Of Life, Learning To Fly, Yet Another Movie, A New Machine Part 1, Terminal Frost, A New Machine Part 2, Sorrow, The Dogs Of War, On The Turning Away, One Of These Days, Time, On The Run, Wish You Were Here, Welcome To The Machine, Us And Them, Money, Another Brick In The Wall Part 2, Comfortably Numb, One Slip, Run Like Hell
Audio Rating: ★★★↙
Miscellaneous: A weird ticking/scratching sound affects **RUN LIKE HELL**, but the rest is good.

Date: 19-11-1987
Location: Frank Erwin Center, University of Texas, Austin, Texas, USA
Track Listing: Shine On You Crazy Diamond, Signs Of Life, Learning To Fly, Yet Another Movie, A New Machine Part 1, Terminal Frost, A New Machine Part 2, Sorrow, The Dogs Of War, On The Turning Away, One Of These Days, Time, On The Run, Wish You Were Here, Welcome To The Machine, Us And Them, Money, Another Brick In The Wall Part 2, Comfortably Numb, One Slip, Run Like Hell
Audio Rating: ★★★★
Miscellaneous: Lovely clear audio, especially on louder tracks; only the vocals lack sufficient presence.

Date: 21-11-1987
Location: Reunion Arena, Reunion Park, Dallas, Texas, USA
Track Listing: Shine On You Crazy Diamond, Signs Of Life, Learning To Fly, Yet Another Movie, A New Machine Part 1, Terminal Frost, A New Machine Part 2, Sorrow, The Dogs Of War, On The Turning Away, One Of These Days, Time, On The Run, Wish You Were Here, Welcome To The Machine, Us And Them, Money, Another Brick In The Wall Part 2, Comfortably Numb, One Slip, Run Like Hell
Audio Rating: ★★★
Miscellaneous: Sound rather muffled.

Date: 22-11-1987
Location: Reunion Arena, Reunion Park, Dallas, Texas, USA
Track Listing: Shine On You Crazy Diamond, Signs Of Life, Learning To Fly, Yet Another Movie, A New Machine Part 1, Terminal Frost, A New Machine Part 2, Sorrow, The Dogs Of War, On The Turning Away, One Of These Days, Time, On The Run, Wish You Were Here, Welcome To The Machine, Us And Them, Money, Another Brick In The Wall Part 2, Comfortably Numb, One Slip, Run Like Hell
Audio Rating: ★★★↙
Miscellaneous: After **RUN LIKE HELL** Gilmour says, 'Thanks you very much! Thank you very much, good night! Hope to see some of you tomorrow night.' They played three nights in Dallas but there seem to be bootlegs for only two of them; this was the second night of three.

Date: 26-11-1987
Location: Los Angeles Memorial Sports Arena, Los Angeles, California, USA
Track Listing: Shine On You Crazy Diamond, Signs Of Life, Learning To Fly, Yet Another Movie, A New Machine Part 1, Terminal Frost, A New Machine Part 2, Sorrow, The Dogs Of War, On The Turning Away, One Of These Days, Time, On The Run, Wish You Were Here, Welcome To The Machine, Us And Them, Money, Another Brick In The Wall Part 2, Comfortably Numb, One Slip, Run Like Hell
Audio Rating: ★★★★
Miscellaneous: One of the most frequently played venues by Pink Floyd, having previously performed there on the *Wish You Were Here* and *The Wall* tours. (For the *Division Bell* tour they bypassed Los Angeles, instead playing nearby Pasadena. For the *Animals* tour, after police violence in 1975, they played Anaheim.)

Date: 27-11-1987
Location: Los Angeles Memorial Sports Arena, Los Angeles, California, USA
Track Listing: Shine On You Crazy Diamond, Signs Of Life, Learning To Fly, Yet Another Movie, A New Machine Part 1, Terminal Frost, A New Machine Part 2, Sorrow, The Dogs Of War, On The Turning Away, One Of These Days, Time, On The Run, Wish You Were Here, Welcome To The Machine, Us And Them, Money, Another Brick In The Wall Part 2, Comfortably Numb, One Slip, Run Like Hell
Audio Rating: ★★★
Miscellaneous: Recorder a bit overloaded when things get loud, so clarity is best during quiet moments, but even then it still sounds quite distant.

Date: 28-11-1987
Location: Los Angeles Memorial Sports Arena, Los Angeles, California, USA
Track Listing: Shine On You Crazy Diamond, Signs Of Life, Learning To Fly, Yet Another Movie, A New Machine Part 1, Terminal Frost, A New Machine Part 2, Sorrow, The Dogs Of War, On The Turning Away, One Of These Days, Time, On The Run, Wish You Were Here, Welcome To The Machine, Us And Them, Money, Another Brick In The Wall Part 2, Comfortably Numb, One Slip, Run Like Hell
Audio Rating: ★★★★↙
Miscellaneous: Excellent audio clarity, and the enthusiastic but not overpowering audience makes it sound very real.

Date: 30-11-1987
Location: Los Angeles Memorial Sports Arena, Los Angeles, California, USA
Track Listing: Shine On You Crazy Diamond, Signs Of Life, Learning To Fly, Yet Another Movie, A New Machine Part 1, Terminal Frost, A New Machine Part 2, Sorrow, The Dogs Of War, On The Turning Away, One Of These Days, Time, On The Run, Wish You Were Here, Welcome To The Machine, Us And Them, Money, Another Brick In The Wall Part 2, Comfortably Numb, One Slip, Run Like Hell
Audio Rating: ★★★↙
Miscellaneous: 'One Slip yeah! Woooh!' says someone recorded for posterity as the song

begins. There's also a very rare bit of jamming at the end of **WELCOME TO THE MACHINE**.

Date: 01-12-1987
Location: Los Angeles Memorial Sports Arena, Los Angeles, California, USA
Track Listing: Shine On You Crazy Diamond, Signs Of Life, Learning To Fly, Yet Another Movie, A New Machine Part 1, Terminal Frost, A New Machine Part 2, Sorrow, The Dogs Of War, On The Turning Away, One Of These Days, Time, On The Run, Wish You Were Here, Welcome To The Machine, Us And Them, Money, Another Brick In The Wall Part 2, Comfortably Numb, One Slip, Run Like Hell
Audio Rating: ★★★♪
Miscellaneous: The fifth night in Los Angeles. **SORROW** and **WELCOME TO THE MACHINE** cut out at the very end, while **RUN LIKE HELL** fades out about two-thirds through.

Date: 03-12-1987
Location: Oakland Coliseum Arena, Oakland, California, USA
Track Listing: Shine On You Crazy Diamond, Signs Of Life, Learning To Fly, Yet Another Movie, A New Machine Part 1, Terminal Frost, A New Machine Part 2, Sorrow, The Dogs Of War, On The Turning Away, One Of These Days, Time, On The Run, Wish You Were Here, Welcome To The Machine, Us And Them, Money, Another Brick In The Wall Part 2, Comfortably Numb, One Slip, Run Like Hell
Audio Rating: ★★★★
Miscellaneous: Another excellent sounding recording, with guitars especially crisp.

Date: 04-12-1987
Location: Oakland Coliseum Arena, Oakland, California, USA
Track Listing: Shine On You Crazy Diamond, Signs Of Life, Learning To Fly, Yet Another Movie, A New Machine Part 1, Terminal Frost, A New Machine Part 2, Sorrow, The Dogs Of War, On The Turning Away, One Of These Days, Time, On The Run, Wish You Were Here, Welcome To The Machine, Us And Them, Money, Another Brick In The Wall Part 2, Comfortably Numb, One Slip, Run Like Hell
Audio Rating: ★★★
Miscellaneous: Gilmour: 'Thank you, good evening, welcome! Alright, thank you. We're gonna do a bunch of songs from our new record in the first half tonight. There'll be tons of old ones later on, okay? This is "Yet Another Movie".' When Gilmour refers to classic Floyd tracks as 'old ones' it's a bit dispiriting.

Date: 05-12-1987
Location: Oakland Coliseum Arena, Oakland, California, USA
Track Listing: Shine On You Crazy Diamond, Signs Of Life, Learning To Fly, Yet Another Movie, A New Machine Part 1, Terminal Frost, A New Machine Part 2, Sorrow, The Dogs Of War, On The Turning Away, One Of These Days, Time, On The Run, Wish You Were Here, Welcome To The Machine, Money, Another Brick In The Wall Part 2, Comfortably Numb
Audio Rating: ★★★♪
Miscellaneous: **SHINE ON YOU CRAZY DIAMOND** fades in about twenty seconds into the song. **WELCOME TO THE MACHINE** cuts off towards the end, while **US AND THEM**, **ONE SLIP**, and **RUN LIKE HELL** are missing.

Date: 06-12-1987
Location: Oakland Coliseum Arena, Oakland, California, USA
Track Listing: Shine On You Crazy Diamond, Signs Of Life, Learning To Fly, Yet Another Movie, A New Machine Part 1, Terminal Frost, A New Machine Part 2, Sorrow, The Dogs Of War, On The Turning Away, One Of These Days, Time, On The Run, Wish You Were Here, Welcome To The Machine, Us And Them, Money, Another Brick In The Wall Part 2, Comfortably Numb, One Slip, Run Like Hell
Audio Rating: ★★★★
Miscellaneous: Very good audio.

Date: 08-12-1987
Location: Kingdome, Seattle, Washington, USA
Track Listing: Shine On You Crazy Diamond, Signs Of Life, Learning To Fly, Yet Another Movie, A New Machine Part 1, Terminal Frost, A New Machine Part 2, Sorrow, The Dogs Of War, On The Turning Away, One Of These Days, Time, On The Run, Wish You Were Here, Welcome To The Machine, Us And Them, Money, Another Brick In The Wall Part 2, Comfortably Numb, One Slip, Run Like Hell
Audio Rating: ★★★★
Miscellaneous: Also nice and crisp.

Date: 10-12-1987
Location: Pacific National Exhibition Coliseum, Vancouver, British Columbia, Canada

Track Listing: Shine On You Crazy Diamond, Signs Of Life, Learning To Fly, Yet Another Movie, A New Machine Part 1, Terminal Frost, A New Machine Part 2, Sorrow, The Dogs Of War, On The Turning Away, One Of These Days, Time, On The Run, Wish You Were Here, Welcome To The Machine, Us And Them, Money, Another Brick In The Wall Part 2, Comfortably Numb, One Slip, Run Like Hell
Audio Rating: ★★★★
Miscellaneous: End of the North American tour (first leg), then seven weeks off. No sense of tiredness or end-of-tour emotion from the band or from Gilmour's stage patter, although the performance and sound are great.

1988

Date: 22-01-1988
Location: Western Springs Stadium, Auckland, New Zealand
Track Listing: Shine On You Crazy Diamond, Signs Of Life, Learning To Fly, Yet Another Movie, A New Machine Part 1, Terminal Frost, A New Machine Part 2, Sorrow, The Dogs Of War, On The Turning Away, One Of These Days, Time, On The Run, Wish You Were Here, Welcome To The Machine, Us And Them, Money, Another Brick In The Wall Part 2, Comfortably Numb, One Slip, Run Like Hell
Audio Rating: ★★★♩
Miscellaneous: First and only time in New Zealand, and the start of a mammoth eight-month leg from the Antipodes to Norway to Spain to California. **A NEW MACHINE PART 2** and **MONEY** fade out at the end of each song.

Date: 27-01-1988
Location: Sydney Entertainment Centre, Sydney, Australia
Track Listing: Shine On You Crazy Diamond, Signs Of Life, Learning To Fly, Yet Another Movie, A New Machine Part 1, Terminal Frost, A New Machine Part 2, Sorrow, The Dogs Of War, On The Turning Away, One Of These Days, Time, On The Run, Wish You Were Here, Welcome To The Machine, Us And Them, Money, Another Brick In The Wall Part 2, Comfortably Numb, One Slip, Run Like Hell
Audio Rating: ★★★♩
Miscellaneous: The start of a remarkable ten-night stretch at the Sydney Entertainment Centre, which held 'only' 13,000 people but was the largest concert venue in Sydney until 1999. The group's first time playing Australia since two shows in August 1971.

Date: 28-01-1988
Location: Sydney Entertainment Centre, Sydney, Australia
Track Listing: Shine On You Crazy Diamond (Fade In), Signs Of Life, Learning To Fly, Yet Another Movie, A New Machine Part 1, Terminal Frost, A New Machine Part 2, Sorrow, The Dogs Of War, On The Turning Away, One Of These Days (Fade In), Time, On The Run, Wish You Were Here, Welcome To The Machine, Us And Them, Money, Another Brick In The Wall Part 2, Comfortably Numb, One Slip, Run Like Hell
Audio Rating: ★★★♩
Miscellaneous: **SHINE ON YOU CRAZY DIAMOND** fades in at 'Come on you raver, you seer of visions', thus missing about 80 per cent of it. **THE DOGS OF WAR** similarly fades out towards the end of the vocal section, and **ONE OF THESE DAYS** fades in about ninety seconds in.

Date: 30-01-1988
Location: Sydney Entertainment Centre, Sydney, Australia
Track Listing: Shine On You Crazy Diamond, Signs Of Life, Learning To Fly, Yet Another Movie, A New Machine Part 1, Terminal Frost, A New Machine Part 2, Sorrow, The Dogs Of War, On The Turning Away, One Of These Days, Time, On The Run, Wish You Were Here, Welcome To The Machine, Us And Them, Money, Another Brick In The Wall Part 2, Comfortably Numb, One Slip, Run Like Hell
Audio Rating: ★★★
Miscellaneous: Echoey and distant-sounding. Quieter moments are okay.

Date: 01-02-1988
Location: Sydney Entertainment Centre, Sydney, Australia
Track Listing: Shine On You Crazy Diamond, Signs Of Life, Learning To Fly, Yet Another Movie, A New Machine Part 1, Terminal Frost, A New Machine Part 2, Sorrow, The Dogs Of War, On The Turning Away, One Of These Days, Time, On The Run, Wish You Were Here, Welcome To The Machine, Us And Them, Money, Another Brick In The Wall Part 2, Comfortably Numb, One Slip, Run Like Hell
Audio Rating: ★★★♩

Miscellaneous: Band sounds very quiet at points, for example during the quiet section of **MONEY**.

Date: 03-02-1988
Location: Sydney Entertainment Centre, Sydney, Australia
Track Listing: Shine On You Crazy Diamond, Signs Of Life, Learning To Fly, Yet Another Movie, A New Machine Part 1, Terminal Frost, A New Machine Part 2, Sorrow, The Dogs Of War, On The Turning Away, One Of These Days, Time, On The Run, Wish You Were Here, Welcome To The Machine, Us And Them, Money, Another Brick In The Wall Part 2, Comfortably Numb, One Slip, Run Like Hell
Audio Rating: ★★★♪
Miscellaneous: 'Thank you! Well thanks again very much!'

Date: 11-02-1988
Location: Thebarton Oval, Adelaide, Australia
Track Listing: Shine On You Crazy Diamond, Signs Of Life, Learning To Fly, Yet Another Movie, A New Machine Part 1, Terminal Frost, A New Machine Part 2, Sorrow, The Dogs Of War, On The Turning Away, One Of These Days, Time, On The Run, Wish You Were Here, Welcome To The Machine, Us And Them, Money, Another Brick In The Wall Part 2, Comfortably Numb, One Slip, Run Like Hell
Audio Rating: ★★★
Miscellaneous: **SHINE ON YOU CRAZY DIAMOND** fades in at 'Now there's a look in your eyes', so there's only about one-third of it here.

Date: 13-02-1988
Location: National Tennis Centre, Melbourne, Australia
Track Listing: Shine On You Crazy Diamond, Signs Of Life, Learning To Fly, Yet Another Movie, A New Machine Part 1, Terminal Frost, A New Machine Part 2, Sorrow (Fade Out)
Audio Rating: ★★♪
Miscellaneous: The start of eight nights in Melbourne. Only goes up to **SORROW**, which fades out during Gilmour's concluding guitar solo.

Date: 15-02-1988
Location: National Tennis Centre, Melbourne, Australia
Track Listing: Shine On You Crazy Diamond, Signs Of Life, Learning To Fly, Yet Another Movie, A New Machine Part 1, Terminal Frost, A New Machine Part 2, Sorrow, The Dogs Of War, On The Turning Away, One Of These Days, Time, On The Run, Wish You Were Here, Welcome To The Machine, Us And Them, Money, Another Brick In The Wall Part 2, Comfortably Numb, One Slip, Run Like Hell
Audio Rating: ★★★★
Miscellaneous: Two noticeable tape flip edits, at 7:37 during **SORROW** and at 7:09 during **MONEY**.

Date: 17-02-1988
Location: National Tennis Centre, Melbourne, Australia
Track Listing: Shine On You Crazy Diamond, Signs Of Life, Learning To Fly, Yet Another Movie, A New Machine Part 1, Terminal Frost, A New Machine Part 2, Sorrow, The Dogs Of War, On The Turning Away, One Of These Days, Time, On The Run, Wish You Were Here, Welcome To The Machine, Us And Them, Money, Another Brick In The Wall Part 2, Comfortably Numb, One Slip, Run Like Hell
Audio Rating: ★★★
Miscellaneous: Murky sound except at quiet instrumental moments (for example, the start of **WISH YOU WERE HERE**).

Date: 19-02-1988
Location: National Tennis Centre, Melbourne, Australia
Track Listing: Shine On You Crazy Diamond, Signs Of Life, Learning To Fly, Yet Another Movie, A New Machine Part 1, Terminal Frost, A New Machine Part 2, Sorrow, The Dogs Of War, On The Turning Away, One Of These Days, Time, On The Run, Wish You Were Here, Welcome To The Machine, Us And Them, Money, Another Brick In The Wall Part 2, Comfortably Numb
Audio Rating: ★★★♪
Miscellaneous: No encores, so no **ONE SLIP** or **RUN LIKE HELL**.

Date: 02-03-1988
Location: Budokan Grand Hall, Tokyo, Japan
Track Listing: Shine On You Crazy Diamond, Signs Of Life, Learning To Fly, Yet Another Movie, A New Machine Part 1, Terminal Frost, A New Machine Part 2, Sorrow, The Dogs Of War, On The Turning Away, One Of These

Days, Time, The Great Gig In The Sky, Wish You Were Here, Welcome To The Machine, Us And Them, Money, Another Brick In The Wall Part 2, Comfortably Numb, One Slip, Run Like Hell
Audio Rating: ★★★★✩
Miscellaneous: First time in Japan since 1972. **THE GREAT GIG IN THE SKY** gets added to the setlist here. Audio is terrific.

Date: 03-03-1988
Location: Budokan Grand Hall, Tokyo, Japan
Track Listing: Shine On You Crazy Diamond, Signs Of Life, Learning To Fly, Yet Another Movie, A New Machine Part 1, Terminal Frost, A New Machine Part 2, Sorrow, The Dogs Of War, On The Turning Away, One Of These Days, Time, The Great Gig In The Sky, Wish You Were Here, Welcome To The Machine, Us And Them, Money, Another Brick In The Wall Part 2, Comfortably Numb, One Slip, Run Like Hell
Audio Rating: ★★★★
Miscellaneous: **SHINE ON YOU CRAZY DIAMOND** fades in after four minutes or so, when 'Syd's Theme' is played. Reputedly the same taper as the previous gig, and almost as impressive audio quality.

Date: 04-03-1988
Location: Yoyogi Olympic Pool, Tokyo, Japan
Track Listing: Shine On You Crazy Diamond, Signs Of Life, Learning To Fly, Yet Another Movie, A New Machine Part 1, Terminal Frost, A New Machine Part 2, Sorrow, The Dogs Of War, On The Turning Away, One Of These Days, Time, The Great Gig In The Sky, Wish You Were Here, Welcome To The Machine, Us And Them, Money, Another Brick In The Wall Part 2, Comfortably Numb, One Slip, Run Like Hell
Audio Rating: ★★★
Miscellaneous: Standard gig, average audio quality.

Date: 05-03-1988
Location: Yoyogi Olympic Pool, Tokyo, Japan
Track Listing: Shine On You Crazy Diamond, Signs Of Life, Learning To Fly, Yet Another Movie, A New Machine Part 1, Terminal Frost, A New Machine Part 2, Sorrow, The Dogs Of War, On The Turning Away, One Of These Days, Time, The Great Gig In The Sky, Wish You Were Here, Welcome To The Machine, Us And Them, Money, Another Brick In The Wall Part 2, Comfortably Numb, One Slip, Run Like Hell
Audio Rating: ★★★★

Miscellaneous: Good clarity but a touch too bassy.

Date: 06-03-1988
Location: Yoyogi Olympic Pool, Tokyo, Japan
Track Listing: Shine On You Crazy Diamond, Signs Of Life, Learning To Fly, Yet Another Movie, A New Machine Part 1, Terminal Frost, A New Machine Part 2, Sorrow, The Dogs Of War, On The Turning Away, One Of These Days, Time, The Great Gig In The Sky, Wish You Were Here, Welcome To The Machine, Us And Them, Money, Another Brick In The Wall Part 2, Comfortably Numb, One Slip, Run Like Hell
Audio Rating: ★★★★✩
Miscellaneous: Great sound quality.

Date: 08-03-1988
Location: Joh Hall, Osaka, Japan
Track Listing: Shine On You Crazy Diamond, Signs Of Life, Learning To Fly, Yet Another Movie, A New Machine Part 1, Terminal Frost, A New Machine Part 2, Sorrow, The Dogs Of War, On The Turning Away, One Of These Days, Time, The Great Gig In The Sky, Wish You Were Here, Welcome To The Machine, Us And Them, Money, Another Brick In The Wall Part 2, Comfortably Numb, One Slip, Run Like Hell
Audio Rating: ★★✩
Miscellaneous: Very muffled sounding, as though the microphone was inside a jacket or bag.

Date: 09-03-1988
Location: Joh Hall, Osaka, Japan
Track Listing: Shine On You Crazy Diamond, Signs Of Life, Learning To Fly, Yet Another Movie, A New Machine Part 1, Terminal Frost, A New Machine Part 2, Sorrow, The Dogs Of War, On The Turning Away, One Of These Days, Time, The Great Gig In The Sky, Wish You Were Here, Welcome To The Machine, Us And Them, Money, Another Brick In The Wall Part 2, Comfortably Numb, One Slip, Run Like Hell
Audio Rating: ★★★✩
Miscellaneous: A bit too bright.

Date: 11-03-1988
Location: Rainbow Hall, Nagoya, Japan
Track Listing: Shine On You Crazy Diamond, Signs Of Life, Learning To Fly, Yet Another Movie, A New Machine Part 1, Terminal Frost, A New Machine Part 2, Sorrow, The Dogs Of War, On The Turning Away, One Of These

Days, Time, The Great Gig In The Sky, Wish You Were Here, Welcome To The Machine, Us And Them, Money, Another Brick In The Wall Part 2, Comfortably Numb, One Slip, Run Like Hell
Audio Rating: ★★★★★
Miscellaneous: A few tape flips mean the taper missed the start of **SORROW** and a section two-thirds through **WELCOME TO THE MACHINE**.

Date: 15-04-1988
Location: Memorial Coliseum, Los Angeles, California, USA
Track Listing: Shine On You Crazy Diamond, Signs Of Life, Learning To Fly, Yet Another Movie, A New Machine Part 1, Terminal Frost, A New Machine Part 2, Sorrow, The Dogs Of War, On The Turning Away, One Of These Days, Time, On The Run, The Great Gig In The Sky, Wish You Were Here, Welcome To The Machine, Us And Them, Money, Another Brick In The Wall Part 2, Comfortably Numb, One Slip, Run Like Hell
Audio Rating: ★★★
Miscellaneous: Five weeks off before another North American leg. Audio has a slight hiss noticeable during quieter moments but pretty good otherwise, if you don't mind the whooping and the hollering.

Date: 18-04-1988
Location: Mile High Stadium, Denver, Colorado, USA
Track Listing: Shine On You Crazy Diamond, Signs Of Life, Learning To Fly, Yet Another Movie, A New Machine Part 1, Terminal Frost, A New Machine Part 2, Sorrow, The Dogs Of War, On The Turning Away, One Of These Days, Time, On The Run, The Great Gig In The Sky, Wish You Were Here, Welcome To The Machine, Us And Them, Money, Another Brick In The Wall Part 2, Comfortably Numb, One Slip, Run Like Hell
Audio Rating: ★★★★★
Miscellaneous: A few cuts here and there, most notable at the end of **US AND THEM**, and **RUN LIKE HELL** only lasts a minute – while Gilmour is still teasing the audience before the songs begins. Audio is, however, excellent.

Date: 20-04-1988
Location: Hughes University, California State University at Sacramento, California, USA
Track Listing: Shine On You Crazy Diamond, Signs Of Life, Learning To Fly, Yet Another Movie, A New Machine Part 1, Terminal Frost, A New Machine Part 2, Sorrow, The Dogs Of War, On The Turning Away, One Of These Days, Time, On The Run, The Great Gig In The Sky, Wish You Were Here, Welcome To The Machine, Us And Them, Money, Another Brick In The Wall Part 2, Comfortably Numb, One Slip, Run Like Hell
Audio Rating: ★★★
Miscellaneous: Sound wavers a little. A slight cut at the very end of **COMFORTABLY NUMB**.

Date: 22-04-1988
Location: Oakland Coliseum Arena, Oakland, California, USA
Track Listing: Shine On You Crazy Diamond, Signs Of Life, Learning To Fly, Yet Another Movie, A New Machine Part 1, Terminal Frost, A New Machine Part 2, Sorrow, The Dogs Of War, On The Turning Away, One Of These Days, Time, On The Run, The Great Gig In The Sky, Wish You Were Here, Welcome To The Machine, Us And Them, Money, Another Brick In The Wall Part 2, Comfortably Numb, One Slip, Run Like Hell
Audio Rating: ★★★
Miscellaneous: Muffled sound.

Date: 23-04-1988
Location: Oakland Coliseum Arena, Oakland, California, USA
Track Listing: Shine On You Crazy Diamond, Signs Of Life, Learning To Fly, Yet Another Movie, A New Machine Part 1, Terminal Frost, A New Machine Part 2, Sorrow, The Dogs Of War, On The Turning Away, One Of These Days, Time, On The Run, The Great Gig In The Sky, Wish You Were Here, Welcome To The Machine, Us And Them, Money, Another Brick In The Wall Part 2, Comfortably Numb, One Slip, Run Like Hell
Audio Rating: ★★★★
Miscellaneous: A second night in Oakland.

Date: 25-04-1988
Location: Municipal Stadium, Phoenix, Arizona, USA
Track Listing: Shine On You Crazy Diamond, Signs Of Life, Learning To Fly, Yet Another Movie, A New Machine Part 1, Terminal Frost, A New Machine Part 2, Sorrow, The Dogs Of War, On The Turning Away, One Of These Days, Time, On The Run, The Great Gig In The Sky, Wish You Were Here, Welcome To The

Machine, Us And Them, Money, Another Brick In The Wall Part 2, Comfortably Numb, One Slip, Run Like Hell
Audio Rating: ★★★
Miscellaneous: Standard gig, nothing to report. Makes you wonder how the band keep doing it.

Date: 26-04-1988
Location: Municipal Stadium, Phoenix, Arizona, USA
Track Listing: Shine On You Crazy Diamond, Signs Of Life, Learning To Fly, Yet Another Movie, A New Machine Part 1, Terminal Frost, A New Machine Part 2, Sorrow, The Dogs Of War, On The Turning Away, One Of These Days, Time, On The Run, The Great Gig In The Sky, Wish You Were Here, Welcome To The Machine, Us And Them, Money, Another Brick In The Wall Part 2, Comfortably Numb, One Slip, Run Like Hell
Audio Rating: ★★★↙
Miscellaneous: **THE GREAT GIG IN THE SKY** and **ONE SLIP** cut off abruptly once they are finished.

Date: 28-04-1988
Location: Texas Stadium, Irving, Texas, USA
Track Listing: Shine On You Crazy Diamond, Signs Of Life, Learning To Fly, Yet Another Movie, A New Machine Part 1, Terminal Frost, A New Machine Part 2, Sorrow, The Dogs Of War, On The Turning Away, One Of These Days, Time, On The Run, The Great Gig In The Sky, Wish You Were Here, Welcome To The Machine, Us And Them, Money, Another Brick In The Wall Part 2, Comfortably Numb, One Slip, Run Like Hell
Audio Rating: ★★★
Miscellaneous: The taper includes a funny story of being caught with recording equipment, kicked out, buying a ticket from a scalper outside, returning to his seat and startling his friend in the next seat, who had witnessed the whole thing.

Date: 30-04-1988
Location: Citrus Bowl, Orlando, Florida, USA
Track Listing: The Dogs Of War, On The Turning Away, One Of These Days, Time, On The Run, The Great Gig In The Sky, Wish You Were Here, Welcome To The Machine, Us And Them, Money, Another Brick In The Wall Part 2, Comfortably Numb, One Slip

Audio Rating: ★↙
Miscellaneous: Truncated recording. Probably as well, the audio is awful.

Date: 04-05-1988
Location: Carter-Finchley Stadium, North Carolina State University, Raleigh, North Carolina, USA
Track Listing: Shine On You Crazy Diamond, Signs Of Life, Learning To Fly, Yet Another Movie, A New Machine Part 1, Terminal Frost, A New Machine Part 2, Sorrow, The Dogs Of War, On The Turning Away, One Of These Days, Time, On The Run, The Great Gig In The Sky, Wish You Were Here, Welcome To The Machine, Us And Them, Money, Another Brick In The Wall Part 2, Comfortably Numb, One Slip, Run Like Hell
Audio Rating: ★★↙
Miscellaneous: More poor audio.

Date: 06-05-1988
Location: Foxboro Stadium, Foxboro, Boston, Massachusetts, USA
Track Listing: Shine On You Crazy Diamond, Signs Of Life, Learning To Fly, Yet Another Movie, A New Machine Part 1, Terminal Frost, A New Machine Part 2, Sorrow, The Dogs Of War, On The Turning Away, One Of These Days, Time, On The Run, The Great Gig In The Sky, Wish You Were Here, Welcome To The Machine, Us And Them, Money, Another Brick In The Wall Part 2, Comfortably Numb, One Slip, Run Like Hell
Audio Rating: ★★★
Miscellaneous: Includes half of **TIME** instead of **ONE OF THESE DAYS**.

Date: 08-05-1988
Location: Foxboro Stadium, Foxboro, Boston, Massachusetts, USA
Track Listing: Shine On You Crazy Diamond, Signs Of Life, Learning To Fly, Yet Another Movie, A New Machine Part 1, Terminal Frost, A New Machine Part 2, Sorrow, The Dogs Of War, On The Turning Away, One Of These Days, Time, On The Run, The Great Gig In The Sky, Wish You Were Here, Welcome To The Machine, Us And Them, Money, Another Brick In The Wall Part 2, Comfortably Numb, One Slip, Run Like Hell
Audio Rating: ★★★★
Miscellaneous: There is a tape flip at 9.36 in **SORROW**, noticeable as a short cut in the song.

Date: 11-05-1988
Location: Stade Du Parc Olympique, Montreal, Quebec, Canada
Track Listing: Shine On You Crazy Diamond, Signs Of Life, Learning To Fly, Yet Another Movie, A New Machine Part 1, Terminal Frost, A New Machine Part 2, Sorrow, The Dogs Of War, On The Turning Away, One Of These Days, Time, On The Run, The Great Gig In The Sky, Wish You Were Here, Welcome To The Machine, Us And Them, Money, Another Brick In The Wall Part 2, Comfortably Numb, One Slip, Run Like Hell
Audio Rating: ★★★
Miscellaneous: A return to Olympic Park of the 1977 *Animals* tour and the Roger Waters spitting incident. **A NEW MACHINE PART 2** is missing part of the track, and runs to only twenty-six seconds (although on the album it only reaches forty-one seconds). Audio quite distant, muffled and echoey, and the audience is very loud.

Date: 13-05-1988
Location: Canadian National Exhibition Stadium, Toronto, Ontario, Canada
Track Listing: Shine On You Crazy Diamond, Signs Of Life, Learning To Fly, Yet Another Movie, A New Machine Part 1, Terminal Frost, A New Machine Part 2, Sorrow, The Dogs Of War, On The Turning Away, One Of These Days, Time, On The Run, The Great Gig In The Sky, Wish You Were Here, Welcome To The Machine, Us And Them, Money, Another Brick In The Wall Part 2, Comfortably Numb, One Slip, Run Like Hell
Audio Rating: ★★★★★
Miscellaneous: Fantastic audio quality, could be a live album release.

Date: 15-05-1988
Location: Veterans Stadium, Philadelphia, Pennsylvania, USA
Track Listing: Shine On You Crazy Diamond, Signs Of Life, Learning To Fly, Yet Another Movie, A New Machine Part 1, Terminal Frost, A New Machine Part 2, Sorrow, The Dogs Of War, On The Turning Away, One Of These Days, Time, On The Run, The Great Gig In The Sky, Wish You Were Here, Welcome To The Machine, Us And Them, Money, Another Brick In The Wall Part 2, Comfortably Numb, One Slip, Run Like Hell
Audio Rating: ★★★★
Miscellaneous: You can hear people arguing and shouting, for example at the start of **WISH YOU WERE HERE** and just after, when people are screaming 'Sit down!' and a guy roars 'Sit down you bimbo!', maybe at a girl sitting on her boyfriend's shoulders and blocking the view.

Date: 16-05-1988
Location: Veterans Stadium, Philadelphia, Pennsylvania, USA
Track Listing: Shine On You Crazy Diamond, Signs Of Life, Learning To Fly, Yet Another Movie, A New Machine Part 1, Terminal Frost, A New Machine Part 2, Sorrow, The Dogs Of War, On The Turning Away, One Of These Days, Time, On The Run, The Great Gig In The Sky, Wish You Were Here, Welcome To The Machine, Us And Them, Money, Another Brick In The Wall Part 2, Comfortably Numb, One Slip, Run Like Hell
Audio Rating: ★★★✦
Miscellaneous: A bit hissy and overly bright, and slightly marred by yellers in the audience.

Date: 18-05-1988
Location: University of Northern Iowa Dome, Cedar Falls, Iowa, USA
Track Listing: Shine On You Crazy Diamond, Signs Of Life, Learning To Fly, Yet Another Movie, A New Machine Part 1, Terminal Frost, A New Machine Part 2, Sorrow, The Dogs Of War, On The Turning Away, One Of These Days, Time, On The Run, The Great Gig In The Sky, Wish You Were Here, Welcome To The Machine, Us And Them, Money, Another Brick In The Wall Part 2, Comfortably Numb, One Slip, Run Like Hell
Audio Rating: ★★★✦
Miscellaneous: Audio clear but lacks body – you have to turn your speaker all the way up to hear it.

Date: 20-05-1988
Location: Camp Randall Stadium, University of Madison-Wisconsin, Madison, Wisconsin, USA
Track Listing: Shine On You Crazy Diamond, Signs Of Life, Learning To Fly, Yet Another Movie, A New Machine Part 1, Terminal Frost, A New Machine Part 2, Sorrow, The Dogs Of War, On The Turning Away, One Of These Days, Time, On The Run, The Great Gig In The Sky, Wish You Were Here, Welcome To The Machine, Us And Them, Money, Another Brick

In The Wall Part 2, Comfortably Numb, One Slip, Run Like Hell
Audio Rating: ★★★
Miscellaneous: During **ANOTHER BRICK IN THE WALL PART 2**, Gilmour sings, 'Hey asshole, leave them kids alone!' Wonder what caused it?*

Date: 21-05-1988
Location: Rosemont Horizon, Rosemont, Chicago, Illinois, USA
Track Listing: Shine On You Crazy Diamond, Signs Of Life, Learning To Fly, Yet Another Movie, A New Machine Part 1, Terminal Frost, A New Machine Part 2, Sorrow, The Dogs Of War, On The Turning Away, One Of These Days, Time, On The Run, The Great Gig In The Sky, Wish You Were Here, Welcome To The Machine, Us And Them, Money, Another Brick In The Wall Part 2, Comfortably Numb, One Slip, Run Like Hell
Audio Rating: ★★★✦
Miscellaneous: Clear but distant-sounding.

Date: 22-05-1988
Location: Rosemont Horizon, Rosemont, Chicago, Illinois, USA
Track Listing: Shine On You Crazy Diamond, Signs Of Life, Learning To Fly, Yet Another Movie, A New Machine Part 1, Terminal Frost, A New Machine Part 2, Sorrow, The Dogs Of War, On The Turning Away, One Of These Days, Time, On The Run, The Great Gig In The Sky, Wish You Were Here, Welcome To The Machine, Us And Them, Money, Another Brick In The Wall Part 2, Comfortably Numb, One Slip, Run Like Hell
Audio Rating: ★★★
Miscellaneous: A bit less distant sounding than the previous gig, with a raucous crowd. Wonder if Gilmour ever wanted to 'do a Roger'.

Date: 24-05-1988
Location: Hubert H. Humphrey Metrodome, Minneapolis, Minnesota, USA
Track Listing: Shine On You Crazy Diamond, Signs Of Life, Learning To Fly, Yet Another Movie, A New Machine Part 1, Terminal Frost, A New Machine Part 2, Sorrow, The Dogs Of War, On The Turning Away, One Of These Days, Time, On The Run, The Great Gig In The Sky, Wish You Were Here, Welcome To The Machine, Us And Them, Money, Another Brick In The Wall Part 2, Comfortably Numb, One Slip, Run Like Hell
Audio Rating: ★★★✦
Miscellaneous: Acoustics for the Metrodome have been described as 'iffy at best'.† The sound here is accordingly pretty murky except at quiet moments.

Date: 26-05-1988
Location: Arrowhead Stadium, Kansas City, Missouri, USA
Track Listing: Shine On You Crazy Diamond, Signs Of Life, Learning To Fly, Yet Another Movie, A New Machine Part 1, Terminal Frost, A New Machine Part 2, Sorrow, The Dogs Of War, On The Turning Away, One Of These Days, Time, On The Run, The Great Gig In The Sky, Wish You Were Here, Welcome To The Machine, Us And Them, Money, Another Brick In The Wall Part 2, Comfortably Numb, One Slip, Run Like Hell
Audio Rating: ★★★
Miscellaneous: Kansas City is, of course, in the state of Missouri, not Kansas as some Pink Floyd books have reported.

Date: 28-05-1988
Location: Ohio State University Stadium, Columbus, Ohio, USA
Track Listing: Shine On You Crazy Diamond, Signs Of Life, Learning To Fly, Yet Another Movie, A New Machine Part 1, Terminal Frost, A New Machine Part 2, Sorrow, The Dogs Of War, On The Turning Away, One Of These Days, Time, On The Run, The Great Gig In The Sky, Wish You Were Here, Welcome To The Machine, Us And Them, Money, Another Brick In The Wall Part 2, Comfortably Numb, One Slip, Run Like Hell
Audio Rating: ★★✦

---

* In 1997 he told *The Daily Telegraph* about his disillusion with the progressive Steiner schools, which left his children two or three years behind in their reading and writing abilities. 'The school had its good aspects, but overall, the system seemed slack. I found the children's knowledge was very patchy, and their school reports, which consisted only of praise, gave me little idea of how they were really doing.' (*Daily Telegraph*, 10 August 1997).

† web.archive.org/web/20140101183105/http://blogs.citypages.com/gimmenoise/2013/12/the_metrodomes_musical_memories_a_look_back.php

Miscellaneous: Distant, echoey and murky. **SORROW** cuts out just after 'Time pass, river roll' and starts again at 'A grim intimation of what is to be'. **ON THE RUN** comes in about halfway through, **US AND THEM** cuts out immediately the song ends and **MONEY** comes in at 'It's a gas'.

Date: 30-05-1988
Location: Three Rivers Stadium, Pittsburgh, Pennsylvania, USA
Track Listing: Shine On You Crazy Diamond, Signs Of Life, Learning To Fly, Yet Another Movie, A New Machine Part 1, Terminal Frost, A New Machine Part 2, Sorrow, On The Turning Away, One Of These Days, Time, On The Run, The Great Gig In The Sky, Wish You Were Here, Welcome To The Machine, Us And Them, Money, Another Brick In The Wall Part 2, Comfortably Numb, One Slip, Run Like Hell
Audio Rating: ★★★
Miscellaneous: 'We want Floyd! We want Floyd! We want Floyd!' the audience are shouting before the show starts, and they remain vociferous throughout. There's a power failure at the end of **SORROW** (at 8.46), with Gilmour saying 'Oh well – I think someone forgot to put some money in the meter, I think we're probably just about right to go. It'll only take a minute and then we'll start something else – that was just getting boring anyway', and consequently the band skip **THE DOGS OF WAR**. Before **COMFORTABLY NUMB** Dave asks the audience, 'Did you like our pig?'

Date: 03-06-1988
Location: Giants Stadium, East Rutherford, New Jersey, USA
Track Listing: Shine On You Crazy Diamond, Signs Of Life, Learning To Fly, Yet Another Movie, A New Machine Part 1, Terminal Frost, A New Machine Part 2, Sorrow, The Dogs Of War, On The Turning Away, One Of These Days, Time, On The Run, The Great Gig In The Sky, Wish You Were Here, Welcome To The Machine, Us And Them, Money, Another Brick In The Wall Part 2, Comfortably Numb, One Slip, Run Like Hell
Audio Rating: ★
Miscellaneous: Very poor sound.

Date: 04-06-1988
Location: Giants Stadium, East Rutherford, New Jersey, USA
Track Listing: Shine On You Crazy Diamond, Signs Of Life, Learning To Fly, Yet Another Movie, A New Machine Part 1, Terminal Frost, A New Machine Part 2, Sorrow, The Dogs Of War, On The Turning Away, One Of These Days, Time, On The Run, The Great Gig In The Sky, Wish You Were Here, Welcome To The Machine, Us And Them, Money, Another Brick In The Wall Part 2, Comfortably Numb, One Slip, Run Like Hell
Audio Rating: ★★
Miscellaneous: There is a fifteen-second gap from a tape flip in **SORROW** at 9:23 and a fifteen-second gap in **MONEY** at 3:06.

Date: 10-06-1988
Location: Stade De La Beaujoire, Nantes, France
Track Listing: Shine On You Crazy Diamond, Signs Of Life, Learning To Fly, Yet Another Movie, A New Machine Part 1, Terminal Frost, A New Machine Part 2, Sorrow, The Dogs Of War, On The Turning Away, One Of These Days, Time, On The Run, The Great Gig In The Sky, Wish You Were Here, Welcome To The Machine, Us And Them, Money, Another Brick In The Wall Part 2, Comfortably Numb, One Slip, Run Like Hell
Audio Rating: ★★★
Miscellaneous: Just six days after the last American gig, the band are in France. They are really soldiering on. Loud moments more effective than quiet passages, which struggle to be heard clearly.

Date: 13-06-1988
Location: Stadion Feyenoord, Rotterdam, Netherlands
Track Listing: Shine On You Crazy Diamond, Signs Of Life, Learning To Fly, Yet Another Movie, A New Machine Part 1, Terminal Frost, A New Machine Part 2, Sorrow, The Dogs Of War, On The Turning Away, One Of These Days, Time, On The Run, The Great Gig In The Sky, Wish You Were Here, Welcome To The Machine, Us And Them, Money, Another Brick In The Wall Part 2, Comfortably Numb, One Slip, Run Like Hell
Audio Rating: ★★
Miscellaneous: No **A NEW MACHINE PART 1**, **TERMINAL FROST**, or **A NEW MACHINE PART 2**.

Date: 14-06-1988
Location: Stadion Feyenoord, Rotterdam, Netherlands
Track Listing: Shine On You Crazy Diamond, Signs Of Life, Learning To Fly, Yet Another Movie, A New Machine Part 1, Terminal Frost, A New Machine Part 2, Sorrow, The Dogs Of War, On The Turning Away, One Of These Days, Time, On The Run, The Great Gig In The Sky, Wish You Were Here, Welcome To The Machine, Us And Them, Money, Another Brick In The Wall Part 2, Comfortably Numb, One Slip, Run Like Hell
Audio Rating: ★★★★✩
Miscellaneous: Same setlist as the previous night, but much better audio quality.

Date: 16-06-1988
Location: Reichstagsgelande, West Berlin, West Germany
Track Listing: Shine On You Crazy Diamond, Signs Of Life, Learning To Fly, Yet Another Movie, A New Machine Part 1, Terminal Frost, A New Machine Part 2, Sorrow, The Dogs Of War, On The Turning Away, One Of These Days, Time, On The Run, The Great Gig In The Sky, Wish You Were Here, Welcome To The Machine, Us And Them, Money, Another Brick In The Wall Part 2, Comfortably Numb, One Slip, Run Like Hell
Audio Rating: ★★★★
Miscellaneous: **A NEW MACHINE PART 1**, **TERMINAL FROST** and **A NEW MACHINE PART 2** restored to setlist.

Date: 18-06-1988
Location: Maimarktgelande, Mannheim, West Germany
Track Listing: Shine On You Crazy Diamond, Signs Of Life, Learning To Fly, Yet Another Movie, A New Machine Part 1, Terminal Frost, A New Machine Part 2, Sorrow, The Dogs Of War, On The Turning Away, One Of These Days, Time, On The Run, The Great Gig In The Sky, Wish You Were Here, Welcome To The Machine, Us And Them, Money, Another Brick In The Wall Part 2, Comfortably Numb, One Slip, Run Like Hell
Audio Rating: ★★★✩
Miscellaneous: **A NEW MACHINE PART 1**, **TERMINAL FROST** and **A NEW MACHINE PART 2** withdrawn again.

Date: 21-06-1988
Location: Place d'Armes, Chateau De Versailles, France
Track Listing: Shine On You Crazy Diamond, Signs Of Life, Learning To Fly, Yet Another Movie, A New Machine Part 1, Terminal Frost, A New Machine Part 2, Sorrow, The Dogs Of War, On The Turning Away, One Of These Days, Time, On The Run, The Great Gig In The Sky, Wish You Were Here, Welcome To The Machine, Us And Them, Money, Another Brick In The Wall Part 2, Comfortably Numb, One Slip, Run Like Hell
Audio Rating: ★★★
Miscellaneous: The Place d'Armes is a fan-shaped square in front of the Palace of Versailles. For a Francophile like Gilmour, it must have been an amazing venue to play. Some fireworks mark the end of the concert.

Date: 22-06-1988
Location: Place d'Armes, Chateau De Versailles, France
Track Listing: Shine On You Crazy Diamond, Signs Of Life, Learning To Fly, Yet Another Movie, A New Machine Part 1, Terminal Frost, A New Machine Part 2, Sorrow, The Dogs Of War, On The Turning Away, One Of These Days, Time, On The Run, The Great Gig In The Sky, Wish You Were Here, Welcome To The Machine, Us And Them, Money, Another Brick In The Wall Part 2, Comfortably Numb, One Slip, Run Like Hell
Audio Rating: ★★★✩
Miscellaneous: Gilmour after **LEARNING TO FLY**: 'Thank you, merci beaucoup, bon soir!' Similar patter just before **COMFORTABLY NUMB**, as always introducing the 'last' song ('la dernière chanson') of the show. You can set your watch by him.

Date: 25-06-1988
Location: Niedersachsenstadion, Hannover, West Germany
Track Listing: Shine On You Crazy Diamond, Signs Of Life, Learning To Fly, Yet Another Movie, A New Machine Part 1, Terminal Frost, A New Machine Part 2, Sorrow, The Dogs Of War, On The Turning Away, One Of These Days, Time, On The Run, The Great Gig In The Sky, Wish You Were Here, Welcome To The Machine, Us And Them, Money, Another Brick In The Wall Part 2, Comfortably Numb, One Slip, Run Like Hell

Audio Rating: ★★★
Miscellaneous: Quieter moments hard to hear properly.

Date: 27-06-1988
Location: Westfalenhalle, Dortmund, West Germany
Track Listing: Shine On You Crazy Diamond, Signs Of Life, Learning To Fly, Yet Another Movie, A New Machine Part 1, Terminal Frost, A New Machine Part 2, Sorrow, The Dogs Of War, On The Turning Away, One Of These Days, Time, On The Run, The Great Gig In The Sky, Wish You Were Here, Welcome To The Machine, Us And Them, Money, Another Brick In The Wall Part 2, Comfortably Numb, One Slip, Run Like Hell
Audio Rating: ★★★↗
Miscellaneous: The start of three nights in Dortmund.

Date: 28-06-1988
Location: Westfalenhalle, Dortmund, West Germany
Track Listing: Shine On You Crazy Diamond, Signs Of Life, Learning To Fly, Yet Another Movie, A New Machine Part 1, Terminal Frost, A New Machine Part 2, Sorrow, The Dogs Of War, On The Turning Away, One Of These Days, Time, On The Run, The Great Gig In The Sky, Wish You Were Here, Welcome To The Machine, Us And Them, Money, Another Brick In The Wall Part 2, Comfortably Numb, One Slip, Run Like Hell
Audio Rating: ★★★↗
Miscellaneous: Noticeable how European audiences clap along to the beat and sing rather than whooping and yelling and whistling, as in North America.

Date: 29-06-1988
Location: Westfalenhalle, Dortmund, West Germany
Track Listing: Shine On You Crazy Diamond, Signs Of Life, Learning To Fly, Yet Another Movie, A New Machine Part 1, Terminal Frost, A New Machine Part 2, Sorrow, The Dogs Of War, On The Turning Away, One Of These Days, Time, On The Run, The Great Gig In The Sky, Wish You Were Here, Welcome To The Machine, Us And Them, Money, Another Brick In The Wall Part 2, Comfortably Numb, One Slip, Run Like Hell
Audio Rating: ★★★
Miscellaneous: Murkier than the last two nights.

Date: 01-07-1988
Location: Praterstadion, Vienna, Austria
Track Listing: Shine On You Crazy Diamond, Signs Of Life, Learning To Fly, Yet Another Movie, Sorrow, The Dogs Of War, On The Turning Away, One Of These Days, Time, On The Run, The Great Gig In The Sky, Wish You Were Here, Welcome To The Machine, Us And Them, Money, Another Brick In The Wall Part 2, Comfortably Numb, One Slip, Run Like Hell
Audio Rating: ★★★↗
Miscellaneous: **A NEW MACHINE PART 1**, **TERMINAL FROST** and **A NEW MACHINE PART 2** dropped again. Recording includes some of the soundcheck. So much clapping.

Date: 03-07-1988
Location: Olympiastadion, Munich, West Germany
Track Listing: Shine On You Crazy Diamond, Signs Of Life, Learning To Fly, Yet Another Movie, Sorrow, The Dogs Of War, On The Turning Away, One Of These Days, Time, On The Run, The Great Gig In The Sky, Wish You Were Here, Welcome To The Machine, Us And Them, Money, Another Brick In The Wall Part 2, Comfortably Numb, One Slip, Run Like Hell
Audio Rating: ★★
Miscellaneous: Sounds like it was recorded inside a bag.

Date: 06-07-1988
Location: Stadio Comunale, Turin, Italy
Track Listing: Shine On You Crazy Diamond, Signs Of Life, Learning To Fly, Yet Another Movie, A New Machine Part 1, Terminal Frost, A New Machine Part 2, Sorrow, The Dogs Of War, On The Turning Away, One Of These Days, Time, On The Run, The Great Gig In The Sky, Wish You Were Here, Welcome To The Machine, Us And Them, Money, Another Brick In The Wall Part 2, Comfortably Numb, One Slip, Run Like Hell
Audio Rating: ★★★
Miscellaneous: **SORROW** fades out just as the song is ending.

Date: 08-07-1988
Location: Stadio Alberto Braglia, Modena, Italy
Track Listing: Shine On You Crazy Diamond, Signs Of Life, Learning To Fly, Yet Another

Movie, A New Machine Part 1, Terminal Frost, A New Machine Part 2, Sorrow, The Dogs Of War, On The Turning Away, One Of These Days, Time, On The Run, The Great Gig In The Sky, Wish You Were Here, Welcome To The Machine, Us And Them, Money, Another Brick In The Wall Part 2, Comfortably Numb, One Slip, Run Like Hell
Audio Rating: ★★★★✯
Miscellaneous: Fantastic sound, one of the best 1988 shows. Lots of sonic detail.

Date: 09-07-1988
Location: Stadio Alberto Braglia, Modena, Italy
Track Listing: Shine On You Crazy Diamond, Signs Of Life, Learning To Fly, Yet Another Movie, A New Machine Part 1, Terminal Frost, A New Machine Part 2, Sorrow, The Dogs Of War, On The Turning Away, One Of These Days, Time, On The Run, The Great Gig In The Sky, Wish You Were Here, Welcome To The Machine, Us And Them, Money, Another Brick In The Wall Part 2, Comfortably Numb, One Slip, Run Like Hell
Audio Rating: ★★★
Miscellaneous: A reversion to very moderate sound quality after the last gig's excellence.

Date: 11-07-1988
Location: Stadio Flaminio, Rome, Italy
Track Listing: Shine On You Crazy Diamond, Signs Of Life, Learning To Fly, Yet Another Movie, A New Machine Part 1, Terminal Frost, A New Machine Part 2, Sorrow, The Dogs Of War, On The Turning Away, One Of These Days, Time, On The Run, The Great Gig In The Sky, Wish You Were Here, Welcome To The Machine, Us And Them, Money, Another Brick In The Wall Part 2, Comfortably Numb, One Slip, Run Like Hell
Audio Rating: ★★★★
Miscellaneous: Fans singing 'Allez-oh-oh' as at the beginning of *Pulse* CD2 (before **SPEAK TO ME**). Sound is excellent, just could be a touch more powerful.

Date: 12-07-1988
Location: Stadio Flaminio, Rome, Italy
Track Listing: Shine On You Crazy Diamond, Signs Of Life, Learning To Fly, Yet Another Movie, A New Machine Part 1, Terminal Frost, A New Machine Part 2, Sorrow, The Dogs Of War, On The Turning Away, One Of These Days, Time, On The Run, The Great Gig In The Sky, Wish You Were Here, Welcome To The Machine, Us And Them, Money, Another Brick In The Wall Part 2, Comfortably Numb, One Slip, Run Like Hell
Audio Rating: ★★★★
Miscellaneous: Audio sounds very similar to the previous night so very likely to be the same taper. There's a maybe one or two minute gap between the end of **COMFORTABLY NUMB** and the beginning of **ONE SLIP**.

Date: 15-07-1988
Location: Stade Charles-Berty, Grenoble, France
Track Listing: Shine On You Crazy Diamond, Signs Of Life, Learning To Fly, Yet Another Movie, A New Machine Part 1, Terminal Frost, A New Machine Part 2, Sorrow, The Dogs Of War, On The Turning Away, One Of These Days, Time, On The Run, The Great Gig In The Sky, Wish You Were Here, Welcome To The Machine, Us And Them, Money, Another Brick In The Wall Part 2, Comfortably Numb, One Slip, Run Like Hell
Audio Rating: ★★★✯
Miscellaneous: Sound of nearby audience at times nearly overpowering. Fortunately they clap more than yell.

Date: 17-07-1988
Location: Stade Charles-Ehrmann, Nice, France
Track Listing: Shine On You Crazy Diamond, Signs Of Life, Learning To Fly, Yet Another Movie, A New Machine Part 1, Terminal Frost, A New Machine Part 2, Sorrow, The Dogs Of War, On The Turning Away, One Of These Days, Time, On The Run, The Great Gig In The Sky, Wish You Were Here, Welcome To The Machine, Us And Them, Money, Another Brick In The Wall Part 2, Comfortably Numb, One Slip, Run Like Hell
Audio Rating: ★★★★★✯
Miscellaneous: Lots of sound captured from nearby audience again.

Date: 20-07-1988
Location: Estadio De Sarria, Barcelona, Spain
Track Listing: Shine On You Crazy Diamond, Signs Of Life, Learning To Fly, Yet Another Movie, A New Machine Part 1, Terminal Frost, A New Machine Part 2, Sorrow, The Dogs Of War, On The Turning Away, One Of These Days, Time, On The Run, The Great Gig In The

Sky, Wish You Were Here, Welcome To The Machine, Us And Them, Money, Another Brick In The Wall Part 2, Comfortably Numb, One Slip, Run Like Hell
Audio Rating: ★★★
Miscellaneous: Gilmour, after **LEARNING TO FLY**: 'Muchas gracias ... that's about all I've learned.'

Date: 22-07-1988
Location: Estadio Vicente Calderon, Madrid, Spain
Track Listing: Shine On You Crazy Diamond, Signs Of Life, Learning To Fly, Yet Another Movie, A New Machine Part 1, Terminal Frost, A New Machine Part 2, Sorrow, The Dogs Of War, On The Turning Away, One Of These Days, Time, On The Run, The Great Gig In The Sky, Wish You Were Here, Welcome To The Machine, Us And Them, Money, Another Brick In The Wall Part 2, Comfortably Numb, One Slip, Run Like Hell
Audio Rating: ★★♪
Miscellaneous: Sound initially very muted but improves as the show goes on.

Date: 24-07-1988
Location: Espace Richter, Montpellier, France
Track Listing: Shine On You Crazy Diamond, Signs Of Life, Learning To Fly, Yet Another Movie, A New Machine Part 1, Terminal Frost, A New Machine Part 2, Sorrow, The Dogs Of War, On The Turning Away, One Of These Days, Time, On The Run, The Great Gig In The Sky, Wish You Were Here, Welcome To The Machine, Us And Them, Money, Another Brick In The Wall Part 2, Comfortably Numb, One Slip, Run Like Hell
Audio Rating: ★★★★♪
Miscellaneous: Excellent audio, the bass drum really thumps and you can hear Wright's keyboards too.

Date: 26-07-1988
Location: St Jakob Stadium, Basel, Switzerland
Track Listing: Shine On You Crazy Diamond, Signs Of Life, Learning To Fly, Yet Another Movie, Sorrow, The Dogs Of War, On The Turning Away, One Of These Days, Time, On The Run, The Great Gig In The Sky, Wish You Were Here, Welcome To The Machine, Us And Them, Money, Another Brick In The Wall Part 2, Comfortably Numb, One Slip, Run Like Hell

Audio Rating: ★★★
Miscellaneous: A NEW MACHINE PART 1, TERMINAL FROST and A NEW MACHINE PART 2 benched again.

Date: 28-07-1988
Location: Stadium Nord, Villeneuve d'Ascq, Lille, France
Track Listing: Shine On You Crazy Diamond, Signs Of Life, Learning To Fly, Yet Another Movie, A New Machine Part 1, Terminal Frost, A New Machine Part 2, Sorrow, The Dogs Of War, On The Turning Away, One Of These Days, Time, On The Run, The Great Gig In The Sky, Wish You Were Here, Welcome To The Machine, Us And Them, Money, Another Brick In The Wall Part 2, Comfortably Numb, One Slip, Run Like Hell
Audio Rating: ★★★♪
Miscellaneous: Nearby fans again overly prominent.

Date: 31-07-1988
Location: Gentofte Stadion, Copenhagen, Denmark
Track Listing: Shine On You Crazy Diamond, Signs Of Life, Learning To Fly, Yet Another Movie, Sorrow, The Dogs Of War, On The Turning Away, One Of These Days, Time, On The Run, The Great Gig In The Sky, Wish You Were Here, Welcome To The Machine, Us And Them, Money, Another Brick In The Wall Part 2, Comfortably Numb, One Slip, Run Like Hell
Audio Rating: ★★★
Miscellaneous: A NEW MACHINE PART 1, TERMINAL FROST and A NEW MACHINE PART 2 benched yet again.

Date: 01-08-1988
Location: Annabel's Disco and Nightclub, Copenhagen, Denmark
Track Listing: Respect, Can't Get Enough, Blues, My Girl, Rock Steady – Rapper's Delight – Le Freak – Rock Steady, Master Blaster, Superstition
Audio Rating: ★★★★
Miscellaneous: As with the impromptu gig at The World's Club in New York on 11 October 1987, the group cut loose playing some R&B and funk covers and the backing singers get a chance to shine. It's a delight.

Date: 02-08-1988
Location: Valle Hovin, Oslo, Norway
Track Listing: Shine On You Crazy Diamond, Signs Of Life, Learning To Fly, Yet Another Movie, Sorrow, The Dogs Of War, On The Turning Away, One Of These Days, Time, On The Run, The Great Gig In The Sky, Wish You Were Here, Welcome To The Machine, Us And Them, Money, Another Brick In The Wall Part 2, Comfortably Numb, One Slip, Run Like Hell
Audio Rating: ★★★
Miscellaneous: So. Much. Clapping.

Date: 05-08-1988
Location: Wembley Stadium, London
Track Listing: Shine On You Crazy Diamond, Signs Of Life, Learning To Fly, Yet Another Movie, Sorrow, The Dogs Of War, On The Turning Away, One Of These Days, Time, On The Run, The Great Gig In The Sky, Wish You Were Here, Welcome To The Machine, Us And Them, Money, Another Brick In The Wall Part 2, Comfortably Numb, One Slip, Run Like Hell
Audio Rating: ★★★↙
Miscellaneous: These two gigs are the only time the group played Wembley Stadium. Next tour they would prefer to play fourteen nights at Earl's Court. At one of the Wembley shows, Gilmour 'stuck [his] middle finger up' and 'mouthed "Fuck off!"' at a fan who 'was waving a Roger Waters t-shirt from the front row'.*

Date: 06-08-1988
Location: Wembley Stadium, London
Track Listing: Shine On You Crazy Diamond, Signs Of Life, Learning To Fly, Yet Another Movie, Sorrow, The Dogs Of War, On The Turning Away, One Of These Days, Time, On The Run, The Great Gig In The Sky, Wish You Were Here, Welcome To The Machine, Us And Them, Money, Another Brick In The Wall Part 2, Comfortably Numb, One Slip, Run Like Hell
Audio Rating: ★★★★
Miscellaneous: More detailed audio than the night before.

Date: 08-08-1988
Location: Maine Road Stadium, Manchester
Track Listing: Shine On You Crazy Diamond, Signs Of Life, Learning To Fly, Yet Another Movie, Sorrow, The Dogs Of War, On The Turning Away, One Of These Days, Time, On The Run, The Great Gig In The Sky, Wish You Were Here, Welcome To The Machine, Us And Them, Money, Another Brick In The Wall Part 2, Comfortably Numb, One Slip, Run Like Hell
Audio Rating: ★★★↙
Miscellaneous: The gig which Guy Pratt attributes as causing the football casual-psychedelic crossover of the late 1980s,† perhaps best personified by Manchester band the Happy Mondays. Especially their album *Bummed*, which samples copiously from the film *Performance* (1970, but filmed 1968), itself both a gangster film and a psychedelic headfuck.

Date: 12-08-1988
Location: The Coliseum, Richfield, Akron, Ohio, USA
Track Listing: Shine On You Crazy Diamond, Signs Of Life, Learning To Fly, Yet Another Movie, A New Machine Part 1, Terminal Frost, A New Machine Part 2, Sorrow, The Dogs Of War, On The Turning Away, One Of These Days, Time, On The Run, The Great Gig In The Sky, Wish You Were Here, Welcome To The Machine, Us And Them, Money, Another Brick In The Wall Part 2, Comfortably Numb, One Slip, Run Like Hell
Audio Rating: ★★★★
Miscellaneous: A final jaunt to the US for ten shows before they call it a day until 1989. The Coliseum is midway between Akron and Cleveland, but is officially part of Akron County. Akron's most noted musical export is probably Devo.

Date: 16-08-1988
Location: The Palace of Auburn Hills, Detroit, Michigan, USA
Track Listing: Shine On You Crazy Diamond, Signs Of Life, Learning To Fly, Yet Another Movie, A New Machine Part 1, Terminal Frost, A New Machine Part 2, Sorrow, The Dogs Of War, On The Turning Away, One Of These Days, Time, On The Run, The Great Gig In The Sky, Wish You Were Here, Welcome To The Machine, Us And Them, Money, Another Brick In The Wall Part 2, Comfortably Numb, One Slip, Run Like Hell

---

* *Q* magazine, June 1999.

† *The Rockonteurs*, episode 41 (featuring Noel Gallagher).

Audio Rating: ★★★
Miscellaneous: **A NEW MACHINE PART 1**, **TERMINAL FROST** and **A NEW MACHINE PART 2** return to the setlist.

Date: 17-08-1988
Location: The Palace of Auburn Hills, Detroit, Michigan, USA
Track Listing: Shine On You Crazy Diamond, Signs Of Life, Learning To Fly, Yet Another Movie, A New Machine Part 1, Terminal Frost, A New Machine Part 2, Sorrow, The Dogs Of War, On The Turning Away, One Of These Days, Time, On The Run, The Great Gig In The Sky, Wish You Were Here, Welcome To The Machine, Us And Them, Money, Another Brick In The Wall Part 2, Comfortably Numb, One Slip, Run Like Hell
Audio Rating: ★★★
Miscellaneous: **SORROW** has a tape flip towards the end then a further eight seconds just before that mighty riff kicks in to end it all, so it's missing the ending. Quality similar to the night previous, could well be the same taper.

Date: 19-08-1988
Location: Nassau Veterans Memorial Coliseum, Long Island, New York, USA
Track Listing: Shine On You Crazy Diamond, Signs Of Life, Learning To Fly, Yet Another Movie, A New Machine Part 1, Terminal Frost, A New Machine Part 2, Sorrow, The Dogs Of War, On The Turning Away, One Of These Days, Time, On The Run, The Great Gig In The Sky, Wish You Were Here, Welcome To The Machine, Us And Them, Money, Another Brick In The Wall Part 2, Comfortably Numb, One Slip, Run Like Hell
Audio Rating: ★★★↗
Miscellaneous: A return to the location of *The Wall* shows of 1980, for five shows on consecutive nights.

Date: 20-08-1988
Location: Nassau Veterans Memorial Coliseum, Long Island, New York, USA
Track Listing: Shine On You Crazy Diamond, Signs Of Life, Learning To Fly, Yet Another Movie, A New Machine Part 1, Terminal Frost, A New Machine Part 2, Sorrow, The Dogs Of War, On The Turning Away, One Of These Days, Time, On The Run, The Great Gig In The Sky, Wish You Were Here, Welcome To The Machine, Us And Them, Money, Another Brick In The Wall Part 2, Comfortably Numb, One Slip, Run Like Hell
Audio Rating: ★★★
Miscellaneous: Second night. Audio lacks definition, though it hits the high and low notes.

Date: 21-08-1988
Location: Nassau Veterans Memorial Coliseum, Long Island, New York, USA
Track Listing: Shine On You Crazy Diamond, Signs Of Life, Learning To Fly, Yet Another Movie, A New Machine Part 1, Terminal Frost, A New Machine Part 2, Sorrow, The Dogs Of War, On The Turning Away, One Of These Days, Time, On The Run, The Great Gig In The Sky, Wish You Were Here, Welcome To The Machine, Us And Them, Money, Another Brick In The Wall Part 2, Comfortably Numb, One Slip, Run Like Hell
Audio Rating: ★★↗
Miscellaneous: More muffled-sounding than the previous night.

Date: 22-08-1988
Location: Nassau Veterans Memorial Coliseum, Long Island, New York, USA
Track Listing: Shine On You Crazy Diamond, Signs Of Life, Learning To Fly, Yet Another Movie, A New Machine Part 1, Terminal Frost, A New Machine Part 2, Sorrow, The Dogs Of War, On The Turning Away, One Of These Days, Time, On The Run, The Great Gig In The Sky, Wish You Were Here, Welcome To The Machine, Us And Them, Money, Another Brick In The Wall Part 2, Comfortably Numb, One Slip, Run Like Hell
Audio Rating: ★★★
Miscellaneous: Lots and lots of whistling and cheering. During **WISH YOU WERE HERE** the singalong sounds truly inspiring. At other quiet moments, such as **US AND THEM**, it's more distracting.

Date: 23-08-1988
Location: Nassau Veterans Memorial Coliseum, Long Island, New York, USA
Track Listing: Shine On You Crazy Diamond, Signs Of Life, Learning To Fly, Yet Another Movie, A New Machine Part 1, Terminal Frost, A New Machine Part 2, Sorrow, The Dogs Of War, On The Turning Away, One Of These Days, Time, On The Run, The Great Gig In The Sky, Wish You Were Here, Welcome To The

Machine, Us And Them, Money, Another Brick In The Wall Part 2, Comfortably Numb, One Slip, Run Like Hell
Audio Rating: ★★★♪
Miscellaneous: Loud songs really kick it, especially **RUN LIKE HELL**, but quiet sections lack sufficient audio definition.

1989
Date: 13-05-1989
Location: Festivalweise, Werchter, Belgium
Track Listing: Shine On You Crazy Diamond, Signs Of Life, Learning To Fly, Yet Another Movie, A New Machine Part 1, Terminal Frost, A New Machine Part 2, Sorrow, The Dogs Of War, On The Turning Away, One Of These Days, Time, On The Run, The Great Gig In The Sky, Wish You Were Here, Welcome To The Machine, Us And Them, Money, Another Brick In The Wall Part 2, Comfortably Numb, One Slip, Run Like Hell
Audio Rating: ★★★
Miscellaneous: After a nine-month break, the *Momentary Lapse* tour resumes, billed as the 'Another Lapse tour' in a wink-wink admission of its bacchanalian nature. This time it's just a four-month swing around European cities from Lahti in Finland (the only time the group visited that country) to Athens (another first). Gilmour's stage patter is typically inconsequential: 'Thank you very much, good evening, bon soir, and welcome. Oh, you missed us last time so we had to come out again. Right, this is the first show of our next little leg of this tour, couple of months here. Now we're going do a little tune called "Yet Another Movie", from our last album. Take it away.'

Date: 16-05-1989
Location: Arena Di Verona, Verona, Italy
Track Listing: Shine On You Crazy Diamond, Signs Of Life, Learning To Fly, Yet Another Movie, A New Machine Part 1, Terminal Frost, A New Machine Part 2, Sorrow, The Dogs Of War, On The Turning Away, One Of These Days, Time, On The Run, The Great Gig In The Sky, Wish You Were Here, Welcome To The Machine, Us And Them, Money, Another Brick In The Wall Part 2, Comfortably Numb, One Slip, Run Like Hell
Audio Rating: ★★★★
Miscellaneous: You hear the audience go 'Oooh!' when Gilmour plays the first solo in **COMFORTABLY NUMB**.

Date: 17-05-1989
Location: Arena Di Verona, Verona, Italy
Track Listing: Shine On You Crazy Diamond, Signs Of Life, Learning To Fly, Yet Another Movie, A New Machine Part 1, Terminal Frost, A New Machine Part 2, Sorrow, The Dogs Of War, On The Turning Away, One Of These Days, Time, On The Run, The Great Gig In The Sky, Wish You Were Here, Welcome To The Machine, Us And Them, Money, Another Brick In The Wall Part 2, Comfortably Numb
Audio Rating: ★★★
Miscellaneous: Encore songs are missing. Sound is clear but rather tinny.

Date: 18-05-1989
Location: Arena Di Verona, Verona, Italy
Track Listing: Shine On You Crazy Diamond, Signs Of Life, Learning To Fly, Yet Another Movie, A New Machine Part 1, Terminal Frost, A New Machine Part 2, Sorrow, The Dogs Of War, On The Turning Away, One Of These Days, Time, On The Run, The Great Gig In The Sky, Wish You Were Here, Welcome To The Machine, Us And Them, Money, Another Brick In The Wall Part 2, Comfortably Numb, One Slip, Run Like Hell
Audio Rating: ★★♪
Miscellaneous: A third night in Verona, playing at the Verona Theatre built in AD 30!

Date: 20-05-1989
Location: Arena Concerti, Monza, Italy
Track Listing: Shine On You Crazy Diamond, Signs Of Life, Learning To Fly, Yet Another Movie, A New Machine Part 1, Terminal Frost, A New Machine Part 2, Sorrow, The Dogs Of War, On The Turning Away, One Of These Days, Time, On The Run, The Great Gig In The Sky, Wish You Were Here, Welcome To The Machine, Us And Them, Money, Another Brick In The Wall Part 2, Comfortably Numb, One Slip, Run Like Hell
Audio Rating: ★★★★♪
Miscellaneous: Band sometimes barely audible ahead of the crowd.

Date: 22-05-1989
Location: Stadio Comunale Ardenza, Livorno, Italy
Track Listing: Shine On You Crazy Diamond, Signs Of Life, Learning To Fly, Yet Another Movie, A New Machine Part 1, Terminal Frost, A New Machine Part 2, Sorrow, The Dogs Of

War, On The Turning Away, One Of These Days, Time, On The Run, The Great Gig In The Sky, Wish You Were Here, Welcome To The Machine, Us And Them, Money, Another Brick In The Wall Part 2, Comfortably Numb, One Slip, Run Like Hell
Audio Rating: ★★★★
Miscellaneous: Raucous audience, sounds almost American in their enthusiasm.

Date: 26-05-1989
Location: Stadio Simonetta Lamberti, Cava De' Tirreni, Italy
Track Listing: Shine On You Crazy Diamond, Signs Of Life, Learning To Fly, Yet Another Movie, A New Machine Part 1, Terminal Frost, A New Machine Part 2, Sorrow, The Dogs Of War, On The Turning Away, One Of These Days, Time, On The Run, The Great Gig In The Sky, Wish You Were Here, Welcome To The Machine, Us And Them, Money, Another Brick In The Wall Part 2, Comfortably Numb, One Slip, Run Like Hell
Audio Rating: ★★½
Miscellaneous: Includes a few minutes of soundchecking.

Date: 31-05-1989
Location: Olympic Stadium Spiridon Spiros Louis, Athens, Greece
Track Listing: One Of These Days (Cut), Wish You Were Here, Welcome To The Machine, Us And Them, Money, Another Brick In The Wall Part 2, Comfortably Numb, One Slip, Run Like Hell
Audio Rating: ★★★★
Miscellaneous: A first time playing in Greece. A truncated recording of the second set only.

Date: 03-06-1989
Location: Olympic Stadium, Moscow, USSR
Track Listing: Shine On You Crazy Diamond, Signs Of Life, Learning To Fly, Yet Another Movie, A New Machine Part 1, Terminal Frost, A New Machine Part 2, Sorrow, The Dogs Of War, On The Turning Away, One Of These Days, Time, On The Run, The Great Gig In The Sky, Wish You Were Here, Welcome To The Machine, Us And Them, Money, Another Brick In The Wall Part 2, Comfortably Numb, One Slip, Run Like Hell
Audio Rating: ★★★
Miscellaneous: The Moscow gigs which may have been offered to have been paid in timber (see **GET YOUR FILTHY HANDS OFF MY DESERT**). The band played five nights in total: 3-4 and 6-8 June. Audience hugely enthusiastic.

Date: 07-06-1989
Location: Olympic Stadium, Moscow, USSR
Track Listing: Shine On You Crazy Diamond, Signs Of Life, Learning To Fly, Yet Another Movie, A New Machine Part 1, Terminal Frost, A New Machine Part 2, Sorrow, The Dogs Of War, On The Turning Away, One Of These Days, Time, On The Run, The Great Gig In The Sky, Wish You Were Here, Welcome To The Machine, Us And Them, Money, Another Brick In The Wall Part 2, Comfortably Numb, One Slip, Run Like Hell
Audio Rating: ★★★★
Miscellaneous: Another highly enthusiastic audience.

Date: 10-06-1989
Location: Lahden Surhali, Lahti, Finland
Track Listing: Shine On You Crazy Diamond, Signs Of Life, Learning To Fly, Yet Another Movie, A New Machine Part 1, Terminal Frost, A New Machine Part 2, Sorrow, The Dogs Of War, On The Turning Away, One Of These Days, Time, On The Run, The Great Gig In The Sky, Wish You Were Here, Welcome To The Machine, Us And Them (False Start), Us And Them, Technical Difficulties, Money, Another Brick In The Wall Part 2, Comfortably Numb, One Slip, Run Like Hell
Audio Rating: ★★★★
Miscellaneous: Another first, this time playing in Finland. A now-rare false start occurs in **US AND THEM**, where Wright's keyboard introduction seems to go on forever, presumably because of some malfunction with the guitars or drums. After nearly three minutes they give up, with Gilmour suavely asking the audience for its understanding, but manage to resume around three minutes later.

Date: 12-06-1989
Location: Globe Arena, Stockholm, Sweden
Track Listing: Shine On You Crazy Diamond, Signs Of Life, Learning To Fly, Yet Another Movie, A New Machine Part 1, Terminal Frost, A New Machine Part 2, Sorrow, The Dogs Of War, On The Turning Away, One Of These Days, Time, On The Run, The Great Gig In The Sky, Wish You Were Here, Welcome To The

Machine, Us And Them, Money, Another Brick In The Wall Part 2, Comfortably Numb, One Slip, Run Like Hell
Audio Rating: ★★★★↙
Miscellaneous: Recorded from section D12, row 36, apparently. The sound is terrific.

Date: 13-06-1989
Location: Globe Arena, Stockholm, Sweden
Track Listing: Shine On You Crazy Diamond, Signs Of Life, Learning To Fly, Yet Another Movie, A New Machine Part 1, Terminal Frost, A New Machine Part 2, Sorrow, The Dogs Of War, On The Turning Away, One Of These Days, Time, On The Run, The Great Gig In The Sky, Wish You Were Here, Welcome To The Machine, Us And Them, Money, Another Brick In The Wall Part 2, Comfortably Numb, One Slip, Run Like Hell
Audio Rating: ★★★★↙
Miscellaneous: After **ANOTHER BRICK IN THE WALL PART 2**, Gilmour says, 'Thank you, we're going to play a selection of Abba's greatest hits now.' What a japester.

Date: 14-06-1989
Location: Globe Arena, Stockholm, Sweden
Track Listing: Shine On You Crazy Diamond, Signs Of Life, Learning To Fly, Yet Another Movie, A New Machine Part 1, Terminal Frost, A New Machine Part 2, Sorrow, The Dogs Of War, On The Turning Away, One Of These Days, Time, On The Run, The Great Gig In The Sky, Wish You Were Here, Welcome To The Machine, Us And Them, Money, Another Brick In The Wall Part 2, Comfortably Numb, One Slip, Run Like Hell
Audio Rating: ★★★↙
Miscellaneous: A third night in Stockholm.

Date: 16-06-1989
Location: Festweisse Im Stadtpark, Hamburg, West Germany
Track Listing: Shine On You Crazy Diamond, Signs Of Life, Learning To Fly, Yet Another Movie, A New Machine Part 1, Terminal Frost, A New Machine Part 2, Sorrow, The Dogs Of War, On The Turning Away, One Of These Days, Time, On The Run, The Great Gig In The Sky, Wish You Were Here, Welcome To The Machine, Us And Them, Money, Another Brick In The Wall Part 2, Comfortably Numb, One Slip, Run Like Hell
Audio Rating: ★★★★↙

Miscellaneous: One of the best sounding bootlegs from this tour, if you don't mind the audience singing along during **ANOTHER BRICK IN THE WALL PART 2** and **ONE SLIP**.

Date: 18-06-1989
Location: Mungersdorfer Stadion, Cologne, West Germany
Track Listing: Shine On You Crazy Diamond, Signs Of Life, Learning To Fly, Yet Another Movie, A New Machine Part 1, Terminal Frost, A New Machine Part 2, Sorrow, The Dogs Of War, On The Turning Away, One Of These Days, Time, On The Run, The Great Gig In The Sky, Wish You Were Here, Welcome To The Machine, Us And Them, Money, Another Brick In The Wall Part 2, Comfortably Numb, One Slip, Run Like Hell
Audio Rating: ★★★★★↙
Miscellaneous: Another fantastically enthusiastic audience. Sound clear but quite significant hiss.

Date: 20-06-1989
Location: Festhalle, Frankfurt, West Germany
Track Listing: Shine On You Crazy Diamond, Signs Of Life, Learning To Fly, Yet Another Movie, A New Machine Part 1, Terminal Frost, A New Machine Part 2, Sorrow, The Dogs Of War, On The Turning Away, One Of These Days, Time, On The Run, The Great Gig In The Sky, Wish You Were Here, Welcome To The Machine, Us And Them, Money, Another Brick In The Wall Part 2, Comfortably Numb, One Slip, Run Like Hell
Audio Rating: ★★★
Miscellaneous: Rapturous audience.

Date: 21-06-1989
Location: Festhalle, Frankfurt, West Germany
Track Listing: Shine On You Crazy Diamond, Signs Of Life, Learning To Fly, Yet Another Movie, A New Machine Part 1, Terminal Frost, A New Machine Part 2, Sorrow, The Dogs Of War, On The Turning Away, One Of These Days, Time, On The Run, The Great Gig In The Sky, Wish You Were Here, Welcome To The Machine, Us And Them, Money, Another Brick In The Wall Part 2, Comfortably Numb, One Slip, Run Like Hell
Audio Rating: ★★★★
Miscellaneous: German audiences sure like to clap along.

Date: 23-06-1989
Location: Linzer Stadion, Linz, Austria
Track Listing: Shine On You Crazy Diamond, Signs Of Life, Learning To Fly, Yet Another Movie, A New Machine Part 1, Terminal Frost, A New Machine Part 2, Sorrow, The Dogs Of War, On The Turning Away, One Of These Days, Time, On The Run, The Great Gig In The Sky, Wish You Were Here, Welcome To The Machine, Us And Them, Money, Another Brick In The Wall Part 2, Comfortably Numb, One Slip, Run Like Hell
Audio Rating: ★★★⌐
Miscellaneous: Yet another gig.

Date: 25-06-1989
Location: Neckarstadion, Stuttgart, West Germany
Track Listing: Shine On You Crazy Diamond, Signs Of Life, Learning To Fly, Yet Another Movie, Sorrow, The Dogs Of War, On The Turning Away, One Of These Days, Time, On The Run, The Great Gig In The Sky, Wish You Were Here, Welcome To The Machine, Us And Them, Money, Another Brick In The Wall Part 2, Comfortably Numb, One Slip, Run Like Hell
Audio Rating: ★★★
Miscellaneous: A few songs missing from the first set – namely **A NEW MACHINE PART 1, TERMINAL FROST**, and **A NEW MACHINE PART 2**. Or maybe the taper knew the setlist beforehand and decided to omit some songs.

Date: 27-06-1989
Location: Palais Omnisports De Paris-Bercy, Paris, France
Track Listing: Shine On You Crazy Diamond, Signs Of Life, Learning To Fly, Yet Another Movie, A New Machine Part 1, Terminal Frost, A New Machine Part 2, Sorrow, The Dogs Of War, On The Turning Away, One Of These Days, Time, On The Run, The Great Gig In The Sky, Wish You Were Here, Welcome To The Machine, Us And Them, Money, Another Brick In The Wall Part 2, Comfortably Numb, One Slip, Run Like Hell
Audio Rating: ★★★⌐
Miscellaneous: Five nights in Paris, 27-30 June and 1 July. Audio mostly clear but slightly muffled.

Date: 28-06-1989
Location: Palais Omnisports De Paris-Bercy, Paris, France
Track Listing: Shine On You Crazy Diamond, Signs Of Life, Learning To Fly, Yet Another Movie, A New Machine Part 1, Terminal Frost, A New Machine Part 2, Sorrow, The Dogs Of War, On The Turning Away, One Of These Days, Time, On The Run, The Great Gig In The Sky, Wish You Were Here, Welcome To The Machine, Us And Them, Money, Another Brick In The Wall Part 2, Comfortably Numb, One Slip, Run Like Hell
Audio Rating: ★★★⌐
Miscellaneous: 'Merci beaucoup, bon soir!' Gilmour is sadly no great stage raconteur.

Date: 29-06-1989
Location: Palais Omnisports De Paris-Bercy, Paris, France
Track Listing: Shine On You Crazy Diamond, Signs Of Life, Learning To Fly, Yet Another Movie, A New Machine Part 1, Terminal Frost, A New Machine Part 2, Sorrow, The Dogs Of War, On The Turning Away, One Of These Days, Time, On The Run, The Great Gig In The Sky, Wish You Were Here, Welcome To The Machine, Us And Them, Money, Another Brick In The Wall Part 2, Comfortably Numb, One Slip, Run Like Hell
Audio Rating: ★★★
Miscellaneous: Clear but very hissy.

Date: 30-06-1989
Location: Palais Omnisports De Paris-Bercy, Paris, France
Track Listing: Shine On You Crazy Diamond, Signs Of Life, Learning To Fly, Yet Another Movie, A New Machine Part 1, Terminal Frost, A New Machine Part 2, Sorrow, The Dogs Of War, On The Turning Away, One Of These Days, Time, On The Run, The Great Gig In The Sky, Wish You Were Here, Welcome To The Machine, Us And Them, Money, Another Brick In The Wall Part 2, Comfortably Numb, One Slip, Run Like Hell
Audio Rating: ★★⌐
Miscellaneous: Sound is murky.

Date: 01-07-1989
Location: Palais Omnisports De Paris-Bercy, Paris, France
Track Listing: Shine On You Crazy Diamond, Signs Of Life, Learning To Fly, Yet Another Movie, A New Machine Part 1, Terminal Frost, A New Machine Part 2, Sorrow, The Dogs Of War, On The Turning Away, One Of These

Days, Time, On The Run, The Great Gig In The Sky, Wish You Were Here, Welcome To The Machine, Us And Them, Money, Another Brick In The Wall Part 2, Comfortably Numb, One Slip, Run Like Hell
Audio Rating: ★★★
Miscellaneous: Audience (clapping throughout) sound much closer than the band, but the clarity is pretty good.

Date: 04-07-1989
Location: London Arena, Isle of Dogs, London
Track Listing: Shine On You Crazy Diamond, Signs Of Life, Learning To Fly, Yet Another Movie, A New Machine Part 1, Terminal Frost, A New Machine Part 2, Sorrow, The Dogs Of War, On The Turning Away, One Of These Days, Time, On The Run, The Great Gig In The Sky, Wish You Were Here, Welcome To The Machine, Us And Them, Money, Another Brick In The Wall Part 2, Comfortably Numb, One Slip, Run Like Hell
Audio Rating: ★★★♪
Miscellaneous: First of six nights in London. London Arena was a fairly short-lived arena and exhibition centre, opening in 1989 and closing in 2003.

Date: 05-07-1989
Location: London Arena, Isle of Dogs, London
Track Listing: Shine On You Crazy Diamond, Signs Of Life, Learning To Fly, Yet Another Movie, A New Machine Part 1, Terminal Frost, A New Machine Part 2, Sorrow, The Dogs Of War, On The Turning Away, One Of These Days, Time, On The Run, The Great Gig In The Sky, Wish You Were Here, Welcome To The Machine, Us And Them, Money, Another Brick In The Wall Part 2, Comfortably Numb, One Slip, Run Like Hell
Audio Rating: ★★★♪
Miscellaneous: Extremely loud audience clapping throughout the latter numbers, and a great singalong to **WISH YOU WERE HERE**.

Date: 07-07-1989
Location: London Arena, Isle of Dogs, London
Track Listing: Shine On You Crazy Diamond, Signs Of Life, Learning To Fly, Yet Another Movie, A New Machine Part 1, Terminal Frost, A New Machine Part 2, Sorrow, The Dogs Of War, On The Turning Away, One Of These Days, Time, On The Run, The Great Gig In The Sky, Wish You Were Here, Welcome To The Machine, Us And Them, Money, Another Brick In The Wall Part 2, Comfortably Numb, One Slip, Run Like Hell
Audio Rating: ★★★
Miscellaneous: Nothing very notable about this.

Date: 08-07-1989
Location: London Arena, Isle of Dogs, London
Track Listing: Shine On You Crazy Diamond, Signs Of Life, Learning To Fly, Yet Another Movie, A New Machine Part 1, Terminal Frost, A New Machine Part 2, Sorrow, The Dogs Of War, On The Turning Away, One Of These Days, Time, On The Run, The Great Gig In The Sky, Wish You Were Here, Welcome To The Machine, Us And Them, Money, Another Brick In The Wall Part 2, Comfortably Numb, One Slip, Run Like Hell
Audio Rating: ★★♪
Miscellaneous: Sound thin and murky.

Date: 09-07-1989
Location: London Arena, Isle of Dogs, London
Track Listing: Shine On You Crazy Diamond, Signs Of Life, Learning To Fly, Yet Another Movie, A New Machine Part 1, Terminal Frost, A New Machine Part 2, Sorrow, The Dogs Of War, On The Turning Away, One Of These Days, Time, On The Run, The Great Gig In The Sky, Wish You Were Here, Welcome To The Machine, Us And Them, Money, Another Brick In The Wall Part 2, Comfortably Numb, One Slip, Run Like Hell
Audio Rating: ★★
Miscellaneous: Audio very muffled and distant.

Date: 10-07-1989
Location: Goffertpark, Nijmegan, Netherlands
Track Listing: Shine On You Crazy Diamond, Signs Of Life, Learning To Fly, Yet Another Movie, Sorrow, The Dogs Of War, On The Turning Away, One Of These Days, Time, On The Run, The Great Gig In The Sky, Wish You Were Here, Welcome To The Machine, Us And Them, Money, Another Brick In The Wall Part 2, Comfortably Numb, One Slip, Run Like Hell
Audio Rating: ★★★
Miscellaneous: Songs dropped: **A NEW MACHINE PART 1**, **TERMINAL FROST** and **A NEW MACHINE PART 2**.

Date: 12-07-1989
Location: Stade Olympique De La Pontaise, Lausanne, Switzerland

Track Listing: Shine On You Crazy Diamond, Signs Of Life, Learning To Fly, Yet Another Movie, Sorrow, The Dogs Of War, On The Turning Away, One Of These Days, Time, On The Run, The Great Gig In The Sky, Wish You Were Here, Welcome To The Machine, Us And Them, Money, Another Brick In The Wall Part 2, Comfortably Numb, One Slip, Run Like Hell
Audio Rating: ★★★↙
Miscellaneous: **A NEW MACHINE PART 1**, **TERMINAL FROST** and **A NEW MACHINE PART 2** are missing here too.

Date: 15-07-1989
Location: Canale Di San Marco, Piazza San Marco, Venice, Italy
Track Listing: Shine On You Crazy Diamond, Learning To Fly, Yet Another Movie, Round And Around, Sorrow, The Dogs Of War, On The Turning Away, Time, The Great Gig In The Sky, Wish You Were Here, Money, Another Brick In The Wall Part 2, Comfortably Numb, Run Like Hell
Audio Rating: ★★★★★
Miscellaneous: A slightly reduced setlist and some shortened tracks owing to the timing demands of TV, with this broadcast live across the world.* An authorised version of this concert, with even better audio, was released in the *Later Days* boxset in 2019.

1990
Date: 30-06-1990
Location: Knebworth Park, England
Track Listing: Shine On You Crazy Diamond Parts I-V, The Great Gig In The Sky, Wish You Were Here, Sorrow, Money, Comfortably Numb, Run Like Hell
Audio Rating: ★★★★★

---

* 'We had a specific length of show to do; the satellite broadcasting meant we had to get it absolutely precise. We had the list of songs, and we'd shortened them, which we'd never done before. I had a big clock with a red digital read-out on the floor in front of me, and had the start time of each number on a piece of paper. If we were coming near the start time of the next number, I just had to wrap up the one we were on. We had a really good time, but the city authorities who had agreed to provide the services of security, toilets, food, completely reneged on everything they were supposed to do, and then tried to blame all the subsequent problems on us. Lots of twaddle was written about it, even by some nice respectable journalists from the *Guardian* – stuff about our music disturbing the buildings; complete fucking absolute twaddle.' Gilmour in *Q* magazine, September 1990.

Miscellaneous: Performed in the wind and pouring rain of an English summer. Also released in the *Later Days* boxset.

1994
Date: 16-03-1994
Location: Norton Air Force Base, San Bernadino, California, USA (rehearsal)
Track Listing: Shine On You Crazy Diamond, High Hopes, Tune Ups, Breathe, Time, Breathe (Reprise), The Great Gig In The Sky, Lost For Words, Tune Ups, Wish You Were Here (Cross-Faded In), Us And Them, Money, Comfortably Numb
Audio Rating: ★★★
Miscellaneous: The 1994 tour launch was pushed back a few weeks since *The Division Bell* had yet to be released. (It finally came out on 28 March, just two days before the tour officially started.) So the band honed their chops while waiting. With no audience it's naturally very audible, although the sound is a bit rough to be honest.

Date: 30-03-1994
Location: Joe Robbie Stadium, Miami, Florida, USA
Track Listing: Astronomy Domine, Learning To Fly, What Do You Want From Me?, Take It Back, Lost For Words, Sorrow, A Great Day For Freedom, Keep Talking, One Of These Days, Shine On You Crazy Diamond, Breathe, Time, Breathe (Reprise), High Hopes, Wish You Were Here, Another Brick In The Wall Part 2, The Great Gig In The Sky, Us And Them, Money, Comfortably Numb, Hey You, Run Like Hell, Astronomy Domine (Take 1), Astronomy Domine (Take 2)
Audio Rating: ★★★↙
Miscellaneous: Raucous audience, whistling and screeching, sounding very close to the taper, whereas the band sound quite distant. The two takes of **ASTRONOMY DOMINE** at the end are probably taken from the soundcheck.

Date: 03-04-1994
Location: The Alamodome, San Antonio, Texas, USA
Track Listing: Astronomy Domine, Learning To Fly, What Do You Want From Me?, Poles Apart, Sorrow, Take It Back, Lost For Words, Keep Talking, On The Turning Away, Shine On You Crazy Diamond, Breathe In The Air, Time, Breathe In The Air (Reprise), High Hopes,

Wish You Were Here, One Of These Days, The Great Gig In The Sky, Us And Them, Money, Comfortably Numb, Hey You, Run Like Hell
Audio Rating: ★✈
Miscellaneous: Echoey, distant and murky.

Date: 05-04-1994
Location: Rice University Stadium, Houston, Texas, USA
Track Listing: Astronomy Domine, Learning To Fly, What Do You Want From Me?, A Great Day For Freedom, Sorrow, Take It Back, On The Turning Away, Keep Talking, One Of These Days, Shine On You Crazy Diamond, Breathe, Time, High Hopes, Wish You Were Here, Another Brick In The Wall Part 2, The Great Gig In The Sky (Aborted), Money, 'Rain Like Fuck' (Aborted)
Audio Rating: ★★★✈
Miscellaneous: Performed in a Biblical downpour, which forced the band to abort several songs. The 'Run!' chant from **RUN LIKE HELL** therefore becomes 'Rain! Rain! Rain! Rain!', while the instruments and amps stop working at various points throughout. Calling it a day, Gilmour announces, 'Due to circumstances entirely beyond our control, everything appears to have stopped working! So thank you very much for coming, I'm really sorry, but we're going to have to love you and leave you. Good night!' (There's quite a few shouts of 'Bullshit!' from evidently disgruntled fans.) Photos from the gig can be seen on the *Pulse* booklet and look very impressive.

Date: 09-04-1994
Location: Autodromo Hermanos Rodriguez, Mexico City, Mexico
Track Listing: Astronomy Domine, Learning To Fly, What Do You Want From Me?, A Great Day For Freedom, Sorrow, Take It Back, On The Turning Away, Keep Talking, One Of These Days, Shine On Your Crazy Diamond, Breathe, Time, High Times, Wish You Were, Another Brick In The Wall Part 2, The Great Gig In The Sky, Us And Them, Money, Comfortably Numb, Hey You, Run Like Hell
Audio Rating: ★★★
Miscellaneous: First time in Mexico. A bit bright and piercing, lacking low-end frequencies.

Date: 10-04-1994
Location: Autodromo Hermanos Rodriguez, Mexico City, Mexico
Track Listing: Astronomy Domine, Learning To Fly, What Do You Want From Me?, A Great Day For Freedom, Sorrow, Take It Back, Another Brick In The Wall Part 2, Keep Talking, On The Turning Away (Cut), Shine On You Crazy Diamond Parts I-V, Breathe, Time, Breathe (Reprise), High Hopes, Wish You Were Here, One Of These Days, The Great Gig In The Sky, Us And Them, Money, Comfortably Numb, Hey You, Run Like Hell
Audio Rating: ★★✈
Miscellaneous: Tinny sound, but very lively audience.

Date: 14-04-1994
Location: Jack Murphy Stadium, San Diego, California, USA
Track Listing: Astronomy Domine, Learning To Fly, What Do You Want From Me?, A Great Day For Freedom, Sorrow, Take It Back, On The Turning Away, Keep Talking, One Of These Days, Shine On You Crazy Diamond I-V, Breathe, Time, Breathe (Reprise), High Hopes, Wish You Were Here, Another Brick In The Wall Part 2, The Great Gig In The Sky, Us And Them, Money, Comfortably Numb:, Hey You, Run Like Hell
Audio Rating: ★★★✈
Miscellaneous: Back to the USA. The sound is a bit subdued, but the clarity is good. Gilmour struggles to sing the high notes in **A GREAT DAY FOR FREEDOM**.

Date: 16-04-1994
Location: The Rose Bowl, Los Angeles, California, USA
Track Listing: Intro, Astronomy Domine, Learning To Fly, What Do You Want From Me?, Poles Apart, Sorrow, Take It Back, On The Turning Away, Keep Talking, One Of These Days, Shine On You Crazy Diamond I-V, Breathe, Time, High Hopes, Wish You Were Here, Another Brick In The Ball Part 2, The Great Gig In The Sky, Us And Them, Money, Comfortably Numb, Hey You, Run Like Hell
Audio Rating: ★★★★
Miscellaneous: Very good sound. The audience doesn't overpower the quiet parts, as so often during American tours.

Date: 17-04-1994
Location: The Rose Bowl, Pasadena, California, USA
Track Listing: Astronomy Domine, Learning To Fly, What Do You Want From Me?, A Great Day For Freedom, Sorrow, Take It Back, On The Turning Away, Keep Talking, One Of These Days, Shine On You Crazy Diamond I-V, Breathe, Time, Breathe (Reprise), High Hopes, Wish You Were Here, Another Brick In The Wall Part 2, The Great Gig In The Sky, Us And Them, Money, Comfortably Numb, Hey You, Run Like Hell
Audio Rating: ★★★
Miscellaneous: Sound is quite muffled. Another loud audience though.

Date: 20-04-1994
Location: Oakland-Alameda County Coliseum, Oakland, California, USA
Track Listing: Astronomy Domine, Learning To Fly, What Do You Want From Me?, On The Turning Away, Poles Apart, Sorrow, Take It Back, Keep Talking, One Of These Days, Shine On You Crazy Diamond I-V, Breathe, Time, Breathe (Reprise), High Hopes, Wish You Were Here, Another Brick In The Wall Part 2, The Great Gig In The Sky, Us And Them, Money, Comfortably Numb, Hey You, Run Like Hell
Audio Rating: ★★★★
Miscellaneous: First of three nights in Oakland. Good crisp sound.

Date: 21-04-1994
Location: Oakland-Alameda County Coliseum, Oakland, California, USA
Track Listing: Astronomy Domine, Learning To Fly, A Lovely Warm Night, What Do You Want From Me?, On The Turning Away, A Great Day For Freedom, Sorrow, Take It Back, Keep Talking, One Of These Days, Shine On You Crazy Diamond I-V, Breathe, Time, Breathe (Reprise), High Hopes, Wish You Were Here, Another Brick In The Wall Part 2, The Great Gig In The Sky, Us And Them, Money, Comfortably Numb, Thank You Very Much Indeed, Hey You, Run Like Hell, Farewell
Audio Rating: ★★★♪
Miscellaneous: 'Thank you very much, good evening! And a lovely warm night you've given us here tonight, mmm! California in the spring time!' Which is about as loquacious as Gilmour gets.

Date: 22-04-1994
Location: Oakland-Alameda County Coliseum, Oakland, California, USA
Track Listing: Astronomy Domine (Fade In), Learning To Fly, What Do You Want From Me?, On The Turning Away, Poles Apart, Sorrow, Take It Back, Keep Talking, One Of These Days, Shine On You Crazy Diamond I-V, Breathe, Time, Breathe (Reprise), High Hopes, The Great Gig In The Sky, One Slip, Us And Them, Wish You Were Here, Money, Another Brick In The Wall Part 2, Comfortably Numb, Hey You, Run Like Hell
Audio Rating: ★★★
Miscellaneous: Thinner sounding and lacking the detail of previous nights in Oakland. **ONE SLIP** gets its only outing on this tour, which is a little odd with it having previously been an encore.

Date: 24-04-1994
Location: Sun Devil Stadium, Arizona State University, Phoenix, Arizona, USA
Track Listing: Astronomy Domine, Learning To Fly, What Do You Want From Me?, On The Turning Away, Lost For Words, Sorrow, Take It Back, Keep Talking, One Of These Days, Shine On You Crazy Diamond I-V, Breathe, Time, Breathe (Reprise), High Hopes (Fade In), The Great Gig In The Sky, Wish You Were Here, Us And Them, Money, Another Brick In The Wall Part 2 (Fade Out), Comfortably Numb (Fade In), Hey You, Run Like Hell
Audio Rating: ★★★♪
Miscellaneous: **LOST FOR WORDS** is not played again until October.

Date: 28-04-1994
Location: Texas Stadium, Irving, Dallas, Texas, USA
Track Listing: Astronomy Domine, Learning To Fly, What Do You Want From Me?, On The Turning Away, Poles Apart, Sorrow, Take It Back, Keep Talking (Tape Flip), One Of These Days, Shine On You Crazy Diamond I-V, Breathe, Time, Breathe (Reprise), High Hopes, The Great Gig In The Sky, Wish You Were Here (Tape Flip), Us And Them, Money, Another Brick In The Wall Part 2, Comfortably Numb, Hey You, Run Like Hell, Thank You/Goodnight
Audio Rating: ★★★♪
Miscellaneous: A bit distant-sounding. Nearby

fan conversations and cheers are sometimes distracting.

Date: 29-04-1994
Location: Texas Stadium, Irving, Dallas, Texas, USA
Track Listing: Astronomy Domine, Learning To Fly, What Do You Want From Me?, On The Turning Away, Coming Back to Life, Sorrow, Take It Back, Keep Talking, One Of These Days, Shine On You Crazy Diamond I-V, Breathe, Time, Breathe (Reprise), High Hopes, The Great Gig In The Sky, Wish You Were Here, Us And Them, Money, Another Brick In The Wall Part 2, Comfortably Numb (Fade Out), Hey You, Run Like Hell
Audio Rating: ★★★★♪
Miscellaneous: Another rain-soaked performance, with **RUN LIKE HELL** adapted as at Houston on 4 April. Nonetheless, the audio quality is excellent.

Date: 01-05-1994
Location: Legion Field, University of Alabama, Birmingham, Alabama, USA
Track Listing: Astronomy Domine, Learning To Fly, What Do You Want From Me?, On The Turning Away, Coming Back to Life, Sorrow, Take It Back, Keep Talking, One Of These Days, Shine On You Crazy Diamond I-V, Breathe, Time, Breathe (Reprise), High Hopes, The Great Gig In The Sky, Wish You Were Here (Fade In), Us And Them, Money, Another Brick In The Wall Part 2, Comfortably Numb, Audience, Hey You, Run Like Hell
Audio Rating: ★★★
Miscellaneous: A bit thin and hissy-sounding.

Date: 03-05-1994
Location: Bobbie Dodd Stadium, Georgia Institute of Technology, Atlanta, Georgia, USA
Track Listing: Astronomy Domine, Learning To Fly, What Do You Want From Me?, On The Turning Away, Coming Back to Life, Sorrow, Take It Back, Keep Talking, One Of These Days, Shine On You Crazy Diamond I-V, Breathe, Time, Breathe (Reprise), High Hopes, The Great Gig In The Sky, Wish You Were Here, Money, Another Brick In The Wall Part 2, Comfortably Numb, Hey You, Run Like Hell
Audio Rating: ★★♪
Miscellaneous: Very muffled, as though recorded in a bag.

Date: 04-05-1994
Location: Bobbie Dodd Stadium, Georgia Institute of Technology, Atlanta, Georgia, USA
Track Listing: Astronomy Domine, Learning To Fly, What Do You Want From Me?, On The Turning Away, Coming Back to Life, Sorrow, Take It Back, Keep Talking, One Of These Days, Shine On You Crazy Diamond I-V, Breathe, Time, Breathe (Reprise), High Hopes, The Great Gig In The Sky, Wish You Were Here, Us And Them, Money, Another Brick In The Wall Part 2, Comfortably Numb, Hey You, Run Like Hell
Audio Rating: ★★★
Miscellaneous: Louder moments are good, but quieter passages barely make it past the noise of the audience.

Date: 06-05-1994
Location: Tampa Stadium, Tampa, Florida, USA
Track Listing: Astronomy Domine, Learning To Fly, What Do You Want From Me?, On The Turning Away, Take It Back, A Great Day For Freedom, Sorrow, Keep Talking, One Of These Days, Shine On You Crazy Diamond Parts I-V, Breathe/Time, Breathe (Reprise), High Hopes, The Great Gig In The Sky, Wish You Were Here, Us And Them, Money, Another Brick In The Wall Part 2, Comfortably Numb, Hey You, Run Like Hell
Audio Rating: ★★★★♪
Miscellaneous: Very good, crisp audio.

Date: 08-05-1994
Location: Vanderbilt University Stadium, Nashville, Tennessee, USA
Track Listing: Astronomy Domine, Learning To Fly, What Do You Want From Me?, On The Turning Away, Take It Back, Great Day For Freedom, Sorrow, Keep Talking, One Of These Days, Shine On You Crazy Diamonds Parts I-V, (Fade Out), Breathe (Fade In), Time, Breathe (Reprise), High Hopes, The Great Gig in the Sky, Wish You Were Here, Us And Them, Money, Another Brick In The Wall Part 2, Comfortably Numb, Encore Break, Hey You, Run Like Hell
Audio Rating: ★★★
Miscellaneous: Echoey and thin sounding.

Date: 10-05-1994
Location: Carter-Finley Stadium, North Carolina State University, Raleigh, North Carolina, USA
Track Listing: Astronomy Domine, Learning

To Fly, What Do You Want From?, On The Turning Away, Take It Back, A Great Day For Freedom, Sorrow, Keep Talking, One Of These Days, Shine On You Crazy Diamond I-V (Cut), Breathe, Time, Breathe (Reprise), High Hopes, The Great Gig In The Sky, Wish You Were Here, Us And Them, Money, Another Brick In The Wall Part 2, Comfortably Numb, Hey You, Run Like Hell
Audio Rating: ★★★
Miscellaneous: Music and vocals fairly crisp, but quite subdued.

Date: 12-05-1994
Location: Death Valley Stadium, Clemson University, Clemson, South Carolina, USA
Track Listing: Astronomy Domine (Fade In), Learning To Fly, What Do You Want From Me?, On The Turning Away, Take It Back, Poles Apart, Sorrow, Keep Talking, One Of These Days, Shine On You Crazy Diamond, Breathe, Time, Breathe (Reprise), High Hopes, The Great Gig In The Sky, Wish You Were Here, Us And Them, Money, Another Brick In The Wall Part 2, Comfortably Numb, Hey You, Run Like Hell
Audio Rating: ★★
Miscellaneous: Quiet and murky sounding.

Date: 14-05-1994
Location: Louisiana Superdrome, New Orleans, Louisiana, USA
Track Listing: Astronomy Domine, Learning To Fly, What Do You Want From Me?, On The Turning Away, Take It Back, Coming Back To Life, Sorrow, Keep Talking, One Of These Days, Shine On You Crazy Diamond I-V, Breathe, Time, High Hopes, The Great Gig In The Sky, Wish You Were Here, Us And Them, Money, Another Brick In The Wall Part 2, Comfortably Numb, Hey You, Run Like Hell
Audio Rating: ★★★★
Miscellaneous: Excellent audio, both at higher and lower frequencies.

Date: 18-05-1994
Location: Foxboro Stadium, Foxborough, Massachusetts, USA
Track Listing: Astronomy Domine, Learning To Fly, What Do You Want From Me?, On The Turning Away, Coming Back To Life, Sorrow, Take It Back, Keep Talking, One Of These Days, Shine On You Crazy Diamond I-V, Breathe, Time, High Hopes, The Great Gig In The Sky, Wish You Were Here, Us And Them, Money, Another Brick In The Wall Part 2, Comfortably Numb, Hey You, Run Like Hell, Crowd Departing
Audio Rating: ★★♪
Miscellaneous: Foxborough is a small town in Massachusetts (population: 18,618 in 2020), roughly 22 miles south of Boston, but it is home to the multi-purpose stadium hosting the New England Patriots NFL team – then Foxboro Stadium, since 2002 the Gillette Stadium.

Date: 19-05-1994
Location: Foxboro Stadium, Foxborough, Massachusetts, USA
Track Listing: Astronomy Domine, Learning To Fly, What Do You Want From Me?, On The Turning Away, Take It Back, Poles Apart, Sorrow, Keep Talking, One Of These Days, Shine On You Crazy Diamond I-V, Breathe, Time, Breathe (Reprise), High Hopes, The Great Gig In The Sky, Wish You Were Here, Us And Them, Money, Another Brick In The Wall Part 2, Comfortably Numb, Hey You, Run Like Hell
Audio Rating: ★★★
Miscellaneous: A second night in Foxborough. Standard set, average sound quality.

Date: 20-05-1994
Location: Foxboro Stadium, Foxborough, Massachusetts, USA
Track Listing: Astronomy Domine, Learning To Fly, What Do You Want From Me?, On The Turning Away, Take It Back, A Great Day For Freedom, Sorrow, Keep Talking, One Of These Days, Shine On You Crazy Diamond I-V, Breathe, Time, Breathe (Reprise), High Hopes, The Great Gig In The Sky, Wish You Were Here, Us And Them, Money, Another Brick In The Wall Part 2, Comfortably Numb, Audience, Hey You, Run Like Hell, Audience
Audio Rating: ★★★
Miscellaneous: Audio quite subdued, audience rather less so.

Date: 22-05-1994
Location: Stade Du Parc Olympique, Montreal, Quebec, Canada
Track Listing: Introduction, Astronomy Domine, Learning To Fly, What Do You Want From Me?, On The Turning Away, Take It Back, Poles Apart, Sorrow, Keep Talking, One Of These Days, Shine On You Crazy Diamond, Breathe, Time, Breathe (Reprise), High Hopes, The Great

Gig In The Sky, Wish You Were Here, Us And Them, Money, Another Brick In The Wall Part 2, Comfortably Numb, Hey You, Run Like Hell
Audio Rating: ★★★
Miscellaneous: Back to the Olympic Stadium in Montreal again, for three consecutive shows. Crowd raucous as always.

Date: 23-05-1994
Location: Stade Du Parc Olympique, Montreal, Quebec, Canada
Track Listing: Astronomy Domine, Learning To Fly, What Do You Want From Me?, On The Turning Away, Take It Back, A Great Day For Freedom, Sorrow, Keep Talking, One Of These Days, Shine On You Crazy Diamond, Breathe, Time, Breathe (Reprise), High Hopes, The Great Gig In The Sky, Wish You Were Here, Us And Them, Money, Another Brick In The Wall Part 2, Comfortably Numb, Hey You, Run Like Hell
Audio Rating: ★★★↴
Miscellaneous: Some fumbling with the microphone before **ASTRONOMY DOMINE** but it soon settles down. Another quite demented crowd.

Date: 24-05-1994
Location: Stade Du Parc Olympique, Montreal, Quebec, Canada
Track Listing: Astronomy Domine, Learning To Fly, What Do You Want From Me?, On The Turning Away, Coming Back to Life, Sorrow, Take It Back, A Great Day For Freedom, Keep Talking, One Of These Days, Shine On You Crazy Diamond Parts I-V, Breathe, Time, Breathe (Reprise), High Hopes, The Great Gig in the Sky, Wish You Were Here, Us And Them, Money, Another Brick In The Wall Part 2, Comfortably Numb, Hey You, Run Like Hell
Audio Rating: ★★★↴
Miscellaneous: The Quebecois really love the Floyd. The shows in Montreal consistently have the strongest (or at least the most vocal) audience response.

Date: 26-05-1994
Location: Municipal Stadium, Cleveland, Ohio, USA
Track Listing: Astronomy Domine, Learning To Fly, What Do You Want From Me?, On The Turning Away, Take It Back, Poles Apart, Sorrow, Keep Talking, One Of These Days, Shine On You Crazy Diamond I-V, Breathe, Time, Breathe (Reprise), High Hopes, The Great Gig In The Sky, Wish You Were Here, Us And Them, Money, Another Brick In The Wall Part 2, Comfortably Numb, Hey You, Run Like Hell
Audio Rating: ★★↴
Miscellaneous: Weak, distant and muffled at loud moments. Indistinct at quiet moments. Guy Pratt yells 'back to Cleveland' (instead of 'back to mother', of course) during **RUN LIKE HELL**.

Date: 27-05-1994
Location: Municipal Stadium, Cleveland, Ohio, USA
Track Listing: Astronomy Domine, Learning To Fly, What Do You Want From Me?, On The Turning Away, Take It Back, A Great Day For Freedom, Sorrow, Keep Talking, One Of These Days, Shine On You Crazy Diamond I-V, Breathe, Time, Breathe (Reprise), High Hopes, The Great Gig In The Sky, Wish You Were Here, Us And Them, Money, Another Brick In The Wall Part 2, Comfortably Numb, Hey You, Run Like Hell
Audio Rating: ★★
Miscellaneous: Very thin and muffled sound.

Date: 29-05-1994
Location: Ohio State University Stadium, Columbus, Ohio, USA
Track Listing: Audience Noise, Astronomy Domine, Learning To Fly, What Do You Want From Me?, On The Turning Away, Coming Back To Life, Sorrow, Take It Back, Keep Talking, One Of These Days, Shine On You Crazy Diamond, Breathe, Time, Breathe (Reprise), High Hopes, The Great Gig In The Sky, Wish You Were Here, Us And Them, Money, Another Brick In The Wall Part 2, Thank You, Comfortably Numb, Crowd Noise, Hey You, Run Like Hell
Audio Rating: ★★★↴
Miscellaneous: Gilmour teases the crowd with a few chords from 'Ohio' (a song by Crosby, Stills, Nash & Young, about the shootings at Kent State University, Ohio in 1970) at the start of **RUN LIKE HELL**.

Date: 31-05-1994
Location: Three Rivers Stadium, Pittsburgh, Pennsylvania, USA
Track Listing: Astronomy Domine, Learning To Fly, What Do You Want From Me?, On The Turning Away, Coming Back to Life, Sorrow, Take It Back, Keep Talking, One Of

These Days, Shine On You Crazy Diamond I-V, Breathe, Time, Breathe (Reprise), High Hopes, The Great Gig In The Sky, Wish You Were Here, Us And Them, Money, Another Brick In The Wall Part 2, Comfortably Numb, Hey You, Run Like Hell
Audio Rating: ★★★
Miscellaneous: Quite hissy, more evident during quieter moments so songs like **US AND THEM** and the opening of **HIGH HOPES** suffer more. Audience very enthusiastic.

Date: 02-06-1994
Location: Veterans Stadium, Philadelphia, Pennsylvania, USA
Track Listing: Astronomy Domine, Learning To Fly, What Do You Want From Me?, On The Turning Away, Take It Back, Poles Apart, Sorrow, Keep Talking, One Of These Days, Shine On You Crazy Diamond Parts I-V, Breathe, Time, Breathe (Reprise), High Hopes, The Great Gig In The Sky, Wish You Were Here, Us And Them, Money, Another Brick In The Wall Part 2, Comfortably Numb, Hey You, Run Like Hell
Audio Rating: ★★★★♪
Miscellaneous: Excellent sound.

Date: 03-06-1994
Location: Veterans Stadium, Philadelphia, Pennsylvania, USA
Track Listing: Astronomy Domine, Learning To Fly, What Do You Want From Me?, On The Turning Away, Take It Back, A Great Day For Freedom, Sorrow, Keep Talking, One Of These Days, Shine On You Crazy Diamond Parts I-V, Breathe, High Hopes, The Great Gig In The Sky, Wish You Were Here, Us And Them, Money, Another Brick In The Wall Part 2, Comfortably Numb, Encore Break, Hey You, Run Like Hell
Audio Rating: ★★★
Miscellaneous: Audio is a bit thin and colourless.

Date: 04-06-1994
Location: Veterans Stadium, Philadelphia, Pennsylvania, USA
Track Listing: Astronomy Domine, Learning To Fly, What Do You Want From Me?, On The Turning Away, Coming Back To Life, Sorrow, Take It Back, Keep Talking, One Of These Days, Shine On You Crazy Diamond, Breathe, Time, Breathe (Reprise), High Hopes, The Great Gig In The Sky, Wish You Were Here, Us And Them, Money, Another Brick In The Wall Part 2, Comfortably Numb, Hey You, Run Like Hell
Audio Rating: ★★★★♪
Miscellaneous: A third night in Philadelphia. Guy Pratt shouting 'back to Philly' on all three nights.

Date: 06-06-1994
Location: Carrier Dome, Syracuse University, Syracuse, New York, USA
Track Listing: Astronomy Domine, Learning To Fly, What Do You Want From Me?, On The Turning Away, Take It Back, Sorrow, Keep Talking, One Of These Days, Shine On You Crazy Diamond, Speak To Me, Breathe, Time, High Hopes, The Great Gig in the Sky, Wish You Were Here, Us And Them, Money, Another Brick In The Wall Part 2, Comfortably Numb, Encore Cheers (Intro), Hey You, Run Like Hell/Applause
Audio Rating: ★★
Miscellaneous: The Carrier Dome being a college football stadium, Guy Pratt sings 'back to college' during **RUN LIKE HELL**.

Date: 10-06-1994
Location: Yankee Stadium, New York City, New York, USA
Track Listing: Astronomy Domine, Learning To Fly, Welcome To Yankee Stadium, What Do You Want From Me?, On The Turning Away, Poles Apart, Take It Back, Sorrow, Keep Talking, One Of These Days, Shine On You Crazy Diamond Parts I-V, Breathe, Time, Breathe (Reprise), High Hopes, The Great Gig In The Sky, Wish You Were Here, Us And Them, Money, Another Brick In The Wall Part 2, Thank You, Comfortably Numb, Hey You, Run Like Hell
Audio Rating: ★★
Miscellaneous: Sound quite wobbly, especially noticeable during quieter moments. Lots of audience noise too.

Date: 11-06-1994
Location: Yankee Stadium, New York City, New York, USA
Track Listing: Astronomy Domine, Learning To Fly, What Do You Want From Me?, On The Turning Away, Take It Back, Coming Back To Life, Sorrow, Keep Talking, One Of These Days, Shine On You Crazy Diamond Parts I-V, Breathe, Time, Breathe (Reprise), High Hopes, The Great Gig In The Sky, Wish You Were Here,

Us And Them, Money, Another Brick In The Wall Part 2, Comfortably Numb, Hey You, Run Like Hell, Brain Damage, Eclipse
Audio Rating: ★★★↲
Miscellaneous: A very rare additional encore, with **BRAIN DAMAGE** and **ECLIPSE**.

Date: 14-06-1994
Location: Hoosier Dome, Indianapolis, Indiana, USA
Track Listing: Astronomy Domine, Learning To Fly, What Do You Want From Me?, On The Turning Away, Take It Back, A Great Day For Freedom, Sorrow, Keep Talking, One Of These Days, Shine On You Crazy Diamond, Breathe, Time, Breathe (Reprise), High Hopes, The Great Gig In The Sky, Wish You Were Here, Us And Them, Money, Another Brick In The Wall Part 2, Comfortably Numb, Hey You, Run Like Hell
Audio Rating: ★★
Miscellaneous: Very noisy audience, audio thin and wobbly.

Date: 16-06-1994
Location: Cyclone Stadium, Iowa State University, Ames, Iowa, USA
Track Listing: Astronomy Domine, Learning To Fly, What Do You Want From Me?, On The Turning Away, Take It Back, A Great Day For Freedom, Sorrow, Keep Talking, One Of These Days, Shine On You Crazy Diamond I-V, Breathe, Time, Breathe (Reprise), High Hopes, The Great Gig In The Sky, Wish You Were Here, Us And Them, Money, Another Brick In The Wall Part 2, Comfortably Numb, Hey You, Run Like Hell (Cut)
Audio Rating: ★★★↲
Miscellaneous: **RUN LIKE HELL** only lasts forty-two seconds, and doesn't even get past the teasing guitar intro. Audio clear but a bit subdued.

Date: 18-06-1994
Location: Mile High Stadium, Denver, Colorado, USA
Track Listing: Astronomy Domine, Learning To Fly, What Do You Want From Me?, On The Turning Away, Take It Back, Coming Back To Life, Sorrow, Keep Talking, One Of These Days, Shine On You Crazy Diamond, Breathe, Time, Breathe (Reprise), High Hopes, The Great Gig In The Sky, Wish You Were Here, Us And Them, Money, Another Brick In The Wall Part 2, Comfortably Numb, Hey, You, Run Like Hell
Audio Rating: ★★★
Miscellaneous: Sounds like the backing singers are chanting 'Rain! Rain! Rain!' during **RUN LIKE HELL**. Must have been another soggy evening.

Date: 20-06-1994
Location: Arrowhead Stadium, Kansas City, Missouri, USA
Track Listing: Fade In – Astronomy Domine, Learning To Fly, What Do You Want From Me?, On The Turning Away, Poles Apart, Take It Back, Sorrow, Keep Talking, One Of These Days, Shine On You Crazy Diamond, Breathe, Time, Breathe (Reprise), High Hopes, The Great Gig In The Sky, Wish You Were Here, Us And Them, Money, Another Brick In The Wall Part 2, Comfortably Numb, Hey You, Run Like Hell
Audio Rating: ★★★↲
Miscellaneous: This time it's 'back to Kansas in a cardboard box!'

Date: 22-06-1994
Location: Hubert H. Humphrey Metrodome, Minneapolis, Minnesota, USA
Track Listing: Astronomy Domine, Learning To Fly, What Do You Want From Me?, On The Turning Away, Take It Back, Coming Back To Life, Sorrow, Keep Talking, One Of These Days, Set Break, Shine On, You Crazy Diamond, Breathe, Time, Breathe (Reprise), High Hopes, The Great Gig in the Sky, Wish You Were Here, Us And Them, Money, Another Brick In The Wall Part 2, Comfortably Numb, (Break), Hey You, Run Like Hell, End Of Show
Audio Rating: ★★★↲
Miscellaneous: The Metrodome's acoustics are famously poor but this sounds pretty good, especially in the vocals.

Date: 25-06-1994
Location: British Columbia Place Stadium, Vancouver, British Columbia, Canada
Track Listing: Soundscapes, Astronomy Domine, Learning To Fly, What Do You Want From Me?, On The Turning Away, Take It Back, Coming Back To Life, Sorrow, Keep Talking, One Of These Days, Shine On You Crazy Diamond, Breathe, Time, High Hopes, The Great Gig In The Sky, Wish You Were Here, Us And Them, Money, Another Brick In The Wall Part 2, Comfortably Numb, Hey You, Run Like Hell, End Show

Audio Rating: ★★★↙
Miscellaneous: Taper notes that he was as far away from the band as possible, but the sound is still very present and quite detailed, even if there's a lot of audience noise too.

Date: 26-06-1994
Location: British Columbia Place Stadium, Vancouver, British Columbia, Canada
Track Listing: Astronomy Domine, Learning To Fly, What Do You Want From Me?, On The Turning Away, Take It Back, Great Day For Freedom, Sorrow, Keep Talking, One Of These Days, Shine On You Crazy Diamond, Breathe, Time, High Hopes, The Great Gig In The Sky, Wish You Were Here, Us And Them, Money, Another Brick In The Wall Part 2, Comfortably Numb, Hey You, Run Like Hell
Audio Rating: ★★★↙
Miscellaneous: Noisy audience, but it doesn't distract from the music.

Date: 01-07-1994
Location: Winnipeg Stadium, Winnipeg, Manitoba, Canada
Track Listing: Astronomy Domine, Learning To Fly, What Do You Want From Me?, On The Turning Away, Poles Apart, Take It Back, Sorrow, Keep Talking, One Of These Days, Shine On You Crazy Diamond, Breathe, High Hopes, The Great Gig In The Sky, Wish You Were Here, Us And Them, Money, Another Brick In The Wall Part 2, Comfortably Numb, Hey You, Run Like Hell
Audio Rating: ★★↙
Miscellaneous: **TIME** is missing, for unknown reasons. Audio is raw and lacks detail and bandwidth.

Date: 03-07-1994
Location: Camp Randall Stadium, University of Madison-Wisconsin, Madison, Wisconsin, USA
Track Listing: Astronomy Domine, Learning To Fly, Hello Madison, What Do You Want From Me?, On The Turning Away, Take It Back, A Great Day For Freedom, Sorrow, Keep Talking, One Of These Days, Shine On You Crazy Diamond Parts I-V, Breathe, Time, Breathe, High Hopes, The Great Gig In The Sky, Wish You Were Here, Us And Them, Money, Another Brick In The Wall Part 2, Applause, Comfortably Numb, Applause, Hey You, Run Like Hell

Audio Rating: ★★★
Miscellaneous: Almost good but it's a touch muffled, like it was recorded in an open bag. Not a disaster by any means, but the lower frequencies and drums lack clarity.

Date: 05-07-1994
Location: Canadian National Exhibition Stadium, Toronto, Ontario, Canada
Track Listing: Astronomy Domine, Learning To Fly, What Do You Want From Me?, On The Turning Away, Take It Back, Coming Back To Life, Sorrow, Keep Talking, One Of These Days, Shine On You Crazy Diamond I-V, Breathe, Time, Breathe (Reprise), High Hopes, The Great Gig In The Sky, Wish You Were Here, Us And Them, Money, Another Brick In The Wall Part 2, Comfortably Numb, Audience, Hey You, Run Like Hell
Audio Rating: ★★★
Miscellaneous: A touch distant-sounding, especially on quieter songs like **US AND THEM**.

Date: 06-07-1994
Location: Canadian National Exhibition Stadium, Toronto, Ontario, Canada
Track Listing: Announcement, Astronomy Domine (Fade In), Learning To Fly, What Do You Want From Me?, On The Turning Away, Take It Back, Sorrow, Keep Talking, One Of These Days, Shine On You Crazy Diamond Parts I-V (Cut), Breathe, Time, Breathe (Reprise), High Hopes, The Great Gig In The Sky, Wish You Were Here, Us And Them, Money, Another Brick In The Wall Part 2, Comfortably Numb, Hey You, Run Like Hell, Taper Speaks, Taper Speaks (Again), Eclipse/Brain Damage Soundcheck
Audio Rating: ★★↙
Miscellaneous: During the opening announcements, the taper chuckles when it says that recording devices are strictly forbidden – 'Too bad!' **ASTRONOMY DOMINE** comes in during the musical interlude and only lasts two minutes. There's also some excruciatingly bad audio, presumably from a soundcheck of **BRAIN DAMAGE** and **ECLIPSE**.

Date: 07-07-1994
Location: Canadian National Exhibition Stadium, Toronto, Ontario, Canada
Track Listing: Astronomy Domine, Learning To Fly, What Do You Want From Me?, On The Turning Away, Take It Back, A Great Day For

Freedom, Sorrow, Keep Talking, One Of These Days, Shine On You Crazy Diamond, Breathe, Time, The Great Gig In The Sky, Wish You Were Here, Us And Them, Money, Another Brick In The Wall Part 2, Comfortably Numb, Hey You, Run Like Hell
Audio Rating: ★★★★
Miscellaneous: Taper tells of having a shirt with 'small holes cut for each mike to just poke through'. Which is just a rather comical image.

Date: 09-07-1994
Location: Robert F. Kennedy Stadium, Washington D.C., USA
Track Listing: Astronomy Domine, Learning To Fly, What Do You Want From Me?, On The Turning Away, Poles Apart, Take It Back, Sorrow, Keep Talking, One Of These Days, Shine On You Crazy Diamond I-V, Breathe, Time, Breathe (Reprise), High Hopes, The Great Gig In The Sky, Wish You Were Here, Us And Them, Money, Another Brick In The Wall Part 2, Comfortably Numb, Hey You, Run Like Hell
Audio Rating: ★★★½
Miscellaneous: Clear but rather faint.

Date: 10-07-1994
Location: Robert F. Kennedy Stadium, Washington D.C., USA
Track Listing: Astronomy Domine, Learning To Fly, What Do You Want From Me?, On The Turning Away, Take It Back, Coming Back To Life, Sorrow, Keep Talking, One Of These Days, Shine On You Crazy Diamond Parts I-V, Breathe, Time, Breathe (Reprise), High Hopes, The Great Gig In The Sky, Wish You Were Here, Us And Them, Money, Another Brick In The Wall Part 2, Comfortably Numb, Hey You, Run Like Hell
Audio Rating: ★½
Miscellaneous: Very murky and distant-sounding.

Date: 12-07-1994
Location: Soldier Field, Chicago, Illinois, USA
Track Listing: Astronomy Domine, Learning To Fly, What Do You Want From Me?, On The Turning Away, Poles Apart, Sorrow, Take It Back, Keep Talking, One Of These Days, Shine On You Crazy Diamond I-V, Breathe, Time, Breathe (Reprise), High Hopes, The Great Gig In The Sky, One Slip, Us And Them, Wish You Were Here, Money, Another Brick In The Wall Part 2, Comfortably Numb, Hey You, Run Like Hell
Audio Rating: ★★½
Miscellaneous: **ONE SLIP** makes a rare re-occurrence. Audio is very thin-sounding.

Date: 14-07-1994
Location: Pontiac Silverdome, Detroit, Michigan, USA
Track Listing: Astronomy Domine, Learning To Fly, What Do You Want From Me?, On The Turning Away, Poles Apart, Take It Back, Sorrow, Keep Talking, One Of These Days, Shine On You Crazy Diamond, Breathe, Time, Breathe (Reprise), High Hopes, The Great Gig In The Sky, Wish You Were Here, Us And Them Intro, Us And Them, Money, Another Brick In The Wall Part 2, Comfortably Numb, Hey You, Run Like Hell
Audio Rating: ★★★
Miscellaneous: Murky and muffled, but pleasantly loud, so louder songs are effective.

Date: 15-07-1994
Location: Pontiac Silverdome, Detroit, Michigan, USA
Track Listing: Shine On You Crazy Diamond Parts I-V, Learning To Fly, High Hopes, Coming Back To Life, Take It Back, Sorrow, Keep Talking, Another Brick In The Wall Part 2, One Of These Days, Speak To Me, Breathe/On The Run, Time, Breathe (Reprise), The Great Gig In The Sky, Money, Us And Them, Any Colour You Like, Brain Damage, Wish You Were Here, Comfortably Numb, Run Like Hell
Audio Rating: ★★★
Miscellaneous: A slight shift in the setlist, with **SHINE ON YOU CRAZY DIAMOND** opening the show and *Dark Side* comprising the second set. After **ONE OF THESE DAYS**, Gilmour says: 'Thank you very much indeed, thank you! We're gonna take a short break, we'll be back in about fifteen minutes. Thank you very much.' If you didn't know better, you'd think he didn't like being on stage. Audio is quite thin but of decent clarity.

Date: 17-07-1994
Location: Giants Stadium, East Rutherford, New Jersey, USA
Track Listing: Shine On You Crazy Diamond Parts I-V, Learning To Fly, High Hopes, Take It Back, Coming Back To Life, Sorrow, Keep

Talking, Another Brick In The Wall Part 2, One Of These Days, Speak To Me, Breathe, On The Run, Time, Breathe (Reprise), The Great Gig In The Sky, Money, Us And Them, Any Colour You Like, Brain Damage/Eclipse, Wish You Were Here, Comfortably Numb, Run Like Hell
Audio Rating: ★★★
Miscellaneous: Audio clear but lacks body, like listening to AM radio.

Date: 18-07-1994
Location: Giants Stadium, East Rutherford, New Jersey, USA
Track Listing: Shine On You Crazy Diamond Parts I-V, Learning To Fly, High Hopes, Take It Back, Coming Back To Life, Sorrow, Keep Talking, Another Brick In The Wall Part 2, One Of These Days, Speak To Me, Breathe, On The Run, Time, The Great Gig in the Sky, Money, Us And Them, Any Colour You Like, Brain Damage, Eclipse, Wish You Were Here, Comfortably Numb, Run Like Hell
Audio Rating: ★★★★
Miscellaneous: Good clarity, detail and range. You can hear Guy Pratt's supple bass playing quite distinctly, for example.

Date: 22-07-1994
Location: Estadio Jose Alvalade, Lisbon, Portugal
Track Listing: Astronomy Domine, Learning To Fly, What Do You Want From Me?, On The Turning Away, Take It Back, Coming Back To Life, Sorrow, Keep Talking, One Of These Days, Shine On You Crazy Diamond I-V, Breathe, Time, High Hopes, The Great Gig In The Sky, Wish You Were Here, Us And Them, Money, Another Brick In The Wall Part 2, Comfortably Numb, Hey You, Run Like Hell
Audio Rating: ★★★★
Miscellaneous: Just four days from finishing the American leg of the tour, they're in Portugal (for the first time).

Date: 23-07-1994
Location: Estadio Jose Alvalade, Lisbon, Portugal
Track Listing: Shine On You Crazy Diamond I-V, Learning To Fly, What Do You Want From Me?, On The Turning Away, Poles Apart, Take It Back, Sorrow, Keep Talking, One Of These Days, Astronomy Domine, Breathe, Time, Breathe (Reprise), High Hopes, The Great Gig In The Sky, Wish You Were Here, Us And Them, Money, Another Brick In The Wall Part 2, Comfortably Numb, Audience, Hey You, Run Like Hell
Audio Rating: ★★★
Miscellaneous: ASTRONOMY DOMINE unusually opens the second set.

Date: 25-07-1994
Location: Estadio de Anoeta, San Sebastian, Spain
Track Listing: Shine On You Crazy Diamond I-V, Learning To Fly, What Do You Want From Me?, On The Turning Away, Take It Back, A Great Day For Freedom, Sorrow, Keep Talking, One Of These Days, Astronomy Domine, Breathe, Time, High Hopes, The Great Gig In The Sky, Wish You Were Here, Us And Them, Money, Another Brick In The Wall Part 2, Comfortably Numb, Hey You, Run Like Hell
Audio Rating: ★★⁺
Miscellaneous: Murky, especially at quieter moments. Guitars are more detailed than vocals. Guy Pratt forgoes his frequent city-naming in **RUN LIKE HELL**.

Date: 27-07-1994
Location: Estadio Olimpico, Barcelona, Spain
Track Listing: Shine On You Crazy Diamond Parts I-V, Learning To Fly, What Do You Want From Me?, On The Turning Away, Take It Back (Cut), Coming Back To Life, Sorrow, Keep Talking, One Of These Days, Astronomy Domine, Breathe, Time, Breathe (Reprise), High Hopes, The Great Gig In The Sky, Wish You Were Here (Cut), Us And Them, Money, Another Brick In The Wall Part 2, Comfortably Numb, Applause, Hey You, Run Like Hell
Audio Rating: ★★★
Miscellaneous: TAKE IT BACK has a probable tape flip causing a cut at 4.18; it's been cross-faded with another, inferior source, so it's quite obvious.

Date: 30-07-1994
Location: Chateau De Chantilly, Chantilly, France
Track Listing: Shine On You Crazy Diamond, Learning To Fly, What Do You Want From Me?, On The Turning Away, Take It Back, Coming Back To Life, Sorrow, Keep Talking, One Of These Days, Astronomy Domine, Breathe, Time, Breathe (Reprise), High Hopes, The Great Gig In The Sky, Wish You Were Here, Us And Them, Money, Another Brick In

The Wall Part 2, Comfortably Numb, Hey You, Run Like Hell
Audio Rating: ★★★
Miscellaneous: A brief bit of bass noodling at the start of **ONE OF THESE DAYS**, in a rare piece of spontaneity. Clapping from audience is quite distracting, but they're obviously highly appreciative.

Date: 31-07-1994
Location: Chateau De Chantilly, Chantilly, France
Track Listing: Shine On You Crazy Diamond I–V, Learning To Fly, What Do You Want From Me?, On The Turning Away, Poles Apart, Take It Back, Sorrow, Keep Talking, One Of These Days, Astronomy Domine, Breathe, Time, Breathe (Reprise), High Hopes, The Great Gig In The Sky, Wish You Were Here, Us And Them, Money, Another Brick In The Wall Part 2, Applause, Comfortably Numb, Hey You, Run Like Hell
Audio Rating: ★★★♪
Miscellaneous: Chantilly is about 40km from the centre of Paris. Quite strange that there were no gigs in Paris itself during the *Division Bell* tour, given their popularity in France. But then again, in the European leg, they also missed out on Madrid, Brussels, and anywhere in the UK outside London.

Date: 02-08-1994
Location: Müngersdorfer Stadion, Cologne, Germany
Track Listing: Astronomy Domine, Learning To Fly, David Talk, What Do You Want From Me?, Take It Back, A Great Day For Freedom, Sorrow, Keep Talking, One Of These Days, Shine On You Crazy Diamond, Breathe, Time, Breathe (Reprise), High Hopes, The Great Gig In The Sky, Wish You Were Here, Us And Them, Money, Another Brick In The Wall Part 2, Comfortably Numb, Hey You, Run Like Hell
Audio Rating: ★★★♪
Miscellaneous: Standard *Division Bell* set, average audio quality, nothing sticks out. It must take a certain bloody-mindedness to keep playing night after night, tour after tour, year after year.

Date: 04-08-1994
Location: Olympiastadion, Munich, Germany
Track Listing: Astronomy Domine, Learning To Fly, What Do You Want From Me?, On The Turning Away, Take It Back, A Great Day For Freedom, Sorrow, Keep Talking, One Of These Days, Shine On You Crazy Diamond, Breathe, Time, Breathe (Reprise), High Hopes, The Great Gig In The Sky, Wish You Were Here, Us And Them, Money, Another Brick In The Wall Part 2, Comfortably Numb, Hey You, Run Like Hell
Audio Rating: ★★★
Miscellaneous: Too echoey in the quiet moments, though the louder parts come through better (if lacking in detail and clarity). Audience sound absolutely up for it, claps nearly drowning out **RUN FOR HELL**, which is quite an achievement.

Date: 06-08-1994
Location: Fussballstadion, Basel, Switzerland
Track Listing: Shine On You Crazy Diamond, Learning To Fly, High Hopes, Take It Back, Coming Back To Life, Sorrow, Keep Talking, Another Brick In The Wall Part 2, One Of These Days, Speak To Me, Breathe, On The Run, Time, Breathe (Reprise), The Great Gig In The Sky, Money, Us And Them, Any Colour You Like, Brain Damage, Eclipse, Wish You Were Here, Comfortably Numb, Run Like Hell
Audio Rating: ★★★★
Miscellaneous: Audience very audible in their vocal appreciation for the proceedings, sometimes to the point of distraction. Sound is very good, with the delicate guitars at the start of **WISH YOU WERE HERE** and the wailing final guitar solo of **COMFORTABLY NUMB** (for example) captured equally well. A full *Dark Side* second set.

Date: 07-08-1994
Location: Fussballstadion, Basel, Switzerland
Track Listing: Astronomy Domine, Learning To Fly, What Do You Want From Me?, On The Turning Away, Poles Apart, Take It Back, Sorrow, Keep Talking, One Of These Days, Shine On You Crazy Diamond, Breathe, Time, Breathe (Reprise), High Hopes, The Great Gig In The Sky, Wish You Were Here, Us And Them, Money, Another Brick In The Wall Part 2, Comfortably Numb, Audience, Hey You, Run Like Hell
Audio Rating: ★★★★
Miscellaneous: Very good sound quality, despite a slight amount of hiss. Audience audibly clapping along to livelier songs in that

very European way but less in evidence than the previous night.

Date: 09-08-1994
Location: Amphitheatre Du Chateau De Grammont, Montpellier, France
Track Listing: Astronomy Domine (Fade In), Learning To Fly, What Do You Want From Me?, On The Turning Away, Poles Apart, Take It Back, Sorrow, Keep Talking, One Of These Days, Shine On You Crazy Diamond Parts I–V, Breathe, Time, Breathe (Reprise), High Hopes, Wish You Were Here, Us And Them, Money, The Happiest Days Of Our Lives, Another Brick In The Wall Part 2, Comfortably Numb, Hey You, Run Like Hell
Audio Rating: ★★★♪
Miscellaneous: Pretty good clarity but lacking in bass frequencies. **THE GREAT GIG IN THE SKY** is missing for unknown reasons. **ANOTHER BRICK IN THE WALL PART 2** played much later than usual, it usually being played in the first set.

Date: 11-08-1994
Location: Esplanade Des Quinconces, Bordeaux, France
Track Listing: Astronomy Domine, Learning To Fly, What Do You Want From Me?, On The Turning Away, Take It Back, Coming Back To Life, Sorrow, Keep Talking, One Of These Days, Applause, Shine On You Crazy Diamond, Breathe, Time, Breathe (Reprise), High Hopes, The Great Gig In The Sky, Wish You Were Here, Us And Them, Money, Another Brick In The Wall Part 2, Jam, Comfortably Numb, Hey You, Run Like Hell
Audio Rating: ★★★★
Miscellaneous: The Place des Quinconces (not Qinconces as reported in some books) is not a stadium but a city square, and one of the largest in Europe at that. There's a very short jam before **COMFORTABLY NUMB**, as the band mimic the audience's 'Ah-ooh-oh-oh!' chant.

Date: 13-08-1994
Location: Hockenheimring, Hockenheim, Germany
Track Listing: Astronomy Domine, Learning To Fly, What Do You Want From Me?, On The Turning Away, Take It Back, Sorrow, A Great Day For Freedom, Keep Talking, One Of These Days, Shine On You Crazy Diamond, Breathe, Time, High Hopes, The Great Gig In The Sky, Wish You Were Here, Us And Them, Money, Another Brick In The Wall Part 2, Comfortably Numb, Hey You, Run Like Hell
Audio Rating: ★★★★★♪
Miscellaneous: Audience clapping gets quite distracting. Hockenheimring, as Formula One fans will know, is a motor racing circuit.

Date: 16-08-1994
Location: Niedersachsenstadion, Hannover, Germany
Track Listing: Intro, Shine On You Crazy Diamond, Learning To Fly, Take It Back, Sorrow, High Hopes, Keep Talking, Another Brick In The Wall Part 2, One Of These Days, Speak To Me, Breathe, On The Run, Time, Breathe (Reprise), The Great Gig In The Sky, Money, Us And Them, Any Colour You Like, Brain Damage, Eclipse, Wish You Were Here, Comfortably Numb, Run Like Hell
Audio Rating: ★★★★★♪
Miscellaneous: Another *Dark Side* second set.

Date: 17-08-1994
Location: Niedersachsenstadion, Hannover, Germany
Track Listing: Soundscape, Astronomy Domine, Learning To Fly, What Do You Want From Me?, On The Turning Away, Take It Back, Sorrow, Keep Talking, One Of These Days, Shine On You Crazy Diamond, Breathe, Time, Breathe (Reprise), High Hopes, The Great Gig In The Sky, Wish You Were Here, Us And Them, Money, Another Brick In The Wall Part 2, Comfortably Numb, Hey You, Run Like Hell
Audio Rating: ★★★♪
Miscellaneous: Includes the 'Soundscape' played as a warm-up, available on cassette versions of *Pulse*.

Date: 19-08-1994
Location: Lufthafen Wiener Neustadt, Vienna, Austria
Track Listing: Shine On You Crazy Diamond, Learning To Fly, What Do You Want From Me?, On The Turning Away, Take It Back, Coming Back To Life, Sorrow, Keep Talking, One Of These Days, Astronomy Domine, Breathe, Time, Breathe (Reprise), High Hopes, The Great Gig In The Sky, Wish You Were Here, Us And Them, Money, Another Brick In The Wall Part 2, Comfortably Numb, Hey You, Run Like Hell

Audio Rating: ★★★↙
Miscellaneous: Slightly echoey sound, vocals not always entirely clear.

Date: 21-08-1994
Location: Maifeld Am Olympiastadion, Berlin, Germany
Track Listing: Astronomy Domine, Learning To Fly, What Do You Want From Me?, On The Turning Away, Take It Back, A Great Day For Freedom, Sorrow, Keep Talking, One Of These Days, Shine On You Crazy Diamond, Breathe, Time, Breathe (Reprise), High Hopes, The Great Gig In The Sky, Wish You Were Here, Money, Another Brick In The Wall Part 2, Comfortably Numb, Hey You, Run Like Hell
Audio Rating: ★★↙
Miscellaneous: Thin, echoey and hissy. From **BREATHE (REPRISE)** onwards, a static noise starts up that stays for the rest of the concert

Date: 23-08-1994
Location: Parkstadion, Gelsenkirchen, Germany
Track Listing: Soundscape, Astronomy Domine, Learning To Fly, What Do You Want From Me?, On The Turning Away, Poles Apart, Take It Back, Sorrow, Keep Talking, One Of These Days, Shine On You Crazy Diamond Parts I–V, Breathe, Time, High Hopes, The Great Gig in the Sky, Wish You Were Here, Us And Them, Money, Another Brick In The Wall Part 2, Comfortably Numb, Hey You, Run Like Hell
Audio Rating: ★★★★↙
Miscellaneous: Excellent enveloping audio, both for rocking tracks and delicate moments, though the audience is more audible than you might prefer.

Date: 25-08-1994
Location: Parken, Copenhagen, Denmark
Track Listing: Shine On You Crazy Diamond, Learning To Fly, What Do You Want From Me?, On The Turning Away, Take It Back, Coming Back To Life, Sorrow, Keep Talking, One Of These Days, Astronomy Domine, Breathe, Time, Breathe (Reprise), High Hopes, The Great Gig in the Sky, Wish You Were Here, Us And Them, Money, Another Brick In The Wall Part 2, Comfortably Numb, Hey You, Run Like Hell
Audio Rating: ★★★
Miscellaneous: Hissy at quiet moments. Audience can be heard speaking Danish as **ASTRONOMY DOMINE** ramps up.

Date: 27-08-1994
Location: Ullevi Stadion, Gothenburg, Sweden
Track Listing: Astronomy Domine, Learning To Fly, What Do You Want From Me?, On The Turning Away, Take It Back, Sorrow, Keep Talking, One Of These Days, Shine On You Crazy Diamond, Breathe, Time, Breathe (Reprise), High Hopes, The Great Gig in the Sky, Wish You Were Here, Us And Them, Money, Another Brick In The Wall Part 2, Comfortably Numb, Hey You, Run Like Hell
Audio Rating: ★★↙
Miscellaneous: Thin and distant-sounding. **THE HAPPIEST DAYS OF OUR LIVES** is somehow listed but doesn't appear.

Date: 29-08-1994
Location: Valle Hovin Stadion, Oslo, Norway
Track Listing: Astronomy Domine, Learning To Fly, What Do You Want From Me?, On The Turning Away, Take It Back, Coming Back To Life, Sorrow, Keep Talking, One Of These Days, Shine On You Crazy Diamond, Breathe, Time, Breathe (Reprise), High Hopes, The Great Gig In The Sky, Wish You Were Here, Us And Them, Money, Another Brick In The Wall Part 2, Comfortably Numb, Marooned, Run Like Hell
Audio Rating: ★★★★↙
Miscellaneous: Very good sound, really captures the potency of Gilmour's guitar.

Date: 30-08-1994
Location: Valle Hovin, Oslo, Norway
Track Listing: Astronomy Domine, Learning To Fly, What Do You Want From Me?, On The Turning Away, Poles Apart, Take It Back, Sorrow, Keep Talking, One Of These Days, Shine On You Crazy Diamond, Breathe, Time, Breathe (Reprise), High Hopes, The Great Gig in the Sky, Wish You Were Here, Us And Them, Money, Another Brick In The Wall Part 2, Comfortably Numb, Marooned, Run Like Hell
Audio Rating: ★★★
Miscellaneous: **MAROONED** gets played for the only time during the tour (and hence, ever), in place of **HEY YOU**. You can really hear Gilmour stretching for the high notes, via his Digitech whammy. Audio sounds overloaded – the high notes squeal and the bass drum thwonks.

Date: 02-09-1994
Location: Festivalweise, Werchter, Belgium
Track Listing: Shine On You Crazy Diamond

I-V, Learning To Fly, What Do You Want From Me?, On The Turning Away, Take It Back, A Great Day For Freedom, Sorrow, Keep Talking, One Of These Days, Astronomy Domine, Breathe, Time, Breathe (Reprise), High Hopes, The Great Gig In The Sky, Wish You Were Here, Money, Another Brick In The Wall Part 2, Comfortably Numb, Hey You, Run Like Hell
Audio Rating: ★★★♪
Miscellaneous: Gilmour says, 'The legendary Guy Pratt on bass guitar' after **ONE OF THESE DAYS**. No **US AND THEM**, very unusually.

Date: 03-09-1994
Location: Stadion Feyenoord, Rotterdam, Netherlands
Track Listing: Astronomy Domine, Learning To Fly, What Do You Want From Me?, On The Turning Away, Poles Apart, Take It Back, Sorrow, Keep Talking, On The Turning Away, Shine On You Crazy Diamond, Breathe, Time, Breathe (Reprise), High Hopes, The Great Gig in the Sky, Wish You Were Here, Us And Them, Money, Another Brick In The Wall Part 2, Comfortably Numb, Hey You, Run Like Hell
Audio Rating: ★★♪
Miscellaneous: **ONE OF THESE DAYS** is dropped, very unusually. Audio quite wobbly.

Date: 04-09-1994
Location: Stadion Feyenoord, Rotterdam, Netherlands
Track Listing: Shine On You Crazy Diamond, Learning To Fly, Take It Back, Sorrow, Keep Talking, Wish You Were Here, Another Brick In The Wall Part 2, One Of These Days, High Hopes, Speak To Me, Breathe, On The Run, Time, Breathe (Reprise), The Great Gig In The Sky, Money, Us And Them, Any Colour You Like, Brain Damage, Eclipse, Comfortably Numb, Run Like Hell
Audio Rating: ★★★
Miscellaneous: Muffled sound. Another *Dark Side* second set.

Date: 05-09-1994
Location: Stadion Feyenoord, Rotterdam, Netherlands
Track Listing: Shine On You Crazy Diamond, Learning To Fly, Take It Back, Sorrow, High Hopes, Keep Talking, Another Brick In The Wall Part 2, One Of These Days, Speak To Me, Breathe, On The Run, Time, The Great Gig In The Sky, Money, Us And Them, Any Colour You Like, Brain Damage, Eclipse, Comfortably Numb, Wish You Were Here, Run Like Hell
Audio Rating: ★★★
Miscellaneous: A third night in Rotterdam, and another *Dark Side* set. Muffled sound lacking in presence.

Date: 07-09-1994
Location: Strahov Stadion, Prague, Czech Republic
Track Listing: Shine On You Crazy Diamond, Learning To Fly, What Do You Want From Me?, On The Turning Away, Take It Back, A Great Day For Freedom, Sorrow, Coming Back to Life, One Of These Days, Astronomy Domine, Breathe, Time, Breathe (Reprise), High Hopes, The Great Gig In The Sky, Wish You Were Here, Us And Them, Money, Another Brick In The Wall Part 2, Comfortably Numb, Hey You, Run Like Hell
Audio Rating: ★★★
Miscellaneous: Around 120,000 people are thought to have attended this concert. Sound no better than average, though, sounding rather muffled and muddy.

Date: 09-09-1994
Location: Stade De La Meinau, Strasbourg, France
Track Listing: Soundscape, Astronomy Domine, Learning To Fly, What Do You Want From Me?, On The Turning Away, Take It Back, Coming Back To Life, Sorrow, Keep Talking, One Of These Days, Shine On You Crazy Diamond, Breathe, Time, Breathe (Reprise), High Hopes, The Great Gig In The Sky, Wish You Were Here, Us And Them, Money, Another Brick In The Wall Part 2, Comfortably Numb, Thank You, Hey You, Run Like Hell, Outro
Audio Rating: ★★★
Miscellaneous: 'Soundscape' gets another appearance, this time for over sixteen minutes. Sound is murky.

Date: 11-09-1994
Location: Stade Du Gerland, Lyon, France
Track Listing: Shine On You Crazy Diamond Parts I-V, Learning To Fly, What Do You Want From Me?, On The Turning Away, Poles Apart, Take It Back, Sorrow, Keep Talking, One Of These Days, Astronomy Domine, Breathe, Time, Breathe (Reprise), High Hopes, The Great Gig In The Sky, Wish You Were Here, Us And Them, Money, Another Brick In The Wall

Part 2, Comfortably Numb, Hey You, Run Like Hell
Audio Rating: ★★★♪
Miscellaneous: The second guitar solo for **COMFORTABLY NUMB** gets extended, lasting from 4.58 to the end of the song at 11.00 – six solid minutes of soloing. It's incredible.

Date: 13-09-1994
Location: Stadio Delle Alpi, Turin, Italy
Track Listing: Introduction, Astronomy Domine, Learning To Fly, What Do You Want From Me?, On The Turning Away, Take It Back, A Great Day For Freedom, Sorrow, Keep Talking, One Of These Days, Shine On You Crazy Diamond, Breathe, Time, High Hopes, The Great Gig In The Sky, Wish You Were Here, Us And Them, Money, Another Brick In The Wall Part 2, Comfortably Numb, Hey You, Run Like Hell
Audio Rating: ★★★★
Miscellaneous: 'Introduction' is a smidgeon of the 'Soundscape' track. Sound could be more powerful but is very clear, with the audience audible but not overpowering.

Date: 15-09-1994
Location: Stadio Fruili, Udine, Italy
Track Listing: Shine On You Crazy Diamond, Learning To Fly, What Do You Want From Me?, On The Turning Away, Take It Back, Coming Back To Life, Sorrow, Keep Talking, One Of These Days, Astronomy Domine, Breathe, Time, Breathe (Reprise), High Hopes, The Great Gig In The Sky, Wish You Were Here, Us And Them, Money, Another Brick In The Wall Part 2, Comfortably Numb, Hey You, Run Like Hell
Audio Rating: ★★★
Miscellaneous: Sound is thin and lacking bass frequencies.

Date: 17-09-1994
Location: Festa Nazionale Dell' Unita, Modena, Italy
Track Listing: Shine On You Crazy Diamond, Learning To Fly, High Hopes, Take It Back, Coming Back To Life, Sorrow, Keep Talking, Another Brick In The Wall Part 2, One Of These Days, Speak To Me, Breathe, On The Run, Time, Breathe (Reprise), The Great Gig In The Sky, Money, Us And Them, Any Colour You Like, Brain Damage, Eclipse, Wish You Were Here, Comfortably Numb, Run Like Hell
Audio Rating: ★★★★♪
Miscellaneous: A *Dark Side* second set. Sound quality is absolutely terrific but could be more punchy, and the audience might be more evident than you'd prefer. Another mammoth **COMFORTABLY NUMB** solo too.

Date: 19-09-1994
Location: Studi Di Cinecitta, Rome, Italy
Track Listing: Shine On You Crazy Diamond (Cuts), Learning To Fly (Fade In), High Hopes, Take It Back, Coming Back To Life, Sorrow, Keep Talking, Another Brick In The Wall Part 2, One Of These Days, Speak To Me, Breathe, On The Run, Time, Breathe (Reprise), The Great Gig In The Sky, Money, Us And Them, Any Colour You Like, Brain Damage, Eclipse, Wish You Were Here, Comfortably Numb, Run Like Hell
Audio Rating: ★★★
Miscellaneous: A *Dark Side* second set. There's a lot of audience chatter – at the start of **ONE OF THESE DAYS**, when Guy Pratt is teasing the audience with bass flicks, you can hear some guy say, 'This is Shine On You Crazy Diamond!'

Date: 20-09-1994
Location: Studi Di Cinecitta, Rome, Italy
Track Listing: Shine On You Crazy Diamond, Learning To Fly, High Hopes, Take It Back, Coming Back To Life, Sorrow, Keep Talking, Another Brick In The Wall Part 2, One Of These Days, Applause, Speak To Me, Breathe, On The Run, Time, Breathe (Reprise), The Great Gig In The Sky, Money, Us And Them, Any Colour You Like, Brain Damage, Eclipse, Wish You Were Here, Comfortably Numb, Run Like Hell
Audio Rating: ★★♪
Miscellaneous: Another *Dark Side* second set. Audio poor, faint, murky and thin.

Date: 21-09-1994
Location: Studi Di Cinecitta, Rome, Italy
Track Listing: Soundscape, Astronomy Domine, Learning To Fly, What Do You Want From Me?, On The Turning Away, Take It Back, A Great Day For Freedom, Sorrow, Keep Talking, One Of These Days, Shine On You Crazy Diamond, Breathe, Time, Breathe (Reprise), High Hopes, The Great Gig In The Sky, Wish You Were Here, Us And Them,

Money, Another Brick In The Wall Part 2, Comfortably Numb, Hey You, Run Like Hell
Audio Rating: ★★★↙
Miscellaneous: A third night in Rome. Studi Di Cinecitta is a film studio complex, not a stadium. *Roman Holiday*, *The Passion of the Christ* and *The English Patient* were filmed there. Audio clear but lacking detail.

Date: 23-09-1994
Location: Stade Du Gerland, Lyon, France
Track Listing: Shine On You Crazy Diamond, Learning To Fly, High Hopes, Take It Back, Coming Back To Life, Sorrow, Keep Talking, Another Brick In The Wall Part 2, One Of These Days, Speak To Me, Breathe, On The Run, Time, The Great Gig In The Sky, Money, Us And Them, Any Colour You Like, Brain Damage, Eclipse, Wish You Were Here, Comfortably Numb, Run Like Hell
Audio Rating: ★★
Miscellaneous: Another *Dark Side* second set. Sound is thin, fuzzy and wobbly: not good.

Date: 25-09-1994
Location: Stade De La Pontaise, Lausanne, Switzerland
Track Listing: Shine On You Crazy Diamond, Learning To Fly, What Do You Want From Me?, On The Turning Away, Take It Back, Coming Back To Life, Sorrow, Keep Talking, One Of These Days, Astronomy Domine, Breathe, Time, Breathe (Reprise), High Hopes, The Great Gig In The Sky, Wish You Were Here, Us And Them, Money, Another Brick In The Wall Part 2, Comfortably Numb, Hey You, Run Like Hell
Audio Rating: ★★★
Miscellaneous: Another monster **COMFORTABLY NUMB** solo, lasting nearly six minutes, but the audio is weak.

Date: 12-10-1994
Location: Earl's Court Exhibition Hall, London, England
Track Listing: Shine On You Crazy Diamond (Cut)
Audio Rating: ★★★★
Miscellaneous: Show stops one minute into the opening of **SHINE ON YOU CRAZY DIAMOND**. You can hear a thudding sound amidst the audience cheers at around 0.20, which presumably is the stand collapsing. Around ninety people were injured, with three hospitalised.* The show was replaced with a date on 17 October.

Date: 13-10-1994
Location: Earl's Court Exhibition Hall, London, England
Track Listing: Announcer, Gilmour Apology, Shine On You Crazy Diamond, Learning To Fly, What Do You Want From Me?, On The Turning Away, Take It Back, Coming Back To Life, Sorrow, Keep Talking, One Of These Days, One Of These Days, Intermission, Astronomy Domine, Breathe, Time, Breathe (Reprise), High Hopes, The Great Gig In The Sky, Wish You Were Here, Us And Them, Money, Another Brick In The Wall Part 2, Comfortably Numb, Hey You, Run Like Hell
Audio Rating: ★★★
Miscellaneous: The start of Gilmour apology isn't audible because of the audience noise, but he says something like, '... whenever you enjoy the show, make sure that everything is safe and sound for you all tonight. And, ah well, let's get on with it in a few minutes [inaudible] with confidence!'

Date: 14-10-1994
Location: Earl's Court Exhibition Hall, London, England
Track Listing: Shine On You Crazy Diamond, Learning To Fly, High Hopes, Take It Back, A Great Day For Freedom, Sorrow, Keep Talking, Another Brick In The Wall Part 2, One Of These Days, Speak To Me, Breathe, On The Run, Time, Breathe (Reprise), The Great Gig In The Sky, Money, Us And Them, Any Colour You Like, Brain Damage, Eclipse, Wish You Were Here, Comfortably Numb, Run Like Hell
Audio Rating: ★★★↙
Miscellaneous: A *Dark Side* second set. Apart from that, nothing notable. Though you do wonder why the group chose Earl's Court, with a capacity of around 20,000, over stadium shows as in Europe and North

---

* *The Independent*, 14 October 1994 www.independent.co.uk/news/uk/pink-floyd-very-angry-and-upset-over-accident-human-error-could-have-caused-temporary-stand-s-collapse-at-rock-concert-attended-by-15-000-fans-danny-penman-reports-1442784.html. 'Dave' Gilmour is quoted as saying 'The band is very angry and upset. It is extremely fortunate that no one was killed. We want to find out from the management of Earls Court what happened.'

America – perhaps the risk of inclement weather? But ignoring cities like Birmingham, Manchester, Liverpool and Glasgow was also a strange decision, given how they played six locations in both France and Germany.

Date: 15-10-1994
Location: Earl's Court Exhibition Hall, London, England
Track Listing: Soundscape, Astronomy Domine, Learning To Fly, What Do You Want From Me?, On The Turning Away, Take It Back, Coming Back To Life, Sorrow, Keep Talking, One Of These Days, Shine On You Crazy Diamond, Breathe, Time, Breathe (Reprise), High Hopes, The Great Gig In The Sky, Wish You Were Here, Us And Them, Money, Another Brick In The Wall Part 2, Comfortably Numb, Hey You, Run Like Hell
Audio Rating: ★★★
Miscellaneous: Audio rather thin.

Date: 16-10-1994
Location: Earl's Court Exhibition Hall, London, England
Track Listing: Shine On You Crazy Diamond, Learning To Fly, High Hopes, Take It Back, Coming Back To Life, Sorrow, Keep Talking, Another Brick In The Wall Part 2, One Of These Days, Speak To Me, Breathe, On The Run, Time, Breathe (Reprise), The Great Gig In The Sky, Money, Us And Them, Any Colour You Like, Brain Damage, Eclipse, Audience, Wish You Were Here, Comfortably Numb, Run Like Hell
Audio Rating: ★★★★♪
Miscellaneous: Another *Dark Side* second set. Audio is superb, easily on a par with *Pulse*.

Date: 17-10-1994
Location: Earl's Court Exhibition Hall, London, England
Track Listing: Astronomy Domine, Learning To Fly, What Do You Want From Me?, On The Turning Away, Poles Apart, Take It Back, Sorrow, Keep Talking, One Of These Days, Shine On You Crazy Diamond, Breathe, Time, Breathe (Reprise), High Hopes, The Great Gig In The Sky, Wish You Were Here, Us And Them, Money, Another Brick In The Wall Part 2, Comfortably Numb, Hey You, Run Like Hell
Audio Rating: ★★★★
Miscellaneous: The rescheduled concert. Gilmour after **LEARNING TO FLY**: 'Thanks you all coming out tonight after your intimidating experience last week. I should sue someone if I was you. Preferably not me!'

Date: 19-10-1994
Location: Earl's Court Exhibition Hall, London, England
Track Listing: Shine On You Crazy Diamond, Learning To Fly, High Hopes, Lost For Words, A Great Day For Freedom, Keep Talking, Coming Back To Life, Sorrow, Another Brick In The Wall Part 2, One Of These Days, Breathe, Breathe (Continued), On The Run, Time, Breathe (Reprise), The Great Gig In The Sky, Money, Us And Them, Any Colour You Like, Brain Damage, Brain Damage (Continued), Eclipse, Wish You Were Here, Comfortably Numb, Run Like Hell
Audio Rating: ★★♪
Miscellaneous: Back to Earl's Court after a day off. Sound is very thin and echoey. Another *Dark Side* second set. A number of song cuts (for tape exchange?) but you're not missing much.

Date: 20-10-1994
Location: Earl's Court Exhibition Hall, London, England
Track Listing: Dj Intro, Shine On You Crazy Diamond Parts, Learning To Fly, High Hopes, Take It Back, Coming Back To Life, Sorrow, Keep Talking, Another Brick In The Wall Part 2, One Of These Days, Speak To Me, Breathe, On The Run, Time, Breathe (Reprise), The Great Gig In The Sky, Money, Us And Them, Any Colour You Like, Brain Damage, Eclipse, Wish You Were Here, Comfortably Numb, Run Like Hell, Dj Outro
Audio Rating: ★★★★*
Miscellaneous: Was broadcast on BBC Radio 1, hence includes brief introduction and outro from them. Audio is outstanding. Another *Dark Side* second set – did Pink Floyd inaugurate the trend of bands touring older albums?

Date: 21-10-1994
Location: Earl's Court Exhibition Hall, London, England
Track Listing: Intro, Astronomy Domine, Learning To Fly, What Do You Want From Me?, On The Turning Away, Poles Apart, Take It Back, Sorrow, Keep Talking, One Of These Days, Shine On You Crazy Diamond, Breathe, Time, Breathe (Reprise), High Hopes, The

Great Gig In The Sky, Wish You Were Here, Us And Them, Money, Another Brick In The Wall Part 2, Comfortably Numb, Hey You, Run Like Hell
Audio Rating: ★★★
Miscellaneous: Overly bright, lacking bass frequencies. The audience quite often overpowers the music.

Date: 22-10-1994
Location: Earl's Court Exhibition Hall, London, England
Track Listing: Astronomy Domine, Learning To Fly, What Do You Want From Me?, On The Turning Away, Take It Back, A Great Day For Freedom, Sorrow, Keep Talking, One Of These Days, Shine On You Crazy Diamond, Breathe, Time, Breathe (Reprise), High Hopes, The Great Gig In The Sky, Wish You Were Here, Us And Them, Money, Another Brick In The Wall Part 2, Comfortably Numb, Hey You, Run Like Hell
Audio Rating: ★★★
Miscellaneous: Very murky.

Date: 23-10-1994
Location: Earl's Court Exhibition Hall, London, England
Track Listing: Shine On You Crazy Diamond, Learning To Fly, High Hopes, Take It Back, Coming Back To Life, Sorrow, Keep Talking, Another Brick In The Wall Part 2, One Of These Days, Breathe, On The Run, Time, Breathe (Reprise), The Great Gig In The Sky, Money, Us And Them, Any Colour You Like, Brain Damage, Eclipse, Wish You Were Here, Comfortably Numb, Run Like Hell
Audio Rating: ★★✦
Miscellaneous: Another *Dark Side* second set. Everything else routine.

Date: 26-10-1994
Location: Earl's Court Exhibition Hall, London, England
Track Listing: Astronomy Domine, Learning To Fly, What Do You Want From Me?, On The Turning Away, Take It Back, Coming Back To Life, Sorrow, Keep Talking, One Of These Days, Shine On You Crazy Diamond, Breathe, Time, Breathe (Reprise), High Hopes, The Great Gig In The Sky, Wish You Were Here, Us And Them, Money, Another Brick In The Wall Part 2, Comfortably Numb, Hey You, Run Like Hell
Audio Rating: ★★★★
Miscellaneous: Back after two nights off for a final furlong. Sound quality is good, both deep and rich, and few distractions from the audience. The vocals could be more prominent, though, and higher frequencies are lacking.

Date: 27-10-1994
Location: Earl's Court Exhibition Hall, London, England
Track Listing: Intro, Shine On You Crazy Diamond, Learning To Fly, What Do You Want From Me?, On The Turning Away, Take It Back, A Great Day For Freedom, Sorrow, Keep Talking, One Of These Days, Astronomy Domine, Breathe, Time, Breathe (Reprise), High Hopes, The Great Gig In The Sky, Wish You Were Here, Us And Them, Money, Another Brick In The Wall Part 2, Comfortably Numb, Hey You, Run Like Hell
Audio Rating: ★★★✦
Miscellaneous: Slight hiss but brighter than the previous show – maybe too much so.

Date: 28-10-1994
Location: Earl's Court Exhibition Hall, London, England
Track Listing: Shine On You Crazy Diamond, Learning To Fly, High Hopes, Take It Back, Poles Apart, Sorrow, Keep Talking, Another Brick In The Wall Part 2, One Of These Days, Speak To Me, Breathe, On The Run, Time, Breathe (Reprise), The Great Gig In The Sky, Money, Us And Them, Any Colour You Like, Brain Damage, Eclipse, Wish You Were Here, Comfortably Numb, Run Like Hell
Audio Rating: ★★★✦
Miscellaneous: Another *Dark Side* second set. Though they never quite nail the majesty of **ECLIPSE** (though that, of course, was dependent on many overdubs).

Date: 29-10-1994
Location: Earl's Court Exhibition Hall, London, England
Track Listing: Shine On You Crazy Diamond, Learning To Fly, High Hopes, Take It Back, Coming Back To Life, Sorrow, Keep Talking, Another Brick In The Wall Part 2, One Of These Days, Speak To Me, Breathe, On The Run, Time, Breathe (Reprise), The Great Gig In The Sky, Money, Us And Them, Any Colour You Like, Brain Damage, Eclipse, Audience, Wish You Were Here, Comfortably Numb, Run Like Hell

Audio Rating: ★★★✦
Miscellaneous: Clear enough but missing higher-range frequencies gives it a dark shading, especially on quieter moments. Another *Dark Side* second set to finish things off. And there you have it: around 1,160 concerts in twenty-eight years, about half of which have been recorded for posterity. It's a treasure trove of sound and emotion. Most people will only have seen Pink Floyd in their own city or thereabouts, so having documentation of Pink Floyd's live career – which is what sustained the band until *Dark Side* broke through – is of hugely important historical significance.

2005
Date: 02-07-2005
Location: Live 8, Hyde Park, London

Track Listing: Speak To Me, Breathe, Breathe (Reprise), Money, Wish You Were Here, Comfortably Numb
Audio Rating: ★★★★★
Miscellaneous: Twenty-four years after *The Wall* tour, Gilmour-Mason-Waters-Wright reunite at Live 8 for the Make Poverty History charity. The artfully chosen setlist moves from existential awareness to satire to humanity to a soul in both heaven and in hell. It wasn't quite Queen at Live Aid – Pink Floyd rely on the build-up of atmosphere, where Freddie Mercury could go out and grab an audience by the throat – but as a reunion it hit all the right notes, perhaps apart from Gilmour's obvious reluctance to join Waters for a bow. Nonetheless, it was a huge moment for everyone who had grown up with Pink Floyd, and a wonderful way to cap their career.

INTERVIEWS

Guy Pratt

Bassist Guy Pratt toured with Pink Floyd on the *Momentary Lapse* and *Division Bell* tours, and played on *Delicate Sound of Thunder*, *The Division Bell*, *Pulse*, and *The Endless River*. He still tours with Nick Mason as the Saucerful of Secrets band, playing Floyd oldies to audiences around the world. His book *My Bass And Other Animals* is an excellent read, and his podcast with Gary Kemp *The Rockonteurs* is marvellous.

Just looking at the *Delicate Sound* tour, and you coming in – I imagine the Pink Floyd sound techs are some of the best in the world, so can you describe what it was like coming into that?
Well, it all gets a bit blurry now. Firstly, it was surprising how secondary the band came to the staging. How things were for us onstage wasn't really considered, it was all about – I mean, there was no room for my amps, for my cabinets. And I was like 'Where am I supposed to put them?' and they said 'Well, do you have to have them?'. So what they did was – because the stage was made of this sort of grille material, so they could pump smoke through it – I basically had my cabinets slung underneath it.

Really? Oh my God!
And the cabinets they'd supplied me with were 15–inch speakers – the thing with those, they sound amazing once you get 20 feet from them, but closer than that it's just this big muddy thing. So to be honest I wasn't really that aware – apart from having my own tech, Syd, which I'd never had before, so I had to get used to telling him to change my strings and everything, and the fact that any sort of thing you just vaguely thought out loud would just happen immediately. For instance, when I turned up my main bass that I brought with me was by Steinberger – it was the 80s, that's what I was playing. And it was

quite a tatty looking one, and I'd taken the Steinberger sticker off, and replaced it with a Britax seatbelt sticker which had come with an old BMW I'd bought. And of course, that's just not acceptable to Pink Floyd. So nothing was said to me, but I turned up one day and my Steinberger wasn't there, nothing was said. And then three days later it came back – it had been sent back to Steinberger and had all new bits, and a shiny new sticker. And I was like 'What?!?'. I had my old 1964 Jazz Bass, 'Betsy', and I noticed as I was playing that it was quite quiet, the output wasn't great, but the pickups were actually quite noisy. And so I mused out loud to Syd, I thought maybe it'd be an idea to change the pickups in this at some point. I come in the next day and there's brand new EMG active pickups on it! And I was like 'Fuck, man – that's a 1964 Jazz, you don't just put new active pickups in it!'. And I wasn't consulted or anything, it was just done. That was sacrilege. But as a result, it must be said, it is still the best sounding bass guitar.

What I think might surprise people is that the sound on stage was really not great compared to what everyone heard, just because of the way the stage was laid out. I had Gary Wallace right behind me, and he had these massive great monitors which were pointed right at my head. And of course David is everywhere, David's unbelievable. Luckily, Nick was at the front of the stage, so I could just hear him to play. The whole thing was such an ... I'd never known anything like that, what to expect, I was just kind of hanging on. I was fully convinced I was going to be sent home, I had such terrible impostor syndrome – this weird thing of feeling incredibly at home with these people personally, thinking 'This feels like home', as time has shown to be absolutely the case, but on a professional level I though 'You don't get to do this, there's no way'.

Did you listen to the playbacks of the shows on that tour?
Me and Jon Carin used to sit up at night, listening to the playback and thinking what we could do to make it better, there was a lot of that. Straight away, you start doing shows you get people going 'Oh, my God, this sounds amazing, sounds incredible' – but you don't know that, I've never heard a Pink Floyd gig.

It must be like being in the eye of a hurricane – musically, personally, and professionally?
Absolutely, very much that – especially when you're trying to find your feet. And we were all from quite different backgrounds – I'd say Jon was the most similar to me, and also because of his youth, but then you had people like Tim Renwick and Gary Wallace, who are both very much musos. And I kind of thought I was meant to be like them, so I was pretending to like all sorts of fusion music ...

How did the discussion of the setlists go? There's that story of scrapping ECHOES after about eight gigs – were you privy to that, was that a group conversation?
I don't think it would have been then. I think in those early days, obviously it was the old Pink Floyd formula – a big opener, then you've got the new album, and then the greatest hits. I don't think we would have had any input into sets.

There's that story of David saying how the younger musicians don't know how to play by feel, they always want to count bars.
He did remark that the problem with young musicians, with modern musicians is that they just don't know how to integrate. I reminded him of that years later.

On that tour, I've read that everything was very synchronised and quite rigid. But did you have moments where you could cut loose?
Oh definitely. I mean stuff changes; you can't always be the same. The only thing that was kind of strict was the stuff that was linked to film. Very often it'd be the song would start then you can go where you want to go with it. But you know, obviously, because it's not really a matter of being rigid, it's just that you're doing a show like that where you've got those amazing light cues and effects, you've got to stick to that script. And frankly, that's a much better show. People jamming on a stadium stage is not pretty. But if David's soloing at the end of a song, obviously that can be very elastic time.

Did any songs evolve, how they were played over the course of the tour?
Absolutely. But it's one of the things where you can't really – it's very hard to point to what happened, it's a long time ago. But things like all the solos in MONEY, that just came up.

Any other songs you think changed much? Like how you were playing?
Not really – I mean I'd need a setlist in front of me, have a listen to it.

I get the impression from your book and from what David has said, that the *Momentary Lapse* tour was a bit of a party tour.
It was, very – probably to the detriment of the music a bit. That's why I think *Pulse* is an infinitely superior record.

David, Nick and Rick must have had 15 years on you, so I daresay they were a bit more cautious?
Definitely. Yeah, it's terrible when I think about it now, I was appallingly unprofessional. Appallingly. But I was fortunate – I mean, as Dave says it drove him mad the way that I used to get wrecked so much but unfortunately was the most consistent musician in the band. I never missed a note.

That must be really exasperating for everyone else.
Yeah!

So when you're preparing for the tour, what were the rehearsals like? There's that famous comment from David that Rick and Nick were 'catatonic' – was that unfair?
I think it is a bit unfair in that when we started rehearsing, David wasn't there for the first few days. I was dreading David turning up, because I was terrified of him. Terrified. And yeah, they were – I mean, I think Nick was nervous. And so he busied himself with organisation of the tour, rather than the playing. Rick was really just sort of coming out of his shell, he was a quiet man at the best of times. And David having to be leader – I mean, he'd done his solo tour a couple of years before, but he didn't really seem to relish it, which is why in the end Bob Ezrin was brought in, I guess as producer but in a more theatrical sense. He was basically brought in as a director. And terrifying – I remember he once said, 'If anyone's ever stuck for anything, look at Guy – he always knows what's going on'.

I wonder if this was a deliberate ploy by David – to put the onus on Rick to lead you through the rehearsals.
No, he wouldn't have done that.

He's not quite that Machiavellian?
Not at all, no. And as we discovered in the later years, he was actually desperately, desperately fond of Rick. He was there for good reasons.

So onto *The Division Bell*. I think you say in your book that you almost had to beg to take part. Were you joking, or were you really a bit miffed?
Well, they tried to go back to the way they worked up to *Dark Side*, which is where they just went into a rehearsal room. And they actually invited me to those first sessions, which was fantastic but also, you know, socially very, very awkward because I'd literally just hooked up with Gala [Wright's daughter], we'd just been on our first holiday together. Obviously David and Nick were teasing Rick a bit, I mean it was all very good natured. But it was fantastic to be there, because in fact a lot of the time Rick was the most applied person. A lot of the time because David and Nick had just got new Mac laptops, and they were playing with those a lot of the time. We had all the old gear, it was great – the old Vox and Farfisa organ, all that old stuff set up in the studio. So a lot of the time it was just me and Rick sitting around. That's where WEARING THE INSIDE OUT came from. Lots of great stuff from jams – MAROONED came out of that. So it was very productive. But at the end of that, once they got the material together and it came to recording, I said 'Well, what about the bass?' and Dave said 'Well I'll probably do

it' – just because he's used to doing that. And I said 'David, I'm going to look a complete twat if I'm not on this album' and he said 'Oh yeah, alright then', so I played on it.

Nick says in his book that 'Guy's playing tended to change the mood of the music that we had created on our own'. Can you remember how? Can you elaborate on that?
You know, I'm an 80s boy – as David would say, he wishes he could get me to play with one hand behind my back. Now, as an older and wiser man I get it, I would probably be much better in that situation. All I was doing was what 99 out of 100 bass players will do which is play too much, simple as that. And this is also reflected in my work. If you listen, especially on the old Floyd material, you listen to how I play those songs on *Delicate Sound of Thunder* compared to how I play on say, *Remember That Night* or David *Live at Pompeii*. I've grown up, I don't need to stake my claim.

There's that famous quote from Miles Davis about how he liked younger musicians because they would challenge him – were you trying to do that? Or were you just trying to fit into the vibe of the material?
I was trying to fit in, but I was trying to fit in whilst not being a pastiche. It had to be real, what I was playing. I've done lots of work for film and TV, and if you want me to write a pastiche Pink Floyd bassline I can do that in a second, but it's got to be real.

Did you ever get slapped down musically? Do they ever say, 'Come on, less of that, you're being silly'?
The funny thing is, or what's annoying is that yes, I did get slapped down by David – but not until way after the event. But that goes both ways. I remember listening back to some rough mixes of *Pulse* with David, and I did something and he went 'Yeah, I always hated it when you do that'. I mean, why didn't you tell me? And conversely, there's this one little fill I'd added to the last verse of High Hopes, and David said 'Oh, yeah, love it. I love it when you do that'. I wish you'd told me that as well, because every night I'm doing it thinking 'God I hope this is alright!'

In the studio, did they reference other bands? I get the impression that they're very insular when it comes to other music. Did they ever say 'Oh, that sounds a bit like Genesis' or whatever?
No, absolutely not. Well, once or twice but it'd be unusual things. I remember there's one song, I don't like to say which, but David said he practically nicked it from Randy Newman. But that might be a kind of, shall we say he was certainly influenced by Newman.

Was there ever a Roger-shaped hole where the others would be expecting you to play? You'd feel a particular part or style?
[Voice frosts over] No, not at all.

What's it like working on the Astoria? It seems very tranquil, did that come over in the music?
Oh, yeah, definitely, because it's beautiful. I haven't done any band work there with them, it was always me and David and producers in the control room. Which is just lovely, it's a fabulous place to work. I do remember once, David was walking me back to my car, up the garden. and I hadn't done my bass properly and my bass fell out and broke. And I was just too embarrassed to say anything, I just put it back in the case.

Was there any discussion on changing the sound from *A Momentary Lapse of Reason*, you know, because the sound is so much more organic on *The Division Bell*?
I think that just happened, because it started out the three of them working together and it just carried on like that. I would say the key thing really was Rick's involvement, so the old sound would happen. There was a confidence – it was like they'd gone out to prove that they were Pink Floyd.

Moving on to the *Division Bell* tour – were you in from the start of the tour? In terms of preparations?
Well, you say preparations – you have to remember with a thing like that, the thing that sidemen seem to forget is that when you come in, it's actually really quite late in the day. They've actually got bigger things to worry about than the music.

So at what stage do you come in?
By the time we come in, the stage has been designed and so on, you know.

Did you get any input, did you get your speaker cabinets to have their own space that time?
I did this time, yes. The annoying thing was that we now had an incredibly narrow stage, it had no depth to it at all because there was this absolutely brilliant idea where the screen was hidden behind the stage. And it wasn't until a few songs in that it would come up. It was an amazing effect, but for some reason they decided it wasn't working, or they didn't like the way the set was. And so we went back into opening with SHINE ON, and then all the time playing that song you'd have the screen up, so we now have this tiny stage for no reason whatsoever. We could have had 40, 50 feet of depth.

Pink Floyd are not maybe the most active of people on stage though.
No. I think that's the reason that David got Scott Page on the first tour, because he knew he would be someone to move around, take some of the pressure off him. I mean, obviously I ended up doing that kind of thing, David maybe didn't know that when he hired me, all he did was hire a bass player.

The *Division Bell* tour was quite short compared to the *Momentary Lapse* tour, which I think stretched over three years, '87 to '89?
Well, not really. *The Momentary Lapse* tour was initially 13 months, and that was going to be the end of it. The *Another Lapse* tour only came up, I think, because we got asked to play in the USSR, and the only way to get Russia was to come up with a tour to pay for that, because you're obviously not going to make any money in Russia.

Was there less to prove than on the *Momentary Lapse* tour?
On *Division Bell*? I don't know what it was. To me it seemed a terrible shame that we didn't go to Australia or the Far East, I think it was just opening up there. I would have liked to have gone, but I got the feeling the others felt that after the last tour, it was just too long to go on tour. I mean it was still seven months. I'm always sad we never played more places in the UK, that was a shame really, but it was a big ask of people.

My uncles went to see the shows in Germany, rather than go to London.
Ha, that's very Scottish!

For *The Endless River*. Do you know how much redubbing went on? How long did it take you personally?
I went in and worked on a few things. A couple of afternoons at David's place in Brighton. It was actually very funny because David was working with Youth, who is my oldest friend in the world, we started out playing together. It was very, very funny because whenever you put me and him in the studio, it all becomes very schoolyard. He was just, you know, 'Play it again', he was trying to produce me way too. And I'm not going to do anything he says. That's quite funny, I think David quite enjoyed that. So I really wasn't privy to very much, it was just a sort of thing that was going on, it didn't seem particularly urgent or anything. So apart from going in for a couple of afternoons I didn't know much about it. It was all stuff left over from *Division Bell*, a lot of it was the stuff from when we were at Britannia Row, those first two weeks.

I hope to see Saucerful of Secrets at some point, if you're touring next year.
That's the idea. We are. I'd love to go to China.

James Guthrie

James Guthrie was the young hot-shot producer who was asked to produce and engineer *The Wall* (although to his discomfort finding that Bob Ezrin had been asked to do the same job) and later working as sound mixer during the 1980-81 live shows, sound coordinator on *Pink Floyd: The Wall*, and then mixing and producing *Is There Anybody Out There?* There can't be much he doesn't know about the technical side of getting the concept onto album, stage show and movie.

How old were you when you got into engineering and producing records?
Nineteen. I started as a tape operator at Mayfair Studios in London on the 1st October 1973. The studio was located above a small chemist's shop in South Molton Street. There were no schools for engineering and producing in those days. It was an apprenticeship. You had to start at the bottom and work your way up. I was fortunate as they desperately needed a tape op. The maintenance guy had been filling in on sessions until they found someone new. As a result, I was on the machines on my very first evening. I think I had two days off in my first year. Being thrown in at the deep end is shocking, but you learn quickly! After that I moved to Audio International and during that time I began producing. I then helped build and moved to, Utopia Studios. Soon after that I went freelance and I started working with the Floyd on *The Wall* in October of 1978 when I was 24.

What is your formal musical and technical background?
I played guitar in various school bands, but that had to take a back seat when I got on the 'other side of the glass', which was just as well really. My studio training happened 'on the job'. The best way to learn the dynamics of a recording session are to be in it. Initially, I was trained by John Hudson. Afterwards when I moved to Audio International, I learned a great deal from Richard Millard. A great part of this job is that you are always learning. Working all the time was a great asset. You need time to experiment, to push yourself and ultimately to develop a style of your own.

How familiar was Pink Floyd to you when you were asked to work with the band?
Well, SEE EMILY PLAY was always one of my favourites. I bought the single when I was about 13 and went around playing it for all my friends saying, 'You've got to hear this!'

I also knew *Piper*, *More* and *Meddle* pretty well. Like most people, I had probably heard *Dark Side* more than any of the others. I actually became a much bigger Floyd fan by working with them. There's an interesting recognition that happens when you finally work with an artist that you are familiar with. The first time David went out into the studio to sing (we were working on the song arrangements and making new demos), I said, 'can you just sing a bit, a cappella, so I can get a rough idea of level?' He began to sing and suddenly there was that amazing, instantly recognisable voice coming out of the speakers. Oh yeah … I thought to myself, as I got a chill, that voice.

The Wall began as a demo from the band's main writer. How did you react to the demo? The Wall as a whole changed a lot during the time of recording but were there elements or characteristics that remained unchanged throughout?
Roger's original demo was rough, but you could hear the brilliance and the importance of the story. He had written what could have been nearly three albums worth of material that had to be whittled down to two. Some of that material was used on later projects, but our initial challenge was to make things more concise, to more effectively tell the story. Songs like COMFORTABLY NUMB came later as a collaboration, but there were a number of tunes that remained relatively unchanged, such as MOTHER, IS THERE ANYBODY OUT THERE, VERA, BRING THE BOYS, DON'T LEAVE ME NOW and many of the musical themes that recur throughout the album.

Unlike earlier Floyd recordings, the band didn't perform much together and the recordings were high on overdubbing. Was that solely a technical matter or was there an artistic consideration to?
Animals was the last album where they were really playing together as a band in the studio. On *The Wall*, we rehearsed some of the songs in the studio as a band and indeed recorded some of the 'new' demos that way, but ultimately the final recording was done one man at a time. Because we were cutting to a click and 'building' each song from the ground up, there was less reason for everyone to be playing at the same time. A bit of that spontaneity would have been nice, but there were also personal relationships to consider. By the time we got to France, things were fairly regimented. I would work with Roger and David from 10am to 6pm, have dinner and then work with Rick from about 7pm to 1am. Obviously, during the drum recording I worked with Nick in the daytime and then spent the evenings choosing the drum performances and editing them together. The following day I would play the edited drum track for Roger and David and Roger would say, 'Great – on to the bass!'

Incidentally, I've been told that there are numerous sites on the internet claiming that Rick didn't actually play on The Wall album. He lost a lot of the recognition that he deserved because for many of those performances, no one else was in the room, so they started to believe that he hadn't played. I want to correct that misconception and let his fans and family know that Rick played some really great keyboards on the album. Just listen to the Hammond and Rhodes on HEY YOU, the Wurlitzer and fuzz organ on YOUNG LUST, all the pads and Moogs on ANOTHER BRICK 1 & 2, the list goes on.

You ran several studios at once to meet the work schedule. How did you make sure everything fitted in the end? Who had the overview?
Making sure that all the elements of a song knit together properly, regardless of where or when they were recorded is all part of the mixing process. This is a very difficult thing to explain, but it's the responsibility of the mixer and you just do it!

What surprised you the most during the sessions? Can you point out some of the most remarkable things you learned?
Initially, I was shocked at how slowly everything moved! I was used to working really quickly when producing and engineering albums. Suddenly it was like the brakes were on and often it was difficult to get the momentum going. Eventually, I adapted to the Floyd pace. One of the great things about working with this band is that you are allowed time to be creative, to pursue an idea even if it takes some time. The Floyd had a production deal to make their records and the record label never heard anything until it was done. The record was made purely and only by the people in the studio.

I had learned early in my career that it was a good idea to try and not be too attached to the elements in a recording. A certain amount of ruthlessness is required especially during mixing. You may have a very complex vocal section for instance that took three days to record. When you come to mix, you realise that it just doesn't work in the song. There is a natural tendency to try and make it work, to try and force it. You need to be able to remove it and move on. Roger has this ability. I thought I was pretty good at doing that, but he was way ahead of me!

I have great memories of working with David on all the guitar solos. For the majority of the solos it was just David, myself and Phil Taylor in the room. We would make numerous passes, then Dave would take a break and I would combine a solo from all the different performances. He would come back, have a listen and either we would move on to the next piece, or he would have me make one or two changes and then we'd move on. As most guitarists know, David uses a lot of finger vibrato as well as the whammy bar, often at the same time. On the first solo of COMFORTABLY NUMB he was exaggerating the effect quite dramatically. I asked if he thought it was too much and he replied, 'No, I want it to sound drunk!' And there it was.

Everyone knows that David is a great soloist, but not enough is said about his accompaniment, or rhythm playing. I learned a lot about guitar arrangements from working with him on this record. Another great example of this is the Animals album – staggering rhythm guitar parts.

We mixed the album at Producers Workshop in L.A. Their level of professionalism and technology was impressive. They had very strict requirements that the new tape had to meet and would actually listen to a portion of each blank reel before they would allow me to print a mix to it! I would arrive at 9:00am and either John or Ben had been there since 8:00am listening to tape. There would be a stack of rejected ¼' reels about waist high that were going to be sent back to the manufacturer!

What piece of equipment in use was the most unusual – hi tech or lo-fi?
I think more than unusual equipment was the use of unusual spaces. I like to record in various places other than the studio. Britannia Row had a games room on the top floor that had a great live sound to it. I put Nick up there for 'In the Flesh' and also used it as a live chamber for one or two other elements. I also discovered an underground tank next to the swimming pool at Superbear Studios in France, which we hung a speaker and a couple of mics in to use as a chamber.

Apart from that – perhaps the television? We recorded a lot of 'wild' TV onto ¼' and some of it directly to the multitrack. 'Nobody Home' was one take. The Gomer Pyle bit, 'Surprise. Surprise, Surprise!' fell right there, perfectly after Roger's vocal.

Another piece that worked better than expected was the telephone operator. Roger was keen to illustrate the personal disconnect of being on the road. We were in L.A. at Producer's Workshop so I phoned my neighbour, Chris Fitzmorris in London. He had the keys to my flat and I asked him to go there and said that I would call him through an operator. 'No matter how many times I call', I said, 'just pick up the phone, say 'Hello', let the operator speak and then hang up'. I placed a telephone in a soundproof area, got on to an extension phone and started recording to ¼' tape. It took a couple of operators – the first two were a bit abrupt, but the 3rd was perfect. I told her that I wanted to make a collect call to Mrs. Floyd. 'Who's calling?' she asked. 'Mr. Floyd', I replied. Chris's timing was terrific, over and over he would hang up just at the right moment and she became genuinely concerned. 'Is there supposed to be someone there besides your wife?' I was playing her along saying things like 'No! I don't know who that is!' 'What's going on?' and she would try the call again. Unwittingly, she was helping to tell the story. Afterwards I went through the ¼' and edited my voice out, just leaving her and Chris. I sometimes wonder if she ever heard herself on the record.

The basic tracks of *The Wall* were edited by you from several takes. Normal fare on today's digital systems. But wasn't it awfully hard back then?
Well, I had nothing to compare it to! I used to love the challenge of complicated tapes edits. It's really pretty amazing what you can get away with. There are thousands of edits on that album, both 2' and ¼'. The mixing was all manual. No computer automation yet. So you would mix until you made a mistake, or until there was a complicated change-over and if the feel was good, you would reset and make an edit in the ¼'. During the mix, I decided that a drum fill was not working well on COMFORTABLY NUMB. We were running two multitrack machines for the recording, a 16track and a 24track locked together

by a Maglink synchronizer (this was before SMPTE code became the standard), so cutting the tape and the timecode all the way through at this late stage was not an option. I decided to make a window edit. I had heard stories of people doing this but had never seen it. Maybe they were true, maybe just folklore. This made me even more determined to try it. I cut the top eight tracks (the drums) out of the 16 track tape and replaced them with a different performance of Nick's drums. It worked fine. The tape looked like a patchwork quilt, but it sounded fine!

From reading about the making of *The Wall* – the record as well as the live show – I get the feeling that it was a project taking shape while pushing for a new era of technology to begin. The production team seemed to be pushing the recording envelope a lot. Many producers suggest that some of the inventiveness of the analogue era went out when digital recording became the new standard.

I would agree. I'm very grateful to have started when I did. On *The Wall* we didn't have much in the way of outboard gear. Lots of tape delay, a couple of DDL's, a Flanger and the 910 Harmonizer, which had not been out very long. Back then, if you heard a sound in your head, you had to be very creative to work out how you were going to manifest the effect. Now you can just call up virtually any sound on a digital box and the end result is not as satisfying. The song had better be good, because that part of the technology is not really going to impress anyone anymore.

I say 'back then' but just look at what George Martin and Geoff Emerick were doing even earlier with the Beatles! They had even less. That was such a creative time and is still a great source of inspiration. I love the production on 'I Am The Walrus'. When I eventually got to meet Geoff (actually only a few years ago) I immediately said, 'I have to know, how did you get that great vocal sound on John? It sounds like a valve limiter distorting rather than the mic amp, how did you do it?!' He thought for a minute and then said something like, 'I'm not sure, I really don't remember'. Disappointment! Perhaps he just didn't want to tell me, which is fair enough.

Discipline and restraint are important in the studio even if you arrive there after great recklessness. I think there is a tendency nowadays for people just starting out with DAWs to time-correct elements in the recording just because they can. Often this can be at the expense of the groove. Staring at a computer screen all day long can make some people produce records with their eyes rather than their ears. I don't wish to be negative about new technology, just cautious. The great artists, engineers and producers will continue to surprise us with great recordings.

You worked a lot with the four Floyd members individually. Do you remember any particular musical or technical anecdotes from recording with the four? Perhaps something about their characteristics as performers and artists in the studio.
There was always a wealth of diverse talent for each band member to exploit. Whether it's David's musical abilities, Roger's vision, Rick's atmospherics, or Nick's ability to provide precisely the right bed for the song. David tends to concentrate more on musical arrangement, Roger more on the overview – the dramatic impact. But Roger's musical knowledge and ability should not be underestimated. He played some great guitar on the record as well as bass. David also played some great bass as well as his guitar.

When we finished at Superbear Studios, the band took the month of August off. I flew to London with the tapes and went to my old stomping ground of Utopia Studios to rough mix everything. The plan was that I would put everything in sequence and send rough mixes to everyone so they could review the progress. I would then go straight to L.A. in order to prepare for the U.S. sessions and meet everyone there at the end of the month. During the sessions in France, we had recorded the scream that bridges THE HAPPIEST DAYS with ANOTHER BRICK PART 2. For some reason the scream was missing. I couldn't find it on any of the tapes. This seemed like an important transition to me and I wanted it to be on the rough mixes. This is a scream that Roger has done for years and is performed by an inhalation of breath rather than an exhalation – difficult to do and very hard on your throat. Roger was still in the South of France and I called him there. I set up the phone recording system, explained that the scream was missing and asked if he would scream down the phone for me, so we would at least have a rough idea of it on the interim mixes. He did numerous 'takes' over the phone, eventually saying to me, 'I can't do this much longer, you know. My family are giving me very strange looks!' I put the scream in place and we never replaced it in the studio, so the performance on the record is phoned in, from France to the UK.

Do you have favourite tracks from *The Wall* (musically or from a technical point of view)?
I like the way the whole album works, both musically and as a narrative. ANOTHER BRICK 1 stands out to me of the three BRICKS, as I think we managed to capture the atmosphere of youth in the 1940's and the child reminiscing. (Each ANOTHER BRICK IN THE WALL originally had a subtitle rather than a number. In order, they were: 'Reminiscing', 'Education' and 'Drugs'). On Roger's original demo, BRICK 1 was just called 'Reminiscing'. The drones against David's guitars, everything swirling, Rick's sparse but emotional electric piano, all create a great musical bed for Roger's vocal.

HEY YOU is another, with everyone playing beautifully, everything has its place even when the song gets busy. COMFORTABLY NUMB as well. It was a great privilege being able to help capture those performances.

I don't know if you ever go back and listen to your back catalogue, but what is your personal view about *The Wall* today? Does it hold up? Are there elements you would have tackled differently today?
When I was young, I was incredibly critical of everything, and nothing that I did, or pretty much anyone else for that matter, could ever be good enough. Over the years I have tried to temper that reaction, but I'm still a perfectionist. It's funny, I've recently been going through *The Wall* multitrack tapes in order to make some transfers and looking back, I thought to myself, actually, this is pretty good! I'm probably too close to it to judge effectively, but I think it holds up today because the material is so strong. Approaching it today, I would probably push for more rehearsal time and try to cut more of the songs as a band. Also, I wouldn't mind hearing THE TRIAL without all the showy, Kurt Weill arrangement. Something darker, cooler and more sinister might be interesting.

Since *The Wall* line-up of Pink Floyd dissolved, you have worked with the factions of the band on many occasions. Is there, in your view, a musical strain, certain sound characteristics or production values that runs through everything, no matter which of the former members you happen to be involved with?
I think they are musically all a bit different, but together they made that sound. By definition, the solo albums all explore more personal avenues, but having said that, I think that Roger's solo album, *Amused to Death*, is very much a 'Pink Floyd' record, both atmospherically and conceptually. The writing always contains such richly compelling subject matter which is very inspiring from a production point of view. Really, it's a producer/engineer's dream, as there's always so much to explore creatively.

(Thanks to Thomas Ulrik Larsen for permission to use this interview. The above text is copyright Thomas, and not to be used without his express permission.)

Steve Mac

Steve Mac is the singer and guitar player for The Australian Pink Floyd Show, probably the premiere Pink Floyd tribute band. Going since 1988, their sound is the closest approximation to live Floyd out there, with their stage sets similarly closely replicating Pink Floyd, with mirror balls, Mr Disc, an inflatable pig, and also an inflatable kangaroo nicknamed Skippy. I must have seen them six times and each been blown away at the verisimilitude to the Floyd. It's also great how each show has had new aspects to it, keeping it fresh for audiences as well as the band. Perhaps their finest moment was playing at David Gilmour's fiftieth birthday party in 1996, after he had noted that he had never been to a Pink Floyd show as a fan. Steve Mac is originally from Adelaide, while The Aussie Floyd continue to tour the world.

Are you in the UK?
I'm in the UK, yeah, and in my place in the UK, which this is our rehearsal studio that we use, with a pub joined onto it. Can have a beer afterwards, which helps. And [turns the tables on your humble interviewer] I've got some questions for you here actually! What is your favourite Pink Floyd song?

It's probably a draw, between DOGS and ECHOES.
Right, you're a meat and potatoes man after my own heart, because they're my two as well. And then the next tough question, which doesn't have to be related – what's your favourite Pink Floyd album?

Animals.
Animals, right. The rocky one? Cool.

Yeah.
Well, I'm glad you said those – I have an instant affection for you.

Thanks! So, what got you into music? What was it that really struck you first?
I had an elder sister, she got this cheap version of a Hammond organ. She wasn't great on it, but she could knock a few tunes out of it. And that gave me that first interest of how someone can play an instrument. These wizards on television and radio. And she also got an acoustic guitar, funnily enough. And my mum was a big Beatles fan. My dad was a bit old school, but mum was a big Beatles fan. And she loved Ringo, thought he was the star of the band. So I got this drum kit when I was about eight or nine years old. I set it up on Christmas morning, played it all Christmas Day and night. And then I woke up on Boxing Day and it was gone. They couldn't handle it. So they threw it out.

So discussions had been had while you were sleeping.
Yeah, they sent it back and thought 'We just can't handle that'. So that kind of killed that, I think they thought 'He obviously can't keep time or do anything'. So I wanted a guitar, and they refused that. So they kind of said 'No, we don't think … you're going to be too loud' or whatever. So when I was 13, my sister came home after being out with some mates and she just turned up with this album – *Dark Side Of The Moon*. And I'd been in school playing football. It was winter, I was covered in mud and I came in – my parents worked, they weren't home. So I ran a hot bath and I sat in this bath, and unbeknownst to me my sister put Dark Side Of The Moon on my parents' hi–fi system and turned it up really loud. And I just remember hearing all the heartbeat, the screams, the tick–tock, jackhammer, voices and thinking 'What the hell is this?'. And it builds up to this intense scary type of crescendo. It just exploded into BREATHE. Like this liquid rainbow. I just melted in that bath, I was in this beautiful warm bath, this music and I'm just away with the fairies. This was just amazing. And just everything about it, the guitar – I used to muck about doing a bit of slide on my sister's guitar when I could, but she didn't have any plectrums and I didn't know what I was doing. But I just liked the sound of it. There was something about the slide and BREATHE that instantly had a connection to me, and the keyboard sounds, and the whole album – I just lay there and listened to this whole album, which is probably a pretty good place to get your first experience of Pink Floyd, in this warm cocoon. Like those floatation tanks where it's designed to take the gravity away and you're just this head in space, freaking out on Floyd.

So that was my first experience and from then on, I just wanted to hear more. And that's kind of the background of me getting into music. But I didn't actually buy a guitar until I was about 17, 18 when I first got a job, and then I could afford to buy a guitar. My parents refused to buy instruments for us.

Do you remember what that first guitar was?
Yes, it was a Les Paul copy. It was by a brand called Coronet. It was awful to play, really bad. I bought it off of a mate's big brother, he was a KISS fan. But the only reason I bought the Les Paul was because I had David Gilmour's first solo album and I think there's a picture in the sleeve of him playing a Les Paul, or what I thought was a Les Paul. I think that was one of the first and only pictures I've actually ever seen of David Gilmour, that you could find because in little old Adelaide in Australia you just didn't get any media. You didn't see anything on the television.

Were there no rock music magazines or things like that at the time?
Not that I could ever afford to buy or saw. I think the ones my sister got just had, I don't know, David Cassidy in it – it was all a pin–up boys for the girls at the time. They weren't into the serious music, and prog rock was a dirty word.

You grew up in Adelaide – what was the music or cultural scene like there at the time you were growing up? What were the teenagers into?
Back then the Australian Broadcasting Association governed what music was allowed to be played, and what percentage of music. To nurture the very tiny Australian market because the population was so small with so few bands in those days – I think it was 33% of airplay had to be an Australian band, then another 33% was British, and the other 33% was American. That was more or less what we got. So you kind of got the Top 40 from all three countries, which made it unique. But since I've come to England, I've spoken to people and they've educated me with the hits in England, I've realised that we missed out on an awful lot of songs that were big in England. And also there were certain songs that were really big in Australia but just didn't go anywhere in England. Over time I've realised what a weird, unique selection of music that we heard, because of course there was no internet back then so you were totally at the mercy of your radio or the record stores – they wouldn't try and sell loads of those records and ship them all out to Australia, or manufacture them in Australia under licence, because there wasn't a big enough population to support the sales of it.

As for my introduction to Pink Floyd music, there was a kid I met in high school. His family came to Australia and they were going back, it didn't work out and they couldn't afford to ship back all this stuff, and he had this Pink Floyd bootleg collection. And he told me all these stories about Pink Floyd and all the folklore about them – Syd Barrett, what they were like on the road and as people, stuff no–one in Australia had ever heard of. And he left me with this fantastic, small but very eclectic collection of Pink Floyd bootlegs. So he was responsible. And to this day, I cannot remember his name, might have been Alvin but I just can't remember it. I literally knew him for only three days. And he was so relieved that the bootlegs would go to a good home. I met him in the library – I was listening to Pink Floyd on a cassette of The Wall or something, and he noticed it.

That guy was like this angel who just came in and dropped all this on you.
It kind of was. I keep thinking Alvin Stardust – that might have been his nickname. Because he wore these purple flares, and I think that's what they called him. It was probably Syd Barrett!

What else were kids listening to?
We had a programme called Countdown, which was the equivalent of the British Top of the Pops. I had one of those little tape deck recorders, buttons on the front, crap speaker in it, and a microphone. So I used to sit there in front of the TV at 6 o'clock on a Sunday, sit and record Countdown – get your mum and dad, your sister, the dog or whatever to shut up so you could record it without any noise in the background. And then listen to that through the week. But again, that was the Top 10 so that was filtered down, and obviously

it was American, Australian, so we didn't get much English stuff. But what we did get was fantastic.

So you said your mum listened to The Beatles. What other bands were there that you were being exposed to?
Alan Parsons Project. I absolutely loved Alan Parsons Project. Still do, really like all of his stuff. There was a spell where there was The Sweet, Slade, Suzi Quatro, all the stuff when it was a bit more rocky. I kind of got into The Beatles later, because I kind of rebelled against that – because they seemed a bit old and fuddy–duddy, because my mother liked it. And my dad liked Perry Como and Acker Bilk, those kind of people. You kind of go against the grain don't you? You want something that's going to wind your parents up.

So when you picked up the guitar about age 18 – were there places to go and play? Were there grubby little pubs that you could go and play in? Did you have any bands when you were young?
The first time I started to play music with other people was when I was 17, 18, and I met this girl at school that I really had the hots for. She went to this youth group that was with the local church – I've never had any involvement with a church or anything like that, apart from being in Sunday school when I was a kid. But it wasn't until I met this girl and then went to the youth group, and they had quite a few musicians in this group and they'd get up and play music. On a Friday night we'd go camping for the weekend, sit around a campfire. And there was a great drummer and a great guitarist, they were into Lynyrd Skynyrd and Pink Floyd. And we formed a band called Special Envoy, because back then we thought we had some fantastic message that was going to change the world. And we wrote songs, and we played a few covers. And it ended up we just got thrown out of two churches because we were too loud and our guitars were too distorted, so that ended my involvement with the church at that point. But by then I was seeking to play music with fellow minded musicians. Seven, eight years went by and then I was 25, 26. And that's when I saw the ad that Lee Smith placed, the founder of the band.

When was that?
That would have been … if I was 25, that would have been 1987, 88.

Wow, you guys have really been doing that a long time. The first time I saw you was in 1997, you played in Stirling.
Stirling University?

That's right. It was a cracking gig.
Oh, good. Excellent. The Scottish audiences always made us really welcome. They just love, love the Floyd – sing along and know all the words, all the solos.

Scottish, Liverpudlian and Irish audiences, they were just on a different level compared to the rest of the UK back then.

I was going to ask later, but since it's a nice segue – I noticed that quite often the fans at the start of the gig can be very well behaved, very quiet, they just sit there taking it all in. So how do you know when things aren't going well, or maybe even badly?
I think that you can tell things are going really well if they're all still sat there! It's when they just piss off to the bar, or they're talking, not even facing you – turning their backs to talk with their friends and you know you're not really their thing. But I remember doing this show up near the north east of Queensland. We'd just done a gig, and we had this 17 hour drive to get to the next gig and do the show. We'd loaded in at midnight, then got in the car and drove there and turned up at 5pm. And the show was at 7pm, all this gear to load in. And we hadn't slept, we'd just been driving – I drove one of the three vehicles. We were exhausted. We set all this gear up, and this was like at a university. It was a big room, like a big basketball or gymnasium arena. We set up and then the doors opened – and no one came in. And there was just one door at the back of the room that was opened every now and then, there was a pool room in there and it's full of people playing eight ball. And for the whole gig every now and then the door would open and someone would stick their head out with their pool cue while they're waiting for their shot, and they'd look at us and then the door would shut again. I can remember thinking we'd nearly killed ourselves and set all this gear up for that! But you learn to appreciate your audience from experiences like that. Having an audience that is anticipating you, listening for every note, and of course clapping at the end of it – if they're doing all of that it generally goes well. We always try to tidy the set as well, so you leave the more upbeat and familiar 'best of' sets towards the end. And Pink Floyd have so many great songs which can arouse such emotions within people, and by then the beer's kicked in as well. They've had a great night, and they want to let off some steam and forget about their worries, have a good time and enjoy the music.

You've worked with Pete Cornish on your guitar rig. Can you just explain what he does and how he's helped you?
Obviously, Pete Cornish pedals and effects are legendary, world-renowned and he's probably one of the oldest experts and pioneers in the way he builds pedals. That shaped the industry, and really helped so many guitarists and musicians sculpt their sound and what they do. I think I wrote to him originally, and invited him to a show. I was telling him about that whale sound in ECHOES in the middle section. We didn't know how that was achieved – this is before the internet and all the rest of it. So we'd never plugged in a wah pedal back to front.

Yeah, that's how it's done.
I didn't even own a wah pedal. Lee did, but he still didn't figure it out. So we used to play that live, but how do you get those high notes and that long sustain? So I wrote to Pete and just said 'Do you know how to do that?' And he said 'Where are you on tour next?' And coincidentally, we were near where he lived. So he came to a show with his wife, and came up and checked out the rig onstage. And then he invited me after the tour to come back and spend a day or two with him in his workshop. It was really good. I went there the next day for a bit, and he had some equipment from all different musicians, some of his sample stuff. He had some stuff with David's Gilmour's rig that he was putting together and working on, and he said that he could build me this Orca pedal that he'd done a few times for David. So mine had the serial number 0004 on it, and this is the pedal that was going to do the Orca sound, he didn't tell me it was just a wah pedal back–to–front, he said it was some special thing. And you had to modify it and it was all involved. He built this big pedal, which I've actually got it over here at home – it's normally in lockup but I've been working with it recently.

Ah – 'Orca 0004, December '99'.
Yes, so there you go. It's also an A–B switch from my lap steel guitar, and it's got a buffer in it and a little mid–range boost circuit and stuff. Anyway, that's the pedal. So I went down there and he was great, and Linda was great – lovely, lovely couple. They were both showing me the difference between pedals and we played through some that were in there, clients' pedals. And, you know, Pete was obviously there all the time, making sure I was well behaved and protecting his clients' equipment, but he was very accommodating and helpful. And I was picking his brains like, you know, you're on this quest for the Holy Grail, and you're trying to do your best to give David Gilmour sounds the justice they deserve, so you're really hungry for knowledge. My background is in electronics – I'd worked in a repair maintenance workshop for 13 years, so we discussed that, and we kind of had this little bit of camaraderie there. A lot of time with a soldering iron in your hand, you know, so that was really good.

I still speak to Pete, I still get a Christmas card from him every year, it's nice. I've bought a considerable number of pedals off him over the years as well, because they just do what they're supposed to do, they work, and I've never had one fail, ever.

I saw you've added Lorelei McBroom to the band?
She's been with us since 2010. Still with us, going on.

How did that come about? Did you just meet her?
There's mixed stories about that. I know Lorelei has her own version of it, which I'm not going to say is incorrect! But from my memory, I just remember a

manager that we had at the time thought it might be good if we could contact Durga, and see if Durga was interested. Or Durga had written to the management via our website, asking if there was any work going. I'm not entirely sure whether it was through Durga or whether it was through Lorelei, but I remember we ended up paying for Lorelei to go to a studio and to record us her singing GREAT GIG IN THE SKY. And it came back and we thought she sounded great. So I think that's how it began. But as far as the introduction went, I don't know if it was our manager saying he should contact Durga, and I don't know whether he contacted Durga and she was unavailable so then he contacted Lorelei, who fortunately was available.

Well the authenticity that you're getting through all that is just amazing.
Thank you.

All the times I've seen you, you've always been trying to improve and outdo yourself on the visual side. So what's cooking on that side of things? Have you got anything that you're working on?
We have. We've got a few effects that'll be new to the show, and we want to tie it all in with the 2023 *Dark Side Of The Moon* 50th anniversary. So we've got some ideas for that. And because we're in the UK at the end of the year, we might start to develop those different elements of production in the UK as well so we're not coming in cold with it on the Dark Side tour next year. We're always looking into different forms of video content – we have done a lot of work in–house, but we are looking further afield as well, and there's some other artists out there that have their own flavour. And we're looking at some animations to incorporate to give things a new and fresher look. With having a pandemic, and World War Three on the horizon there's a whole different mindset. Obviously all of those lyrics and messages are as relevant today as they were when Pink Floyd wrote them, but it's nice to kind of make the visual content a bit more in keeping with what's going on today.

Have you seen Roger's *This Is Not A Drill* tour? He's really pushing the envelope with the video content that he's doing.
I've only seen the odd clip that people have been putting up on YouTube via Facebook, I haven't had the luxury or privilege of sitting down and seeing the full show of it.

A lot of stuff winds up on YouTube.
I've seen Roger talking about how people say 'I love the music, but I'm not really into all that politics'. And then he says 'Well, if that's your case then bugger off to the bar'.

Yeah, I did find that the last time I saw him, I found he was getting very didactic. It was like 'This is what you should think', you know? But that's Roger.
I must say, because we put on a show, we do often think people are coming to forget their worries, they want to forget how bad the world is. We want to give them some entertainment, we want to give them some thought-provoking stuff that hopefully will make a difference. They'll go away and carry Pink Floyd's message and make the world a better place through their actions, but it's always a balance.

I know we've done shows where we have meet and greets, and quite often we get asked 'Have you seen Roger?' and we say 'Yes we have – have you seen him? And did you enjoy it?'. And some people say 'It was brilliant, all of it'. And some people say 'I really enjoyed it, but I won't go again because it was just too much of a lecture. And it was too heavy going politically'. They had opposing views to Roger and it offended them, so therefore they wouldn't go again. He's alienated a big part of his audience in their opinions, so you hear all those things. But I think of the world in this day and age, and think how many people have the opportunity Roger has, to have a soapbox as big and as widespread as that, that are actually really trying to defend humanity, mankind and human rights. It will be a sad day when Roger isn't there or is not doing it. And who else is going to step up to the plate and do it, be brave enough to do it? He's a dying breed in this overly PC world. It will be a sad day when we lose Roger's defiant stance for mankind. We do need more of it. You know, he does often use the term brothers and sisters., and that is what we all are ultimately, when you get rid of all that bullshit, that's what we are. I don't believe we're all equals, because I don't believe the world is like that. I think we all have the same rights as each other, we should have the same rights as each other. But you know, some people are strong, some are weak, some are fast, some are slow, some are super brainy, some aren't so clever. So we're not all equal as individuals, but we should still have the same rights. And he's fighting for rights.

For sure. Speaking of the pandemic, how did you keep going there during it? Were there a lot of things locked down?
I think financially, we just all had to beg, steal and borrow because for 22 months we couldn't put on any shows, the shows we had scheduled just kept getting rescheduled and kicked on further down the road. It was a good opportunity for us all to realise what we leave behind when we go on tour for eight months of the year or so, so that was a good thing that came out of that, we could really work on home and relationships and those kinds of things, and get all those jobs done around the house that needed to be done. So it was good in that respect, although we just had to be very careful with money of course, because we didn't know – as my dad would say 'It's a long time between drinks', when you didn't know when the next drink was coming. I think all of us, the band and crew

went out to try to keep productive in some aspect, in some way, just for your own sanity, just to feel some worth, because when you feel like the rug's been pulled out from under you and you almost become institutionalised when you've been doing this for so long, you can't really work anywhere else. So it was trying to do things to remind yourself that you could achieve stuff, even though they were non-musical, but everyone did different projects, and I'm happy to say that we all came through it pretty much unscathed. And all the wiser for it, as far as trying to be prepared for the next thing. A good life lesson as well.

On a more cheerful note – what's the biggest gig you've played?
We played a football stadium in Malta, and pretty much the whole city of Malta was there, including the Prime Minister. We had police escorts driven from the airport to the hotels and all that kind of stuff, in limousines, so that was very surreal because we're just a bunch of bonzos from Adelaide who just all of a sudden made good, and then you get treated like royalty. So that was a bit weird, but still a great memory and experience. We've done some big gigs in the ice hockey arenas throughout America and Canada, and we've played some stadiums in Italy, played the O2 in London, the Royal Albert Hall of course. Birmingham Arena, Sheffield Arena, and the Hippodrome and the Glasgow Arena. Some really quite well established and highly respected venues.

Have you played Gdansk?
Have we played Gdansk? I know we've played Prague.

You'll have seen David Gilmour live in Gdansk?
I have. Obviously I wasn't there, but I've got the DVD boxset and collection – and of course, Colin Norfield mixed for it, so I've heard all about it from him, because he's worked with us over the years. I think we came along at the right time, and this kind of thing turned into something with its own momentum, and we've kind of been dragged along by it while working very hard. But it's just been a very fortunate combination of everything, and we've been made welcome in a lot of countries. The demand for Pink Floyd, it just seems to cross cultural differences and national boundaries, it's just worldwide and loved by so many people. What a testament to what they create.

On a similar sort of theme that we touched on earlier, there's quite the ecosystem of all the Floyd tribute bands – there's Mac Floyd, Brit Floyd, I must have seen five or six of them. Are you friendly with them? How does it work between you?
I think in the early days, because – there wasn't that many when we first started, there wasn't many Rolling Stones, or Led Zeppelin, or ABBA tribute bands, you know. But there's tens of thousands of them now, and they have kind of saturated the live market, in every corner of the world. You go now when you're

in a venue, you look at the posters on the wall, and the future acts coming up, it's just so many tribute bands. Some of them are really bad, some of them are great, and some of them are just OK. And you know, there's different levels for different markets. It's fantastic, the public getting to hear the music they love, and people going out and spending money. So that helps the industry and keeps everything ticking over.

But after doing it 34 years, you do look at things very philosophically and realistically, and you realise that you're very lucky yourselves. There's room for everyone out there – and the world's full of people that want to hear it. You can I believe get caught up in looking at your competition, if you want to call it that, and end up looking and analysing what they're doing, and letting it affect what you're doing. So seeing what they're doing, and worrying about it – 'Oh, they've got this, we need to get that, we're changing this, so we've got to'. You can lose sight of who you are. So I just tend to let us all get on with it, and wish you all well, and we're just going to get on and do what we do the way we do it. Life's too short. We're still going great. What's the point? It's like an ex-marriage, isn't it? Why spend your life bitter and hating your ex-wife? It's not going to make you any happier in life. You just got to enjoy what's ahead of you and make the most of it. We don't know how long we've got here.

You should tell Roger and David this.
Ha! Yes, perhaps. I'd love to sit in a room.

Yeah, be the therapist, the counsellor.
I just love both of them dearly and love what they do and what they bring. And if you had two good friends that were tearing each other apart, you'd wish that they could get along, just be happy and enjoy life.

Can you just tell the story of playing at David Gilmour's 50th birthday party? How nervous were you playing the front of the band? Who was there that you recognised?
It was both one of the best moments of our lives, and one of the most terrifying moments of our lives. Coming from our background, we weren't used to hanging out with A-grade celebrities. And I believe there were 500 A-grade celebrities invited to the party. So you were playing to people that you grew up absolutely loving, and respecting and idolising – not only in music, but in comedy and the arts, writers and all kinds of people there, newsreaders I had a lot of respect for.

Where was it held?
It was held at Fulham Town Hall, and there was like a theatre in there, and it was set in a 60s vibe. So they had Persian rugs on the floor, an ice sculpture in the middle, and some people doing body paintings. And the food was magnificent

– I had the best cream cheese and smoked salmon sandwich I've ever had in my life. To this day I've never had a sandwich as good as that, it was incredible. How the other half live! But it was just fantastic. We were kind of told that, you know, we were kind of employed helpers, we need to keep to ourselves so be polite, don't get in anyone's face or anything, and we really wanted to respect that so we did. I do remember having George Harrison sat on the floor in front of me while we were playing through our set, in his 60s outfit, smoking a cigarette the size of a toilet roll – I'm not sure what was in it, but he seemed to be enjoying himself. And there was a magician there, the Bootleg Beatles played there as well, so it was a great night.

How long did you play for?
We played I think about an hour, I have got the setlist somewhere – I do know that we cut a few numbers from it. ANOTHER BRICK IN THE WALL PART 2, HAVE A CIGAR was in it, HEY YOU, SHINE ON YOU CRAZY DIAMOND was in it, MONEY was in it. Possibly RUN LIKE HELL. They were the songs that David chose.

Oh, he chose them?
Yeah. He gave us a list of songs that he asked for, and we played the ones that we knew. It came about because it was him saying to his wife – and she encouraged it to happen – saying that the one thing he regrets is he's never been able to witness a Pink Floyd concert himself, so that's why it came to be part of the entertainment for his birthday party. Of course he got up on stage, coaxed by Rick Wright to get up on stage to play COMFORTABLY NUMB. And he got up on stage and I got on my knees and held my guitar up to him as if it was handing the sword to King Arthur, picking up Excalibur. And he took my guitar and then he looked at my pedal board and he casually said 'So how d'you fly this thing?'. Which I thought was really cool because I'm into aviation in a big way. So I showed him a few sounds, and then he began to twiddle the knobs of my guitar and press buttons. He just turned my guitar rig into the best it's ever sounded, and off he went and played a couple of songs, to the delight of everyone that was there that night. It was great, magical. I was buzzing for days, I couldn't sleep. I got home that night and I just sat on the couch and thought 'I can't believe that just happened'. I've still got the strings and the plectrum that he played on that guitar, and I still use that guitar. It was very, very magical.

You may also enjoy ...

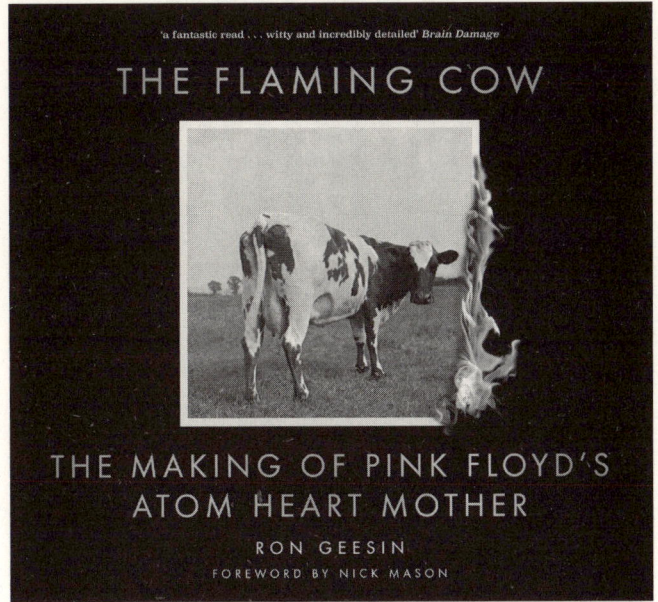

978 0 7509 9574 0

A rare insight into the brilliant but often fraught collaboration between Pink Floyd and composer Ron Geesin, the result of which became known as *Atom Heart Mother*. From the time drummer Nick Mason visited Geesin's damp basement flat in Notting Hill, to the last game of golf between bassist Roger Waters and Geesin, this book is an unflinching account about how one of Pink Floyd's most celebrated compositions came to life.

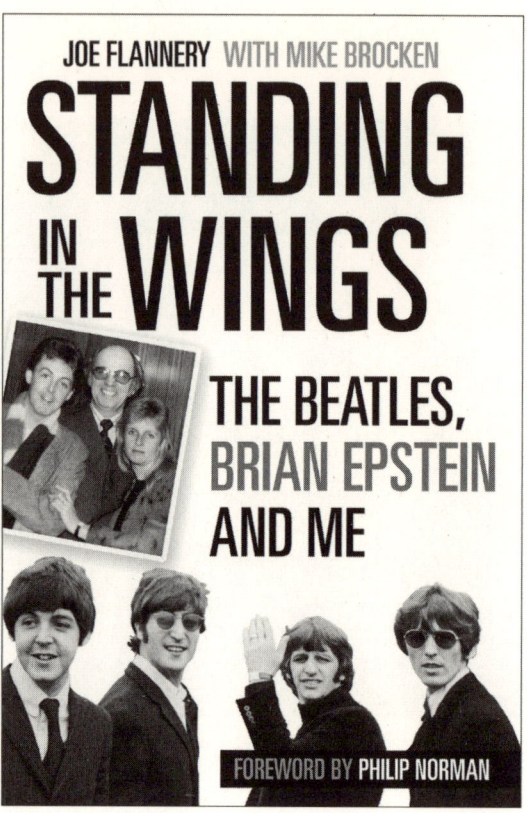

978 0 7509 8760 8

Joe Flannery – described as the 'Secret Beatle' – was the business associate and partner of Brian Epstein and became an integral part of The Beatles' management team during their rise to fame in the early 1960s. *Standing in the Wings* is Flannery's account of this fascinating era.

The destination for history
www.thehistorypress.co.uk

978 1 80399 433 8

Labelled with Love is an odyssey through your record collection and the world beyond it, from the Jazz Age to punk, the civil rights movement to Thatcherism, the Beatles to Britpop, and Ella Fitzgerald to The Ramones.